# Trials of Modernity

## Europe in the World

### THIRD EDITION

## Stacy Burton & Dennis Dworkin

Pearson
Custom
Publishing

PEARSON CUSTOM PUBLISHING
75 Arlington Street, Suite 300, Boston, MA 02116
A Pearson Education Company

# COPYRIGHT ACKNOWLEDGMENTS

# CONTENTS

## SECTION IV
# Romanticism and Industrial Transformation     171

# INTRODUCTION

There are many ways that the readings in this book of original sources in European cultural history can be interpreted. In our view, one of the principal threads is the exploration of the modern experience. On the cover is Edvard Munch's 1893 painting, *The Scream*. The painting, according to the artist, is autobiographical.

> I was tired and ill—I stood looking out across the fjord—the sun was setting—the clouds were colored red—like blood—I felt as though a scream went through nature—I thought I heard a scream—I painted the picture—painted the clouds like real blood. The colors were screaming.

The artist suggests that the painting is about his inner life; and indeed most viewers have emphasized its subjective and psychological qualities as well. It has been interpreted as being about the individual's isolation from others and the world, the fragmentation of the self, and a feeling of anguish about the human condition. *The Scream* is most often thought of as being part of "modern art." This is in part because of when and how it was painted, but also because it captures the anxieties, fears, and apprehensions that many have felt about the world in which we live. We have chosen it because it visually represents the title of this volume: *Trials of Modernity*.

At the same time, the "trials of modernity" are not exhausted by the qualities found in Munch's painting. What modernity is, when it came into existence, and indeed whether it still exists are all questions that resist easy answers. Nor is the nature of the intellectual and cultural movements that have grown up in response to this modern world—modern thought or, more recently, "modernism"—any easier to define. There have been those like Munch who appear anxious and fearful about this world. Frequently this has been accompanied by nostalgia or longing for an unrecoverable past. Yet there have been others who view modernity as being synonymous with "progress" and look forward eagerly to an even better future. Both responses seem characteristic. As the critic Marshall Berman writes: "To be modern is to find ourselves in an environment that promises us adventure, power, joy, growth, transformation of ourselves and the world—and, at the same time, that threatens to destroy everything we have, everything we know, everything we are." Whether Berman's definition is useful is an open question. We hope that the readings we've selected will allow readers to make up their own minds.

Yet the readings are not about modernity in general. As the subtitle suggests—and in our view it is as important as the title—the book is about European culture since 1500. Because some now question why we still need to know about Europe, it seems appropriate to give our own views on the subject. First, it is impossible to understand fully the meaning of American identities without coming to grips with the European traditions which have been so important in shaping them. European society should not be studied instead of other cultures that have shaped the American way of life but in conjunction with them. Second, if we are interested in understanding the modern world there is no better place to start than Europe, where the terms to define this experience were originally established. Given that the process of modernization has been nearly universal, what happened in Europe and how Europeans reacted to it is of great interest.

As we've suggested, "modernity" is not the only theme that runs through the readings in this book. Texts that we've chosen can be interpreted from numerous perspectives. Some of the readings address the question: What is human nature? Are human beings naturally good, or naturally evil? Are they controlled by fate, or responsible for their own destiny? Another dimension of the readings involves the relationship between an individual and his or her society. Here we might ask the questions: What makes a good society? What responsibilities do individuals have to societies, and societies to individuals? Several of the readings explore the relations between men and women. When considering these readings, we might ask: What are—and what could or should be—the relations (social, economic, intellectual, sexual) between men and women? Do women and men differ inherently, or are apparent gender differences socially constructed? If so, what significance should we attach to differences? Why have women traditionally been treated very differently from men? In more than one section, readings explore Europe's connections with other cultures. Several issues are relevant here. Why do human cultures differ and conflict? What are or should be the intellectual, economic, and social relationships between differing cultures? What does it mean to be "civilized" or "enlightened," to be "barbaric" or "primitive"? Why are barbaric acts sometimes perpetrated by apparently civilized societies? The numerous questions that have been asked here are by no means the only possible ones. Students and instructors will certainly come up with their own.

The date given for each text is in almost all cases the date of first publication. Selecting the most representative dates can be difficult, since some texts were written years, even decades, before they were published. William Blake's "Mock on, mock on," for example, comes from a manuscript notebook he kept from about 1790 to 1810, and Olive Schreiner's story "The Buddhist Priest's Wife" was first published thirty years after it was written. We have chosen to use dates of publication since they best reflect when the text entered into public discussion.

This book could not have been produced without the generous contributions of the Western Traditions faculty. We thank Scott Casper for reading drafts of the introduction and Martha Hildreth and Bruce Moran for reading section introductions and suggesting readings for inclusion. Several other faculty members have suggested texts to us or commented on the first edition: Deborah Achtenberg, Viktoria Hertling, Louis Marvick, Gaye McCollum, Thomas Nickles, and Margaret Urie. We thank them all. We would also like to express our gratitude to Phillip Boardman, chair of the Western Traditions program, who has supported our efforts since the project's inception. Finally, we would like to acknowledge the help of Jonathan Conley, who helped us read the proofs.

Stacy Burton
Dennis Dworkin
University of Nevada, Reno

# FOREWORD TO THE THIRD EDITION

The third edition of *Trials of Modernity* represents the most ambitious revision since its original publication in 1996. Undoubtedly the greatest change consists of the nearly forty new selections. The new readings involve a wide range of topics, from the history of science and the idea of nationalism to the meaning of race and life under postmodernity. But the most important reason for the additional texts is suggested by the book's new subtitle: "Europe in the World." The impetus emanates from the growing awareness of how globalization is reshaping the world and our consciousness of it, breaking down boundaries everywhere. In the case of Europe, it is less clear what its definition consists of, or what constitutes its borders; throughout, we have attempted to create an enlarged concept of Europe, Eastern as well as Western. It is also becoming apparent that European culture cannot be understood apart from its global connections. This entails not only taking into account European empires, migrations, and participation in the slave trade. It also means acknowledging the significance of intellectuals and writers from former colonies. Shaped by European institutions and ideas, yet products of their indigenous culture as well, they have made original cultural contributions that are difficult to classify along national lines. In an age characterized by multiculturalism and diaspora peoples—where the borders between cultures are becoming increasingly blurred—we have tried to include authors who move between cultures: Frantz Fanon, born in Martinique, who spent years of his life in France and Algeria; Mohandas K. Gandhi, whose nonviolent assault on British imperialism was rooted in Hindu and Western traditions; Jamaica Kincaid, who settled in New York but evocatively portrays family relationships in her native Antigua; and Ignatius Sancho, who was born on an African slave ship but ended up as a well-known literary figure in eighteenth-century London. In the same spirit, we have added authors from Haiti, Jamaica, Trinidad, and West Africa. In making these additions, we have always had in our minds not only the national discussion on multiculturalism but also the current one at the University of Nevada, Reno. We see these new selections as part of that dialogue.

There are also other, more modest changes to the third edition. There are changes to some readings used in previous editions, notably the updating of older translations and the modification of the selections themselves. A few readings have been dropped—either because of disuse or because others were found that were preferable. The sections that comprise the book have been slightly altered. We have also changed the form of the introductions. Section introductions have been shortened, while each reading now has an introduction of its own. The maps and illustrations have been modified slightly as well.

We could not have put together this reader without the input and advice of our colleagues. In addition to those already acknowledged in the first edition, we would like to thank Guy Axtell, David Fenimore, Elizabeth Swingrover, and Barbara Walker for their suggestions and support.

# SECTION I

# Early Modern Europe: The Reformation and the Emergence of Science

The modern world did not suddenly appear during a specific year, at a particular time, and at a precise place. Nor did medieval society suddenly cease to exist. The transition from a medieval world to a modern one took place over centuries, and it is only with hindsight that we can understand it in these terms. The pace of change was unevenly distributed: different parts of Europe were affected by it at different rates. And the experience of this transition was neither uniform nor homogeneous. Yet beginning in the sixteenth and seventeenth centuries—and according to some historians perhaps even earlier—it is possible to detect social, economic, political, and cultural developments that would reshape European society and consciousness. In retrospect, we can see that they represented the first glimmers of the modern world.

The readings in this section explore two of these developments: the Protestant Reformation and the Scientific Revolution. The immediate event that triggered the Protestant Reformation—the first successful attempt in Western European history to break the monopoly power of the Roman Catholic Church—was the attempt by Pope Leo X to raise money to build St. Peter's Cathedral in Rome by granting papal indulgences, or pardons of sin, in return for appropriate donations to the Church. (The practice of granting indulgences was not new, and there had been objections before.) When in 1517 a papal agent, a Dominican friar named John Tetzel, attempted to raise money through the granting of indulgences in central Germany, Martin Luther, a professor in Old Testament studies at the University of Wittenberg, responded by posting a list of ninety-five theses or propositions on the Castle Church protesting (what he perceived as) a mockery of religious practice. Although it was Luther's response to a specific abuse of church authority that originally provoked the Reformation, his critique had much wider implications, producing a sweeping condemnation of the entire foundation of Roman Catholic authority. It also opened the door for a challenge to political authority as traditionally conceived. Revolutionaries in the English Civil War would later overthrow the monarchy based on their reading of the Bible, recently translated into English.

The second subject of this section—the Scientific Revolution—does not at first glance seem to have much to do with the birth of Protestantism. What possibly could Copernicus's heliocentric view of the universe (the view that the earth revolves around the sun) and Luther's struggle against the Catholic Church have in common?

But if we think about it, despite the very different nature of the concerns of religious reformers and astronomers, they both challenged the received wisdom of the past—the worldview that had held together medieval life. Religious reformers challenged the infallibility of the papacy and the viability of the Roman Catholic Church. Astronomers and the creators of modern physics challenged the medieval view of the universe, the Ptolemaic or geocentric view that held that the earth was the center of the universe. Most important, the pioneers of the new science were more concerned with discovering the underlying laws governing the motion of the heavens than with understanding what the ultimate purpose of the heavens was. They were interested in learning about the 'how' rather than the 'why' of the natural world. Speculation about divine purpose disappeared from proper scientific inquiry.

The Scientific Revolution was not limited to the study of nature. Though the full flowering of political science was an eighteenth-century phenomenon, it was in the early modern world that intellectuals began to conceive of a science of politics based on human beings as they could be observed in practice.

# Niccolò Machiavelli

## *from* THE PRINCE (CA. 1516)

*Niccolò Machiavelli (1469–1527) was from among the wealthiest and most prominent families in Florence, but his father was among its poorest members. In his own words, he "learnt to do without before he learnt to enjoy." Machiavelli held a number of important political and diplomatic posts, beginning with being head of the second chancery of the Florentine Republic at the age of twenty-nine. Though a man of action and a great Florentine patriot, he is best known for his political thought, notably* The Prince, *one of the great meditations on the nature of cold-blooded political power—hence our word 'Machiavellian'. Rather than analyzing the ideal prince, that is, human beings as they should be, Machiavelli anatomizes how princely power is maintained, founded on an idea of human nature as it is. In short,* The Prince *is one of the founding texts of an emerging political science—the scientific revolution applied to politics and the state.*

### XV. THE THINGS FOR WHICH MEN, AND ESPECIALLY PRINCES, ARE PRAISED OR BLAMED

It now remains for us to see how a prince must regulate his conduct towards his subjects or his allies. I know that this has often been written about before, and so I hope it will not be thought presumptuous for me to do so, as, especially in discussing this subject, I draw up an original set of rules. But since my intention is to say something that will prove of practical use to the inquirer, I have thought it proper to represent things as they are in a real truth, rather than as they are imagined. Many have dreamed up republics and principalities which have never in truth been known to exist; the gulf between how one should live and how one does live is so wide that a man who neglects what is actually done for what should be done moves towards self-destruction rather than self-preservation. The fact is that a man who wants to act virtuously in every way necessarily comes to grief among so many who are not virtuous. Therefore if a prince wants to maintain his rule he must be prepared not to be virtuous, and to make use of this or not according to need.

So leaving aside imaginary things about a prince, and referring only to those which truly exist, I say that whenever men are discussed and especially princes (who are more exposed to view), they are judged for various qualities which earn them either praise or condemnation. Some, for example, are held to be generous, and others miserly (I use the Tuscan word rather than the word avaricious: we also call a man who is mean with what he possesses, miserly, whereas avaricious applies also to a man who wants to plunder others). Some are held to be benefactors, others are called grasping; some cruel, some compassionate; one man faithless, another faithful; one man effeminate and cowardly, another fierce and courageous; one man courteous, another proud; one man lascivious, another chaste; one guileless, another crafty; one stubborn, another flexible; one grave, another frivolous; one religious, another sceptical; and so forth. I know everyone will agree that it would be most laudable if a prince possessed all the qualities deemed to be good among those I have enumerated. But, because of conditions in the world, princes cannot have those qualities, or observe them completely. So a prince has of necessity to be so prudent that he knows how to escape the evil reputation attached to those vices which could lose him his state, and how to avoid those vices which are not so dangerous, if he possibly can; but, if he cannot, he need not worry so much about the latter. And then, he must not flinch from being blamed for vices which are necessary for safeguarding the state. This is because, taking everything into account, he will find that some of the things that appear to be virtues will, if he practises them, ruin him, and some of the things that appear to be vices will bring him security and prosperity.

●

## XVII. Cruelty and Compassion; and Whether It Is Better to Be Loved Than Feared, or the Reverse

Taking others of the qualities I enumerated above, I say that a prince must want to have a reputation for compassion rather than for cruelty: none the less, he must be careful that he does not make bad use of compassion. Cesare Borgia was accounted cruel; nevertheless, this cruelty of his reformed the Romagna, brought it unity, and restored order and obedience. On reflection, it will be seen that there was more compassion in Cesare than in the Florentine people, who, to escape being called cruel, allowed Pistoia to be devastated. So a prince must not worry if he incurs reproach for his cruelty so long as he keeps his subjects united and loyal. By making an example or two he will prove more compassionate than those who, being too compassionate, allow disorders which lead to murder and rapine. These nearly always harm the whole community, whereas executions ordered by a prince only affect individuals. A new prince, of all rulers, finds it impossible to avoid a reputation for cruelty, because of the abundant dangers inherent in a newly won state. Vergil, through the mouth of Dido, says:

> *Res dura, et regni novitas me talia cogunt*
> *Moliri, et late fines custode tueri.*

[Harsh necessity, and the newness of my kingdom, force me to do
such things and to guard my frontiers everywhere. *Aeneid* i, 563]

None the less, a prince must be slow to believe allegations and to take action, and must watch that he does not come to be afraid of his own shadow; his behaviour must be tempered by humanity and prudence so that over-confidence does not make him rash or excessive distrust make him unbearable.

Cruelty is fine
if loyalty achieved

From this arises the following question: whether it is better to be loved than feared, or the reverse. The answer is that one would like to be both the one and the other; but because it is difficult to combine them, it is far better to be feared than loved if you cannot be both. One can make this generalization about men: they are ungrateful, fickle, liars, and deceivers, they shun danger and are greedy for profit; while you treat them well, they are yours. They would shed their blood for you, risk their property, their lives, their sons, so long, as I said above, as danger is remote; but when you are in danger they turn away. Any prince who has come to depend entirely on promises and has taken no other precautions ensures his own ruin; friendship which is bought with money and not with greatness and nobility of mind is paid for, but it does not last and it yields nothing. Men worry less about doing an injury to one who makes himself loved than to one who makes himself feared. For love is secured by a bond of gratitude which men, wretched creatures that they are, break when it is to their advantage to do so; but fear is strengthened by a dread of punishment which is always effective.

The prince must none the less make himself feared in such a way that, if he is not loved, at least he escapes being hated. For fear is quite compatible with an absence of hatred; and the prince can always avoid hatred if he abstains from the property of his subjects and citizens and from their women. If, even so, it proves necessary to execute someone, this is to be done only when there is proper justification and manifest reason for it. But above all a prince must abstain from the property of others; because men sooner forget the death of their father than the loss of their patrimony. It is always possible to find pretexts for confiscating someone's property; and a prince who starts to live by rapine always finds pretexts for seizing what belongs to others. On the other hand, pretexts for executing someone are harder to find and they are sooner gone.

However, when a prince is campaigning with his soldiers and is in command of a large army then he need not worry about having a reputation for cruelty; because, without such a reputation, no army was ever kept united and disciplined. Among the admirable achievements of Hannibal is included this: that although he led a huge army, made up of countless different races, on foreign campaigns, there was never any dissension, either among the troops themselves or against their leader, whether things were going well or badly. For this, his inhuman cruelty was wholly responsible. It was this, along with his countless other qualities, which made him feared and respected by his soldiers. If it had not been for his cruelty, his other qualities would not have been enough. The historians, having given little thought to this, on the one hand admire what Hannibal achieved, and on the other condemn what made his achievements possible.

That his other qualities would not have been enough by themselves can be proved by looking at Scipio, a man unique in his own time and through all recorded history. His armies mutinied against him in Spain, and the only reason for this was his excessive leniency, which allowed his soldiers more licence than was good for military discipline. Fabius Maximus reproached him for this in the Senate and called him a corrupter of the Roman legions. Again, when the Locrians were plundered by one of Scipio's officers, he neither gave them satisfaction nor punished his officer's insubordination; and this was all because of his being too lenient by nature. By way of excuse for him some senators argued that many men were better at not making mistakes themselves than at correcting them in others. But in time Scipio's lenient nature would have spoilt his fame and glory had he continued to indulge it during his command; when he lived under orders from the Senate, however, this fatal characteristic of his was not only concealed but even brought him glory.

So, on this question of being loved or feared, I conclude that since some men love as they please but fear when the prince pleases, a wise prince should rely on what he controls, not on what he cannot control. He must only endeavour, as I said, to escape being hated.

—*trans. George Bull*

## Martin Luther

# *from* AN OPEN LETTER TO THE CHRISTIAN NOBILITY OF THE GERMAN NATION CONCERNING THE REFORM OF THE CHRISTIAN ESTATE (1520)

*Martin Luther (1483–1546) can be credited with having launched the Reformation. (See the introduction to this section.) Inspired by his reading of St. Paul and St. Augustine, he held that original sin was inescapable: salvation was unattainable through individual action or 'works'; it was a gift freely given by God to those who lived a life of faith. "An Open Letter to the Christian Nobility of the German Nation Concerning the Reform of the Christian Estate, 1520" demonstrates the sweeping implications of Luther's thought. He in effect dismissed the need for a Roman Catholic Church, for he rejected the idea (central to Catholicism) that an ordained priesthood's administration of the sacraments was necessary for an individual's salvation. Luther supplanted the idea of a priestly hierarchy with a priesthood of all believers, an emphasis on individual responsibility that became a central tenet of the Protestant revolution in religious thought.*

*To His Most Illustrious and Mighty Imperial Majesty,*
*and to the Christian Nobility of the German Nation,*

Grace and power from God, Most illustrious Majesty, and most gracious and dear Lords.

It is not out of sheer forwardness or rashness that I, a single, poor man, have undertaken to address your worships. The distress and oppression which weigh down all the Estate of Christendom, especially of Germany, and which move not me alone, but everyone to cry out time and again, and to pray for help, have forced me even now to cry aloud that God may inspire some one with His Spirit to lend this suffering nation a helping hand. Ofttimes the councils have made some pretence at reformation, but their attempts have been cleverly hindered by the guile of certain men and things have gone from bad to worse. I now intend, by the help of God, to throw some light upon the wiles and wickedness of these men, to the end that when they are known, they may not henceforth be so hurtful and so great a hindrance. God has given us a noble youth to be our head and thereby has awakened great hopes of good in many hearts; wherefore it is meet that we should do our part and profitably use this time of grace.

In this whole matter the first and most important thing is that we take earnest heed not to enter on it trusting in great might or in human reason, even though all power in the world were ours; for God cannot and will not suffer a good work to be begun with trust in our own power or reason. Such works He crushes ruthlessly to earth, as it is written in the xxxiii Psalm, "There is no king saved by the multitude of an host; a mighty man is not delivered by much strength." On this account, I fear, it came to pass of old that the good Emperors Frederick I and II, and many other German emperors were shamefully oppressed and trodden under foot by the popes, although all the world feared them. It may be that they relied on their own might more than on God, and therefore they had to fall. In our own times, too, what was it that raised the blood-thirsty Julius II to such heights? Nothing else, I fear, except that France, the Germans, and Venice relied upon themselves. The children of Benjamin slew forty-two thousand Israelites because the latter relied on their own strength.

That it may not so fare with us and our noble young Emperor Charles, we must be sure that in this matter we are dealing not with men, but with the princes of hell, who can fill the world with war and bloodshed, but whom war and bloodshed do not overcome. We must go at this work despairing of physical force and humbly trusting God; we must seek God's help with earnest prayer, and fix our minds on nothing else than the misery and distress of suffering Christendom, without regard to the deserts of evil men. Otherwise we may start the game with great prospect of success, but when we get well into it the evil spirits will stir up such confusion that the whole world will swim in blood, and yet nothing will come of it. Let us act wisely, therefore, and in the fear of God. The more force we use, the greater our disaster if we do not act humbly and in God's fear. The popes and the Romans have hitherto been able, by the devil's help, to set kings at odds with one another, and they may well be able to do it again, if we proceed by our own might and cunning, without God's help.

## I. The Three Walls of the Romanists

The Romanists, with great adroitness, have built three walls about them, behind which they have hitherto defended themselves in such wise that no one has been able to reform them; and this has been the cause of terrible corruption throughout all Christendom.

First, when pressed by the temporal power, they have made decrees and said that the temporal power has no jurisdiction over them, but, on the other hand, that the spiritual is above the temporal power. Second, when the attempt is made to reprove them out of the Scriptures, they raise the objection that the interpretation of the Scriptures belongs to no one except the pope. Third, if threatened with a council, they answer with the fable that no one can call a council but the pope. . . .

Against the first wall we will direct our first attack.

It is pure invention that pope, bishops, priests and monks are to be called the "spiritual estate"; princes, lords, artisans, and farmers the "temporal estate." That is indeed a fine bit of lying and hypocrisy. Yet no one should be frightened by it; and for this reason—*viz.*, that all Christians are truly of the "spiritual estate," and there is among them no difference at all but that of office, as Paul says in I Corinthians xii, We are all one body, yet every member has its own work, whereby it serves every other, all because we have one baptism, one Gospel, one faith, and are all alike Christians; for baptism, Gospel and faith alone make us "spiritual" and a Christian people. . . .

To make it still clearer. If a little group of pious Christian laymen were taken captive and set down in a wilderness, and had among them no priest consecrated by a bishop, and if there in the wilderness they were to agree in choosing one of themselves, married or unmarried, and were to charge him with the office of baptizing, saying mass, absolving and preaching, such a man would be as truly a priest as though all bishops and popes had consecrated him. That is why in cases of necessity any one can baptize and give absolution, which would be impossible unless we were all priests. This great grace and power of baptism and of the Christian Estate they have well-nigh destroyed and caused us to forget through the canon law. It was in the manner aforesaid that Christians in olden days chose from their number bishops and priests, who were afterwards confirmed by other bishops, without all the show which now obtains. It was thus that Sts. Augustine, Ambrose, and Cyprian became bishops. . . .

From all this it follows that there is really no difference between laymen and priests, princes and bishops, "spirituals" and "temporals," as they call them, except that of office and work, but not of "estate"; for they are all of the same estate,—true priests, bishops, and popes,—though they are not all engaged in the same work, just as all priests and monks have not the same work. This is the teaching of St. Paul in Romans xii and I Corinthians xii, and of St. Peter in I Peter ii, as I have said above, *viz.,* that we are only one body of Christ, the Head, all members one of another. Christ has not two different bodies, one "temporal," the other "spiritual." He is one Head, and He has one body. . . .

See, now, how Christian is the decree which says that the temporal power is not above the "spiritual estate" and may not punish it. That is as much as to say that the hand shall lend no aid when the eye is suffering. Is it not unnatural, not to say unchristian, that one member should not help another and prevent its destruction? Verily, the more honorable the member, the more should the others help. I say then, since the temporal power is ordained of God to punish evildoers and to protect them that do well, it should therefore be left free to perform its office without hindrance through the whole body of Christendom without respect of persons, whether it affect pope, bishops, priests, monks, nuns or anybody else. For if the mere fact that the temporal power has a smaller place among the Christian offices than has the office of preachers or confessors, or of the clergy, then the tailors, cobblers, masons, carpenters, potboys, tapsters, farmers, and all the secular tradesmen, should also be prevented from providing pope, bishops, priests and monks with shoes, clothing, houses, meat and drink, and from paying them tribute. But if these laymen are allowed to do their work unhindered, what do the Roman scribes mean by their laws, with which they withdraw themselves from the jurisdiction of the temporal Christian power, only so that they may be free to do evil and to fulfill what St. Peter has said: "There shall be false teachers among you, and through covetousness shall they with feigned words make merchandise of you."

On this account the Christian temporal power should exercise its office without let or hindrance, regardless whether it be pope, bishop, or priest whom it affects; whoever is guilty, let him suffer. All that the canon law has said to the contrary is sheer invention of Roman presumption. . . .

The second wall is still more flimsy and worthless. They wish to be the only Masters of the Holy Scriptures, even though in all their lives they learn nothing from them. They assume for themselves sole authority, and with insolent juggling of words they would persuade us that the pope, whether he be a bad man or a good man, cannot err in matters of faith; and yet they cannot prove a single letter of it. Hence it comes that so many heretical and unchristian, nay, even unnatural ordinances have a place in the canon law, of which, however, there is no present need to speak. For since they think that the Holy Spirit never leaves them, be they ever so unlearned and wicked, they make bold to decree whatever they will. And if it were true, where would be the need or use of the Holy Scriptures? Let us burn them, and be satisfied with the unlearned lords at Rome, who are possessed of the Holy Spirit,—although He can possess only pious hearts! Unless I had read it myself, I could not have believed that the devil would make such clumsy pretensions at Rome, and find a following.

But, not to fight them with mere words, we will quote the Scriptures. St. Paul says in I Corinthians xiv: "If to anyone something better is revealed, though he be sitting and listening to another in God's Word, then the first, who is speaking, shall hold his peace and give place." What would be the use of this commandment, if we were only to believe him who does the talking or who has the highest seat? Christ also says in John vi, that all Christians shall be taught of God. Thus it may well happen that the pope and his followers are wicked men, and no true Christians, not taught of God, not having true understanding. On the other hand, an ordinary man may have true understanding; why then should we not follow him? Has not the pope erred many times? Who would help Christendom when the pope errs, if we were not to believe another, who had the Scriptures on his side, more than the pope? . . .

Besides, if we are all priests, as was said above, and all have one faith, one Gospel, one sacrament, why should we not also have the power to test and judge what is correct or incorrect in matters of faith? What becomes of the words of Paul in I Corinthians ii: "He that is spiritual judgeth all things, yet he himself is judged of no man," and in II Corinthians iv: "We have all the same Spirit of faith"? Why, then, should not we perceive what squares with faith and what does not, as well as does an unbelieving pope? . . .

The third wall falls of itself when the first two are down. For when the pope acts contrary to the Scriptures, it is our duty to stand by the Scriptures, to reprove him, and to constrain him, according to the word of Christ in Matthew xviii:

> If thy brother sin against thee, go and tell it him between thee and him alone; if he hear thee not, then take with thee one or two more; if he hear them not, tell it to the Church; if he hear not the Church, consider him a heathen.

They have no basis in Scripture for their contention that it belongs to the pope alone to call a council or confirm its actions; for this is based merely upon their own laws, which are valid only in so far as they are not injurious to Christendom or contrary to the laws of God. When the Pope deserves punishment, such laws go out of force, since it is injurious to Christendom not to punish him by means of a council. . . .

Therefore, when necessity demands, and the pope is an offence to Christendom, the first man who is able should, as a faithful member of the whole body, do what he can to bring about a truly free council. No one can do this so well as the temporal authorities, especially since now they also are fellow-Christians, fellow-priests, "fellow-spirituals" fellow-lords over all things, and whenever it is needful or profitable, they should give free course to the office and work in which God has put them above every man. Would it not be an unnatural thing, if a fire broke out in a city, and every body were to stand by and let it burn on and on and consume everything that could burn, for the sole reason that nobody had the authority of the burgomaster, or because, perhaps, the fire broke out in the burgomaster's house? In such case is it not the duty of every citizen to arouse and call the rest? How much more should this be done in the spiritual city of Christ, if a fire of offence breaks out, whether in the papal government, or anywhere else? In the same way, if the enemy attacks a city, he who first rouses the others deserves honour and thanks; why then should he not deserve honour who makes known the presence of the enemy from hell, and awakens the Christians, and calls them together? . . .

Thus I hope that the false, lying terror with which the Romans have this long time made our conscience timid and stupid, has been allayed. They, like all of us, are subject to the temporal sword; they have no power to interpret the Scriptures by mere authority; without learning; they have no authority to prevent a council or, in sheer wantonness, to pledge it, bind it, or take away its liberty; but if they do this, they are in truth in the communion of Antichrist and of the devil, and have nothing at all of Christ except the name.

## II. Abuses to Be Discussed in Councils

We shall now look at the matters which should be discussed in the councils, and with which popes, cardinals, bishops, and all the scholars ought properly to be occupied day and night if they love Christ and His Church. . . .

1. It is a horrible and frightful thing that the ruler of Christendom who boasts himself vicar of Christ and successor of St. Peter, lives in such worldly splendor that in this regard no king nor emperor can equal or approach him, and that he who claims the title of "most holy" and "most spiritual" is more worldly than the world itself. He wears a triple crown, when the greatest kings wear but a single crown; if that is like the poverty of Christ and of St. Peter, then it is a new kind of likeness. When a word is said against it, they cry out "Heresy!" but that is because they do not wish to hear how unchristian and ungodly such a practice is. I think, however, that if the pope were with tears to pray to God he would have to lay aside these crowns, for our God can suffer no pride, and his office is nothing else than this,—daily to weep and pray for Christendom, and to set an example of all humility. . . .

2. What is the use in Christendom of these people who are called the cardinals? I shall tell you. Italy and Germany have many rich monasteries, foundations, benefices, and livings. No better way has been discovered to bring all these to Rome than by creating cardinals and giving them the bishoprics, monasteries, and prelacies, and so overthrowing the worship of God. For this reason we now see Italy a very wilderness—monasteries in ruins, bishoprics devoured, the prelacies and the revenues of all the churches drawn to Rome, cities decayed, land and people laid waste, because

there is no more worship or preaching. Why? The cardinals must have the income. No Turk could have so devastated Italy and suppressed the worship of God.

Now that Italy is sucked dry, they come into Germany, and begin oh so gently. But let us beware, or Germany will soon become like Italy. Already we have some cardinals; what the Romans seek by that the "drunken Germans" are not to understand until we have not a bishopric, a monastery, a living, a benefice, *a heller* or a *pfennig* left. Antichrist must take the treasures of the earth, as it was prophesied. . . .

I advise, however, that the number of cardinals be reduced, or that the pope be made to keep them at his own expense. Twelve of them would be more than enough, and each of them might have an income of a thousand *gulden* a year. How comes it that we Germans must put up with such robbery and such extortion of our property, at the hands of the pope? . . .

3. If ninety-nine parts of the papal court were done away and only the hundredth part allowed to remain, it would still be large enough to give decisions in matters of faith. Now, however, there is such a swarm of vermin yonder in Rome, all boasting that they are "papal," that there was nothing like it in Babylon. These are more than three thousand papal secretaries alone; who will count the other offices, when they are so many that they scarcely can be counted? And they all lie in wait for the prebends and benefices of Germany as wolves lie in wait for the sheep. I believe that Germany now gives much more to the pope at Rome than it gave in former times to the emperors. Indeed, some estimate that every year more than three hundred thousand *gulden* find their way from Germany to Rome, quite uselessly and fruitlessly; we get nothing for it but scorn and contempt. And yet we wonder that princes, nobles, cities, endowments, land, and people are impoverished! We should rather wonder that we still have anything to eat!

*—trans. C. M. Jacobs*

# John Knox

# *from* THE FIRST BLAST OF THE TRUMPET AGAINST THE MONSTROUS REGIMENT OF WOMEN (1558)

*John Knox (1514–1572) is the central figure in the Scottish Reformation, playing a pivotal role in shaping the Church of Scotland's austere moral tone and democratic or presbyterian form of government. Known for his moral intransigence, passionate rhetoric, and relentless polemic, he once said that he would prefer poison to celebrating a single mass. In* The First Blast of the Trumpet Against the Monstrous Regiment of Women, *Knox's argument that women were inherently unsuited to reign over men was neither original nor uncommon for the time. Yet his denunciation of women must be viewed in its political context. It was written when two Catholic monarchs—Mary, Queen of Scots and Mary Tudor—were making it difficult for Protestants to observe their religion in Scotland and England.*

## THE FIRST BLAST TO AWAKEN WOMEN DEGENERATE

To promote a woman to bear rule, superiority, dominion, or empire above any realm, nation, or city, is repugnant to nature; contumely [*an insult*] to God, a thing most contrary to his revealed will and approved ordinance; and finally, it is the subversion of good order, of all equity and justice.

In the probation of this proposition, I will not be so curious as to gather whatsoever may amplify, set forth, or decor the same; but I am purposed, even as I have spoken my conscience in most plain and few words, so to stand content with a simple proof of every member, bringing in for my witness God's ordinance in nature, his plain will revealed in his word. . . .

### *[The Empire of Women is Repugnant to Nature]*

And first, where I affirm the empire of a woman to be a thing repugnant to nature, I mean not only that God, by the order of his creation, has spoiled [*deprived*] woman of authority and dominion, but also that man has seen, proved, and pronounced just causes why it should be. Man, I say, in many other cases, does in this behalf see very clearly. For the causes are so manifest, that they cannot be hid. For who can deny but it is repugnant to nature, that the blind shall be appointed to lead and conduct such as do see? That the weak, the sick, and impotent persons shall nourish and keep the whole and strong? And finally, that the foolish, mad, and frenetic shall govern the discreet, and give counsel to such as be sober of mind? And such be all women, compared unto man in bearing of authority. For their sight in civil regiment is but blindness; their strength, weakness; their counsel, foolishness; and judgment, frenzy, if it be rightly considered.

•

### [The Empire of Women is Contrary to the Revealed Will of God ]

But now to the second part of nature, in the which I include the revealed will and perfect ordinance of God; and against this part of nature, I say, that it does manifestly repugn that any woman shall reign and bear dominion over man. For God, first by the order of his creation, and after by the curse and malediction pronounced against the woman (by reason of her rebellion) has pronounced the contrary.

First, I say, that woman in her greatest perfection was made to serve and obey man, not to rule and command him. As St. Paul does reason in these words: "Man is not of the woman, but the woman of the man. And man was not created for the cause of the woman, but the woman for the cause of man; and therefore ought the woman to have a power upon her head" [1 Cor. 11:8–10] (that is, a cover in sign of subjection). Of which words it is plain that the apostle means, that woman in her greatest perfection should have known that man was lord above her; and therefore that she should never have pretended any kind of superiority above him, no more than do the angels above God the Creator, or above Christ their head. So I say, that in her greatest perfection, woman was created to be subject to man.

But after her fall and rebellion committed against God, there was put upon her a new necessity, and she was made subject to man by the irrevocable sentence of God, pronounced in these words: "I will greatly multiply thy sorrow and thy conception. With sorrow shalt thou bear thy children, and thy will shall be subject to thy man; and he shall bear dominion over thee" (Gen. 3:16). Hereby may such as altogether be not blinded plainly see, that God by his sentence has dejected all women from empire and dominion above man. For two punishments are laid upon her: to wit, a dolour, anguish, and pain, as oft as ever she shall be mother; and a subjection of her self, her appetites, and will, to her husband, and to his will. From the former part of this malediction can neither art, nobility, policy, nor law made by man deliver womankind; but whosoever attains to that honour to be mother, proves in experience the effect and strength of God's word. But (alas!) ignorance of God, ambition, and tyranny have studied to abolish and destroy the second part of God's punishment. For women are lifted up to be heads over realms, and to rule above men at their pleasure and appetites. But horrible is the vengeance which is prepared for the one and for the other, for the promoters and for the persons promoted, except they speedily repent. For they shall be dejected from the glory of the sons of God to the slavery of the devil, and to the torment that is prepared for all such as do exalt themselves against God.

# Elizabeth I, Queen of England

# FIRST SPEECH (1558)
# GOLDEN SPEECH (1601)

*Elizabeth Tudor (1533–1603) became queen of England in 1558 amidst great turmoil. In the eleven years since the death of her father, Henry VIII, England had been ruled first by his young son Edward VI, whose advisors forcibly advanced the Reformation, and then by his daughter Mary Tudor, who vehemently attempted to return England to Catholicism. During Elizabeth's long reign, England weathered constant intrigue and warfare as the monarchs of France and Spain sought to add England to their domains. Pursuing pragmatic solutions to religious conflicts and defeating the Spanish Armada, Elizabeth saw England become more firmly established as a powerful state. Early in her reign, she was pressured to marry and guarantee the succession to the throne. By her death, Elizabeth herself had become the symbol of nationhood, celebrated by poets and artists as Gloriana or the Virgin Queen. In these speeches she describes the relations that obtain between the monarch and the people. The first was given to nobles present when she ascended to the throne; the second, her most celebrated, to Parliament.*

## FIRST SPEECH

My lords, the law of nature moveth me to sorrow for my sister; the burden that is fallen upon me maketh me amazed; and yet, considering I am God's creature, ordained to obey His appointment, I will thereto yield, desiring from the bottom of my heart that I may have assistance of His grace to be the minister of His heavenly will in this office now committed to me. And as I am but one body naturally considered, though by His permission a body politic to govern, so I shall desire you all, my lords (chiefly you of the nobility, everyone in his degree and power), to be assistant to me, that I with my ruling and you with your service may make a good account to almighty God and leave some comfort to our posterity in earth. I mean to direct all my actions by good advice and counsel. And therefore, considering that divers of you be of the ancient nobility, having your beginnings and estates of my progenitors, kings of this realm, and thereby ought in honor to have the more natural care for maintaining of my estate and this commonwealth; some others have been of long experience in governance and enabled by my father of noble memory, my brother, and my late sister to bear office; the rest of you being upon special trust lately called to her service only and trust, for your service considered and rewarded; my meaning is to require of you all nothing more but faithful hearts in such service as from time to time shall be in your powers towards the preservation of me and this commonwealth. And for counsel and advice I shall accept you of my nobility, and such others of you the rest as in consultation I shall think meet and shortly appoint, to the which also, with their advice, I will join to their aid, and for ease of their burden, others meet for my service. And they which I shall not appoint, let them not think the same for any disability in them, but for that I do consider a multitude doth make rather discord and confusion than good counsel. And of my goodwill you shall not doubt, using yourselves as appertaineth to good and loving subjects.

## Golden Speech

Mr. Speaker, we have heard your declaration and perceive your care of our estate by falling into the consideration of a grateful acknowledgment of such benefits as you have received, and that your coming is to present thanks unto us, which I accept with no less joy than your loves can have desire to offer such a present. I do assure you there is no prince that loveth his subjects better, or whose love can countervail our love. There is no jewel, be it of never so rich a price, which I set before this jewel—I mean your loves. For I do more esteem it than any treasure or riches, for that we know how to prize. But love and thanks I count unvaluable, and though God hath raised me high, yet this I count the glory of my crown: that I have reigned with your loves. This makes me that I do not so much rejoice that God hath made me to be a queen, as to be a queen over so thankful a people. Therefore I have cause to wish nothing more than to content the subjects, and that is a duty which I owe. Neither do I desire to live longer days than that I may see your prosperity, and that is my only desire. And as I am that person which still yet under God hath delivered you, so I trust by the almighty power of God that I shall be His instrument to preserve you from envy, peril, dishonor, shame, tyranny, and oppression, partly by means of your intended helps, which we take very acceptable because it manifesteth the largeness of your loves and loyalties unto your sovereign. Of myself I must say this: I never was any greedy, scraping grasper, nor a strait, fast-holding prince, nor yet a waster. My heart was never set on worldly goods, but only for my subjects' good. What you bestow on me, I will not hoard it up, but receive it to bestow on you again. Yea, my own properties I account yours to be expended for your good, and your eyes shall see the bestowing of all for your good. Therefore render unto them from me, I beseech you, Mr. Speaker, such thanks as you imagine my heart yieldeth but my tongue cannot express.

. . . Mr. Speaker, you give me thanks, but I doubt me that I have more cause to thank you all than you me; and I charge you to thank them of the Lower House from me. For had I not received a knowledge from you, I might have fallen into the lapse of an error only for lack of true information. Since I was queen yet did I never put my pen to any grant but that upon pretext and semblance made unto me, it was both good and beneficial to the subject in general, though a private profit to some of my ancient servants who had deserved well. But the contrary being found by experience, I am exceedingly beholding to such subjects as would move the same at the first. And I am not so simple to suppose but that there be some of the Lower House whom these grievances never touched; and for them I think they speak out of zeal to their countries and not out of spleen or malevolent affection, as being parties grieved. And I take it exceedingly gratefully from them, because it gives us to know that no respects or interests had moved them other than the minds they bear to suffer no diminution of our honor and our subjects' love unto us, the zeal of which affection tending to ease my people and knit their hearts unto me, I embrace with a princely care. For above all earthly treasures I esteem my people's love, more than which I desire not to merit. That my grants should be grievous unto my people and oppressions to be privileged under color of our patents, our kingly dignity shall not suffer it. Yea, when I heard it I could give no rest unto my thoughts until I had reformed it. Shall they (think you) escape unpunished that have thus oppressed you, and have been respectless of their duty and regardless of our honor? No, no, Mr. Speaker, I assure you, were it not more for conscience' sake than for any glory or increase of love that I desire, these errors, troubles, vexations, and oppressions done by these varlets and low persons (not worthy the name of subjects) should not escape without condign punishment.

But I perceive they dealt with me like physicians who, ministering a drug, make it more acceptable by giving it a good aromatical savor; or when they give pills, do gild them all over. I have ever used to set the Last Judgment Day before my eyes and so to rule as I shall be judged, to answer before a higher Judge. To whose judgment seat I do appeal that never thought was cherished in my heart that tended not unto my people's good. And now if my kingly bounties have been abused and my grants turned to the hurts of my people, contrary to my will and meaning, or if any in authority under me have neglected or perverted what I have committed to them, I hope God will not lay their culps and offenses to my charge. Who, though there were danger in repealing our grants, yet what danger would I not rather incur for your good than I would suffer them still to continue? I know the title of a king is a glorious title, but assure yourself that the shining glory of princely authority hath not so dazzled the eyes of our understanding but that we well know and remember that we also are to yield an account of our actions before the great Judge.

To be a king and wear a crown is a thing more glorious to them that see it than it is pleasant to them that bear it. For myself, I was never so much enticed with the glorious name of a king or royal authority of a queen as delighted that God hath made me His instrument to maintain His truth and glory, and to defend this kingdom (as I said) from peril, dishonor, tyranny, and oppression. There will never queen sit in my seat with more zeal to my country, care to my subjects, and that will sooner with willingness venture her life for your good and safety, than myself. For it is not my desire to live nor reign longer than my life and reign shall be for your good. And though you have had and may have many princes more mighty and wise sitting in this seat, yet you never had or shall have any that will be more careful and loving. Shall I ascribe anything to myself and my sexly weakness? I were not worthy to live then, and of all most unworthy of the mercies I have had from God, who hath ever yet given me a heart which yet never feared any foreign or home enemy. I speak it to give God the praise as a testimony before you, and not to attribute anything unto myself. For I, O Lord, what am I, whom practices and perils past should not fear? Or what can I do that I should speak for any glory? God forbid. This, Mr. Speaker, I pray you deliver unto the House, to whom heartily recommend me, and so I commit you all to your best fortunes and further counsels; and I pray you, Mr. Comptroller, Mr. Secretary, and you of my Council, that before these gentlemen depart into their countries, you bring them all to kiss my hand.

# Galileo Galilei

## *from* THE STARRY MESSENGER (1610)

*Galileo Galilei (1564–1642), son of a musician, studied philosophy and mathematics and became professor at Pisa and then Padua. His scientific research led to foundational discoveries in astronomy and physics. His early experiments are legendary: he was said to have demonstrated the laws of motion by dropping bodies of different weights from the leaning tower of Pisa. After hearing of a new instrument for seeing distant objects, he experimented with grinding lenses himself until he had designed a telescope capable of furthering astronomical study. With its aid he discovered sunspots and the moons of Jupiter and demonstrated that the moon's light is reflected and its surface mountainous. For these and other discoveries and his public accounts of them, Galileo was appointed professor at the University of Florence and denounced as a heretic. His discoveries provided compelling support of the Copernican theory of the universe, of which Galileo became an open advocate. After years of ecclesiastical conflict over his scientific work, Galileo was ordered to stand trial before the Inquisition in 1633. At the trial he was forced to capitulate and sentenced to permanent house arrest. This selection comes from Galileo's first publication describing his observations.*

Great indeed are the things which in this brief treatise I propose for observation and consideration by all students of nature. I say great, because of the excellence of the subject itself, the entirely unexpected and novel character of these things, and finally because of the instrument by means of which they have been revealed to our senses.

Surely it is a great thing to increase the numerous host of fixed stars previously visible to the unaided vision, adding countless more which have never before been seen, exposing these plainly to the eye in numbers ten times exceeding the old and familiar stars.

It is a very beautiful thing, and most gratifying to the sight, to behold the body of the moon, distant from us almost sixty earthly radii, as if it were no farther away than two such measures—so that its diameter appears almost thirty times larger, its surface nearly nine hundred times, and its volume twenty-seven thousand times as large as when viewed with the naked eye. In this way one may learn with all the certainty of sense evidence that the moon is not robed in a smooth and polished surface but is in fact rough and uneven, covered everywhere, just like the earth's surface, with huge prominences, deep valleys, and chasms.

Again, it seems to me a matter of no small importance to have ended the dispute about the Milky Way by making its nature manifest to the very senses as well as to the intellect. Similarly it will be a pleasant and elegant thing to demonstrate that the nature of those stars which astronomers have previously called "nebulous" is far different from what has been believed hitherto. But what surpasses all wonders by far, and what particularly moves us to seek the attention of all astronomers and philosophers, is the discovery of four wandering stars not known or observed by any man before us. Like Venus and Mercury, which have their own periods about the sun, these have theirs about a certain star that is conspicuous among those already known, which they sometimes precede and sometimes follow, without ever departing from it beyond certain limits. All these facts were discovered and observed by me not many days ago with the aid of a spyglass which I devised, after first being illuminated by divine grace. . . .

About ten months ago a report reached my ears that a certain Fleming had constructed a spyglass by means of which visible objects, though very distant from the eye of the observer, were distinctly seen as if nearby. Of this truly remarkable effect several experiences were related, to which some persons gave credence while others denied them. A few days later the report was confirmed to me in a letter from a noble Frenchman at Paris, Jacques Badovere, which caused me to apply myself wholeheartedly to inquire into the means by which I might arrive at the invention of a similar instrument. This I did shortly afterwards, my basis being the theory of refraction. First I prepared a tube of lead, at the ends of which I fitted two glass lenses, both plane on one side while on the other side one was spherically convex and the other concave. Then placing my eye near the concave lens I perceived objects satisfactorily large and near, for they appeared three times closer and nine times larger than when seen with the naked eye alone. Next I constructed another one, more accurate, which represented objects as enlarged more than sixty times. Finally, sparing neither labor nor expense, I succeeded in constructing for myself so excellent an instrument that objects seen by means of it appeared nearly one thousand times larger and over thirty times closer than when regarded with our natural vision.

It would be superfluous to enumerate the number and importance of the advantages of such an instrument at sea as well as on land, But forsaking terrestrial observations, I turned to celestial ones, and first I saw the moon from as near at hand as if it were scarcely two terrestrial radii away. After that I observed often with wondering delight both the planets and the fixed stars, and since I saw these latter to be very crowded, I began to seek (and eventually found) a method by which I might measure their distances apart.

•

Now let us review the observations made during the past two months, once more inviting the attention of all who are eager for true philosophy to the first steps of such important contemplations. Let us speak first of that surface of the moon which faces us. For greater clarity I distinguish two parts of this surface, a lighter and a darker; the lighter part seems to surround and to pervade the whole hemisphere, while the darker part discolors the moon's surface like a kind of cloud, and makes it appear covered with spots. Now those spots which are fairly dark and rather large are plain to everyone and have been seen throughout the ages; these I shall call the "large" or "ancient" spots, distinguishing them from others that are smaller in size but so numerous as to occur all over the lunar surface, and especially the lighter part. The latter spots had never been seen by anyone before me. From observations of these spots repeated many times I have been led to the opinion and conviction that the surface of the moon is not smooth, uniform, and precisely spherical as a great number of philosophers believe it (and the other heavenly bodies) to be, but is uneven, rough, and full of cavities and prominences, being not unlike the face of the earth, relieved by chains of mountains and deep valleys.

•

There is another thing which I must not omit, for I beheld it not without a certain wonder; this is that almost in the center of the moon there is a cavity larger than all the rest, and perfectly round in shape. I have observed it near both first and last quarters, and have tried to represent it as correctly as possible in the second of the above figures. As to light and shade, it offers the same appearance as would a region like Bohemia if that were enclosed on all sides by very lofty mountains arranged exactly in a circle. Indeed, this area on the moon is surrounded by such enormous peaks that the bounding edge adjacent to the dark portion of the moon is seen to be bathed in sunlight before the boundary of light and shadow reaches halfway across the same space. As in other spots, its shaded portion faces the sun while its lighted part is toward the dark side of the moon; and for a third time I draw attention to this as a very cogent proof of the ruggedness and unevenness that pervades all the bright region of the moon. Of these spots, moreover, those are always darkest which touch the boundary line between light and shadow, while those farther off appear both smaller and less dark, so that when the moon ultimately becomes full (at opposition to the sun), the shade of the cavities is distinguished from the light of the places in relief by a subdued and very tenuous separation.

•

But here I foresee that many persons will be assailed by uncertainty and drawn into a grave difficulty, feeling constrained to doubt a conclusion already explained and confirmed by many phenomena. If that part of the lunar surface which reflects sunlight more brightly is full of chasms (that is, of countless prominences and hollows), why is it that the western edge of the waxing moon, the eastern edge of the waning moon, and the entire periphery of the full moon are not seen to be uneven, rough, and wavy? On the contrary they look as precisely round as if they were drawn with a compass; and yet the whole periphery consists of that brighter lunar substance which we have declared to be filled with heights and chasms. In fact not a single one of the great spots extends to the extreme periphery of the moon, but all are grouped together at a distance from the edge.

Now let me explain the twofold reason for this troublesome fact, and in turn give a double solution to the difficulty. In the first place, if the protuberances and cavities in the lunar body existed only along the extreme edge of the circular periphery bounding the visible hemisphere, the moon might (indeed, would necessarily) look to us almost like a toothed wheel, terminated by a warty or wavy edge. Imagine, however, that there is not a single series of prominences arranged only along the very circumference, but a great many ranges of mountains together with their valleys and canyons disposed in ranks near the edge of the moon, and not only in the hemisphere visible to us but everywhere near the boundary line of the two hemispheres. Then an eye viewing them from afar will not be able to detect the separation of prominences by cavities, because the intervals between the mountains located in a given circle or a given chain will be hidden by the interposition of other heights situated in yet other ranges. This will be especially true if the eye of the observer is placed in the same straight line with the summits of these elevations. Thus on earth the summits of several mountains close together appear to be situated in one plane if the spectator is a long way off and is placed at an equal elevation. Similarly in a rough sea the tops of the waves seem to lie in one plane, though between one high crest and another there are many gulfs and chasms of such depth as not only to hide the hulls but even the bulwarks, masts, and rigging of stately ships. Now since there are many chains of mountains and chasms on the moon in addition to those around its periphery, and since the eye, regarding these from a great distance, lies nearly in the plane of their summits, no one need wonder that they appear as arranged in a regular and unbroken line.

To the above explanation another may be added; namely, that there exists around the body of the moon, just as around the earth, a globe of some substance denser than the rest of the aether. This may serve to receive and reflect the sun's radiations without being sufficiently opaque to prevent our seeing through it, especially when it is not illuminated. Such a globe, lighted by the sun's rays, makes the body of the moon appear larger than it really is, and if it were thicker it would be able to prevent our seeing the actual body of the moon. And it actually is thicker near the circumference of the moon; I do not mean in an absolute sense, but relatively to the rays of our vision, which cut it obliquely there. Thus it may obstruct our vision, especially when it is lighted, and cloak the lunar periphery that is exposed to the sun.

—*trans. Stillman Drake*

# Francis Bacon

# *from* NOVUM ORGANUM (1620)

*The Englishman Francis Bacon (1561–1626) combined the dual role of statesman and philosopher. As a statesman, Bacon was a leading government official during the reign of James I: he was solicitor general, attorney general, privy counsellor, Lord Keeper, and Lord Chancellor. He was also convicted of accepting bribes from office suitors and was fined, imprisoned, and banished from Parliament and the court. As a thinker, he is best known as one of the major forces in developing the inductive method in the sciences, the view that scientific understanding can only come from careful and ongoing observation of specific occurrences. Bacon discusses this idea in the "New Organon," a series of aphorisms which were part of a larger work,* Great Renewal. *Bacon saw* Great Renewal *as representing a "total reconstruction of the sciences, arts, and all human knowledge."*

## APHORISMS CONCERNING THE INTERPRETATION OF NATURE AND THE KINGDOM OF MAN

I. Man, being the servant and interpreter of Nature, can do and understand so much and so much only as he has observed in fact or in thought in the course of nature: beyond this he neither knows anything nor can do anything.

II. Neither the naked hand nor the understanding left to itself can effect much. It is by instruments and helps that the work is done, which are as much wanted for the understanding as for the hand. And as the instruments of the hand either give motion or guide it, so the instruments of the mind supply either suggestions for the understanding or cautions.

III. Human knowledge and human power meet in one; for where the cause is not known the effect cannot be produced. Nature to be commanded must be obeyed; and that which in contemplation is as the cause is in operation as the rule.

IV. Towards the effecting of works, all that man can do is to put together or put asunder natural bodies. The rest is done by nature working within.

VI. It would be an unsound fancy and self-contradictory to expect that things which have never yet been done can be done except by means which have never yet been tried.

XI. As the sciences which we now have do not help us in finding out new works, so neither does the logic which we now have help us in finding out new sciences.

XII. The logic now in use serves rather to fix and give stability to the errors which have their foundations in commonly received notions than to help the search after truth. So it does more harm than good.

XVIII. The discoveries which have hitherto been made in the sciences are such as lie close to vulgar notions, scarcely beneath the surface. In order to penetrate into the inner and further recesses of nature, it is necessary that both notions and axioms be derived from things by a more sure and guarded way; and that a method of intellectual operation be introduced altogether better and more certain.

XIX. There are and can be only two ways of searching into and discovering truth. The one flies from the senses and particulars to the most general axioms, and from these principles, the truth of which it takes for settled and immovable, proceeds to judgment and to the discovery of the middle axioms. And this way is now in fashion. The other derives axioms from the senses and particulars, rising by a gradual and unbroken ascent, so that it arrives at the most general axioms last of all. This is the true way, but as yet untried.

XXII. Both ways set out from the senses and particulars, and rest in the highest generalities; but the difference between them is infinite. For the one just glances at experiment and particulars in passing, the other dwells duly and orderly among them. The one, again, begins at once by establishing certain abstract and useless generalities, the other rises by gradual steps to that which is prior and better known in the order of nature.

XXXI. It is idle to expect any great advancement in science from the superinducing and engrafting of new things upon old. We must begin anew from the very foundations, unless we would revolve forever in a circle with mean and contemptible progress.

XXXV. It was said by Borgia of the expedition of the French into Italy, that they came with chalk in their hands to mark out their lodgings, not with arms to force their way in. I in like manner would have my doctrine enter quietly into the minds that are fit and capable of receiving it; for confutations cannot be employed, when the difference is upon first principles and very notions and even upon forms of demonstration.

XXXVI. One method of delivery alone remains to us; which is simply this: we must lead men to the particulars themselves, and their series and order; while men on their side must force themselves for awhile to lay their notions by and begin to familiarize themselves with facts.

XXXVII. The doctrine of those who have denied that certainty could be attained at all, has some agreement with my way of proceeding at the first setting out; but they end in being infinitely separated and opposed. For the holders of that doctrine assert simply that nothing can be known; I also assert that not much can be known in nature by the way which is now in use. But then they go on to destroy the authority of the senses and understanding; whereas I proceed to devise and supply helps for the same.

XXXVIII. The idols and false notions which are now in possession of the human understanding, and have taken deep root therein, not only so beset men's minds that truth can hardly find entrance, but even after entrance is obtained, they will again in the very instauration of the science meet and trouble us, unless men being fore-warned of the danger fortify themselves as far as may be against their assaults.

XXXIX. There are four classes of Idols which beset men's minds. To these for dis-tinction's sake I have assigned names, calling the first class *Idols of the Tribe;* the sec-ond, *Idols of the Cave;* the third, *Idols of the Marketplace;* the fourth, *Idols of the Theatre.*

XL. The formation of ideas and axioms by true induction is no doubt the proper remedy to be applied for the keeping off and clearing away of idols. To point them out, however, is of great use; for the doctrine of Idols is to the Interpretation of Nature what the doctrine of the refutation of Sophisms is to common Logic.

XLI. The Idols of the Tribe have their foundation in human nature itself, and in the tribe or race of men. For it is a false assertion that the sense of man is the measure of things. On the contrary, all perceptions as well of the sense as of the mind are according to the measure of the universe. And the human understanding is like a false mirror, which, receiving rays irregularly, distorts and discolours the nature of things by mingling its own nature with it.

XLII. The Idols of the Cave are the idols of the individual man. For every one (besides the errors common to human nature in general) has a cave or den of his own, which refracts and discolors the light of nature; owing either to his own proper and peculiar nature; or to his education and conversation with others; or to the reading of books, and the authority of those whom he esteems and admires; or to the differences of impressions, accordingly as they take place in a mind preoccupied and predisposed or in a mind indifferent and settled; or the like. So that the spirit of man (according as it is meted out to different individuals) is in fact a thing variable and full of perturbation, and governed as it were by chance. Whence it was observed by Heraclitus that men look for sciences in their own lesser worlds, and not in the greater or common world.

XLIII. There are also Idols formed by the intercourse and association of men with each other, which I call Idols of the Marketplace, on account of the commerce and consort of men there. For it is by discourse that men associate; and words are imposed according to the apprehension of the vulgar. And therefore the ill and unfit choice of words wonderfully obstructs the understanding. Nor do the definitions or explanations wherewith in some things learned men are wont to guard and defend themselves, by any means set the matter right. But words plainly force and overrule the understanding, and throw all into confusion, and lead men away into numberless empty controversies and idle fancies.

XLIV. Lastly, there are Idols which have immigrated into men's minds from the various dogmas of philosophies, and also from wrong laws of demonstration. These I call Idols of the Theatre; because in my judgment all the received systems are but so many stage-plays, representing worlds of their own creation after an unreal and scenic fashion. Nor is it only of the systems now in vogue, or only of the ancient sects and philosophies, that I speak; for many more plays of the same kind may yet be com-posed and in like artificial manner set forth; seeing that errors the most widely differ-ent have nevertheless causes for the most part alike. Neither again do I mean this only of entire systems, but also of many principles and axioms in science, which by tradi-tion, credulity, and negligence have come to be received.

*—trans. J. Spedding*

# Gerrard Winstanley and others

## from A DECLARATION FROM THE POOR OPPRESSED PEOPLE OF ENGLAND (1649)

*The English Civil War (1640–1660) produced a civil war between Parliament and the Crown, the trial and execution of Charles I, and the protectorate of Oliver Cromwell (the only time in English history when there was no monarch). For some, it was a time when the world was turned upside down. If any group embodied this feeling of inversion, it was the Diggers, who in 1649–50 cultivated common land south of London in defiance of the principle of private property, which they held to be in violation of God's laws. Their leader was Gerrard Winstanley (1609–1660), a cloth merchant, who continued, following the dispersal of the Digger's colony, to represent their communist ideas two hundred years before Marx. In the selection below, Winstanley argues that the legal claims of the nobility were based on murder and theft and that the meek should inherit the earth. "For the earth . . . was made to be a common storehouse of livelihood to all mankind, friend and foe, without exception."*

We whose names are subscribed do in the name of all the poor oppressed people in England declare unto you that call yourselves lords of manors and lords of the land that in regard the King of righteousness, our maker, hath enlightened our hearts so far as to see that the earth was not made purposely for you to be lords of it, and we to be your slaves, servants and beggars; but it was made to be a common livelihood to all, without respect of persons: and that your buying and selling of land and the fruits of it, one to another, is the cursed thing, and was brought in by war; which hath and still does establish murder and theft in the hands of some branches of mankind over others, which is the greatest outward burden and unrighteous power that the creation groans under. For the power of enclosing land and owning property was brought into the creation by your ancestors by the sword; which first did murder their fellow-creatures, men, and after plunder or steal away their land, and left this land successively to you, their children. And therefore, though you did not kill or thieve, yet you hold that cursed thing in your hand by the power of the sword; and so you justify the wicked deeds of your fathers; and that sin of your fathers shall be visited upon the head of you and your children, to the third and fourth generation, and longer too, till your bloody and thieving power be rooted out of the land.

And further, in regard the King of righteousness hath made us sensible of our burdens, and the cries of groanings of our hearts are come before him: we take it as a testimony of love from him, that our hearts begin to be freed from slavish fear of men, such as you are; and that we find resolutions in us, grounded upon the inward law of love one towards another, to dig and plough up the commons and waste lands through England; and that our conversation shall be so unblameable that your laws shall not reach to oppress us any longer, unless you by your laws will shed the innocent blood that runs in our veins.

For though you and your ancestors got your property by murder and theft, and you keep it by the same power from us that have an equal right to the land with you by the righteous law of creation, yet we shall have no occasion of quarreling (as you do) about that disturbing devil, called particular property. For the earth, with all her fruits of corn, cattle and such like, was made to be a common storehouse of livelihood to all mankind, friend and foe, without exception.

And to prevent all your scrupulous objections, know this, that we must neither buy nor sell; money must not any longer (after our work of the earth's community is advanced) be the great god that hedges in some, and hedges out others. For money is but part of the earth: and surely, the righteous creator, who is King, did never ordain that unless some of the mankind do bring that mineral (silver and gold) in their hands to others of their own kind, that they should neither be fed, nor be clothed. No surely, for this was the project of tyrant-flesh (which landlords are branches of) to set his image upon money. And they make this unrighteous law, that none should buy or sell, eat or be clothed or have any comfortable livelihood among men, unless they did bring his image stamped upon gold or silver in their hands.

•

For after our work of the earthly community is advanced, we must make use of gold and silver, as we do of other metals, but not to buy and sell withal; for buying and selling is the great cheat that robs and steals the earth one from another. It is that which makes some lords, others beggars, some rulers, others to be ruled; and makes great murderers and thieves to be imprisoners and hangers of little ones, or of sincere-hearted men.

And while we are made to labour the earth together, with one consent and willing mind; and while we are made free that every one, friend and foe, shall enjoy the benefit of their creation, that is, to have food and raiment from the earth, their mother; and every one subject to give account of his thoughts, words and actions to none, but to the one only righteous judge and Prince of Peace; the spirit of righteousness that dwells, and that is now rising up to rule in, every creature and in the whole globe. We say, while we are made to hinder no man of his privileges given him in his creation, equal to one as to another; what law then can you make to take hold upon us, but laws of oppression and tyranny, that shall enslave or spill the blood of the innocent? And so yourselves, your judges, lawyers and justices, shall be found to be the greatest transgressors in and over mankind.

But to draw nearer to declare our meaning, what we would have and what we shall endeavour to the uttermost to obtain, as moderate and righteous reason directs us; seeing we are made to see our privileges, given us in our creation, which have hitherto been denied to us and our fathers since the power of the sword began to rule and the secrets of the creation have been locked up under the traditional, parrot-like speaking from the universities and colleges for scholars, and since the power of the murdering and thieving sword, formerly as well as now of late years, hath set up a government and maintains that government; for what are prisons, and putting others to death, but the power of the sword to enforce people to that government which was got by conquest and sword and cannot stand of itself, but by the same murdering power? That government, that is got over people by the sword and kept by the sword, is not set up by the King of righteousness to be his law, but by covetousness, the great god of the world; who hath been permitted to reign for a time, times and dividing of time, and his government draws to the period of the last term of his allotted time. And then the nations shall see the glory of that government that shall rule in righteousness, without either sword or spear;

And seeing further the power of righteousness in our hearts, seeking the livelihood of others as well as ourselves, hath drawn forth our bodies to begin to dig and plough in the commons and waste land for the reasons already declared;

And seeing and finding ourselves poor, wanting food to feed upon while we labour the earth to cast in seed and to wait till the first crop comes up; and wanting ploughs, carts, corn and such materials to plant the commons withal, we are willing to declare our condition to you, and to all that have the treasury of the earth locked up in your bags, chests and barns, and will offer up nothing to this public treasury; but will rather see your fellow-creatures starve for want of bread, that have an equal right to it with yourselves by the law of creation. But this by the way we only declare to you and to all that follow the subtle art of buying and selling the earth with her fruits, merely to get the treasury thereof into their hands, to lock it up from them to whom it belongs; that so such covetous, proud, unrighteous, selfish flesh may be left without excuse in the day of judgment.

And therefore the main thing we aim at, and for which we declare our resolutions to go forth and act, is this: to lay hold upon, and as we stand in need to cut and fell and make the best advantage we can of the woods and trees that grow upon the commons, to be a stock for ourselves and our poor brethren, through the land of England, to plant the commons withal; and to provide us bread to eat, till the fruit of our labours in the earth bring forth increase. And we shall meddle with none of your properties (but what is called commonage) till the spirit in you make you cast up your lands and goods, which were got and still is kept in your hands by murder and theft; and then we shall take it from the spirit that hath conquered you, and not from our swords, which is an abominable and unrighteous power, and a destroyer of the creation. But the Son of Man comes not to destroy, but to save.

And we are moved to send forth this declaration abroad, to give notice to every one whom it concerns, in regard we hear and see that some of you, that have been lords of manors, do cause the trees and woods that grow upon the commons, which you pretend a royalty unto, to be cut down and sold for your own private use; whereby the common land, which your own mouths do say belongs to the poor, is impoverished, and the poor oppressed people robbed of their rights; while you give them cheating words by telling some of our poor oppressed brethren that those of us that have begun to dig and plough up the commons will hinder the poor; and so blind their eyes, that they see not their privilege, while you and the rich freeholders make the most profit of the commons, by your over-stocking of them with sheep and cattle; and the poor that have the name to own the commons have the least share therein. Nay, they are checked by you if they cut wood, heath, turf or furzes in places about the common where you disallow.

Therefore we are resolved to be cheated no longer, nor be held under the slavish fear of you no longer, seeing the earth was made for us as well as for you. And if the common land belongs to us who are the poor oppressed, surely the woods that grow upon the commons belong to us likewise? Therefore we are resolved to try the uttermost in the light of reason to know whether we shall be free men or slaves. If we lie still and let you steal away our birthrights, we perish; and if we petition we perish also, though we have paid taxes, given free-quarter and ventured our lives to preserve the nation's freedom as much as you, and therefore by the law of contract with you, freedom in the land is our portion as well as yours, equal with you. And if we strive for freedom, and your murdering, governing laws destroy us, we can but perish.

Therefore we require and we resolve to take both common land and common words to be a livelihood for us, and look upon you as equal with us, not above us, knowing very well that England, the land of our nativity, is to be a common treasury of livelihood to all, without respect of persons.

•

For we say our purpose is to take those common woods to sell them, now at first to be a stock for ourselves, and our children after us, to plant and manure the common land withal. For we shall endeavour by our righteous acting not to leave the earth any longer entangled unto our children by self-seeking proprietors; but to leave it a free store-house and common treasury to all, without respect of persons. And this we count is our duty, to endeavour to the uttermost, every man in his place (according to the National Covenant which the Parliament set forth)* a reformation, to preserve the people's liberties, one as well as another: as well those as have paid taxes and given free-quarter, as those that have either borne the sword or taken our monies to dispose of them for public use. For if the reformation must be according to the Word of God, then every one is to have the benefit and freedom of his creation, without respect of persons. We count this our duty, we say, to endeavour to the uttermost, and so shall leave those that rise up to oppose us without excuse in their day of judgment; and our precious blood, we hope, shall not be dear to us, to be willingly laid down at the door of a prison, or foot of a gallows, to justify this righteous cause, if those that have taken our money from us, and promised to give us freedom for it, should turn tyrants against us: for we must not fight, but suffer.

•

And we hope we may not doubt (at least we expect) that they that are called the great council and powers of England, who so often have declared themselves, by promises and covenants, and confirmed them by multitude of fasting days and devout protestations to make England a free people, upon condition they would pay monies and adventure their lives against the successor of the Norman conqueror, under whose oppressing power England was enslaved: and we look upon that freedom promised to be the inheritance of all, without respect of persons. And this cannot be, unless the land of England be freely set at liberty from proprietors, and

*The Solemn League and Covenant was adopted by Parliament on 25 September 1643.

become a common treasury to all her children, as every portion of the land of Canaan was the common livelihood of such and such a tribe, and of every member in that tribe, without exception, neither hedging in any, nor hedging out.

•

And thus in love we have declared the purpose of our hearts plainly, without flattery, expecting love and the same sincerity from you, without grumbling or quarrelling, being creatures of your own image and mould, intending no other matter herein but to observe the law of righteous action, endeavouring to shut out of the creation the cursed thing, called particular property, which is the cause of all wars, bloodshed, theft and enslaving laws, that hold the people under misery.

Signed for and in the behalf of all the poor oppressed people of England and the whole world.

[Forty-five signatures]

# Thomas Hobbes

## *from* LEVIATHAN (1651)

*A thinker who bridges the two worlds of the Reformation and the Scientific Revolution is Thomas Hobbes (1588–1679), one of the first modern political philosophers and one of the founders of the emerging field of political science. Hobbes embraced the scientific method and was an admirer of approaches drawn from pure mathematics. In his major work,* Leviathan, *Hobbes's political vision—an argument for the necessity of a strong ruler and state—was shaped by his living through the seventeenth-century English Civil War, an event whose origins are in part attributable to the Reformation in England a hundred years before. Because of his aristocratic associations, Hobbes was forced to flee England and live in Paris, where he tutored the exiled, future king of England, Charles II, in mathematics. Hobbes's experience of decades of violence and bloodshed helped shape his ideas about the proper role of government and the state.*

### THE INTRODUCTION

Nature, the art whereby God hath made and governs the world, is by the *art* of man, as in many other things, so in this also imitated, that it can make an artificial animal. For seeing life is but a motion of limbs, the beginning whereof is in some principal part within; why may we not say that all *automata* (engines that move themselves by springs and wheels as doth a watch) have an artificial life? For what is the *heart,* but a *spring;* and the *nerves,* but so many *strings;* and the *joints,* but so many *wheels,* giving motion to the whole body, such as was intended by the artificer? *Art* goes yet further, imitating that rational and most excellent work of Nature, *man.* For by art is created that great LEVIATHAN called a COMMONWEALTH, or STATE, in Latin, CIVITAS, which is but an artificial man, though of greater stature and strength than the natural, for whose protection and defence it was intended; and in which the *sovereignty* is an artificial *soul,* as giving life and motion to the whole body; the *magistrates* and other *officers* of judicature and execution, artificial *joints; reward* and *punishment,* by which fastened to the seat of the sovereignty every joint and member is moved to perform his duty, are the *nerves,* that do the same in the body natural; the *wealth* and *riches* of all the particular members are the *strength; salus populi,* the *people's safety,* its *business; counsellors,* by whom all things needful for it to know are suggested unto it, are the *memory; equity,* and *laws,* an artificial *reason* and *will; concord, health; sedition, sickness;* and *civil war, death.* Lastly, the *pacts* and *covenants,* by which the parts of this body politic were at first made, set together, and united, resemble that *fiat,* or the *let us make man,* pronounced by God in creation.

# CHAPTER XIII

## *Of the Natural Condition of Mankind as Concerning Their Felicity, and Misery*

Nature hath made men so equal in the faculties of the body, and mind; as that though there be found one man sometimes manifestly stronger in body, or of quicker mind than another; yet when all is reckoned together, the difference between man, and man, is not so considerable, as that one man can thereupon claim to himself any benefit, to which another may not pretend, as well as he. For as to the strength of body, the weakest has strength enough to kill the strongest, either by secret machination, or by confederacy with others, that are in the same danger with himself.

And as to the faculties of the mind, setting aside the arts grounded upon words, and especially that skill of proceeding upon general, and infallible rules, called science; which very few have, and but in few things; as being not a native faculty, born with us; nor attained, as prudence, while we look after somewhat else, I find yet a greater equality amongst men, than that of strength. For prudence, is but experience; which equal time, equally bestows on all men, in those things they equally apply themselves unto. That which may perhaps make such equality incredible, is but a vain conceit of one's own wisdom, which almost all men think they have in a greater degree, than the vulgar; that is, than all men but themselves, and a few others, whom by fame, or for concurring with themselves, they approve. For such is the nature of men, that howsoever they may acknowledge many others to be more witty, or more eloquent, or more learned; yet they will hardly believe there be many so wise as themselves; for they see their own wit at hand, and other men's at a distance. But this proveth rather that men are in that point equal, than unequal. For there is not ordinarily a greater sign of the equal distribution of any thing, than that every man is contented with his share.

From this equality of ability, ariseth equality of hope in the attaining of our ends. And therefore if any two men desire the same thing, which nevertheless they cannot both enjoy, they become enemies; and in the way to their end, which is principally their own conservation, and sometimes their delectation only, endeavour to destroy or subdue one another. And from hence it comes to pass, that where an invader hath no more to fear; than another man's single power; if one plant, sow, build, and possess a convenient seat, others may probably be expected to come prepared with forces united, to dispossess, and deprive him, not only of the fruit of his labour, but also of his life, or liberty. And the invader again is in the like danger of another.

And from this diffidence of one another, there is no way for any man to secure himself, so reasonable, as anticipation; that is, by force, or wiles, to master the persons of all men he can, so long, till he see no other power great enough to endanger him; and this is no more than his own conservation requireth, and is generally allowed. Also because there be some, that taking pleasure in contemplating their own power in the acts of conquest, which they pursue farther than their security requires; if others, that otherwise would be glad to be at ease within modest bounds, should not by invasion increase their power, they would not be able, long time, by standing only on their defence, to subsist. And by consequence, such augmentation of dominion over men being necessary to a man's conservation, it ought to be allowed him.

Again, men have no pleasure, but on the contrary a great deal of grief, in keeping company, where there is no power able to over-awe them all. For every man looketh that his companion should value him, at the same rate he sets upon himself: and upon all signs of contempt, or undervaluing, naturally endeavours, as far as he dares (which amongst them that have no common power to keep them in quiet, is far enough to make them destroy each other), to extort a greater value from his contemners, by damage; and from others, by the example.

So that in the nature of man, we find three principal causes of quarrel. First, competition; secondly, diffidence; thirdly, glory.

The first, maketh men invade for gain; the second, for safety; and the third, for reputation. The first use violence, to make themselves masters of other men's persons, wives, children, and cattle; the second, to defend them; the third, for trifles, as a word, a smile, a different opinion, and any other sign of undervalue, either direct in their persons, or by reflection in their kindred, their friends, their nation, their profession, or their name.

Hereby, it is manifest, that during the time men live without a common power to keep them all in awe, they are in that condition which is called war; and such a war, as is of every man, against every man. For WAR, consisteth not in battle only, or the act of fighting; but in a tract of time, wherein the will to contend by battle is sufficiently known; and therefore the notion of *time,* is to be considered in the nature of war; as it is in the nature of weather. For as the nature of foul weather, lieth not in a shower or two of rain; but in an inclination thereto of many days together; so the nature of war, consisteth not in actual fighting; but in the known disposition thereto, during all the time there is no assurance to the contrary. All other time is PEACE.

Whatsoever therefore is consequent to a time of war, where every man is enemy to every man; the same is consequent to the time, wherein men live without other security, than what their own strength, and their own invention shall furnish them withal. In such condition, there is no place for industry; because the fruit thereof is uncertain; and consequently no culture of the earth; no navigation, nor use of the commodities that may be imported by sea; no commodious building; no instruments of moving, and removing, such things as require much force; no knowledge of the face of the earth; no account of time; no arts; no letters; no society; and which is worst of all, continual fear, and danger of violent death; and the life of man, solitary, poor, nasty, brutish, and short.

It may seem strange to some man, that has not well weighed these things; that Nature should thus dissociate, and render men apt to invade, and destroy one another; and he may therefore, not trusting to this inference, made from the passions, desire perhaps to have the same confirmed by experience. Let him therefore consider with himself, when taking a journey, he arms himself, and seeks to go well accompanied; when going to sleep, he locks his doors; when even in his house he locks his chests; and this when he knows there will be laws, and public officers, armed, to revenge all injuries shall be done him; what opinion he has of his fellow subjects, when he rides armed; of his fellow citizens, when he locks his doors; and of his children, and servants, when he locks his chests. Does he not there as much accuse mankind by his actions, as I do by my words? But neither of us accuse man's nature in it. The desires, and other passions of man, are in themselves no sin. No more are the actions, that proceed from those passions, till they know a law that forbids them: which till laws be made they cannot know: nor can any law be made, till they have agreed upon the person that shall make it.

It may peradventure be thought, there was never such a time, nor condition of war as this, and I believe it was never generally so, over all the world: but there are many places, where they live so now. For the savage people in many places of America, except the government of small families, the concord whereof dependeth on natural lust, have no government at all; and live at this day in that brutish manner, as I said before. Howsoever, it may be perceived what manner of life there would be, where there were no common power to fear, by the manner of life, which men that have formerly lived under a peaceful government, use to degenerate into, in a civil war.

But there had never been any time, wherein particular men were in a condition of war one against another; yet in all times kings and persons of sovereign authority, because of their independency, are in continual jealousies, and in the state and posture of gladiators; having their weapons pointing, and their eyes fixed on one another; that is, their forts, garrisons, and guns upon the frontiers of their kingdoms; and continual spies upon their neighbours; which is a posture of war. But because they uphold thereby, the industry of their subjects; there does not follow from it, that misery, which accompanies the liberty of particular men.

To this war of every man, against every man, this also is consequent; that nothing can be unjust. The notions of right and wrong, justice and injustice, have there no place. Where there is no common power, there is no law; where no law, no injustice. Force, and fraud, are in war the two cardinal virtues. Justice, and injustice, are none of the faculties neither of the body, or mind. If they were, they might be in a man that were alone in the world, as well as his senses, and passions. They are qualities, that relate to men in society, not in solitude. It is consequent also to the same condition that there be no propriety [property], no dominion, no *mine* and *thine* distinct; but only that to be every man's that he can get; and for so long, as he can keep it. And thus much for the ill condition, which man by mere nature is actually placed in; though with a possibility to come out of it, consisting partly in the passions, partly in his reason.

The passions that incline men to peace, are fear of death; desire of such things as are necessary to commodious living; and a hope by their industry to obtain them. And reason suggesteth convenient articles of peace, upon which men may be drawn to agreement. These articles, are they, which otherwise are called the Laws of nature, whereof I shall speak more particularly, in the two following chapters.

## CHAPTER XIV

### *Of the First and Second Natural Laws, and of Contracts*

The RIGHT OF NATURE, which writers commonly call *jus naturale,* is the liberty each man hath, to use his own power, as he will himself, for the preservation of his own nature; that is to say, of his own life; and consequently, of doing any thing, which in his own judgement, and reason, he shall conceive to be the aptest means thereunto.

By LIBERTY, is understood, according to the proper signification of the word, the absence of external impediments; which impediments, may oft take away part of a man's power to do what he would; but cannot hinder him from using the power left to him, according as his judgement, and reason shall dictate to him.

A LAW OF NATURE, *lex naturalis,* is a precept or general rule, found out by reason, by which a man is forbidden to do that, which is destructive of his life, or taketh away the means of preserving the same, and to omit that, by which he thinketh it may be best preserved. For though they that speak of this subject, use to confound *jus,* and *lex, right* and *law;* yet they ought to be distinguished; because RIGHT, consisteth in liberty to do, or to forbear; whereas LAW determineth, and bindeth to one of them: so that law, and right, differ as much, as obligation and liberty; which in one and the same matter are inconsistent.

And because the condition of man, as hath been declared in the precedent chapter, is a condition of war of every one against every one: in which case every one is governed by his own reason; and there is nothing he can make use of, that may not be a help unto him, in preserving his life against his enemies; it followeth, that in such a condition, every man has a right to every thing; even to one another's body. And therefore, as long as this natural right of every man to every thing endureth, there can be no security to any many, how strong or wise soever he be, of living out the time, which nature ordinarily alloweth men to live. And consequently it is a precept, or general rule. of reason, *that every man, ought to endeavour peace, as far as he has hope of obtaining it; and when he cannot obtain it, that he may seek, and use, all helps and advantages of war.* The first branch of which rule, containeth the first and fundamental law of nature; which is, *to seek peace and follow it.* The second, the sum of the right of nature; which is, *by all means we can, to defend ourselves.*

From this fundamental law of nature, by which men are commanded to endeavour peace, is derived this second law; *that a man be willing, when others are so too, as farforth, as for peace, and defence of himself he shall think it necessary, to lay down this right to all things; and be contented with so much liberty against other men, as he would allow other men against himself.* For as long as every man holdeth this right, of doing anything he liketh, so long are all men in the condition of war. But if other men will not lay down their right, as well as he; then there is no reason for any one, to divest himself of his: for that were to expose himself to peace, which no man is bound to, rather than to dispose himself to peace. This is that law of the Gospel: *whatsoever you require that others should do to you, that do ye to them.* And that law of all men, *quod tibi fieri non vis, alteri ne feceris.*

To *lay* down a man's right to anything, is to *divest* himself of the *liberty,* of hindering another of the benefit of his own right to the same. For he that renounceth, or passeth away his right, giveth not to any other man a right which he had not before; because there is nothing to which every man had not right by nature: but only standeth out of his way, that he may enjoy his own original right, without hindrance from him; not without hindrance from another. So that the effect which redoundeth to one man, by another man's defect of right, is but so much diminution of impediments to the use of his own right original.

Right is laid aside, either by simply renouncing it, or by transferring it to another. By *simply* RENOUNCING; when he cares not to whom the benefit thereof redoundeth. By TRANSFERRING, when he intendeth the benefit thereof to some certain person or persons. And when a man has in either manner abandoned, or granted away his right, then is he said to be OBLIGED, or BOUND, not to hinder those, to whom such right is granted, or abandoned, from the benefit of it: and that he *ought,* and it is DUTY, not to make void that voluntary act of his own: and that such hindrance is INJUSTICE and INJURY, as being *sine jure;* the right being before renounced, or transferred. So that *injury,* or *injustice,* in the controversies of the world, is somewhat like to that, which in the disputations of scholars is called *absurdity.* For as it is there called an absurdity, to contradict what one maintained in the beginning: so in the world, it is called injustice, and injury, voluntarily to undo that, which from the beginning he had voluntarily done. The way by which a man either simply renounceth or transferreth his right, is a declaration, or signification, by some voluntary and sufficient sign, or signs, that he doth so renounce, or transfer; or hath so renounced, or transferred the same, to him that accepteth it. And these signs are either words only, or actions only; or, as it happeneth most often, both words, and actions. And the same are the BONDS, by which men are bound, and obliged: bonds, that have their strength, not from their own nature, for nothing is more easily broken than a man's word, but from fear of some evil consequence upon the rupture.

Whensoever a man transferreth his right, or renounceth it; it is either in consideration of some right reciprocally transferred to himself; or for some other good he hopeth for thereby. For it is a voluntary act: and of the voluntary acts of every man the object is some *good to himself.* And therefore there be some rights, which no man can be understood by any words, or other signs, to have abandoned, or transferred. At first a man cannot lay down the right of resisting them, that assault him by force, to take away his life; because he cannot be understood to aim thereby, at any good to himself. The same may be said of wounds, and chains, and imprisonment; both because there is no benefit consequent to such patience; as there is to the patience of suffering another to be wounded, or imprisoned: as also because a man cannot tell, when he seeth men proceed against him by violence, whether they intend his death or not. And lastly the motive, and end for which this renouncing, and transferring of right is introduced, is nothing else but the security of a man's person, in his life, and in the means of so preserving life, as not to be weary of it. And therefore if a man by words, or other signs, seem to despoil himself of the end, for which those signs were intended; he is not to be understood as if he meant it, or that it was his will; but that he was ignorant of how such words and actions were to be interpreted.

The mutual transferring of right, is that which men call CONTRACT. . . .

If a covenant be made, wherein neither of the parties perform presently, but trust one another; the condition of mere nature, which is a condition of war of every man against every man, upon any reasonable suspicion, it is void: but if there be a common power set over them both, with right and force sufficient to compel performance, it is not void. For he that performeth first, has no assurance the other will perform after; because the bonds of words are too weak, to bridle men's ambition, avarice, anger, and other passions, without the fear of some coercive power; which in the condition of mere nature, where all men are equal, and judges of the justness of their own fears, cannot possibly be supposed. And therefore he which performeth first, does but betray himself to his enemy; contrary to the right, he can never abandon, of defending his life, and means of living.

But in a civil estate, where there's a power set up to constrain those that would otherwise violate their faith, that fear is no more reasonable; and for that cause, he which by the covenant is to perform first, is obliged so to do. . . .

The force of words, being, as I have formerly noted, too weak to hold men to the performance of their covenants; there are in man's nature, but two imaginable helps to strengthen it. And those are either a fear of the consequences of breaking their word; or a glory, or pride in appearing not to need to break it. This latter is a generosity too rarely found to be presumed on, especially in the pursuers of wealth, command, or sensual pleasure; which are the greatest part of mankind. The passion to be reckoned upon, is fear. . . .

# Chapter XV

## Of Other Laws of Nature

From that law of nature, by which we are obliged to transfer to another, such rights, as being retained, hinder the peace of mankind, there followeth a third; which is this, *that men perform their covenants made:* without which covenants are in vain, and but empty words; and the right of all men to all things remaining, we are still in the condition of war.

And in this law of nature consisteth the fountain and original of JUSTICE. For where no covenant hath preceded, there hath no right been transferred, and every man has right to every thing; and consequently, no action can be unjust. But when a covenant is made, then to break it is *unjust;* and the definition of INJUSTICE, is no other than *the not performance of covenant.* And whosoever is not unjust, is *just.*

But because covenants of mutual trust, where there is a fear of not performance on either part, as hath been said in the former chapter, are invalid; though the original of justice be the making of covenants; yet injustice actually there can be none, till the cause of such fear be taken away; which while men are in the natural condition of war, cannot be done. Therefore before the names of just, and unjust can have place, there must be some coercive power, to compel men equally to the performance of their covenants, by the terror of some punishment, greater than the benefit they expect by the breach of their covenant; and to make good that propriety, which by mutual contract men acquire, in recompense of the universal right they abandon: and such power there is none before the erection of a commonwealth. And this is also to be gathered out of the ordinary definition of justice in the Schools: for they say, that *justice is the constant will of giving to every man his own.* And therefore where there is no *own,* that is no propriety, there is no injustice; and where there is no coercive power erected, that is, where there is no commonwealth, there is no propriety; all men having right to all things: therefore where there is no commonwealth, there nothing is unjust. So that the nature of justice, consisteth in keeping of valid covenants: but the validity of covenants begins not but with the constitution of a civil power, sufficient to compel men to keep them: and then it is also that propriety begins.

# Chapter XVII

## Of the Causes, Generation, and Definition of a Commonwealth

The final cause, end, or design of men, who naturally love liberty, and dominion over others, in the introduction of that restraint upon themselves, in which we see them live in commonwealths, is the foresight of their own preservation, and of a more contented life thereby; that is to say, of getting themselves out from that miserable condition of war which is necessarily consequent, as hath been shown in Chapter XIII, to the natural passions of men, when there is no visible power to keep them in awe, and tie them by fear of punishment to the performance of their covenants, and observation of those laws of nature set down in the fourteenth and fifteenth chapters.

For the laws of nature, *as justice, equity, modesty, mercy,* and, in sum, *doing to others, as we would be done to,* of themselves, without the terror of some power, to cause them to be observed, are contrary to our natural passions that carry us to partiality, pride, revenge, and the like. And covenants, without the sword, are but words, and of no strength to secure a man at all. Therefore notwithstanding the laws of nature, which every one hath then kept, when he has the will to keep them, when he can do it safely, if there be no power erected, or not great enough for our security; every man will, and may lawfully rely on his own strength and art, for caution against all other men. And in all places, where men have lived by small families, to rob and spoil one another, has been a trade, and so far from being reputed against the law of nature, that the greater spoils they gained, the greater was their honour; and men observed no other laws therein, but the laws of honour; that is, to abstain from cruelty, leaving to men their lives, and instruments of husbandry. And as small families did then; so now do cities and kingdoms which are but greater families, for their own security, enlarge their dominions, upon all pretences of danger, and fear of invasion, or assistance that may be given to invaders, and endeavour as much as they can to subdue, or weaken their neighbours, by open force, and secret arts, for want of other caution, justly; and are remembered for it in after ages with honour.

Nor is it the joining together of a small number of men, that gives them this security; because in small numbers, small actions on the one side or the other, make the advantage of strength so great, as is sufficient to carry the victory; and therefore gives encouragement to an invasion. The multitude sufficient to confide in for our security, is not determined by any certain number, but by comparison with the enemy we fear; and is then sufficient, when the odds of the enemy is not of so visible and conspicuous moment, to determine the event of war, as to move him to attempt.

And be there never so great a multitude; yet if their actions be directed according to their particular judgements, and particular appetites, they can expect thereby no defence, nor protection, neither against a common enemy, nor against the injuries of one another. For being distracted in opinions concerning the best use and application of their strength, they do not help but hinder one another; and reduce their strength by mutual opposition to nothing: whereby they are easily, not only subdued by a very few that agree together; but also when there is no common enemy, they make war upon each other, for their particular interests. For if we could suppose a great multitude of men to consent in the observation of justice, and other laws of nature, without a common power to keep them all in awe; we might as well suppose all mankind to do the same; and then there neither would be, nor need to be any civil government, or commonwealth at all; because there would be peace without subjection.

Nor is it enough for the security, which men desire should last all the time of their life, that they be governed, and directed by one judgement, for a limited time; as in one battle, or one war. For though they obtain a victory by their unanimous endeavour against a foreign enemy; yet afterwards, when either they have no common enemy, or he that by one part is held for an enemy, is by another part held for a friend, they must needs by the difference of their interest dissolve, and fall again into a war amongst themselves.

It is true, that certain living creatures, as bees, and ants, live sociably one with another, which are therefore by Aristotle numbered amongst political creatures; and yet have no other direction, than their particular judgments and appetites; nor speech, whereby one of them can signify to another, what he thinks expedient for the common benefit: and therefore some man may perhaps desire to know, why mankind cannot do the same. To which I answer,

First, that men are continually in competition for honour and dignity, which these creatures are not; and consequently amongst men there ariseth on that ground, envy, and hatred, and finally war; but amongst these not so.

Secondly, that amongst these creatures, the common good differeth not from the private; and being by nature inclined to their private, they procure thereby the common benefit. But man, whose joy consisteth in comparing himself with other men, can relish nothing but what is eminent.

Thirdly, that these creatures, having not, as man, the use of their reason, do not see, nor think they see any fault, in the administration of their common business; whereas amongst men, there are very many, that think themselves wiser, and abler to govern the public, better than the rest; and these strive to perform and innovate, one this way, another that way, and thereby bring it into distraction and civil war.

Fourthly, that these creatures, though they have some use of voice, in making known to one another their desires, and other affections; yet they want that art of words, by which some men can represent to others, that which is good, in the likeness of evil; and evil, in the likeness of good; and augment, or diminish the apparent greatness of good and evil; discontenting men and, troubling their peace at their pleasure.

Fifthly, irrational creatures cannot distinguish between *injury,* and *damage;* and therefore as long as they be at ease, they are not offended with their fellows; whereas man is then most troublesome, when he is most at ease: for then it is that he loves to shew his wisdom, and control the actions of them that govern the commonwealth.

Lastly, the agreement of these creatures is natural; that of men, is by covenant only, which is artificial: and therefore it is no wonder if there be somewhat else required, besides covenant, to make their agreement constant and lasting; which is a common power, to keep them in awe, and to direct their actions to the common benefit.

The only way to erect such a common power, as may be able to defend them from the invasion of foreigners, and the injuries of one another, and thereby to secure them in such sort, as that by their own industry, and by the fruits of the earth, they may nourish themselves and live contentedly; is to confer all their power and strength upon one man, or upon one assembly of men, that may reduce all their wills, by plurality of voices, unto one will: which is as much as to say, to appoint one man, or assembly of men, to bear their person; and every one to own, and acknowledge himself to be author of whatsoever he that so beareth their person, shall act, or cause to be acted, in those things which concern the common peace and safety; and therein to submit their wills, every one to his will, and their judgements, to his judgement. This is more than consent, or concord; it is a real unity of them all, in one and the same person, made by covenant of every man with every man, in such manner, as if every man should say to every man: *I authorise and give up my right of governing myself, to this man, or to this assembly of men, on this condition, that thou give up thy right to him, and authorise all his actions in like manner.* This done, the multitude so united in one person is called a COMMONWEALTH, in Latin, CIVITAS. This is the generation of that great LEVIATHAN, or rather, to speak more reverently, of that *mortal god,* to which we owe, under the *immortal God,* our peace and defence. For by this authority, given him by every particular man in the commonwealth, he hath the use of so much power and strength conferred on him, that by terror thereof, he is enabled to perform the wills of them all, to peace at home, and mutual aid against their enemies abroad. And in him consisteth the essence of the commonwealth; which, to define it, is *one person of whose acts a great multitude, by mutual covenants one with another, have made themselves every one the author, to the end he may use the strength and means of them all, as he shall think expedient, for their peace and common defence.*

And he that carrieth this person, is called SOVEREIGN, and said to have *sovereign power;* and every one besides, his SUBJECT.

# Margaret Lucas Cavendish

## *from* PHILOSOPHICAL LETTERS (1664)
## *from* GROUNDS OF NATURAL PHILOSOPHY (1668)

*Margaret Lucas (1623–1673) joined the English court as an attendant to the queen in 1643, during the English Civil War. In exile with other royalists, she met and married William Cavendish, Marquis of Newcastle, a wealthy noble and patron who served as governor to the heir to the throne, the future Charles II. (Cavendish appointed philosopher Thomas Hobbes as tutor to the prince.) The marriage was unusual: Lucas had no dowry and Cavendish, thirty years her senior, was of much higher social rank. They lived in Paris and Antwerp until the Restoration of the monarchy in 1660, when they returned to England. At a time when women who wrote for publication were deemed eccentric, Margaret Cavendish actively sought an audience for her ideas. She published poetry, romances, philosophical speculations, scientific essays, utopian fiction, a memoir, and a biography of her husband. In the first selection here, she reflects on the work of Descartes, whom she had met; in the second, she analyzes the relation between mind and body.*

### *FROM* PHILOSOPHICAL LETTERS: OR, MODEST REFLECTIONS
#### *XXXVI*

MADAM,

That all other animals, besides man, want reason, your author [Descartes] endeavours to prove in his *Discourse of Method,* where his chief argument is, that other animals cannot express their mind, thoughts or conceptions, either by speech or any other signs, as man can do: For, says he, "it is not for want of the organs belonging to the framing of words, as we may observe in parrots and pies, which are apt enough to express words they are taught, but understand nothing of them." My answer is, that one man expressing his mind by speech or words to another, doth not declare by it his excellency and supremacy above all other creatures, but for the most part more folly, for a talking man is not so wise as a contemplating man. But by reason other creatures cannot speak or discourse with each other as men, or make certain signs, whereby to express themselves as dumb and deaf men do, should we conclude they have neither knowledge, sense, reason, or intelligence? Certainly, this is a very weak argument; for one part of a man's body, as one hand, is not less sensible than the other, nor the heel less sensible than the heart, nor the leg less sensible than the head, but each part hath its sense and reason, and so consequently its sensitive and rational knowledge; and although they cannot talk or give intelligence to each other by speech, nevertheless each hath its own peculiar and particular knowledge, just as each particular man has his own particular knowledge, for one man's knowledge is not another man's knowledge; and if there be such a peculiar and particular knowledge in every several part of one animal creature, as man, well may there be such in creatures of different kinds and sorts: But this particular knowledge belonging to each creature, doth not prove that there is no intelligence at all betwixt them, no more than the want of human knowledge doth prove the want of reason; for reason is the rational part of matter, and makes perception, observation, and intelligence different in every creature, and every sort of creatures, according to their proper natures, but perception, observation and intelligence do not make reason, reason being the cause, and they the effects. Wherefore though other creatures have not the speech, nor mathematical rules and demonstrations, with other arts and sciences, as men; yet may their perceptions and observations be as wise as men's and they may have as much intelligence and commerce betwixt each other, after their own manner and way, as men have after theirs: To which I leave them and man to his conceited prerogative and excellence, resting,

Madam,

Your faithful Friend,
and Servant.

## *FROM* GROUNDS OF NATURAL PHILOSOPHY

### The Fifth Part.
### Chap. I.

#### Of MAN.

Now I have discoursed, in the former Parts, after a general manner, of *Animals:* I will, in the following Chapters, speak more particularly of that sort we named *Mankind;* who believe (being ignorant of the Nature of other Creatures) that they are the most knowing of all Creatures; and yet a *whole Man* (as I may say for expression-sake) doth not know all the Figurative Motions belonging either to his Mind, or Body: for, he doth not generally know every particular Action of his Corporeal Motions, as, How he was framed, or formed, or perfected. Nor doth he know every particular Motion that occasions his present Consistence, or Being: Nor every particular Digestive, or Nourishing Motion: Nor, when he is sick, the particular Irregular Motion that causes his Sickness. Nor do the Rational Motions in the Head, know always the Figurative Actions of those of the Heel. In short, (as I said) Man doth not generally know every particular Part, or Corporeal Motion, either of Mind, or Body: Which proves, Man's Natural Soul is not inalterable, or individable, and uncompoundable.

### Chap. II.
### Of the variety of Man's Natural Motions.

There is abundance of varieties of Figurative Motions in Man: As, first, There are several Figurative Motions of the Form and Frame of Man, as of his Innate, Interior, and Exterior Figurative Parts. Also, there are several Figures of his several Perceptions, Conceptions, Appetite, Digestions, Reparations, and the like. There are also several

Figures of several Postures of his several Parts; and a difference of his Figurative Motions, or Parts, from other Creatures; all which are Numberless: And yet all these different Actions are proper to the Nature of MAN.

### Chap. V.
### Of the several Perceptions amongst the several Parts of MAN.

There being infinite several Corporeal Figurative Motions, or Actions of Nature, there must of necessity be infinite several Self-knowledges and Perceptions: but I shall only, in this Part of my Book, treat of the Perception proper to Mankind: And first, of the several and different Perceptions, proper for the several and different Parts: for, though every Part and Particle of a Man's Body, is perceptive; yet, every particular Part of a Man, is not generally perceived; for, the Interior Parts do not generally perceive the Exterior; nor the Exterior, generally or perfectly, the Interior; and yet, both Interior and Exterior Corporeal Motions, agree as one Society; for, every Part, or Corporeal Motion, knows its own Office; like as Officers in a Common-wealth, although they may not be acquainted with each other, yet they know their Employments: So every particular Man in a Common-wealth, knows his own Employment, although he knows not every Man in the Common-wealth. The same do the Parts of a Man's Body, and Mind. But, if there be any Irregularity, or Disorder in a Common-wealth, every Particular is disturbed, perceiving a Disorder in the Common-wealth. The same amongst the Parts of a Man's Body; and yet many of those Parts do not know the particular Cause of that general Disturbance. As for the Disorders, they may proceed from some Irregularities; but for Peace, there must be a general Agreement, that is, every Part must be Regular.

### Chap. VI.
### Of Divided and Composed Perceptions.

As I have formerly said, There is in Nature both Divided and Composed Perceptions; and for proof, I will mention Man's Exterior Perceptions; As for example, Man hath a Composed Perception of Seeing, Hearing, Smelling, Tasting, and Touching; whereof every several sort is composed, though after different manners, or ways; and yet are divided, being several sorts of Perceptions, and not all one Perception. Yet again, they are all Composed, being united as proper Perceptions of one Man; and not only so, but united to perceive the different Parts of one Object: for, as Perceptions are composed of Parts, so are Objects; and as there are different Objects, so there are different Perceptions; but it is not possible for a Man to know all the several sorts of Perceptions proper to every Composed Part of his Body or Mind, much less of others.

### Chap. VII.
### Of the Ignorances of the several Perceptive Organs.

As I said, That every several composed Perception, was united to the proper use of their whole Society, as one Man; yet, every several Perceptive Organ of Man is ignorant of each other; as the Perception of Sight is ignorant of that of Hearing; the Perception of Hearing, is ignorant of the Perception of Seeing; and the Perception of Smelling is ignorant of the Perceptions of the other two, and those of Scent, and the same of Tasting, and Touching: Also, every Perception of every particular Organ, is different; but some sorts of Human Perceptions require some distance between them and the Object: As for example, The Perception of Sight requires certain Distances, as also

Magnitudes; whereas the Perception of Touch requires a Joyning-Object, or Part. But this is to be noted, That although these several Organs are not perfectly, or thoroughly acquainted; yet in the Perception of the several parts of one Object, they do all agree to make their several Perceptions, as it were by one Act, at one point of time.

### Chap. XV.
### Of the Agreeing, or Disagreeing, of the Sensitive and Rational Parts of Human Creatures.

There is, for the most part, a general agreement between the Rational and Sensitive Parts of Human Creatures; not only in their particular, but general actions; only the Rational are the Designing-parts; and the Sensitive, the Labouring parts: As for proof, The Mind designs to go to such, or such Foreign Parts, or Places; upon which design the Sensitive Parts will labour to execute the Mind's intention, so as the whole Sensitive Body labours to go to the designed place, without the Mind's further Concern: for, the Mind takes no notice of every action of the Sensitive parts; neither of those of the Eyes, Ears; or of the Leggs, or feet; nor of their perceptions: for, many times, the Mind is busied in some Conception, Imagination, Fancy, or the like; and yet the Sensitive Parts execute the Mind's Design exactly. But, for better proof, When as the Sensitive parts are sick, weak, or defective, through some irregularities, the Sensitive parts cannot execute the Mind's Design: also, when the Sensitive parts are careless, they oft mistake their way; or when they are irregularly opposed, or busied about some Appetite, they will not obey the Mind's desire; all which are different degrees of Parts. But, as it is amongst the particular parts of a Society; so, many times, between several Societies; for, sometimes, the Sensitive parts of two Men will take no notice of each other: As for example, When two men speak together, one man regards not what the other says; so many times, the Sensitive parts regard not the Propositions of the Rational; but then the Sensitive is not perfectly regular.

### Chap. XVI.
### Of the Power of the Rational; or rather, of the Indulgency of the Sensitive.

The Rational Corporeal Motions, being the purest, most free, and so most active, have great power over the Sensitive; as to perswade, or command them to obedience: As for example, When a man is studying about some Inventions of Poetical Fancies, or the like; though the Sensitive Corporeal Motions, in the Sensitive Organs, desire to desist from patterning of Objects, and would move towards sleep; yet the Rational will not suffer them, but causes them to work, *viz.* to write, or to read, or do some other Labour: Also, when the Rational Mind is merry, it will cause the Leggs to dance, the Organs of the Voice to sing, the Mouth to speak, to eat, to drink, and the like: If the Mind moves to sadness, it causes the Eyes to weep, the Lungs to sigh, the Mouth to speak words of Complaint. Thus the Rational Corporeal Motions of the Mind, will occasion the Senses to watch, to work, or to sport and play. But mistake me not; for I do not mean, the Senses are bound to obey the Rational Designs; for, the Sensitive Corporeal Motions, have as much freedom of Self-moving, as the Rational: for, the Command of the Rational, and the Obedience of the Sensitive, is rather an Agreement, than a Constraint: for, in many cases, the Sensitive will not agree, and so not obey: also, in many cases, the Rational submits to the Sensitive: also, the Rational sometimes will be irregular; and, on the other side, sometimes the Sensitive will be irregular, and the Rational regular; and sometimes both irregular.

## Chap. XVII.
### Of Human Appetites and Passions.

The Sensitive Appetites, and the Rational Passions do so resemble each other, as they would puzzle the most wise Philosopher to distinguish them; and there is not only a Resemblance, but, for the most part, a sympathetical Agreement between the Appetites, and the Passions; which strong conjunction, doth often occasion disturbances to the whole life of Man; with endless Desires, unsatiable Appetites, violent Passions, unquiet Humors, Grief, Pain, Sadness, Sickness, and the like; through which, Man seems to be more restless, than any other Creature: but, whether the cause be in the Manner, or Form of Man's Composition, or occasioned by some Irregularities; I will leave to those who are wiser than I, to judg. But this is to be noted, That the more Changes and Alterations the Rational and Sensitive Motions make, the more variety of Passions and Appetites the Man hath: also, the quicker Wit, man hath. But, as all the Human Senses are not bound to one Organ; so all Knowledges are not bound to one Sense, no more than all the Parts of Matter to the composition of one particular Creature: but, by some of the Rational and Sensitive actions, we may perceive the difference of some of the Sensitive and Rational actions; as, Sensitive Pain, Rational Grief; Sensitive Pleasure, Rational delight; Sensitive Appetite, Rational Desire; which are sympathetical actions of the Rational and Sensitive Parts: Also, through sympathy, Rational Passions will occasion Sensitive Appetites; and Appetites, the like Passions.

# Isaac Newton

## *from* THE MATHEMATICAL PRINCIPLES OF NATURAL PHILOSOPHY (1687)

*Isaac Newton (1642–1727) was an eccentric and remote individual who was as interested in mysticism and the occult as he was in modern science. His* The Mathematical Principles of Natural Philosophy, *in which he sets forth the theory of universal gravitation, is among the most original and path-breaking works in the history of science. The importance of the book is that Newton is able to explain the movement of bodies in both heaven and earth on the basis of a universal set of laws, three involving their motion and one their attraction towards each other. Yet if Newton's mechanics was path-breaking, it is also a culmination of over two hundred years of scientific exploration, building on the labors of scientists such as Nicolaus Copernicus, Tycho Brahe, Johannes Kepler, and Galileo. Similarly, Newton's description of the scientific method builds on the work of thinkers such as Francis Bacon, while offering an extension of these ideas as well.*

## THE RULES OF REASONING IN PHILOSOPHY

*Rule I.* We are to admit no more causes of natural things, than such as are both true and sufficient to explain their appearances.

To this purpose the philosophers say, that Nature does nothing in vain, and more is in vain, when less will serve; for Nature is pleased with simplicity, and affects not the pomp of superfluous causes.

*Rule II.* Therefore to the same natural effects we must, as far as possible, assign the same causes.

As to respiration in a man, and in a beast; the descent of stones in Europe and in America; the light of our culinary fire and of the sun; the reflection of light in the earth, and in the planets.

*Rule III.* The qualities of bodies, which admit neither intension nor remission of degrees, and which are found to belong to all bodies within reach of our experiments, are to be esteemed the universal qualities of all bodies whatsoever.

For since the qualities of bodies are only known to us by experiments, we are to hold for universal, all such as universally agree with experiments; and such as are not liable to diminution, can never be quite taken away. We are certainly not to relinquish the evidence of experiments for the sake of dreams and vain fictions of our own devising; nor are we to recede from the analogy of Nature, which is wont to be simple, and always consonant to itself. We no other way know the extension of bodies, than by our senses, nor do these reach it in all bodies; but because we perceive extension in all that are sensible, therefore we ascribe it universally to all others, also. That abundance of bodies are hard we learn by experience. And because the hardness of the whole arises from the hardness of the parts, we therefore justly infer the hardness of the undivided particles not only of the bodies we feel but of all others. That all bodies are impenetrable, we gather not from reason, but from sensation. The bodies which we handle we find impenetrable, and thence conclude impenetrability to be a universal property of all bodies whatsoever. That all bodies are moveable, and endowed with certain powers (which we called the forces of inertia) or persevering in their motion or in their rest, we only infer from the like properties observed in the bodies which we have seen. The extension, hardness, impenetrability, mobility, and force of inertia of the whole, result from the extension, hardness, impenetrability, mobility, and forces of inertia of the parts: and thence we conclude that the least particles of all bodies to be also all extended, and hard, and impenetrable, and moveable, and endowed with their proper forces of inertia. And this is the foundation of all philosophy. Moreover, that the divided but contiguous particles of bodies may be separated from one another, is a matter of observation: and, in the particles that remain undivided, our minds are able to distinguish yet lesser parts, as is mathematically demonstrated. But whether the parts so distinguished, and not yet divided, may, by the powers of nature, be actually divided and separated from one another, we cannot certainly determine. Yet had we the proof of but one experiment, that any undivided particle, in breaking a hard and solid body, suffered a division, we might by virtue of this rule, conclude, that the undivided as well as the divided particles, may be divided and acually separated into infinity.

Lastly, if it universally appears, by experiments and astronomical observations, that all bodies about the earth, gravitate toward the earth; and that in proportion to the quantity of matter which they severally contain; that the moon likewise, according to the quantity of its matter, gravitates toward the earth; that on the other hand our sea gravitates toward the moon; and all the planets mutually one toward another; and the comets in like manner towards the sun; we must, in consequence of this rule, universally allow, that all bodies whatsoever are endowed with a principle of mutual gravitation. For the argument from the appearances concludes with more force for the universal gravitation of all bodies, than for the impenetrability, of which among those in the celestial regions, we have no experiments, nor any manner of observation. Not that I affirm gravity to be essential to all bodies. By their inherent force I mean nothing but their force of inertia. This is immutable. Their gravity is diminished as they recede from the earth.

*Rule IV.* In experimental philosophy we are to look upon propositions collected by general induction from phenomena as accurately or very nearly true, notwithstanding any contrary hypotheses that may be imagined, till such time as other phenomena occur, by which they may either be made more acurate, or liable to exceptions.

This rule we must follow that the argument of induction may not be evaded by hypotheses.

# SECTION II

# Travel, Exploration, and Conflict Between Cultures

Encounters with other cultures, both within Europe and around the globe, played a significant role in the shaping of European ideas, social practices, and political and economic systems. The outline of these encounters, at least politically and economically, is familiar. In 1500, to the south of Europe lay the Ottoman Empire, which had conquered the remains of the Byzantine empire and taken its capital, Constantinople, in 1453. To the east lay Russia, little-known and thought generally to be uncivilized. Beyond were India, China, Africa, all known to Europeans only in sketchy, often fantastic terms. By late in the next century, the Ottoman Empire stretched from Morocco to the Persian gulf and from the Crimea almost to Vienna. European powers were concerned, first about the threat of invasion (Ottoman armies besieged Vienna in 1683), and later (especially in the nineteenth century) about the increasing power of imperial Russia in Europe and the East and the political effects of the gradual dissolution of the Ottoman Empire.

What lay west of Europe was also poorly known in 1500, though that changed dramatically in the centuries that followed as Europeans explored the area they called the 'New World', conquered the local inhabitants with the aid of technological advantages and disease, and established their own settlements. By the eighteenth century several European states—especially Spain, Britain, France, and the Netherlands—had substantial empires in the New World, with territory in Africa and India as well. As independence movements in the Americas contested European rule in the late eighteenth and nineteenth centuries, European states expanded their empires to the east and south, claiming political and economic dominance over much of Africa, India, and Asia.

Encounters such as these were affected by European assumptions about other cultures and provided images, practices, experiences and ideas that affected European cultures in return. Speculation about other peoples was hardly new, of course, but became increasingly common and important as exploration abroad increased, trade networks expanded, imperial rivalries intensified, and travel to other countries within Europe and around the globe became easier. At home and abroad, in philosophical essays, letters, novels, and histories, Europeans wrote about other cultures, often as a means of defining—or celebrating—their own national and cultural identities or explaining their political dominance. Ancient Greeks had defined themselves in contrast to other peoples, whom they commonly referred to as 'barbarians'; Christians in

Europe had characterized others, especially Moslems, as 'infidels'. As part of their program to create a unified Spanish state—which they envisioned as a wholly Catholic state—Isabella and Ferdinand had expelled all Jews and Moslems from Spain in 1492. At the same time, ironically, their financial support of the exploratory voyages of Christopher Columbus helped to bring peoples hitherto unknown in Europe into the European cultural consciousness. In early modern Europe, the social mores, art forms, and ideas of cultures foreign to one's own—English, Russian or Greek as well as African, Chinese, or Indian—continued both to fascinate and to disturb.

Directly and indirectly, then, Europeans considered questions such as these: What accounts for differences between cultures? Are some cultures better than others? What does it mean to be 'civilized'? Is slavery acceptable, or wrong? Does technological superiority prove cultural superiority? Is it just for one people to govern another? What are, and what should be, the relations between different peoples, cultures, and nationalities? As the texts in this and later sections demonstrate, the situations in which these questions have been addressed in the last five hundred years have varied enormously.

It is ironically appropriate that independence movements around the globe in the nineteenth and twentieth centuries found in European ideas some of their most powerful arguments against imperial domination. With the growth of empires abroad came the spread of European cultural institutions, which served to disseminate and claim the superiority of European modes of thought. In the two centuries following the American and French revolutions, as opposition to European rule in Latin America, India, and Africa grew, intellectuals and revolutionaries around the globe would invoke the Enlightenment ideals about liberty and equality that had helped to inspire those earlier revolutions. Schooled in European ideas, they would make strategic and philosophical use of them in impassioned arguments against empire.

# Christopher Columbus

# LETTER (1493)

*When Christopher Columbus (1451–1506) set sail from the Canary Islands in 1492 under the flag of Spain, his goal was to find a western route to South and East Asia, rather than the world (new to Europeans) that he 'discovered'. His goal was to convert the people of the East to Christianity. More important, he sought a sea route to the East—a cheaper way of transporting its riches than the land routes across Asia. Over a twelve-year period Columbus made four voyages that took him to the Caribbean and Central and South America. A letter written by Columbus during the first voyage provides an occasion to enter into the current debate over Columbus's achievement. Should he be seen as a great navigator who contributed to the expanding wealth of Europe and made possible European migrations to the new world? Or was he deeply flawed and ruthless, responsible for the oppression of native peoples?*

Sir:

As I know that you will have pleasure of the great victory which our Lord hath given me in my voyage, I write you this, by which you shall know that, in twenty days I passed over to the Indies with the fleet which the most illustrious King and Queen, our Lords, gave me: where I found very many islands peopled with inhabitants beyond number. And, of them all, I have taken possession for their Highnesses, with proclamation and the royal standard displayed; and I was not gainsaid. On the first which I found, I put the name San Salvador, in commemoration of His high Majesty, who marvellously hath given all this: the Indians call it Guanahani. The second I named the Island of Santa Maria de Concepcion, the third Ferrandina, the fourth Isabella, the fifth La Isla Juana [Cuba]; and so for each one a new name. When I reached Juana, I followed its coast west-wardly, and found it so large that I thought it might be the mainland province of Cathay. And as I did not thus find any towns and villages on the seacoast, save small hamlets with the people whereof I could not get speech, because they all fled away forthwith, I went on farther in the same direction, thinking I should not miss of great cities or towns. And at the end of many leagues, seeing that there was no change, and that the coast was bearing me northwards, whereunto my desire was contrary since the winter was already confronting us, I formed the purpose of making from thence to the South, and as the wind also blew against me, I determined not to wait for other weather and turned back as far as a port agreed upon; from which I sent two men into the country to learn if there were a king, or any great cities. They travelled for three days, and found interminable small villages and a numberless population, but nought of ruling authority; wherefore they returned. I understood sufficiently from other Indians whom I had already taken, that this land, in its continuousness, was an island; and so I followed its coast eastwardly for a hundred and seven leagues as far as where it terminated; from which headland I saw another island to the east, ten or eight leagues distant from this, to which I at once gave the name La Spañola. And I proceeded thither, and followed the northern coast, as with La Juana, eastwardly for a hundred and seventy-eight great leagues in a direct easterly course, as with La Juana. The which, and all the others, are very large to an excessive degree, and this extremely so. In it, there are many havens on the seacoast, incomparable with any others that I know in Christendom, and plenty of rivers so good and great that it is a marvel. The lands thereof are high, and in it are very many ranges of hills, and most lofty mountains incomparably beyond the Island of Centrefrei; all most beautiful in a thousand shapes, and all accessible, and full of trees of a thousand kinds, so lofty that they seem to reach the sky. And I am assured that they never lose their foliage; as may be imagined, since I saw them as green and as beautiful as they are in Spain during May. And some of them were in flower, some in fruit, some in another stage according to their kind. And the nightingale was singing, and other birds of a thousand sorts, in the month of November, round about the way that I was going. There are palm-trees of six or eight species, wondrous to see for their beautiful variety; but so are the other trees, and fruits, and plants therein. There are wonderful pinegroves, and very large plains of verdure, and there is honey, and many kinds of birds, and many various fruits. In the earth there are many mines of metals; and there is a population of incalculable number. Spañola is a marvel; the mountains and hills, and plains and fields, and land, so beautiful and rich for planting and sowing, for breeding cattle of all sorts, for building of towns and villages. There could be no believing, without seeing, such harbours as are here, as well as the many and great rivers, and excellent waters, most of which contain gold. In the trees and fruits and plants, there are great differences from those of Juana. In this, there are many spiceries, and great mines of gold and other metals. The people of this island, and of all the others that I have found and seen or not seen, all go naked, men and women, just as their mothers bring them forth; although some women cover a single place with the leaf of a plant, or a cotton something which they make for that purpose. They have no iron or steel, nor any weapons; nor are they fit thereunto; not because they be not a well-formed people and of fair stature, but that they are most wondrously timorous. They have no other weapons than the stems of reeds in their seeding state, on the end of which they fix little sharpened stakes. Even these, they dare not use; for many times has it happened that I sent two or three men ashore to some village to parley, and countless numbers of them sallied forth, but as soon as they saw those approach, they fled away in such wise that even a father would not wait for his son. And this was not because any hurt had ever been done to any of them:—on the contrary, at every headland where I have gone and been able to hold speech with them, I gave them of everything which I had, as well cloth as many other things, without accepting aught therefor; but such they are, incurably timid. It is true that since they have become more assured, and are losing that terror, they are artless and generous with what they have, to such a degree as no one would believe but he who had seen it. Of anything they have, if it be asked for, they never say no, but do rather invite the person to accept it, and show as much lovingness as though they would give their hearts. And whether it be a thing of value, or one of little worth, they are straightways content with whatsoever trifle of whatsoever kind may be given them in return for it. I forbade that anything so worthless as fragments of broken platters, and pieces of broken glass, and strap-buckles, should be given them; although when they were able to get such things they seemed to think they had the best jewel in the world, for it was the hap of a sailor to get, in exchange for a strap, gold to the weight of two and a half castellanos, and others much more for other things of far less value; while for new blancas they gave every thing they had, even though it were the worth of two or three gold castellanos, or one or two arrobas of spun cotton. They took even pieces of broken barrelhoops, and gave whatever they had, like senseless brutes; insomuch that it seemed to me ill. I forbade it, and I gave gratuitously a thousand useful things that I carried, in order that they may conceive affection, and furthermore may be made Christians; for they are inclined to the love and service of their Highnesses and of all the Castilian nation, and they strive to combine in giving us things which they have in abundance, and of which we are in need. And they know no sect, or idolatry save that they all believe that power and goodness are in the sky, and they believed very firmly that I, with these ships and crew, came from the sky; and in such opinion, they received me at every place where I landed, after they had lost their terror. And this comes not because they are ignorant; on the contrary, they are men of very subtle wit, who navigate all those seas, and who give a marvellously good account of everything—but because they never saw men wearing clothes or the like of our ships. And as soon as I arrived in the Indies, in the first island that I found, I took some of them by force, to the intent that they should learn our speech and give me information of what there was in those parts. And so it was, that very soon they understood us and we them, what by speech or what by signs; and those Indians have been of much service. To this day I carry them with me who are still of the opinion that I come from heaven, as appears from much conversation which they have had with me. And they were the first to proclaim it wherever I arrived; and the others went running from house to house and to the neighbouring villages, with loud cries of "Come! come to see the people from heaven!" Then, as soon as their minds were reassured about us, every one came, men as well as women, so that there remained none behind, big or little; and they all brought something to eat and drink, which they gave with wondrous lovingness. They have in all the islands very many canoes, after the manner of rowing-galleys, some larger, some smaller; and a good many are larger than a galley of eighteen benches. They are not so wide, because they are made of a single log of timber, but a galley could not keep up with them in rowing, for their motion is a thing beyond belief. And with these, they navigate through all those islands which are numberless, and ply their traffic. I have seen some of those canoes with seventy and eighty men in them, each one with his oar. In all those islands, I saw not much diversity in the looks of the people, or in their manners and language; but they all understand each other, which is a thing of singular towardness for what I hope their Highnesses will determine, as to making them conversant with our holy faith, unto which they are well disposed. I have already told how I had gone a hundred and seven leagues, in a straight line from West to East, along the seacoast of the

Island of Juana; according to which itinerary, I can declare that that island is larger than England and Scotland combined; as, over and above those hundred and seven leagues, there remains for me, on the western side, two provinces whereto I did not go—one of which they call Anan, where the people are born with tails—which provinces cannot be less in length than fifty or sixty leagues, according to what may be understood from the Indians with me, who know all the islands. This other, Española, has a greater circumference than the whole of Spain from Colibre in Catalunya, by the seacoast, as far as Fuente Ravia in Biscay; since, along one of its four sides, I went for a hundred and eighty-eight great leagues in a straight line from West to East. This is a land to be desired,—and once seen, never to be relinquished—in which—although, indeed, I have taken possession of them all for their Highnesses, and all are more richly endowed than I have skill and power to say, and I hold them all in the name of their Highnesses who can dispose thereof as much and as completely as of the kingdoms of Castile—in this Española, in the place most suitable and best for its proximity to the gold mines, and for traffic with the continent, as well on this side as on the further side of the Great Can, where there will be great commerce and profit, I took possession of a large town which I named the city of Navidad. And I have made fortifications there, and a fort which by this time will have been completely finished and I have left therein men enough for such a purpose, with arms and artillery, and provisions for more than a year, and a boat, and a man who is master of all sea-craft for making others; and great friendship with the King of that land, to such a degree that he prided himself on calling and holding me as his brother. And even though his mind might change towards attacking those men, neither he nor his people know what arms are, and go naked. As I have already said, they are the most timorous creatures there are in the world, so that the men who remain there are alone sufficient to destroy all that land, and the island is without personal danger for them if they know how to behave themselves. It seems to me that in all those islands, the men are all content with a single wife; and to their chief or king they give as many as twenty. The women, it appears to me, do more work than the men. Nor have I been able to learn whether they held personal property, for it seemed to me that whatever one had, they all took shares of, especially of eatable things. Down to the present, I have not found in those islands any monstrous men, as many expected, but on the contrary all the people are very comely; nor are they black like those in Guinea, but have flowing hair; and they are not begotten where there is an excessive violence of the rays of the sun. It is true that the sun is there very strong, notwithstanding that it is twenty-six degrees distant from the equinoctial line. In those islands, where there are lofty mountains, the cold was very keen there, this winter; but they endure it by being accustomed thereto, and by the help of the meats which they eat with many and inordinately hot spices. Thus I have not found, nor had any information of monsters, except of an island which is here the second in the approach to the Indies, which is inhabited by a people whom, in all the islands, they regard as very ferocious, who eat human flesh. These have many canoes with which they run through all the islands of India, and plunder and take as much as they can. They are no more ill-shaped than the others, but have the custom of wearing their hair long, like women; and they use bows and arrows of the same reedstems, with a point of wood at the top, for lack of iron which they have not. Amongst those other tribes who are excessively cowardly, these are ferocious; but I hold them as nothing more than the others. These are they who have to do with the women of Matremonio—which is the first island that is encountered in the passage from Spain to the Indies—in which there are no men. Those women practise no female usages, but have bows and arrows of reeds such as above mentioned; and they arm and cover themselves with plates of copper of which they have much. In another island, which they assure me is larger than Española, the people have no hair. In this, there is incalculable gold; and concerning these and the rest I bring Indians with me as witnesses. And in conclusion, to speak only of what has been done in this voyage, which has been so hastily performed, their Highnesses may see that I shall give them as much gold as they may need, with very little aid which their Highnesses will give me; spices and cotton at once, as much as their Highnesses will order to be shipped, and as much as they shall order to be shipped of mastic—which till now has never been found except in Greece, in the island of Xio, and the Seignory sells it for what it likes; and aloe-wood as much as they shall order to be shipped; and slaves as many as they shall order to be shipped— and these shall be from idolaters. And I believe that I have discovered rhubarb and cinnamon, and I shall find that the men whom I am leaving there will have discovered a thousand other things of value; as I made no delay at any point, so long as the wind gave me an opportunity of sailing, except only in the town of Navidad till I had left things safely arranged and well established. And in truth I should have done much more if the ships had served me as well as might reasonably have been expected. This is enough; and thanks to eternal God our Lord who gives to all those who walk His way, victory over things which seem impossible; and this was signally one such, for although men have talked or written of those lands, it was all by conjecture, without confirmation from eyesight, importing just so much that the hearers for the most part listened and judged that there was more fable in it than anything actual, however trifling. Since thus our Redeemer has given to our most illustrious King and Queen, and to their famous kingdoms, this victory in so high a matter, Christendom should take gladness therein and make great festivals, and give solemn thanks to the Holy Trinity for the great exaltation they shall have by the conversion of so many peoples to our Holy faith; and next for the temporal benefit which will bring hither refreshment and profit, not only to Spain, but to all Christians. This briefly, in accordance with the facts. Dated on the caravel, off the Canary Islands, the 15 February of the year 1493.

At your command,

The Admiral

—*trans. J. B. Thacher*

# Michel de Montaigne

## *from* ESSAYS (1572)

*M*ichel de Montaigne (1533–1592), a French aristocrat from Bordeaux, created the literary essay as a form for introspection. As a young man, he studied the law and spent time at court; in 1571, however, after his father's death, he retired to his estate to pursue intellectual life. Drawing on both life experiences and extensive reading, he wrote three volumes of essays in which he endeavored to strip away surface opinions and get at the core of human nature and society. His topics range from human emotions to the great Latin authors to philosophical speculations. Montaigne was intrigued by European accounts of the peoples of the 'New World' and found in them a stark contrast to the violent Wars of Religion between Catholics and Protestants that divided France during most of his life. In "On the Cannibals" he turns a critical eye toward Europeans, asking how they distinguish between 'barbarian' and 'civilized' peoples and why they think themselves to be among the latter.

---

### ON THE CANNIBALS

When King Pyrrhus crossed into Italy, after noting the excellent formation of the army which the Romans had sent ahead towards him he said, 'I do not know what kind of Barbarians these are' (for the Greeks called all foreigners Barbarians) 'but there is nothing barbarous about the ordering of the army which I can see!' The Greeks said the same about the army which Falminius brought over to their country, as did Philip when he saw from a hill-top in his kingdom the order and plan of the Roman encampment under Publius Sulpicius Galba.[1] We should be similarly wary of accepting common opinions; we should judge them by the ways of reason not by popular vote.

I have long had a man with me who stayed some ten or twelve years in that other world which was discovered in our century when Villegaignon made his landfall and named it *La France Antartique*.[2] This discovery of a boundless territory seems to me

---

1. Plutarch, *Life of Pyrrhus* and *Life of Flaminius*.
2. Durand de Villegagnon struck land, in Brazil, in 1557. Cf. *Lettres sur la navigation du chevalier de Villegaignon es terres de l'Amérique,* Paris, 1557, by an author who calls himself simply N.B.

worthy of reflection. I am by no means sure that some other land may not be discovered in the future, since so many persons, greater than we are, were wrong about this one! I fear that our eyes are bigger than our bellies, our curiosity more[3] than we can stomach. We grasp at everything but clasp nothing but wind.

That man of mine was a simple, rough fellow—qualities which make for a good witness: those clever chaps notice more things more carefully but are always adding glosses; they cannot help changing their story a little in order to make their views triumph and be more persuasive; they never show you anything purely as it is: they bend it and disguise it to fit in with their own views. To make their judgement more credible and to win you over they emphasize their own side, amplify it and extend it. So you need either a very trustworthy man or else a man so simple that he has nothing in him on which to build such false discoveries or make them plausible; and he must be wedded to no cause. Such was my man; moreover on various occasions he showed me several seamen and merchants whom he knew on that voyage. So I am content with what he told me, without inquiring what the cosmographers have to say about it.

What we need is topographers who would make detailed accounts of the places which they had actually been to. But because they have the advantage of visiting Palestine, they want to enjoy the right of telling us tales about all the rest of the world! I wish everyone would write only about what he knows—not in this matter only but in all others. A man may well have detailed knowledge or experience of the nature of one particular river or stream, yet about all the others he knows only what everyone else does; but in order to trot out his little scrap of knowledge he will write a book on the whole of physics! From this vice many great inconveniences arise.

Now to get back to the subject, I find (from what has been told me) that there is nothing savage or barbarous about those peoples, but that every man calls barbarous anything he is not accustomed to; it is indeed the case that we have no other criterion of truth or right-reason than the example and form of the opinions and customs of our own country. There we always find the perfect religion, the perfect polity, the most developed and perfect way of doing anything! Those 'savages' are only wild in the sense that we call fruits wild when they are produced by Nature in her ordinary course; whereas it is fruit which we have artificially perverted and misled from the common order which we ought to call savage. It is in the first kind that we find their true, vigorous, living, most natural and most useful properties and virtues, which we have bastardized in the other kind by merely adapting them to our corrupt tastes. Moreover, there is a delicious savour which even our taste finds excellent in a variety of fruits produced in those countries without cultivation: they rival our own. It is not sensible that artifice should be reverenced more than Nature, our great and powerful Mother. We have so overloaded the richness and beauty of her products by our own ingenuity that we have smothered her entirely. Yet wherever her pure light does shine, she wondrously shames our vain and frivolous enterprises:

> *Et veniunt ederæ sponte sua melius,*
> *Surgit et in solis formosior arbutus antris,*
> *Et volucres nulla dulcius arte canunt.*

3. '80: our bellies, *as they say, applying it to those whose appetite and hunger make them desire more meat than they can manage: I fear that we too have* curiosity far *more . . .*

[Ivy grows best when left untended; the strawberry tree flourishes more beautifully in lonely grottoes, and birds sing the sweeter for their artlessness.][4]

All our strivings cannot even manage to reproduce the nest of the smallest little bird, with its beauty and appropriateness to its purpose; we cannot even reproduce the web of the wretched spider. Plato says that all things are produced by nature, fortune or art, the greatest and fairest by the first two, the lesser and least perfect by the last.[5]

Those peoples, then, seem to me to be barbarous only in that they have been hardly fashioned by the mind of man, still remaining close neighbours to their original state of nature. They are still governed by the laws of Nature and are only very slightly bastardized by ours; but their purity is such that I am sometimes seized with irritation at their not having been discovered earlier, in times when there were men who could have appreciated them better than we do. It irritates me that neither Lycurgus nor Plato had any knowledge of them, for it seems to me that what experience has taught us about those peoples surpasses not only all the descriptions with which poetry has beautifully painted the Age of Gold[6] and all its ingenious fictions about Man's blessed early state, but also the very conceptions and yearnings of philosophy. They could not even imagine a state of nature so simple and so pure as the one we have learned about from experience; they could not even believe that societies of men could be maintained with so little artifice, so little in the way of human solder. I would tell Plato that those people have no trade of any kind, no acquaintance with writing, no knowledge of numbers, no terms for governor or political superior, no practice of subordination or of riches or poverty, no contracts, no inheritances, no divided estates, no occupation but leisure, no concern for kinship—except such as is common to them all—no clothing, no agriculture, no metals, no use of wine or corn. Among them you hear no words for treachery, lying, cheating, avarice, envy, backbiting or forgiveness. How remote from such perfection would Plato find that Republic which he thought up—'viri a diis recentes' [men fresh from the gods].[7]

*Hos natura modos primum dedit.*

[These are the ways which Nature first ordained.][8]

In addition they inhabit a land with a most delightful countryside and a temperate climate, so that, from what I have been told by my sources, it is rare to find anyone ill there;[9] I have been assured that they never saw a single man bent with age, toothless, blear-eyed or tottering. They dwell along the sea-shore, shut in to landwards by great lofty mountains, on a stretch of land some hundred leagues in width. They have fish and flesh in abundance which bear no resemblance to ours; these they eat simply cooked. They were so horror-struck by the first man who brought a horse

4. Propertius, I, ii, 10–12.
5. Plato, *Laws,* X, 888A–B.
6. Cf. Elizabeth Armstrong, *Ronsard and the Age of Gold,* Cambridge, 1968.
7. Seneca, *Epist. moral.,* XC, 44. (This epistle is a major defence of the innocence of natural man before he was corrupted by philosophy and progress.)
8. Virgil, *Georgics,* II, 208.
9. One of Montaigne's sources was Simon Goulart's *Histoire du Portugal,* Paris, 1587, based on a work by Bishop Jeronimo Osorio (da Fonseca) and others.

there and rode it that they killed him with their arrows before they could recognize him, even though he had had dealings with them on several previous voyages. Their dwellings are immensely long, big enough to hold two or three hundred souls; they are covered with the bark of tall trees which are fixed into the earth, leaning against each other in support at the top, like some of our barns where the cladding reaches down to the ground and acts as a side. They have a kind of wood so hard that they use it to cut with, making their swords from it as well as grills to cook their meat. Their beds are woven from cotton and slung from the roof like hammocks on our ships; each has his own, since wives sleep apart from their husbands. They get up at sunrise and have their meal for the day as soon as they do so; they have no other meal but that one. They drink nothing with it, like those Eastern peoples who, according to Suidas,[10] only drink apart from meals. They drink together several times a day, and plenty of it. This drink is made from a certain root and has the colour of our claret. They always drink it lukewarm; it only keeps for two or three days, it tastes a bit sharp, is in no ways heady and is good for the stomach; for those who are not used to it it is laxative but for those who are, it is a very pleasant drink. Instead of bread they use a certain white product resembling coriander-cakes. I have tried some: it tastes sweet and somewhat insipid.

They spend the whole day dancing; the younger men go off hunting with bow and arrow. Meanwhile some of the women-folk are occupied in warming up their drink: that is their main task. In the morning, before their meal, one of their elders walks from one end of the building to the other, addressing the whole barnful of them by repeating one single phrase over and over again until he has made the rounds, their building being a good hundred yards long. He preaches two things only: bravery before their enemies and love for their wives. They never fail to stress this second duty, repeating that it is their wives who season their drink and keep it warm. In my own house, as in many other places, you can see the style of their beds and rope-work as well as their wooden swords and the wooden bracelets with which they arm their wrists in battle, and the big open-ended canes to the sound of which they maintain the rhythm of their dances. They shave off all their hair, cutting it more cleanly than we do, yet with razors made of only wood or stone. They believe in the immortality of the soul: souls which deserve well of the gods dwell in the sky where the sun rises; souls which are accursed dwell where it sets. They have some priests and prophets or other, but they rarely appear among the people since they live in the mountains. When they do appear they hold a great festival and a solemn meeting of several villages—each of the barns which I have described constituting a village situated about one French league distant from the next. The prophet then addresses them in public, exhorting them to be virtuous and dutiful, but their entire system of ethics contains only the same two articles: resoluteness in battle and love for their wives. He foretells what is to happen and the results they must expect from what they undertake; he either incites them to war or deflects them from it, but only on condition that if he fails to divine correctly and if things turn out other than he foretold, then if they can catch him—he is condemned as a false prophet and hacked to pieces. So the prophet who gets it wrong once is seen no more.

---

10. Suidas, *Historica, caeteraque omnia quae ad cognitionem rerum spectant*, Basle, 1564.

Prophecy is a gift of God.[11] That is why abusing it should be treated as a punishable deceit. Among the Scythians, whenever their soothsayers got it wrong they were shackled hand and foot and laid in ox-carts full of bracken where they were burned.[12] Those who treat subjects under the guidance of human limitations can be excused if they have done their best; but those who come and cheat us with assurances of powers beyond the natural order and then fail to do what they promise, should they not be punished for it and for the foolhardiness of their deceit?

These peoples have their wars against others further inland beyond their mountains; they go forth naked, with no other arms but their bows and their wooden swords sharpened to a point like the blades of our pig-stickers. Their steadfastness in battle is astonishing and always ends in killing and bloodshed: they do not even know the meaning of fear or flight. Each man brings back the head of the enemy he has slain and sets it as a trophy over the door of his dwelling. For a long period they treat captives well and provide them with all the comforts which they can devise; afterwards the master of each captive summons a great assembly of his acquaintances; he ties a rope to one of the arms of his prisoner and holds him by it, standing a few feet away for fear of being caught in the blows, and allows his dearest friend to hold the prisoner the same way by the other arm: then, before the whole assembly, they both hack at him with their swords and kill him. This done, they roast him and make a common meal of him, sending chunks of his flesh to absent friends. This is not as some think done for food—as the Scythians used to do in antiquity—but to symbolize ultimate revenge, As a proof of this, when they noted that the Portuguese who were allied to their enemies practised a different kind of execution on them when taken prisoner—which was to bury them up to the waist, to shoot showers of arrows at their exposed parts and then to hang them—they thought that these men from the Other World, who had scattered a knowledge of many a vice throughout their neighbourhood and who were greater masters than they were of every kind of revenge, which must be more severe than their own; so they began to abandon their ancient method and adopted that one. It does not sadden me that we should note the horrible barbarity in a practice such as theirs: what does sadden me is that, while judging correctly of their wrong-doings we should be so blind to our own. I think there is more barbarity in eating a man alive than in eating him dead; more barbarity in lacerating by rack and torture a body still fully able to feel things, in roasting him little by little and having him bruised and bitten by pigs and dogs (as we have not only read about but seen in recent memory, not among enemies in antiquity but among our fellow-citizens and neighbours—and, what is worse, in the name of duty and religion) than in roasting him and eating him after his death.

Chrysippus and Zeno, the leaders of the Stoic school, certainly thought that there was nothing wrong in using our carcasses for whatever purpose we needed, even for food—as our own forebears did when, beleaguered by Caesar in the town of Alesia, they decided to relieve the hunger of the besieged with the flesh of old men, women and others who were no use in battle:

> *Vascones, fama est, alimentis talibus usi*
> *Produxere animas.*

11. Cf. Cicero, *De divinatione*, I, i.1; I Peter 1:2; I Corinthians 12:20; 13:2.
12. Herodotus, *History*, IV, lxix.

[By the eating of such food it is notorious that the Gascons prolonged their lives.][13]

And our medical men do not flinch from using corpses in many ways, both internally and externally, to cure us.[14] Yet no opinion has ever been so unruly as to justify treachery, disloyalty, tyranny and cruelty, which are everyday vices in us. So we can indeed call those folk barbarians by the rules of reason but not in comparison with ourselves, who surpass them in every kind of barbarism. Their warfare is entirely noble and magnanimous; it has as much justification and beauty as that human malady allows: among them it has no other foundation than a zealous concern for courage. They are not striving to conquer new lands, since without toil or travail they still enjoy that bounteous Nature who furnishes them abundantly with all they need, so that they have no concern to push back their frontiers. They are still in that blessed state of desiring nothing beyond what is ordained by their natural necessities: for them anything further is merely superfluous. The generic term which they use for men of the same age is 'brother'; younger men they call 'sons'. As for the old men, they are the 'fathers' of everyone else; they bequeath all their goods indivisibly, to all these heirs in common, there being no other entitlement than that with which Nature purely and simply endows all her creatures by bringing them into this world. If the neighbouring peoples come over the mountains to attack them and happen to defeat them, the victors' booty consists in fame and in the privilege of mastery in virtue and valour: they have no other interest in the goods of the vanquished and so return home to their own land, which lacks no necessity; nor do they lack that great accomplishment of knowing how to enjoy their mode-of-being in happiness and to be content with it. These people do the same in their turn, they require no other ransom from their prisoners-of-war than that they should admit and acknowledge their defeat—yet there is not one prisoner in a hundred years who does not prefer to die rather than to derogate from the greatness of an invincible mind by look or by word; you cannot find one who does not prefer to be killed and eaten than merely to ask to be spared. In order to make their prisoners love life more they treat them generously in every way,[15] but occupy their thoughts with the menaces of the death awaiting all of them, of the tortures they will have to undergo and of the preparations being made for it, of limbs to be lopped off and of the feast they will provide. All that has only one purpose: to wrench some weak or unworthy word from their lips or to make them wish to escape, so as to enjoy the privilege of having frightened them and forced their constancy.[16]

Indeed, if you take it the right way, true victory[17] consists in that alone:

*victoria nulla est*
*Quam quæ confessos animo quoque subjugat hostes.*

[There is no victory unless you subjugate the minds of the enemy and make them admit defeat.][18]

---

13. Sextus Empiricus, *Hypotyposes,* III, xxiv; Caesar, *Gallic Wars,* VII, lvii–lviii; Juvenal, *Satires,* XV, 93–4.
14. Mummies were imported for use in medicines. (Othello's handkerchief was steeped in 'juice of mummy.')
15. '80: generously in every way, *and furnish them with all the comforts they can devise* but . . .
16. '80: their *virtue and their* constancy . . .
17. '80: true *and solid* victory . . .
18. Claudian, *De sexto consulatu Honorii,* 248–9.

In former times those warlike fighters the Hungarians never pressed their advantage beyond making their enemy throw himself on their mercy. Once having wrenched this admission from him, they let him go without injury or ransom, except at most for an undertaking never again to bear arms against them.[19]

Quite enough of the advantages we do gain over our enemies are mainly borrowed ones not truly our own. To have stronger arms and legs is the property of a porter not of Valour; agility is a dead and physical quality, for it is chance which causes your opponent to stumble and which makes the sun dazzle him; to be good at fencing is a matter of skill and knowledge which may light on a coward or a worthless individual. A man's worth and reputation lie in the mind and in the will: his true honour is found there. Bravery does not consist in firm arms and legs but in firm minds and souls: it is not a matter of what our horse or our weapons are worth but of what we are. The man who is struck down but whose mind remains steadfast, *'si succiderit, de genu pugnat'* [if his legs give way, then on his knees doth he fight];[20] the man who relaxes none of his mental assurance when threatened with imminent death and who faces his enemy with inflexible scorn as he gives up the ghost is beaten by Fortune not by us: he is slain but not vanquished.[21] Sometimes it is the bravest who may prove most unlucky. So there are triumphant defeats rivalling victories; Salamis, Plataea, Mycale and Sicily are the fairest sister-victories which the Sun has ever seen, yet they would never dare to compare their combined glory with the glorious defeat of King Leonidas and his men at the defile of Thermopylae.[22] Who has ever run into battle with a greater desire and ambition for victory than did Captain Ischolas when he was defeated? Has any man ever assured his safety more cleverly or carefully than he assured his destruction?[23] His task was to defend against the Arcadians a certain pass in the Peleponnesus. He realized that he could not achieve this because of the nature of the site and of the odds against him, concluding that every man who faced the enemy must of necessity die in the battlefield; on the other hand he judged it unworthy of his own courage, of his greatness of soul and of the name of Sparta to fail in his duty; so he chose the middle path between these two extremes and acted thus: he saved the youngest and fittest soldiers of his unit to serve for the defence of their country and sent them back there. He then determined to defend that pass with men whose loss would matter less and who would, by their death, make the enemy purchase their breakthrough as dearly as possible. And so it turned out. After butchering the Arcadians who beset them on every side, they were all put to the sword. Was ever a trophy raised to a victor which was not better due to those who were vanquished? True victory lies in your role in the conflict, not in coming through safely: it consists in the honour of battling bravely not battling through.

To return to my tale, those prisoners, far from yielding despite all that was done to them during the two or three months of their captivity, maintain on the contrary a joyful countenance: they urge their captors to hurry up and put them to the test; they defy them, insult them and reproach them for cowardice and for all the battles they

---

19. Nicolas Chalcocondylas (tr. Blaise de Vigenère), *De la décadence de l'empire grec,* V, ix.
20. Seneca, *De constantia,* II.
21. '80: by us: *he is vanquished in practice but not by reason; it is his bad luck which we may indict not his cowardice.* Sometimes . . .
22. Cf. Cicero, *Tusc. disput.,* I, xli, 100 for the glory of Leonidas' death in the defile of Thermopylae.
23. Diodorus Siculus, XV, xii.

have lost against their country. I have a song made by one such prisoner which contains the following: Let them all dare to come and gather to feast on him, for with him they will feast on their own fathers and ancestors who have served as food and sustenance for his body. 'These sinews,' he said, 'this flesh and these veins—poor fools that you are—are your very own; you do not realize that they still contain the very substance of the limbs of your forebears: savour them well, for you will find that they taste of your very own flesh!' There is nothing 'barbarous' in the contriving of that topic. Those who tell how they die and who describe the act of execution show the prisoners spitting at their killers and pulling faces at them. Indeed, until their latest breath, they never stop braving them and defying them with word and look. It is no lie to say that these men are indeed savages—by our standards; for either they must be or we must be: there is an amazing gulf between their souls and ours.[24]

The husbands have several wives: the higher their reputation for valour the more of them they have. One beautiful characteristic of their marriages is worth noting: just as our wives are zealous in thwarting our love and tenderness for other women, theirs are equally zealous in obtaining them for them. Being more concerned for their husband's reputation than for anything else, they take care and trouble to have as many fellow-wives as possible, since that is a testimony to their husband's valour.

—Our wives will scream that that is a marvel, but it is not: it is a virtue proper to matrimony, but at an earlier stage. In the Bible Leah, Rachel, Sarah and the wives of Jacob all made their fair handmaidens available to their husbands; Livia, to her own detriment, connived at the lusts of Augustus, and Stratonice the consort of King Deiotarus not only provided her husband with a very beautiful chambermaid who served her but carefully brought up their children and lent a hand in enabling them to succeed to her husband's rank.[25]

—Lest anyone should think that they do all this out of a simple slavish subjection to convention or because of the impact of the authority of their ancient customs without any reasoning or judgement on their part, having minds so dulled that they could never decide to do anything else, I should cite a few examples of what they are capable of.

Apart from that war-song which I have just given an account of, I have another of their songs, a love-song, which begins like this:

> O Adder, stay: stay O Adder! From your colours
>    let my sister take the pattern for a girdle
>    she will make for me to offer to my love;
> So may your beauty and your speckled hues be for
>    ever honoured above all other snakes.

This opening couplet serves as the song's refrain. Now I know enough about poetry to make the following judgement: not only is there nothing 'barbarous' in this conceit but it is thoroughly anacreontic.[26] Their language incidentally is a pleasant one with an agreeable sound and has terminations[27] rather like Greek.

---

24. '80: their *constancy* and ours . . .
25. Standard examples: cf. Tiraquellus, *De legibus connubialibus,* XIII, 35, for all these un-jealous wives. (But Leah and Sarah were in fact Jacob's wives.)
26. Anacreon was the great love-poet of Teos (fl. 540 B.C.).
27. '80: their language *is the pleasantest language in the world; its* sound *is agreeable to the ear* and has terminations . . .

Three such natives, unaware of what price in peace and happiness they would have to pay to buy a knowledge of our corruptions, and unaware that such commerce would lead to their downfall—which I suspect to be already far advanced—pitifully allowing themselves to be cheated by their desire for novelty and leaving the gentleness of their regions to come and see ours, were at Rouen at the same time as King Charles IX.[28] The King had a long interview with them: they were shown our manners, our ceremonial and the layout of a fair city. Then someone asked them what they thought of all this and wanted to know what they had been most amazed by. They made three points; I am very annoyed with myself for forgetting the third, but I still remember two of them. In the first place they said (probably referring to the Swiss Guard) that they found it very odd that all those full-grown bearded men, strong and bearing arms in the King's entourage, should consent to obey a boy rather than choosing one of themselves as a Commander; secondly—since they have an idiom in their language which calls all men 'halves' of one another—that they had noticed that there among us men fully bloated with all sorts of comforts while their halves were begging at their doors, emaciated with poverty and hunger: they found it odd that those destitute halves should put up with such injustice and did not take the others by the throat or set fire to their houses.

I had a very long talk with one of them (but I used a stupid interpreter who was so bad at grasping my meaning and at understanding my ideas that I got little joy from it). When I asked the man (who was a commander among them, our sailors calling him a king) what advantage he got from high rank, he told me that it was to lead his troops into battle; asked how many men followed him, he pointed to an open space to signify as many as it would hold—about four or five thousand men; questioned whether his authority lapsed when the war was over, he replied that he retained the privilege of having paths cut for him through the thickets in their forests, so that he could easily walk through them when he visited villages under his sway.

Not at all bad, that.—Ah! But they wear no breeches . . .

28. In 1562, when Rouen was retaken by Royalist forces.

# Richard Hakluyt

## *from* THE PRINCIPAL NAVIGATIONS, VOYAGES, TRAFFIQUES AND DISCOVERIES OF THE ENGLISH NATION (1598–1600)

*Richard Hakluyt (1551?–1616) studied at Oxford, where he read many records of travel and exploration, took religious orders, and later lectured on geography. Hakluyt combined a scholarly interest in travel with practical politics, drawing on his expertise in geography to further England's economic and political purposes. His first book,* Divers Voyages Touching the Discovery of America *(1582), compiled various earlier accounts in order to document what was known about the New World and make a case for English expansion abroad.* The Principal Navigations, Voyages, Traffiques and Discoveries of the English Nation, *Hakluyt's major work, celebrates the accomplishments of English travelers and explorers, particularly sixteenth-century explorers such as Martin Frobisher and Sir Francis Drake. It also provides eyewitness information about travel routes, politics, customs, and natural resources to aid future European trade expeditions and explorers who might journey beyond the edges of the mapped world.*

### [PREFACE TO THE SECOND EDITION, 1598]

Having for the benefit and honour of my country zealously bestowed so many years, so much travail and cost, to bring antiquities smothered and buried in dark silence, to light, and to preserve certain memorable exploits of late years by our English nation achieved, from the greedy and devouring jaws of oblivion: to gather likewise, and as it were to incorporate into one body the torn and scattered limbs of our ancient and late navigations by sea, our voyages by land, and traffics of merchandise by both: I do this second time (friendly reader) presume to offer unto thy view this discourse. For the bringing of which into this homely and rough-hewn shape, which here thou seest, what restless nights, what painful days, what heat, what cold I have endured; how many long and chargeable journeys I have travelled; how many famous libraries I have searched into; what variety of ancient and modern writers I have perused, what expenses I have not spared; and yet what fair opportunities of private gain, preferment, and ease I have neglected. Howbeit, the honour and benefit of this Commonweal wherein I live and breathe hath made all difficulties seem easy.

Be it granted that the renowned Portugal Vasco da Gama traversed the main ocean southward of Africa. Did not Richard Chancellor and his mates perform the like, northward of Europe? Suppose that Columbus that noble and high-spirited Genoese escried unknown lands to the westward of Europe and Africa: did not the valiant English knight Sir Hugh Willoughby; did not the famous pilots Stephen Burrough, Arthur Pet, and Charles Jackman accost Novaya Zemlya to the north of Europe and Asia? Howbeit you will say perhaps, not with the like golden success, not with such deductions of colonies, nor attaining of conquests. True it is, that our success hath not been correspondent unto theirs: yet in this our attempt the uncertainty of finding was far greater, and the difficulty and danger of searching was no whit less.

Into what dangers and difficulties they plunged themselves, I tremble to recount. For first they were to expose themselves unto the rigour of the stern and uncouth northern seas, then they were to sail by the ragged and perilous coast of Norway, to frequent the unhaunted shores of Finmark, to double the dreadful and misty North Cape, and as it were to open and unlock the sevenfold mouth of Dvina. Unto what drifts of snow and mountains of ice even in June, July, and August, unto what hideous over-falls, uncertain currents, dark mists and fogs, and divers other fearful inconveniences they were subject and in danger of, I wish you rather to learn out of the voyages of Sir Hugh Willoughby, Stephen Burrough, Arthur Pet and the rest. . . .

## The new navigation and discovery of the kingdom of Moscovy, by the northeast, in the year 1553: enterprised by Sir Hugh Willoughby knight, and performed by Richard Chancellor pilot major of the voyage.

At what time our merchants perceived the commodities and wares of England to be in small request with the countries and people about us, and near to us, and that those merchandises were now neglected, and the price thereof abated, certain grave citizens of London, and men careful for the good of their country, began to think with themselves, how this mischief might be remedied.

Seeing that the wealth of the Spaniards and Portuguese, by the discovery and search of new trades and countries was marvellously increased, supposing the same to be a course and mean for them also to obtain the like, they thereupon resolved upon a new and strange navigation. After much speech and conference together, it was at last concluded that three ships should be prepared and furnished out, for the search and discovery of the northern part of the world, to open a way and passage to our men for travel to new and unknown kingdoms. Every man willing to be of the society, should disburse the portion of twenty and five pounds apiece: so that in short time by this means the sum of six thousand pounds being gathered, the three ships were bought, newly built and trimmed. Whereas they afore determined to have the eastern part of the world sailed unto, and yet that the sea towards the same was not open, whereas yet it was doubtful whether there were any passage yea or no, they resolved to victual the ships for eighteen months, six months victual to sail to the place, so much more to remain there if the extremity of the winter hindered their return, and so much more also for the time of their coming home.

One Sir Hugh Willoughby a most valiant gentleman, and well born, very earnestly requested to have that care and charge committed unto him. At last they concluded and appointed him the admiral. And for the government of the other ships, one Richard Chancellor, a man of great estimation for many good parts of wit in him, was elected. By the twentieth day of May, the captains and mariners should take shipping, and depart from Radcliffe upon the ebb, if it pleased God. They having saluted their acquaintance, one his wife, another his children, another his kinsfolks, and having weighed anchor, they departed with the turning of the water, and sailing easily, came first to Greenwich. The greater ships are towed down with boats, and oars, and the mariners being all apparelled in watchet or sky coloured cloth, made way with diligence. And being come near to Greenwich (where the Court then lay), presently upon the news, the courtiers came running out, and the common people flocked together, standing very thick upon the shore: the Privy Council, they looked out at the windows of the Court, and the rest ran up to the tops of the towers: the ships hereupon discharged their ordnance. One stood in the poop of the ship, and by his gesture bids farewell to his friends in the best manner he could. Another walks upon the hatches, another climbs the shrouds, another stands upon the mainyard, and another in the top of the ship. To be short, it was a very triumph. They departed and came to Harwich: at the last, with a good wind they hoisted up sail, and committed themselves to the sea, giving their last adieu to their native country, which they knew not whether they should ever return to see again or not.

Sir Hugh Willoughby, a man of good foresight called together the chiefest men of the other ships. They conclude and agree, that if any great tempest should arise at any time, and happen to disperse and scatter them, every ship should endeavour his best to go to Wardhouse, a haven or castle of some name in the kingdom of Norway, and that they that arrived there first in safety, should stay and expect the coming of the rest.

The very same day in the afternoon, about four of the clock, so great a tempest suddenly arose, and the seas were so outrageous, that the ships could not keep their intended course, but some were perforce driven one way, and some another way, to their great peril and hazard. The said admiral bearing all his sails, was carried away with so great force and swiftness, that not long after he was quite out of sight, and the third ship also was dispersed and lost us. The ship boat of the admiral was overwhelmed in the sight and view of the manners of the *Bonaventure*.

Now Richard Chancellor with his ship and company being thus left alone, shapeth his course for Wardhouse in Norway, there to expect and abide the arrival of the rest of the ships. Having stayed there the space of seven days, and looked in vain for their coming, he determined at length to proceed alone in the purposed voyage. As he was preparing himself to depart, he fell in company and speech with certain Scottishmen, who began earnestly to dissuade him from the further prosecution of the discovery, by amplifying the dangers which he was to fall into. But he persuading himself that a man of valour could not commit a more dishonourable part than for fear of danger to avoid and shun great attempts, was nothing at all changed or discouraged, remaining steadfast and immutable in his first resolution: determining either to bring that to pass which was intended, or else to die the death.

As for them which were with Master Chancellor in his ship, they were resolute. When they saw their desire and hope of the arrival of the rest of the ships to be every day more and more frustrated, they provided to sea again, and Master Chancellor held on his course towards that unknown part of the world, and sailed so far, that he came at last to the place where he found no night at all, but a continual light and brightness of the sun shining clearly upon the huge and mighty sea. At length it pleased God to bring them into a certain great bay, whereinto they entered. Looking every way about them, they espied afar off a certain fisher boat, which Master Chancellor, accompanied with a few of his men, went towards. They being amazed by the strange greatness of his ship, began presently to avoid and to flee: but he still following them at last overtook them, they (being in great fear, as men half-dead) prostrated themselves before him, offering to kiss his feet: but he (according to his great and singular courtesy,) looked pleasantly upon them, comforting them by signs and gestures, refusing those duties and reverences of theirs, and taking them up in all loving sort from the ground. And it is strange to consider how much favour afterwards in that place, this humanity of his did purchase to himself. For they spread a report abroad of the arrival of a strange nation, of a singular gentleness and courtesy: whereupon the common people came together offering to these new-come guests victuals freely, and not refusing to traffic with them, except they had been bound by a certain religious use and custom, not to buy any foreign commodities, without the knowledge and consent of the king.

This country was called Russia, or Moscovy, and Ivan Vasilivich (which was at that time their King's name) ruled and governed far and wide in those places. And the barbarous Russians asked likewise of our men whence they were: whereunto answer was made, that they were Englishmen sent into those coasts, from the most excellent King Edward the Sixth, having from him in commandment certain things to deliver to their king, and seeking nothing else but his amity and friendship, and traffic with his people, whereby they doubted not, but that great commodity and profit would grow to the subjects of both kingdoms.

They secretly sent a message to the Emperor, to certify him of the arrival of a strange nation, and withall to know his pleasure concerning them. He granted liberty to his subjects to bargain and traffic with them: and further promised, that if it would please them to come to him, he himself would bear the whole charges of post horses. So Master Chancellor began his journey, which was very long and most troublesome, wherein he had the use of certain sleds, which in that country are very common, the people almost not knowing any other manner of carriage, the cause whereof is the exceeding hardness of the ground congealed in the winter time by the force of the cold, which in those places is very extreme and horrible. After much ado and great pains taken in this long and weary journey (for they had travelled very near fifteen hundred miles), Master Chancellor came at last to Moscow, the chief city of the kingdom, and the seat of the king.

The whole country is plain and champaign, and a few hills in it: and towards the north it hath very large and spacious woods, wherein is great store of fir trees, a wood very necessary, and fit for the building of houses: there are also wild beasts bred in those woods, as bears and black wolves. When the winter doth once begin there it doth still more and more increase by a perpetuity of cold: neither doth that cold slack, until the force of the sunbeams doth dissolve the cold, and make glad the earth. Our mariners which we left in the ship in the meantime to keep it, in their going up only from their cabins to the hatches, had their breath oftentimes so suddenly taken away, that they eftsoons fell down as men very nearly dead, so great is the sharpness of that cold climate.

The empire and government of the king is very large, and his wealth at this time exceeding great. The city of Moscow is the chiefest of all the rest. Our men say, that in bigness it is as great as the City of London, with the suburbs thereof. There are many and great buildings in it, but for beauty and fairness nothing comparable to ours. Their streets and ways are not paved with stone as ours are: the walls of their houses are of wood: the roofs for the most part are covered with shingle boards.

After they had remained about twelve days in the city, there was then a messenger sent unto them, to bring them to the King's house: within the gates of the court, there sat a very honourable company of courtiers, to the number of one hundred, all apparelled in cloth of gold, down to their ankles: being conducted into the chamber of presences our men began to wonder at the majesty of the Emperor: his seat was aloft, in a very royal throne, having on his head a diadem, or crown of gold, apparelled with a robe all of goldsmith's work, and in his hand he held a sceptre garnished, and beset with precious stones. On one side of him stood his chief Secretary, on the other side, the great Commander, both of them arrayed also in cloth of gold: and then there sat the council of one hundred and fifty in number, all in like sort arrayed.

Master Chancellor being therewithall nothing dismayed, saluted, and did his duty to the Emperor, after the manner of England, and withall, delivered unto him the letters of our king, Edward the Sixth.

Next unto Moscow, the City of Novgorod is reputed the chiefest of Russia: the chiefest and greatest market town of all Moscovy. This town excels all the rest in the commodities of flax and hemp: it yields also hides, honey, and wax. The Flemings there sometimes had a house of merchandise, but by reason that they used ill dealing there, they lost their privileges. Those Flemings hearing of the arrival of our men in those parts, wrote their letters to the Emperor against them, accusing them for pirates and rovers, wishing him to detain and imprison them. Which things when they were known of our men, they conceived fear, that they should never have returned home. But the Emperor believing rather the King's letters, which our men brought, than the lying and false suggestions of the Flemings, used no ill entreaty towards them.

The north parts of Russia yield very rare and precious skins: and amongst the rest, those principally, which we call sables, worn about the necks of our noblewomen and ladies: it hath also martins' skins, white, black, and red fox skins, skins of hares, and ermines, and others, as beavers, minxes and minivers. They use to boil the water of the sea, whereof they make very great store of salt.

They maintain the opinions of the Greek Church. In their private houses they have images for their household saints: he that comes into his neighbour's house doth first salute his saints, although he see them not. For the articles of our faith, and the Ten Commandments, no man, or at the least very few of them do either know them or can say them: their opinion is that such secret and holy things as they are should not rashly and imprudently be communicated with the common people. Concerning the Latin, Greek and Hebrew tongues, they are altogether ignorant.

There is a certain part of Moscovy bordering upon the countries of the Tartars, wherein those Moscovites that dwell are very great idolaters. The common houses of the country are everywhere built of beams of fir tree. The form and fashion of their houses in all places is four squares with strait and narrow windows, whereby with a transparent casement made or covered with skin like to parchment they receive the light. They have stoves wherein in the morning they make a fire, and the same fire doth either moderately warm, or make very hot the whole house.

These are the things most excellent Queen, which your subjects newly returned from Russia have brought home concerning the state of that country.

# Mary Wortley Montagu

## LETTERS (1716–1718)

*Mary Wortley Montagu (1689–1762) accompanied her husband to Constantinople, where he had been sent as ambassador from England. The journey took them through central Europe and across the Balkans, scarred by decades of fighting between armies of the Holy Roman and Ottoman empires, to Constantinople. Two years later she returned to England by way of Tunis and France. During the course of her travels she wrote long descriptive letters to her sister the Countess of Mar, the poet Alexander Pope, and others in which she measured English ideas about everything from the Austrian court to the secrets of the Turkish harem against her experiences. She also reported on the Turkish practice of inoculation for smallpox, then unknown in England. The letters circulated widely in English social circles when they were first written, and years later Wortley Montagu prepared them for publication. Despite objections from her daughter, who shared the assumption of her class that women should not be known as authors, the book appeared within a year of her death.*

---

### TO THE COUNTESS OF B. [BRISTOL].

#### *Nuremberg, Aug. 22, O.S. [1716].*

After five days travelling post, I am sure I could sit down to write on no other occasion, but to tell my dear Lady _____, that I have not forgot her obliging command, of sending her some account of my travels.

I have already passed a large part of Germany, have seen all that is remarkable in Cologne, Frankfort, Wurtsburg, and this place; and 'tis impossible not to observe the difference between the free towns and those under the government of absolute princes, as all the little sovereigns of Germany are. In the first, there appears an air of commerce and plenty. The streets are well built, and full of people, neatly and plainly dressed. The shops loaded with merchandise, and the commonalty clean and cheerful. In the other, a sort of shabby finery, a number of dirty people of quality tawdered out; narrow nasty streets out of repair, wretchedly thin of inhabitants, and above half of the common sort asking alms. I cannot help fancying one under the figure of a handsome clean Dutch citizen's wife, and the other like a poor town lady of pleasure, painted and ribboned out in her head-dress, with tarnished silver-laced shoes and a ragged under-petticoat, a miserable mixture of vice and poverty.

They have sumptuary laws in this town, which distinguish their rank by their dress, and prevent the excess which ruins so many other cities, and has a more agreeable effect to the eye of a stranger than our fashions. I think, after the Archbishop of Cambray having declared for them, I need not be ashamed to own, that I wish these laws were in force in other parts of the world. When one considers impartially the merits of a rich suit of clothes in most places, the respect and the smiles of favour that it procures, not to speak of the envy and the sighs it occasions (which is very often the principal charm to the wearer), one is forced to confess, that there is need of an uncommon understanding to resist the temptation of pleasing friends and mortifying rivals; and that it is natural to young people to fall into a folly, which betrays them to that want of money which is the source of a thousand basenesses. What numbers of men have begun the world with generous inclinations, that have afterwards been the instruments of bringing misery on a whole people, being led by a vain expence into debts, that they could clear no other way but by the forfeit of their honour, and which they would never have contracted, if the respect the many pay to habits was fixed by law only to a particular colour or cut of plain cloth! These reflections draw after them others that are too melancholy. I will make haste to put them out of your head by the farce of relics, with which I have been entertained in all the Romish churches.

The Lutherans are not quite free from these follies. I have seen here, in the principal church, a large piece of the cross set in jewels, and the point of the spear, which they told me, very gravely, was the same that pierced the side of our Saviour. But I was particularly diverted in a little Roman Catholic church which is permitted here, where the professors of that religion are not very rich, and consequently cannot adorn their images in so rich a manner as their neighbours. For, not to be quite destitute of all finery, they have dressed up an image of our Saviour over the altar in a fair full-bottomed wig very well powdered. I imagine I see your ladyship stare at this article, of which you very much doubt the veracity; but, upon my word, I have not yet made use of the privilege of a traveller; and my whole account is writ with the same plain sincerity of heart, with which I assure you that I am, dear madam, your ladyship's, &c.

## To the Countess of _____ [Mar].

### *Vienna, Sept. 14, O.S. [1716].*

Though I have so lately troubled you, my dear sister, with a long letter, yet I will keep my promise in giving you an account of my first going to court.

In order to that ceremony, I was squeezed up in a gown, and adorned with a gorget and the other implements thereunto belonging: a dress very inconvenient, but which certainly shews the neck and shape to great advantage. I cannot forbear in this place giving you some description of the fashions here, which are more monstrous and contrary to all common sense and reason, than 'tis possible for you to imagine. They build certain fabrics of gauze on their heads about a yard high, consisting of three or four stories, fortified with numberless yards of heavy ribbon. The foundation of this structure is a thing they call a *Bourle* which is exactly of the same shape and kind, but about four times as big, as those rolls our prudent milk-maids make use of to fix their pails upon. This machine they cover with their own hair, which they mix with a great deal of false, it being a particular beauty to have their heads too large to go into a moderate tub. Their hair is prodigiously powdered, to conceal the mixture, and set out with three or four rows of bodkins (wonderfully large, that stick [out] two or three inches from their hair), made of diamonds, pearls, red, green, and yellow stones, that it certainly requires as much art and experience to carry the load upright, as to dance upon May-day with the garland. Their whalebone petticoats outdo ours by several yards circumference, and cover some acres of ground.

You may easily suppose how much this extraordinary dress sets off and improves the natural ugliness with which God Almighty has been pleased to endow them all generally. Even the lovely empress herself is obliged to comply, in some degree, with these absurd fashions, which they would not quit for all the world. I had a private audience (according to ceremony) of half an hour, and then all the other ladies were permitted to come [and] make their court. I was perfectly charmed with the empress: I cannot, however, tell you that her features are regular; her eyes are not large, but have a lively look, full of sweetness; her complexion the finest I ever saw; her nose and forehead well made, but her mouth has ten thousand charms that touch the soul. When she smiles, 'tis with a beauty and sweetness that forces adoration. She has a vast quantity of fine fair hair; but then her person!—one must speak of it poetically to do it rigid justice; all that the poets have said of the mien of Juno, the air of Venus, come not up to the truth. The Graces move with her; the famous statues of Medecis was not formed with more delicate proportions; nothing can be added to the beauty of her neck and hands. Till I saw them, I did not believe there were any in nature so perfect, and I was almost sorry that my rank here did not permit me to kiss them; but they are kissed sufficiently; for every body that waits on her pays that homage at their entrance, and when they take leave.

When the ladies were come in, she sat down to Quinze. I could not play at a game I had never seen before, and she ordered me a seat at her right hand, and had the goodness to talk to me very much, with that grace so natural to her. I expected every moment, when the men were to come in to pay their court; but this drawing-room is very different from that of England; no man enters it but the old grand-master, who comes in to advertize the empress of the approach of the emperor. His imperial majesty did me the honour of speaking to me in a very obliging manner; but he never speaks to any of the other ladies; and the whole passes with a gravity and air of ceremony that has something very formal in it.

## To the Countess of _____ [Mar].

### Blankenburg, Dec. 17, O.S. [1716].

You will not forgive me, if I do not say something of Hanover; I cannot tell you that the town is either large or magnificent. The opera-house, which was built by the late Elector, is much finer than that of Vienna. I was very sorry that the ill weather did not permit me to see Hernhausen in all its beauty; but, in spite of the snow, I thought the gardens very fine. I was particularly surprised at the vast number of orange trees, much larger than I have ever seen in England, though this climate is certainly colder. But I had more reason to wonder that night at the king's table. There was brought to him from a gentleman of this country, two large baskets full of ripe oranges and lemons of different sorts, many of which were quite new to me; and, what I thought worth all the rest, two ripe ananas, which, to my taste, are a fruit perfectly delicious. You know they are naturally the growth of Brazil, and I could not imagine how they could come there but by enchantment. Upon enquiry, I learnt that they have brought their stoves to such perfection, they lengthen the summer as long as they please, giving to every plant the degree of heat it would receive from the sun in its native soil. The effect is very near the same; I am surprised we do not practise in England so useful an invention.

This reflection naturally leads me to consider our obstinacy in shaking with cold six months in the year, rather than make use of stoves, which are certainly one of the greatest conveniences of life; and so far from spoiling the form of a room, they add very much to the magnificence of it, when they are painted and gilt, as at Vienna, or at Dresden, where they are often the shape of china jars, statues, or fine cabinets, so naturally represented, they are not to be distinguished. If ever I return, in defiance to the fashion, you shall certainly see one in the chamber of,

Dear sister, &c.

## To the Countess of _____ [Mar].

### *Peterwaradin, Jan. 30, O.S. [1717]*

. . . Leaving Comora on the other side [of] the river, we went the eighteenth to Nosmuhl, a small village, where, however, we made shift to find tolerable accommodation. We continued two days travelling between this place and Buda, through the finest plains in the world, as even as if they were paved, and extremely fruitful; but for the most part desert and uncultivated, laid waste by the long war between the Turk and emperor, and the more cruel civil war occasioned by the barbarous persecution of the Protestant religion by the Emperor Leopold. That prince has left behind him the character of an extraordinary piety, and was naturally of a mild merciful temper; but, putting his conscience into the hands of a Jesuit, he was more cruel and treacherous to his poor Hungarian subjects, than ever the Turk has been to the Christians; breaking, without scruple, his coronation oath, and his faith, solemnly given in many public treaties. Indeed, nothing can be more melancholy than, travelling through Hungary, reflecting on the former flourishing state of that kingdom, and seeing such a noble spot of earth almost uninhabited. This is also the present circumstances of Buda (where we arrived very early the twenty-second), once the royal seat of the Hungarian kings, where their palace was reckoned one of the most beautiful buildings of the age, now wholly destroyed, no part of the town having been repaired since the last siege, but the fortifications and the castle, which is the present residence of the governor-general Ragule, an officer of great merit. He came immediately to see us, and carried us in his coach to his house, where I was received by his lady with all possible civility and magnificently entertained.

## To Mr. P. [Pope].

### *Belgrade, Feb. 12, O.S. [1717].*

. . . This little digression has interrupted my telling you we passed over the fields of Carlowitz, where the last great victory was obtained by Prince Eugene over the Turks. The marks of that glorious bloody day are yet recent, the field being strewed with the skulls and carcases of unburied men, horses, and camels. I could not look without horror, on such numbers of mangled human bodies, and reflect on the injustice of war, that makes murder not only necessary but meritorious. Nothing seems to be a plainer proof of the irrationality of mankind (whatever fine claims we pretend to reason) than the rage with which they contest for a small spot of ground, when such large parts of fruitful earth lie quite uninhabited. It is true, custom has now made it unavoidable; but can there be a greater demonstration of want of reason, than a custom being firmly established, so plainly contrary to the interest of man in general? I am a good deal inclined to believe Mr. Hobbes, that the state of nature is a state of war; but thence I conclude human nature not rational, if the word reason means common sense, as I suppose it does. I have a great many admirable arguments to support this reflection; but I won't trouble you with them, but return, in a plain style, to the history of my travels.

## To the Lady.

### *Adrianople, April 1, O.S. [1717].*

I am now got into a new world, where everything I see appears to me a change of scene; and I write to your ladyship with some content of mind, hoping at least that you will find the charm of novelty in my letters, and no longer reproach me, that I tell you nothing extraordinary.

I won't trouble you with a relation of our tedious journey; but I must not omit what I saw remarkable at Sophia, one of the most beautiful towns in the Turkish empire, and famous for its hot baths, that are resorted to both for diversion and health. I stopped here one day on purpose to see them. Designing to go *incognita,* I hired a Turkish coach. These voitures are not at all like ours, but much more convenient for the country, the heat being so great that glasses would be very troublesome. . . .

. . . I went to the bagnio about ten o'clock. It was already full of women. It is built of stone, in the shape of a dome, with no windows but in the roof, which gives light enough. There were five of these domes joined together, the outmost being less than the rest, and serving only as a hall, where the portress stood at the door. Ladies of quality generally give this woman the value of a crown or ten shillings; and I did not forget that ceremony. The next room is a very large one paved with marble, and all round it, raised, two sofas of marble, one above another. There were four fountains of cold water in this room, falling first into marble basins, and then running on the floor in little channels made for that purpose, which carried the streams into the next room, something less than this, with the same sort of marble sofas, but so hot with steams of sulphur proceeding from the baths joining to it, it was impossible to stay there with one's clothes on. The two other domes were the hot baths, one of which had cocks of cold water turning into it, to temper it to what degree of warmth the bathers have a mind to.

I was in my travelling habit, which is a riding dress, and certainly appeared very extraordinary to them. Yet there was not one of them that shewed the least surprise or impertinent curiosity, but received me with all the obliging civility possible. I know no European court where the ladies would have behaved themselves in so polite a manner to a stranger. I believe in the whole, there were two hundred women, and yet none of those disdainful smiles, or satiric whispers, that never fail in our assemblies when any body appears that is not dressed exactly in the fashion. They repeated over and over to me, "Uzelle, pék uzelle," which is nothing but Charming, very charming.—The first sofas were covered with cushions and rich carpets, on which sat the ladies; and on the second, their slaves behind them, but without any distinction of rank by their dress, all being in the state of nature, that is, in plain English, stark naked, without any beauty or defect concealed. Yet there was not the least wanton smile or immodest gesture amongst them. They walked and moved with the same majestic grace which Milton describes of our general mother. There were many amongst them as exactly proportioned as ever any goddess was drawn by the pencil of Guido or Titian,—and most of their skins shiningly white, only adorned by their beautiful hair divided into many tresses, hanging on their shoulders, braided either with pearl or ribbon, perfectly representing the figures of the Graces.

I was here convinced of the truth of a reflection I had often made, that if it was the fashion to go naked, the face would be hardly observed. I perceived that the ladies with the finest skins and most delicate shapes had the greatest share of my admiration, though their faces were sometimes less beautiful than those of their companions. To tell you the truth, I had wickedness enough to wish secretly that Mr. Jervas could have been there invisible. I fancy it would have very much improved his art, to see so many fine women naked, in different postures, some in conversation, some working, others drinking coffee or sherbet, and many negligently lying on their cushions, while their slaves (generally pretty girls of seventeen or eighteen) were employed in braiding their hair in several pretty fancies. In short, it is the women's coffee-house, where all the news of the town is told, scandal invented, &c.—They generally take this diversion once a-week, and stay there at least four or five hours, without getting cold by immediate coming out of the hot bath into the cold room, which was very surprising to me. The lady that seemed the most considerable among them, entreated me to sit by her, and would fain have undressed me for the bath. I excused myself with some difficulty. They being all so earnest in persuading me, I was at last forced to open my shirt, and shew them my stays; which satisfied them very well, for, I saw, they believed I was so locked up in that machine, that it was not in my own power to open it, which contrivance they attributed to my husband.—I was charmed with their civility and beauty, and should have been very glad to pass more time with them; but Mr. W____[Wortley] resolving to pursue his journey the next morning early, I was in haste to see the ruins of Justinian's church, which did not afford me so agreeable a prospect as I had left, being little more than a heap of stones.

Adieu, madam: I am sure I have now entertained you with an account of such a sight as you never saw in your life, and what no book of travels could inform you of. 'Tis no less than death for a man to be found in one of these places.

## To Mrs. S. C_____ [Miss Sarah Chiswell].

### *Adrianople, April 1, O.S. [1717].*

*A propos* of distempers, I am going to tell you a thing that I am sure will make you wish yourself here. The small-pox, so fatal, and so general amongst us, is here entirely harmless by the invention of *ingrafting*, which is the term they give it. There is a set of old women who make it their business to perform the operation every autumn, in the month of September, when the great heat is abated. People send to one another to know if any of their family has a mind to have the small-pox: they make parties for this purpose, and when they are met (commonly fifteen or sixteen together), the old woman comes with a nut-shell full of the matter of the best sort of small-pox, and asks what veins you please to have opened. She immediately rips open that you offer to her with a large needle (which gives you no more pain than a common scratch), and puts into the vein as much venom as can lie upon the head of her needle, and after binds up the little wound with a hollow bit of shell; and in this manner opens four or five veins. The Grecians have commonly the superstition of opening one in the middle of the forehead, in each arm, and on the breast, to mark the sign of the cross; but this has a very ill effect, all these wounds leaving little scars, and is not done that those that are not superstitious, who choose to have them in the legs, or that part of the arm that is concealed. The children or young patients play together all the rest of the day, and are in perfect health to the eighth. Then the fever begins to seize them, and they keep their beds two days, very seldom three. They have very rarely above twenty or thirty in their faces, which never mark; and in eight days' time they are as well as before their illness. Where they are wounded, there remain running sores during the distemper, which I don't doubt is a great relief to it. Every year thousands undergo this operation; and the French embassador says pleasantly, that they take the small-pox here by way of diversion, as they take the waters in other countries. There is no example of any one that has died in it; and you may believe I am very well satisfied of the safety of this experiment, since I intend to try it on my dear little son.

I am patriot enough to take pains to bring this useful invention into fashion in England; and I should not fail to write to some of our doctors very particularly about it, if I knew any one of them that I thought had virtue enough to destroy such a considerable branch of their revenue for the good of mankind. But that distemper is too beneficial to them not to expose to all their resentment the hardy wight that should undertake to put an end to it. Perhaps, if I live to return, I may, however, have courage to war with them. Upon this occasion admire the heroism in the heart of your friend, &c.

## To the Lady _____.

### Belgrade Village, June 17, O.S. [1717].

I heartily beg your ladyship's pardon; but I really could not forbear laughing heartily at your letter, and the commissions you are pleased to honour me with.

You desire me to buy you a Greek slave, who is to be mistress of a thousand good qualities. The Greeks are subjects, and not slaves. Those who are to be bought in that manner, are either such as are taken to war, or stolen by the Tartars from Russia, Circassia, or Georgia, and are such miserable, awkward, poor wretches, you would not think any of them worthy to be your housemaids. 'Tis true that many thousands were taken in the Morea; but they have been, most of them, redeemed by the charitable contributions of the Christians, or ransomed by their own relations at Venice. The fine slaves that wait upon the great ladies, or serve the pleasures of the great men, are all bought at the age of eight or nine years old, and educated with great care, to accomplish them in singing, dancing, embroidery, &c. They are commonly Circassians, and their patron never sells them, except it is as a punishment for some very great fault. If ever they grow weary of them, they either present them to a friend, or give them their freedom. Those that are exposed to sale at the markets are always either guilty of some crime, or so entirely worthless that they are of no use at all. I am afraid you will doubt the truth of this account, which I own is very different from our common notions in England; but it is no less truth for all that.

Your whole letter is full of mistakes from one end to the other. I see you have taken your ideas of Turkey from that worthy author Dumont, who has written with equal ignorance and confidence. 'Tis a particular pleasure to me here, to read the voyages to the Levant, which are generally so far removed from truth, and so full of absurdities, I am very well diverted with them. They never fail giving you an account of the women, whom 'tis certain they never saw, and talking very wisely of the genius of the men, into whose company they are never admitted; and very often describe mosques, which they dare not peep into. The Turks are very proud, and will not converse with a stranger they are not assured is considerable in his own country. I speak of the men of distinction; for, as to the ordinary fellows, you may imagine what ideas their conversation can give of the general genius of the people . . .

## TO MRS. T. [THISTLETHWAYTE].

### *Pera of Constantinople, Jan. 4, O.S. [1718].*

. . . To say the truth, I am, at this present writing, not very much turned for the recollection of what is diverting, my head being wholly filled with the preparations necessary for the increase of my family, which I expect every day. You may easily guess at my uneasy situation. But I am, however, in some degree comforted, by the glory that accrues to me from it, and a reflection on the contempt I should otherwise fall under. You won't know what to make of this speech: but, in this country, it is more despicable to be married and not fruitful, than it is with us to be fruitful before marriage. They have a notion, that, whenever a woman leaves off bringing children, it is because she is too old for that business, whatever her face says to the contrary, and this opinion makes the ladies here so ready to make proofs of their youth, (which is as necessary, in order to be a received beauty, as it is to shew the proofs of nobility, to be admitted knight of Malta,) that they do not content themselves with using the natural means, but fly to all sorts of quackeries, to avoid the scandal of being past childbearing, and often kill themselves by them. Without any exaggeration, all the women of my acquaintance that have been married ten years, have twelve or thirteen children; and the old ones boast of having had five-and-twenty or thirty a-piece, and are respected according to the number they have produced. Whey they are with child, it is their common expression to say, They hope God will be so merciful to them to send two this time; and when I have asked them sometimes, How they expected to provide for such a flock as they desire? they answered, That the plague will certainly kill half of them; which, indeed, generally happens, without much concern to the parents, who are satisfied with the vanity of having brought forth so plentifully.

The French embassadress is forced to comply with this fashion as well as myself. She has not been here much above a year, and has lain in once, and is big again. What is most wonderful is, the exemption they seem to enjoy from the curse entailed on the sex. They see all company the day of their delivery, and, at the fortnight's end, return visits, set out in their jewels and new clothes. I wish I may find the influence of the climate in this particular. But I fear I shall continue an Englishwoman in that affair. . . .

But, having entertained you with things I don't like, it is but just I should tell you something that pleases me. The climate is delightful in the extremest degree. I am now sitting, this present fourth of January, with the windows open, enjoying the warm shine of the sun, while you are freezing over a sad sea-coal fire; and my chamber set out with carnations, roses, and jonquils, fresh from my garden. I am also charmed with many points of the Turkish law, to our shame be it spoken, better designed and better executed than ours; particularly, the punishment of convicted liars (triumphant criminals in our country, God knows): They are burnt in the forehead with a hot iron, being proved the authors of any notorious falsehood. How many white foreheads should we see disfigured, how many fine gentlemen would be forced to wear their wigs as low as their eyebrows, were this law in practice with us! I should go on to tell you many other parts of justice, but I must send for my midwife.

## To Mr. P_____.

I have been running about Paris at a strange rate with my sister, and strange sights have we seen. They are, at least, strange sights to me, for after having been accustomed to the gravity of the Turks, I can scarcely look with an easy and familiar aspect at the levity and agility of the airy phantoms that are dancing about me here, and I often think that I am at a puppet-shew amidst the representations of real life. I stare prodigiously, but nobody remarks it, for every body stares here; staring is à la mode—there is a stare of attention and *intérêt,* a stare of curiosity, a stare of expectation, a stare of surprise, and it would greatly amuse you to see what trifling objects excite all this staring. This staring would have rather a solemn kind of air, were it not alleviated by grinning, for at the end of a stare there comes always a grin, and very commonly the entrance of a gentleman or a lady into a room is accompanied with a grin, which is designed to express complacence and social pleasure, but really shews nothing more than a certain contortion of muscles that must make a stranger laugh really, as they laugh artificially. The French grin is equally remote from the cheerful serenity of a smile, and the cordial mirth of an honest English horse-laugh. I shall not perhaps stay here long enough to form a just idea of French manners and characters, though this, I believe, would require but little study, as there is no great depth in either. It appears, on a superficial view, to be a frivolous, restless, and agreeable people. . . .

# Jonathan Swift

# A MODEST PROPOSAL (1729)

*Jonathan Swift (1667–1745) is one of the greatest satirists to have written in the English language and is best known for* Gulliver's Travels. *Swift was an Anglo-Irish Protestant, educated at Trinity College, Dublin and Oxford University. He was ordained as a minister in the Anglican Church in 1695. While living in England, Swift cast his political sails with the Tories, the champions of the Anglican Church and the traditional monarchy, acting as their chief political pamphleteer. When their political opponents, the Whigs, emerged in 1714 as the preferred political party of the incoming monarch George I, Swift returned to Ireland. He became Dean of St. Patrick's Cathedral and became known as an important voice in Irish affairs. In "A Modest Proposal," Swift produces a remarkable satire on a deadly serious subject: the devastating poverty of Catholic Irish peasants and their shabby treatment by their Protestant landlords.*

## A MODEST PROPOSAL FOR PREVENTING THE CHILDREN OF POOR PEOPLE IN IRELAND FROM BEING A BURDEN TO THEIR PARENTS OR COUNTRY, AND FOR MAKING THEM BENEFICIAL TO THE PUBLIC

It is a melancholy object to those who walk through this great town or travel in the country, when they see the streets, the roads, and cabin doors, crowded with beggars of the female sex, followed by three, four, or six children, all in rags and importuning every passenger for an alms. These mothers, instead of being able to work for their honest livelihood, are forced to employ all their time in strolling to beg sustenance for their helpless infants: who as they grow up either turn thieves for want of work, or leave their dear native country to fight for the Pretender in Spain, or sell themselves to the Barbadoes.

I think it is agreed by all parties that this prodigious number of children in the arms, or on the backs, or at the heels of their mothers, and frequently of their fathers, is in the present deplorable state of the kingdom a very great additional grievance; and, therefore, whoever could find out a fair, cheap, and easy method of making these children sound, useful members of the commonwealth, would deserve so well of the public as to have his statue set up for a preserver of the nation.

But my intention is very far from being confined to provide only for the children of professed beggars; it is of a much greater extent, and shall take in the whole number of infants at a certain age who are born of parents in effect as little able to support them as those who demand our charity in the streets.

As to my own part, having turned my thoughts for many years upon this important subject, and maturely weighed the several schemes of other projectors, I have always found them grossly mistaken in the computation. It is true, a child just dropped from its dam may be supported by her milk for a solar year, with little other nourishment; at most not above the value of 2s., which the mother may certainly get, or the value in scraps, by her lawful occupation of begging; and it is exactly at one year old that I propose to provide for them in such a manner as instead of being a charge upon their parents or the parish, or wanting food and raiment for the rest of their lives, they shall on the contrary contribute to the feeding, and partly to the clothing, of many thousands.

There is likewise another great advantage in my scheme, that it will prevent those voluntary abortions, and that horrid practice of women murdering their bastard children, alas! too frequent among us! sacrificing the poor innocent babes I doubt more to avoid the expense than the shame, which would move tears and pity in the most savage and inhuman breast.

The number of souls in this kingdom being usually reckoned one million and a half, of these I calculate there may be about two hundred thousand couples whose wives are breeders; from which number I subtract thirty thousand couples who are able to maintain their own children, although I apprehend there cannot be so many, under the present distresses of the kingdom; but this being granted, there will remain an hundred and seventy thousand breeders. I again subtract fifty thousand for those women who miscarry, or whose children die by accident or disease within the year. There only remains one hundred and twenty thousand children of poor parents annually born: the question therefore is, how this number shall be reared and provided for, which, as I have already said, under the present situation of affairs, is utterly impossible by all the methods hitherto proposed. For we can neither employ them in handicraft or agriculture; we neither build houses (I mean in the country) nor cultivate land: they can very seldom pick up a livelihood by stealing, till they arrive at six years old, except where they are of towardly parts, although I confess they learn the rudiments much earlier, during which time, they can however be properly looked upon only as probationers, as I have been informed by a principal gentleman in the county of Cavan, who protested to me that he never knew above one or two instances under the age of six, even in a part of the kingdom so renowned for the quickest proficiency in that art.

I am assured by our merchants, that a boy or a girl before twelve years old is no salable commodity; and even when they come to this age they will not yield above three pounds, or three pounds and half-a-crown at most on the exchange; which cannot turn to account either to the parents or kingdom, the charge of nutriment and rags having been at least four times that value.

I shall now therefore humbly propose my own thoughts, which I hope will not be liable to the least objection.

I have been assured by a very knowing American of my acquaintance in London, that a young healthy child well nursed is at a year old a most delicious, nourishing, and wholesome food, whether stewed, roasted, baked, or boiled; and I make no doubt that it will equally serve in a fricassee or a ragout.

I do therefore humbly offer it to public consideration that of the hundred and twenty thousand children already computed, twenty thousand may be reserved for breed, whereof only one-fourth part to be males; which is more than we allow to sheep, black cattle or swine; and my reason is, that these children are seldom the fruits of marriage, a circumstance not much regarded by our savages, therefore one male will be sufficient to serve four females. That the remaining hundred thousand may, at a year old, be offered in the sale to the persons of quality and fortune through the kingdom; always advising the mother to let them suck plentifully in the last month, so as to render them plump and fat for a good table. A child will make two dishes at an entertainment for friends; and when the family dines alone, the fore or hind quarter will make a reasonable dish, and seasoned with a little pepper or salt will be very good boiled on the fourth day, especially in winter.

I have reckoned upon a medium that a child just born will weigh 12 pounds, and in a solar year, if tolerably nursed, increaseth to 28 pounds.

I grant this food will be somewhat dear, and therefore very proper for landlords, who, as they have already devoured most of the parents, seem to have the best title to the children.

Infant's flesh will be in season throughout the year, but more plentiful in March, and a little before and after; for we are told by a grave author, an eminent French physician, that fish being a prolific diet, there are more children born in Roman Catholic countries about nine months after Lent than at any other season; therefore, reckoning a year after Lent, the markets will be more glutted than usual, because the number of popish infants is at least three to one in this kingdom: and therefore it will have one other collateral advantage, by lessening the number of papists among us.

I have already computed the charge of nursing a beggar's child (in which list I reckon all cottagers, laborers, and four-fifths of the farmers) to be about two shillings per annum, rags included; and I believe no gentleman would repine to give ten shillings for the carcass of a good fat child, which, as I have said, will make four dishes of excellent nutritive meat, when he hath only some particular friend or his own family to dine with him. Thus the squire will learn to be a good landlord, and grow popular among his tenants; the mother will have eight shillings net profit, and be fit for work till she produces another child.

Those who are more thrifty (as I must confess the times require) may flay the carcass; the skin of which artificially dressed will make admirable gloves for ladies, and summer boots for fine gentlemen.

As to our city of Dublin, shambles may be appointed for this purpose in the most convenient parts of it, and butchers we may be assured will not be wanting; although I rather recommend buying the children alive, and dressing them hot from the knife, as we do roasting pigs.

A very worthy person, a true lover of his country, and whose virtues I highly esteem, was lately pleased in discoursing on this matter to offer a refinement upon my scheme. He said that many gentlemen of this kingdom, having of late destroyed their deer, he conceived that the want of venison might be well supplied by the bodies of young lads and maidens, not exceeding fourteen years of age nor under twelve; so great a number of both sexes in every country being now ready to starve for want of work and service; and these to be disposed of by their parents, if alive, or otherwise by their nearest relations. But with due deference to so excellent a friend and so deserving a patriot, I cannot be altogether in his sentiments; for as to the males, my American acquaintance assured me, from frequent experience, that their flesh was generally tough and lean, like that of our schoolboys by continual exercise, and their taste disagreeable; and to fatten them would not answer the charge. Then as to the females, it would, I think, with humble submission be a loss to the public, because they soon would become breeders themselves; and besides, it is not improbable that some scrupulous people might be apt to censure such a practice (although indeed very unjustly), as a little bordering upon cruelty; which, I confess, hath always been with me the strongest objection against any project, however so well intended.

But in order to justify my friend, he confessed that this expedient was put into his head by the famous Psalmanazar, a native of the island Formosa, who came from thence to London above twenty years ago, and in conversation told my friend, that in his country when any young person happened to be put to death, the executioner sold the carcass to persons of quality as a prime dainty; and that in his time the body of a plump girl of fifteen, who was crucified for an attempt to poison the emperor, was sold to his imperial majesty's prime minister of state, and other great mandarins of the court, in joints from the gibbet, at four hundred crowns. Neither indeed can I deny, that if the same use were made of several plump young girls in this town, who without one single groat to their fortunes cannot stir abroad without a chair, and appear at playhouse and assemblies in foreign fineries which they never will pay for, the kingdom would not be the worse.

Some persons of a desponding spirit are in great concern about that vast number of poor people, who are aged, diseased, or maimed, and I have been desired to employ my thoughts what course may be taken to ease the nation of so grievous an encumbrance. But I am not in the least pain upon that matter, because it is very well known that they are every day dying and rotting by cold and famine, and filth and vermin, as fast as can be reasonably expected. And as to the young laborers, they are now in as hopeful a condition; they cannot get work, and consequently pine away for want of nourishment, to a degree that if at any time they are accidentally hired to common labor, they have not strength to perform it; and thus the country and themselves are happily delivered from the evils to come.

I have too long digressed, and therefore shall return to my subject. I think the advantages by the proposal which I have made are obvious and many, as well as of the highest importance.

For first, as I have already observed, it would greatly lessen the number of papists, with whom we are yearly overrun, being the principal breeders of the nation as well as our most dangerous enemies; and who stay at home on purpose with a design to deliver the kingdom to the Pretender, hoping to take their advantage by the absence of so many good protestants, who have chosen rather to leave their country than stay at home and pay tithes against their conscience to an Episcopal curate.

Secondly, The poorer tenants will have something valuable of their own, which by law may be made liable to distress and help to pay their landlord's rent, their corn and cattle being already seized, and money a thing unknown.

Thirdly, Whereas the maintenance of an hundred thousand children, from two years old and upward, cannot be computed at less than ten shillings a-piece per annum, the nation's stock will be thereby increased fifty thousand pounds per annum, beside the profit of a new dish introduced to the tables of all gentlemen of fortune in the kingdom who have any refinement in taste. And the money will circulate among ourselves, the goods being entirely of our own growth and manufacture.

Fourthly, The constant breeders, beside the gain of eight shillings sterling per annum by the sale of their children, will be rid of the charge of maintaining them after the first year. Fifthly, This food would likewise bring great custom to taverns; where the vintners will certainly be so prudent as to procure the best receipts for dressing it to perfection, and consequently have their houses frequented by all the fine gentlemen, who justly value themselves upon their knowledge in good eating: and a skilful cook, who understands how to oblige his guests, will contrive to make it as expensive as they please.

Sixthly, This would be a great inducement to marriage, which all wise nations have either encouraged by rewards or enforced by laws and penalties. It would increase the care and tenderness of mothers toward their children, when they were sure of a settlement for life to the poor babes, provided in some sort by the public, to their annual profit instead of expense. We should see an honest emulation among the married women, which of them could bring the fattest child to the market. Men would become as fond of their wives during the time of their pregnancy as they are now of their mares in foal, their cows in calf, their sows when they are ready to farrow; nor offer to beat or kick them (as is too frequent a practice) for fear of a miscarriage.

Many other advantages might be enumerated. For instance, the addition of some thousand carcasses in our exportation of barreled beef, the propagation of swine's flesh, and improvement in the art of making good bacon, so much wanted among us by the great destruction of pigs, too frequent at our tables; which are no way comparable in taste or magnificence to a well-grown, fat, yearling child, which roasted whole will make a considerable figure at a lord mayor's feast or any other public entertainment. But this and many others I omit, being studious of brevity.

Supposing that one thousand families in this city would be constant customers for infants flesh, besides others who might have it at merry meetings, particularly weddings and christenings: I compute that Dublin would take off annually about twenty thousand carcasses, and the rest of the kingdom (where probably they will be sold somewhat cheaper) the remaining eighty thousand.

I can think of no one that will possibly be raised against this proposal, unless it should be urged that the number of people will be thereby much lessened in the kingdom. This I freely own, and it was indeed one principal design in offering it to the world. I desire the reader will observe, that I calculated my remedy for this one individual Kingdom of Ireland, and for no other that ever was, is, or, I think, ever can be upon earth. Therefore let no man talk to me of other expedients: Of taxing our absentees at five shillings a pound: Of using neither clothes, nor household furniture, except what is our own growth and manufacture: Of utterly rejecting the materials and instruments that promote foriegn luxury: Of curing the expensiveness of pride, vanity, idleness, and gaming in our women: Of introducing a vein of parsimony, prudence, and temperance: Of learning to love our country, wherein we differ even from Laplanders, and the inhabitants of Tompinamboo: Of quitting our animosities and factions, nor act any longer like the Jews, who were murdering one another at the very moment their city was taken: Of being a little cautious not to sell our country and consciences for nothing: Of teaching landlords to have at least one degree of mercy towards their tenants. Lastly, of putting a spirit of honesty, industry, into our shopkeepers, who, if a resolution could now be taken to buy only our native goods, would immediately unite to cheat and exact upon us in the price, the measure and goodness, nor could ever yet be brought to make one fair proposal of just dealing, though often and ernestly invited to it.

Therefore I repeat, let no man talk to me of these and the like expedients, till he hath at least a glimpse of hope that there will ever be some hearty and sincere attempt to put them in practice. But as to myself, having been wearied out for many years with offering vain, idle, visionary thoughts, and at length utterly dispairing of success, I fortunately fell upon this proposal, which as it is wholly new, so it hath something solid and real, of no expense and little trouble, full in our own power, and whereby we can incur no danger in disobliging England. For this kind of commodity will not bear exportation, the flesh being of too tender a consistence to admit a long continuance in salt, although perhaps I could name a country that would be glad to eat up our whole nation without it.

After all, I am not so violently bent upon my own opinion as to reject any offer proposed by wise men, which shall be found equally innocent, cheap, easy, and effectual. But before something of that kind shall be advanced in contradiction to my scheme, and offering a better, I desire the author or authors will be pleased maturely to consider two points. First, as things now stand, how they will be able to find food and raiment for an hundred thousand useless mouths and backs. And secondly, there being a round million of creatures in human figure throughout this kingdom, whose whole subsistence put into a common stock would leave them in debt two millions of pounds sterling, adding those who are beggars by profession to the bulk of farmers, cottagers, and laborers, with their wives and children who are beggars in effect: I desire those politicians who dislike my overture, and may perhaps be so bold as to attempt an answer, that they will first ask the parents of these mortals, whether they would not at this day think it a great happiness to have been sold for food, at a year old in the manner I prescribe, and thereby have avoided such a perpetual scene of misfortunes as they have since gone through by the oppression of landlords, the impossibility of paying rent without money or trade, the want of common sustenance, with neither house nor clothes to cover them from the inclemencies of the weather, and the most inevitable prospect of entailing the like or greater miseries upon their breed for ever.

I profess, in the sincerity of my heart, that I have not the least personal interest in endeavoring to promote this necessary work, having no other motive than the public good of my country, by advancing our trade, providing for infants, relieving the poor, and giving some pleasure to the rich. I have no children by which I can propose to get a single penny; the youngest being nine years old, and my wife past child-bearing.

# Charles de Secondat, Baron de Montesquieu

## *from* THE SPIRIT OF LAWS (1748)

*Charles de Secondat, Baron de Montesquieu (1689–1755), trained as a lawyer but devoted his life to literary and philosophical pursuits. His first publication,* Persian Letters *(1721), a novel composed of letters written by Persians traveling in Europe, appeared anonymously. Using a fictional device popular among eighteenth-century European writers—including Jonathan Swift and Françoise de Graffigny—he commented satirically on the excesses of his own society and political order by contrasting them with others, real or imagined. Montesquieu revisited the topic of cultural and political differences more earnestly a few decades later in* The Spirit of Laws, *a philosophical treatise on government influenced by the Enlightenment emphasis on reason and science. One of his arguments is that different political systems are appropriate in different times and places, depending on variables such as social customs, religion and tradition, and climate: the best government conforms to the temperament of the people governed. In the section included here, he speculates about the relationship between climate, national character, and laws.*

## Book XIV

### *Of Laws in Relation to the Nature of the Climate*

#### 1. —General Idea

If it be true that the temper of the mind and the passions of the heart are extremely different in different climates, the laws ought to be in relation both to the variety of those passions and to the variety of those tempers.

#### 2. —Of the Difference of Men in Different Climates

Cold air constringes the extremities of the external fibres of the body;[1] this increases their elasticity, and favours the return of the blood from the extreme parts to the heart. It contracts[2] those very fibres; consequently it increases also their force. On the contrary, warm air relaxes and lengthens the extremes of the fibres; of course it diminishes their force and elasticity.

1. This appears even in the countenance: in cold weather people look thinner.
2. We know that it shortens iron.

People are therefore more vigorous in cold climates. Here the action of the heart and the reaction of the extremities of the fibres are better performed, the temperature of the humours is greater, the blood moves more freely towards the heart, and reciprocally the heart has more power. This superiority of strength must produce various effects; for instance, a greater boldness, that is, more courage; a greater sense of superiority, that is, less desire of revenge; a greater opinion of security, that is, more frankness, less suspicion, policy, and cunning. In short, this must be productive of very different tempers. Put a man into a close, warm place, and for the reasons above given he will feel a great faintness. If under this circumstance you propose a bold enterprise to him, I believe you will find him very little disposed towards it; his present weakness will throw him into despondency; he will be afraid of everything, being in a state of total incapacity. The inhabitants of warm countries are, like old men, timorous; the people in cold countries are, like young men, brave. If we reflect on the late wars,[3] which are more recent in our memory, and in which we can better distinguish some particular effects that escape us at a greater distance of time, we shall find that the northern people, transplanted into southern regions,[4] did not perform such exploits as their countrymen, who, fighting in their own climate, possessed their full vigour and courage.

This strength of the fibres in northern nations is the cause that the coarser juices are extracted from their aliments. Hence two things result: one, that the parts of the chyle or lymph are more proper, by reason of their large surface, to be applied to and to nourish the fibres; the other, that they are less proper, from their coarseness, to give a certain subtilty to the nervous juice. Those people have therefore large bodies and but little vivacity.

The nerves that terminate from all parts in the cutis form each a nervous bundle; generally speaking, the whole nerve is not moved, but a very minute part. In warm climates, where the cutis is relaxed, the ends of the nerves are expanded and laid open to the weakest action of the smallest objects. In cold countries the cutis is constringed and the papillae compressed: the miliary glands are in some measure paralytic; and the sensation does not reach the brain, except when it is very strong and proceeds from the whole nerve at once. Now, imagination, taste, sensibility, and vivacity depend on an infinite number of small sensations.

I have observed the outermost part of a sheep's tongue, where, to the naked eye, it seems covered with papillae. On these papillae I have discerned through a microscope small hairs, or a kind of down; between the papillae were pyramids shaped towards the ends like pincers. Very likely these pyramids are the principal organ of taste.

I caused the half of this tongue to be frozen, and observing it with the naked eye I found the papillae considerably diminished: even some rows of them were sunk into their sheath. The outermost part I examined with the microscope, and perceived no pyramids. In proportion as the frost went off, the papillae seemed to the naked eye to rise, and with the microscope the miliary glands began to appear.

This observation confirms what I have been saying, that in cold countries the nervous glands are less expanded: they sink deeper into their sheaths, or they are sheltered from the action of external objects; consequently they have not such lively sensations.

In cold countries they have very little sensibility for pleasure; in temperate countries, they have more; in warm countries, their sensibility is exquisite. As climates are

3. Those for the succession to the Spanish monarchy.
4. For instance, in Spain.

distinguished by degrees of latitude, we might distinguish them also in some measure by those of sensibility. I have been at the opera in England and in Italy, where I have seen the same pieces and the same performers; and yet the same music produces such different effects on the two nations: one is so cold and phlegmatic, and the other so lively and enraptured, that it seems almost inconceivable.

It is the same with regard to pain, which is excited by the laceration of some fibre of the body. The Author of nature has made it an established rule that this pain should be more acute in proportion as the laceration is greater: now it is evident that the large bodies and coarse fibres of the people of the north are less capable of laceration than the delicate fibres of the inhabitants of warm countries; consequently the soul is there less sensible of pain. You must flay a Muscovite alive to make him feel.

From this delicacy of organs peculiar to warm climates it follows that the soul is most sensibly moved by whatever relates to the union of the two sexes: here everything leads to this object.

In northern climates scarcely has the animal part of love a power of making itself felt. In temperate climates, love, attended by a thousand appendages, endeavours to please by things that have at first the appearance, though not the reality, of this passion. In warmer climates it is liked for its own sake, it is the only cause of happiness, it is life itself.

In southern countries a machine of a delicate frame but strong sensibility resigns itself either to a love which rises and is incessantly laid in a seraglio, or to a passion which leaves women in a greater independence, and is consequently exposed to a thousand inquietudes. In northern regions a machine robust and heavy finds pleasure in whatever is apt to throw the spirits into motion, such as hunting, travelling, war, and wine. If we travel towards the north, we meet with people who have few vices, many virtues, and a great share of frankness and sincerity. If we draw near the south, we fancy ourselves entirely removed from the verge of morality; here the strongest passions are productive of all manner of crimes, each man endeavouring, let the means be what they will, to indulge his inordinate desires. In temperate climates we find the inhabitants inconstant in their manners, as well as in their vices and virtues: the climate has not a quality determinate enough to fix them.

The heat of the climate may be so excessive as to deprive the body of all vigour and strength. Then the faintness is communicated to the mind; there is no curiosity, no enterprise, no generosity of sentiment; the inclinations are all passive; indolence constitutes the utmost happiness; scarcely any punishment is so severe as mental employment; and slavery is more supportable than the force and vigour of mind necessary for human conduct.

### 3. —Contradiction in the Tempers of Some Southern Nations

The Indians[5] are naturally a pusillanimous people; even the children[6] of Europeans born in India lose the courage peculiar to their own climate. But how shall we reconcile this with their customs and penances so full of barbarity? The men voluntarily

5. "One hundred European soldiers," says Tavernier, "would without any great difficulty beat a thousand Indian soldiers."
6. Even the Persians who settle in the Indies contract in the third generation the indolence and cowardice of the Indians. See Bernier on the Mogul, tom. i. p. 182.

undergo the greatest hardships, and the women burn themselves: here we find a very odd compound of fortitude and weakness.

Nature, having framed those people of a texture so weak as to fill them with timidity, has formed them at the same time of an imagination so lively that every object makes the strongest impression upon them. That delicacy of organs which renders them apprehensive of death contributes likewise to make them dread a thousand things more than death: the very same sensibility induces them to fly and dare all dangers.

As a good education is more necessary to children than to such as have arrived at maturity of understanding, so the inhabitants of those countries have much greater need than the European nations of a wiser legislator. The greater their sensibility, the more it behoves them to receive proper impressions, to imbibe no prejudices, and to let themselves be directed by reason.

At the time of the Romans the inhabitants of the north of Europe were destitute of arts, education, and almost of laws; and yet the good sense annexed to the gross fibres of those climates enabled them to make an admirable stand against the power of Rome, till the memorable period in which they quitted their woods to subvert that great empire.

### 4. —Cause of the Immutability of Religion, Manners, Customs, and Laws in the Eastern Countries

If to that delicacy of organs which renders the eastern nations so susceptible of every impression you add likewise a sort of indolence of mind, naturally connected with that of the body, by means of which they grow incapable of any exertion or effort, it is easy to comprehend that when once the soul has received an impression it cannot change it. This is the reason that the laws, manners, and customs,[7] even those which seem quite indifferent, such as their mode of dress, are the same to this very day in eastern countries as they were a thousand years ago.

### 5. —That Those are Bad Legislators Who Favour the Vices of the Climate, and Good Legislators Who Oppose Those Vices

The Indians believe that repose and non-existence are the foundation of all things, and the end in which they terminate. Hence they consider entire inaction as the most perfect of all states, and the object of their desires. To the Supreme Being they give the title of immovable.[8] The inhabitants of Siam believe that their utmost happiness[9] consists in not being obliged to animate a machine, or to give motion to a body.

In those countries where the excess of heat enervates and exhausts the body, rest is so delicious, and motion so painful, that this system of metaphysics seems natural; and Foe,[10] the legislator of the Indies, was directed by his own sensations when he placed mankind in a state extremely passive; but his doctrine arising from the laziness of the climate favoured it also in its turn; which has been the source of an infinite deal of mischief.

7. We find by a fragment of Nicolaus Damascenus, collected by Constantine Porphyrogenitus, that it was an ancient custom in the East to strangle a governor who had given any displeasure; it was in the time of the Medes.
8. Panamanack: See Kircher.
9. La Loubiere, Relation of Siam, p. 446.
10. Foe endeavoured to reduce the heart to a mere vacuum: "We have eyes and ears, but perfection consists in neither seeing nor hearing; a mouth, hand, &c., but perfection requires that these members should be inactive." This is taken from the dialogue of a Chinese philosopher, quoted by Father Du Halde, tom. iii.

The legislators of China were more rational when, considering men not in the peaceful state which they are to enjoy hereafter, but in the situation proper for discharging the several duties of life, they made their religion, philosophy, and laws all practical. The more the physical causes incline mankind to inaction, the more the moral causes should estrange them from it.

### 10. —Of the Laws in Relation to the Sobriety of the People

In warm countries the aqueous part of the blood loses itself greatly by perspiration;[11] it must therefore be supplied by a like liquid. Water is there of admirable use; strong liquors would congeal the globules[12] of blood that remain after the transuding of the aqueous humour.

In cold countries the aqueous part of the blood is very little evacuated by perspiration. They may therefore make use of spirituous liquors, without which the blood would congeal. They are full of humours; consequently strong liquors, which give a motion to the blood, are proper for those countries.

The law of Mahomet, which prohibits the drinking of wine, is therefore fitted to the climate of Arabia: and indeed, before Mahomet's time, water was the common drink of the Arabs. The law[13] which forbade the Carthaginians to drink wine was a law of the climate; and, indeed, the climate of those two countries is pretty nearly the same.

Such a law would be improper for cold countries, where the climate seems to force them to a kind of national intemperance, very different from personal ebriety. Drunkenness predominates throughout the world, in proportion to the coldness and humidity of the climate. Go from the equator to the north pole, and you will find this vice increasing together with the degree of latitude. Go from the equator again to the south pole, and you will find the same vice travelling south,[14] exactly in the same proportion.

It is very natural that where wine is contrary to the climate, and consequently to health, the excess of it should be more severely punished than in countries where intoxication produces very few bad effects to the person, fewer to the society. and where it does not make people frantic and wild, but only stupid and heavy. Hence those laws[15] which inflicted a double punishment for crimes committed in drunkenness were applicable only to a personal, and not to a national, ebriety. A German drinks through custom, and a Spaniard by choice.

In warm countries the relaxing of the fibres produces a great evacuation of the liquids, but the solid parts are less transpired. The fibres, which act but faintly, and have very little elasticity, are not much impaired; and a small quantity of nutritious juice is sufficient to repair them; for which reason they eat very little.

It is the variety of wants in different climates that first occasioned a difference in the manner of living, and this gave rise to a variety of laws. Where people are very

11. "My body is a sieve; scarcely have I swallowed a pint of water, but I see it transude like dew out of all my limbs, even to my fingers' ends. I drink ten pints a day, and it does me no manner of harm."— Berniers Travels, tom. ii. p. 261.

12. In the blood there are red globules, fibrous parts, white globules and water, in which the whole swims.

13. Plato, book II. of Laws; Aristotle, of the care of domestic affairs; Eusebius's Evangelical Preparation, book XII. chap. xvii.

14. This is seen in the Hottentots, and the inhabitants of the most southern part of Chile.

15. As Pittacus did, according to Aristotle, *Polit.* lib I. cap. iii. He lived in a climate where drunkenness is not a national vice.

communicative there must be particular laws, and others where there is but little communication.

### 13. —Effects Arising from the Climate of England

In a nation so distempered by the climate as to have a disrelish of everything, nay, even of life, it is plain that the government most suitable to the inhabitants is that in which they cannot lay their uneasiness to any single person's charge, and in which, being under the direction rather of laws than of the prince, it is impossible for them to change the government without subverting the laws themselves.

And if this nation has likewise derived from the climate a certain impatience of temper, which renders them incapable of bearing the same train of things for any long continuance, it is obvious that the government above mentioned is the fittest for them.

This impatience of temper is not very considerable of itself; but it may become so when joined with courage.

It is quite a different thing from levity, which makes people undertake or drop a project without cause; it borders more upon obstinacy, because it proceeds from so lively a sense of misery that it is not weakened even by the habit of suffering.

This temper in a free nation is extremely proper for disconcerting the projects of tyranny,[16] which is always slow and feeble in its commencement, as in the end it is active and lively: which at first only stretches out a hand to assist, and exerts afterwards a multitude of arms to oppress.

Slavery is ever preceded by sleep. But a people who find no rest in any situation, who continually explore every part, and feel nothing but pain, can hardly be lulled to sleep.

Politics are a smooth file, which cuts gradually, and attains its end by a slow progression. Now the people of whom we have been speaking are incapable of bearing the delays, the details, and the coolness of negotiations: in these they are more unlikely to succeed than any other nation; hence they are apt to lose by treaties what they obtain by their arms.

### 14. —Other Effects of the Climate

Our ancestors, the ancient Germans, lived in a climate where the passions were extremely calm. Their laws decided only in such cases where the injury was visible to the eye, and went no farther. And as they judged of the outrages done to men from the greatness of the wound, they acted with no other delicacy in respect to the injuries done to women. The laws of the Alemans[17] on this subject is very extraordinary. If a person uncovers a woman's head, he pays a fine of fifty sous; if he uncovers her leg up to the knee, he pays the same; and double from the knee upwards. One would think that the law measured the insults offered to women as we measure a figure in geometry; it did not punish the crime of the imagination, but that of the eye. But upon the migration of a German nation into Spain, the climate soon found a necessity for different laws. The law of the Visigoths inhibited the surgeons to bleed a free woman, except either her father, mother, brother, son, or uncle was present. As the imagina-

16. Here I take this word for the design of subverting the established power, and especially that of democracy; this is the signification in which it was understood by the Greeks and Romans.
17. Chap. lviii. 1 and 2.

tion of the people grew warm, so did that of the legislators; the law suspected everything when the people had become suspicious.

These laws had, therefore, a particular regard for the two sexes. But in their punishments they seem rather to humour the revengeful temper of private persons than to administer public justice. Thus, in most cases, they reduced both the criminals to be slaves to the offended relatives or to the injured husband; a free-born woman[18] who had yielded to the embraces of a married man was delivered up to his wife to dispose of her as she pleased. They obliged the slaves,[19] if they found their master's wife in adultery, to bind her and carry her to her husband; they even permitted her children to be her accusers, and her slaves to be tortured in order to convict her. Thus their laws were far better adapted to refine, even to excess, a certain point of honour than to form a good civil administration. We must not, therefore, be surprised if Count Julian was of opinion that an affront of that kind ought to be expiated by the ruin of his king and country; we must not be surprised if the Moors, with such a conformity of manners, found it so easy to settle and to maintain themselves in Spain, and to retard the fall of their empire.

## 15. —Of the Different Confidence Which the Laws Have in the People, According to the Difference of Climates

The people of Japan are of so stubborn and perverse a temper that neither their legislators nor magistrates can put any confidence in them: they set nothing before their eyes but judgments, menaces, and chastisements; every step they take is subject to the inquisition of the civil magistrate. Those laws which out of five heads of families establish one as a magistrate over the other four; those laws which punish a family or a whole ward for a single crime; those laws, in fine, which find nobody innocent where one may happen to be guilty, are made with a design to implant in the people a mutual distrust, and to make every man the inspector, witness, and judge of his neighbour's conduct.

On the contrary, the people of India are mild,[20] tender, and compassionate. Hence their legislators repose great confidence in them. They have established[21] very few punishments; these are not severe, nor are the rigorously executed. They have subjected nephews to their uncles, and orphans to their guardians, as in other countries they are subjected to their fathers; they have regulated the succession by the acknowledged merit of the successor. They seem to think that every individual ought to place entire confidence in the good nature of his fellow-subjects.[22]

They enfranchise their slaves without difficulty, they marry them, they treat them as their children.[23] Happy climate which gives birth to innocence, and produces a lenity in the laws!

—*trans. Thomas Nugent*

18. Law of the Visigoths, book III. tit. 4, 9.
19. Ibid. book III. tit. 4, 6.
20. See Bernier, tom. ii. p. 140.
21. See in the 14th Collection of the Edifying Letters, p. 403, the principal laws or customs of the inhabitants of the peninsula on this side the Ganges.
22. See Edifying Letters, IX. 378.
23. I had once thought that the lenity of slavery in India had made Diodorus say that there was neither master nor slave in that country; but Diodorus has attributed to the whole continent of India what, according to Strabo, lib. XV., belonged only a particular nation.

# Olaudah Equiano

## *from* THE INTERESTING NARRATIVE OF THE LIFE OF OLAUDAH EQUIANO, OR GUSTAVUS VASSA, THE AFRICAN (1789)

*Olaudah Equiano (1750–1797), originally kidnapped and enslaved by fellow West Africans, was sent to the West Indies, where he was befriended by a master and was eventually freed. Along the way, he converted to Christianity, received an education, and traveled widely. As a freeman, he settled in England, becoming one of the leading spokesmen and activists for the abolition of slavery. Equiano's* The Interesting Narrative, *which went through one American and eight English editions following its publication, provides a compelling firsthand account of the cruelties of slavery. He was true to his African past, while condemning those Africans who sold their own people. He condemned the slave owners of Jamaica, while paying tribute to those English men and women of his adopted country who treated him with kindness and respect. In thinking about this reading, examine the illustration of Equiano found elsewhere in this book. How does the artist represent him?*

Such is the imperfect sketch my memory has furnished me with of the manners and customs of a people among whom I first drew my breath. And here I cannot forbear suggesting what has long struck me forcibly, namely, the strong analogy which even by this sketch, imperfect as it is, appears to prevail in the manners and customs of my countrymen, and those of the Jews, before they reached the Land of Promise, and particularly the patriarchs, while they were yet in that pastoral state which is described in Genesis—an analogy, which alone would induce me to think that the one people had sprung from another. Indeed this is the opinion of Dr. Gill, who, in his commentary on Genesis, very ably deduces the pedigree of the Africans from Afer and Afra, the descendants of Abraham by Keturah his wife and concubine, (for both these titles are applied to her). It is also conformable to the sentiments of Dr. John Clarke, formerly Dean of Sarum, in his Truth of the Christian Religion: both these authors concur in ascribing to us this original. The reasonings of these gentlemen are still further confirmed by the Scripture Chronology of the Rev. Arthur Bedford; and if any further corroboration were required, this resemblance in so many respects is a strong evidence in support of the opinion. Like the Israelites in their primitive state, our government was conducted by our chiefs, our judges, our wise men, and elders; and the head of a family with us enjoyed a similar authority over his household with that which is ascribed to Abraham and the other patriarchs. The law of retaliation obtained almost universally with us as with them; and even their religion appeared to have shed upon us a ray of its glory, though broken and spent in its passage, or eclipsed by the cloud with which time, tradition, and ignorance might have enveloped it: for we had our circumcision (a rule I believe peculiar to that people): we had also our sacrifices and burnt-offerings, our washings and purifications, on the same occasions as they had.

As to the difference of colour between the Eboan Africans and the modern Jews, I shall not presume to account for it. It is a subject which has engaged the pens of men of both genius and learning, and is far above my strength. The most able and Reverend Mr. T. Clarkson, however, in his much-admired Essay on the Slavery and Commerce of the Human Species, has ascertained the cause, in a manner that at once solves every objection on that account, and, on my mind at least, has produced the fullest conviction. I shall therefore refer to that performance for the theory, contenting myself with extracting a fact as related by Dr. Mitchel. "The Spaniards, who have inhabited America, under the torrid zone, for any time, are become as dark coloured as our native Indians of Virginia, *of which I myself have been a witness.* There is also another instance of a Portuguese settlement at Mitomba, a river in Sierra Leona, where the inhabitants are bred from a mixture of the first Portuguese discoverers with the natives, and are now become, in their complexion, and in the woolly quality of their hair, *perfect negroes,* retaining however a smattering of the Portuguese language."

These instances, and a great many more which might be adduced, while they shew how the complexions of the same persons vary in different climates, it is hoped may tend also to remove the prejudice that some conceive against the natives of Africa on account of their colour. Surely the minds of the Spaniards did not change with their complexions! Are there not causes enough to which the apparent inferiority of an African may be ascribed, without limiting the goodness of God, and supposing he forbore to stamp understanding on certainly his own image, because "carved in ebony?" Might it not naturally be ascribed to their situation? When they come among Europeans, they are ignorant of their language, religion, manners, and customs. Are any pains taken to teach them these? Are they treated as men? Does not slavery itself depress the mind, and extinguish all its fire, and every noble sentiment? But, above all, what advantages do not a refined people possess over those who are rude and uncultivated? Let the polished and haughty European recollect that *his* ancestors were once, like the Africans, uncivilized, and even barbarous. Did Nature make *them* inferior to their sons? and should *they too* have been made slaves? Every rational mind answers, No. Let such reflections as these melt the pride of their superiority into sympathy for the wants and miseries of their sable brethren, and compel them to acknowledge, that understanding is not confined to feature or colour. If, when they look round the world, they feel exultation, let it be tempered with benevolence to others, and gratitude to God, "who hath made of one blood all nations of men for to dwell on all the face of the earth; and whose wisdom is not our wisdom, neither are our ways his ways."

●

The first object which saluted my eyes when I arrived on the coast was the sea, and a slave-ship, which was then riding at anchor, and waiting for its cargo. These filled me with astonishment, which was soon converted into terror, which I am yet at a loss to describe, nor the then feelings of my mind. When I was carried on board I was immediately handled, and tossed up, to see if I were sound, by some of the crew; and I was now persuaded that I had gotten into the world of bad spirits, and that they were going to kill me. Their complexions too differing so much from ours, their long hair, and the language they spoke, which was very different from any I had ever heard, united to confirm me in this belief. Indeed, such were the horrors of my views and fears at the moment, that, if ten thousand worlds had been my own, I would have freely parted with them all to have exchanged my condition with that of the meanest slave in my own country. When I looked round the ship too, and saw a large furnace of copper boiling, and a multitude of black people of every description chained together, every one of their countenances expressing dejection and sorrow, I no longer doubted of my fate, and, quite overpowered with horror and anguish, I fell motionless on the deck and fainted. When I recovered a little, I found some black people about me, who I believed were some of those who brought me on board, and had been receiving their pay; they talked to me in order to cheer me, but all in vain. I asked them if we were not to be eaten by those white men with horrible looks, red faces, and long hair. They told me I was not; and one of the crew brought me a small portion of spirituous liquor in a wine glass; but, being afraid of him, I would not take it out of his hand. One of the blacks therefore took it from him and gave it to me, and I took a little down my palate, which, instead of reviving me, as they thought it would, threw me into the greatest consternation at the strange feeling it produced, having never tasted any such liquor before. Soon after this, the blacks who brought me on board went off, and left me abandoned to despair. I now saw myself deprived of all chance of returning to my native country, or even the least glimpse of hope of gaining the shore, which I now considered as friendly; and I even wished for my former slavery in preference to my present situation, which was filled with horrors of every kind, still heightened by my ignorance of what I was to undergo. I was not long suffered to indulge my grief; I was soon put down under the decks, and there I received such a salutation in my nostrils as I had never experienced in my life; so that with the loathsomeness of the stench, and crying together, I became so sick and low that I was not able to eat, nor had I the least desire to taste any thing. I now wished for the last friend, Death, to relieve me; but soon, to my grief, two of the white men offered me eatables; and, on my refusing to eat, one of them held me fast by the hands, and laid me across, I think, the windlass, and tied my feet, while the other flogged me severely. I had never experienced any thing of this kind before; and although, not being used to the water, I naturally feared that element the first time I saw it; yet, nevertheless, could I have got over the nettings, I would have jumped over the side, but I could not; and, besides, the crew used to watch us very closely who were not chained down to the decks, lest we should leap into the water; and I have seen some of these poor African prisoners most severely cut for attempting to do so, and hourly whipped for not eating. This indeed was often the case with myself. In a little time after, amongst the poor chained men, I found some of my own nation, which in a small degree gave ease to my mind. I inquired of these what was to be done with us? they gave me to understand we were to be carried to these white people's country to work for them. I then was a little relieved, and thought, if it were no worse than working, my situation was not so desperate: but still I feared I should be put to death, the white people looked and acted, as I thought, in so savage a manner; for I had never seen among any people such instances of brutal cruelty; and this was not only shewn towards us blacks, but also to some of the whites themselves. One white man in particular I saw, when we were permitted to be on deck, flogged so unmercifully with a large rope near the foremast, that he died in consequence of it; and they tossed him over the side as they would have done a brute. This made me fear these people the more; and I expected nothing less than to be treated in the same manner. At last, when the ship we were in had got in all her cargo, they made ready with many fearful noises, and we were all put under deck, so that we could not see how they managed the vessel. But this disappointment was the least of my sorrow. The stench of the hold while we were on the coast was so intolerably loathsome, that it was dangerous to remain there for any time, and some of us had been permitted to stay on the deck for the fresh air; but now that the whole ship's cargo were confined together, it became absolutely pestilential. The closeness of the place, and the heat of the climate, added to the number in the ship, which was so crowded that each had scarcely room to turn himself, almost suffocated us. This produced copious perspirations, so that the air soon became unfit for respiration, from a variety of loathsome smells, and brought on a sickness among the slaves, of which many died, thus falling victims to the improvident avarice, as I may call it, of their purchasers. This wretched situation was again aggravated by the galling of the chains, now become insupportable; and the filth of the necessary tubs, into which the children often fell, and were almost suffocated. The shrieks of the women, and the groans of the dying, rendered the whole a scene of horror almost inconceivable. Happily perhaps for myself I was soon reduced so low here that it was thought necessary to keep me almost always on deck; and from my extreme youth I was not put in fetters. In this situation I expected every hour to share the fate of my companions, some of whom were almost daily brought upon deck at the point of death, which I began to hope would soon put an end to my miseries. Often did I think many of the inhabitants of the deep much more happy than myself; I envied them the freedom they enjoyed, and as often wished I could change my condition for theirs. Every circumstance I met with served only to render my state more painful, and heighten my apprehensions, and my opinions of the cruelty of the whites. One day they had taken a number of fishes; and when they had killed and satisfied themselves with as many as they thought fit, to our astonishment who were on the deck, rather than give any of them to us to eat, as we expected, they tossed the remaining fish into the sea again, although we begged and prayed for some as well as we could, but in vain; and some of my countrymen, being pressed by hunger, took an opportunity, when they thought no one saw them, of trying to get a little privately; but they were discovered, and the attempt procured them some very severe floggings.

●

. . . At last we came in sight of the island of Barbadoes, at which the whites on board gave a great shout, and made many signs of joy to us. We did not know what to think of this; but as the vessel drew nearer we plainly saw the harbour, and other ships of different kinds and sizes: and we soon anchored amongst them off Bridge Town. Many merchants and planters now came on board, though it was in the evening. They put us in separate parcels, and examined us attentively. They also made us jump, and pointed to the land, signifying we were to go there. We thought by this we should be eaten by these ugly men, as they appeared to us; and, when soon after we were all put down under the deck again; there was much dread and trembling among us, and nothing but bitter cries to be heard all the night from these apprehensions, insomuch that at last the white people got some old slaves from the land to pacify us. They told us we were not to be eaten, but to work, and were soon to go to land, where we should see many of our country people. This report eased us much; and sure enough, soon after we were landed, there came to us Africans of all languages. . . . We were not many days in the merchant's custody before we were sold after their usual manner, which is this:—On a signal given, (as the beat of a drum), the buyers rush as once into the yard where the slaves are confined, and make choice of that parcel they like best. The noise and clamour with which this is attended, and the eagerness visible in the countenances of the buyers, serve not a little to increase the apprehension of the terrified Africans, who may well be supposed to consider them as the ministers of that destruction to which they think themselves devoted. In this manner, without scruple, are relations and friends separated, most of them never to see each other again. I remember in the vessel in which I as brought over, in the men's apartment, there were several brothers, who, in the sale, were sold in different lots; and it was very moving on this occasion to see and hear their cries at parting. O, ye nominal Christians! might not an African ask you, learned you this from your God? who says unto you, Do unto all men as you would men should do unto you? Is it not enough that we are torn from our country and friends to toil for your luxury and lust of gain? Must every tender feeling to be likewise sacrificed to your avarice? Are the dearest friends and relations, now rendered more dear by their separation from their kindred, still to be parted from each other, and thus prevented from cheering the gloom of slavery with the small comfort of being together and mingling their sufferings and sorrow? Why are parents to lose their children, brothers their sisters, or husbands their wives? Surely this is a new refinement in cruelty, which, while it has no advantage to atone for it, thus aggravates distress, and adds fresh horrors even to the wretchedness of slavery.

●

It was now between three and four years since I first came to England, a great part of which I had spent at sea; so that I became inured to that service, and began to consider myself as happily situated; for my master treated me always extremely well; and my attachment and gratitude to him were very great. From the various scenes I had beheld on ship-board, I soon grew a stranger to terror of every kind, and was, in that respect at least, almost an Englishman. I have often reflected with surprise that I never felt half the alarm at any of the numerous dangers I have been in, that I was filled with at the first sight of the Europeans, and at every act of theirs, even the most trifling, when I first came among them, and for some time afterwards. That fear, however, which was the effect of my ignorance, wore away as I began to know them. I could now speak English tolerably well, and I perfectly understood every thing that was said. I now not only felt myself quite easy with these new countrymen, but relished their society and manners. I no longer looked upon them as spirits, but as men superior to us; and therefore I had the stronger desire to resemble them; to imbibe their spirit, and imitate their manners; I therefore embraced every occasion of improvement; and every new thing that I observed I treasured up in my memory. I had long wished to be able to read and write; and for this purpose I took every opportunity to gain instruction, but had made as yet very little progress. However, when I went to London with my master, I had soon an opportunity of improving myself, which I gladly embraced. Shortly after my arrival, he sent me to wait upon the Miss Guerins, who had treated me with much kindness when I was there before; and they sent me to school.

While I was attending these ladies, their servants told me I could not go to heaven, unless I was baptized. This made me very uneasy; for I had now some faint idea of a future state: accordingly I communicated my anxiety to the eldest Miss Guerin, with whom I was become a favourite, and pressed her to have me baptized; when, to my great joy, she told me I should. She had formerly asked my master to let me be baptized, but he had refused; however, she now insisted on it; and he, being under some obligation to her brother, complied with her request; so I was baptized at St. Margaret's church, Westminster, in February 1759, by my present name.

# The Enlightenment
# and the French Revolution

The English poet Alexander Pope once considered the impact of Newton on the intellectual life of his time. He wrote:

> Nature and Nature's laws lay hid in Night.
> God said, "Let Newton be," and all was light.

These lines powerfully convey the awe that eighteenth-century intellectuals felt about Newton's achievement. In four elegant laws, he seemed to explain the underlying principles of all matter and motion. The secrets of the universe had been unlocked; and if Newton was not God himself, he was surely one of his appointed messengers.

Eighteenth-century thinkers believed that what Newton had achieved for physical nature could also be accomplished for 'human nature,' that is, in the social sciences. By fusing abstract reasoning and empirical investigation in the manner of Newton, they could discover the laws underpinning human society and consequently refashion political and social institutions in accordance with them. The intellectual movement embodying this viewpoint is the Enlightenment, arguably the first modern movement in Western thought. Enlightenment thinkers wanted to uproot (what they perceived as) hundreds of years of darkness—centuries of superstition, arbitrary custom, and church tyranny—and create a society grounded in rational principles. Many were not philosophers in the usual sense, but social critics and writers interested in reaching an expanding, frequently middle-class audience with a growing interest in public affairs. Enlightenment thinkers were as likely to write novels as philosophical treatises. They acted as advisers to monarchs and emperors, although their advice was not necessarily followed. Their views were spread through the growing eighteenth-century publishing business and the thriving literary societies, clubs, and salons of the time. Given the wider public role that they fashioned for themselves, Enlightenment thinkers have sometimes been described as *philosophes,* writers and social critics who were as interested in transforming the world as understanding it.

The Enlightenment thinkers, especially in France, used the tools of rational critique to campaign for the reform of political and social institutions. Yet probably few of them imagined that their ideas would inspire the French Revolution, a tumultuous event that overthrew the monarchy, redrew the political map, and plunged Europe into war for nearly a generation. The Enlightenment did not cause the French Revolution, but it is hard to picture it without it. The English historian Christopher Hill once wrote: "Revolutions are not made without ideas, but they are not made by intellectuals. Steam is essential to driving a railway engine; but neither a locomotive nor a permanent way can be built without steam." The Enlightenment was the steam of the revolutionary engine of France.

The Age of the Enlightenment and the French Revolution took place at the height of the African slave trade, which saw between seven and ten million Africans (the majority from West Africa) sent to the Americas between the second half of the sixteenth century and 1867. During the eighteenth century an average of forty-five thousand slaves a year were exported. While it has been customary to see slavery and its ramifications as being distinct from intellectual and cultural history, more recently historians have tended to see them as being intertwined. Not only were many Enlightenment thinkers preoccupied with issues having to do with race, but also significant numbers of Africans (many of whom had attained their freedom) lived in Europe, including those regarded at the time as significant writers. It is estimated that 5,000 Africans lived in London at the century's end (out of a population of 780,000). The French Revolution also felt the impact of the spread of slavery. In the French colony of Haiti, revolutionary ideas and turmoil contributed to the end of slavery in 1794 and independence a decade later.

# John Locke

## *from* AN ESSAY ON HUMAN UNDERSTANDING (1690)
## *from* OF CIVIL GOVERNMENT (1690)

*T*he Englishman John Locke (1632–1704) is not, strictly speaking, part of the Enlightenment. He is more properly viewed as a harbinger of the movement and one of its formative influences. Locke is perhaps best known for his influence on political thought. His contention in Of Civil Government *that people have the right to change their government when their liberty and property are threatened is one of the ideas that influenced the American founding fathers, especially Thomas Jefferson. Yet Locke also played a central role in shaping eighteenth-century epistemological debates. His* An Essay On Human Understanding *represents a refutation of Descartes's notion that innate ideas in the mind exist independently of experience. He argues that the mind at birth is a* tabula rasa, *a blank slate devoid of any content or ideas, and that it acquires ideas from 'experience'— either through 'sensation', sensory perception of the world, or 'reflection', the process whereby the mind reflects on its own operations.*

### *FROM* AN ESSAY ON HUMAN UNDERSTANDING

#### *Chapter 2. No Innate Principles in the Mind*

1. *The way shown how we come by any knowledge, sufficient to prove it not innate.*—It is an established opinion amongst some men, that there are in the understanding certain *innate principles;* some primary notions, *(koinai ennoiai),* characters, as it were stamped upon the mind of man, which the soul receives in its very first being, and brings into the world with it. It would be sufficient to convince unprejudiced readers of the falseness of this supposition, if I should only show (as I hope I shall in the following parts of this discourse) how men, barely by the use of their natural faculties, may attain to all the knowledge they have, without the help of any innate impressions; and may arrive at certainty, without any such original notions or principles. For I imagine any one will easily grant, that it would be impertinent to suppose the ideas of colours innate in a creature to whom God hath given sight, and a power to receive them by the eyes from external objects; and no less unreasonable would it be to attribute several truths to the impressions of nature and innate characters, when we

may observe in ourselves faculties fit to attain as easy and certain knowledge of them as if they were originally imprinted on the mind.

But because a man is not permitted without censure to follow his own thoughts in the search of truth, when they lead him ever so little out of the common road, I shall set down the reasons that made me doubt of the truth of that opinion, as an excuse for my mistake, if I be in one; which I leave to be considered by those who, with me, dispose themselves to embrace truth wherever they find it.

2. *General assent the great argument.*—There is nothing more commonly taken for granted, than that there are certain *principles,* both *speculative* and *practical* (for they speak of both), universally agreed upon by all mankind; which therefore, they argue, must needs be the constant impressions which the souls of men receive in their first beings and which they bring into the world with them, as necessarily and really as they do any of their inherent faculties.

3. *Universal consent proves nothing innate.*—This argument, drawn from universal consent, has this misfortune in it, that if it were true in matter of fact, that there were certain truths wherein all mankind agreed, it would not prove them innate, if there can be any other way shown, how men may come to that universal agreement in the things they do consent in; which I presume may be done.

4. *"What is, is,"* and *"It is impossible for the same Thing to be and not to be,"* not *universally assented to.*—But, which is worse, this argument of universal consent which is made use of to prove innate principles, seems to me a demonstration that there are none such; because there are none to which all mankind give an universal assent. I shall begin with the speculative, and instance in those magnified principles of demonstration, "Whatsoever is, is," and "It is impossible for the same thing to be and not to be"; which, of all others, I think have the most allowed title to innate. These have so settled a reputation of maxims universally received, that it will no doubt be thought strange if any one should seem to question it. But yet I take liberty to say, that these propositions are so far from having an universal assent, that there are a great part of mankind to whom they are not so much as known.

5. *Not on the mind naturally imprinted, because not known to children, idiots, &c.*—For, first, it is evident, that all children and idiots have not the least apprehension or thought of them: and the want of that is enough to destroy that universal assent, which must needs be the necessary concomitant of all innate truths: it seeming to me near a contradiction to say, that there are truths imprinted on the soul which it perceives or understands not; imprinting, if it signify anything, being nothing else but the making certain truths to be perceived. No proposition can be said to be in the mind which it never yet knew, which it was never yet conscious of. For if any one may, then, by the same reason, all propositions that are true, and the mind is capable ever of assenting to, may be said to be in the mind, and to be imprinted; since if any one can be said to be in the mind, which it never yet knew, it must be only because it is capable of knowing it; and so the mind is of all truths it ever shall know. Nay, thus truths may be imprinted on the mind which it never did, nor ever shall know: for a man may live long, and die at last in ignorance of many truths which his mind was capable of knowing, and that with certainty. So that if the capacity of knowing be the natural impression contended for, all the truths a man ever comes to know will, by this account, be every one of them innate: and this great point will amount to no more, but only to a very high improper way of speaking. But then, to

what end such contest for certain innate maxims? If truths can be imprinted on the understanding without being perceived, I can see no difference there can be between any truths the mind is *capable* of knowing in respect of their original: they must all be innate, or all adventitious; in vain shall a man go about to distinguish them. He therefore that talks of innate notions in the understanding, cannot (if he intend thereby any distinct sort of truths) mean such truths to be in the understanding as it never perceived, and is yet wholly ignorant of. For if these words "to be in the understanding" have any propriety, they signify to be understood. If therefore these two propositions: "Whatsoever is, is," and, "It is impossible for the same thing to be, and not to be," are by nature imprinted, children cannot be ignorant of them; infants, and all that have souls, must necessarily have them in their understandings, know the truth of them, and assent to it . . . .

## Book II
### Chapter 1. Of Ideas in General and Their Original

1. *Idea is the object of thinking.*—Every man being conscious to himself that he thinks, and that which his mind is applied about whilst thinking being the ideas that are there, it is past doubt that men have in their minds several ideas, such as are those expressed by the words, "whiteness, hardness, sweetness, thinking, motion, man, elephant, army, drunkenness," and others. It is in the first place then to be enquired, How he comes by them?

I know it is a received doctrine, that men have native ideas and original characters stamped upon their minds in their very first being. This opinion I have at large examined already; and, I suppose, what I have said in the foregoing Book will be much more easily admitted, when I have shown whence the understanding may get all the ideas it has, and by what ways and degrees they may come into the mind; for which I shall appeal to every one's own observation and experience.

2. *All ideas come from sensation or reflection.*—Let us then suppose the mind to be, as we say, white paper, void of all characters, without any ideas; how comes it to be furnished? Whence comes it by that vast store, which the busy and boundless fancy of man has painted on it with an almost endless variety? Whence has it all the materials of reason and knowledge? To this I answer, in one word, from EXPERIENCE; in that all our knowledge is founded, and from that it ultimately derives itself. Our observation, employed either about external sensible objects, or about the internal operations of our minds, perceived and reflected on by ourselves, is that which supplies our understandings with all the materials of thinking. These two are the foundations of knowledge, from whence all the ideas we have or can naturally have, do spring.

3. *The objects of sensation one source of ideas.*—First, our senses, conversant about particular sensible objects, do convey into the mind several distinct perceptions of things, according to those various ways wherein those objects do affect them; and thus we come by those ideas we have of yellow, white, heat, cold, soft, hard, bitter, sweet, and all those which we call sensible qualities; which when I say the senses convey into the mind, I mean, they from external objects convey into the mind what produces there those perceptions. This great source of most of the ideas we have, depending wholly upon our senses, and derived by them to the understanding, I call, SENSATION.

4. *The operations of our minds the other source of them.*—Secondly, the other fountain, from which experience furnishes the understanding with ideas, is the perception

of the operations of our mind within us, as it is employed about the ideas it has got: which operations, when the soul comes to reflect on and consider, do furnish the understanding with another set of ideas which could not be had from things without: and such are perception, thinking, doubting, believing, reasoning, knowing, willing, and all the different actings of our own minds; which we being conscious of, and observing in ourselves, do from these receive into our understanding as distinct ideas, as we do from bodies affecting our senses. This source of ideas every man has wholly in himself: and though it be not sense, as having nothing to do with external objects, yet it is very like it, and might properly enough be called internal sense. But as I call the other Sensation, so I call this REFLECTION, the ideas it affords being such only as the mind gets by reflecting on its own operations within itself. By Reflection, then, in the following part of this discourse, I would be understood to mean that notice which the mind takes of its own operations, and the manner of them, by reason whereof there come to be ideas of these operations in the understanding. These two, I say, viz., external material things as the objects of Sensation, and the operations of our own minds within as the objects of Reflection are, to me, the only originals from whence all our ideas take their beginnings. The term *operations* here, I use in a large sense, as comprehending not barely the actions of the mind about its ideas, but some sort of passions arising sometimes from them, such as is the satisfaction or uneasiness arising from any thought.

5. *All our ideas are of the one or the other of these.*—The understanding seems to me not to have the least glimmering of any ideas which it doth not receive from one of these two. *External objects* furnish the mind with the ideas of sensible qualities, which are all those different perceptions they produce in us; and *the mind* furnishes the understanding with ideas of its own operations. These, when we have taken a full survey of them, and their several modes, combinations, and relations, we shall find to contain all our whole stock of ideas; and that we have nothing in our minds which did not come in one of these two ways. Let any one examine his own thoughts, and thoroughly search into his understanding, and then let him tell me, whether all the original ideas he has there, are any other than of the objects of his senses, or of the operations of his mind considered as objects of his reflection; and how great a mass of knowledge soever he imagines to be lodged there, he will, upon taking a strict view, see that he has not any idea in his mind but what one of these two have imprinted, though perhaps with infinite variety compounded and enlarged by the understanding, as we shall see hereafter.

6. *Observable in children.*—He that attentively considers the state of a child at his first coming into the world, will have little reason to think him stored with plenty of ideas that are to be the matter of his future knowledge. It is by degrees he comes to be furnished with them: and though the ideas of obvious and familiar qualities themselves before the memory begins to keep a register of time and order, yet it is often so late before some unusual qualities come in the way, that there are few men that cannot recollect the beginning of their acquaintance with them: and if it were worth while, no doubt a child might be so ordered as to have but a very few even of the ordinary ideas till he were grown up to a man. But all that are born into the world being surrounded with bodies that perpetually and diversely affect them, variety of ideas, whether care be taken about it or no, are imprinted on the minds of children. Light and colours are busy and at hand everywhere when the eye is but open; sounds and some tangible qualities fail not to solicit their proper senses, and force an entrance to

the mind; but yet I think it will be granted easily, that if a child were kept in a place where he never saw any other but black and white till he were a man, he would have no more ideas of scarlet or green, than he that from his childhood never tasted an oyster or a pineapple has of those particular relishes.

7. *Men are differently furnished with these according to the different objects they converse with.*—Men then come to be furnished with fewer or more simple ideas from without, according as the objects they converse with afford greater or less variety; and from the operations of their minds within, according as they more or less reflect on them. For, though he that contemplates the operations of his mind cannot but have plain and clear ideas of them; yet, unless he turn his thoughts that way, and considers them *attentively,* he will no more have clear and distinct ideas of all the operations of his mind, and all that may be observed therein, than he will have all the particular ideas of any landscape, or of the parts and motions of a clock, who will not turn his eyes to it, and with attention heed all the parts of it. The picture or clock may be so placed, that they may come in his way every day; but yet he will have but a confused idea of all the parts they are made up of, till he applies himself with attention to consider them each in particular.

8. *Ideas of reflection later, because they need attention.*—And hence we see the reason why it is pretty late before most children get ideas of the operations of their own minds; and some have not any very clear or perfect ideas of the greatest part of them all their lives. Because, though they pass there continually, yet, like floating visions, they make not deep impressions enough to leave in the mind clear, distinct, lasting ideas, till the understanding turns inward upon itself, reflects on its own operations, and makes them the object of its own contemplation. Children, when they come first into it, are surrounded with a world of new things, which, by a constant solicitation of their senses, draw the mind constantly to them, forward to take notice of new, and apt to be delighted with the variety of changing objects. Thus the first years are usually employed and diverted in looking abroad. Men's business in them is to acquaint themselves with what is to be found without; and so, growing up in a constant attention to outward sensations, seldom make any considerable reflection on what passes within them till they come to be of riper years; and some scarce ever at all.

9. *The soul begins to have ideas when it begins to perceive.*—To ask, at what time a man has first any ideas, is to ask when he begins to perceive; having ideas, and perception, being the same thing. I know it is an opinion, that the soul always thinks; and that it has the actual perception of ideas in itself constantly, as long as it exists; and that actual thinking is as inseparable from the soul, as actual extension is from the body; which if true, to enquire after the beginning of a man's ideas is the same as to enquire after the beginning of his soul. For by this account, soul and its ideas, as body and its extension, will begin to exist both at the same time.

## FROM OF CIVIL GOVERNMENT
### Book II, Chapter 1

I think it may not be amiss to set down what I take to be political power; that the power of a magistrate over a subject may be distinguished from that of a father over his children, a master over his servants, a husband over his wife, and a lord over his slave. All which distinct powers happening sometimes together in the same man, if he be considered under these different relations, it may help us to distinguish these powers one from another, and show the difference betwixt a ruler of a commonwealth, a father of a family, and a captain of a galley.

Political power, then, I take to be a right of making laws with penalties of death, and consequently all less penalties, for the regulating and preserving of property, and of employing the force of the community, in the execution of such laws, and in the defence of the commonwealth from foreign injury; and all this only for the public good.

## Chapter 2
### Of the State of Nature

To understand political power right, and derive it from its original, we must consider what state all men are naturally in, and that is, a state of perfect freedom to order their actions and dispose of their possessions and persons, as they think fit, within the bounds of the law of nature; without asking leave, or depending upon the will of any other man.

A state also of equality wherein all the power and jurisdiction is reciprocal, no one having more than another; there being nothing more evident, than that creatures of the same species and rank, promiscuously born to all the same advantages of nature, and the use of the same faculties, should also be equal one amongst another without subordination or subjection; unless the lord and master of them all should, by any manifest declaration of his will, set one above another, and confer on him, by an evident and clear appointment, an undoubted right to dominion and sovereignty. . . .

But though this be a state of liberty, yet it is not a state of license: though man in that state have an uncontrollable liberty to dispose of his person or possessions, yet he has not liberty to destroy himself, or so much as any creature in his possession, but where some nobler use than its bare preservation calls for it. The state of nature has a law of nature to govern it, which obliges every one: and reason, which is that law, teaches all mankind, who will but consult it, that being all equal and independent, no one ought to harm another in his life, health, liberty, or possessions: for men being all the workmanship of one omnipotent and infinitely wise Maker; all the servants of one sovereign master, sent into the world by his order, and about his business; they are his property, whose workmanship they are, made to last during his, not another's pleasure: and being furnished with like faculties, sharing all in one community of nature, there cannot be supposed any such subordination among us, that may authorize us to destroy another, as if we were made for one another's uses, as the inferior ranks of creatures are for ours. Every one, as he is bound to preserve himself, and not to quit his station wilfully, so by the like reason, when his own preservation comes not in competition, ought he, as much as he can, to preserve the rest of mankind, and may not, unless it be to do justice to an offender, take away or impair the life, or what tends to the preservation of life, the liberty, health, limb, or goods of another.

And that all men may be restrained from invading others' rights, and from doing hurt to one another, and the law of nature be observed, which willeth the peace and preservation of all mankind, the execution of the law of nature is, in that state, put into every man's hands, whereby every one has a right to punish the transgressors of that law to such a degree as may hinder its violation: for the law of nature would, as all other laws that concern men in this world, be in vain, if there were nobody that in the state of nature had a power to execute the law, and thereby preserve the innocent and restrain offenders. And if any one in the state of nature may punish another for any evil he has done, every one may do so: for in that state of perfect equality where naturally there is no superiority or jurisdiction of one over another, what any may do in prosecution of that law, every one must needs have a right to do.

And thus, in the state of nature, "one man comes by a power over another"; but yet no absolute or arbitrary power, to use a criminal, when he has got him in his hands, according to the passionate heats, or boundless extravagancy of his own will; but only to retribute to him, so far as calm reason and conscience dictate, what is proportionate to his transgression; which is so much as may serve for reparation and restraint: for these two are the only reasons, why one man may lawfully do harm to another, which is that we call punishment. In transgressing the law of nature, the offender declares himself to live by another rule than that of reason and common equity, which is that measure God has set to the actions of men, for their mutual security; and so he becomes dangerous to mankind, the tie, which is to secure them from injury and violence, being slighted and broken by him. Which being a trespass against the whole species, and the peace and safety of it, provided for by the law of nature; every man upon this score, by the right he hath to preserve mankind in general, may restrain, or, where it is necessary, destroy things noxious to them, and so may bring such evil on any one, who hath transgressed that law, as may make him repent the doing of it, and thereby deter him, and by his example others, from doing the like mischief. And in this case, and upon this ground, "every man hath a right to punish the offender, and be executioner of the law of nature."

### Chapter 3
### *Of the State of War*

The state of war is a state of enmity and destruction: and therefore declaring by word or action, not a passionate and hasty but a sedate settled design upon another man's life, puts him in a state of war with him against whom he has declared such an intension, and so has exposed his life to the other's power to be taken away by him, or any one that joins with him in his defence, and espouses his quarrel; it being reasonable and just, I should have a right to destroy that which threatens me with destruction; for, by the fundamental law of nature, man being to be preserved as much as possible, when all cannot be preserved, the safety of the innocent is to be preferred: and one may destroy a man who makes war upon him, or has discovered an enmity to his being, for the same reason that he may kill a wolf or a lion; because such men are not under the ties of the common law of reason, have no other rule, than that of force and violence, and so may be treated as beasts of prey, those dangerous and noxious creatures, that will be sure to destroy him whenever he falls into their power.

And hence it is, that he who attempts to get another man in to his absolute power, does thereby put himself into a state of war with him; it being to be understood as a declaration of a design upon his life: for I have reason to conclude, that he who would get me into his power without my consent, would use me as he pleased when he got me there, and destroy me too when he had a fancy to it; for nobody can desire to have me in his absolute power, unless it be to compel me by force to that which is against the right of my freedom, *i.e.,* make me a slave. To be free from such force is the only security of my preservation; and reason bids me look on him, as an enemy to my preservation, who would take away that freedom which is the fence to it; so that he who makes an attempt to enslave me, thereby puts himself into a state of war with me. He that, in the state of nature, would take away the freedom that belongs to any one in that state, must necessarily be supposed to have a design to take away everything else, that freedom being the foundation of all the rest: as he that, in the state of society, would take away the freedom belonging to those of that society or commonwealth, must be supposed to design to take away from them every thing else, and so be looked on as in a state of war.

This makes it lawful for a man to kill a thief, who has not in the least hurt him, nor declared any design upon his life, any farther than, by the use of force, so to get him in his power, as to take away his money, or what he pleases, from him; because using force, where he has no right, to get me into his power, let his pretence be what it will, I have no reason to suppose, that he, who would take away my liberty, would not, when he had me in his power, take away every thing else. And therefore it is lawful for me to treat him as one who has put himself into a state of war with me, *i.e.,* kill him if I can; for to that hazard does he justly expose himself, whoever introduces a state of war, and is aggressor in it.

And here we have the plain "difference between the state of nature and the state of war," which however some men have confounded, are as far distant as a state of peace, goodwill, mutual assistance and preservation, and a state of enmity, malice, violence and mutual destruction, are one from another. Men living together according to reason, without a common superior on earth, with authority to judge between them, is properly the state of nature. But force, or a declared design of force, upon the person of another where there is no common superior on earth to appeal to for relief, is the state of war: and it is the want of such an appeal gives a man the right of war even against an aggressor, though he be in society and a fellow-subject.

*Chapter 4*
*Of Slavery*

The natural liberty of man is to be free from any superior power on earth, and not to be under the will or legislative authority of man, but to have only the law of nature for his rule. The liberty of man, in society, is to be under no other legislative power, but that established, by consent, in the commonwealth; nor under the dominion of any will, or restraint of any law, but what that legislative shall enact, according to the trust put in it. Freedom then is not what Sir Robert Filmer* tells us, "a liberty for every one to do what he lists, to live as he pleases, and not be tied by any laws": but freedom of men under government is, to have a standing rule to live by, common to every one of that society, and made by the legislative power erected in it; a liberty to follow my own will in all things, where the rule prescribes not; and not to be subject to the inconstant, uncertain, unknown, arbitrary will of another man: as freedom of nature is, to be under no other restraint but the law of nature.

This freedom from absolute, arbitrary power, is so necessary to, and closely joined with a man's preservation, that he cannot part with it, but by what forfeits his preservation and life together.

---

* [English political theorist and a defender of the divine right of kings (c. 1598–1653) —*Ed.*]

*Chapter 5*
*Of Property*

God, who hath given the world to men in common, hath also given them reason to make use of it to the best advantage of life, and convenience. The earth, and all that is therein, is given to men for the support and comfort of their being. And though all the fruits it naturally produces, and beasts it feeds, belong to mankind in common, as they are produced by the spontaneous hand of nature; and nobody has originally a private dominion, exclusive of the rest of mankind, in any of them, as they are thus in their natural state; yet being given for the use of men, there must of necessity be a means to appropriate them some way or other, before they can be of any use, or at all beneficial to any particular man. The fruit, or venison, which nourishes the wild Indian, who knows no enclosure, and is still a tenant in common, must be his, and so his, *i.e.,* a part of him, that another can no longer have any right to it, before it can do him any good for the support of his life.

Though the earth, and all inferior creatures, be common to all men, yet every man has a property in his own person: this nobody has any right to but himself. The labour of his body, and the work of his hands, we may say, are properly his. Whatsoever then he removes out of the state that nature hath provided, and left it in, he hath mixed his labour with, and joined it to something that is his own, and thereby makes it his property. It being by him removed from the common state nature hath placed it in, it hath by his labour something annexed to it, that excludes the common right of other men. For this labour being the unquestionable property of the labourer, no man but he can have a right to what that is once joined to, at least where there is enough, and as good, left in common for others.

He that is nourished by the acorns he picked up under an oak, or the apples he gathered by the trees in the wood, has certainly appropriated them to himself. Nobody can deny but the nourishment is his. I ask then, when did they begin to be his? when he digested? or when he eat? or when he boiled? or when he brought them home? or when he picked them up? and it is plain, if the first gathering made them not his, nothing else could. That labour put a distinction between them and common: that added something to them more than nature, the common mother of all, had done and so they became his private right. And will any one say he had no right to those acorns or apples he thus appropriated, because he had not the consent of all mankind to make them his? was it a robbery thus to assume to himself what belonged to all in common? If such a consent as that was necessary, man had starved, notwithstanding the plenty God had given him. We see in commons, which remain so by compact, that it is the taking any part of what is common, and removing it out of the state nature leaves it in, which begins the property; without which the common is of no use. And the taking of this or that part does not depend on the express consent of all the commoners. Thus the grass my horse has bit; the turfs my servant has cut; and the ore I have digged in any place, where I have a right to them in common with others, become my property; without the assignation or consent of any body. The labour that was mine, removing them out of that common state they were in, hath fixed my property in them.

●

It will perhaps be objected to this, that "if gathering the acorns, or other fruits of the earth, &c. makes a right to them, then any one may engross as much as he will." To which I answer. Not so. The same law of nature, that does by this means give us property, does also bound this property too. "God has given us all things richly" I Tim. vi. 17, is the voice of reason confirmed by inspiration. But how far has he given it us? To enjoy. As much as any one can make use of to any advantage of life before it spoils, so much he may by his labour fix a property in: whatever is beyond this is more than his share, and belongs to others. Nothing was made by God for man to spoil or destroy. And thus, considering the plenty of natural provisions there was a long time in the world, and the few spenders; and to how small a part of that provision the industry of one man could extend itself; and engross it to the prejudice of others; especially keeping within the bounds, set by reason, of what might serve for his use; there could be then little room for quarrels or contentions about property so established.

But the chief matter of property being now not the fruits of the earth, and the beasts that subsist on it, but the earth itself; as that which takes in, and carries with it all the rest; I think it is plain, that property in that too is acquired as the former. As much land as a man tills, plants, improves, cultivates, and can use the product of, so much is his property. He by his labour does, as it were, enclose it from the common. Nor will it invalidate his right, to say every body else has an equal title to it, and therefore he cannot appropriate, he cannot enclose, without the consent of all his fellow commoners, all mankind. God, when he gave the world in common to all mankind, commanded man also to labour, and the penury of his condition required it of him. God and his reason commanded him to subdue the earth, *i.e.,* improve it for the benefit of life, and therein lay out something upon it that was his own, his labour. He that, in obedience to this command of God, subdued, tilled, and sowed any part of it, thereby annexed to it something that was his property, which another had no title to, nor could without injury take from him.

•

Nor is it so strange, as perhaps before consideration it may appear, that the property of labour should be able to over-balance the community of land; for it is labour indeed that put the difference of value on every thing; and let any one consider what the difference is between an acre of land planted with tobacco or sugar, sown with wheat or barley, and an acre of the same land lying in common, without any husbandry upon it, and he will find, that the improvement of labour makes the far greater part of the value. I think it will be but a very modest computation to say, that of the products of the earth useful to the life of man, nine-tenths are the effects of labour; nay, if we will rightly estimate things as they come to our use, and cast up the several expenses about them, what in them is purely owing to nature, and what to labour, we shall find, that in most of them ninety-nine hundredths are wholly to be put on the account of labour.

### Chapter 7
### Of Political or Civil Society

Whenever . . . any number of men are so united into one society, as to quit everyone his executive power of the law of nature, and to resign it to the public, there and there only is a political, or civil society. And this is done, wherever any number of men, in the state of nature, enter into society to make one people, one body politic, under one supreme government; or else when any one joins himself to, and incorporates with any government already made: for hereby he authorizes the society, or, which is all one, the legislative thereof, to make laws for him, as the public good of the society shall require; to the execution whereof, his own assistance (as to his own degrees) is due. And this puts men out of a state of nature into that of a commonwealth, by setting up a judge on earth, with authority to determine all the controversies, and redress the injuries that may happen to any member of the commonwealth: which judge is the legislative, or magistrate appointed by it. And wherever there are any number of men, however associated, that have no such decisive power to appeal to, there they are still in the state of nature.

Hence it is evident, that absolute monarchy, which by some men is counted the only government in the world, is indeed inconsistent with civil society, and so can be no form of civil government at all; for the end of civil society being to avoid and remedy these inconveniences of the state of nature, which necessarily follow from every man being judge in his own case, by setting up a known authority, to which every one of that society may appeal upon any injury received, or controversy that may arise, and which every one of the society ought to obey; wherever any persons are, who have not such an authority to appeal to for the decision of any difference between them, there those persons are still in the state of nature and so is every absolute prince, in respect of those who are under his dominion.

For he being supposed to have all, both legislative and executive power in himself alone, there is no judge to be found, no appeal lies open to any one, who may fairly and indifferently, and with authority decide, and from whose decision relief and redress may be expected of any injury or inconveniency that may be suffered from the prince, or by his order: so that such a man, however intitled, czar, or grand seignior; or how you please, is as much in the state of nature, with all under his dominion, as he is with the rest of mankind: for wherever any two men are, who have no standing rule, and common judge of appeal to on earth, for the determination of controversies of right betwixt them, there they are still in the state of nature, and under all the inconveniences of it, with only this woeful difference to the subject, or rather slave of an absolute prince; that whereas in the ordinary state of nature he has a liberty to judge of his right, and, according to the best of his power, to maintain it; now whenever his property is invaded by the will and order of his monarch, he has not only no appeal, as those in society ought to have, but, as if he were degraded from the common state of rational creatures, is denied a liberty to judge of, or to defend his right; and so is exposed to all the misery and inconveniences, that a man can fear from one, who being in the unrestrained state of nature, is yet corrupted with flattery, and armed with power.

For he that thinks absolute power purifies men's blood, and corrects the baseness of human nature, need read but the history of this or any other age, to be convinced of the contrary.

## Chapter 8
### Of the Beginning of Political Societies

Men being, as has been said, by nature, all free, equal, and independent, no one can be put out of this estate, and subjected to the political power of another, without his own consent. The only way, whereby any one divests himself of his natural liberty, and puts on the bonds of civil society, is by agreeing with other men to join and unite into a community, for their comfortable, safe, and peaceable living one amongst another, in a secure enjoyment of their properties, and a greater security against any, that are not of it. This any number of men may do, because it injures not the freedom of the rest: they are left as they were in the liberty of the state of nature. When any number of men have so consented to make one community or government, they are thereby presently incorporated, and make one body politic, wherein the majority have a right to act and conclude the rest.

For when any number of men have, by the consent of every individual, made a community, they have thereby made that community one body, with a power to act as one body, which is only by the will and determination of the majority: for that which acts any community, being only the consent of the individuals of it, and it being necessary to that which is one body to move one way; it is necessary the body should move that way whither the greater force carries it, which is the consent of the majority: or else it is impossible it should act or continue one body, one community, which the consent of every individual that united into it, agreed that it should; and so every one is bound by that consent to be concluded by the majority. And therefore we see, that in assemblies, impowered to act by positive laws, where no number is set by that positive law which impowers them, the act of the majority passes for the act of the whole, and of course determines; as having, by the law of nature and reason, the power of the whole.

And thus every man, by consenting with others to make one body politic under one government, puts himself under an obligation, to every one of that society, to submit to the determination of the majority, and to be concluded by it; or else this original compact, whereby he with others incorporate into one society, would signify nothing, and be no compact, if he be left free, and under no other ties than he was in before in the state of nature.

### Chapter 9
### Of the Ends of Political Society and Government

If man in the state of nature be so free, as has been said; if he be absolute lord of his own person and possessions, equal to the greatest, and subject to nobody, why will he part with his freedom? why will he give up his empire, and subject himself to the dominion and control of any other power? To which it is obvious to answer, that though in the state of nature he hath such a right, yet the enjoyment of it is very uncertain, and constantly exposed to the invasion of others; for all being kings as much as he, every man his equal, and the greater part no strict observers of equity and justice, the enjoyment of the property he has in this state is very unsafe, very unsecure. This makes him willing to quit a condition, which however free, is full of fears and continual dangers: and it is not without reason, that he seeks out, and is willing to join in society with others, who are already united, or have a mind to unite, for the mutual preservation of their lives, liberties, and estates, which I call by the general name, property.

The great and chief end, therefore, of men's uniting into commonwealths, and putting themselves under government, is the preservation of their property. To which in the state of nature there are many things wanting.

First, There wants an established, settled, known law, received and allowed by common consent to be the standard of right and wrong, and the common measure to decide all controversies between them; for though the law of nature be plain and intelligible to all rational creatures; yet men being biassed by their interest, as well as ignorant for want of studying it, are not apt to allow of it as a law binding to them in the application of it to their particular cases.

Secondly, In the state of nature there wants a known and indifferent judge, with authority to determine all differences according to the established law: for every one in that state being both judge and executioner of the law of nature, men being partial to themselves, passion and revenge is very apt to carry them too far, and with too much heat, in their own cases; as well as negligence and unconcernedness, to make them too remiss in other men's.

Thirdly, In the state of nature, there often wants power to back and support the sentence when right, and to give it due execution. They who by any injustice offend, will seldom fail, where they are able, by force to make good their injustice; such resistance many times makes the punishment dangerous, and frequently destructive, to those who attempt it.

Thus mankind, notwithstanding all the privileges of the state of nature, being but in an ill condition, while they remain in it, are quickly driven into society. Hence it comes to pass that we seldom find any number of men live any time together in this state. The inconveniences that they are therein exposed to, by the irregular and uncertain exercise of the power every man has of punishing the transgressions of others, make them take sanctuary under the established laws of government, and therein seek the preservation of their property. It is this makes them so willingly give up every one his single power of punishing, to be exercised by such alone, as shall be appointed to it amongst them; and by such rules as the community, or those authorized by them to that purpose, shall agree on. And in this we have the original right of both the legislative and executive power, as well as of the governments and societies themselves.

●

But though men, when they enter into society give up the equality, liberty, and executive power they had in the state of nature, into the hands of the society, to be so far disposed of by the legislature, as the good of the society shall require; yet it being only with an intention in every one the better to preserve himself, his liberty and property; (for no rational creature can be supposed to change his condition with an intention to be worse) the power of the society or legislative constituted by them, can never be supposed to extend farther, than the common good; but is obliged to secure every one's property, by providing against those three defects above mentioned, that made the state of nature so unsafe and uneasy. And so whoever has the legislative or supreme power of any commonwealth, is bound to govern by established standing laws, promulgated and known to the people, and not by extemporary decrees; by indifferent and upright judges, who are to decide controversies by those laws; and to employ the force of the community at home, only in the execution of such laws; or abroad to prevent or redress foreign injuries, and secure the community from inroads and invasion. And all this to be directed to no other end, but the peace, safety, and public good of the people.

### Chapter 13
### *Of the Subordination of the Powers of the Commonwealth*

Though in a constituted commonwealth, standing upon its own basis, and acting according to its own nature, that is, acting for the preservation of the community, there can be but one supreme power, which is the legislative, to which all the rest are and must be subordinate; yet the legislative being only a fiduciary power to act for certain ends, there remains still "in the people a supreme power to remove or alter the legislative," when they find the legislative act contrary to the trust reposed in them: for all power given with trust for the attaining an end, being limited by that end; whenever that end is manifestly neglected or opposed, the trust must necessarily be forfeited, and the power devolve into the hands of those that gave it, who may place it anew where they shall think best for their safety and security. And thus the community perpetually retains a supreme power of saving themselves from the attempts and designs of any body, even of their legislators, whenever they shall be so foolish, or so wicked, as to try and carry on designs against the liberties and properties of the subject: for no man, or society of men, having a power to deliver up their preservation, or consequently the means of it, to the absolute will and arbitrary dominion of another; whenever any one shall go about to bring them into such a slavish condition, they will always have a right to preserve what they have not a power to part with; and to rid themselves of those who invade this fundamental, sacred, and unalterable law of self-preservation, for which they entered into society. And thus the community may be said in this respect to be always the supreme power.

*Chapter 19*
*Of the Dissolution of Government*

The reason why men enter into society, is the preservation of their property; and the end why they choose and authorize a legislative is, that there may be laws made, and rules set, as guards and fences to the properties of all the members of the society: to limit the power, and moderate the dominion, of every part and member of the society: for since it can never be supposed to be the will of the society, that the legislature should have a power to destroy that which every one designs to secure by entering into society, and for which the people submitted themselves to legislators of their own making; whenever the legislators endeavor to take away and destroy the property of the people, or to reduce them to slavery under arbitrary power, they put themselves into a state of war with the people, who are thereupon absolved from any farther obedience, and are left to the common refuge, which God hath provided for all men, against force and violence. Whensoever therefore the legislative shall transgress this fundamental rule of society; and either by ambition, fear, folly or corruption, endeavour to grasp themselves or put into the hands of any other, an absolute power over the lives, liberties, and estates of the people, by this breach of trust they forfeit the power the people had put into their hands for quite contrary ends, and it devolves to the people, who have a right to resume their original liberty, and, by the establishment of a new legislative, (such as they shall think fit) provide for their own safety and security, which is the end for which they are in society. What I have said here, concerning the legislative in general holds true also concerning the supreme executor, who having a double trust put in him, both to have a part in the legislative, and the supreme execution of the law, acts against both, when he goes about to set up his own arbitrary will as the law of the society. He acts also contrary to his trust, when he either employs the force, treasure, and offices of the society to corrupt the representatives, and gain them to his purposes; or openly pre-engages the electors, and prescribes to their choice, such, whom he has, by solicitations, threats, promises, or otherwise, won to his designs: and employs them to bring in such, who have promised before-hand what to vote, and what to enact. Thus to regulate candidates and electors, and new-model the ways of election, what is it but to cut up the government by the roots, and poison the very fountain of public security?

●

But it will be said, this hypothesis lays a ferment for frequent rebellion. To which I answer,

First, no more than any other hypothesis: for when the people are made miserable, and find themselves exposed to the ill-usage of arbitrary power, cry up their governors as much as you will, for sons of Jupiter; let them be sacred or divine, descended, or authorized from heaven; give them out for whom or what you please, the same will happen. The people generally ill-treated, and contrary to right, will be ready upon any occasion to ease themselves of a burden that sits heavy upon them. They will wish, and seek for the opportunity, which in the change, weakness, and accidents of human affairs, seldom delays long to offer itself. He must have lived but a little while in the world, who has not seen examples of this in his time; and he must have read very little, who cannot produce examples of it in all sorts of governments in the world.

Secondly, I answer, such revolutions happen not upon every little mismanagement in public affairs. Great mistakes in the ruling part, many wrong and inconvenient laws, and all the slips of human frailty, will be borne by the people without mutiny or murmur. But if a long train of abuses, prevarications, and artifices, all tending the same way, make the design visible to the people, and they cannot but feel what they lie under, and see whither they are going; it is not to be wondered, that they should then rouse themselves, and endeavor to put the rule into such hands which may secure to them the ends for which government was at first erected.

●

Whosoever uses force without right, as every one does in society, who does it without law, puts himself into a state of war with those against whom he so used it; and in that state all former ties are cancelled, all other rights cease, and every one has a right to defend himself, and to resist the aggressor.

## *from* OF NATIONAL CHARACTERS (1748)

## *from* AN ESSAY ON THE NATURE AND IMMUTABILITY OF TRUTH, IN OPPOSITION TO SOPHISTRY AND SKEPTICISM (1770)

*D*avid Hume (1711–1776)—a philosopher, historian, economist, and essayist—was an important contributor to the tradition of philosophical empiricism. He was a key figure in the Scottish Enlightenment, which for a brief time made Edinburgh one of the intellectual capitals of Europe. In this excerpt from "Of National Characters," Hume's belief in human evolution is the basis for his belief that Negroes and "in general all other species of men" are "naturally inferior to the whites." While many of Hume's contemporaries would have endorsed such racist arguments, James Beattie's (1725–1803) critique suggests that such beliefs were not universal. Perhaps Hume paid attention to what Beattie was saying. In the 1776 edition of the text the passage was modified.

### *FROM* OF NATIONAL CHARACTERS

The human mind is of a very imitative nature; nor is it possible for any set of men to converse often together, without acquiring a similitude of manners, and communicating to teach other their vices as well as virtues. The propensity to company and society is strong in all rational creatures; and the same disposition, which gives us this propensity, makes us enter deeply into each other's sentiments, and causes like passions and inclinations to run, as it were, by contagion, through that whole club or knot of companions. Where a number of men are united into one political body, the occasions of their intercourse must be so frequent, for defense, commerce and government, that, together with the same speech or language, they must acquire a resemblance in their manners, and have a common or national character, as well as a personal one, peculiar to each individual. Now though nature produces all kinds of temper and understanding in great abundance, it does not follow, that she always produces them in like proportions and that in every society the ingredients of industry and indolence, valour and cowardice, humanity and brutality, wisdom and folly, will be mixed after the same manner. In the infancy of society, if any of these disposi-tions be found in greater abundance than the rest, it will naturally prevail in the com-positions and give a tincture to the national character . . .

If the characters of men depended on the air and climate, the degrees of heat and cold should naturally be expected to have a mighty influence; since nothing has a greater effect on all plants and irrational animals. And indeed there is some reason to think, that all the nations, which live beyond the polar circles or between the tropics, are inferior to the rest of the species, and are incapable of all the higher attainments of the human mind. The poverty and misery of the northern inhabitants of the globe, and the indolence of the southern from their few necessities, may, perhaps, account for this remarkable difference, without our having recourse to physical causes. This however is certain, that the characters of nations are very promiscuous in the temper-ate climates, and that almost all the general observations, which have been formed of the more southern or more northern people in these climates, are found to be uncer-tain and fallacious. [In a footnote:] I am apt to suspect the negroes and in general all other species of men (for there are four or five different kinds) to be naturally inferior to the whites. There never was a civilized nation of any other complexion than white, nor even any individual eminent either in action or speculation. No ingenious manu-factures amongst them, no arts, no sciences. On the other hand, the most rude and barbarous of the whites, such as the ancient Germans, the present Tartars, have still something eminent about them, in their valour, form of government, or some other particular. Such a uniform and constant difference could not happen, in so many countries and ages if nature had not made an original distinction between these breeds of men. Not to mention our colonies, there are negroe slaves dispersed all over Europe, of whom none ever discovered any symptoms of ingenuity; though low people without education will start up amongst us and distinguish themselves in every pro-fession. In Jamaica, indeed, they talk of one negroe as a man of parts and learning; but it is likely he is admired for slender accomplishments, like a parrot who speaks a few words plainly [end of footnote] . . .

## *FROM* AN ESSAY ON THE NATURE AND IMMUTABILITY OF TRUTH, IN OPPOSITION TO SOPHISTRY AND SKEPTICISM

That I may not be thought a blind admirer of antiquity, I would crave the reader's indulgence for one short digression more, in order to put him in mind of an impor-tant error in morals, inferred from partial and inaccurate experience, by no less a per-son than Aristotle himself. He argues "That men of little genius, and great bodily strength, are by nature destined to serve, and those of better capacity, to command; that the natives of Greece, and of some other countries, being naturally superior in genius, have a natural right to empire; and that the rest of mankind, being naturally stupid, are destined to labour and slavery." This reasoning is now, alas! of little advan-tage to Aristotle's countrymen, who have for many ages been doomed to that slavery, which, in his judgment, nature had destined them to impose on others; and many nations whom he would have consigned to everlasting stupidity, have shown them-selves equal in genius to the most exalted of humankind. It would have been more worthy of Aristotle to have inferred man's natural and universal right to liberty from that natural and universal passion with which man desires it, and from the salutary consequences to learning, to virtue, and to every human improvement, of which it never fails to be productive. He wanted perhaps, to desire some excuse for servitude; a practice which to their eternal reproach, both Greeks and Romans tolerated even in the days of their glory.

Mr Hume argues that nearly in the same manner in regard to the superiority of white man over black. "I am apt to suspect," says he, "the negroes and in general all the other species of man (for there are four or five different kinds) to be naturally inferior to the whites. There never was a civilized nation of any other complexion than white, nor even any individual eminent either in action or speculation. No ingenious manufactures among them, no arts, no sciences. There are negro-slaves dispersed all over Europe, of whom none ever discovered any symptoms of ingenuity." These assertions are strong, but I know not whether they have anything else to recommend them. For, first, though true they would not prove the point in question, except were it also proved, that the Africans and Americans, even though arts and sciences were introduced among them, would still remain unsusceptible to cultivation. The inhabitants of Great Britain and France were as savage 2,000 years ago as those of Africa and America are to this day. To civilize a nation is a work requires a long time to accomplish. And one may as well say of an infant, that he can never become a man, as of a nation now barbarous, that it can never be civilized. Secondly, of the facts here asserted, no man could have sufficient evidence, except from a personal acquaintance with all the negroes that now are, or ever were, on the face of the earth. These people write no histories, and all of the reports of all the travellers that ever visited them, will not amount to anything like a proof of what is here affirmed. But, thirdly, we know that these assertions are not true. The empires of Peru and Mexico could not have been governed, nor the metropolis of the latter built after so singular a manner, in the middle of a lake, without men eminent both for action and speculation. Every body has heard of the magnificence, good government, and ingenuity, of the ancient Peruvians. The Africans and Americans are known to have many ingenious manufactures and arts among them, which even Europeans would find it no easy matter to imitate. Sciences indeed they have none; because they have no letters, but in oratory, some of them, particularly the Indians of the Five Nations, are said to be greatly our superiors. It will be readily allowed that the condition of a slave is not favourable to genius of any kind; and yet, the negro-slaves dispersed over Europe, have often discovered symptoms of ingenuity, notwithstanding their unhappy circumstances. They become excellent handicraftsmen, and practical musicians, and indeed learn everything their masters are at pains to teach them, perfidy and debauchery not excepted. That a negro-slave, who can neither read nor write, nor speak any European language, who is not permitted to do anything but what his master commands, and who has not a friend on earth, but is universally considered and treated as if he were of a specifies inferior to the human—that such a creature should so distinguish himself among Europeans, as to be talked of throughout the world for a man of genius, is surely no reasonable expectation. To suppose him of an inferior species, because he does not thus distinguish himself, is just as rational as to suppose any private European of an inferior species, because he has not raised himself to the condition of royalty.

It is easy to see with what views some modern authors throw out these hints to prove the natural inferiority of the Negroes. But let every friend of humanity pray, that they may be disappointed. Britons are famous for generosity, a virtue in which it is easy for them to excel both the Romans and Greeks. Let it never be said, that slavery is countenanced by the bravest, and most generous people on earth; by a people who are animated with that heroic passion, the love of liberty, beyond all nations ancient or modern; and the fame of whose toilsome, but unwearied perseverance, in vindicating, at the expense of life and fortune, the sacred rights of mankind will strike terror into the hearts of sycophants and tyrants, and excite the admiration and gratitude of all good men to the latest posterity.

*Jean-Jacques Rousseau*

# *from* DISCOURSE ON THE ORIGIN AND FOUNDATIONS OF INEQUALITY AMONG MEN (1755)

*Jean-Jacques Rousseau (1712–1778), one of the most provocative figures of the Enlightenment, was a citizen of Geneva who spent much of his life in France. The* Discourse on Inequality, *his second major treatise, was originally entered in a competition at the Dijon Academy on the question: "What is the origin of inequality among men and is it warranted by natural law?" Rousseau pursues familiar themes about the distinction between civilization and barbarism and the proper nature of civil society by outlining a history of human development from a primitive state to the kind of class society found in eighteenth-century Europe. 'Civilization,' he argues, produces inequality, greed, and a frenetic pace of life, the opposite of what he envisions as the better life of the 'noble savage', who "breathes only peace and freedom" and "wishes only to live and remain idle." Rousseau did not win the competition, but his ideas proved to be extremely influential. He would continue to work out these themes in later works including* The Social Contract *(1762), in which he argued against feudalism in favor of the rights of all men.*

*Question proposed by the Dijon Academy*

'What is the origin of the inequality among men, and is it authorized by natural law?'

•

What exactly is the object of discourse? To pinpoint that moment in the progress of things when, with right succeeding violence, nature was subjected to the law; to explain by what sequence of prodigious events the strong could resolve to serve the weak, and the people to purchase imaginary repose at the price of real happiness.

The philosophers who have examined the foundations of society have all felt it necessary to go back to the state of nature, but none of them has succeeded in getting there. Some have not hesitated to attribute to men in that state of nature the concept of just and unjust, without bothering to show that they must have had such a concept, or even that it would be useful to them. Others have spoken of the natural right each has to keep and defend what he owns without saying what they mean by 'own'. Others again, starting out by giving the stronger authority over the weaker, promptly introduce government, without thinking of the time that must have elapsed before the words 'authority' and 'government' could have had any meaning among men. Finally, all these philosophers talking ceaselessly of need, greed, oppression, desire and pride have transported into the state of nature concepts formed in society. They speak of savage man and they depict civilized man. It has not even entered the heads of most of our philosophers to doubt that the state of nature once existed, yet it is evident from reading the Scriptures that the first man, having received the light of reason and precepts at once from God, was not himself in the state of nature; and giving the writings of Moses that credence which every Christian philosopher owes them, one must deny that even before the Flood men were in the pure state of nature, unless they relapsed into it through some extraordinary event—a paradox that would be troublesome to uphold and altogether impossible to prove.

Let us begin by setting aside all the facts, because they do not affect the question. One must not take the kind of research which we enter into as the pursuit of truths of history, but solely as hypothetical and conditional reasonings, better fitted to clarify the nature of things than to expose their actual origin; reasonings similar to those used every day by our physicists to explain the formation of the earth. Religion commands us to believe that since God himself withdrew men from the state of nature they are unequal because he willed that they be; but it does not forbid us to make conjectures, based solely on the nature of man and the beings that surround him, as to what the human race might have become if it had been abandoned to itself. This is what is asked of me and what I propose to examine in this discourse.

O Man, to whatever country you belong and whatever your opinions, listen: here is your history as I believe I have read it, not in the books of your fellow men who are liars but in Nature which never lies. Everything which comes from her will be true; there will be nothing false except that which I have intermixed, unintentionally, of my own. The times of which I am going to speak are very remote—how much you have changed from what you were! It is, so to say, the life of your species that I am going to describe, in the light of the qualities which you once received and which your culture and your habits have been able to corrupt but not able to destroy. There is, I feel, an age at which the individual would like to stand still; you are going to search for the age at which you would wish your whole species had stood still. Discontented with your present condition for reasons which presage for your unfortunate posterity even greater discontent, you will wish perhaps you could go backwards in time—and this feeling must utter the eulogy of your first ancestors, the indictment of your contemporaries, and the terror of those who have the misfortune to live after you.

•

The body of a savage being the only instrument he knows, he puts it to all sorts of uses of which our bodies, for lack of practice, are incapable; our equipment deprives us of that strength and agility which necessity obliges him to acquire. If he had had an axe, would his wrist have been able to break such solid branches? If he had had a sling, would his hand have been able to throw a stone with such speed? If he had had a ladder, would he have been able to climb a tree so nimbly? If he had had a horse, would he have been able to run so fast? Let the civilized man gather all his machines around him, and no doubt he will easily beat the savage; but if you would like to see an even more unequal match, pit the two together naked and unarmed, and you will soon see the advantages of having all one's forces constantly at one's command, of being always prepared for any eventuality, and of always being, so to speak, altogether complete in oneself.

●

On the question of sickness I shall not repeat the vain and empty declamations against medicine that are uttered by most people when they are healthy, but I will ask whether there is any solid evidence for concluding that in the country where medicine is most rudimentary the average life of men is shorter than it is in the country where the art is cultivated with the greatest care; and how indeed could that be the case if we bring upon ourselves more diseases than medicine can furnish remedies? The extreme inequality of our ways of life, the excess of idleness among some and the excess of toil among others, the ease of stimulating and gratifying our appetites and our senses, the over-elaborate foods of the rich, which inflame and overwhelm them with indigestion, the bad food of the poor, which they often go without altogether, so that they over-eat greedily when they have the opportunity; those late nights, excesses of all kinds, immoderate transports of every passion, fatigue, exhaustion of mind, the innumerable sorrows and anxieties that people in all classes suffer, and by which the human soul is constantly tormented: these are the fatal proofs that most of our ills are of our own making, and that we might have avoided nearly all of them if only we had adhered to the simple, unchanging and solitary way of life that nature ordained for us. If nature destined us to be healthy, I would almost venture to assert that the state of reflection is a state contrary to nature, and that the man who meditates is a depraved animal. When we think of the good constitution of savages—at least of those we have not corrupted with our strong liquors—and reflect that they have almost no disorders except wounds and old age, we are almost prompted to believe that we could write the history of human illness by following the history of civilized societies. Such at least was the opinion of Plato, who deduced from the fact that certain remedies were used or approved by Podalirius and Machaon at the siege of Troy, that the various sicknesses which could be provoked by these remedies, were not then known to mankind.*

With so few sources of illness, man in the state of nature has little need for remedies, and even less for physicians; the human race is, in this respect, in no worse a condition than any other species; and we can easily learn from hunters whether they find sick animals in the field. Assuredly, they find many which have received serious wounds that have healed very well, which have had bones or even limbs broken and restored by no other surgeon than time and by no other regimen than their ordinary life, without being any the less perfectly healed, as a result of not having been tormented with incisions, poisoned with drugs or wasted by fasting. In short, however useful medicine well administered may be for us, it is certain that if a sick savage abandoned to himself has nothing to hope for except from nature, conversely he has nothing to fear except from his sickness, all of which makes his situation very often preferable to our own.

Let us therefore beware of confusing savage man with the man we have before our eyes. Nature treats every animal abandoned to her care with a partiality which seems to prove how jealous she is of that right. The horse, the cat, the bull and even the ass are for the most part larger and all have a more robust constitution, more

*Paracelus reports that dieting, so necessary today, was first invented by Hippocrates (See Plato's *Republic*, *III*, 405d and Homer's *Iliad, XI*, 639).

vigour, more strength and more spirit in the forest than under our roofs; they lose half those advantages on becoming domesticated, and one might say that all our efforts to care for and feed these animals have only succeeded in making them degenerate. The same is true even of man himself; in becoming sociable and a slave, he grows feeble, timid, servile; and his soft and effeminate way of life completes the enervation both of his strength and his courage. Furthermore, the difference between savage and the domesticated man must be greater than the difference between wild and tame animals, for since men and beasts are treated equally by nature, all the commodities which man gives himself beyond those he gives to the animals he tames, are so many particular factors that make him degenerate more appreciably.

●

I know we are constantly being told that nothing is more miserable than man in the state of nature; and if it is true, as I think I have proved, that it is only after many centuries that man could have had either the desire or the opportunity to quit that state, this is a charge to bring against nature and not against him whom nature has so constituted. But if I understand correctly the term 'miserable', it is a word that has no meaning or signifies only a painful deprivation and state of suffering in body or soul. Now I would be pleased to have it explained to me what kind of misery can be that of a free being whose heart is at peace and whose body is in health? I ask which—civilized or natural life—is the more liable to become unbearable to those who experience it? We see around us people who nearly all complain and several of whom indeed deprive themselves of their existence as far as they are able; and the joint sanction of divine and human law hardly suffices to halt this disorder. I ask if anyone has ever heard of a savage in a condition of freedom even dreaming of complaining about his life and killing himself? Let it be judged with less pride on which side the real misery lies. Nothing, on the contrary could be as miserable as a savage man dazzled by enlightenment, tormented by passions, and arguing about a state different from his own. It is thanks to a very wise Providence that the faculties which were potential in him should have become actual only with the opportunity of using them, so that they were neither superfluous nor onerous before their time, nor late in appearing and useless when the need arose. In instinct alone man had all he needed for living in a state of nature; in cultivated reason he has what is necessary only for living in society.

Above all, let us not conclude with Hobbes that man is naturally evil just because he has no idea of goodness, that he is vicious for want of any knowledge of virtue, that he always refuses to do his fellow-men services which he does not believe he owes them, or that on the strength of the right he reasonably claims to things he needs, he foolishly imagines himself to be the sole proprietor of the whole universe. Hobbes saw very clearly the defects of all modern definitions of natural right, but the conclusions he drew from his own definition show that his own concept of natural right is equally defective. Reasoning on his own principles, that writer ought to have said that the state of nature, being the state where man's care for his own preservation is least prejudicial to that of others, is the one most conducive to peace and the most suited to mankind. Hobbes said precisely the opposite as a result of introducing, illogically, into the savage man's care for his own preservation the need to satisfy a multitude of passions which are the product of society and which have made laws necessary.

●

Such is the pure movement of nature, prior to all reflection; such is the force of natural pity, which the utmost depravity of morals is hardly able to destroy—for we see daily in our theatres men being moved, even weeping at the suffering of a wretch who, were they in the tyrant's place would only increase the torments of his enemy.* Mandeville well realized that men, despite all their morality, would never have been any better than monsters if nature had not given them pity to support reason, but he failed to see that all the social virtues which he denies in men flow from this quality alone. In fact, what are generosity, mercy and humanity but compassion applied to the weak, to the guilty or to the human race in general? Benevolence, and even friendship, correctly understood, is only the outcome of constant compassion directed towards a particular object; for is desiring that a person should not suffer other than desiring that he should be happy? Even if it were true that pity is no more than a feeling that puts us in the place of the sufferer, a feeling that is obscure but strong in savage man, and developed but weak in civilized man, what difference would this make to my argument, except to give it more force? In fact, pity becomes all the more intense as the perceiving animal identifies itself more intimately with the suffering animal. Now it is clear that this identification must have been infinitely closer in the state of nature than in the state of reasoning. It is reason which breeds pride and reflection which fortifies it; reason which turns man inward into himself; reason which separates him from everything which troubles or affect him. It is philosophy which isolates a man, and prompts him to say in secret at the sight of another suffering: 'Perish if you will; I am safe.' No longer can anything but dangers to society in general disturb the tranquil sleep of the philosopher or drag him from his bed. A fellow-man may with impunity be murdered under his window, for the philosopher has only to put his hands over his ears and argue a little with himself to prevent nature, which rebels inside him, from making him identify himself with the victim of the murderer. The savage man entirely lacks this admirable talent, and for want of wisdom and reason he always responds recklessly to the first promptings of human feelings. In riots or fights in the streets it is always the populace that gathers round; the prudent man departs; it is the ill-bred mob, the market-women who separate the combatants and prevent superior people from killing one another.

It is therefore very certain that pity is a natural sentiment which, by moderating in each individual the activity of self-love, contributes to the mutual preservation of the whole species. It is pity which carries us without reflection to the aid of those we see suffering; it is pity which in the state of nature takes the place of laws, morals and virtues, with the added advantage that no one there is tempted to disobey its gentle

---

*They are like the bloodthirsty Sulla, who was so sensitive to sufferings he had not caused, or like Alexander of Pherae, who did not dare attend the performance of any tragedy, lest he be seen sobbing with Andromache and Priam, although he could listen without emotion to the cries of all the citizens whose throats were cut daily on his orders: 'Tenderness of heart is the gift Nature declares she gave to the human race with the gift of tears'

> (Mollissima corda
> Humano generi dare se natura fatetur
> Quae lacrimas dedit)
> Juvenal, Satires, XV, 131 [Added to Edition of 1782].

voice; it will always dissuade a robust savage from robbing a weak child or a sick old man of his hard-won sustenance if he has hope of finding his own elsewhere; it is pity which, in place of that noble maxim of rational justice 'Do unto others as you would have them do unto you', inspires all men with this other maxim of natural goodness, much less perfect but perhaps more useful: 'Do good to yourself with as little possible harm to others.' In a word, it is to this natural feeling, rather than to subtle arguments, that we must look for the origin of that repugnance which every man would feel against doing evil, even independently of the maxims of education. Although it may be proper for Socrates and other minds of that class to acquire virtue through reason, the human race would long since have ceased to exist if its preservation had depended only on the reasoning of the individuals who compose it.

•

If I have dwelled so long on the hypothesis of this primitive condition, it is because, having ancient errors and inveterate prejudices to eliminate, I thought I ought to dig down to the roots, and provide a picture of the true state of nature, to show to what extent inequality, even in its natural form, is far from having in that state as much reality and influence as our writers claim.

In fact, it is easy to see that among the differences which distinguish between men that several are taken to be natural which are solely the product of habit and of the various ways of life that man adopts in society. Thus a robust or a delicate temperament, together with the strength or weakness attaching to it, often derives from the manly or the effeminate manner in which one has been raised rather than from the original constitution of the body. The same is true of the powers of the mind; and not only does education establish a difference between cultivated minds and those which are not, but it increases the differences among cultivated minds in proportion to their culture; for when a giant and a dwarf walk the same road, every step each takes gives an extra advantage to the giant. Now if we compare the prodigious diversity of upbringings and of ways of life which prevail among the different classes in the civil state with the simplicity and uniformity of animal and savage life, where everyone eats the same foods, lives in the same style and does exactly the same things, it will be understood how much less the difference between man and man must be in the state of nature than it is in society, and how much natural inequality must be increased in the human species through the effects of instituted inequality.

•

Having proved that inequality is hardly perceived in the state of nature, and that its influence there is almost nil, it remains for me to explain its origin and its progress in the successive developments of the human mind. After having shown that *improvability,* the social virtues and other faculties that natural man received as potentialities could never have developed by themselves, that in order to develop they needed the fortuitous concurrence of several alien causes which might never have arisen and without which man would have remained forever in his primitive condition, I must now consider and bring together the different chance factors which have succeeded in improving human reason while worsening the human species, making man wicked while making him sociable, and carrying man and the world from their remote beginnings to the point at which we now behold them.

Since the events I have to describe might have happened in several ways, I admit I can make the choice between those possibilities only by means of conjecture; but beside the fact that those conjectures become rational when they are the most probable that can be inferred from the nature of things and constitute the only means one can have for discovering the truth, the conclusions I want to deduce from mine will not thereby be conjectural, since, on the basis of the principles I have established, it would be impossible to formulate any other system which would not yield the same results and from which I could not draw identical conclusions.

## Part Two

The first man who, having enclosed a piece of land, thought of saying 'This is mine' and found people simple enough to believe him, was the true founder of civil society. How many crimes, wars, murders; how much misery and horror the human race would have been spared if someone had pulled up the stakes and filled in the ditch and cried out to his fellow men: 'Beware of listening to this impostor. You are lost if you forget that the fruits of the earth belong to everyone and that the earth itself belongs to no one!' But is it highly probable that by this time things had reached a point beyond which they could not go on as they were; for the idea of prosperity, depending on many prior ideas which could only have arisen in successive stages, was not formed all at once in the human mind. It was necessary for men to make much progress, to acquire much industry and knowledge, to transmit and increase it from age to age, before arriving at this final stage of the state of nature. Let us therefore look farther back, and try to review from a single perspective the slow succession of events and discoveries in their most natural order.

•

Difficulties soon presented themselves and man had to learn to overcome them. The height of trees, which prevented him from reaching their fruits; the competition of animals seeking to nourish themselves on the same fruits; the ferocity of animals who threatened his life—all this obliged man to apply himself to bodily exercises; he had to make himself agile, fleet of foot, and vigorous in combat. Natural weapons—branches of trees and stones—were soon found to be at hand. He learned to overcome the obstacles of nature, to fight when necessary against other animals, to struggle for his subsistence even against other men, or to indemnify himself for what he was forced to yield to the stronger.

•

Those first slow developments finally enabled men to make more rapid ones. The more the mind became enlightened, the more industry improved. Soon, ceasing to doze under the first tree, or to withdraw into caves, men discovered that various sorts of hard sharp stones could serve as hatchets to cut wood, dig the soil, and make huts out of the branches, which they learned to cover with clay and mud. This was the epoch of a first revolution, which established and differentiated families, and which introduced property of a sort from which perhaps even then many quarrels and fights were born. However, as the strongest men were probably the first to build themselves huts which they felt themselves able to defend, it is reasonable to believe that the weak found it quicker and safer to imitate them rather than try to dislodge them; and as for those who already possessed huts, no one would readily venture to appropriate his neighbour's, not so much because it did not belong to him as because it would be no use to him and because he could not seize it without exposing himself to a very lively fight with the family which occupied it.

The first movements of the heart were the effect of this new situation, which united in a common dwelling husbands and wives, fathers and children; the habit of living together generated the sweetest sentiments known to man, conjugal love and paternal love. Each family became a little society, all the better united because mutual affection and liberty were its only bonds; at this stage also the first differences were established in ways of life of the two sexes which had hitherto been identical. Women became more sedentary and accustomed themselves to looking after the hut and the children while men went out to seek their common subsistence. The two sexes began, in living a rather softer life, to lose something of their ferocity and their strength; but if each individual became separately less able to fight wild beasts, all, on the other hand, found it easier to group tougher to resist them jointly.

This new condition, with its solitary and simple life, very limited in its needs, and very few instruments invented to supply them, left men to enjoy a great deal of leisure, which they used to procure many sorts of commodities unknown to their fathers; and this was the first yoke they imposed on themselves, without thinking about it, and the first source of the evils they prepared for their descendants. For not only did such commodities continue to soften both body and mind, they almost lost through habitual use their power to please, and as they had at the same time degenerated into actual needs, being deprived of them became much more cruel than the possession of them was sweet; and people were unhappy in losing them without being happy in possessing them.

•

To the extent that ideas and feelings succeeded one another, and the heart and mind were exercised, the human race became more sociable, relationships became more extensive and bonds tightened. People grew used to gathering together in front of their huts or around a large tree; singing and dancing, true progeny of love and leisure, became the amusement, or rather the occupation, of idle men and women thus assembled. Each began to look at the others and to want to be looked at himself; and public esteem came to be prized. He who sang or danced the best; he who was the most handsome, the strongest, the most adroit or the most eloquent became the most highly regarded, and this was the first step towards inequality and at the same time towards vice. From those first preferences there arose, on the one side, vanity and scorn, on the other, shame and envy, and the fermentation produced by these new leavens finally produced compounds fatal to happiness and innocence.

As soon as men learned to value one another and the idea of consideration was formed in their minds, everyone claimed a right to it, and it was no longer possible for anyone to be refused consideration without affront. This gave rise to the first duties of civility, even among savages: and henceforth every intentional wrong became an outrage, because together with the hurt which might result from the injury, the offended party saw an insult to his person which was often more unbearable than the hurt itself. Thus, as everyone punished the contempt shown him by another in a manner proportionate to the esteem he accorded himself, revenge became terrible, and men grew bloodthirsty and cruel. This is precisely the stage reached by most of the savage peoples known to us; and it is for lack of having sufficiently distinguished between different ideas and seen how far those peoples already are from the first state of nature that so many authors have hastened to conclude that man is naturally cruel and needs civil institutions to make him peaceable, whereas in truth nothing is more peaceable than man in his primitive state; placed by nature at an equal distance from the stupidity of brutes and the fatal enlightenment of civilized man, limited equally by reason and instinct to defending himself against evils which threaten him, he is retrained by natural pity from doing harm to anyone, even after receiving harm himself: for according to the wise Locke: 'Where there is no property, there is no injury.'

But it must be noted that society's having come into existence and relations among individuals having been already established meant that men were required to have qualities different from those they possessed from their primitive constitution; morality began to be introduced into human actions, and each man, prior to laws, was the sole judge and avenger of the offenses he had received, so that the goodness suitable to the pure state of nature was no longer that which suited nascent society; it was necessary for punishments to be more severe to the extent that opportunities for offense became more frequent; and the terror of revenge had to serve in place of the restraint of laws. Thus although men had come to have less fortitude, and their natural pity had suffered some dilution, this period of the development of human faculties, the golden mean between the indolence of the primitive state and the petulant activity of our own pride, must have been the happiest epoch and the most lasting. The more we reflect on it, the more we realize that this state was the least subject to revolutions, and the best for man; and that man can have left it only as the result of some fatal accident, which, for the common good, ought never to have happened. The example of savages, who have almost always been found at this point of development, appears to confirm that the human race was made to remain there always; to confirm that this state was the true youth of the world, and that all subsequent progress has been so many steps in appearance towards the improvement of the individual, but so many steps in reality towards the decrepitude of the species.

As long as men were content with their rustic huts, as long as they confined themselves to sewing their garments of skins with thorns or fish-bones, and adorning themselves with feathers or shells, to painting their bodies with various colours, to improving or decorating their bows and arrows; and to using sharp stones to make a few fishing canoes or crude musical instruments; in a word, so long as they applied themselves only to work that one person could accomplish alone and to arts that did not require the collaboration of several hands, they lived as free, healthy, good and happy men so far as they could be according to their nature and they continued to enjoy among themselves the sweetness of independent intercourse; but from the instant one man needed the help of another, and it was found to be useful for one man to have provisions enough for two, equality disappeared, property was introduced, work became necessary, and vast forests were transformed into pleasant fields which had to be watered with the sweat of men, and where slavery and misery were soon seen to germinate and flourish with the crops.

•

From the cultivation of the land, its division necessarily followed, and from property once recognized arose the first rules of justice: for in order to render each his own, each must be able to have something; moreover, as men began to direct their eyes towards the future and all saw that they had some goods to lose, there was no one who did not fear reprisals against himself for the injuries he might do to another. This origin is all the more natural, in that it is impossible to conceive of the idea of property arising from anything other than manual labour, for one cannot see what besides his own labour a man can add to things he has not actually made in order to appropriate them. It is his labour alone which, in giving the cultivator the right to the product of the land he has tilled, gives him in consequence the right to the land itself, at least until the harvest, which, being repeated from year to year, brings about a continued occupation, easily transformed into property. Grotius says that when the ancients gave Ceres the title of Legislatrix, and the festival celebrated in her honour the name of Thesmophoria, they implied that the division of the earth had produced a new sort of right: that is to say, the right to property different from the one derived from natural law.

Things in this state might have remained equal if talents had been equal, and if, for example, the use of iron and the consumption of foodstuffs had always exactly balanced each other, but this equilibrium, which nothing maintained, was soon broken: the stronger did more productive work, the more adroit did better work, the more ingenious devised ways of abridging his labour: the farmer had greater need of iron or the smith greater need of wheat, and with both working equally, the one earned plenty while the other had hardly enough to live on. It is thus that natural inequality merges imperceptibly with inequality of ranks, and the differences between men, increased by differences of circumstance, make themselves more visible and more permanent in their effects, and begin to exercise a correspondingly large influence over the destiny of individuals.

●

Behold, then, all our faculties developed, memory and imagination brought into play, pride stimulated, reason made active and the mind almost at the point of the perfection of which it is capable. Behold all the natural qualities called into action, the rank and destiny of each man established, not only as to the quantity of his possessions and his power to serve or to injure, but as to the intelligence, beauty, strength, skill, merit or talents; and since these qualities were the only ones that could attract consideration it soon became necessary either to have them or to feign them. It was necessary in one's own interest to seem to be other than one was in reality. Being and appearance became two entirely different things, and from this distinction arose insolent ostentation, deceitful cunning and all the vices that follow in their train. From another point of view, behold man, who was formerly free and independent, diminished as a consequence of a multitude of new wants into subjection, one might say, to the whole of nature and especially to his fellow men, men of whom he has become the slave, in a sense, even in becoming their master; for if he is rich he needs their services; if he is poor he needs their aid; and even a middling condition does not enable him to do without them. He must therefore seek constantly to interest others in his lot and make them see an advantage, either real or apparent, for themselves in working for his benefit; all of which makes him devious and artful with some, imperious and hard towards others, and compels him to treat badly the people he needs if he cannot make them fear him and does not judge it in his interest to be of service to them. Finally, a devouring ambition, the burning passion to enlarge one's relative fortune, not so much from real need as to put oneself ahead of others, inspires in all men a dark propensity to injure one another, a secret jealousy which is all the more dangerous in that it often assumes the mask of benevolence in order to do its deeds in greater safety; in a word, there is competition and rivalry on the one hand, conflicts of interest on the other, and always the hidden desire to gain an advantage at the expense of other people. All these evils are the main effects of property and the inseparable consequences of nascent inequality.

•

All ran towards their chains believing that they were securing their liberty; for although they had reason enough to discern the advantages of a civil order, they did not have experience enough to foresee the dangers. Those most capable of predicting the abuses were precisely those who expected to profit from them; and even the wisest saw that men must resolve to sacrifice one part of their freedom in order to preserve the other, even as a wounded man has his arm cut off to save the rest of his body.

Such was, or must have been, the origin of society and of laws, which put new fetters on the weak and gave new powers to the rich, which irretrievably destroyed natural liberty, established for all time the law of property and inequality, transformed adroit usurpation into irrevocable right, and for the benefit of a few ambitious men subjected the human race thenceforth to labour, servitude and misery. It is easy to see how the foundation of one society made the establishment of all the rest unavoidable, and how, being faced with united forces, it was necessary for others to unite in turn. Societies, as they multiplied and spread, soon came to cover the whole surface of the earth, and it was no longer possible to find a single corner of the universe where one might free oneself from the yoke and withdraw one's head from beneath the sword, often precariously held, which every man saw perpetually hanging over him.

•

If we follow the progress of inequality in these different revolutions, we shall find that the establishment of law and the right of property was the first stage, the institution of magistrates the second, and the transformation of legitimate into arbitrary power the third and last stage. Thus, the status of rich and poor was authorized by the first epoch, that of strong and weak by the second, and by the third that of master and slave, which is the last degree of inequality, and the stage to which all the others finally lead until new revolutions dissolve the government altogether or bring it back to legitimacy.

To understand the necessity of this progress, we must consider less the motives for the establishment of the body politic than the way in which that body performs in action and the disadvantages it introduces, for the vices which make social institutions necessary are the same vices which make the abuse of those institutions inevitable. Leaving aside the unique case of Sparta, where the laws concerned mainly the education of children and where Lycurgus established morals so well that it was almost unnecessary to add laws, laws, being in general less strong than passions, restrain men without changing them; so that it would be easy to prove that any government which, without being corrupted or degenerate, worked perfectly according to the ends of its institution, would have been instituted unnecessarily, and that a country where nobody evaded the laws or exploited the magistracy would need neither laws nor magistrates.

Political distinctions necessarily introduce civil distinctions. The growing inequality between the people and its chiefs is soon reproduced between individuals, and is modified there in a thousand ways according to passions, talents and circumstances. The magistrate cannot usurp illegitimate power without enrolling clients to whom he is forced to yield some part of it. Besides, citizens allow themselves to be oppressed only so far as they are impelled by a blind ambition; and fixing their eyes below rather than above themselves, come to love domination more than independence, and agree to wear chains for the sake of imposing chains on others in turn. It is difficult to reduce to obedience a man who has no wish to command, and the most adroit politician could not enslave men whose only wish was to be free; on the other hand, inequality extends easily among ambitious and cowardly souls, who are always ready to run the risks of fortune and almost indifferent as to whether they command or obey, according to fortune's favour. Thus there must have come a time when the eyes of the people were so dazzled that their leaders had only to say to the least of men: 'Be great, with all your posterity', and at once that man appeared great in the eyes of the world as well as in his own eyes and his descendants exalted themselves all the more in proportion to their distance from him; the more remote and uncertain the cause, the greater the effect; the more idlers who could be counted in a family, the more illustrious it became.

●

What reflection teaches on this subject is perfectly confirmed by observation; savage man and civilized man differ so much in the bottom of their hearts and inclinations that that which constitutes the supreme happiness of the one would reduce the other to despair. The savage man breathes only peace and freedom; he desires only to live and stay idle, and even the *ataraxia* of the Stoic does not approach his proud indifference towards every other object. Civil man, on the contrary, being always active, sweating and restless, torments himself endlessly in search of ever more laborious occupations; he works himself to death, he even runs towards the grave to put himself into shape to live, or renounces life in order to acquire immortality. He pays court to great men he loathes and to rich men he despises; he spares nothing to secure the honour of serving them; he boasts vaingloriously of his own baseness and of their patronage, and being proud of his slavery he speaks with disdain of those who have not the honour of sharing it. What a spectacle for a Carib would be the arduous and envied labours of a European minister! How many cruel deaths would not that indolent savage prefer to the horrors of such a life, which often is not even sweetened by the satisfaction of doing good? In order for him to understand the motives of anyone assuming so many cares, it would be necessary for the words 'power' and 'reputation' to have a meaning for his mind; he would have to know that there is a class of men who attach importance to the gaze of the rest of the world, and who know how to be happy and satisfied with themselves on the testimony of others rather than on their own. Such is, in fact, the true cause of all these differences: the savage lives within himself; social man lives always outside himself; he knows how to live only in the opinion of others, it is, so to speak, from their judgment alone that he derives the sense of his own existence. It is not my subject here to show how such a disposition gives birth to so much indifference to good and evil coupled with such beautiful talk about morality; or how, as everything is reduced to appearances, everything comes to be false and warped, honour, friendship, virtue, and often even vices themselves, since in the end men discover the secret of boasting about vices; or show how, as a result of always asking others what we are and never daring to put the question to ourselves in the midst of so much philosophy, humanity, civility and so many sublime maxims, we have only façades, deceptive and frivolous, honour without virtue, reason without wisdom, and pleasure without happiness. It is enough for me to have proved that this is not at all the original state of men, and that it is only the spirit of society together with the inequality that society engenders which changes and corrupts in this way all our natural inclinations.

I have tried to set out the origin and progress of inequality, the establishment and the abuse of political societies, to the extent that these things can be deduced from the nature of man by the light of reason alone, independently of the sacred dogmas which give to sovereign authority the sanction of divine right. It follows from this exposition that inequality, being almost non-existent in the state of nature, derives its force and its growth from the development of our faculties and the progress of the human mind, and finally becomes fixed and legitimate through the institution of property and laws. It follows furthermore that that moral inequality, authorized by positive law alone, is contrary to natural right, whenever it is not matched in exact proportion with physical inequality—a distinction which sufficiently determines what we ought to think of that form of inequality which prevails among all civilized peoples; for it is manifestly contrary to the law of nature, however defined, that a child should govern an old man, that an imbecile should lead a wise man, and that a handful of people should gorge themselves with superfluities while the hungry multitude goes in want of necessities.

— *trans. Maurice Cranston*

# Adam Smith

## *from* INQUIRY INTO THE NATURE AND CAUSES OF THE WEALTH OF NATIONS (1776)

*Scottish by birth, Adam Smith (1723–1790) is, of course, well known as one of the founders of economics. Less known is his connection to the Enlightenment. Just as Newton sought to understand the laws of motion, Smith attempted to uncover the laws of economic behavior. Like other Enlightenment thinkers, he believed that knowledge of these laws was a precondition for bringing the world into harmony with them. Smith extended the thought of the eighteenth-century French physiocrats, a group of economic thinkers who advocated the ending of feudal or artificial controls on land use in order to liberate productive capacity. In* An Inquiry into the Nature and Causes of the Wealth of Nations, *Smith argues that restrictions on agriculture, manufacture, and trade in the form of monopolies, tariffs, and other controls are an impediment to maximizing productive capacity; he also believes that the verdict of the market is ultimately the best economic policy. In Smith's view, individuals in isolation, seeking to satisfy their own passions and desires, would ultimately produce the best social result as if "led by an invisible hand."*

## CHAPTER 7

### *Of the Natural and Market Price of Commodities*

There is in every society or neighbourhood an ordinary or average rate both of wages and profit in every different employment of labour and stock. This rate is naturally regulated, as I shall show hereafter, partly by the general circumstances of the society, their riches or poverty, their advancing, stationary, or declining condition; and partly by the particular nature of each employment.

There is likewise in every society or neighbourhood an ordinary or average rate of rent, which is regulated too, as I shall shew hereafter, partly by the general circumstances of the society or neighbourhood in which the land is situated, and partly by the natural or improved fertility of the land.

These ordinary or average rates may be called the natural rates of wages, profit, and rent, at the time and place in which they commonly prevail.

When the price of any commodity is neither more nor less than what is sufficient to pay the rent of the land, the wages of the labour, and the profits of the stock employed in raising, preparing, and bringing it to market, according to their natural rates, the commodity is then sold for what may be called its natural price.

The commodity is then sold precisely for what it is worth, or for what it really costs the person who brings it to market; for though in common language what is called the prime cost of any commodity does not comprehend the profit of the person who is to sell it again, yet if he sells it at a price which does not allow him the ordinary rate of profit in his neighbourhood, he is evidently a loser by the trade; since by employing his stock in some other way he might have made that profit. His profit, besides, is his revenue, the proper fund of his subsistence. As, while he is preparing and bringing the goods to market, he advances to his workmen their wages, or their subsistence; so he advances to himself, in the same manner, his own subsistence, which is generally suitable to the profit which he may reasonably expect from the sale of his goods. Unless they yield him this profit, therefore, they do not repay him what they may very properly be said to have really cost him.

Though the price, therefore, which leaves him this profit, is not always the lowest at which a dealer may sometimes sell his goods, it is the lowest at which he is likely to sell them for any considerable time; at least where there is perfect liberty, or where he may change his trade as often as he pleases.

The actual price at which any commodity is commonly sold is called its market price. It may either be above, or below, or exactly the same with its natural price.

The market price of every particular commodity is regulated by the proportion between the quantity which is actually brought to market, and the demand of those who are willing to pay the natural price of the commodity, or the whole value of the rent, labour, and profit, which must be paid in order to bring it thither. Such people may be called the effectual demanders, and their demand the effectual demand; since it may be sufficient to effectuate the bringing of the commodity to market. It is different from the absolute demand. A very poor man may be said in some sense to have a demand for a coach and six; he might like to have it; but his demand is not an effectual demand, as the commodity can never be brought to market in order to satisfy it.

When the quantity of any commodity which is brought to market falls short of the effectual demand, all those who are willing to pay the whole value of the rent, wages, and profit, which must be paid in order to bring it thither, cannot be supplied with the quantity which they want. Rather than want it altogether, some of them will be willing to give more. A competition will immediately begin among them, and the market price will rise more or less above the natural price, according as either the greatness of the deficiency, or the wealth and wanton luxury of the competitors, happen to animate more or less the eagerness of the competition. Among competitors of equal wealth and luxury the same deficiency will generally occasion a more or less eager competition, according as the acquisition of the commodity happens to be of more or less importance to them. Hence the exorbitant price of the necessities of life during the blockade of a town or in a famine.

When the quantity brought to market exceeds the effectual demand, it cannot be all sold to those who are willing to pay the whole value of the rent, wages and profit, which must be paid in order to bring it thither. Some part must be sold to those who are willing to pay less, and the low price which they give for it must reduce the price of the whole. The market price will sink more or less below the natural price, according as the greatness of the excess increases more and less the competition of the sellers, or according as it happens to be more or less important to them to get immediately rid of the commodity. The same excess in the importation of perishable, will occasion a much greater competition than in that of durable commodities; in the importation of oranges, for example, than in that of old iron.

When the quantity brought to market is just sufficient to supply the effectual demand and no more, the market price naturally comes to be either exactly, or as nearly as can be judged of, the same with the natural price. The whole quantity upon hand can be disposed of for this price, and cannot be disposed of for more. The competition of the different dealers obliges them all to accept of this price, but does not oblige them to accept of less. . . .

## CHAPTER 2

### *Of Restraints Upon the Importation from Foreign Countries of Such Goods as Can Be Produced at Home*

. . . every individual who employs his capital in the support of domestic industry, necessarily endeavors so to direct that industry, that its produce may be of the greatest possible value.

The produce of industry is what it adds to the subject or materials upon which it is employed. In proportion as the value of this produce is great or small, so will likewise be the profits of the employer. But it is only for the sake of profit that any man employs a capital in the support of industry; and he will always, therefore, endeavor to employ it in the support of that industry of which the produce is likely to be of the greatest value, or to exchange for the greatest quantity either of money or of other goods.

But the annual revenue of every society is always precisely equal to the exchangeable value of the whole annual produce of its industry, or rather is precisely the same thing with the exchangeable value. As every individual, therefore, endeavours as much as he can both to employ his capital in the support of domestic industry, and so to direct that industry that its produce may be of the greatest value; every individual necessarily labours to render the annual revenue of the society as great as he can. He generally, indeed, neither intends to promote the public interest, nor knows how much he is promoting it. By preferring the support of domestic to that of foreign industry, he intends only his own security; and by directing that industry in such a manner as its produce may be of the greatest value, he intends only his own gain, and he is in this, as in many other cases, led by an invisible hand to promote an end which was no part of his intention. Nor is it always the worse for the society that it was no part of it. By pursuing his own interest he frequently promotes that of the society more effectually than when he really intends to promote it. I have never known much good done by those who affected to trade for the public good. It is an affectation, indeed, not very common among merchants, and very few words need be employed in dissuading them from it. . . .

It is thus that every system which endeavours, either, by extraordinary encouragements, to draw towards a particular species of industry a greater share of the capital of the society than what would naturally go to it; or, by extraordinary restraints, to force from a particular species of industry some share of the capital which would otherwise be employed in it; is in reality subversive of the great purpose which it means to promote. It retards, instead of accelerating, the progress of the society towards real wealth and greatness: and diminishes, instead of increasing, the real value of the annual produce of its land and labour.

All systems either of preference or of restraint, therefore, being thus completely taken away, the obvious and simple system of natural liberty establishes itself of its own accord. Every man, as long as he does not violate the laws of justice, is left perfectly free to pursue his own interest his own way, and to bring both his industry and capital into competition with those of any other man, or order of men. The sovereign is completely discharged from a duty, in the attempting to perform which he must always be exposed to innumerable delusions, and for the proper performance of which no human wisdom or knowledge could ever be sufficient; the duty of superintending the industry of private people, and of directing it towards the employments most suitable to the interest of the society. According to the system of natural liberty, the sovereign has only three duties to attend to; three duties of great importance, indeed, but plain and intelligible to common understandings; first, the duty of protecting the society from the violence and invasion of other independent societies; secondly, the duty of protecting, as far as possible, every member of the society from the injustice or oppression of every other member of it, or the duty of establishing an exact administration of justice; and thirdly, the duty of erecting and maintaining certain public works and certain public institutions, which it can never be for the interest of any individual, or small number of individuals, to erect and maintain; because the profit could never repay the expense to any individual or small number of individuals, though it may frequently do much more than repay it to a great society. . . .

# Ignatius Sancho

## *from* LETTERS (1778)

*Ignatius Sancho (1729–1780) was born on a slave ship in the Middle Passage from Africa to the Americas. His mother died soon after he was born, and his father chose suicide over slavery. The two-year old Sancho was brought to England where he served as a domestic servant. As he grew older, he was encouraged by a patron to pursue reading and self-improvement. Overcoming numerous obstacles and disappointments, Sancho married, had six children, and opened up a small shop in London frequented by numerous prominent people. He began to carry on a correspondence with many of them, including the author Lawrence Sterne. Following Sancho's death, his friends published a collection of his letters, in part to pay tribute to his memory but also to protest the perception that blacks were inferior. In the letter chosen for this anthology, Sancho pleads with a young man to be more compassionate towards the indigenous peoples of India, reminding him that the English corrupted them. He writes as both an insider and outsider to English culture. He was the first Afro-Briton to receive an entry in the British* Dictionary of National Biography.

---

## TO MR. J[ACK] W[INGRAVE]

Your good father insists on my scribbling a sheet of absurdities, and gives me a notable reason for it, that is, 'Jack will be pleased with it.'—Now be it known to you—I have a respect both for father and son—yea for the whole family, who are every soul (that I have the honour or pleasure to know any thing of) tinctured—and leavened with all the obsolete goodness of old times—so that a man runs some hazard in being seen in the W[ingrav]e's society of being biassed to Christianity.—I never see your poor Father—but his eyes betray his feelings—for the hopeful youth in India—a tear of joy dancing upon the lids—is a plaudit not to be equalled this side death!—See the effects of right-doing, my worthy friend—continue in the tract of rectitude—and despise poor paltry Europeans—titled—Nabobs.—Read your Bible—as day follows night, God's blessing follows virtue—honour—and riches bring up the rear—and the end is peace.—Courage, my boy—I have done preaching.—Old folks love to seem wise—and if you are silly enough to correspond with grey hairs—take the consequence.—I have had the pleasure of reading most of your letters, through the kindness of your father.—Youth is naturally prone to vanity—such is the weakness of Human Nature, that pride has a fortress in the best of hearts—I know no person that possesses a better than Johnny W[ingrav]e—but although flattery is poison to youth, yet truth obliges me to confess that your correspondence betrays no symptom of vanity—but teems with truths of an honest affection—which merits praise—and commands esteem.

In some one of your letters which I do not recollect—you speak (with honest indignation) of the treachery and chicanery of the Natives*.—My good friend, you should remember from whom they learnt those vices:—the first christian visitors found them a simple, harmless people—but the cursed avidity for wealth urged these first visitors (and all the succeeding ones) to such acts of deception—and even wanton cruelty—that the poor ignorant Natives soon learnt to turn the knavish—and diabolical arts which they too soon imbibed—upon their teachers.

I am sorry to observe that the practice of your country (which as a resident I love—and for its freedom—and for the many blessings I enjoy in it—shall ever have my warmest wishes—prayers—and blessings); I say it is with reluctance, that I must observe your country's conduct has been uniformly wicked in the East—West-Indies—and even on the coast of Guinea.—The grand object of English navigators—indeed of all christian navigators—is money—money—money—for which I do not pretend to blame them—Commerce was meant by the goodness of the Deity to diffuse the various goods of the earth into every part—to unite mankind in the blessed chains of brotherly love—society—and mutual dependence:—the enlightened Christian should diffuse the riches of the Gospel of peace—with the commodities of his respective land—Commerce attended with strict honesty—and with Religion for its companion—would be a blessing to every shore it touched at.—In Africa, the poor wretched natives—blessed with the most fertile and luxuriant soil—are rendered so much the more miserable for what Providence meant as a blessing:—the Christians' abominable traffic for slaves—and the horrid cruelty and treachery of the petty Kings—encouraged by their Christian customers—who carry them strong liquors—to enflame their national madness—and powder—and bad fire-arms—to furnish them with the hellish means of killing and kidnapping.—But enough—it is a subject that sours my blood—and I am sure will not please the friendly bent of your social affections.—I mentioned these only to guard my friend against being too hasty in condemning the knavery of a people who bad as they may be—possibly—were made worse—by their Christian visitors.—Make human nature thy study—wherever thou resident—whatever the religion—or the complexion—study their hearts.—Simplicity, kindness, and charity be thy guide—with these even Savages will respect you—and God will bless you!

Your father—who sees every improvement of his boy with delight—observes that your hand-writing is much for the better—in truth, I think it as well as any

---

* Extracts of two letters from Mr. W[ingrav]e to his Father, dated Bombay, 1776 and 1777

1776. I have introduced myself to Mr. G—, who behaved very friendly in giving me some advice, which was very necessary, as the inhabitants, who are chiefly Blacks, are a set of canting, deceitful people, and of whom one must have great caution.

1777. I am now thoroughly convinced, that the account which Mr. G— gave me of the natives of this country is just and true, that they are a set of deceitful people, and have not such a word as Gratitude in their language, neither do they know what it is—and as to their dealings in trade, they are like unto Jews.

modest man can wish:—if my long epistles do not frighten you—and I live till the return of next spring—perhaps I shall be enabled to judge how much you are improved since your last favour:—write me a deal about the natives—the soil and produce—the domestic and interior manners of the people—customs—prejudices—fashions—and follies.—Alas! we have plenty of the two last here—and what is worse, we have politics—and a detestable Brother's war—where the right hand is hacking and hewing the left—whilst Angels weep at our madness—and Devils rejoice at the ruinous prospect.

Mr. R[ush] and the ladies are well.—Johnny R[ush] has favoured me with a long letter—he is now grown familiar with danger—and can bear the whistling of bullets—the cries and groans of the human species—the roll of drums—clangor of trumpets—shouts of combatants—and thunder of cannon—all these he can bear with solider-like fortitude—with now and then a secret wish for the society of his London friends—in the sweet blessed security—of peace—and friendship.

This, young man, is my second letter—I have wrote till I am stupid, I perceive—I ought to have found it out two pages back.—Mrs. Sancho joins me in good wishes—I join her in the same—in which double sense believe me,

Yours, &c. &c.

I. SANCHO

Very short Postscript

It is with sincere pleasure I hear you have a lucrative establishment—which will enable you to appear and act with decency—your good sense will naturally lead you to proper œconomy—as distant from frigid parsimony, as from a heedless extravagancy—but as you may possibly have some time to spare upon your hands for necessary recreation—give me leave to obtrude my poor advice.—I have heard it more than once observed of fortunate adventurers—they have come home enriched in purse—but wretchedly barren in intellects—the mind, my dear Jack, wants food—as well as the stomach—why then should not one wish to increase in knowledge as well as money?—Young says—"Books are fair Virtue's advocates, and friends"—now my advice is—to preserve about 20*l.* a year for two or three seasons—by which means you may gradually form a useful, elegant, little library—suppose now the first year you send the order—and the money to your father—for the following books—which I recommend from my own superficial knowledge as useful.—A man should know a little of Geography—History, nothing more useful, or pleasant.

Robertson's Charles the 5th, 4 vols.
Goldsmith's History of Greece, 2 vols.
Ditto, of Rome, 2 vols.
Ditto, of England, 4 vols.

Two small volumes of Sermons useful—and very sensible—by one Mr. Williams, a dissenting minister—which are as well as fifty—for I love not a multiplicity of doctrines—a few plain tenets—easy—simple—and directed to the heart—are better than volumes of controversial nonsense.—Spectators—Guardians—and Tatlers—you have of course.—Young's Night-Thoughts—Milton—and Thomson's Seasons were my summer companions—for near twenty years—they mended my heart—they improved my veneration to the Deity—and increased my love to my neighbours.

You have to thank God for strong natural parts—a feeling humane heart—you write with sense and judicious discernment—improve yourself, my dear Jack, that if it should please God to return you to your friends with the fortune of a man in upper rank, the embellishments of your mind may be ever considered as greatly superior to your riches—and only inferior to the goodness of your heart. I give you the above as a sketch—your father and other of your friends will improve upon it in the course of time—I do indeed judge that the above is enough at first—in conformity with the old adage—"A few Books and a few Friends, and those well chosen."

Adieu, Yours,

I. SANCHO

# Immanuel Kant

# WHAT IS ENLIGHTENMENT? (1784)

*The German philosopher Immanuel Kant (1724–1804) was arguably the most important philosopher of the eighteenth century, enormously influential on the history of aesthetics, ethics, and epistemology (the theory of knowledge). In "What Is Enlightenment?" he attempts to define the principal characteristics of his age. Kant's reflections are reminiscent of Pope's contrast between darkness and light quoted at the beginning of the introduction to this section. He suggests that motto of the period is "Have courage to use your own reason!" It is an age distinguished from previous historical epochs by its refusal to accept traditional authority at face value. Though Kant believes that open discussions are necessary to advance enlightenment, he is worried that they could possibly undermine state authority and, as a result, social stability. Such concerns are voiced in his second motto: "Argue as much as you will, and about what you will, only obey!" It is well worth considering whether these two mottos represent compatible aims.*

Enlightenment is man's release from his self-incurred tutelage. Tutelage is man's inability to make use of his understanding without direction from another. Self-incurred is this tutelage when its cause lies not in lack of reason but in lack of resolution and courage to use it without direction from another. *Sapere aude!* "Have courage to use your own reason!"—that is the motto of enlightenment.

Laziness and cowardice are the reasons why so great a portion of mankind, after nature has long since discharged them from external direction *(naturaliter maiorennes)*, nevertheless remains under lifelong tutelage, and why it is so easy for others to set themselves up as their guardians. It is so easy not to be of age. If I have a book which understands for me, a pastor who has a conscience for me, a physician who decides my diet, and so forth, I need not trouble myself. I need not think, if I can only pay—others will readily undertake the irksome work for me.

That the step to competence is held to be very dangerous by the far greater portion of mankind (and by the entire fair sex)—quite apart from its being arduous—is seen to by those guardians who have so kindly assumed superintendence over them. After the guardians have first made their domestic cattle dumb and have made sure that these placid creatures will not dare take a single step without the harness of the cart to which they are tethered, the guardians then show them the danger which threatens if they try to go alone. Actually, however, this danger is not so great, for by falling a few times they would finally learn to walk alone. But an example of this failure makes them timid and ordinarily frightens them away from all further trials.

For any single individual to work himself out of the life under tutelage which has become almost his nature is very difficult. He has come to be fond of this state, and he is for the present really incapable of making use of his reason, for no one has ever let him try it out. Statutes and formulas, those mechanical tools of the rational employment or rather misemployment of his natural gifts, are the fetters of an everlasting tutelage. Whoever throws them off makes only an uncertain leap over the narrowest ditch because he is not accustomed to that kind of free motion. Therefore, there are few who have succeeded by their own exercises of mind both in freeing themselves from incompetence and in achieving a steady pace.

But that the public should enlighten itself is more possible; indeed, if only freedom is granted, enlightenment is almost sure to follow. For there will always be some independent thinkers, even among the established guardians of the great masses, who, after throwing off the yoke of tutelage from their own shoulders, will disseminate the spirit of the rational appreciation of both their own worth and every man's vocation for thinking for himself. But be it noted that the public, which has first been brought under this yoke by their guardians, forces the guardians themselves to remain bound when it is incited to do so by some of the guardians who are themselves capable of some enlightenment—so harmful is it to implant prejudices, for they later take vengeance on their cultivators or on their descendants. Thus the public can only slowly attain enlightenment. Perhaps a fall of personal despotism or of avaricious or tyrannical oppression may be accomplished by revolution, but never a true reform in ways of thinking. Rather, new prejudices will serve as well as old ones to harness the great unthinking masses.

For this enlightenment, however, nothing is required but freedom, and indeed the most harmless among all the things to which this term can properly be applied. It is the freedom to make public use of one's reason at every point. But I hear on all sides, "Do not argue!" The officer says: "Do not argue but drill!" The tax collector: "Do not argue but pay!" The cleric: "Do not argue but believe!" Only one prince in the world says, "Argue as much as you will, and about what you will, but obey!" Everywhere there is restriction on freedom.

Which restriction is an obstacle to enlightenment, and which is not an obstacle but a promoter of it? I answer: The public use of one's reason must always be free, and it alone can bring about enlightenment among men. The private use of reason, on the other hand, may often be very narrowly restricted without particularly hindering the progress of enlightenment. By the public use of one's reason I understand the use which a person makes of it as a scholar before the reading public. Private use I call that which one may make of it in a particular civil post or office which is entrusted to him. Many affairs which are conducted in the interest of the community require a certain mechanism through which some members of the community must passively conduct themselves with an artificial unanimity, so that the government may direct them to public ends, or at least prevent them from destroying those ends. Here argument is certainly not allowed—one must obey. But so far as a part of the mechanism regards himself at the same time as a member of the whole community or of a society of world citizens, and thus in the role of a scholar who addresses the public (in the proper sense of the word) through his writings, he certainly can argue without hurting the affairs for which he is in part responsible as a passive member. Thus it would be ruinous for an officer in service to debate about the suitability or utility of a command given to him by his superior; he must obey. But the right to make remarks on errors in the military service and to lay them before the public for judgment cannot equitably be refused him as a scholar. The citizen cannot refuse to pay the taxes imposed on him; indeed, and impudent complaint at those levied on him can be punished as a scandal (as it could occasion general refractoriness). But the same person nevertheless does not act contrary to his duty as a citizen when, as a scholar, he publicly expresses his thoughts on the inappropriateness or even the injustice of these levies. Similarly a clergyman is obligated to make his sermon to his pupils in catechism and his congregation conform to the symbol of the church which he serves, for he has been accepted on this condition. But as a scholar he has complete freedom, even the calling, to communicate to the public all his carefully tested and well-meaning thoughts on that which is erroneous in the symbol and to make suggestions for the better organization of the religious body and church. In doing this there is nothing that could be laid as a burden on his conscience. For what he teaches as a consequence of his office as a representative of the church, this he considers something about which he has no freedom to teach according to his own lights; it is something which he is appointed to propound at the dictation of and in the name of another. He will say, "Our church teaches this or that; those are the proofs which it adduces." He thus extracts all practical uses for his congregation from statutes to which he himself would not subscribe with full conviction but to the enunciation of which he can very well pledge himself because it is not impossible that truth lies hidden in them, and, in any case, there is at least nothing in them contradictory to inner religion. For if he believed he had found such in them, he could not conscientiously discharge the duties of his office; he would have to give it up. The use, therefore, which an appointed teacher makes of his reason before his congregation is merely private, because this congregation is only a domestic one (even if it be a large gathering); with respect to it, as a priest, he is not free, nor can he be free, because he carries out the orders of another. But as a scholar, whose writings speak to his public, the world, the clergyman in the public use of his reason enjoys an unlimited freedom to use his own reason and to speak in his own person. That the guardians of the people (in spiritual things) should themselves be incompetent is an absurdity which amounts to the eternalization of absurdities.

But would not a society of clergymen, perhaps a church conference or venerable classis (as they call themselves among the Dutch), be justified in obligating itself by oath to a certain unchangeable symbol in order to enjoy an unceasing guardianship over each of its members and thereby over the people as a whole, and even to make it eternal? I answer that this is altogether impossible. Such a contract, made to shut off all further enlightenment from the human race, is absolutely null and void even if confirmed by the supreme power, by parliaments, and by the most ceremonious of peace treaties. An age cannot bind itself and ordain to put the succeeding one into such a condition that it cannot extend its (at best very occasional) knowledge, purify itself of errors, and progress in general enlightenment. That would be a crime against human nature, the proper destination of which lies precisely in this progress; and the descendants would be fully justified in rejecting those decrees as having been made in an unwarranted and malicious manner.

The touchstone of everything that can be concluded as a law for a people lies in the question whether the people could have imposed such a law on itself. Now such a religious compact might be possible for a short and definitely limited time, as it were, in expectation of a better. One might let every citizen, and especially the clergyman, in the role of scholar, make his comments freely and publicly, i.e., through writing, on the erroneous aspects of the present institution. The newly introduced order might last until insight into the nature of these things had become so general and widely approved that through uniting their voices (even if not unanimously) they could bring a proposal to the throne to take those congregations under protection which had united into a changed religious organization according to their better ideas, without, however, hindering others who wish to remain in the order. But to unite in permanent religious institution which is not to be subject to doubt before the public even in the lifetime of one man, and thereby to make a period of time fruitless in the progress of mankind toward improvement, thus working to the disadvantage of posterity—that is absolutely forbidden. For himself (and only for a short time) a man may postpone enlightenment in what he ought to know, but to renounce it for himself and even more to renounce it for posterity is to injure and trample on the rights of mankind.

And what a people may not decree for itself can even less be decreed for them by a monarch, for his lawgiving authority rests on his uniting the general public will in his own. If he only sees to it that all true or alleged improvements stand together with civil order, he can leave it to his subjects to do what they find necessary for their spiritual welfare. This is not his concern, though it is incumbent on him to prevent one of them from violently hindering another in determining and promoting this welfare to the best of his ability. To meddle in these matters lowers his own majesty, since by the writings in which his subjects seek to present their views he may evaluate his own governance. He can do this when, with deepest understanding, he lays upon himself the reproach, *Caesar non est supra grammaticos.* Far more does he injure his own majesty when he degrades his supreme power by supporting the ecclesiastical despotism of some tyrants in his state over his other subjects.

If we are asked, "Do we now live in an *enlightened age?*" the answer is, "No," but we do live in an *age of enlightenment*. As things now stand, much is lacking which prevents men from being, or easily becoming, capable of correctly using their own reason in religious matters with assurance and free from outside direction. But, on the other hand, we have clear indications that the field has not been opened wherein men may freely deal with these things and that the obstacles to general enlightenment or the release from self-imposed tutelage are gradually being reduced. In this respect, this is the age of enlightenment, or the century of Frederick.

A prince who does not find it unworthy of himself to say that he holds it to be his duty to prescribe nothing to men in religious matters but to give them complete freedom while renouncing the haughty name of *tolerance,* is himself enlightened and deserves to be esteemed by the grateful world and posterity as the first, at least from the side of government, who divested the human race of its tutelage and left each man free to make use of his reason in matters of conscience. Under him venerable ecclesiastics are allowed, in the role of scholars, and without infringing on their official duties, freely to submit for public testing their judgments and views which here and there diverge from the established symbol. And an even greater freedom is enjoyed by those who are restricted by no official duties. This spirit of freedom spreads beyond this land, even to those in which it must struggle with external obstacles erected by a government which misunderstands its own interest. For an example gives evidence to such a government that in freedom there is not the least cause for concern about public peace and the stability of the community. Men work themselves gradually out of barbarity if only intentional artifices are not made to hold them in it.

I have placed the main point of enlightenment—the escape of men from their self-incurred tutelage—chiefly in matters of religion because our rulers have no interest in playing the guardian with respect to the arts and sciences and also because religious incompetence is not only the most harmful but also the most degrading of all. But the manner of thinking of the head of a state who favors religious enlightenment goes further, and he sees that there is no danger to his lawgiving in allowing his subjects to make public use of their reason and to publish their thoughts on a better formulation of his legislation and even their open-minded criticisms of the laws already made. Of this we have a shining example wherein no monarch is superior to him whom we honor.

But only one who is himself enlightened, is not afraid of shadows, and has a numerous and well-disciplined army to assure public peace, can say: "Argue as much as you will, and about what you will, only obey!" A republic could not dare say such a thing. Here is shown a strange and unexpected trend in human affairs in which almost everything, looked at in the large, is paradoxical. A greater degree of civil freedom appears advantageous to the freedom of mind of the people, and yet it places inescapable limitations upon it; a lower degree of civil freedom, on the contrary, provides the mind with room for each man to extend himself to his full capacity. As nature has uncovered from under this hard shell the seed for which she most tenderly cares—the propensity and vocation to free thinking—this gradually works back upon the character of the people, who thereby gradually become capable of managing freedom; finally, it affects the principles of government, which finds it to its advantage to treat men, who are now more than machines, in accordance with their dignity.

—*trans. Lewis White Beck*

# Emmanuel Sieyès

## *from* WHAT IS THE THIRD ESTATE? (1789)

*In 1788 France was bankrupt, a result of nearly a century of wars with its chief rival Britain, and could not continue in its existing form. Backed to the wall, the monarchy called the Estates-General, a representative assembly of the three French estates—the clergy, the nobility, and everyone else (comprising the bourgeoisie and the peasantry). The leaders of the three estates disagreed about how the assembly should be structured. The representatives of the first two estates—the clergy and the nobility—argued that each estate should vote separately and receive one vote. This was of great benefit to them, since the leaders of the clergy were largely from the nobility, and thus they could always veto the will of the Third Estate. The leaders of the Third Estate, which had the same number of representatives as the other two combined, wanted the assembly to meet as a single body which voted by 'head' rather than by 'order'.*

*It is at this point that Emmanuel (Abbé) Sieyès (1748–1836), a clergyman and political theorist, entered the debate. In "What Is the Third Estate?" Sieyès argues that the Third Estate's demands are too timid. Insofar as it represents more than ninety percent of the French people, it comprises the nation: not only because it is the vast majority of the population, but also because it is responsible for the material and intellectual output of France. He advocates that the Third Estate constitute itself as a national assembly. While it would be an exaggeration to say that Sieyès was responsible for starting the French Revolution, his political vision was realized in June 1789. When Louis XVI attempted to bar the Estates-General from meeting, the representatives of the Third Estate gathered together at the tennis courts of Versailles, declared themselves a national assembly, and pledged to meet as a body until France had a written constitution. The French Revolution had begun.*

---

The plan of this pamphlet is very simple. We have three questions to ask:

1st.   What is the third estate? Everything.
2nd.   What has it been heretofore in the political order? Nothing.
3rd.   What does it demand? To become something therein. We shall see if the answers are correct. Then we shall examine the measures that have been tried and those which must be taken in order that the third estate may in fact become *something*. Thus we shall state:

4th. What the ministers have *attempted,* and what the privileged classes themselves *propose* in its favor.

5th. What *ought* to have been done.

6th. Finally, what *remains* to be done in order that the third estate may take its rightful place.

## CHAPTER I

### *The Third Estate Is a Complete Nation*

What are the essentials of national existence and prosperity? *Private* enterprise and *public* functions.

Private enterprise may be divided into four classes: 1st. Since earth and water furnish the raw material for man's needs, the first class will comprise all families engaged in agricultural pursuits. 2nd. Between the original sale of materials and their consumption or use, further workmanship, more or less manifold, adds to these materials a second value, more or less compounded. Human industry thus succeeds in perfecting the benefits of nature and in increasing the gross produce twofold, ten-fold, one hundredfold in value. Such is the work of the second class. 3rd. Between production and consumption, as well as among the different degrees of production, a group of intermediate agents, useful to producers as well as to consumers, comes into being; these are the dealers and merchants. . . . 4th. In addition to these three classes of industrious and useful citizens concerned with goods for consumption and use, a society needs many private undertakings and endeavors which are *directly* useful or agreeable to the *individual.* This fourth class includes from the most distinguished scientific and liberal professions to the least esteemed domestic services. Such are the labors which sustain society. Who performs them? The third estate.

Public functions likewise under present circumstances may be classified under four well known headings: the Sword, the Robe, the Church, and the Administration. It is unnecessary to discuss them in detail in order to demonstrate that the third estate everywhere constitutes nineteen-twentieths of them, except that it is burdened with all that is really arduous, with all the tasks that the privileged order refuses to perform. Only the lucrative and honorary positions are held by members of the privileged order . . . nevertheless they have dared lay the order of the third estate under an interdict. They have said to it: "Whatever be your services, whatever your talents, you shall go thus far and no farther. It is not fitting that you be honored."

It suffices here to have revealed that the alleged utility of a privileged order to public service is only a chimera; that without it, all that is arduous in such service is performed by the third estate; that without it, the higher positions would be infinitely better filled; that they naturally ought to be the lot of and reward for talents and recognized services; and that if the privileged classes have succeeded in usurping all the lucrative and honorary positions, it is both an odious injustice to the majority of citizens and a treason to the commonwealth.

Who, then, would dare to say that the third estate has not within itself all that is necessary to constitute a complete nation? It is the strong and robust man whose one arm remains enchained. If the privileged order were abolished, the nation would be not something less but something more. Thus, what is the third estate? Everything; but an everything shackled and oppressed. What would it be without the privileged order? Everything; but an everything free and flourishing. Nothing can progress without it; everything would proceed infinitely better without the others. It is not sufficient to have demonstrated that the privileged classes, far from being useful to the nation, can only enfeeble and injure it; it is necessary, moreover, to prove that the nobility does not belong to the social organization at all; that, indeed, it may be a *burden* upon the nation, but that it would not know how to constitute a part thereof. . . .

What is a nation? a body of associates living under a *common* law and represented by the same *legislature*.

Is it not exceedingly clear that the noble order has privileges, exemptions, even rights separate from the rights of the majority of citizens? Thus it deviates from the common order, from the common law. Thus its civil rights already render it a people apart in a great nation. It is indeed *imperium in imperio.*

Also, it enjoys its political rights separately. It has its own representatives, who are by no means charged with representing the people. Its deputation sits apart; and when it is assembled in the same room with the deputies of ordinary citizens, it is equally true that its representation is essentially distinct and separate; it is foreign to the nation in principle, since its mandate does not emanate from the people, and in aim, since its purpose is to defend not the general but a special interest.

The third estate, then, comprises everything appertaining to the nation; and whatever is not the third estate may not be regarded as being of the nation. What is the third estate? Everything!

## CHAPTER III

### *What Does the Third Estate Demand? To Become Something*

. . . The true petitions of this order may be appreciated only through the authentic claims directed to the government by the large municipalities of the kingdom. What is indicated therein? That the people wishes to be *something,* and, in truth, the very least that is possible. It wishes to have real representatives in the Estates General, that is to say, deputies *drawn from its order,* who are competent to be interpreters of its will and defenders of its interests. But what will it avail it to be present at the Estates General if the predominating interest there is contrary to its own! Its presence would only consecrate the oppression of which it would be the eternal victim. Thus, it is indeed certain that it cannot come to vote at the Estates General unless it is to have in that body *an influence at least equal to that of the privileged classes;* and it demands a number of representatives equal to that of the first two orders together. Finally, this equality of representation would become completely illusory if every chamber voted separately. The third estate demands, then, that votes be taken *by head and not by order.* This is the essence of those claims so alarming to the privileged classes, because they believed that thereby the reform of abuses would become inevitable. The real intention of the third estate is to have an influence in the Estates General equal to that of the privileged classes. I repeat, can it ask less? And is it not clear that if its influence therein is less than equality, it cannot be expected to emerge from its political nullity and become *something*?

But what is indeed unfortunate is that the three articles constituting the demand of the third estate are insufficient to give it this equality of influence which it cannot, in reality, do without. In vain will it obtain an equal number of representatives drawn from its order; the influence of the privileged classes will establish itself and dominate even in the sanctuary of the third estate. . . .

## Chapter VI

*What Remains to Be Done. Development of Some Principles*

. . . The third estate must perceive in the trend of opinions and circumstances that it can hope for nothing except from its own enlightenment and courage. Reason and justice are in its favor; . . . there is no longer time to work for the conciliation of parties. What accord can be anticipated between the energy of the oppressed and the rage of the oppressors?

They have dared pronounce the word secession. They have menaced the King and the people. Well! Good God! How fortunate for the nation if this so desirable secession might be made permanently! How easy it would be to dispense with the privileged classes! How difficult to induce them to be citizens! . . .

In vain would they close their eyes to the revolution which time and force of circumstances have effected; it is none the less real. Formerly the third estate was serf, the noble order everything. Today the third estate is everything, the nobility but a word. . . .

In such a state of affairs, what must the third estate do if it wishes to gain possession of its political rights in a manner beneficial to the nation? There are two ways of attaining this objective. In following the first, the third estate must assemble apart: it will not meet with the nobility and the clergy at all; it will not remain with them, either by *order* or by *head*. I pray that they will keep in mind the enormous difference between the assembly of the third estate and that of the other two orders. The first represents 25,000,000 men, and deliberates concerning the interests of the nation. The two others, were they to unite, have the powers of only about 200,000 individuals and think only of their privileges. The third estate alone, they say, cannot constitute the *Estates General*. Well! So much the better! It will form a *National Assembly*. . . .

—*trans. John Hall Stewart*

# THE DECLARATION OF THE RIGHTS OF MAN AND OF THE CITIZEN (1789)

*Olympe de Gouges*

# THE DECLARATION OF THE RIGHTS OF WOMAN (1791)

The Declaration of the Rights of Man and of the Citizen *is the classic statement of the French Revolution's principles—liberty, equality, and fraternity. Passed by the National Assembly, it was modeled on the English and American Bill of Rights as well as statements of rights in American state constitutions. A critical response to the text is* The Declaration of the Rights of Woman. *Its author Olympe de Gouges (1748–1793) argued that the transformation of the Revolution had left the unequal position of women untouched. Influenced by Rousseau's political thought, yet rejecting Rousseau's belief that the sexes were unequal, she argued that men and women were equal in the state of nature and accordingly should be so in the French Republic. Significantly, de Gouges addressed her demands for women's rights to Marie Antoinette, the Queen of France, rather than King Louis XVI or the National Assembly.*

## THE DECLARATION OF THE RIGHTS OF MAN AND OF THE CITIZEN

The representatives of the French people, organized as a National Assembly, believing that the ignorance, neglect, or contempt of the rights of man are the sole cause of public calamities and of the corruption of governments, have determined to set forth in a solemn declaration the natural, inalienable, and sacred rights of man, in order that this declaration, being constantly before all the members of the social body, shall remind them continually of their rights and duties; in order that the acts of the legislative power, as well as those of the executive power, may be compared at any moment with the objects and purposes of all political institutions and may thus be more respected; and, lastly, in order that the grievances of the citizens, based hereafter upon simple and incontestable principles, shall tend to the maintenance of the constitution and redound to the happiness of all. Therefore the National Assembly recognizes and proclaims, in the presence and under the auspices of the Supreme Being, the following rights of man and of the citizen:

1. Men are born and remain free and equal in rights. Social distinctions may be founded only upon the general good.

2. The aim of all political association is the preservation of the natural and imprescriptible rights of man. These rights are liberty, property, security, and resistance to oppression.

3. The principle of all sovereignty resides essentially in the nation. No body nor individual may exercise any authority which does not proceed directly from the nation.

4. Liberty consists in the freedom to do everything which injures no one else; hence the exercise of the natural rights of each man has no limits except those which assure to the other members of the society the enjoyment of the same rights. These limits can only be determined by law.

5. Law can only prohibit such actions as are hurtful to society. Nothing may be prevented which is not forbidden by law, and no one may be forced to do anything not provided for by law.

6. Law is the expression of the general will. Every citizen has a right to participate personally, or through his representative, in its formation. It must be the same for all, whether it protects or punishes. All citizens, being equal in the eyes of the law, are equally eligible to all dignities and to all public positions and occupations, according to their abilities, and without distinction except that of their virtues and talents.

7. No person shall be accused, arrested, or imprisoned except in the cases and according to the forms prescribed by law. Any one soliciting, transmitting, executing, or causing to be executed, any arbitrary order, shall be punished. But any citizen summoned or arrested in virtue of the law shall submit without delay, as resistance constitutes an offense.

8. The law shall provide for such punishments only as are strictly and obviously necessary, and no one shall suffer punishment except it be legally inflicted in virtue of a law passed and promulgated before the commission of the offense.

9. As all persons are held innocent until they shall have been declared guilty, if arrest shall be deemed indispensable, all harshness not essential to the securing of the prisoner's person shall be severely repressed by law.

10. No one shall be disquieted on account of his opinions, including his religious views, provided their manifestation does not disturb the public order established by law.

11. The free communication of ideas and opinions is one of the most precious of the rights of man. Every citizen may, accordingly, speak, write, and print with freedom, but shall be responsible for such abuses of this freedom as shall be defined by law.

12. The security of the rights of man and of the citizen requires public military forces. These forces are, therefore, established for the good of all and not for the personal advantage of those to whom they shall be intrusted.

13. A common contribution is essential for the maintenance of the public forces and for the cost of administration. This should be equitably distributed among all the citizens in proportion to their means.

14. All the citizens have a right to decide, either personally or by their representatives, as to the necessity of the public contribution; to grant this freely; to know to what uses it is put; and to fix the proportion, the mode of assessment and of collection and the duration of the taxes.

15. Society has the right to require of every public agent an account of his administration.

16. A society in which the observance of the law is not assured, nor the separation of powers defined, has no constitution at all.

17. Since property is an inviolable and sacred right, no one shall be deprived thereof except where public necessity, legally determined, shall clearly demand it, and then only on condition that the owner shall have been previously and equitably indemnified.

## DECLARATION OF THE RIGHTS OF WOMAN AND THE FEMALE CITIZEN

Man, are you capable of being just? It is a woman who poses the question; you will not deprive her of that right at least. Tell me, what gives you sovereign empire to oppress my sex? Your strength? Your talents? Observe the Creator in his wisdom; survey in all her grandeur that nature with whom you seem to want to be in harmony, and give me, if you dare, an example of this tyrannical empire. Go back to animals, consult the elements, study plants, finally glance at all the modifications of organic matter, and surrender to the evidence when I offer you the means; search, probe, and distinguish, if you can, the sexes in the administration of nature. Everywhere you will find them mingled; everywhere they cooperate in harmonious togetherness in this immortal masterpiece.

Man alone has raised his exceptional circumstances to a principle. Bizarre, blind, bloated with science and degenerated—in a century of enlightenment and wisdom—into the crassest ignorance, he wants to command as a despot a sex which is in full possession of its intellectual faculties; he pretends to enjoy the Revolution and to claim his rights to equality in order to say nothing more about it.

For the National Assembly to decree in its last sessions, or in those of the next legislature:

### Preamble

Mothers, daughters, sisters [and] representatives of the nation demand to be constituted into a national assembly. Believing that ignorance, omission, or scorn for the rights of woman are the only causes of public misfortunes and of the corruption of governments, [the women] have resolved to set forth in a solemn declaration the natural, inalienable, and sacred rights of woman in order that this declaration, constantly exposed before all the members of the society; will ceaselessly remind them of their rights and duties; in order that the authoritative acts of women and the authoritative acts of men may be at any moment compared with and respectful of the purpose of all political institutions; and in order that citizens' demands, henceforth based on simple and incontestable principles, will always support the constitution, good morals, and the happiness of all.

Consequently, the sex that is as superior in beauty as it is in courage during the sufferings of maternity recognizes and declares in the presence and under the auspices of the Supreme Being, the following Rights of Woman and of Female Citizens.

### Article I

Woman is born free and lives equal to man in her rights. Social distinctions can be based only on the common utility.

## Article II

The purpose of any political association is the conservation of the natural and impre-scriptible rights of woman and man; these rights are liberty, property, security, and especially resistance to oppression.

## Article III

The principle of all sovereignty rests essentially with the nation, which is nothing but the union of woman and man; no body and no individual can exercise any authority which does not come expressly from it [the nation].

## Article IV

Liberty and justice consist of restoring all that belongs to others; thus, the only limits on the exercise of the natural rights of woman are perpetual male tyranny; these lim-its are to be reformed by the laws of nature and reason.

## Article V

Laws of nature and reason proscribe all acts harmful to society; everything which is not prohibited by these wise and divine laws cannot be prevented, and no one can be constrained to do what they do not command.

## Article VI

The law must be the expression of the general will; all female and male citizens must contribute either personally or through their representatives to its formation; it must be the same for all: male and female citizens, being equal in the eyes of the law, must be equally admitted to all honors, positions, and public employment according to their capacity and without other distinctions besides those of their virtues and talents.

## Article VII

No woman is an exception; she is accused, arrested, and detained in cases determined by law. Women, like men, obey this rigorous law.

## Article VIII

The law must establish only those penalties that are strictly and obviously necessary, and no one can be punished except by virtue of a law established and promulgated prior to the crime and legally applicable to women.

## Article IX

Once any woman is declared guilty, complete rigor is [to be] exercised by the law.

## Article X

No one is to be disquieted for his very basic opinions; woman has the right to mount the scaffold; she must equally have the right to mount the rostrum, provided that her demonstrations do not disturb the legally established public order.

## Article XI

The free communication of thoughts and opinions is one of the most precious rights of woman, since that liberty assures the recognition of children by their fathers. Any female citizen thus may say freely, I am the mother of a child which belongs to you, without being forced by a barbarous prejudice to hide the truth; [an exception may be made] to respond to the abuse of this liberty in cases determined by the law.

## Article XII

The guarantee of the rights of woman and the female citizen implies a major benefit; this guarantee must be instituted for the advantage of all, and not for the particular benefit of those to whom it is entrusted.

## Article XIII

For the support of the public force and the expenses of administration, the contributions of woman and man are equal; she shares all the duties [*corvées*] and all the painful tasks; therefore, she must have the same share in the distribution of positions, employment, offices, honors and jobs [*industrie*].

## Article XIV

Female and male citizens have the right to verify, either by themselves or through their representatives, the necessity of the public contribution. This can only apply to women if they are granted an equal share, not only of wealth, but also of public administration, and in the determination of the proportion, the base, the collection, and the duration of the tax.

## Article XV

The collectivity of women, joined for tax purposes to the aggregate of men, has the right to demand an accounting of his administration from any public agent.

## Article XVI

No society has a constitution without the guarantee of rights and the separation of powers; the constitution is null if the majority of individuals comprising the nation have not cooperated in drafting it.

## Article XVII

Property belongs to both sexes whether united or separate; for each it is an inviolable and sacred right; no one can be deprived of it, since it is the true patrimony of nature, unless the legally determined public need obviously dictates it, and then only with a just and prior indemnity.

## Postscript

Woman, wake up; the tocsin of reason is being heard throughout the whole universe; discover your rights. The powerful empire of nature is no longer surrounded by prejudice, fanaticism, superstition, and lies. The flame of truth has dispersed all the clouds of folly and usurpation. Enslaved man has multiplied his strength and needs recourse to yours to break his chains. Having become free, he has become unjust to his companion. Oh, women! When will you cease to be blind? What advantage have you received from the Revolution? A more pronounced scorn, a more marked disdain. In the centuries of corruption you ruled only over the weakness of men. The reclamation of your patrimony, based on the wise decrees of nature—what have you to dread from such a fine undertaking?

—*trans. Darline Gay Levy, Harriet Branson Applewhite, and Mary Durham Johnson*

# Edmund Burke

## *from* REFLECTIONS ON THE FRENCH REVOLUTION (1790)

*In England, the French Revolution gave rise to a major political debate between those who supported it and those who were its critics, a debate which had implication for English politics as well. For the Irish-born politician Edmund Burke (1729–1797) the Revolution was a colossal blunder. In one of the classic statements of conservative political theory,* Reflections on the French Revolution, *Burke rejects the idea that a political system could be recast on the basis of Enlightenment rationality. He argues that a nation is like a body. It develops over time, is continually changing and evolving, and could reform itself only in terms of its own historical traditions. He does not deny that France faces a crisis, but he believes that a revolution is a breach of faith with all those who have lived before it and all those who were yet to be born. Implicit in Burke's argument is a defense of the English constitution, which is not a written document but an accumulation of centuries of legal tradition.*

---

. . . You will observe, that from Magna Charta to the Declaration of Right, it has been the uniform policy of our constitution to claim and assert our liberties, as an *entailed inheritance* derived to us from our forefathers, and to be transmitted to our posterity; as an estate specially belonging to the people of this kingdom, without any reference whatever to any other more general or prior right. By this means our constitution preserves a unity in so great a diversity of its parts. We have an inheritable crown; an inheritable peerage; and a House of Commons and a people inheriting privileges, franchises, and liberties, from a long line of ancestors.

This policy appears to me to be the result of profound reflection; or rather the happy effect of following nature, which is wisdom without reflection, and above it. A spirit of innovation is generally the result of a selfish temper, and confined views. People will not look forward to posterity, who never look backward to their ancestors. Besides, the people of England well know, that the idea of inheritance furnishes a sure principle of conservation, and a sure principle of transmission; without at all excluding a principle of improvement. It leaves acquisition free; but it secures what it acquires. Whatever advantages are obtained by a state proceeding on these maxims, are locked fast as in a sort of family settlement; grasped as in a kind of mortmain for ever. By a constitutional policy, working after the pattern of nature, we receive, we hold, we transmit our government and our privileges, in the same manner in which we enjoy and transmit our property and our lives. The institutions of policy, the goods of fortune, the gifts of providence, are handed down to us, and from us, in the same course and order. Our political system is placed in a just correspondence and symmetry with the order of the world, and with the mode of existence decreed to a permanent body composed of transitory parts; wherein, by the disposition of a stupendous wisdom, moulding together the great mysterious incorporation of the human race, the whole, at one time, is never old, or middle-aged, or young, but, in a condition of unchangeable constancy, moves on through the varied tenor of perpetual decay, fall, renovation, and progression. Thus, by preserving the method of nature in the conduct of the state, in what we improve, we are never wholly new; in what we retain, we are never wholly obsolete. By adhering in this manner and on those principles to our forefathers, we are guided not by the superstition of antiquarians, but by the spirit of philosophic analogy. In this choice of inheritance we have given to our frame of polity the image of a relation in blood; binding up the constitution of our country with our dearest domestic ties; adopting our fundamental laws into the bosom of our family affections; keeping inseparable, and cherishing with the warmth of all their combined and mutually reflected charities, our state, our hearths, our sepulchres, and our altars. . . .

You might, if you pleased, have profited of our example, and have given to your recovered freedom a correspondent dignity. Your privileges, though discontinued, were not lost to memory. Your constitution, it is true, whilst you were out of possession, suffered waste and dilapidation; but you possessed in some parts the walls, and, in all, the foundations, of a noble and venerable castle. You might have repaired those walls; you might have built on those old foundations. Your constitution was suspended before it was perfected; but you had the elements of a constitution very nearly as good as could be wished. In your old states you possessed that variety of parts corresponding with the various descriptions of which your community was happily composed; you had all that combination, and all that opposition of interests, you had that action and counteraction, which, in the natural and in the political world, from the reciprocal struggle of discordant power, draws out the harmony of the universe. These opposed and conflicting interests, which you considered as so great a blemish in your old and in our present constitution, interpose a salutary check to all precipitate resolutions. They render deliberation a matter not of choice, but of necessity; they make all change a subject of *compromise,* which naturally begets moderation; they produce *temperaments* preventing the sore evil of harsh, crude, unqualified reformations; and rendering all the headlong exertions of arbitrary power, in the few or in the many for ever impracticable. Through that diversity of members and interests, general liberty had as many securities as there were separate views in the several orders; whilst by pressing down the whole by the weight of a real monarchy, the separate parts would have been prevented from warping, and starting from their allotted places.

You had all these advantages in your ancient states; but you chose to act as if you had never been moulded into civil society; and had everything to begin anew. You began ill, because you began by despising everything that belonged to you. You set up your trade without a capital. If the last generations of your country appeared without much lustre in your eyes, you might have passed them by, and derived your claims from a more early race of ancestors. Under a pious predilection for those ancestors, your imaginations would have realized in them a standard of virtue and wisdom, beyond the vulgar practice of the hour: and you would have risen with the example to whose imitation you aspired. Respecting your forefathers, you would have been taught to respect yourselves. You would not have chosen to consider the French as a people of yesterday, as a nation of low-born servile wretches until the emancipating year of 1789. . . .

Compute your gains: see what is got by those extravagant and presumptuous speculations which have taught your leaders to despise all their predecessors, and all their contemporaries, and even to despise themselves, until the moment in which they became truly despicable. By following those false lights, France has bought undisguised calamities at a higher price than any nation has purchased the most unequivocal blessings! France has bought poverty by crime! France has not sacrificed her virtue to her interest, but she has abandoned her interest, that she might prostitute her virtue. All other nations have begun the fabric of a new government, or the reformation of an old, by establishing originally, or by enforcing with greater exactness, some rites or other of religion. All other people have laid the foundations of civil freedom in severer manners, and a system of a more austere and masculine morality. France, when she let loose the reins of regal authority, doubled the license of a ferocious dissoluteness in manners, and of an insolent irreligion in opinions and practices; and has extended through all ranks of life, as if she were communicating some privilege, or laying open some secluded benefit, all the unhappy corruptions that usually were the disease of wealth and power. This is one of the new principles of equality in France. . . .

It is said, that twenty-four millions ought to prevail over two hundred thousand. True; if the constitution of a kingdom be a problem of arithmetic. This sort of discourse does well enough with the lamp-post for its second: to men who *may* reason calmly, it is ridiculous. The will of the many, and their interest, must very often differ; and great will be the difference when they make an evil choice. A government of five hundred country attornies and obscure curates is not good for twenty- four millions of men, though it were chosen by eight and forty million; nor is it the better for being guided by a dozen of persons of quality, who have betrayed their trust in order to obtain that power. At present, you seem in everything to have strayed out of the high road of nature. The property of France does not govern it. Of course property is destroyed, and rational liberty has no existence. All you have got for the present is a paper circulation, and a stock-jobbing constitution: and, as to the future, do you seriously think that the territory of France, upon the republican system of eighty-three independent municipalities, (to say nothing of the parts that compose them,) can ever be governed as one body, or can ever be set in motion by the impulse of one mind? . . .

It is now sixteen or seventeen years since I saw the queen of France, then the dauphiness, at Versailles; and surely never lighted on this orb, which she hardly seemed to touch, a more delightful vision. I saw her just above the horizon, decorating and cheering the elevated sphere she just began to move in,—glittering like the morning-star, full of life, and splendour, and joy. Oh! what a revolution! and what a heart must I have to contemplate without emotion that elevation and that fall! Little did I dream when she added titles of veneration to those of enthusiastic, distant, respectful love, that she should ever be obliged to carry the sharp antidote against disgrace concealed in that bosom; little did I dream that I should have lived to see such disasters fallen upon her in a nation of gallant men, in a nation of men of honour, and of cavaliers. I thought ten thousand swords must have leaped from their scabbards to avenge even a look that threatened her with insult. But the age of chivalry is gone. That of sophisters, economists, and calculators, has succeeded; and the glory of Europe is extinguished for ever. Never, never more shall we behold that generous loyalty to rank and sex, that proud submission, that dignified obedience, that subordination of the heart, which kept alive, even in servitude itself, the spirit of an exalted freedom. The unbought grace of life, the cheap defence of nations, the nurse of manly sentiment and heroic enterprise, is gone! It is gone, that sensibility of principle, that charity of honor, which felt a stain like a wound, which inspired courage whilst it mitigated ferocity, which ennobled whatever it touched, and under which vice itself lost half its evil, by losing all its grossness.

This mixed system of opinion and sentiment had its origin in the ancient chivalry; and the principle, though varied in its appearance by the varying state of human affairs, subsisted and influenced through a long succession of generations, even to the time we live in. If it should ever be totally extinguished, the loss I fear will be great. It is this which has given its character to modern Europe. It is this which has distinguished it under all its forms of government, and distinguished it to its advantage, from the states of Asia, and possibly from those states which flourished in the most brilliant periods of the antique world. It was this, which, without confounding ranks, had produced a noble equality, and handed it down through all the gradations of social life. It was this opinion which mitigated kings into companions, and raised private men to be fellows with kings. Without force or opposition, it subdued the fierceness of pride and power; it obliged sovereigns to submit to the soft collar of social esteem, compelled stern authority to submit to elegance, and gave a dominating vanquisher of laws to be subdued by manners.

But now all is to be changed. All the pleasing illusions, which made power gentle and obedience liberal, which harmonized the different shades of life, and which, by a bland assimilation, incorporated into politics the sentiments which beautify and soften private society, are to be dissolved by this new conquering empire of light and reason. All the decent drapery of life is to be rudely torn off. All the superadded ideas, furnished from the wardrobe of a moral imagination, which the heart owns, and the understanding ratifies, as necessary to cover the defects of our naked, shivering nature, and to raise it to dignity in our own estimation, are to be exploded as a ridiculous, absurd, and antiquated fashion.

On this scheme of things, a king is but a man, a queen is but a woman; a woman is but an animal, and an animal not of the highest order. All homage paid to the sex in general as such, and without distinct views, is to be regarded as romance and folly. Regicide, and parricide, and sacrilege, are but fictions of superstition, corrupting jurisprudence by destroying its simplicity. The murder of a king, or a queen, or a bishop, or a father, are only common homicide; and if the people are by any chance, or in any way, gainers by it, a sort of homicide much the most pardonable, and into which we ought not to make too severe a scrutiny.

On the scheme of this barbarous philosophy, which is the offspring of cold hearts and muddy understandings, and which is as void of solid wisdom as it is destitute of all taste and elegance, laws are to be supported only by their own terrors, and by the concern which each individual may find in them from his own private speculations, or can spare to them from his own private interests. . . .

# Mary Wollstonecraft

## *from* VINDICATION OF THE RIGHTS OF WOMAN (1792)

*M*ary Wollstonecraft (1757–1797), one of the pioneers of modern feminism, lived her life in defiance of the conventions of her time. She lived with the radical political thinker William Godwin and only married him after she became pregnant. She died eleven days after giving birth to her second daughter, Mary, the future author of Frankenstein. Her response to Burke's attack on the French Revolution, A Vindication of the Rights of Woman, is one of the first classics of feminist thought. For Wollstonecraft, the problem with the French Revolution is not that it takes place, but that it does not go far enough. The Revolution proclaims "the rights of man," but what it really means is the rights of men. Whereas previously the privileged classes had oppressed the great majority of the population, in revolutionary France one half of the population now dominates the other half. Wollstonecraft, drawing upon Enlightenment rationalism, argues that only if men and women are political and social equals can they develop the mutual respect that is necessary to create universal harmony.

---

To account for, and excuse the tyranny of man, many ingenious arguments have been brought forward to prove, that the two sexes, in the acquirement of virtue, ought to aim at attaining a very different character; or, to speak explicitly, women are not allowed to have sufficient strength of mind to acquire what really deserves the name of virtue. Yet it should seem, allowing them to have souls, that there is but one way appointed by Providence to lead *mankind* to either virtue or happiness.

If then women are not a swarm of ephemeron triflers, why should they be kept in ignorance under the specious name of innocence? Men complain, and with reason, of the follies and caprices of our sex, when they do not keenly satirise our headstrong passions and grovelling vices. Behold, I should answer, the natural effect of ignorance! The mind will ever be unstable that has only prejudices to rest on, and the current will run with destructive fury when there are no barriers to break its force. Women are told from their infancy, and taught by the example of their mothers, that a little knowledge of human weakness, justly termed cunning, softness of temper, *outward* obedience, and a scrupulous attention to a puerile kind of propriety, will obtain for them the protection of man; and should they be beautiful, everything else is needless, for at least twenty years of their lives. . . .

How grossly do they insult us who thus advise us only to render ourselves gentle, domestic brutes! For instance, the winning softness so warmly and frequently recommended, that governs by obeying. What childish expressions, and how insignificant is the being—can it be an immortal one?—who will condescend to govern by such sinister methods? "Certainly," says Lord Bacon, "man is of kin to the beasts by his body; and if he be not of kin to God by his spirit, he is a base and ignoble creature!" Men, indeed, appear to me to act in a very unphilosophical manner, when they try to secure the good conduct of women by attempting to keep them always in a state of childhood. Rousseau was more consistent when he wished to stop the progress of reason in both sexes, for if men eat of the tree of knowledge, women will come in for a taste; but, from the imperfect cultivation which their understandings now receive, they only attain a knowledge of evil. . . .

. . . the most perfect education, in my opinion, is such an exercise of the understanding as is best calculated to strengthen the body and form the heart. Or, in other words, to enable the individual to attain such habits of virtue as will render it independent. In fact, it is a farce to call any being virtuous whose virtues do not result from the exercise of its own reason. This was Rousseau's opinion respecting men; I extend it to women, and confidently assert that they have been drawn out of their sphere by false refinement, and not by an endeavour to acquire masculine qualities. Still the regal homage which they receive is so intoxicating, that until the manners of the times are changed, and formed on more reasonable principles, it may be impossible to convince them that the illegitimate power which they obtain by degrading themselves is a curse, and that they must return to nature and equality if they wish to secure the placid satisfaction that unsophisticated affections impart. But for this epoch we must wait—wait perhaps till kings and nobles, enlightened by reason, and, preferring the real dignity of man to childish state, throw off their gaudy hereditary trappings; and if then women do not resign the arbitrary power of beauty—they will prove that they have *less* mind than man.

I may be accused of arrogance; still I must declare what I firmly believe, that all the writers who have written on the subject of female education and manners, from Rousseau to Dr. Gregory, have contributed to render women more artificial, weak characters, than they would otherwise have been; and consequently, more useless members of society. I might have expressed this conviction in a lower key, but I am afraid it would have been the whine of affectation, and not the faithful expression of my feelings, of the clear result which experience and reflection have led me to draw. When I come to that division of the subject, I shall advert to the passages that I more particularly disapprove of, in the works of the authors I have just alluded to; but it is first necessary to observe that my objection extends to the whole purport of those books, which tend, in my opinion, to degrade one-half of the human species, and render women pleasing at the expense of every solid virtue. . . .

Many are the causes that, in the present corrupt state of society, contribute to enslave women by cramping their understandings and sharpening their senses. One, perhaps, that silently does more mischief than all the rest, is their disregard of order.

To do everything in an orderly manner is a most important precept, which women, who, generally speaking, receive only a disorderly kind of education, seldom attend to with that degree of exactness that men, who from their infancy are broken into method, observe. This negligent kind of guesswork—for what other epithet can be used to point out the random exertions of a sort of instinctive common sense never brought to the test of reason?—prevents their generalizing matters of fact; so they do today what they did yesterday, merely because they did it yesterday.

This contempt of the understanding in early life has more baneful consequences than is commonly supposed; for the little knowledge which women of strong minds attain is, from various circumstances, of a more desultory kind than the knowledge of men, and it is acquired more by sheer observations on real life than from comparing what has been individually observed with the results of experience generalized by speculation. Led by their dependent situation and domestic employments more into society, what they learn is rather by snatches; and as learning is with them in general only a secondary thing, they do not pursue any one branch with that persevering ardour necessary to give vigour to the faculties and clearness to the judgment. In the present state of society a little learning is required to support the character of a gentle-man, and boys are obliged to submit to a few years of discipline. But in the education of women, the cultivation of the understanding is always subordinate to the acquire-ment of some corporeal accomplishment. Even when enervated by confinement and false notions of modesty, the body is prevented from attaining that grace and beauty which relaxed half-formed limbs never exhibit. Besides, in youth, their faculties are not brought forward by emulation; and having no serious scientific study, if they have natural sagacity, it is turned too soon on life and manners. They dwell on effects and modifications, without tracing them back to causes; and complicated rules to adjust behaviour are a weak substitute for simple principles.

As a proof that education gives this appearance of weakness to females, we may instance the example of military men, who are, like them, sent into the world before their minds have been stored with knowledge, or fortified by principles. The conse-quences are similar; soldiers acquire a little superficial knowledge, snatched from the muddy current of conversation, and from continually mixing with society, they gain what is termed a knowledge of the world; and this acquaintance with manners and customs has frequently been confounded with a knowledge of the human heart. But can the crude fruit of casual observation, never brought to the test of judgment, formed by comparing speculation and experience, deserve such a distinction? Sol-diers, as well as women, practise the minor virtues with punctilious politeness. Where is then the sexual difference, when the education has been the same? All the differ-ence that I can discern arises from the superior advantage of liberty which enables the former to see more of life.

It is wandering from my present subject, perhaps, to make a political remark; but as it was produced naturally by the train of my reflections, I shall not pass it silently over.

Standing armies can never consist of resolute robust men; they may be well-disciplined machines, but they will seldom contain men under the influence of strong passions, or with very vigorous faculties; and as for any depth of understanding, I will venture to affirm that it is as rarely to be found in the army as amongst women. And the cause, I maintain, is the same. It may be further observed that officers are also par-ticularly attentive to their persons, fond of dancing, crowded rooms, adventures, and ridicule. Like the *fair* sex, the business of their lives is gallantry; they were taught to please, and they only live to please. Yet they do not lose their rank in the distinction of sexes, for they are still reckoned superior to women, though in what their superior-ity consists, beyond what I have just mentioned, it is difficult to discover.

The great misfortune is this, that they both acquire manners before morals, and a knowledge of life before they have from reflection any acquaintance with the grand ideal outline of human nature. The consequence is natural. Satisfied with common nature, they become a prey to prejudices, and taking all their opinions on credit, they blindly submit to authority. So that if they have any sense, it is a kind of instinctive glance that catches proportions, and decides with respect to manners, but fails when arguments are to be pursued below the surface, or opinions analysed.

May not the same remark be applied to women? Nay, the argument may be carried still further, for they are both thrown out of a useful station by the unnatural distinctions established in civilized life. Riches and hereditary honours have made cyphers of women to give consequence to the numerical figure; and idleness has produced a mixture of gallantry and despotism into society, which leads the very men who are the slaves of their mistresses to tyrannize over their sisters, wives, and daughters. This is only keeping them in rank and file, it is true. Strengthen the female mind by enlarging it, and there will be an end to blind obedience; but as blind obedience is ever sought for by power, tyrants and sensualists are in the right when they endeavour to keep woman in the dark, because the former only want slaves, and the latter a plaything. The sensualist, indeed, has been the most dangerous of tyrants, and women have been duped by their lovers, as princes by their ministers, whilst dreaming that they reigned over them. . . .

Youth is the season for love in both sexes; but in those days of thoughtless enjoyment provision should be made for the more important years of life, when reflection takes place of sensation. But Rousseau, and most of the male writers who have followed his steps, have warmly indicated that the whole tendency of female education ought to be directed to one point—to render them pleasing.

Let me reason with the supporters of this opinion who have any knowledge of human nature. Do they imagine that marriage can eradicate the habitude of life? The woman who has only been taught to please will soon find that her charms are oblique sunbeams, and that they cannot have much effect on her husband's heart when they are seen every day, when the summer is passed and gone. Will she then have sufficient native energy to look into herself for comfort, and cultivate her dormant faculties? or is it not more rational to expect that she will try to please other men, and, in the emotions raised by the expectation of new conquests, endeavour to forget the mortification her love or pride has received? When the husband ceases to be a lover, and the time will inevitably come, her desire of pleasing will then grow languid, or become a spring of bitterness; and love, perhaps, the most evanescent of all passions, gives place to jealousy or vanity. . . .

. . . How then can the great art of pleasing be such a necessary study? it is only useful to a mistress. The chaste wife and serious mother should only consider her power to please as the polish of her virtues, and the affection of her husband as one of the comforts that render her task less difficult, and her life happier. But, whether she be loved or neglected, her first wish should be to make herself respectable, and not to rely for all her happiness on a being subject to like infirmities with herself.

The worthy Dr. Gregory fell into a similar error. I respect his heart, but entirely disapprove of his celebrated *Legacy to his Daughters*.

He advises them to cultivate a fondness for dress, because a fondness for dress, he asserts, is natural to them. I am unable to comprehend what either he or Rousseau mean when they frequently use this indefinite term. If they told us that in a pre-existent state the soul was fond of dress, and brought this inclination with it into a new body, I should listen to them with a half-smile, as I often do when I hear a rant about innate elegance. But if he only meant to say that the exercise of the faculties will produce this fondness, I deny it. It is not natural; but arises, like false ambition in men, from a love of power.

Dr. Gregory goes much further; he actually recommends dissimulation, and advises an innocent girl to give the lie to her feelings, and not dance with spirit, when gaiety of heart would make her feet eloquent without making her gestures immodest. In the name of truth and common sense, why should not one woman acknowledge that she can take more exercise than another? or, in other words, that she has a sound constitution; and why, to damp innocent vivacity, is she darkly to be told that men will draw conclusions which she little thinks of? Let the libertine draw what inference he pleases; but, I hope, that no sensible mother will restrain the natural frankness of youth by instilling such indecent cautions. . . .

Women ought to endeavour to purify their hearts; but can they do so when their uncultivated understandings make them entirely dependent on their senses for employment and amusement, when no noble pursuits set them above the little vanities of the day, or enable them to curb the wild emotions that agitate a reed, over which every passing breeze has power? To gain the affections of a virtuous man, is affectation necessary? Nature has given woman a weaker frame than man; but, to ensure her husband's affections, must a wife, who, by the exercise of her mind and body whilst she was discharging the duties of a daughter, wife, and mother, has allowed her constitution to retain its natural strength, and her nerves a healthy tone,—is she, I say, to condescend to use art, and feign a sickly delicacy, in order to secure her husband's affection? Weakness may excite tenderness, and gratify the arrogant pride of man; but the lordly caresses of a protector will not gratify a noble mind that pants for and deserves to be respected. Fondness is a poor substitute for friendship!

In a seraglio, I grant, that all these arts are necessary; the epicure must have his palate tickled, or he will sink into apathy; but have women so little ambition as to be satisfied with such a condition? Can they supinely dream life away in the lap of pleasure, or the languor of weariness, rather than assert their claim to pursue reasonable pleasures, and render themselves conspicuous by practising the virtues which dignify mankind? . . .

Besides, the woman who strengthens her body and exercises her mind will, by managing her family and practising various virtues, become the friend, and not the humble dependent of her husband; and if she, by possessing such substantial qualities, merit his regard, she will not find it necessary to conceal her affection, nor to pretend to an unnatural coldness of constitution to excite her husband's passions. . . .

Nature, or, to speak with strict propriety, God, has made all things right; but man has sought him out many inventions to mar the work. . . .

If, I say, for I would not impress by declamation when Reason offers her sober light, if they be really capable of acting like rational creatures, let them not be treated like slaves; or, like the brutes who are dependent on the reason of man, when they associate with him; but cultivate their minds, give them the salutary sublime curb of principle, and let them attain conscious dignity by feeling themselves only dependent on God. Teach them, in common with man, to submit to necessity; instead of giving, to render them more pleasing, a sex to morals.

Further, should experience prove that they cannot attain the same degree of strength of mind, perseverance, and fortitude, let their virtues be the same in kind, though they may vainly struggle for the same degree; and the superiority of man will be equally clear, if not clearer; and truth, as it is a simple principle, which admits of no modification, would be common to both. Nay the order of society, as it is at present regulated, would not be inverted, for woman would then only have the rank that reason assigned her, and arts could not be practised to bring the balance even, much less to turn it.

These may be termed Utopian dreams. Thanks to that Being who impressed them on my soul, and gave me sufficient strength of mind to dare to exert my own reason, till, becoming dependent only on Him for the support of my virtue, I view, with indignation, the mistaken notions that enslave my sex.

I love man as my fellow; but his sceptre, real or usurped, extends not to me, unless the reason of an individual demands my homage; and even then the submission is to reason, and not to man. In fact, the conduct of an accountable being must be regulated by the operations of its own reason; or on what foundation rests the throne of God?

It appears to me necessary to dwell on these obvious truths, because females have been insulated, as it were; and while they have been stripped of the virtues that should clothe humanity, they have been decked with artificial graces that enable them to exercise a short-lived tyranny. Love, in their bosoms, taking place of every nobler passion, their sole ambition is to be fair, to raise emotion instead of inspiring respect; and this ignoble desire, like the servility in absolute monarchies, destroys all strength of character. Liberty is the mother of virtue, and if women be, by their very constitution, slaves, and not allowed to breathe the sharp invigorating air of freedom, they must ever languish like exotics, and be reckoned beautiful flaws in nature. Let it also be remembered, that they are the only flaw.

As to the argument respecting the subjection in which the sex has ever been held, it retorts on man. The many have always been enthralled by the few; and monsters, who scarcely have shown any discernment of human excellence, have tyrannized over thousands of their fellow-creatures. Why have men of superior endowments submitted to such degradation? For, is it not universally acknowledged that kings, viewed collectively, have ever been inferior, in abilities and virtue, to the same number of men taken from the common mass of mankind—yet have they not, and are they not still treated with a degree of reverence that is an insult to reason? China is not the only country where a living man has been made a God. . . .

I shall not pursue this argument any further than to establish an obvious inference, that as sound politics diffuse liberty, mankind, including woman, will become more wise and virtuous.

. . . A man when he enters any profession has his eye steadily fixed on some future advantage (and the mind gains great strength by having all its efforts directed to one point), and, full of his business, pleasure is considered as mere relaxation; whilst women seek for pleasure as the main purpose of existence. In fact, from the education, which they receive from society, the love of pleasure may be said to govern them all; but does this prove that there is a sex in souls? It would be just as rational to declare that the courtiers in France, when a destructive system of despotism had formed their character, were not men, because liberty, virtue, and humanity, were sacrificed to pleasure and vanity. Fatal passions, which have ever domineered over the *whole* race! . . .

In short, women, in general, as well as the rich of both sexes, have acquired all the follies and vices of civilization, and missed the useful fruit. It is not necessary for me always to premise, that I speak of the condition of the whole sex, leaving exceptions out of the question. Their senses are inflamed, and their understandings neglected, consequently they become the prey of their senses, delicately termed sensibility, and are blown about by every momentary gust of feeling. Civilized women are, therefore, so weakened by false refinement, that, respecting morals, their condition is much below what it would be were they left in a state nearer to nature. Ever restless and anxious, their over-exercised sensibility not only renders them uncomfortable themselves, but troublesome, to use a soft phrase, to others. All their thoughts turn on things calculated to excite emotion and feeling, when they should reason, their conduct is unstable, and their opinions are wavering—not the wavering produced by deliberation or progressive views, but by contradictory emotions. By fits and starts, they are warm in many pursuits; yet this warmth, never concentrated into perseverance, soon exhausts itself; exhaled by its own heat, or meeting with some other fleeting passion, to which reason has never given any specific gravity, neutrality ensues. Miserable, indeed, must be that being whose cultivation of mind has only tended to inflame its passions! A distinction should be made between inflaming and strengthening them. The passions thus pampered, whilst the judgment is left unformed, what can be expected to ensue? Undoubtedly, a mixture of madness and folly!

This observation should not be confined to the *fair* sex; however, at present, I only mean to apply it to them.

Novels, music, poetry, and gallantry, all tend to make women the creatures of sensation, and their character is thus formed in the mould of folly during the time they are acquiring accomplishments, the only improvement they are excited, by their station in society, to acquire. This overstretched sensibility naturally relaxes the other powers of the mind, and prevents intellect from attaining that sovereignty which it ought to attain to render a rational creature useful to others, and content with its own station; for the exercise of the understanding, as life advances, is the only method pointed out by nature to calm the passions.

Satiety has a very different effect, and I have often been forcibly struck by an emphatical description of damnation; when the spirit is represented as continually hovering with abortive eagerness round the defiled body, unable to enjoy anything without the organs of sense. Yet, to their senses, are women made slaves, because it is by their sensibility that they obtain present power.

And will moralists pretend to assert that this is the condition in which one-half of the human race should be encouraged to remain with listless inactivity and stupid acquiescence? Kind instructors! what were we created for? To remain, it may be said, innocent; they mean in a state of childhood. We might as well never have been born, unless it were necessary that we should be created to enable man to acquire the noble privilege of reason, the power of discerning good from evil, whilst we lie down in the dust from whence we were taken, never to rise again.

It would be an endless task to trace the variety of meannesses, cares, and sorrows, into which women are plunged by the prevailing opinion, that they were created rather to feel than reason, and that all the power they obtain must be obtained by their charms and weakness:

> Fine by defect, and amiably weak!

And, made by this amiable weakness entirely dependent, excepting what they gain by illicit sway, on man, not only for protection, but advice, is it surprising that, neglecting the duties that reason alone points out, and shrinking from trials calculated to strengthen their minds, they only exert themselves to give their defects a graceful covering, which may serve to heighten their charms in the eye of the voluptuary, though it sink them below the scale of moral excellence.

Fragile in every sense of the word, they are obliged to look up to man for every comfort. In the most trifling danger they cling to their support, with parasitical tenacity, piteously demanding succour; and their *natural* protector extends his arm, or lifts up his voice, to guard the lovely trembler—from what? Perhaps the frown of an old cow, or the jump of a mouse; a rat would be a serious danger. In the name of reason, and even common sense, what can save such beings from contempt; even though they be soft and fair.

These fears, when not affected, may produce some pretty attitudes; but they show a degree of imbecility which degrades a rational creature in a way women are not aware of—for love and esteem are very distinct things.

I am fully persuaded that we should hear of none of these infantine airs, if girls were allowed to take sufficient exercise, and not confined in close rooms till their muscles are relaxed, and their powers of digestion destroyed. To carry the remark still further, if fear in girls, instead of being cherished, perhaps created, were treated in the same manner as cowardice in boys, we should quickly see women with more dignified aspects. It is true, they could not then with equal propriety be termed the sweet flowers that smile in the walk of man; but they would be more respectable members of society, and discharge the important duties of life by the light of their own reason. "Educate women like men," says Rousseau, "and the more they resemble our sex the less power will they have over us." This is the very point I aim at. I do not wish them to have power over men; but over themselves.

In the same strain have I heard men argue against instructing the poor; for many are the forms that aristocracy assumes. "Teach them to read and write," say they, "and you take them out of the station assigned them by nature." An eloquent Frenchman has answered them, I will borrow his sentiments. "But they know not, when they make man a brute, that they may expect every instant to see him transformed into a ferocious beast. Without knowledge there can be no morality."

Ignorance is a frail base for virtue! Yet, that it is the condition for which woman was organized, has been insisted upon by the writers who have most vehemently argued in favour of the superiority of man; a superiority not in degree, but offence; though, to soften the argument, they have laboured to prove, with chivalrous generosity, that the sexes ought not to be compared; man was made to reason, woman to feel: and that together, flesh and spirit, they make the most perfect whole, by blending happily reason and sensibility into one character. . . .

I come round to my old argument: if woman be allowed to have an immortal soul, she must have, as the employment of life, an understanding to improve. And when, to render the present state more complete, though everything proves it to be but a fraction of a mighty sum, she is incited by present gratification to forget her grand destination, nature is counteracted, or she was born only to procreate and rot. Or, granting brutes of every description a soul, though not a reasonable one, the exercise of instinct and sensibility may be the step which they are to take, in this life, towards the attainment of reason in the next; so that through all eternity they will lag behind man, who, why we cannot tell, had the power given him of attaining reason in his first mode of existence. . . .

## *from* PROCLAMATION (1793)

## *from* LETTER TO THE DIRECTORY (1797)

## *from* REGULATIONS REGARDING FIELD LABOR (1800)

*T*he French Revolution's impact was not only felt in Europe. As European powers went to war with revolutionary France, the conflict extended to the colonies as well. Within this colonial theater, one of the most extraordinary figures was Toussaint L'Ouverture (1743–1803). A freed slave and a fervent Catholic, Toussaint was responsible for emancipating the slaves of Haiti (St. Domingue) and creating a short-lived, black-governed French protectorate. The following excerpts represent three different aspects of Toussaint's political life and thought. The two proclamations of 1793 suggest the religious underpinnings of Toussaint's thought and his indebtedness to the ideas of the French Revolution. In his letter to the Directory (the French revolutionary government) he defends the violent actions of blacks that were condemned by the French general Vienot Vaulanc. He argues that the actions of blacks were no different than those of the French revolutionaries themselves. If the Revolution produced violence in France, should not the authorities show understanding towards a nation whose people had been deprived of freedom, education, and civilization? In the final extract, "Regulations Respecting Field Labor," we see Toussaint's efforts at reconciling individual freedom and economic and political survival. Fearful that the end of slavery would mean economic ruin and political instability, he felt compelled to restrict the movement of laborers.

### PROCLAMATION OF 25 AUGUST 1793

Having been the first to champion your cause, it is my duty to continue to labour for it. I cannot permit another to rob me of the initiative. Since I have begun, I will know how to conclude. Join me and you will enjoy the rights of freemen sooner than any other way. Neither whites nor mulattoes have formulated my plans; it is to the Supreme Being alone that I owe my inspiration. We have begun, we have carried on, we will know how to reach the goal.

### PROCLAMATION OF 29 AUGUST 1793

Brothers and Friends:

I am Toussaint L'Ouverture. My name is perhaps known to you. I have undertaken to avenge you. I want liberty and equality to reign throughout St. Domingue. I am working towards that end. Come and join me, brothers, and combat by our side for the same cause.

## LETTER TO THE DIRECTORY, 28 OCTOBER 1797

Citizen Directors,

At the moment when I thought I had just rendered eminent service to the Republic and to my fellow citizens, when I had just proven my recognition of the justice of the French people toward us, when I believed myself worthy of the confidence that the Government had placed in me and which I will never cease to merit, a speech was made in the *Corps Legislatif* during the meeting of 22 May 1797 by Vienot Vaublanc . . . and, while going through it, I had the sorrow of seeing my intentions slandered on every page and the political existence of my brothers threatened.

A similar speech from the mouth of a man whose fortune had been momentarily wiped out by the revolution in St. Domingue would not surprise me, the loser has the right to complain up to a certain point, but what must profoundly affect me is that the *Corps Legislatif* could have approved and sanctioned such declamations, which are so unsuitable to the restoration of our tranquility; which, instead of spurring the field-negroes to work, can only arouse them by allowing them to believe that the representatives of the French people were their enemies.

In order to justify myself in your eyes and in the eyes of my fellow citizens, whose esteem I so eagerly desire, I am going to apply myself to refuting the assertions of citizen Vaublanc . . . and . . . prove that the enemies of our liberty have only been motivated in this event by a spirit of personal vengeance and that the public interest and respect for the Constitution have been continually trampled under foot by them. . . .

> *Second Assertion:* "Everyone is agreed in portraying the Colony in the most shocking state of disorder and groaning under the military government. And what a military government! In whose hands is it confined? In that of ignorant and gross negroes, incapable of distinguishing between unrestrained license and austere liberty." . . .

This shocking disorder in which the Commission found St. Domingue was not the consequence of the liberty given to the blacks but the result of the uprising of thirty Ventôse [the Villate affair], for, prior to this period, order and harmony reigned in all Republican territory as far as the absence of laws would allow. All citizens blindly obeyed the orders of General Laveaux; his will was the national will for them, and they submitted to him as a man invested with the authority emanating from the generous nation that had shattered their chains.

If, upon the arrival of the Commission, St. Domingue groaned under a military government, this power was not in the hands of the blacks; they were subordinate to it, and they only executed the orders of General Laveaux. These were the blacks who, when France was threatened with the loss of this Colony, employed their arms and their weapons to conserve it, to reconquer the greatest part of its territory that treason had handed over to the Spanish and English. . . . These were the blacks who, with the good citizens of the other two colors, flew to the rescue of General Laveaux in the

Villate Affair and who, by repressing the audacious rebels who wished to destroy the national representation, restored it to its rightful depository.

Such was the conduct of those blacks in whose hands citizen Vienot Vaublanc said the military government of St. Domingue found itself, such are those negroes he accuses of being ignorant and gross; undoubtedly they are, because without education there can only be ignorance and grossness. But must one impute to them the crime of this educational deficiency or, more correctly, accuse those who prevented them by the most atrocious punishments from obtaining it? And are only civilized people capable of distinguishing between good and evil, of having notions of charity and justice? The men of St. Domingue have been deprived of an education; but even so, they no longer remain in a state of nature, and because they haven't arrived at the degree of perfection that education bestows, they do not merit being classed apart from the rest of mankind, being confused with animals. . . .

Undoubtedly, one can reproach the inhabitants of St. Domingue, including the blacks, for many faults, even terrible crimes. But even in France, where the limits of sociability are clearly drawn, doesn't one see its inhabitants, in the struggle between despotism and liberty, going to all the excesses for which the blacks are reproached by their enemies? The fury of the two parties has been equal in St. Domingue; and if the excesses of the blacks in these critical moments haven't exceeded those committed in Europe, must not an impartial judge pronounce in favor of the former? Since it is our enemies themselves who present us as ignorant and gross, aren't we more excusable than those who, unlike us, were not deprived of the advantages of education and civilization? Surrounded by fierce enemies, oft cruel masters; without any other support than the charitable intentions of the friends of freedom in France, of whose existence we were hardly aware; driven to excessive errors by opposing parties who were rapidly destroying each other; knowing, at first, only the laws of the Mother-Country that favored the pretensions of our enemies and, since our liberty, receiving only the semi-yearly or yearly instructions of our government, and no assistance, but almost always slanders or diatribes from our old oppressors—how can we not be pardoned some moments of ill-conduct, some gross faults, of which we were the first victims? Why, above all, reflect upon unreproachable men, upon the vast majority of the blacks, the faults of the lesser part, who, in time, had been reclaimed by the attentions of the majority to order and respect for the superior authorities? . . .

## Regulations Respecting Field Labor

Citizens,

After putting an end to the war in the South, our first duty has been to return thanks to the Almighty; which we have done with a zeal becoming so great a blessing: Now, Citizens, it is necessary to consecrate all our moments to the prosperity of St. Domingo, to the public tranquillity, and consequently, to the welfare of our fellow citizens.

But, to attain this end in an effectual manner, all the civil and military officers must make it their business, every one in their respective department, to perform the duties of their offices with devotion and attachment to the public welfare.

You will easily conceive, Citizens, that Agriculture is the support of Government; since it is the foundation of Commerce and Wealth, the source of Arts and

Industry, it keeps everybody employed, as being the mechanism of all Trades. And, from the moment that every individual becomes useful, it creates public tranquillity; disturbances disappear together with idleness, by which they are commonly generated, and everyone peaceably enjoys the fruits of his industry.

Officers civil and military, this is what you must aim at; such is the plan to be adopted, which I prescribe to you; and I declare in the most peremptory manner, that it shall be enforced: My country demands this salutary step; I am bound to it by my office, and the security of our liberties demands it imperiously.

But in order to secure our liberties, which are indispensable to our happiness, every individual must be usefully employed, so as to contribute to the public good, and the general tranquillity.

Considering that the soldier, who has sacred duties to perform, as being the safeguard of the people, and in perpetual activity, to execute the orders of his Chief, either for maintaining interior tranquillity, or for fighting abroad the enemies of the country, is strictly subordinate to his superior officers; and as it is of great importance that overseers, drivers and field-negroes, who in like manner have their superiors, should conduct themselves as officers, subalterns, and soldiers in whatever may concern them.

•

I do most peremptorily order as follows:

*Art. 1.* All overseers, drivers, and field-negroes are bound to observe, with exactness, submission, and obedience, their duty in the same manner as soldiers.

*Art. 2.* All overseers, drivers, and field-labourers, who will not perform with assiduity the duties required of them, shall be arrested and punished as severely as soldiers deviating from their duty. After which punishment, if the offender be an overseer, he shall be enlisted in one of the regiments of the army in St. Domingo. If a driver, he shall be dismissed from his employment and placed among the field-negroes, without ever being permitted to act as a driver again. And, if a common-labourer, he shall be punished with the same severity as a private soldier, according to his guilt.

*Art. 3.* All field-labourers, men and women, now in a state of idleness, living in towns, villages, and on other plantations than those to which they belong, with an intention to evade work, even those of both sexes who have not been employed in field labour since the revolution, are required to return immediately to their respective plantations, if, in the course of eight days from the promulgation of this present regulation, they shall not produce sufficient proof to the commanding officers in the place of their residence of their having some useful occupation or means of livelihood; but it is to be understood that being a servant is not to be considered a useful occupation; in consequence whereof, those amongst the laborers who have quitted their plantations in order to hire themselves, shall return thereto, under the personal responsibility of those with whom they live in that capacity. By the term "an useful occupation" is meant, what enables a man to pay a contribution to the State.

*Art. 4.* This measure, indispensable to the public welfare, positively prescribes to all those of either sex that are not labourers to produce the proofs of their having an occupation or profession sufficient to gain their livelihood, and that they can afford to pay a contribution to the Republic. Otherwise, and in default thereof, all those who shall be found in contravention hereto, shall be instantly arrested, and if they are found guilty they shall be drafted into one of the regiments of the army, if not, they shall be sent to the field and compelled to work. This measure, which is to be strictly enforced, will put a stop to the idle habit of wandering about, since it will oblige everyone to be usefully employed.

*Art. 5.* Parents are earnestly entreated to attend to their duty towards their children; which is, to make them good citizens; for that purpose they must instruct them in good morals, in the Christian religion, and the fear of God. Above all, exclusive of this education, they must be brought up in some specific business or profession to enable them not only to earn their living, but also to contribute to the expences of the Government.

*— trans. George F. Tyson, Jr.*

# Romanticism
# and Industrial Transformation

The several decades following the French Revolution found Europe in the midst of social, economic, and political transformations more profound, and profoundly hurried, than anything in historical memory. While these transformations reshaped societies and governments across Europe, Great Britain, the first nation to become industrialized, serves as a prototype—and harbinger of things to come—for other nations. The growth of industry and spread of its attendant social consequences in Britain were debated impassionedly among politicians, philosophers, writers, and advocates for the poor in the British Isles and on the continent. Rapid urbanization resulted in unsanitary slums and increased crime, while the shift to large factories from smaller workplaces left workers with very little say concerning the conditions in which they worked. At the same time, industrialization was providing an increasingly comfortable life for the growing middle classes, particularly for those with capital, who could become extremely wealthy through manufacturing, railroads, shipping, and banking. And in England, as elsewhere, male members of the propertied middle class could vote, unlike working-class men; women did not begin to have access to the vote in most European nations until after the Great War.

The movement in the arts known as Romanticism accentuated the contradictions of industrial transformation. Romanticism began in opposition to the pre-eminence of reason, science, and logic—and denigration of feeling and imagination—in Enlightenment thought. Inspired by the ideals of the French Revolution and the philosophies of Rousseau and Kant, Romantic writers in Germany, England, and other nations turned to organic rather than mechanical categories for understanding, focused on spiritual insight and emotion in place of 'factual' knowledge, and venerated genius rather than reason and empirical study. Whereas eighteenth-century rationalists had imagined God as a watchmaker, the Romantics envisioned deity as a cosmic poet and artist. Abandoning the eighteenth-century emphasis on classical aesthetic forms, reason, and restraint, the Romantics turned to nature, the exotic, and the supernatural, finding in them a greater creative freedom necessary for the full expression of human nature. Romanticism's heady emphasis on individual experience and the imagination occurs at a time when each seems threatened by profound social change.

From very divergent vantage points, European writers in the first half of the nineteenth century considered what their rapidly changing nations were, might become, and ought to be. Some saw industrial and urban developments as dangerous, others as evidence of Europe's greatness: a range of responses is evident in the readings in this section. While the Romantic poets decried what they saw as a loss of authenticity in life, other thinkers turned their attention to the practical and philosophical realities of the bourgeois, industrialized, urban societies in which they lived. What, they asked, would provide the common ground in these societies? What ideas or images would serve to promote and further national unity? Was the basis of the nation its political state, its culture and language, or its commercial interests?

The overwhelming social and cultural consequences of economic and political transformation inspired everything from fiery political debate to books defining how women and men in different social classes should behave and what they ought to read. As the middle classes became increasingly prosperous, their interests began to be allied with those of the aristocracy; as the working classes struggled with desperate poverty, crowded living conditions, and dangerous workplaces, they became increasingly restless and politicized. The condition of the poor in industrialized nations was much discussed, first in England and then on the continent. Great cities, busy factories, railroads, and empires made some men wealthy, but their wealth came from the work of thousands of working men and women in conditions that many found appalling. Civilization had always required people to surrender some freedoms, but many now asked if modernization cost too many too much. Benjamin Disraeli, a man of letters and politician who later became prime minister of Britain, warned in his 1846 novel *Sybil* that Britain was becoming "Two Nations." The class divisions he described would soon prove fertile ground for advocates of a workers' revolution.

# Johann Gottfried von Herder

## *from* MATERIALS FOR THE PHILOSOPHY OF THE HISTORY OF MANKIND (1784)

*Nationalism was a product of the French Revolution, which held that the people were the foundation of the nation. They were citizens, rather than subjects, who had rights and responsibilities. But France was relatively homogeneous with a long history as a unified state. In Germany, as in most of the rest of Europe, the situation was dramatically different. The lives of peoples of different ethnic, religious, and cultural backgrounds were interwoven, and they lived under a wide variety of governmental forms—empires, principalities, independent cities, and so forth. A pivotal thinker in framing German nationalist thought was Johann Gottfried von Herder (1744–1803), a critic, theologian, and philosopher, who was a harbinger of the Romantic movement. Herder's view of the nation, as articulated in* Materials for the Philosophy of the History of Mankind, *stresses its organic and cultural character as embodied in folklore, popular traditions, religion, and language. In his view, the Germans must be true to their own traditions rather than mingling with others and experiencing a "protracted intellectual servitude."*

Nature has sketched with mountain ranges which she fashioned and with streams which she caused to flow from them the rough but substantial outline of the whole history of man. One height produced nations of hunters, thus supporting and rendering necessary a savage state; another, more extended and mild, afforded a field to shepherd peoples and supplied them with tame animals; a third made agriculture easy and needful; while a fourth led to fishing and navigation and at length to trade. The structure of the earth, in its natural variety and diversity, rendered all such distinguishing conditions inescapable. Seas, mountain ranges and rivers are the most natural boundaries not only of lands but also of peoples, customs, languages and empires, and they have been, even in the greatest revolutions in human affairs, the directing lines or limits of world history. If otherwise mountains had arisen, rivers flowed, or coasts trended, then how very different would mankind have scattered over this tilting place of nations. . . .

Nature brings forth families; the most natural state therefore is also one people, with a national character of its own. For thousands of years this character preserves itself within the people and, if the native princes concern themselves with it, it can be cultivated in the most natural way: for a people is as much a plant of nature as is a family, except that it has more branches. Nothing therefore seems more contradictory to the true end of governments than the endless expansion of states, the wild confusion of races and nations under one scepter. An empire made up of a hundred peoples and 120 provinces which have been forced together is a monstrosity, not a state-body.

What is the supreme law which we note in all great historical events? In my opinion, it is this: that, in every part of our earth, all possible development is determined in part by the position and the necessities of the locality, in part by circumstances and the opportunities of the age, and in part by the inborn and self-nourishing character of the peoples. . . . All events in the human sphere, like all productions of nature, are decreed solely by time, locality, and national character, in short by the coordination of all the forces of life in their most positive individuality.

Active human powers are the springs of human history, and, as man originates from and in one race, so his body, education, and mode of thinking are genetic. Hence that striking national character, which, deeply imprinted on the most ancient peoples, is unequivocally displayed in all their operations on the earth. As the mineral water derives its component parts, its operative power, and its flavor from the soil through which it flows, so the ancient character of peoples arose from the family features, the climate, the way of life and education, the early actions and employments, that were peculiar to them. The manners of the fathers took deep root and became the internal prototype of the descendants. The mode of thinking of the Jews, which is best known to us from their writings and actions, may serve as an example: both in the land of their fathers and in the midst of other nations they remain as they were, and even when mixed with other peoples they may be distinguished for some generations onward. It was and is the same with all other peoples of antiquity—Egyptians, Chinese, Arabs, Hindus, etc. The more secluded they lived, nay frequently the more they were oppressed, the more their character was confirmed, so that, if every one of these nations had remained in its place, the earth might have been regarded as a garden where in one plot one human national plant, in another, another, bloomed in its proper form and nature, where in this corner one kind of national animal, in that, another, pursued its course according to its instincts and character. . . .

Has a people anything dearer than the speech of its fathers? In its speech resides its whole thought-domain, its tradition, history, religion, and basis of life, all its heart and soul. To deprive a people of its speech is to deprive it of its one eternal good. . . . As God tolerates all the different languages in the world, so also should a ruler not only tolerate but honor the various languages of his peoples. . . . The best culture of a people cannot be expressed through a foreign language; it thrives on the soil of a nation most beautifully, and, I may say, it thrives only by means of the nation's inherited and inheritable dialect. With language is created the heart of a people; and is it not a high concern, amongst so many peoples—Hungarians, Slavs, Rumanians, etc.—to plant seeds of well-being for the far future and in the way that is dearest and most appropriate to them? . . .

The savage who loves himself, his wife, and his child with quiet joy and glows with limited activity for his tribe as for his own life is, it seems to me, a more genuine being than that cultured shade who is enchanted by the shadow of his whole species. . . . In his poor hut, the former finds room for every stranger, receives him as a brother with impartial good humor and never asks whence he came. The inundated heart of the idle cosmopolitan is a home for no one. . . .

No greater injury can be inflicted on a nation than to be robbed of her national character, the peculiarity of her spirit and her language. Reflect on this and you will perceive our irreparable loss. Look about you in Germany for the character of the nation, for their own particular cast of thought, for their own peculiar vein of speech; where are they? Read Tacitus; there you will find their character: "The tribes of Germany, who never degrade themselves by mingling with others, form a peculiar, unadulterated, original nation, which is its own archetype. Even their physical development is universally uniform, despite the large numbers of the people," and so forth. Now look about you and say: "The tribes of Germany have been degraded by mingling with others; they have sacrificed their natural disposition in protracted intellectual servitude; and, since they have, in contrast to others, imitated a tyrannical prototype for a long time, they are, among all the nations of Europe, the least true to themselves." . . .

If Germany were only guided by the forces of the age, by the leading strings of her own culture, our intellectual disposition would doubtless be poor and restricted; but it would be true to our own soil, fashioned upon its own model, and not so misshapen and cast down. . . .

*William Blake*

# SELECTED POEMS

THE LAMB (1789); THE TYGER (1794); LONDON (1794); MOCK ON, MOCK ON, VOLTAIRE, ROUSSEAU (CA. 1800)

*William Blake (1757–1827) published his first volume of poetry while still a student of engraving at the Royal Academy in London. After opening his own print shop in 1784, he devised an original way to combine verbal and visual art in what he called "illuminated printing": he engraved his books, with each plate capable of containing both poetic text and illustration (see, for example, the reproduction of "London" in this reader). Over the next twenty years he published philosophical tracts, collections of lyric poetry, and epics and worked out his own cosmology in a series of books dealing with prophecy and myth. Influenced by the French Revolution, Romanticism, and his own mystic inclinations, Blake combined lyricism with intense feeling and poetry with social commentary, particularly in his best-known collection,* Songs of Innocence and of Experience *(1794), from which "The Lamb," "The Tyger," and "London" are taken.*

## THE LAMB (1789)

Little Lamb who made thee
Dost thou know who made thee
Gave thee life & bid thee feed.
By the stream & o'er the mead;
Gave thee clothing of delight,
Softest clothing wooly bright;
Gave thee such a tender voice,
Making all the vales rejoice!
Little Lamb who made thee
Dost thou know who made thee

Little Lamb I'll tell thee,
Little Lamb I'll tell thee!
He is called by thy name,
For he calls himself a Lamb:
He is meek & he is mild,
He became a little child:

176

I a child & thou a lamb,
We are called by his name.
Little Lamb God bless thee.
Little Lamb God bless thee.

## THE TYGER (1794)

Tyger Tyger, burning bright,
In the forests of the night,
What immortal hand or eye,
Could frame thy fearful symmetry?

In what distant deeps or skies
Burnt the fire of thine eyes!
On what wings dare he aspire?
What the hand, dare seize the fire?

And what shoulder, & what art,
Could twist the sinews of thy heart?
And when thy heart began to beat,
What dread hand? & what dread feet?

What the hammer? what the chain,
In what furnace was thy brain?
What the anvil? what dread grasp,
Dare its deadly terrors clasp?

When the stars threw down their spears
And water'd heaven with their tears:
Did he smile his work to see?
Did he who made the Lamb make thee?

Tyger, Tyger burning bright,
In the forests of the night:
What immortal hand or eye,
Dare frame thy fearful symmetry?

## LONDON (1794)

I wander thro' each charter'd street,
Near where the charter'd Thames does flow,
And mark in every face I meet
Marks of weakness, marks of woe.

In every cry of every Man,
In every Infants cry of fear,
In every voice: in every ban,
The mind-forg'd manacles I hear.

How the Chimney-sweepers cry
Every blackning Church appalls;

And the hapless Soldiers sigh
Runs in blood down Palace walls.

But most thro' midnight streets I hear
How the youthful Harlots curse
Blasts the new-born Infants tear,
And blights with plagues the Marriage hearse.

## Mock on, mock on, Voltaire, Rousseau (ca. 1800)

Mock on, mock on, Voltaire, Rousseau;
Mock on, mock on: 'tis all in vain!
You throw the sand against the wind,
And the wind blows it back again.

And every sand becomes a gem
Reflected in the beams divine;
Blown back they blind the mocking eye,
But still in Israel's paths they shine.

The atoms of Democritus
And Newton's particles of light
Are sands upon the Red Sea shore,
Where Israel's tents do shine so bright.

# William Wordsworth

## SELECTED POEMS

### THE TABLES TURNED (1798); LINES COMPOSED A FEW MILES ABOVE TINTERN ABBEY (1798)

## *from* PREFACE *TO* LYRICAL BALLADS (1800)

*William Wordsworth (1770–1850) was born in the Lake District in the north of England. Deeply sympathetic with the ideals of the French Revolution and unhappy in London, he returned to the country, where he set up house with his sister Dorothy and formed a poetic partnership with another young poet, Samuel Taylor Coleridge. In 1798 the two poets published an anonymous collection entitled* Lyrical Ballads; *a second edition appeared in 1800. In Wordsworth's poems, the natural world functions as a site in which poets can reflect upon themselves and their society, often finding in rural life a truthfulness that seems uncorrupted by the hurried pace and hypocrisy of the cities. In the preface to the second edition, Wordsworth calls for a new kind of poetry to be written in the language of the common man rather than in the stylized forms of the eighteenth century. His impassioned description of poetry is one of the best-known statements of Romanticism's celebration of nature, individual experience, and the imagination.*

### THE TABLES TURNED

*An Evening Scene on the Same Subject*

Up! up! my friend, and quit your books;
Or surely you'll grow double:
Up! up! my friend, and clear your looks;
Why all this toil and trouble?

The sun, above the mountain's head,
A freshening lustre mellow
Through all the long green fields has spread,
His first sweet evening yellow.

Books! 'tis a dull and endless strife:
Come, hear the woodland linnet,
How sweet his music! on my life,
There's more of wisdom in it.

And hark! how blithe the throstle sings!
He, too, is no mean preacher:
Come forth into the light of things,
Let nature be your teacher.

She has a world of ready wealth,
Our minds and hearts to bless—
Spontaneous wisdom breathed by health,
Truth breathed by cheerfulness.

One impulse from a vernal wood
May teach you more of man,
Of moral evil and of good,
Than all the sages can.

Sweet is the lore which nature brings;
Our meddling intellect
Mis-shapes the beauteous forms of things:—
We murder to dissect.

Enough of science and of art;
Close up those barren leaves;
Come forth, and bring with you a heart
That watches and receives.

# LINES

*Composed a Few Miles Above Tintern Abbey on Revisiting the Banks
of the Wye During a Tour, July 13, 1798*

Five years have past; five summers, with the length
Of five long winters! and again I hear
These waters, rolling from their mountain-springs
With a soft inland murmur.—Once again
Do I behold these steep and lofty cliffs,
That on a wild secluded scene impress
Thoughts of more deep seclusion; and connect
The landscape with the quiet of the sky.
The day is come when I again repose
Here, under this dark sycamore, and view
These plots of cottage-ground, these orchard-tufts,
Which at this season, with their unripe fruits,
Are clad in one green hue, and lose themselves
'Mid groves and copses. Once again I see
These hedge-rows, hardly hedge-rows, little lines
Of sportive wood run wild: these pastoral farms,
Green to the very door; and wreaths of smoke
Sent up, in silence, from among the trees!
With some uncertain notice, as might seem
Of vagrant dwellers in the houseless woods,
Or of some hermit's cave, where by his fire

The hermit sits alone.
                    These beauteous forms,
Through a long absence, have not been to me
As is a landscape to a blind man's eye:
But oft, in lonely rooms, and 'mid the din
Of towns and cities, I have owed to them
In hours of weariness, sensations sweet,
Felt in the blood, and felt along the heart;
And passing even into my purer mind,
With tranquil restoration:—feelings too
Of unremembered pleasure: such, perhaps,
As have no slight or trivial influence
On that best portion of a good man's life,
His little, nameless, unremembered, acts
Of kindness and of love. Nor less, I trust,
To them I may have owed another gift,
Of aspect more sublime; that blessed mood,
In which the burthen of the mystery,
In which the heavy and the weary weight
Of all this unintelligible world,
Is lightened:—that serene and blessed mood,
In which the affections gently lead us on,—
Until, the breath of this corporeal frame
And even the motion of our human blood
Almost suspended, we are laid asleep
In body, and become a living soul:
While with an eye made quiet by the power
Of harmony, and the deep power of joy,
We see into the life of things.
                   If this
Be but a vain belief, yet, oh! how oft—
In darkness and amid the many shapes
Of joyless daylight; when the fretful stir
Unprofitable, and the fever of the world,
Having hung upon the beatings of my heart—
How oft, in spirit, have I turned to thee,
O sylvan Wye! thou wanderer thro' the woods,
How often has my spirit turned to thee!
   And now, with gleams of half-extinguished thought,
With many recognitions dim and faint,
And somewhat of a sad perplexity,
The picture of the mind revives again:
While here I stand, not only with the sense
Of present pleasure, but with pleasing thoughts
That in this moment there is life and food
For future years. And so I dare to hope,
Though changed, no doubt, from what I was when first

I came among these hills; when like a roe
I bounded o'er the mountains, by the sides
Of the deep rivers, and the lonely streams,
Wherever nature led: more like a man
Flying from something that he dreads, than one
Who sought the thing he loved. For nature then
(The coarser pleasures of my boyish days,
And their glad animal movements all gone by)
To me was all in all.—I cannot paint
What then I was. The sounding cataract
Haunted me like a passion; the tall rock,
The mountain, and the deep and gloomy wood,
Their colours and their forms, were then to me
An appetite; a feeling and a love,
That had no need of a remoter charm,
By thought supplied, nor any interest
Unborrowed from the eye.—That time is past,
And all its aching joys are now no more,
And all its dizzy raptures. Not for this
Faint I, nor mourn nor murmur; other gifts
Have followed; for such loss, I would believe,
Abundant recompense. For I have learned
To look on nature, not as in the hour
Of thoughtless youth; but hearing oftentimes
The still, sad music of humanity,
Nor harsh nor grating, though of ample power
To chasten and subdue. And I have felt
A presence that disturbs me with the joy
Of elevated thoughts; a sense sublime
Of something far more deeply interfused,
Whose dwelling is the light of setting suns,
And the round ocean and the living air,
And the blue sky, and in the mind of man:
A motion and a spirit, that impels
All thinking things, all objects of all thought,
And rolls through all things. Therefore am I still
A lover of the meadows and the woods,
And mountains; and of all that we behold
From this green earth; of all the mighty world
Of eye, and ear,—both what they half create,
And what perceive; well pleased to recognise
In nature and the language of the sense
The anchor of my purest thoughts, the nurse,
The guide, the guardian of my heart, and soul
Of all my moral being.
                              Nor perchance,
If I were not thus taught, should I the more

Suffer my genial spirits to decay:
For thou art with me here upon the banks
Of this fair river; thou my dearest Friend,
My dear, dear friend; and in thy voice I catch
The language of my former heart, and read
My former pleasures in the shooting lights
Of thy wild eyes. Oh! yet a little while
May I behold in thee what I was once,
My dear, dear sister! and this prayer I make,
Knowing that Nature never did betray
The heart that loved her; 'tis her privilege,
Through all the years of this our life, to lead
From joy to joy: for she can so inform
The mind that is within us, so impress
With quietness and beauty, and so feed
With lofty thoughts, that neither evil tongues,
Rash judgments, nor the sneers of selfish men,
Nor greetings where no kindness is, nor all
The dreary intercourse of daily life,
Shall e'er prevail against us, or disturb
Our cheerful faith, that all which we behold
Is full of blessings. Therefore let the moon
Shine on thee in thy solitary walk;
And let the misty mountain-winds be free
To blow against thee: and, in after years,
When these wild ecstasies shall be matured
Into a sober pleasure; when thy mind
Shall be a mansion for all lovely forms,
Thy memory be as a dwelling-place
For all sweet sounds and harmonies; oh! then,
If solitude, or fear, or pain, or grief
Should be thy portion, with what healing thoughts
Of tender joy wilt thou remember me,
And these my exhortations! Nor, perchance—
If I should be where I no more can hear
Thy voice, nor catch from thy wild eyes these gleams
Of past existence—wilt thou then forget
That on the banks of this delightful stream
We stood together; and that I, so long
A worshipper of Nature, hither came
Unwearied in that service; rather say
With warmer love—oh! with far deeper zeal
Of holier love. Nor wilt thou then forget,
That after many wanderings, many years
Of absence, these steep woods and lofty cliffs,
And this green pastoral landscape, were to me
More dear, both for themselves and for thy sake!

## *from* Preface *to* Lyrical Ballads

The principal object, then, which I proposed to myself in these poems was to choose incidents and situations from common life, and to relate or describe them, throughout, as far as was possible, in a selection of language really used by men; and, at the same time, to throw over them a certain colouring of imagination, whereby ordinary things should be presented to the mind in an unusual way; and, further, and above all, to make these incidents and situations interesting by tracing in them, truly though not ostentatiously, the primary laws of our nature: chiefly, as far as regards the manner in which we associate ideas in a state of excitement. Low and rustic life was generally chosen, because in that condition, the essential passions of the heart find a better soil in which they can attain their maturity, are less under restraint, and speak a plainer and more emphatic language; because in that condition of life our elementary feelings co-exist in a state of greater simplicity, and, consequently, may be more accurately contemplated, and more forcibly communicated; because the manners of rural life germinate from those elementary feelings; and, from the necessary character of rural occupations, are more easily comprehended; and are more durable; and lastly, because in that condition the passions of men are incorporated with the beautiful and permanent forms of nature. The language, too, of these men is adopted (purified indeed from what appear to be its real defects, from all lasting and rational causes of dislike or disgust) because such men hourly communicate with the best objects from which the best part of language is originally derived; and because, from their rank in society and the sameness and narrow circle of their intercourse, being less under the influence of social vanity they convey their feelings and notions in simple and unelaborated expressions. Accordingly, such a language, arising out of repeated experience and regular feelings, is a more permanent, and a far more philosophical language, than that which is frequently substituted for it by poets, who think that they are conferring honour upon themselves and their art, in proportion as they separate themselves from the sympathies of men, and indulge in arbitrary and capricious habits of expression, in order to furnish food for fickle tastes, and fickle appetites, of their own creation.[1]

I cannot, however, be insensible of the present outcry against the triviality and meanness both of thought and language, which some of my contemporaries have occasionally introduced into their metrical compositions; and I acknowledge, that this defect, where it exists, is more dishonorable to the writer's own character than false refinement or arbitrary innovation, though I should contend at the same time that it is far less pernicious in the sum of its consequences. From such verses the poems in these volumes will be found distinguished at least by one mark of difference, that each of them has a worthy *purpose*. Not that I mean to say, that I always began to write with a distinct purpose formally conceived; but I believe that my habits of meditation have so formed my feelings, as that my descriptions of such objects as strongly excite those feelings, will be found to carry along with them a *purpose*. If in this opinion I am mistaken, I can have little right to the name of a poet. For all good poetry is the spontaneous overflow of powerful feelings: but though this be true, poems to which any value can be attached, were never produced on any variety of subjects but by a man who, being possessed of more than usual organic sensibility, had also thought long and deeply. For our

---

[1]It is worth while here to observe that the affecting parts of Chaucer are almost always expressed in language pure and universally intelligible even to this day [Wordsworth's note].

continued influxes of feeling are modified and directed by our thoughts, which are indeed the representatives of all our past feelings; and, as by contemplating the relation of these general representatives to each other we discover what is really important to men, so, by the repetition and continuance of this act, our feelings will be connected with important subjects, till at length, if we be originally possessed of much sensibility, such habits of mind will be produced, that, by obeying blindly and mechanically the impulses of those habits, we shall describe objects, and utter sentiments, of such a nature and in such connection with each other, that the understanding of the being to whom we address ourselves, if he be in a healthful state of association, must necessarily be in some degree enlightened, and his affections ameliorated.

•

Taking up the subject, then, upon general grounds, let me ask, what is meant by the word Poet? What is a Poet? To whom does he address himself? And what language is to be expected from him?—He is a man speaking to men: a man, it is true, endowed with more lively sensibility, more enthusiasm and tenderness, who has a greater knowledge of human nature, and a more comprehensive soul, than are supposed to be common among mankind; a man pleased with his own passions and volitions, and who rejoices more than other men in the spirit of life that is in him; delighting to contemplate similar volitions and passions as manifested in the goings-on of the Universe, and habitually impelled to create them where he does not find them. To these qualities he has added a disposition to be affected more than other men by absent things as if they were present; an ability of conjuring up in himself passions, which are indeed far from being the same as those produced by real events, yet (especially in those parts of the general sympathy which are pleasing and delightful) do more nearly resemble the passions produced by real events, than anything which, from the motions of their own minds merely, other men are accustomed to feel in themselves:—whence, and from practice, he has acquired a greater readiness and power in expressing what he thinks and feels, and especially those thoughts and feelings which, by his own choice, or from the structure of his own mind, arise in him without immediate external excitement.

But whatever portion of this faculty we may suppose even the greatest Poet to possess, there cannot be a doubt that the language which it will suggest to him must often, in liveliness and truth, fall short of that which is uttered by men in real life, under the actual pressure of those passions, certain shadows of which the Poet thus produces, or feels to be produced, in himself.

However exhalted a notion we would wish to cherish of the character of a Poet, it is obvious, that while he describes and imitates passions, his employment is in some degree mechanical, compared with the freedom and power of real and substantial action and suffering. So that it will be the wish of the Poet to bring his feelings near to those of the persons whose feelings he describes, nay, for short spaces of time, perhaps, to let himself slip into an entire delusion, and even confound and identify his own feelings with theirs; modifying only the language which is thus suggested to him by a consideration that he describes for a particular purpose, that of giving pleasure. Here, then, he will apply the principle of selection which has been already insisted upon. He will depend upon this for removing what would otherwise be painful or disgusting in the passion; he will feel that there is no necessity to trick out or to elevate nature: and, the more industriously he applies this principle, the deeper will be his faith that no words, which *his* fancy or imagination can suggest, will be to be compared with those which are the emanations of reality and truth.

But it may be said by those who do not object to the general spirit of these remarks, that, as it is impossible for the Poet to produce upon all occasions language as exquisitely fitted for the passion as that which the real passion itself suggests, it is proper that he should consider himself as in the situation of a translator, who does not scruple to substitute excellencies of another kind for those which are unattainable by him; and endeavours occasionally to surpass his original, in order to make some amends for the general inferiority to which he feels that he must submit. But this would be to encourage idleness and unmanly despair. Further, it is the language of men who speak of what they do not understand; who talk of Poetry as of a matter of amusement and idle pleasure; who will converse with us as gravely about a *taste* for Poetry, as they express it, as if it were a thing as indifferent as a taste for rope-dancing, or Frontiniac or Sherry. Aristotle, I have been told, has said, that Poetry is the most philosophic of all writing: it is so: its object is truth, not individual and local, but general, and operative; not standing upon external testimony, but carried alive into the heart by passion; truth which is its own testimony, which gives competence and confidence to the tribunal to which it appeals, and receives them from the same tribunal. Poetry is the image of man and nature. The obstacles which stand in the way of the fidelity of the Biographer and Historian, and of their consequent utility, are incalculably greater than those which are to be encountered by the Poet who comprehends the dignity of his art. The Poet writes under one restriction only, namely, the necessity of giving immediate pleasure to a human Being possessed of that information which may be expected from him, not as a lawyer, a physician, a mariner, an astronomer, or a natural philosopher, but as a Man. Except this one restriction, there is no object standing between the Poet and the image of things; between this, and the Biographer and Historian, there are a thousand.

Nor let this necessity of producing immediate pleasure be considered as a degradation of the Poet's art. It is far otherwise. It is an acknowledgment of the beauty of the universe, an acknowledgment the more sincere, because not formal, but indirect; it is a task light and easy to him who looks at the world in the spirit of love: further, it is a homage paid to the native and naked dignity of man, to the grand elementary principle of pleasure, by which he knows, and feels, and lives, and moves. We have no sympathy but what is propagated by pleasure: I would not be misunderstood; but wherever we sympathise with pain, it will be found that the sympathy is produced and carried on by subtle combinations with pleasure. We have no knowledge, that is, no general principles drawn from the contemplation of particular facts, but what has been built up by pleasure, and exists in us by pleasure alone. The Man of science, the Chemist and Mathematician, whatever difficulties and disgusts they may have had to struggle with, know and feel this. However painful may be the objects with which the Anatomist's knowledge is connected, he feels that his knowledge is pleasure; and where he has no pleasure he has no knowledge. What then does the Poet? He considers man and the objects that surround him as acting and re-acting upon each other, so as to produce an infinite complexity of pain and pleasure; he considers man in his own nature and in his ordinary life as contemplating this with a certain quantity of immediate knowledge, with certain convictions, intuitions, and deductions, which from habit acquire the quality of intuitions; he considers him as looking upon this complex scene of ideas and sensations, and finding everywhere objects that immediately excite in him sympathies which, from the necessities of his nature, are accompanied by an overbalance of enjoyment.

To this knowledge which all men carry about with them, and to these sympathies in which, without any other discipline than that of our daily life, we are fitted to take delight, the Poet principally directs his attention. He considers man and nature as essentially adapted to each other, and the mind of man as naturally the mirror of the fairest and most interesting properties of nature. And thus the Poet, prompted by this feeling of pleasure, which accompanies him through the whole course of his studies, converses with general nature, with affections akin to those, which, through labour and length of time, the Man of science has raised up in himself, by conversing with those particular parts of nature which are the objects of his studies. The knowledge both of the Poet and the Man of science is pleasure; but the knowledge of the one cleaves to us as a necessary part of our existence, our natural and unalienable inheritance; the other is a personal and individual acquisition, slow to come to us, and by no habitual and direct sympathy connecting us with our fellow-beings. The Man of science seeks truth as a remote and unknown benefactor; he cherishes and loves it in his solitude: the Poet, singing a song in which all human beings join with him, rejoices in the presence of truth as our visible friend and hourly companion. Poetry is the breath and finer spirit of all knowledge; it is the impassioned expression which is in the countenance of all Science. Emphatically may it be said of the Poet, as Shakespeare hath said of man, "that he looks before and after." He is the rock of defence for human nature; an upholder and preserver, carrying everywhere with him relationship and love. In spite of difference of soil and climate, of language and manners, of laws and customs: in spite of things silently gone out of mind, and things violently destroyed; the Poet binds together by passion and knowledge the vast empire of human society, as it is spread over the whole earth, and over all time. The objects of the Poet's thoughts are everywhere; though the eyes and senses of man are, it is true, his favourite guides, yet he will follow wheresoever he can find an atmosphere of sensation in which to move his wings. Poetry is the first and last of all knowledge—it is as immortal as the heart of man. If the labours of Men of science should ever create any material revolution, direct or indirect, in our condition, and in the impressions which we habitually receive, the Poet will sleep then no more than at present; he will be ready to follow the steps of the Man of science, not only in those general indirect effects, but he will be at his side, carrying sensation into the midst of the objects of the science itself. The remotest discoveries of the Chemist, the Botanist, or Mineralogist, will be as proper objects of the Poet's art as any upon which it can be employed, if the time should ever come when these things shall be familiar to us, and the relations under which they are contemplated by the followers of these respective sciences shall be manifestly and palpably material to us as enjoying and suffering beings. If the time should ever come when what is now called science, thus familiarised to men, shall be ready to put on, as it were, a form of flesh and blood, the Poet will lend his divine spirit to aid the transfiguration, and will welcome the Being thus produced, as a dear and genuine inmate of the household of man.—It is not, then, to be supposed that any one, who holds that sublime notion of Poetry which I have attempted to convey, will break in upon the sanctity and truth of his pictures by transitory and accidental ornaments, and endeavour to excite admiration of himself by arts, the necessity of which must manifestly depend upon the assumed meanness of his subject.

What has been thus far said applies to Poetry in general; but especially to those parts of composition where the Poet speaks through the mouths of his characters; and upon this point it appears to authorise the conclusion that there are few persons of good sense, who would not allow that the dramatic parts of composition are defective, in proportion as they deviate from the real language of nature, and are coloured by a diction of the Poet's own, either peculiar to him as an individual Poet or belonging simply to Poets in general; to a body of men who, from the circumstance of their compositions being in metre, it is expected will employ a particular language.

It is not, then, in the dramatic parts of composition that we look for this distinction of language; but still it may be proper and necessary where the Poet speaks to us in his own person and character. To this I answer by referring the Reader to the description before given of a Poet. Among the qualities there enumerated as principally conducing to form a Poet, is implied nothing differing in kind from other men, but only in degree. The sum of what was said is, that the Poet is chiefly distinguished from other men by a greater promptness to think and feel without immediate external excitement, and a greater power in expressing such thoughts and feelings as are produced in him in that manner. But these passions and thoughts and feelings are the general passions and thoughts and feelings of men. And with what are they connected? Undoubtedly with our moral sentiments and animal sensations, and with the causes which excite these; with the operations of the elements, and the appearances of the visible universe; with storm and sunshine, with the revolutions of the seasons, with cold and heat, with loss of friends and kindred, with injuries and resentments, gratitude and hope, with fear and sorrow. These, and the like, are the sensations and objects which the Poet describes, as they are the sensations of other men, and the objects which interest them. The Poet thinks and feels in the spirit of human passions. How, then, can his language differ in any material degree from that of all other men who feel vividly and see clearly? It might be *proved* that it is impossible. But supposing that this were not the case, the Poet might then be allowed to use a peculiar language when expressing his feelings for his own gratification, or that of men like himself. But Poets do not write for Poets alone, but for men. Unless therefore we are advocates for that admiration which subsists upon ignorance, and that pleasure which arises from hearing what we do not understand, the Poet must descend from this supposed height; and, in order to excite rational sympathy, he must express himself as other men express themselves. To this it may be added, that while he is only selecting from the real language of men, or, which amounts to the same thing, composing, accurately in the spirit of such selection, he is treading upon safe ground, and we know what we are to expect from him. Our feelings are the same with respect to metre; for, as it may be proper to remind the Reader, the distinction of metre is regular and uniform, and not, like that which is produced by what is usually called POETIC DICTION, arbitrary, and subject to infinite caprices upon which no calculation whatever can be made. In the one case, the Reader is utterly at the mercy of the Poet, respecting what imagery or diction he may choose to connect with the passion; whereas, in the other, the metre obeys certain laws, to which the Poet and Reader both willingly submit because they are certain, and because no interference is made by them with the passion, but such as the concurring testimony of ages has shown to heighten and improve the pleasure which co-exists with it.

# Georg Wilhelm Friedrich Hegel

## *from* THE PHILOSOPHY OF HISTORY
## (CA. 1822–1824)

*G*. *W.F. Hegel (1770–1831), one of the more imposing figures in the history of German phi-losophy, was professor at Heidelberg and then Berlin. His central project was to articulate a systematic way of comprehending human life, a means of understanding orderly processes underlying the chaotic surface of history. To this end, Hegel developed the concept of the dialectic: a given state, or initial thesis, produces a reaction in response, or antithesis, which in turn produces a resolution of opposites, or synthesis, which eventually becomes the next thesis. His interest in history was thus not in the particulars of specific events, but in large-scale metaphysical questions about how historical developments occur and how, philosophically, they might be explained. In* The Philosophy of History, *a book drawn from his university lectures, Hegel proposes a broad pattern for human history from its infancy in the Orient to its old age in the Europe of his own time.*

The History of the World travels from East to West, for Europe is absolutely the end of History, Asia the beginning. The History of the World has an East κατ' ἐξοχήν; (the term East in itself is entirely relative), for although the Earth forms a sphere, History performs no circle round it, but has on the contrary a determinate East, viz., Asia. Here rises the outward physical Sun, and in the West it sinks down: here consentaneously rises the Sun of self-consciousness, which diffuses a nobler brilliance. The History of the World is the discipline of the uncontrolled natural will, bringing it into obedience to a Universal principle and conferring subjective freedom. The East knew and to the present day knows only that *One* is Free; the Greek and Roman world, that *some* are free; the German World knows that *All* are free. The first political form therefore which we observe in History, is *Despotism,* the second *Democracy* and *Aristocracy,* the third *Monarchy.*

To understand this division we must remark that as the State is the universal spiritual life, to which individuals by birth sustain a relation of confidence and habit, and in which they have their existence and reality—the first question is, whether their actual life is an unreflecting use and habit combining them in this unity, or whether its constituent individuals are reflective and personal beings having a properly subjective and independent existence. In view of this, *substantial* [objective] freedom must be distinguished from *subjective* freedom. Substantial freedom is the abstract undeveloped Reason implicit in volition, proceeding to develop itself in the State. But in this phase of Reason there is still wanting personal insight and will, that is, subjective freedom; which is realized only in the Individual, and which constitutes the reflection of the Individual in his own conscience. Where there is merely substantial freedom, commands and laws are regarded as something fixed and abstract, to which the subject holds himself in absolute servitude. These laws need not concur with the desire of the individual, and the subjects are consequently like children, who obey their parents without will or insight of their own. But as subjective freedom arises, and man descends from the contemplation of external reality into his own soul, the contrast suggested by reflection arises, involving the Negation of Reality. The drawing back from the actual world forms *ipso facto* an antithesis, of which one side is the absolute Being—the Divine—the other the human subject as an individual. In that immediate, unreflected consciousness which characterizes the East, these two are not yet distinguished. The substantial world is distinct from the individual, but the antithesis has not yet created a schism between [absolute and subjective] Spirit.

The first phase—that with which we have to begin—is the *East*. Unreflected consciousness—substantial, objective, spiritual existence—forms the basis; to which the subjective will first sustains a relation in the form of faith, confidence, obedience. In the political life of the East we find a realized rational freedom, developing itself without advancing to *subjective* freedom. It is the childhood of History. Substantial forms constitute the gorgeous edifices of Oriental *Empires* in which we find all rational ordinances and arrangements, but in such a way, that individuals remain as mere accidents. These revolve round a centre, round the sovereign, who, as patriarch—not as despot in the sense of the *Roman* Imperial Constitution—stands at the head. For he has to enforce the moral and substantial: he has to uphold those essential ordinances which are already established; so that what among us belongs entirely to subjective freedom, here proceeds from the entire and general body of the State. The glory of Oriental conception is the One Individual as that substantial being to which all belongs, so that no other individual has a separate existence, or mirrors himself in his subjective freedom. All the riches of imagination and Nature are appropriated to that dominant existence in which subjective freedom is essentially merged; the latter looks for its dignity *not* in itself, but in that absolute object. All the elements of a complete State—even subjectivity—may be found there, but not yet harmonized with the grand substantial being. For outside the One Power—before which nothing can maintain an independent existence—there is only revolting caprice, which, beyond the limits of the central power, roves at will without purpose or result. Accordingly we find the wild hordes breaking out from the Upland—failing upon the countries in question, and laying them waste, or settling down in them, and giving up their wild life; but in all cases resultlessly lost in the central substance. This phase of Substantiality, since it has not taken up its antithesis into itself and overcome it, directly divides itself into two elements. On the one side we see duration, stability—Empires belonging to mere space, as it were [as distinguished from Time]—unhistorical History;—as for example, in China, the State based on the Family relation;—a paternal Government, which holds together the constitution by its provident care, its admonitions, retributive or rather disciplinary inflictions;—a prosaic Empire, because the antithesis of Form, viz., Infinity, Ideality, has not yet asserted itself. On the other side, the

Form of Time stands contrasted with this spatial stability. The States in question, without undergoing any change in themselves, or in the principle of their existence, are constantly changing their position towards each other. They are in ceaseless conflict, which brings on rapid destruction. The opposing principle of individuality enters into these conflicting relations; but it is itself as yet only unconscious, merely natural Universality—Light, which is not yet the light of the personal soul. This History, too (*i.e.,* of the struggles before-mentioned) is, for the most part, really *unhistorical,* for it is only the repetition of the same majestic ruin. The new element, which in the shape of bravery, prowess, magnanimity, occupies the place of the previous despotic pomp, goes through the same circle of decline and subsidence. This subsidence is therefore not really such, for through all this restless change no advance is made. History passes at this point—and only outwardly, *i.e.,* without connection with the previous phase—to Central Asia. Continuing the comparison with the ages of the individual man, this would be the boyhood of History, no longer manifesting the repose and trustingness of the child, but boisterous and turbulent. The Greek World may then be compared with the period of adolescence, for here we have individualities forming themselves. This is the *second* main principle in human History. Morality is, as in Asia, a principle; but it is morality impressed on individuality, and consequently denoting the free volition of Individuals. Here, then, is the Union of the Moral with the subjective Will, or the Kingdom of *Beautiful Freedom,* for the Idea is united with a plastic form. It is not yet regarded abstractedly, but immediately bound up with the Real, as in a beautiful work of Art; the Sensuous bears the stamp and expression of the Spiritual. This Kingdom is consequently true Harmony; the world of the most charming, but perishable or quickly passing bloom: it is the natural, unreflecting observance of what is *becoming*—not yet true *Morality.* The individual will of the Subject adopts unreflectingly the conduct and habit prescribed by Justice and the Laws. The Individual is therefore in unconscious unity with the Idea—the social weal. That which in the East is divided into two extremes—the substantial as such, and the individuality absorbed in it—meets here. But these distinct principles are only *immediately* in unity, and consequently involve the highest degree of contradiction; for this æsthethic Morality has not yet passed through the struggle of subjective freedom, in its second birth, its *palingenesis;* it is not yet purified to the standard of the free subjectivity that is the essence of true morality.

The third phase is the realm of abstract Universality (in which the Social aim absorbs all individual aims): it is the *Roman State,* the severe labors of the *Manhood* of History. For true manhood acts neither in accordance with the caprice of a despot, nor in obedience to a graceful caprice of its own; but works for a general aim, one in which the individual perishes and realizes his own private object only in that general aim. The State begins to have all abstract existence, and to develop itself for a definite object, in accomplishing which its members have indeed a share, but not a complete and concrete one [calling their whole being into play]. Free *individuals* are sacrificed to the severe demands of the *National* objects, to which they must surrender themselves in this service of abstract generalization. The Roman State is not a repetition of such a State of Individuals as the Athenian Polis was. The geniality and joy of soul that existed there have given place to harsh and rigorous toil. The interest of History is detached from individuals, but these gain for themselves abstract, formal Universality. The Universal subjugates the individuals; they have to merge their own interests in it; but in return the abstraction which they themselves embody—that is to say, their personality—is recognized: in their individual capacity they become persons with definite rights as such. In the same sense as individuals may be said to be incorporated in the abstract idea of Person, *National Individualities* (those of the Roman Provinces) have also to experience this fate: in this form of Universality their concrete forms are crushed, and incorporated with it as a homogeneous and indifferent mass. Rome becomes a Pantheon of all deities, and of all Spiritual existence, but these divinities and this Spirit do not retain their proper vitality.—The development of the State in question proceeds in two directions. On the one hand, as based on reflection—abstract Universality—it has the express outspoken antithesis in itself: it therefore essentially involves in itself the struggle which that antithesis supposes; with the necessary issue, that individual caprice—the purely contingent and thoroughly worldly power of *one despot*—gets the better of that abstract universal principle. At the very outset we have the antithesis between the Aim of the State as the abstract universal principle on the one hand, and the abstract personality of the individual on the other hand. But when subsequently, in the historical development, individuality gains the ascendant, and the breaking up of the community into its component atoms can only be restrained by external compulsion, then the subjective might of *individual despotism* comes forward to play its part, as if summoned to fulfil this task. For the mere abstract compliance with Law implies on the part of the subject of law the supposition that he has not attained to self-organization and self-control; and this principle of obedience, instead of being hearty and voluntary, has for its motive and ruling power only the arbitrary and contingent disposition of the individual; so that the latter is led to seek consolation for the loss of his freedom in exercising and developing his private right. This is the purely *worldly* harmonization of the antithesis. But in the next place, the pain inflicted by Despotism begins to be felt, and Spirit driven back into its utmost depths, leaves the godless world, seeks for a harmony in itself, and begins now an inner life—a complete concrete subjectivity, which possesses at the same time a substantiality that is not grounded in mere external existence. Within the soul therefore arises the *Spiritual* pacification of the struggle, in the fact that the individual personality, instead of following its own capricious choice, is purified and elevated into universality;—a subjectivity that of its own free will adopts principles tending to the good of all—reaches, in fact, a divine personality. To that worldly empire, this Spiritual one wears a predominant aspect of opposition, as the empire of a subjectivity that has attained to the knowledge of itself—itself in its essential nature—the Empire of Spirit in its full sense.

The *German* world appears at this point of development—the fourth phase of World-History. This would answer in the comparison with the periods of human life to its *Old Age*. The Old Age of *Nature* is weakness; but that of *Spirit* is its perfect maturity and *strength*, in which it returns to unity with itself, but in its fully developed character as *Spirit*.—This fourth phase begins with the Reconciliation presented in Christianity; but only in the germ, without national or political development. We must therefore regard it as commencing rather with the enormous contrast between the spiritual, religious principle, and the barbarian Real World. For Spirit as the consciousness of in inner World is, at the commencement, itself still in an abstract form. All that is *secular* is consequently given over to rudeness and capricious violence. The *Mohammedan* principle—the enlightenment of the Oriental World—is the first to contravene this barbarism and caprice. We find it developing itself later and more rapidly than Christianity; for the latter needed eight centuries to grow up into a political form. But that principle of the German World which we are now discussing, attained concrete reality only in the history of the German Nations. The contrast of the Spiritual principle animating the *Ecclesiastical* State, with the rough and wild barbarism of the *Secular* State, is here likewise present. The Secular *ought* to be in harmony with the Spiritual principle, but we find nothing more than the *recognition* of that obligation. The Secular power forsaken by the Spirit, must in the first instance vanish in presence of the Ecclesiastical [as representative of Spirit]; but while this latter degrades itself to rnere secularity, it loses its influence with the loss of its proper character and vocation. From this corruption of the Ecclesiastical element—that is, of the Church—results the higher form of rational thought. Spirit once more driven back upon itself, produces its work in an intellectual shape, and becomes capable of realizing the Ideal of Reason from the Secular principle alone. Thus it happens, that in virtue of elements of Universality, which have the principle of Spirit as their basis, the empire of Thought is established actually and concretely. The antithesis of Church and State vanishes. The Spiritual becomes reconnected with the Secular, and develops this latter as an independently organic existence. The State no longer occupies a position of real inferiority to the Church, and is no longer subordinate to it. The latter asserts no prerogative, and the Spiritual is no longer an element foreign to the State. Freedom has found the means of realizing its Ideal—its true existence. This is the ultimate result which the process of History is intended to accomplish, and we have to traverse in detail the long track which has been thus cursorily traced out. Yet length of Time is something entirely relative, and the element of Spirit is Eternity. Duration, properly speaking, cannot be said to belong to it.

—*trans. J. Sibree*

# Johann Wolfgang von Goethe

## *from* THE THEORY OF A WORLD LITERATURE (CA. 1827–1830)

*Johann Wolfgang von Goethe (1749–1832) was a prolific poet, playwright, novelist, and philosopher of aesthetics. He was extraordinarily influential in literary and aesthetic circles in Germany and across Europe. His first novel,* The Sorrows of Young Werther *(1774), was immensely popular, and its protagonist became a model of the romantic sensibility: young enthusiasts dressed like Werther, read the books he read, and even committed suicide as he had. Goethe's major dramatic work,* Faust *(1808, 1832), on which he worked for decades, re-created the old story of selling one's soul to the devil in exchange for knowledge and power. Goethe found poetic inspiration in traditional German folk sources and in the classical heritage he had experienced directly while traveling in Italy. The ideas about world literature he expressed late in life reflect both his belief in distinct national differences and his ideal of a world literature in which "free spiritual intercourse" could occur across cultural boundaries.*

## I (1827)

Everywhere we hear and read of the progress of the human race, of the broader view of international and human relations. Since it is not my office here to define or qualify these broad generalities, I shall merely acquaint my friends with my conviction that there is being formed a universal world-literature, in which an honorable rôle is reserved for us Germans. All the nations review our work; they praise, censure, accept, and reject, imitate and misrepresent us, open or close their hearts to us. All this we must accept with equanimity, since this attitude, taken as a whole, is of great value to us.

We experience the same thing from our own countrymen, and why should the nations agree among themselves if fellow-citizens do not understand how to unite and coöperate with each other? In a literary sense we have a good start of the other nations; they will always be learning to prize us more, even if they only show it by borrowing from us without thanks, and making use of us without giving recognition of the fact.

As the military and physical strength of a nation develops from its internal unity and cohesion, so must its aesthetic and ethical strength grow gradually from a similar unanimity of feeling and ideas. This, however, can only be accomplished with time. I look back as a coöperator in this work over many years and reflect how a German literature has been brought together out of heterogeneous, if not conflicting, elements,—a literature which for that reason is only peculiarly *one* in the sense that it is composed in *one* language,—which, however, out of a variety of wholly different talents and abilities, minds and actions, criticisms and undertakings, gradually draws out to the light of day the true inner soul of a people.

## II (1827)

My sanguine suggestion that our present active epoch with its increasing communication between the nations might soon hope for a world-literature has been taken up by chance by our neighbors of the west, who indeed can accomplish great things in this same direction. They express themselves on the subject in the following manner:

### Le Globe, *Tome V., No. 91.*

"Every nation indeed, when its turn comes, feels that tension which, like the attractive power of physical bodies, draws one towards the other, and eventually will unite in one universal sympathy all the races of which humanity consists. The endeavor of scholars to understand one another and compare one another's work is by no means new; the Latin language in former times has provided an admirable vehicle for this purpose. But however they labored and strove, the barriers by which peoples were separated began to divide them also, and hurt their intellectual intercourse. The instrument of which they made use could only satisfy a certain range and course of ideas, so that they touched each other only through the intellect, instead of directly through the feelings and through poetry. Travel, the study of languages, periodical literature, have taken the place of that universal language, and establish many intimate and harmonious relations which *it* could never cultivate. Even the nations that devote themselves chiefly to trade and industry are most concerned with this exchange of ideas. England, whose home activity is so tremendous, whose life is so busy, that it seems as if it would be able to study nothing but itself, at the present time is showing a symptom of this need and desire to broaden its connection with the outside world and widen its horizon. Its Reviews, with which we are already familiar, are not enough for them; two new periodicals, devoted especially to foreign literature, and coöperating together towards that end, are to appear regularly."

•

Left to itself every literature will exhaust its vitality, if it is not refreshed by the interest and contributions of a foreign one. What naturalist does not take pleasure in the wonderful things that he sees produced by reflection in a mirror? Now what a mirror in the field of ideas and morals means, every one has experienced in himself, and once his attention is aroused, he will understand how much of his education he owes to it.

## III (1828)

•

These journals, as they win an ever wider public, will contribute in the most effective way towards that universal world-literature for which we are hoping. Only, we repeat, the idea is not that the nations shall think alike, but that they shall learn how to understand each other, and, if they do not care to love one another, at least that they will learn to tolerate one another. Several societies now exist for the purpose of making the British Isles acquainted with the continent, and are working effectively and with a practical unanimity of opinion. We continentals can learn from them the intellectual background of the time across the channel, what they are thinking and what their judgments about things are. On the whole, we acknowledge gladly that they go about the work with intense seriousness, with industry and tolerance and general good-will. The result for us will be that we shall be compelled to think again of our own recent literature, which we have in some measure already put to one side, and to consider and examine it anew. . . .

# IV (1829)

### *More About a World Literature*

### The Difficulties

If a world-literature, such as is inevitable with the ever-increasing facility of communication, is to be formed in the near future, we must expect from it nothing more and nothing different from what it can and does accomplish.

The wide world, extensive as it is, is only an expanded fatherland, and will, if looked at aright, be able to give us no more than what our home soil can endow us with also. What pleases the crowd spreads itself over a limitless field, and, as we already see, meets approval in all countries and regions. The serious and intellectual meets with less success, but those who are devoted to higher and more profitable things will learn to know each other more quickly and more intimately. For there are everywhere in the world such men, to whom the truth and the progress of humanity are of interest and concern. But the road which they pursue, the pace which they keep, is not to everybody's liking; the particularly aggressive wish to advance faster, and so turn aside, and prevent the furthering of that which they could promote. The serious-minded must therefore form a quiet, almost secret, company, since it would be futile to set themselves against the current of the day; rather must they manfully strive to maintain their position till the flood has past. Their principal consolation, and indeed encouragement, such men must find in the fact that truth is serviceable. If they can discover this relation, and exhibit its meaning and influence in a vital way, they will not fail to produce a powerful effect, indeed one that will extend over a range of years.

### The Encouragements

Since it is often profitable to present to the reader not one's bald thought, but rather to awaken and stimulate his own thinking, it may be useful to recall the above observation which I had occasion to write down some time ago.

The question whether this or that occupation to which a man devotes himself is useful recurs often enough in the course of time, and must come before us especially at this time when it is no longer permitted to any one to live quietly according to his tastes, satisfied, moderate, and without demands upon him. The external world is so importunate and exciting that each one of us is threatened with being carried away in the whirlpool. In order to satisfy his own needs, each one sees himself compelled to attend almost instantaneously to the requirements of others; and the question naturally arises whether he has any skill or readiness to satisfy these pressing duties. There seems to be nothing left to us to say than that only the purest and strictest egoism can save us; but this must be a self-conscious resolution, thoroughly felt and calmly expressed.

Let each one ask himself for what he is best fitted, and let him cultivate this most ardently and wisely in himself and for himself; let him consider himself successively as apprentice, as journeyman, as older journeyman, and finally, but with the greatest of circumspection, as master.

If he can, with discriminating modesty, increase his demands on the external world only with the growth of his own capabilities, thus insinuating himself into the world's good graces by being useful, then he will attain his purpose step by step, and if he succeeds in reaching the highest level, will be able to influence men and things with ease.

Life, if he studies it closely, will teach him the opportunities and the hindrances which present or intrude themselves upon him; but this much the man of practical wisdom will always have before his eyes:—To tire oneself out for the sake of the favor of to-day brings no profit for to-morrow or after.

### Other Considerations

Every nation has peculiarities by which it is distinguished from the others, and it is by these distinguishing traits that nations are also attracted to and repelled from one another. The external expressions of these inner idiosyncrasies appear to the others in most cases strikingly disagreeable, or, if endurable, merely amusing. This is why, too, we always respect a nation less than it deserves. The inner traits, on the other hand, are not known or recognized, by foreigners or even by the nation itself; for the inner nature of a whole nation, as well as the individual man, works all unconsciously. At the end we wonder, we are astounded, at what appears.

These secrets I do not pretend to know, much less to have the cleverness to express them if I did. Only this much will I say,—that, so far as my insight goes, the characteristic intellectual and spiritual activity of the French is now at its height again, and for that reason will exercise soon again a great influence on the civilized world. I would gladly say more, but it leads too far; one has to be so detailed in order to be understood, and to make acceptable what one has to say.

It was not merely permissible but highly admirable that a society of Germans was formed for the special purpose of studying German poetry; since these persons, as cultured men acquainted with the other fields of German literature and politics both generally and in detail, were well qualified to select and judge works of belles-lettres and use them as a basis for intellectual, as well as pleasurable and stimulating, conversation.

Some one may say that the best literature of a nation cannot be discovered or recognized, unless one brings home to one's mind the whole complex of its circumstances and social conditions. Something of all this can be obtained from the papers, which give us enough detailed information of public affairs. But this is not enough; we must add to it what foreigners in their critical journals and reviews are accustomed to say about themselves and about other nations, particularly the Germans,—their ideas and opinions, their interest in and reception of our productions.

•

French poetry, like French literature, is not distinct in spirit from the life and passions of the nation as a whole. In recent times it appears naturally always as the "Opposition," and summons every genius to make the most of his talent in resisting the "powers that be," which since they are endowed with force do not need to be intellectual or spiritual.

If we follow this verse, which reveals so much, we see deep down into the soul of the nation, and from the way in which they judge us, more or less favorably, we can at the same time learn to judge ourselves. And it can do no harm to have some one make us think about ourselves. . . .

## V (1830)

There has been talk for some time of a general world-literature, and indeed not without justice. For the nations, after they had been shaken into confusion and mutual conflict by the terrible wars, could not return to their settled and independent life again without noticing that they had learned many foreign ideas and ways, which they had unconsciously adopted, and had come to feel here and there previously unrecognized spiritual and intellectual needs. Out of this arose the feeling of neighborly relations, and, instead of shutting themselves up as before, they gradually came to desire the adoption of some sort of more or less free spiritual intercourse.

This movement, it is true, has lasted only a short time, but still long enough to start considerable speculation, and to acquire from it, as one must always from any kind of foreign trade, both profit and enjoyment.

*—trans. Randolph S. Bourne*

# Andrew Ure

## *from* THE PHILOSOPHY
## OF MANUFACTURES (1835)

*Andrew Ure (1778–1857), born into a wealthy Scottish family, was professor of chemistry at a college in Glasgow and then a research chemist for the British government. His* A Dictionary of Chemistry *became a standard reference work on the subject. Like other scientifically minded Victorians, he was keenly interested in industrial processes and their social effects. In* The Philosophy of Manufactures, or, an Exposition of the Scientific, Moral, and Commercial Economy of the Factory System of Great Britain, *he reports that he found "the scene of industry . . . always exhilarating," advocates safe industrial practices, and argues that workers benefit from factories more than they suffer. Ure's book apparently found an interested audience: the following selection comes from the third edition, which appeared posthumously in 1861.*

---

. . . When the wandering savage becomes a citizen, he renounces many of his dangerous pleasures in return for tranquility and protection. He can no longer gratify at will a revengeful spirit upon his foes, nor seize with violence a neighbor's possessions. In like manner, when the handicraftsman exchanges hard work with fluctuating employment and pay, for continuous work of a lighter kind with steady wages, he must necessarily renounce his old prerogative of stopping when he pleases, because he would thereby throw the whole establishment into disorder. Of the amount of injury resulting from the violation of the rules of automatic labor he can hardly ever be the proper judge; just as mankind at large can never fully estimate the evils consequent upon an infraction of God's moral law. Yet the factory operative, little versant in the great operations of political economy, currency, and trade, and actuated too often by an invidious feeling toward the capitalist who animates his otherwise torpid talents, is easily persuaded by artful demagogues, that his sacrifice of time and skill is beyond proportion of his recompense, or that fewer hours of industry would be an ample equivalent for his wages. This notion seems to have taken an early and inveterate hold of the factory mind, and to have been riveted from time to time by the leaders of those secret combinations, so readily formed among a peculiar class of men, concentrated in masses within a narrow range of country.

Instead of repining as they have done at the prosperity of their employers, and concerting odious measures to blast it, they should, on every principle of gratitude and self-interest, have rejoiced at the success resulting from their labors, and by regularity and skill have recommended themselves to monied men desirous of engaging in a profitable concern, and of procuring qualified hands to conduct it. Thus good workmen would have advanced their condition to that of overlookers, managers, and partners in new mills, and have increased at the same time the demand for their companions' labor in the market. It is only by an undisturbed progression of this kind that the rate of wages can be permanently raised or upheld. Had it not been for the violent collisions and interruptions resulting from erroneous views among the operatives, the factory system would have developed still more rapidly and beneficially for all concerned than it has, and would have exhibited still more frequently gratifying examples of skilful workmen becoming opulent proprietors. Every misunderstanding either repels capital altogether, or diverts it from flowing, for a time, in the channels of trade liable to strikes.

No master would wish to have any wayward children to work within the walls of his factory, who do not mind their business without beating, and he therefore usually fines and turns away any spinners who are known to maltreat their assistants. Hence, ill-usage of any kind is a very rare occurrence. I have visited many factories, both in Manchester and in the surrounding districts, during a period of several months, entering the spinning rooms, unexpectedly, and often alone, at different times of day, and I never saw a single instance of corporal chastisement inflicted on a child, nor indeed did I ever see children in ill-humor. They seemed to be always cheerful and alert, taking pleasure in the light play of their muscles—enjoying the mobility natural to their age. The scene of industry, far from exciting sad emotions in my mind, was always exhilarating. It was delightful to observe the nimbleness with which they pieced the broken ends, as the mule-carriage began to recede from the fixed roller-beam, and to see them at leisure, after a few seconds' exercise of their tiny fingers, to amuse themselves in any attitude they chose, till the stretch and winding-on were once more completed. The work of these lively elves seemed to resemble a sport, in which habit gave them a pleasing dexterity. Conscious of their skill, they were delighted to show it off to any stranger. As to exhaustion by the day's work, they evinced no trace of it on emerging from the mill in the evening, for they immediately began to skip about any neighboring play-ground, and to commence their little amusements with the same alacrity as boys issuing from a school. It is moreover my firm conviction, that if children are not ill-used by bad parents or guardians, but receive in food and raiment the full benefit of what they earn, they would thrive better in our modern factories than if left alone in apartments too often ill-aired, damp and cold.

Of all the modern prejudices that exist with regard to factory labor, there is none more unfounded than that which ascribes to it excessive tedium and irksomeness above other occupations, owing to its being carried on in conjunction with the "unceasing motion of the steam-engine." In an establishment for spinning or weaving cotton, all the hard work is performed by the steam-engine, which leaves for the attendant no hard labor at all, and literally nothing to do in general; but at intervals to perform some delicate operation, such as joining threads that break, taking the cops off the spindles, etc. And it is so far from being true that the work in a factory is incessant, because the motion of the steam-engine is incessant, that the labor is not incessant on that very account, because it is performed in conjunction with the steam-engine. Of all manufacturing employments, those are by far the most irksome and incessant in which steam-engines are not employed, as in lace-running and stocking-weaving, and the way to prevent an employment from being incessant is to introduce a steam-engine into it. . . .

The factory system, then, instead of being detrimental to the comfort of the laboring population, is its grand Palladium; for the more complicated and extensive the machinery required for any manufacture, the less risk is there of its agents being injured by the competition of foreign manufactures, and the greater inducement and ability has the mill-owner to keep up the wages of his work-people. The main reason why they are so high is, that they form a small part of the value of the manufactured article, so that if reduced too low by a sordid master, they would render his operatives less careful, and thereby injure the quality of their work more than could be compensated by saving in wages. . . .

The most recent, and perhaps most convincing, evidence regarding the healthiness of factory children is that given in the official report of Mr. Harrison, the inspecting surgeon appointed for the mills of Preston and its vicinity. There are 1,656 under 18 years of age, of whom 952 are employed in spinning-rooms, 468 in carding rooms, 128 at power-looms, and 108 in winding, skewering cops, etc. "I have made very particular inquiries respecting the health of every child whom I have examined, and I find that the average annual sickness of each child is not more than four days; at least, that not more than four days on an average are lost by each child in a year, in consequence of sickness. This includes disorders of every kind, for the most part induced by causes wholly unconnected with factory labor. I have been not a little surprised to find so little sickness which can fairly be attributed to mill work. I have met with very few children who have suffered from injuries occasioned by machinery; and the protection, especially in new factories, is so complete, that accidents will, I doubt not, speedily become rare. I have not met with a single instance out of the 1,656 children whom I have examined, of deformity, that is referable to factory labor. It must be admitted, that factory children do not present the same blooming robust appearance as is witnessed among children who labor in the open air, but I question if they are not more exempt from acute diseases, and do not, on the average, suffer less sickness than those who are regarded as having more healthy employments. The average age at which the children of this district enter the factories is ten years and two months; and the average age of all the young persons together is fourteen years."

# *from* THE WOMEN OF ENGLAND: THEIR SOCIAL DUTIES AND DOMESTIC HABITS (1839)

*Sarah Stickney Ellis (1799–1872) was raised a Quaker and became an essayist and writer of advice manuals whose work was widely read by members of England's middle classes. After joining the Congregationalists in 1837, Ellis became involved in the temperance movement. In the 1840s, following the great success of* The Women of England: Their Social Duties and Domestic Habits *(and its sequels,* The Daughters of England, The Mothers of England, *and* The Wives of England*) she established a girls' school to further advocate her theories of proper feminine education. To Ellis, the separate private and public spheres of an increasingly affluent Victorian society were evidence of the nation's industriousness and moral character. In this selection she argues that middle-class women, now less burdened by the menial work necessary to sustain day-to-day existence, should turn their attention from frivolous diversions or public affairs to the creation of domestic comforts. It is women's duty to serve as exemplars of virtue and moral excellence.*

Every country has its peculiar characteristics, not only of climate and scenery, of public institutions, government, and laws; but every country has also its *moral characteristics,* upon which is founded its true title to a station, either high or low, in the scale of nations. . . .

. . . It is not . . . from the aristocracy of the land that the characteristics of English women should be taken. . . . Neither is it entirely amongst the indigent and most laborious of the community, that we can with propriety look for those strong features of nationality, which stamp the moral character of different nations. . . .

In looking around, then, upon our "nation of shop-keepers," we readily perceive that by dividing society into three classes, as regards what is commonly called rank, the middle class must include so vast a portion of the intelligence and moral power of the country at large, that it may not improperly be designated the pillar of our nation's strength, its base being the important class of the laborious poor, and its rich and highly ornamental capital, the ancient nobility of the land. In no other country is society thus beautifully proportioned, and England should beware of any deviation from the order and symmetry of her national column. . . .

. . . It is, then, strictly speaking, to those who belong to that great mass of the population of England which is connected with trade and manufactures;—or, in order to make the application more direct, to that portion of it who are restricted to the services of from one to four domestics,—who, on the one hand, enjoy the advantages of a liberal education, and, on the other, have no pretension to family rank. . . .

It is from the class of females above described, that we naturally look for the highest tone of moral feeling, because they are at the same time removed from the pressing necessities of absolute poverty, and admitted to the intellectual privileges of the great: and thus, while they enjoy every facility in the way of acquiring knowledge, it is their still higher privilege not to be exempt from the domestic duties which call forth the best energies of the female character. . . .

It is perhaps the nearest approach we can make toward any thing like a definition of what is most striking in the characteristics of the women of England, to say, that the nature of their domestic circumstances is such as to invest their characters with the threefold recommendation of *promptitude in action, energy of thought, and benevolence of feeling.* With all the responsibilities of family comfort and social enjoyment resting upon them, and unaided by those troops of menials who throng the halls of the affluent and the great, they are kept alive to the necessity of making their own personal exertions conducive to the great end of promoting the happiness of those around them. . . .

"What shall I do to gratify myself—to be admired—or to vary the tenor of my existence?" are not the questions which a woman of right feelings asks on first awaking to the avocations of the day. Much more congenial to the highest attributes of woman's character, are inquiries such as these: "How shall I endeavor through this day to turn the time, the health, and the means permitted me to enjoy, to the best account? Is anyone sick, I must visit their chamber without delay, and try to give their apartment an air of comfort, by arranging such things as the wearied nurse may not have thought of. Is any one about to set off on a journey, I must see that the early meal is spread, to prepare it with my own hands, in order that the servant, who was working late last night, may profit by unbroken rest. Did I fail in what was kind or considerate to any of the family yesterday; I will meet her this morning with a cordial welcome, and show, in the most delicate way I can, that I am anxious to atone for the past. Was any one exhausted by the last day's exertion, I will be an hour before them this morning, and let them see that their labor is so much in advance. Or, if nothing extraordinary occurs to claim my attention, I will meet the family with a consciousness that, being the least engaged of any member of it, I am consequently the most at liberty to devote myself to the general good of the whole, by cultivating cheerful conversation, adapting myself to the prevailing tone of feeling, and leading those who are least happy, to think and speak of what will make them more so."

. . . Good household management, conducted on this plan, is indeed a science well worthy of attention. It comprises so much, as to invest it with an air of difficulty on the first view; but no woman can reasonably complain of incapability, because nature has endowed the sex with perceptions so lively and acute, that where benevolence is the impulse, and principle the foundation upon which they act, experience will soon teach them by what means they may best accomplish the end they have in view. . . .

The domestic woman, moving in a comparatively limited circle, is not necessarily confined to a limited number of ideas, but can often expatiate upon subjects of mere local interest with a vigor of intellect, a freshness of feeling, and a liveliness of fancy, which create in the mind of the uninitiated stranger, a perfect longing to be admitted into the home associations from whence are derived such a world of amusement, and so unfailing a relief from the severer duties of life. . . .

Above all other characteristics of the women of England, the strong moral feeling pervading even their most trifling and familiar actions, ought to be mentioned as most conducive to the maintenance of that high place which they so justly claim in the society of their native land. . . . The women of England are not surpassed by those of any other country for their clear perception of the right and the wrong of common and familiar things, for their reference to principle in the ordinary affairs of life, and for their united maintenance of that social order, sound integrity, and domestic peace, which constitute the foundation of all that is most valuable in the society of our native land.

Much as I have said of the influence of the domestic habits of my country-women, it is, after all, to the prevalence of religious instruction, and the operation of religious principle upon the heart, that the consistent maintenance of their high tone of moral character is to be attributed. . . . Women are said to be more easily brought under this influence than men; and we consequently see, in places of public worship, and on all occasions in which religious object is the motive for exertion, a greater proportion of women than men. . . .

If . . . all was confusion and neglect at home—filial appeals unanswered—domestic comforts uncalculated—husbands, sons, and brothers referred to servants for all the little offices of social kindness, in order that the ladies of the family might hurry away at the appointed time to some committee-room, scientific lecture, or public assembly: however laudable the object for which they met, there would be sufficient cause why their cheeks should be mantled with the blush of burning shame . . . which those whose charity has not begun at home, ought never to appropriate to themselves.

It is a widely mistaken notion to suppose that the sphere of usefulness recommended here, is a humiliating and degraded one. . . . With [some women] it is a favorite plea, brought forward in extenuation of their own uselessness, that they have no influence—that they are not leading women—that society takes no note of them. . . .

It is an important consideration, that from such women as these, myriads of immortal beings derive that early bias of character, which under Providence decides their fate, not only in this world, but in the world to come. And yet they flutter on, and say they have no influence—they do not aspire to be leading women—they are in society but as grains of sand on the sea-shore. Would they but pause one moment to ask how will this plea avail them, when as daughters without gratitude, friends without good faith, wives without consideration, and mothers without piety, they stand before the bar of judgment, to render an account of the talents committed to their trust! . . .

Amongst this unpretending class are found striking and noble instance of women, who apparently feeble and insignificant, when called into action by pressing and peculiar circumstances, can accomplish great and glorious purposes, supported and carried forward by that most valuable of all faculties—*moral power*. And just in proportion as women cultivate this faculty (under the blessing of heaven) . . . is their influence over their fellow-creatures, and consequently their power of doing good.

It is not to be presumed that women *possess* more moral power than men, but happily for them, such are their early impressions, associations, and general position in the world, that their moral feelings are less liable to be impaired by the pecuniary objects which too often constitute the chief end of man, and which, even under the limitations of better principle, necessarily engage a large portion of his thoughts. . . .

How often has man returned to his home with a mind confused by the many voices, which in the mart, the exchange, or the public assembly, have addressed themselves to his inborn selfishness or his worldly pride; and while his integrity was shaken, and his resolution gave way beneath the pressure of apparent necessity, or the insidious pretences of expediency, he has stood corrected before the clear eye of woman, as it looked directly to the naked truth, and detected the lurking evil of the specious act he was about to commit. Nay, so potent may have become this secret influence, that he may have borne it about with him like a kind of second conscience, for mental reference, and spiritual counsel, in moments of trial: and when the snares of the world were around him, and temptations from within and without have bribed over the witness in his own bosom, he has thought of the humble monitress who sat alone, guarding the fireside comforts of his distant home; and the remembrance of her character, clothed in moral beauty, has scattered the clouds before his mental vision, and sent him back to that beloved home, a wiser and a better man.

# Mrs. Smart, Mrs. Britton, and Mary Hunt

## *from* Reports of Special Assistant Poor Law Commissioners on the Employment of Women and Children in Agriculture (1843)

*The Poor Law Commissioners were charged with overseeing the disbursement of government relief to the destitute in nineteenth-century Britain. Guided by the notion that poverty was a reflection of moral failing, the laws under which they operated required the poor to be hard working and thus deserving in order to receive aid. The Commissioners' duties included the regulation of workhouses and the establishment of special commissions to inquire into the living circumstances and working conditions of the poor. Mrs. Smart, Mrs. Britton, and Mary Hunt, residents of Wiltshire, each testified before special assistant Poor Law Commissioners during a 1843 inquiry regarding the employment of women and children in agriculture.*

### MRS. SMART, CALNE, WILTSHIRE

I went out leasing (gleaning) this autumn for three weeks, and was very lucky: I got six bushels of corn. I got up at two o'clock in the morning, and got home at seven at night. My other girls, aged 10, 15, and 18, went with me. We leased in the neighbourhood, and sometimes as far as seven miles off.

I have had 13 children, and have brought seven up. I have been accustomed to work in the fields at hay-time and harvest. Sometimes I have had my mother, and sometimes my sister, to take care of the children, or I could not have gone out. I have gone to work at seven in the morning till six in the evening; in harvest sometimes much later, but it depends on circumstances. Women with a family cannot be ready so soon as the men, and must be home earlier, and therefore they don't work so many hours. In making hay I have been strained with the work: I have felt it sometimes for weeks; so bad sometimes I could not get out of my chair. In leasing, in bringing home the corn, I have hurt my head, and have been made deaf by it. Often, out of the hay-fields, myself and my children have come home with our things quite wet through: I have gone to bed for an hour for my things to get a little dry, but have had to put them on again when quite wet. My health is very good now.

I generally had 10d. a-day, sometimes as much as 1s. a-day. My husband earns 15s. a-week, but his employment is not regular. Our boys are brought up to their father's work.

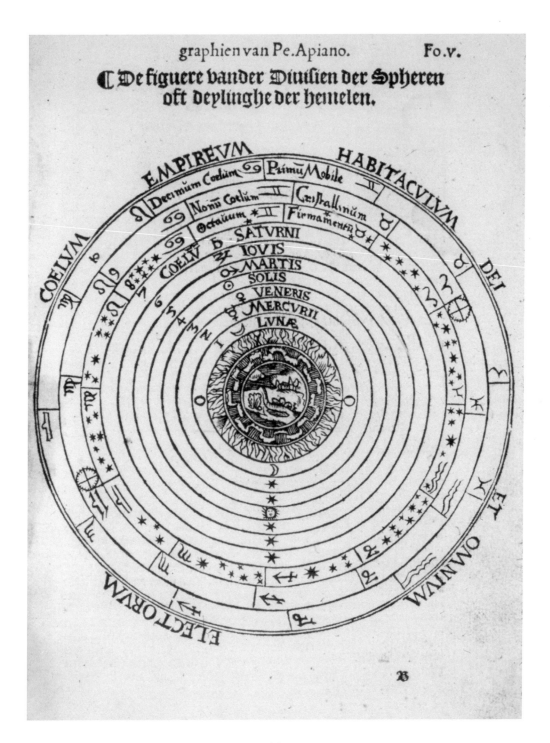

(a)

The Copernican heliocentric worldview challenged the geocentric cosmology associated with Ptolemy. Note that Copernicus, like his forebears, still believes that the orbits of the planets are circular and uniform.

*Cosmographica,* by Petrus Apianus, courtesy of the Library of Congress, Rare Books Collection.

net, in quo terram cum orbe lunari tanquam epicyclo contineri diximus. Quinto loco Venus nono mense reducitur. Sextum deniq; locum Mercurius tenet, octuaginta dierum spacio circū currens. In medio uero omnium residet Sol. Quis enim in hoc

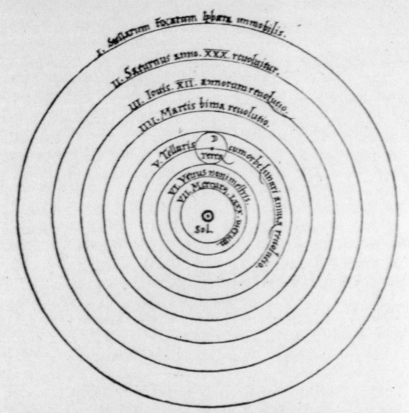

pulcherimo templo lampadem hanc in alio uel meliori loco po neret, quàm unde totum simul possit illuminare. Siquidem non inepte quidam lucernam mundi, alij mentem, alij rectorem uo= cant. Trimegistus uisibilem Deum, Sophoclis Electra intuentē omnia. Ita profecto tanquam in solio regali Sol residens circum agentem gubernat Astrorum familiam. Tellus quoq; minime fraudatur lunari ministerio, sed ut Aristoteles de animalibus ait, maximā Luna cū terra cognatio nē habet. Concipit interea à Sole terra, & impregnatur annuo partu. Inuenimus igitur sub hac

(b)

*De Revolutionibus Orbium Coelestium,* by Nicolaus Copernicus, courtesy of the Library of Congress, Rare Books Collection.

Fifteenth-century Europeans could only imagine what peoples in other parts of the world were like.

*Illustration of the Fabulous Races of Humankind,* courtesy of Sint-Baafskathedral, Ghent, Belgium.

A Catholic caricature depicts Martin Luther as a seven-headed monster—the different heads representing him as a hypocrite, a fanatic, and a Barabbas (an allusion to the criminal whom Pontius Pilate freed at the time he sentenced Jesus to death).

*Title Page of a Pamphlet by Johannes Cochlaeus,* courtesy of the British Library.

Seventeenth-century Europeans often idealized "primitive" life in the Americas.

*Illustration of an Idealized Couple from L'Amerique Historique,* courtesy of *Bibliotech Magazine*, Paris, France.

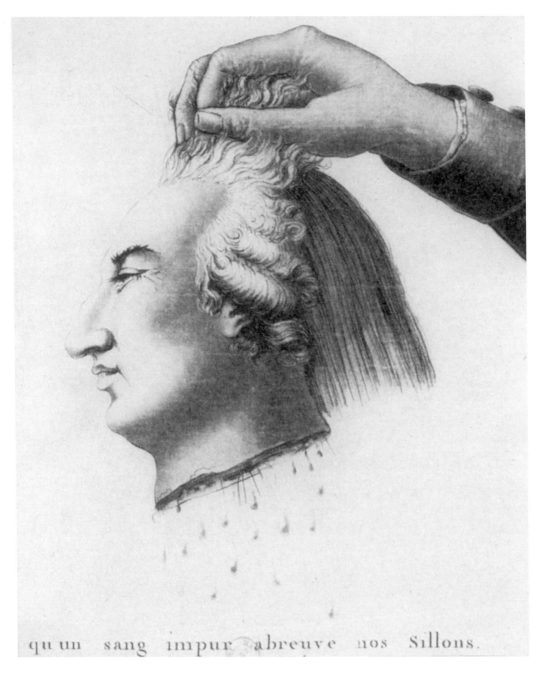

qu un sang impur abreuve nos Sillons.

The Aristocracy loses its head in the French Revolution.

*Matter for Thought for Crowned Jugglers,* courtesy of Bibliotech Nationale, Paris.

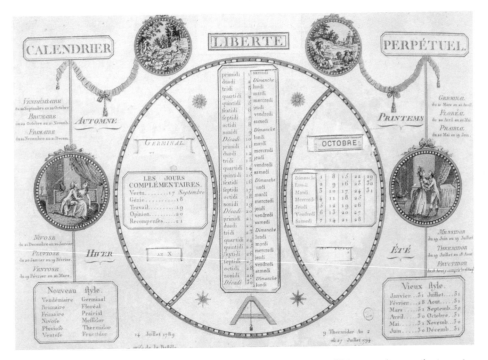

Believing that the French Revolution transformed the nature of history, the revolutionaries created a new calendar based on the rhythms of agricultural life. Here the two calendars are compared.

*Revolutionary Calendar, France, 1790s,* courtesy of Musée Carnavalet, Paris.

The eighteenth-century French architect Claude-Nicolas Ledoux creates a plan for a factory town founded on a salt works. It represents the Enlightenment preoccupation with rational order and harmony.

*Vue Perspective de la Ville de Chaux (after 1775),* by Claude-Nicolas Ledoux, courtesy of Art Resource.

Equiana, author of *The Interesting Narrative*, simultaneously proclaims himself to be an African and a Christian.

*Olaudah Equiano,* courtesy of the British Museum.

# LONDON

I wander thro' each charter'd street,
Near where the charter'd Thames does flow
And mark in every face I meet
Marks of weakness, marks of woe.

In every cry of every Man,
In every Infants cry of fear,
In every voice; in every ban,
The mind-forg'd manacles I hear

How the Chimney-sweepers cry
Every blackning Church appalls,
And the hapless Soldiers sigh
Runs in blood down Palace walls

But most thro' midnight streets I hear
How the youthful Harlots curse
Blasts the new born Infants tear
And blights with plagues the Marriage hearse

An artist as well as a poet, William Blake created illustrated editions of his poetry.

*London,* by William Blake, courtesy of the Houghton Library, Harvard University.

(a)

(b)

The pernicious effects of alcohol on working-class families are vividly portrayed by the middle-class reformer and illustrator, George Cruikshank.

(c)

Three illustrations from a series of eight titled *The Bottle*, by George Cruikshank, courtesy of Radio Times Hulton Picture Library, London.

Queen Victoria and Prince Albert buy into the Victorian ideal of domestic life.

*Queen Victoria and Prince Albert at Windsor with the Princess Royal,* by Edwin Lanseer, courtesy of the Royal Collection, Windsor Palace.

Housing the Great Exhibition of 1851 (the first World's Fair), the Crystal Palace is the first building made from iron and glass and put together from prefabricated parts.

*The Crystal Palace, London,* by Joseph Paxton, courtesy of E. Galloway.

The connection between capitalism and imperialism in late nineteenth-century Britain is brought home in this advertisement for Pears' Soap.

British advertisement: *Pears' Soap in the Soudan, courtesy of Mansell Collection, England.*

Cecil Rhodes' imperialist ambition to link by railway British holdings from Cairo to Capetown is satirized in this cartoon: "The Rhodes Colossus."

Punch cartoon: *The Rhodes Colossus,* courtesy of the Warder Collection.

Though the recruitment of women for munitions work was seen as a temporary measure, gender roles had already begun to shift prior to the First World War.

British recruiting poster: *On Her Their Lives Depend*, courtesy of the Imperial War Museum, London.

*George V Inspecting Model Trenches Near Sailly,* courtesy of the Imperial War Museum, London.

During the First World War, idealized images of battle were quickly eroded by the realities of trench warfare.

*A Trench on the Somme,* courtesy of the Imperial War Museum, London

The building containing the Bauhaus School of Architecture and Design is a classic expression of modernist functionalism.

*Bauhaus, Dessau,* by Walter Gropius, courtesy of Art Resource.

The surrealist artist Max Ernst's manipulation of a nineteenth-century plate is an attack on middle-class prudery and suggests the movement's affinity with Freudian psychoanalysis.

Plate from *Une Semaine de Bonte,* by Max Ernst, courtesy of DACS.

Marcel Duchamp's act of satirical desecration of the West's most famous painting is emblematic of the loss of faith following World War I.

*L.H.O.O.Q.*, by Marcel Duchamp, courtesy of Art Resource.

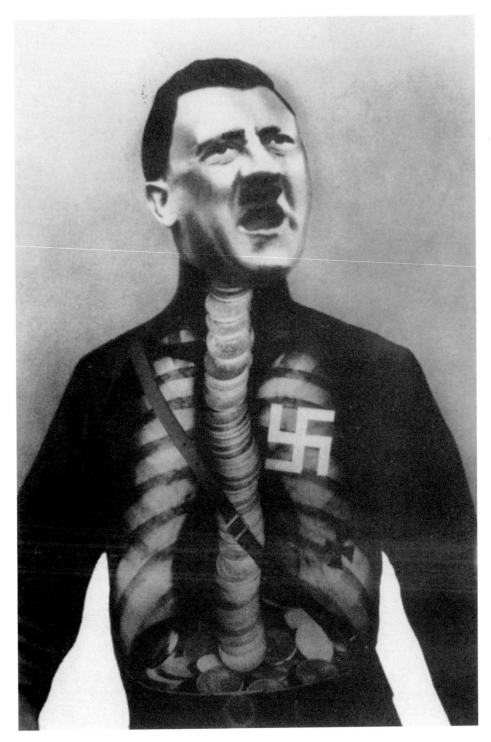

For the Marxist artist John Heartfield, Hitler might represent himself as a man of the people, but underneath he was a front for German capitalism.

*Adolf, the Superman: Swallows Gold and Spouts Junk,* by John Heartfield, courtesy of Akademie der Kunste, Berlin.

Picasso's *Guernica* depicts the outrage many Europeans felt following the Fascists' bombing of civilians during the Spanish Civil War.

*Guernica,* by Pablo Picasso, courtesy of Art Resource.

The classical design of the House of German Art embodies the Third Reich's belief that it was the culmination of the Western Tradition.

*House of German Art, Munich,* by Paul Ludwig Troost, courtesy of Art Resource.

Stalin's removal in Prague proclaims the end of Communism.

*Stalin removed in Prague,* courtesy of the BBC Photographic Library.

Richard Hamilton's collage satirizes the rampant consumerism of the 1950s.

*Just What Is It That Makes Today's Homes So Different, So Appealing?* by Richard Hamilton, courtesy of the Bridgeman Art Library, New York.

We pay 7£ a-year rent for our cottage and large garden. There are three rooms in the cottage; two bed-rooms, in which we have three beds; and we find great difficulty in sleeping our family. When we wash our sheets, we must have them dry again by night. In the garden we raise plenty of potatoes. We have about a shilling's worth of neat a-week; a pig's milt sometimes; a pound or three-quarters of a pound of suet. Seven gallons of bread a-week; sometimes a little pudding on a Sunday. I can cook a little. I was, before I married, housemaid, and afterwards cook in a family.

## Mrs. Britton, Calne, Wiltshire

I am 41 years old; I have lived at Calne all my life. I went to school till I was eight years old, when I went out to look after children. At ten years old I went to work at a factory in Calne, where I was till I was 26. I have been married 15 years. My husband is an agricultural labourer. I have seven children, all boys. The oldest is fourteen. The youngest three-quarters of a year old. My husband is a good workman, and does most of his work by the lump, and earns from 9s. to 10s. a-week pretty constantly, but finds his own tools,—his wheelbarrow, which cost 1£, pickaxe, which cost 3s., and scoop, which cost 3s.

I have worked in the fields, and when I went out I left the children in the care of the oldest boy, and frequently carried the baby with me, as I could not go home to nurse it. I have worked at hay-making and at harvest, and at other times in weeding and keeping the ground clean. I generally work from half-past seven till five, or half-past. When at work in the spring I have received 10d. a day, but that is higher than the wages of women in general; 8d. or 9d. is more common. My master always paid 10d. When working I never had any beer, and I never felt the want of it. I never felt that my health was hurt by the work. Hay-making is hard work, very fatiguing, but it never hurt me. Working in the fields is not such hard work as working in the factory. I am always better when I can get out to work in the fields. I intend to do so next year if I can. Last year I could not go out, owing to the birth of the baby. My eldest boy gets a little to do; but don't earn more than 9d. a-week; he has not enough to do. My husband has 40 lugs of land, for which he pays 10s. a-year. We grow potatoes and a few cabbages, but not enough for our family; for that we should like to have forty lugs more. We have to buy potatoes. One of the children is a cripple, and the [Poor Law] guardians allow us two gallons of bread a-week for him. We buy two gallons more, according as the money is. Nine people can't do with less than four gallons of bread a-week. We could eat much more bread if we could get it; sometimes we can afford only one gallon a-week. We very rarely buy butcher's fresh meat, certainly not oftener than once a-week, and not more than sixpenny worth. I like my husband to have a bit of meat, now he has left off drinking. I buy ½ lb. butter a-week, 1 oz. tea, ½ lb. sugar. The rest of our food is potatoes, with a little fat. The rent of our cottage is 1s.6d. a-week; there are two rooms in it. We all sleep in one room, under the tiles. Sometimes we receive private assistance, especially in clothing. Formerly my husband was in the habit of drinking, and everything went bad. He used to beat me. I have often gone to bed, I and my children, without supper, and have had no breakfast the next morning, and frequently no firing. My husband attended a lecture on teetotalism one evening about two years ago, and I have reason to bless that evening. My husband has never touched a drop of drink since. He has been better in health, getting stouter, and has behaved like a good husband to me ever since. I have been much more comfortable, and the children happier. He works better than he did. He can mow better, and that is hard work, and he does not mind being laughed at by the other men for not drinking. I send my eldest boy to Sunday school; them that are younger go to the day school. My eldest boy never complains of work hurting him. My husband now goes regularly to church: formerly he could hardly be got there.

## Mary Hunt, Studley, Wiltshire

I am in my fiftieth year. I have had 12 children, and, if it please God, I shall very soon have my 13th. I was left early without father and mother, with a crippled brother, whom I had to help to support. I began to work in the fields at 16. I had to work very hard, and got a good deal of lump-work. I have earned as much as 2s.6d. a-day at digging, but I was always considered as a very hard worker. I married at 22, and had to put up with a good deal with a young family; and have often had only salt and potatoes for days together. I was always better when out at work in the fields; and as for hard work I never was hurt by it. I have carried half a sack of peas to Chippenham, four miles, when I have been large in the family way. I have known what it is to work hard.

I think it a much better thing for mothers to be at home with their children; they are much better taken care of, and other things go on better. I have always left my children to themselves, and, God be praised! nothing has ever happened to them, though I have thought it dangerous. I have many a time come home, and have thought it a mercy to find nothing has happened to them. It would be much better if mothers could be at home, but they must work. Bad accidents often happen. I always hold to it to put children out early, and to bring them up to work; they do better. Families are better altogether when children go out regularly; the children are better than when kept at home getting into all sorts of mischief.

# Friedrich Engels

## *from* THE CONDITION OF THE WORKING CLASS IN ENGLAND (1844)

*Friedrich Engels (1820–1895), whose father owned a textile factory in Prussia and was partner in a cotton plant in Britain, became one of the great critics of the human price of industrialization. Engels began reading the work of leftist intellectuals and the philosopher Hegel while a business apprentice and became persuaded that the necessary consequence of the dialectic was socialism. In the 1840s, he moved to Manchester to work for the family enterprises and study advanced industrial society and its class conflict firsthand. This led to his first major publication,* The Condition of the Working Class in England, *and, eventually, to a life-long political partnership with Karl Marx. Together, they wrote the* Communist Manifesto. *Engels found the achievements of industry impressive but their social costs staggering: "One realizes," he observed, "that these Londoners have been forced to sacrifice the best qualities of their human nature, to bring to pass all the marvels of civilisation which crowd their city." Eventually a partner in his father's business, Engels used his private income to help support Marx's research in philosophy and economics and his political work.*

---

Such, in brief, is the history of English industrial development in the past sixty years, a history, which has no counterpart in the annals of humanity. Sixty, eighty years ago, England was a country like every other, with small towns, few and simple industries, and a thin but *proportionally* large agricultural population. Today it is a country like no other, with a capital of two and a half million inhabitants; with vast manufacturing cities; with an industry that supplies the world, and produces almost everything by means of the most complex machinery; with an industrious, intelligent, dense population, of which two-thirds are employed in trade and commerce, and composed of classes wholly different; forming, in fact, with other customs and other needs, a different nation from the England of those days. The industrial revolution is of the same importance for England as the political revolution is for France, and the philosophical revolution for Germany; and the difference between England in 1760 and in 1844 is at least as great as that between France, under the *ancient régime* and during the revolution of July. But the mightiest result of this industrial transformation is the English proletariat.

. . . The rapid extension of manufacture demanded hands, wages rose, and troops of workmen migrated from the agricultural districts to the towns. Population multiplied enormously, and nearly all the increase took place in the proletariat. . . . Thus arose the great manufacturing and commercial cities of the British Empire, in which at least three-fourths of the population belong to the working-class, while the lower middle-class consists only of small shopkeepers, and very very few handicrafts-men. For, though the rising manufacture first attained importance by transforming tools into machines, work-rooms into factories, and consequently, the toiling lower middle-class into the toiling proletariat, and the former large merchants into manu-facturers, though the lower middle-class was thus early crushed out, and the popula-tion reduced to the two opposing elements, workers and capitalists, this happened outside of the domain of manufacture proper, in the province of handicraft and retail trade as well. In the place of the former masters and apprentices, came great capital-ists and working-men who had no prospect of rising above their class. Handiwork was carried on after the fashion of factory work, the division of labour was strictly applied, and small employers who could not compete with great establishments were forced down into the proletariat. At the same time the destruction of the former organization of handwork, and the disappearance of the lower middle-class deprived the working-man of all possibility of rising into the middle-class himself. Hitherto he had always had the prospect of establishing himself somewhere as master artificer, perhaps employing journeymen and apprentices; but now, when master artificers were crowded out by manufacturers, when large capital had become necessary for car-rying on work independently, the working-class became, for the first time, an inte-gral, permanent class of the population, whereas it had formerly often been merely a transition leading to the bourgeoisie. Now, he who was born to toil had no other prospect than that of remaining a toiler all his life. Now, for the first time, therefore, the proletariat was in a position to undertake an independent movement.

In this way were brought together those vast masses of working-men who now fill the whole British Empire, whose social condition forces itself every day more and more upon the attention of the civilized world. The condition of the working-class is the condition of the vast majority of the English people. The question: What is to become of those destitute millions, who consume today what they earned yesterday; who have created the greatness of England by their inventions and their toil; who become with every passing day more conscious of their might, and demand, with daily increasing urgency, their share of the advantages of society?—This, since the Reform Bill, has become the national question. All Parliamentary debates, of any importance, may be reduced to this; and, though the English middle-class will not as yet admit it, though they try to evade this great question, and to represent their own particular interests as the truly national ones, their action is utterly useless. With every session of Parliament, the working-class gains ground, the interests of the middle-class diminish in importance; and, in spite of the fact that the middle-class is the chief, in fact, the only power in Parliament, the last session of 1844 was a contin-uous debate upon subjects affecting the working-class, the Poor Relief Bill, the Fac-tory Act, the Masters' and Servants' Act; . . .

In spite of all this, the English middle-class, especially the manufacturing class, which is enriched directly by means of the poverty of the workers, persists in ignoring this poverty. This class, feeling itself the mighty representative class of the nation, is ashamed to lay the sore spot of England bare before the eyes of the world; will not confess, even to itself, that the workers are in distress, because it, the property-holding, manufacturing class, must bear the moral responsibility for this distress. Hence the scornful smile which intelligent Englishmen (and they, the middle-class alone are known on the Continent) assume when any one begins to speak of the condition of the working-class; hence the utter ignorance on the part of the whole middle-class of everything which concerns the workers; hence the ridiculous blunders which men of this class, in and out of Parliament, make when the position of the proletariat comes under discussion; hence the absurd freedom from anxiety, with which the middle-class dwells upon a soil that is honeycombed, and may any day collapse, the speedy collapse of which is as certain as a mathematical or mechanical demonstration; hence the miracle that the English have as yet no single book upon the condition of their workers, although they have been examining and mending the old state of things no one knows how many years. Hence also the deep wrath of the whole working-class, from Glasgow to London, against the rich, by whom they are systematically plundered and mercilessly left to their fate, a wrath which before too long a time goes by, a time almost within the power of man to predict, must break out into a Revolution in comparison with which the French Revolution, and the year 1794, will prove to have been child's play.

A town, such as London, where a man may wander for hours together without reaching the beginning of the end, without meeting the slightest hint which could lead to the inference that there is open country within reach, is a strange thing. This colossal centralization, this heaping together of two and a half millions of human beings at one point, has multiplied the power of this two and a half millions a hundredfold; has raised London to the commercial capital of the world, created the giant docks and assembled the thousand vessels that continually cover the Thames. I know nothing more imposing than the view which the Thames offers during the ascent from the sea to London Bridge. The masses of buildings, the wharves on both sides, especially from Woolwich upwards, the countless ships along both shores, crowding ever closer and closer together, until, at last, only a narrow passage remains in the middle of the river, a passage through which hundreds of steamers shoot by one another; all this is so vast, so impressive, that a man cannot collect himself, but is lost in the marvel of England's greatness before he sets foot upon English soil.

But the sacrifices which all this has cost become apparent later. After roaming the streets of the capital a day or two, making headway with difficulty through the human turmoil and the endless lines of vehicles, after visiting the slums of the metropolis, one realizes for the first time that these Londoners have been forced to sacrifice the best qualities of their human nature, to bring to pass all the marvels of civilization which crowd their city; that a hundred powers which slumbered within them have remained inactive, have been suppressed in order that a few might be developed more fully and multiply through union with those of others. The very turmoil of the streets has something repulsive, something against which human nature rebels. The hundreds of thousands of all classes and ranks crowding past each other, are they not all human beings with the same qualities and powers, and with the same interest in being happy? And have they not, in the end, to seek happiness in the same way, by the same means? And still they crowd by one another as though they had nothing in common, nothing to do with one another, and their only agreement is the tacit one, that each keep to his own side of the pavement, so as not to delay the opposing streams of the crowd, while it occurs to no man to honour another with so much as a glance. The brutal indifference, the unfeeling isolation of each in his private interest becomes the more repellent and offensive, the more these individuals are crowded together, within a limited space. And, however much one may be aware that this isolation of the individual, this narrow self-seeking is the fundamental principle of our society everywhere, it is nowhere so shamelessly barefaced, so self-conscious as just here in the crowding of the great city. The dissolution of mankind into monads of which each one has a separate principle and a separate purpose, the world of atoms, is here carried out to its utmost extreme.

Hence it comes, too, that the social war, the war of each against all, is here openly declared. . . . [P]eople regard each other only as useful objects; each exploits the other, and the end of it all is, that the stronger treads the weaker under foot, and that the powerful few, the capitalists, seize everything for themselves, while to the weak many, the poor, scarcely a bare existence remains.

What is true of London, is true of Manchester, Birmingham, Leeds, is true of all great towns. Everywhere barbarous indifference, hard egotism on one hand, and nameless misery on the other, everywhere social warfare, every man's house in a state of siege, everywhere reciprocal plundering under the protection of the law, and all so shameless, so openly avowed that one shrinks before the consequences of our social state as they manifest themselves here undisguised, and can only wonder that the whole crazy fabric still hangs together.

Every great city has one or more slums, where the working-class is crowded together. True, poverty often dwells in hidden alleys close to the palaces of the rich; but, in general, a separate territory has been assigned to it, where, removed from the sight of the happier classes, it may struggle along as it can. These slums are pretty equally arranged in all the great towns of England, the worst houses in the worst quarters of the towns; usually one or two-storied cottages in long rows, perhaps with cellars used as dwellings, almost always irregularly built. These houses of three or four rooms and a kitchen form, throughout England, some parts of London excepted, the general dwellings of the working-class. The streets are generally unpaved, rough, dirty, filled with vegetable and animal refuse, without sewers or gutters, but supplied with foul, stagnant pools instead. Moreover, ventilation is impeded by the bad, confused method of building of the whole quarter, and since many human beings here live crowded into a small space, the atmosphere that prevails in these working-men's quarters may readily be imagined. Further, the streets serve as drying grounds in fine weather; lines are stretched across from house to house, and hung with wet clothing.

—*trans. Mrs. F. Kelley Wischnewetzky*

# Matthew Arnold

## *from* CULTURE AND ANARCHY (1869)

*Matthew Arnold (1822–1888), son of an influential educational reformer, studied at Oxford and became a man of letters and an inspector of schools. His poetry brought him election to a professorship at Oxford, but his greatest influence was as a literary and cultural critic concerned with the growing—and increasingly influential—Victorian middle class. His work as a school inspector required Arnold to travel extensively and brought him into contact with middle-class citizens in every part of England. What he saw concerned him greatly: they were, he declared, materialistic, narrow-minded, smug, and uninformed "Philistines." Unfamiliar with the great works of ancient and modern cultures, they were ill-prepared to assume the responsibilities of governing society or advancing civilization. Cultural critics, Arnold argued, bore the responsibility "to learn and propagate the best that is known and thought in the world, and thus to establish a current of fresh and true ideas." In* Culture and Anarchy, *Arnold issues a call for enlightenment: it would be through educating the middle class in the best that is known and thought, not through industry, that modern society would be improved.*

### I. SWEETNESS AND LIGHT

The disparagers of culture make its motive curiosity; sometimes, indeed, they make its motive mere exclusiveness and vanity. The culture which is supposed to plume itself on a smattering of Greek and Latin is a culture which is begotten by nothing so intellectual as curiosity; it is valued either out of sheer vanity and ignorance, or else as an engine of social and class distinction, separating its holder, like a badge or title, from other people who have not got it. No serious man would call this *culture,* or attach any value to it, as culture, at all. . . .

If culture . . . is a study of perfection, and of harmonious perfection, general perfection, and perfection which consists in becoming something rather than in having something, in an inward condition of the mind and spirit, not in an outward set of circumstances,—it is clear that culture, instead of being the frivolous and useless thing . . . has a very important function to fulfil for mankind. And this function is particularly important in our modern world, of which the whole civilisation is, to a much greater degree than the civilisation of Greece and Rome, mechanical and external, and tends constantly to become more so. But above all in our own county has culture a weighty part to perform, because here that mechanical character, which civilisation tends to take everywhere, is shown in the most eminent degree. Indeed nearly all the characters of perfection, as culture teaches us to fix them, meet in this country with some powerful tendency which thwarts them and sets them at defiance. The idea of perfection as an *inward* condition of the mind and spirit is at variance with the mechanical and material civilisation in esteem with us, and nowhere, as I have said, so much in esteem as with us. The idea of perfection as a *general* expansion of the human family is at variance with our strong individualism, our hatred of all limits to the unrestrained swing of the individual's personality, our maxim of "every man for himself." The idea of perfection as an *harmonious* expansion of human nature is at variance with our want of flexibility, with our inaptitude for seeing more than one side of a thing, with our intense energetic absorption in the particular pursuit we happen to be following. . . .

Wealth, again, that end to which our prodigious works for material advantage are directed,—the commonest of commonplaces tells us how men are always apt to regard wealth as a precious end in itself; and certainly they have never been so apt thus to regard it as they are in England at the present time. Never did people believe anything more firmly, than nine Englishmen out of ten at the present day believe that our greatness and welfare are proved by our being so very rich. Now, the use of culture is that it helps us, by means of its spiritual standard of perfection, to regard wealth as but machinery, and not only to say as a matter of words that we regard wealth as but machinery, but really to perceive and feel that it is so. If it were not for this purging effect wrought upon our minds by culture, the whole world, the future as well as the present, would inevitably belong to the Philistines. The people who believe most that our greatness and welfare are proved by our being very rich, and who most give their lives and thoughts to becoming rich, are just the very people whom we call the Philistines. Culture says: "Consider these people, then, their way of life, their habits, their manners, the very tones of their voice; look at them attentively; observe the literature they read, the things which give them pleasure, the words which come forth out of their mouths, the thoughts which make the furniture of their minds; would any amount of wealth be worth having with the condition that one was to become just like these people by having it?" And thus culture begets a dissatisfaction which is of the highest possible value in stemming the common tide of men's thoughts in a wealthy and industrial community, and which saves the future, as one may hope, from being vulgarised, even if it cannot save the present. . . .

It is by thus making sweetness and light to be characters of perfection, that culture is of like spirit with poetry, follows one law with poetry. I have called religion a more important manifestation of human nature than poetry, because it has worked on a broader scale for perfection, and with greater masses of men. But the idea of beauty and of a human nature perfect on all its sides, which is the dominant idea of poetry, is a true and invaluable idea, though it has not yet had the success that the idea of conquering the obvious faults of our animality, and of a human nature perfect on the moral side, which is the dominant idea of religion, has been enabled to have; and it is destined, adding to itself the religious idea of a devout energy, to transform and govern the other. The best art and poetry of the Greeks, in which religion and poetry are one, in which the idea of beauty and of a human nature perfect on all sides adds to itself a religious and devout energy, and works in the strength of that, is on this account of such surpassing interest and instructiveness for us, though it was,—as, having regard to the human race in general, and, indeed, having regard to the Greeks themselves, we must own,—a premature attempt, an attempt which for success needed the moral and religious fibre in humanity to be more braced and developed than it had yet been. But Greece did not err in having the idea of beauty, harmony, and complete human perfection, so present and paramount; it is impossible to have this idea too present and paramount; only the moral fibre must be braced too. And we, because we have braced the moral fibre, are not on that account in the right way, if at the same time the idea of beauty, harmony, and complete human perfection, is wanting or misapprehended amongst us; and evidently it *is* wanting or misapprehended at present. And when we rely as we do on our religious organisations, which in themselves do not and cannot give us this idea, and think we have done enough if we make them spread and prevail, then, I say, we fall into our common fault of over-valuing machinery. . . .

I have said that the new and more democratic force which is now superseding our old middle-class liberalism cannot yet be rightly judged. It has its main tendencies still to form. We hear promises of its giving us administrative reform, law reform, reform of education, and I know not what; but those promises come rather from its advocates, wishing to make a good plea for it and to justify it for superseding middle-class liberalism, than from clear tendencies which it has itself yet developed. But meanwhile it has plenty of well-intentioned friends against whom culture may with advantage continue to uphold steadily its ideal of human perfection; that this is *an inward spiritual activity, having for its characters increased sweetness, increased light, increased life, increased sympathy.* Mr. Bright, who has a foot in both worlds, the world of middle-class liberalism and the world of democracy, but who brings most of his ideas from the world of middle-class liberalism in which he was bred, always inclines to inculcate that faith in machinery to which, as we have seen, Englishmen are so prone, and which has been the bane of middle-class liberalism. He complains with a sorrowful indignation of people who "appear to have no proper estimate of the value of the franchise;" he leads his disciples to believe,—what the Englishman is always too ready to believe,—that the having a vote, like the having a large family, or a large business, or large muscles, has in itself some edifying and perfecting effect upon human nature. Or else he cries out to the democracy,—"the men," as he calls them, "upon whose shoulders the greatness of England rests,"—he cries out to them: "See what you have done! I look over this country and see the cities you have built, the railroads you have made, the manufactures you have produced, the cargoes which freight the ships of the greatest mercantile navy the world has ever seen! I see that you have converted by your labours what was once a wilderness, these islands, into a fruitful garden; I know that you have created this wealth, and are a nation whose name is a word of power throughout all the world." . . . But teaching the democracy to put its trust in achievements of this kind is merely training them to be Philistines to take the place of the Philistines whom they are superseding; and they too, like the middle class, will be encouraged to sit down at the banquet of the future without having on a wedding garment, and nothing excellent can then come from them. Those who know their besetting faults, those who have watched them and listened to them, or those who will read the instructive account recently given of them by one of themselves, the *Journeyman Engineer,* will agree that the idea which culture sets before us of perfection,—an increased spiritual activity, having for its characters increased sweetness, increased light, increased life, increased sympathy,—is an idea which the new democracy needs far more than the idea of the blessedness of the franchise, or the wonderfulness of their own industrial performances. . . .

The pursuit of perfection, then, is the pursuit of sweetness and light. He who works for sweetness works in the end for light also; he who works for light works in the end for sweetness also. But he who works for sweetness and light united, works to make reason and the will of God prevail. He who works for machinery, he who works for hatred, works only for confusion. Culture looks beyond machinery, culture hates hatred; culture has but one great passion, the passion for sweetness and light. Yes, it has one yet greater!—the passion for making them *prevail*. It is not satisfied till we *all* come to a perfect man; it knows that the sweetness and light of the few must be imperfect until the raw and unkindled masses of humanity are touched with sweetness and light. If I have not shrunk from saying that we must work for sweetness and light, so neither have I shrunk from saying that we must have a broad basis, must have sweetness and light for as many as possible. Again and again I have insisted how those are the happy moments of humanity, how those are the marking epochs of a people's life, how those are the flowering times for literature and art and all the creative power of genius, when there is a *national* glow of life and thought, when the whole of society is in the fullest measure permeated by thought, sensible to beauty, intelligent and alive. Only it must be *real* thought and *real* beauty; *real* sweetness and *real* light. Plenty of people will try to give the masses, as they call them, an intellectual food prepared and adapted in the way they think proper for the actual condition of the masses. The ordinary popular literature is an example of this way of working on the masses. Plenty of people will try to indoctrinate the masses with the set of ideas and judgments constituting the creed of their own profession or party. Our religious and political organisations give an example of this way of working on the masses. I condemn neither way; but culture works differently. It does not try to teach down to the level of inferior classes; it does not try to win them for this or that sect of its own, with ready-made judgments and watchwords. It seeks to do away with classes; to make all live in an atmosphere of sweetness and light, and use ideas, as it uses them itself, freely,—to be nourished and not bound by them.

# SECTION V

# Materialism, Evolution, Nationalism, Imperialism

Questions about human societies continued to preoccupy many people through the second half of the nineteenth century and into the twentieth. Faced with the profound social changes resulting from the French and industrial revolutions and influenced by Enlightenment rationalism, scientists and philosophers developed theories to explain the origins and functioning of human societies, to account for differences between various cultures and societies, and to improve them. In the eighteenth century, French thinkers had conceived the idea of the encyclopedia, a series of texts that would sum up human knowledge; in the early nineteenth century the German philosopher Hegel had constructed a universal theory of history in which all human history was understood as a dialectical progression from primitive to philosophically sophisticated cultures. Asking "what is the ultimate design of the World?" Hegel responded that "the History of the world is none other than the progress of the consciousness of Freedom; a process whose development according to the necessity of its nature, it is our business to investigate."

Hegel's statement is a useful introduction to the concerns of nineteenth-century philosophers, scientists, and politicians. From differing points of view and with widely varied purposes, many sought to understand both the exact particulars of the world and the underlying laws of nature or society—what later thinkers would call the grand narratives—that would explain them. Some, such as Hegel, were primarily interested in explaining history and society in terms of abstract principles. Others, such as the French philosopher Auguste Comte, founder of Positivism, were primarily interested in using precise observation and description to obtain exact knowledge. Still others, including Karl Marx, had more pressing purposes in mind. As Marx wrote in his "Theses on Feuerbach" in 1845: "The philosophers have only *interpreted* the world, in various ways; the point, however, is to *change* it." Each of these impulses—to understand the world, to know it precisely, and to transform it—can be traced through the selections that follow. One of the striking features of these writers is their confidence—both in their ideas and in the capacity of science and philosophy to explain the major dilemmas of human life and, in doing so, make it possible for men and women to change the world.

The most powerful political ideology in late nineteenth- and early twentieth-century Europe was nationalism. Through conquest, economic alliance, or dynastic marriage, states had often linked together people who spoke different languages and histories. In the mid-nineteenth century, however, the idea that states should be founded on nations—nation-states "naturally" composed of people sharing a common language, culture, and history—became immensely popular. Culturally, nationalism was an outgrowth of romanticism, which had celebrated folk art forms over more cosmopolitan practices. Philosophically, it was an after-effect of the ideals of the French Revolution, and politically it was a local response to Napoleon's ambitious attempt to dominate the entire continent. When applied to human societies, evolutionary theory appeared as though it might complement nationalism by explaining the differences between cultures that philosophers had discussed for centuries. To some, it suggested scientific, even moral justifications for class societies and European imperialism: perhaps the rich were inherently superior to the poor, and perhaps Europeans were more evolved than peoples in other parts of the world. To others, crude applications of evolutionary theory to contemporary ethnic and colonial conflicts provided a pseudo-scientific veneer to racism.

Nationalist ideas were influential throughout Europe, taking different forms as circumstances varied. The power of the vast Habsburg Empire, for example, was seriously weakened both by conflict between the Magyar nobles of Hungary and the dominant Austrians, who spoke German, and by Pan-Slavic movements hoping to unite all Slavic peoples in a single nation. In Ireland, resistance to British rule intensified, leading eventually to partition and the establishment of the Irish Free State in 1922. In Italy and Germany—terms that originally referred to geographic locations divided into numerous small states and principalities—nationalist fervor helped lead to a unified Kingdom of Italy in the 1860s and to the German Empire in the 1870s. As nationalist sentiments fed anti-Semitism, European Jews began to advocate the need for a Jewish state.

Nationalism also affected the ways imperialism was understood at home: part of Britain's national pride, for example, rested on the fact that it was the British *Empire,* upon which the sun never set. While the primary motivations for imperialism were economic and political, notions of cultural superiority drawn from romantic nationalism, social Darwinism, religious ideology, and other sources served to explain and justify European rule abroad. Imperialism was, however, the subject of much debate in Europe. In the nineteenth century, disagreements tended to focus on the purpose of empire and on competing interests, strategies, and practices in support of imperialism. Following the Great War, discussion turned to the very different matter of whether Europe should, or could, continue to rule most of the world.

# Karl Marx

# Preface *to* Toward a Critique of Political Economy (1859)

*Karl Marx (1818–1883), born into a middle-class, German Jewish family that had converted to Christianity, studied philosophy and jurisprudence at the Universities of Bonn and Berlin. After completing his doctoral dissertation, he wrote for an opposition newspaper and intellectual journals. As Marx recounts in this Preface, a summary of his early work, when the newspaper was suppressed under Prussian censorship laws he moved to Paris and then, banished by the French government, to Brussels. There Marx and Friedrich Engels, with whom he collaborated for nearly forty years, drafted their materialist conception of history. Hegel and other idealists, they argued, erred dramatically in supposing that ideas are the central force in human history. Marx and Engels turned idealism on its head, arguing that the real dialectic of human history is grounded in material reality instead:*

> *In direct contrast to German philosophy which descends from heaven to earth, here we ascend from earth to heaven. That is to say, we do not set out from what men say, imagine, conceive, nor from men as narrated, thought of, imagined, conceived, in order to arrive at men in the flesh. We set out from real, active men, and on the basis of their real life-process we demonstrate the development of the ideological reflexes and echoes of this life-process.*

> *Marx lived in London from 1849 until his death, working on an exhaustive analysis of political economy, writing for the* New York Daily Tribune, *and corresponding with participants in workers' movements across Europe.*

---

I examine the system of bourgeois economy in the following order: *capital, landed property, wage-labour; the State, foreign trade, world market.* The economic conditions of existence of the three great classes into which modern bourgeois society is divided are analysed under the first three headings; the interconnection of the other three headings is self-evident. The first part of the first book, dealing with Capital, comprises the following chapters: 1. The commodity; 2. Money or simple circulation; 3. Capital in general. The present part consists of the first two chapters. The entire material lies before me in the form of monographs, which were written not for publication but for self-clarification at widely separated periods; their remoulding into an integrated whole according to the plan I have indicated will depend upon circumstances.

A general introduction, which I had drafted, is omitted, since on further consideration it seems to me confusing to anticipate results which still have to be substantiated, and the reader who really wishes to follow me will have to decide to advance from the particular to the general. A few brief remarks regarding the course of my study of political economy may, however, be appropriate here.

Although I studied jurisprudence, I pursued it as a subject subordinated to philosophy and history. In the year 1842–43, as editor of the *Rheinische Zeitung*, I first found myself in the embarrassing position of having to discuss what is known as material interests. The deliberations of the Rhenish Landtag on forest thefts and the division of landed property; the official polemic started by Herr von Schaper, then Oberpräsident of the Rhine Province, against the *Rheinische Zeitung* about the condition of the Moselle peasantry, and finally the debates on free trade and protective tariffs caused me in the first instance to turn my attention to economic questions. On the other hand, at that time when good intentions "to push forward" often took the place of factual knowledge, an echo of French socialism and communism, slightly tinged by philosophy, was noticeable in the *Rheinische Zeitung*. I objected to this dilettantism, but at the same time frankly admitted in a controversy with the *Allgemeine Augsburger Zeitung* that my previous studies did not allow me to express any opinion on the content of the French theories. When the publishers of the *Rheinische Zeitung* conceived the illusion that by a more compliant policy on the part of the paper it might be possible to secure the abrogation of the death sentence passed upon it, I eagerly grasped the opportunity to withdraw from the public stage to my study.

The first work which I undertook to dispel the doubts assailing me was a critical reexamination of the Hegelian philosophy of law; the introduction to this work being published in the *Deutsch-Französische Jahrbücher* issued in Paris in 1844. My inquiry led me to the conclusion that neither legal relations nor political forms could be comprehended whether by themselves or on the basis of a so-called general development of the human mind, but that on the contrary they originate in the material conditions of life, the totality of which Hegel, following the example of English and French thinkers of the eighteenth century, embraces within the term "civil society"; that the anatomy of this civil society, however, has to be sought in political economy. The study of this, which I began in Paris, I continued in Brussels, where I moved owing to an expulsion order issued by M. Guizot. The general conclusion at which I arrived and which, once reached, became the guiding principle of my studies can be summarised as follows. In the social production of their existence, men inevitably enter into definite relations, which are independent of their will, namely relations of production appropriate to a given stage in the development of their material forces of production. The totality of these relations of production constitutes the economic structure of society, the real foundation, on which arises a legal and political superstructure and to which correspond definite forms of social consciousness. The mode of production of material life conditions the general process of social, political and intellectual life. It is not the consciousness of men that determines their existence, but their social existence that determines their consciousness. At a certain stage of development, the material productive forces of society come into conflict with the existing relations of production or—this merely expresses the same thing in legal terms—with the property relations within the framework of which they have operated hitherto. From forms of development of the productive forces these relations turn into their fetters. Then begins an era of social revolution. The changes in the economic foundation lead sooner or later to the transformation of the whole immense superstructure. In studying such transformations it is always necessary to distinguish between the material transformation of the economic conditions of production, which can be determined with the precision of natural science, and the legal, political, religious, artistic or philosophic—in short, ideological forms in which men become conscious of this conflict and fight it out. Just as one does not judge an individual by what he thinks about himself, so one cannot judge such a period of transformation by its consciousness, but, on the contrary, this consciousness must be explained from the contradictions of material life, from the conflict existing between the social forces of production and the relations of production. No social order is ever destroyed before all the productive forces for which it is sufficient have been developed, and new superior relations of production never replace older ones before the material conditions for their existence have matured within the framework of the old society. Mankind thus inevitably sets itself only such tasks as it is able to solve, since closer examination will always show that the problem itself arises only when the material conditions for its solution are already present or at least in the course of formation. In broad outline, the Asiatic, ancient, feudal and modern bourgeois modes of production may be designated as epochs marking progress in the economic development of society. The bourgeois mode of production is the last antagonistic form of the social process of production—antagonistic not in the sense of individual antagonism but of an antagonism that emanates from the individuals' social conditions of existence—but the productive forces developing within bourgeois society create also the material conditions for a solution of this antagonism. The prehistory of human society accordingly closes with this social formation.

Frederick Engels, with whom I maintained a constant exchange of ideas by correspondence since the publication of his brilliant essay on the critique of economic categories (printed in the *Deutsch-Französische Jahrbücher*), arrived by another road (compare his *Lage der arbeitenden Klasse in England*) at the same result as I, and when in the spring of 1845 he too came to live in Brussels, we decided to set forth together our conception as opposed to the ideological one of German philosophy, in fact to settle accounts with our former philosophical conscience. The intention was carried out in the form of a critique of post-Hegelian philosophy. The manuscript, two large octavo volumes, had long ago reached the publishers in Westphalia when we were informed that owing to changed circumstances it could not be printed. We abandoned the manuscript to the gnawing criticism of the mice all the more willingly since we had achieved our main purpose—self-clarification. Of the scattered works in which at that time we presented one or another aspect of our views to the public, I shall mention only the *Manifesto of the Communist Party,* jointly written by Engels and myself, and a *Discours sur le libre échange,* which I myself published. The salient points of our conception were first outlined in an academic, although polemical, form in my *Misère de la philosophie . . .* , this book which was aimed at Proudnon appeared in 1847. The publication of an essay on *Wage-Labour* written in German in which I combined the lectures I had held on this subject at the German Workers' Association in Brussels, was interrupted by the February Revolution and my forcible removal from Belgium in consequence.

The publication of the *Neue Rheinische Zeitung* in 1848 and 1849 and subsequent events cut short my economic studies, which I could only resume in London in 1850. The enormous amount of material relating to the history of political economy assembled in the British Museum, the fact that London is a convenient vantage point for the observation of bourgeois society, and finally the new stage of development which this society seemed to have entered with the discovery of gold in California and Australia, induced me to start again from the very beginning and to work carefully through the new material. These studies led partly of their own accord to apparently quite remote subjects on which I had to spend a certain amount of time. But it was in particular the imperative necessity of earning my living which reduced the time at my disposal. My collaboration, continued now for eight years, with the *New York Tribune,* the leading Anglo-American newspaper, necessitated an excessive fragmentation of my studies, for I wrote only exceptionally newspaper correspondence in the strict sense. Since a considerable part of my contributions consisted of articles dealing with important economic events in Britain and on the Continent, I was compelled to become conversant with practical detail which, strictly speaking, lie outside the sphere of political economy.

This sketch of the course of my studies in the domain of political economy is intended merely to show that my views—no matter how they may be judged and how little they conform to the interested prejudices of the ruling classes—are the outcome of conscientious research carried on over many years. At the entrance to science, as at the entrance to hell, the demand must be made:

> *Qui si convien lasciare ogni sospetto*
> *Ogni viltà convien che qui sia morta.*

"Here must be abandoned all distrust, All cowardice must here be dead."
(Dante, *Inferno* 3:13)

—*trans. S. W. Ryazanskaya*

# Charles Darwin

## *from* THE ORIGIN OF SPECIES (1859)
## *from* THE DESCENT OF MAN (1871)

*Charles Darwin (1809–1882) traveled around the world at 22, helping to survey the coast of South America, taking notes on animals and plants, and observing local cultures. In 1859 he published what many would consider the century's single most significant book,* The Origin of Species, *in which he laid out in precise detail a theory of evolution. Drawing upon years of research, Darwin advanced the idea of natural selection to account for variation in nature and implied that the human species had evolved from more primitive forms (he would say this directly only later, in* The Descent of Man*). While recognizing that evolution challenged traditional religious views of the world, he also found it compatible with the idea of a Creator. Darwin saw evolution as the grand narrative that explained the development of the natural world and, presumably, of the social world as well:*

> *There is grandeur in this view of life, with its several powers, having been origi-nally breathed into a few forms or into one; and that, whilst this planet has gone cycling on according to the fixed law of gravity, from so simple a beginning end-less forms most beautiful and most wonderful have been, and are being, evolved.*

## *FROM* THE ORIGIN OF SPECIES

Nothing is easier than to admit in words the truth of the universal struggle for life, or more difficult—at least I have found it so—than constantly to bear this conclusion in mind. Yet, unless it be thoroughly engrained in the mind, the whole economy of nature, with every fact on distribution, rarity, abundance, extinction, and variation, will be dimly seen or quite misunderstood. We behold the face of nature bright with gladness, we often see superabundance of food; we do not see or we forget, that the birds which are idly singing round us mostly live on insects or seeds, and are thus constantly destroying life; or we forget how largely these songsters, or their eggs, or their nestlings, are destroyed by birds and beasts of prey; we do not always bear in mind, that, though food may be now superabundant, it is not so at all seasons of each recurring year. . . .

A struggle for existence inevitably follows from the high rate at which all organic beings tend to increase. Every being, which during its natural lifetime produces several eggs or seeds, must suffer destruction during some period of its life, and during some season or occasional year, otherwise, on the principle of geometrical increase, its numbers would quickly become so inordinately great that no country could support the product. Hence, as more individuals are produced than can possibly survive, there must in every case be a struggle for existence, either one individual with another of the same species, or with the individuals of distinct species, or with the physical conditions of life. It is the doctrine of Malthus applied with manifold force to the whole animal and vegetable kingdoms; for in this case there can be no artificial increase of food, and no prudential restraint from marriage. Although some species may be now increasing, more or less rapidly, in numbers, all cannot do so, for the world would not hold them.

There is no exception to the rule that every organic being naturally increases at so high a rate that, if not destroyed, the earth would soon be covered by the progeny of a single pair. Even slow-breeding man has doubled in twenty-five years, and at this rate, in less than a thousand years, there would literally not be standing-room for his progeny. Linnaeus has calculated that if an annual plant produced only two seeds—and there is no plant so unproductive as this—and their seedlings next year produced two, and so on, then in twenty years there would be a million plants. The elephant is reckoned the slowest breeder of all known animals, and I have taken some pains to estimate its probable minimum rate of natural increase; it will be safest to assume that it begins breeding when thirty years old, and goes on breeding till ninety years old, bringing forth six young in the interval, and surviving until one hundred years old; if this be so, after a period of from 740 to 750 years there would be nearly nineteen million elephants alive, descended from the first pair.

But we have better evidence on this subject than mere theoretical calculations, namely, the numerous recorded cases of the astonishingly rapid increase of various animals in a state of nature, when circumstances have been favourable to them during two or three following seasons. Still more striking is the evidence from our domestic animals of many kinds which have run wild in several parts of the world; if the statements of the rate of increase of slow-breeding cattle and horses in South America, and latterly in Australia, had not been well authenticated, they would have been incredible. So it is with plants; cases could be given of introduced plants which have become common throughout whole islands in a period of less than ten years. Several of the plants, such as the cardoon and a tall thistle, which are now the commonest over the wide plains of La Plata, clothing square leagues of surface almost to the exclusion of every other plant, have been introduced from Europe; and there are plants which now range in India, as I hear from Dr. Falconer, from Cape Comorin to the Himalaya, which have been imported from America since its discovery. In such cases, and endless others could be given, no one supposes, that the fertility of animals or plants has been suddenly and temporarily increased in any sensible degree. The obvious explanation is that the conditions of life have been highly favourable, and that there has consequently been less destruction of the old and young, and that nearly all the young have been enabled to breed. Their geometrical ratio of increase, the result of which never fails to be surprising, simply explains their extraordinarily rapid increase and wide diffusion in their new homes.

In a state of nature almost every full-grown plant annually produces seeds, and amongst animals there are very few which do not annually pair. Hence we may confidently assert, that all plants and animals are tending to increase at a geometrical ratio,—that all would rapidly stock every station in which they could anyhow exist— and that this geometrical tendency to increase must be checked by destruction at some period of life. Our familiarity with the larger domestic animals tends, I think, to mislead us: we see no great destruction falling on them, but we do not keep in mind that thousands are annually slaughtered for food, and that in a state of nature an equal number would have somehow to be disposed of.

The only difference between organisms which annually produce eggs or seeds by the thousand, and those which produce extremely few, is, that the slow-breeders would require a few more years to people, under favourable conditions, a whole district, let it be ever so large. The condor lays a couple of eggs and the ostrich a score, and yet in the same country the condor may be the more numerous of the two; the Fulmar petrel lays but one egg, yet it is believed to be the most numerous bird in the world. One fly deposits hundreds of eggs, and another, like the hippobosca, a single one; but this difference does not determine how many individuals of the two species can be supported in a district. A large number of eggs is of some importance to those species which depend on a fluctuating amount of food, for it allows them rapidly to increase in number. But the real importance of a large number of eggs or seeds is to make up for much destruction at some period of life; and this period in the great majority of cases is an early one. If an animal can in any way protect its own eggs or young, a small number may be produced, and yet the average stock be fully kept up; but if many eggs or young are destroyed, many must be produced, or the species will become extinct. It would suffice to keep up the full number of a tree, which lived on an average for a thousand years, if a single seed were produced once in a thousand years, supposing that this seed were never destroyed, and could be ensured to germinate in a fitting place. So that, in all cases, the average number of any animal or plant depends only indirectly on the number of its eggs or seeds.

In looking at Nature, it is most necessary to keep the foregoing considerations always in mind—never to forget that every single organic being may be said to be striving to the utmost to increase in numbers; that each lives by a struggle at some period of its life; that heavy destruction inevitably falls either on the young or old, during each generation or at recurrent intervals. Lighten any check, mitigate the destruction ever so little, and the number of the species will almost instantaneously increase to any amount.

The causes which check the natural tendency of each species to increase are most obscure. Look at the most vigorous species; by as much as it swarms in numbers, by so much will it tend to increase still further. We know not exactly what the checks are even in a single instance. Nor will this surprise any one who reflects how ignorant we are on this head, even in regard to mankind, although so incomparably better known than any other animal. This subject of the checks to increase has been ably treated by several authors, and I hope in a future work to discuss it at considerable length, more especially in regard to the feral animals of South America. Here I will make only a few remarks, just to recall to the reader's mind some of the chief points. Eggs or very young animals seem generally to suffer most, but this is not invariably the case. With plants there is a vast destruction of seeds, but, from some observations which I have made it appears that the seedlings suffer most from germinating in ground already thickly stocked with other plants. Seedlings, also, are destroyed in vast numbers by various enemies; for instance, on a piece of ground three feet long and two wide, dug and cleared, and where there could be no choking from other plants, I marked all the seedlings of our native weeds as they came up, and out of 357 no less than 295 were destroyed, chiefly by slugs and insects. If turf which has long been mown, and the case would be the same with turf closely browsed by quadrupeds, be let to grow, the more vigorous plants gradually kill the less vigorous, though fully grown plants; thus out of twenty species growing on a little plot of mown turf (three feet by four) nine species perished, from the other species being allowed to grow up freely.

The amount of food for each species of course gives the extreme limit to which each can increase; but very frequently it is not the obtaining food, but the serving as prey to other animals, which determines the average number of species. Thus, there seems to be little doubt that the stock of partridges, grouse, and hares on any large estate depends chiefly on the destruction of vermin. If not one head of game were shot during the next twenty years in England, and, at the same time, if no vermin were destroyed, there would, in all probability, be less game than at present, although hundreds of thousands of game animals are now annually shot. On the other hand, in some cases, as with the elephant, none are destroyed by beasts of prey; for even the tiger in India most rarely dares to attack a young elephant protected by its dam. . . .

Many cases are on record showing how complex and unexpected are the checks and relations between organic beings, which have to struggle together in the same country. . . .

[I give an] instance showing how plants and animals, remote in the scale of nature, are bound together by a web of complex relations. I shall hereafter have occasion to show that the exotic Lobelia fulgens is never visited in my garden by insects, and consequently, from its peculiar structure, never sets a seed. Nearly all our orchidaceous plants absolutely require the visits of insects to remove their pollen-masses and thus to fertilise them. I find from experiments that humble-bees are almost indispensable to the fertilisation of the heartsease (Violo tricolor), for other bees do not visit this flower. I have also found that the visits of bees are necessary for the fertilisation of some kinds of clover; for instance, 20 heads of Dutch clover (Trifolium repens) yielded 2,290 seeds, but 20 other heads protected from bees produced not one. Again, 100 heads of red clover (T. pratense) produced 2,700 seeds, but the same number of protected heads produced not a single seed. Humble-bees alone visit red clover, as other bees cannot reach the nectar. It has been suggested that moths may fertilise the clovers; but I doubt whether they could do so in the case of the red clover, from their weight not being sufficient to depress the wing petals. Hence we may infer as highly probable that, if the whole genus of humble-bees became extinct or very rare in England, the heartsease and red clover would become very rare, or wholly disappear. The number of humble-bees in any district depends in a great measure upon the number of field-mice, which destroy their combs and nests; and Col. Newman, who has long attended to the habits of humble-bees, believes that "more than two-thirds of them are thus destroyed all over England." Now the number of mice is largely dependent, as every one knows, on the number of cats; and Col. Newman says, "Near villages and small towns I have found the nests of humble-bees more numerous than elsewhere, which I attribute to the number of cats that destroy the mice." Hence it is quite credible that the presence of a feline animal in large numbers in a district might determine, through the intervention first of mice and then of bees, the frequency of certain flowers in that district! . . .

If under changing conditions of life organic beings present individual differences in almost every part of their structure, and this cannot be disputed; if there be, owing to their geometrical rate of increase, a severe struggle for life at some age, season, or year, and this certainly cannot be disputed; then, considering the infinite complexity of the relations of all organic beings to each other and to their conditions of life, causing an infinite diversity in structure, constitution, and habits, to be advantageous to them, it would be a most extraordinary fact if no variations had ever occurred useful to each being's own welfare, in the same manner as so many variations have occurred useful to man. But if variations useful to any organic being ever do occur, assuredly individuals thus characterised will have the best chance of being preserved in the struggle for life; and from the strong principle of inheritance, these will tend to produce offspring similarly characterised. This principle of preservation, or the survival of the fittest, I have called Natural Selection. It leads to the improvement of each creature in relation to its organic and inorganic conditions of life; and consequently, in most cases, to what must be regarded as an advance in organisation. Nevertheless, low and simple forms will long endure if well fitted for their simple conditions of life.

Natural selection, on the principle of qualities being inherited at corresponding ages, can modify the egg, seed, or young, as easily as the adult. Amongst many animals, sexual selection will have given its aid to ordinary selection, by assuring to the most vigorous and best adapted males the greatest number of offspring. Sexual selection will also give characters useful to the males alone, in their struggles or rivalry with other males; and these characters will be transmitted to one sex or to both sexes, according to the form of inheritance which prevails.

Whether natural selection has really thus acted in adapting the various forms of life to their several conditions and stations, must be judged by the general tenor and balance of evidence given in the following chapters. But we have already seen how it entails extinction; and how largely extinction has acted in the world's history, geology plainly declares. Natural selection, also, leads to divergence of character; for the more organic beings diverge in structure, habits, and constitution, by so much the more can a large number be supported on the area—of which we see proof by looking to the inhabitants of any small spot, and to the productions naturalised in foreign lands. Therefore, during the modification of the descendants of any one species, and during the incessant struggle of all species to increase in numbers, the more diversified the descendants become, the better will be their chance of success in the battle for life. Thus the small differences distinguishing varieties of the same species, steadily tend to increase, till they equal the greater differences between species of the same genus, or even of distinct genera.

We have seen that it is the common, the widely-diffused and widely-ranging species, belonging to the larger genera within each class, which vary most; and these tend to transmit to their modified offspring that superiority which now makes them dominant in their own countries. Natural selection, as has just been remarked, leads to divergence of character and to much extinction of the less improved and intermediate forms of life. On these principles, the nature of the affinities, and the generally well-defined distinctions between the innumerable organic beings in each class throughout the world, may be explained. It is a truly wonderful fact—the wonder of which we are apt to overlook from familiarity—that all animals and all plants throughout all time and space should be related to each other in groups, subordinate to groups, in the manner which we everywhere behold—namely, varieties of the same species most closely related, species of the same genus less closely and unequally related, forming sections and subgenera, species of distinct genera much less closely related, and genera related in different degrees, forming subfamilies, families, orders, subclasses and classes. The several subordinate groups in any class cannot be ranked in a single file, but seem clustered round points, and these round other points, and so on in almost endless cycles. If species had been independently created, no explanation would have been possible of this kind of classification; but it is explained through inheritance and the complex action of natural selection, entailing extinction and divergence of character. . . .

The affinities of all the beings of the same class have sometimes been represented by a great tree. I believe this simile largely speaks the truth. The green and budding twigs may represent existing species; and those produced during former years may represent the long succession of extinct species. At each period of growth all the grow-ing twigs have tried to branch out on all sides, and to overtop and kill the surround-ing twigs and branches, in the same manner as species and groups of species have at all times overmastered other species in the great battle for life. The limbs divided into great branches, and these into lesser and lesser branches, were themselves once, when the tree was young, budding twigs; and this connection of the former and present buds by ramifying branches may well represent the classification of all extinct and liv-ing species in groups subordinate to groups. Of the many twigs which flourished when the tree was a mere bush, only two or three, now grown into great branches, yet survive and bear the other branches; so with the species which lived during long-past geological periods, very few have left living and modified descendants. From the first growth of the tree, many a limb and branch has decayed and dropped off; and these fallen branches of various sizes may represent those whole orders, families, and genera which have now no living representatives, and which are known to us only in a fossil state. As we here and there see a thin straggling branch springing from a fork low down in a tree, and which by some chance has been favoured and is still alive on its summit, so we occasionally see an animal like the Ornithorhynchus or Lepidosiren, which in some small degree connects by its affinities two large branches of life, and which has apparently been saved from fatal competition by having inhabited a pro-tected station. As buds give rise by growth to fresh buds, and these, if vigorous, branch out and overtop on all sides many a feebler branch, so by generation I believe it has been with the Great Tree of Life, which fills with its dead and broken branches the crust of the earth, and covers the surface with its everbranching and beautiful ramifications. . . .

It is interesting to contemplate an entangled bank, clothed with many plants of many kinds, with birds singing on the bushes, with various insects flitting about, and with worms crawling through the damp earth, and to reflect that these elaborately con-structed forms, so different from each other, and dependent on each other in so com-plex a manner, have all been produced by laws acting around us. These laws, taken in the largest sense, being Growth with Reproduction; Inheritance which is almost implied by reproduction; Variability from the indirect and direct action of the external conditions of life, and from use and disuse; a Ratio of Increase so high as to lead to a Struggle for Life, and as a consequence to Natural Selection, entailing Divergence of Character and the Extinction of less-improved forms. Thus, from the war of nature, from famine and death, the most exalted object which we are capable of conceiving, namely, the production of the higher animals, directly follows. There is grandeur in this view of life, with its several powers, having been originally breathed into a few forms or into one; and that, whilst this planet has gone cycling on according to the fixed law of gravity, from so simple a beginning endless forms most beautiful and most wonderful have been, and are being, evolved.

## *FROM* THE DESCENT OF MAN

### *Chapter XXI*
### *General Summary and Conclusion*

. . . The main conclusion arrived at in this work, and now held by many naturalists who are well competent to form a sound judgment, is that man is descended from some less highly-organized form. The grounds upon which this conclusion rests will never be shaken, for the close similarity between man and the lower animals in embryonic development, as well as in innumerable points of structure and constitution, both of high, and of the most trifling importance—the rudiments which he retains, and the abnormal reversions to which he is occasionally liable—are facts which cannot be disputed. They have long been known, but until recently they told us nothing with respect to the origin of man. Now, when viewed by the light of our knowledge of the whole organic world, their meaning is unmistakable. The great principle of evolution stands up clear and firm, when these groups of facts are considered in connection with others, such as the mutual affinities of the members of the same group, their geographical distribution in past and present times, and their geological succession. It is incredible that all these facts should speak falsely. He who is not content to look, like a savage, at the phenomena of Nature as disconnected, cannot any longer believe that man is the work of a separate act of creation. He will be forced to admit that the close resemblance of the embryo of man to that, for instance, of a dog—the construction of his skull, limbs, and whole frame, independently of the uses to which the parts may be put, on the same plan with that of other mammals—the occasional reappearance of various structures, for instance, of several distinct muscles, which man does not normally possess, but which are common to the Quadrumana—and a crowd of analogous facts—all point in the plainest manner to the conclusion that man is the co-descendant with other mammals of a common progenitor.

[This] conclusion . . . that man is descended from some lowly-organized form, will, I regret to think, be highly distasteful to many persons. But there can hardly be a doubt that we are descended from barbarians. The astonishment which I felt on first seeing a party of Fuegians on a wild and broken shore will never be forgotten by me, for the reflection at once rushed into my mind—such were our ancestors. These men were absolutely naked and bedaubed with paint, their long hair was tangled, their mouths frothed with excitement, and their expression was wild, startled, and distrustful. They possessed hardly any arts, and, like wild animals, lived on what they could catch; they had no government, and were merciless to every one not of their own small tribe. He who has seen a savage in his native land will not feel much shame, if forced to acknowledge that the blood of some more humble creature flows in his veins. For my own part, I would as soon be descended from that heroic little monkey, who braved his dreaded enemy in order to save the life of his keeper; or from that old baboon, who, descending from the mountains, carried away in triumph his young comrade from a crowd of astonished dogs—as from a savage who delights to torture his enemies, offers up bloody sacrifices, practises infanticide without remorse, treats his wives like slaves, knows no decency, and is haunted by the grossest superstitions.

Man may be excused for feeling some pride at having risen, though not through his own exertions, to the very summit of the organic scale; and the fact of his having thus risen, instead of having been aboriginally placed there, may give him hopes for a still higher destiny in the distant future. But we are not here concerned with hopes or fears, only with the truth as far as our reason allows us to discover it. I have given the evidence to the best of my ability; and we must acknowledge, as it seems to me, that man with all his noble qualities, with sympathy which feels for the most debased, with benevolence which extends not only to other men but to the humblest living creature, with his godlike intellect which has penetrated into the movements and constitution of the solar system—with all these exalted powers—Man still bears in his bodily frame the indelible stamp of his lowly origin.

# Richard Burton

# *from* Two Trips to Gorilla Land (1876)

*Richard Burton (1821–1890) was one of the most celebrated nineteenth-century travelers. Fluent in over twenty languages, well-read in history and ethnography, and audacious, Burton wrote many lengthy accounts of peoples he visited and places he explored. His* Personal Narrative of a Pilgrimage to Al-Madinah and Meccah *(1855), for example, recounts his pilgrimage to Mecca disguised as a Moslem and contains extensive ethnographic and political information seldom accessible to Europeans. Though a supporter of imperialism, Burton was often very critical of Britain's policies in Africa. In* Two Trips to Gorilla Land and the Cataracts of the Congo *(1876), written shortly after fighting between the coastal Fanti and the inland Ashanti had threatened colonial stations, Burton argues that British policy in West Africa is a failure because the ill-informed politicians who make it lack expert knowledge of local cultures. Burton's own claimed expertise, however, betrays the racial biases of his day: though he opposes slavery, he sees African emigration as desirable both to provide manual laborers for a European civilization he deems superior and to put an end to warfare between local tribes.*

After a languid conviction during the last half-century of owning some ground upon the West Coast of Africa, England has been rudely aroused by a little war which will have large consequences. The causes that led to the 'Ashantee Campaign' . . . may be broadly laid down as general incuriousness, local mismanagement, and the operation of unprincipled journalism.

It is not a little amusing to hear the complaints of the public that plain truth about the African has not been told. I could cite more than one name that has done so. But what was the result? We were all soundly abused by the negrophile; the multitude cared little about reading 'unpopular opinions'; and then, when the fullness of time came, it turned upon us, and rent us, and asked why we had not spoken freely concerning Ashanti and Fanti, and all the herd. My *Wanderings in West Africa* is a case in point: so little has it been read, that a President of the Royal Geographical Society could state, "If Fantees are cowardly and lazy, Krumen are brave"; the latter being the most notorious poltroons on the West African seaboard.

The hostilities on the Gold Coast might have been averted with honour to ourselves at any time between 1863 and 1870, by a Colonial Office mission and a couple of thousand pounds. I need hardly say what has been the case now. The first steps were taken with needless disasters, and the effect has been far different from what we intended or what was advisable. For a score of years we [travellers] have been advising the English statesman not to despise the cunning of barbarous tribes, never to attempt finessing with Asiatic or African; to treat these races with perfect sincerity and truthfulness. I have insisted, and it is now seen with what reason, that every attempt at deception, at asserting the 'thing which is not', will presently meet with the reward it deserves. I can only regret that my counsels have not made themselves heard.

Yet this ignoble war between barbarous tribes whom it has long been the fashion to pet, this poor scuffle between the breechloader and the Birmingham trade musket, may yet in one sense do good. It must perforce draw public attention to the West Coast of Africa, and raise the question, 'What shall we do with it?' My humble opinion, expressed early in 1865 to the Right Honourable Mr. Adderley, has ever been this. If we are determined not to follow the example of the French, the Dutch, the Portuguese, and the Spaniard, and not to use the country as a convict station, resolving to consume, as it were, our crime at home, we should also resolve to retain only a few ports and forts, without territory, at points commanding commerce, after the fashion of Lusitanians in the old heroic days. The export slave-trade is now dead and buried; the want of demand must prevent its revival; and free emigration has yet to be created. As Mr. Bright rightly teaches strong places and garrisons are not necessary to foster trade and to promote the success of missions. The best proof on the West African Coast is to be found in the so-called Oil Rivers, where we have never held a mile of ground, and where our commerce prospers most. The great 'Tribune' will forgive my agreeing in opinion with him when he finds that we differ upon one most important point. It is the merchant, not the garrison, that causes African wars. If the home authorities would avoid a campaign, let them commit their difficulty to a soldier, not to a civilian.

The chronic discontent of the so-called 'civilized' Africa, the contempt of the rulers if not of the rule, and the bitter hatred between the three races, white, black, and black-white, fomented by many an unprincipled print, which fills its pocket with coin of cant and Christian charity, will end in even greater scandals than the last disreputable war. If the *damnosa licentia* be not suppressed—and where are the strong hands to suppress it?—we may expect to see the scenes of Jamaica revived with improvements at Sierra Leone. However unwilling I am to cut off any part of our great and extended empire, to renew anywhere, even in Africa, the process of dismemberment . . . it is evident to me that English occupation of the West African Coast has but slightly forwarded the cause of humanity, and that upon the whole it has proved a remarkable failure.

We can be wise in time.

•

All who believe in "progress" are socially antislavers, as we all are politically Republicans. But between the two extremes, between despotism, in which society is regimented like an army, and liberty, where all men are theoretically free and equal, there are infinite shades of solid rule and government which the wisdom of nations adapts to their wants. The medium of constitutional monarchy or hereditary presidentship recommends itself under existing circumstances to the more advanced peoples, and with good reason; we nowhere find a prevalence of those manly virtues, disinterestedness and self-sacrifice to the "respublica," which rendered the endurance of ancient republics possible. Rome could hardly have ruled the world for centuries had her merchants supplied Carthage with improved triremes or furnished the Parthians with the latest style of weapons. We must be wise and virtuous before we can hope to be good republicans, and man in the mass is not yet "homo sapiens;" he is not wise, and certainly he is not virtuous.

The present state of Africa suggests two questions concerning the abolition of the export slave-trade, which must be kept essentially distinct from domestic servitude. The first is, "Does the change benefit the negro?" Into this extensive subject I do not propose to enter, contenting myself with recording a negative answer. But upon the second, "Is the world ready for its abolition?" I would offer a few remarks. They will be ungrateful to that small but active faction which has laboured so long and so hard to misinform the English public concerning Africa, and which is as little fitted to teach anything about the African as to legislate for Mongolian Tartary. It has prevailed for a time to the great injury of the cause, and we cannot but see its effects in almost every step taken by the Englishman, civilian or soldier, who lands his British opinions and prejudices on the West Coast, and who, utterly ignoring the fact that the African, as far as his small interests are concerned, is one of the clearest sighted of men, unhesitatingly puts forth addresses and proclamations which he would not think of submitting to Europeans. But I have faith in my countrymen. If there be any nation that deserves to be looked upon as the arbiter of public opinion in Europe, it is England proper, which, to the political education of many generations, adds an innate sense of moderation, of justice, and of fair play, and a suspicion of extreme measures however theoretically perfect, which do not exist elsewhere. Heinrich Heine expressed this idea after his Maccabean fashion, "Ask the stupidest Englishman a question of politics, and he will say something clever; ask the cleverest Englishman a question of religion and he will say something stupid." Hence the well-wishers of England can feel nothing but regret when they find her clear and cold light of reason obscured, as it has been, upon the negro question by the mists and clouds of sentimental passion, and their first desire is to see this weakness pass away.

I unhesitatingly assert—and all unprejudiced travellers will agree with me—that the world still wants the black hand. Enormous tropical regions yet await the clearing and the draining operations by the lower races, which will fit them to become the dwelling-place of civilized man.

But slave-exportation is practically dead; we would not revive it, nor indeed could we, the revival would be a new institution, completely in disaccord with the spirit of the age. It is for us to find something which shall take its place, and which shall satisfy the just aspirations of those who see their industry and energy neutralized by want of labour. I need hardly say that all requirements would be met by negro-emigration; and that not only Africa, but the world of the east as well as of the west, call for some measure of the kind. The "cooly" from Hindostan may in time become a valuable article, but it will be long before he can be induced to emigrate in sufficient numbers: the Chinese will be a mistake when the neglected resources of the mighty

"Central Empire," mineral and others, shall be ready to be developed, as they soon must, under the supervision of Europeans. It remains only for us to draw upon the great labour-bank of Negro-land.

A bonâ fide emigration, a free *engagé* system, would be a boon to Western and Inner Africa, where the tribes live in an almost continual state of petty warfare. The anti-slavers and the abolitionists, of course, represent this to be the effect of the European trade in man's flesh and blood; but it prevails, and has ever prevailed, and long will prevail, even amongst peoples which have never sent a head of negro to the coast. And there is a large class of men captured in battle, and a host of those condemned to death by savage superstition, whose lives can be saved only by their exportation, which, indeed, is the African form of transportation. "We believe," says the Abbé Proyart (1776), "that the father sells his son and the prince his subjects; *he* only who has lived among them can know that it is not even lawful for a man to sell his slave, if he be born in the country, unless he have incurred that penalty by certain crimes specified by law."

It will be objected that any scheme of the kind must be so involved in complicated difficulties that it cannot fail to degenerate into the old export slave-trade. This I deny. Admitting that such must at first be its tendency, I am persuaded that the details can so be controlled as to secure the use without the abuse. Women and children, for instance, should never be allowed on board ship, unless accompanying husbands and parents. Those who speak some words of a foreign tongue, English, French, Spanish, or Portuguese, and on the eastern coast Hindostani, might lead the way, to be followed in due time by the wilder races. Probably the best ground for the trial would be the Island of Zanzibar, where we can completely control its operations. And what should lend us patience and courage to meet and to beat down all difficulties is the consideration that success will be the sole possible means, independent of El Islam, of civilizing, or rather of humanizing, the Dark Continent. The excellent Abbé Proyart begins his "History of Loango" with the wise and memorable words: "Touching the Africans, these people have vices,—what people is exempt from vice? But, were they even more wicked and more vicious, they would be so much the more entitled to the commiseration and good offices of their fellow-men, and, should the missionary despair of making them Christians, men ought still to endeavour to make them men."

•

I have thus attempted to trace a picture of the Congo River in the latter days of the slave-trade, and of its lineal descendant, "L'Immigration Africaine." The people at large are satisfied, and the main supporters of the traffic—the chiefs, the "medicine-men," and the white traders—have at length been powerless to arrest its destruction.

And here we may quote certain words of wisdom from the "Congo Expedition" in 1816: "It is not to be expected that the effects of abolition will be immediately perceptible; on the contrary, it will probably require more than one generation to become apparent: *for effects, which have been the consequence of a practice of three centuries, will certainly continue long after the cause is removed.*" The allusion in the sentence which I have italicized, is of course, to the American exportation—domestic slavery must date from the earliest ages. These sensible remarks conclude with advocating "colonization in the cause of civilization;" a process which at present cannot be too strongly deprecated.

That the Nzadi is capable of supplying something better than slaves may be shown by a list of what its banks produce. Merolla says in 1682: "Cotton here is to be gathered in great abundance, and the shrubs it grows on are so prolific, that they never almost leave sprouting." Captain Tuckey declares "the only vegetable production at Boma of any consequence in commerce is cotton, which grows wild most luxuriantly, but the natives have ceased to gather it since the English have left off trading to the river." I will not advocate tobacco, cotton and sugar; they are indigenous, it is true, but their cultivation is hardly fitted to the African in Africa. Copper in small quantities has been brought from the interior, but the mineral resources of the wide inland regions are wholly unknown. If reports concerning mines on the plateau be trustworthy, there will be a rush of white hands, which must at once change, and radically change, all the conditions of the riverine country. Wax might be supplied in large quantities; the natives, however, have not yet learnt to hive their bees. Ivory was so despised by the slave-trade, that it was sent from the upper Congo to Mayumba and the other exporting harbours; demand would certainly produce a small but regular supply.

●

When time shall be ripe for a bonâ fide emigration, the position of Boma, at the head of the delta, a charming station, with healthy air and delicious climate, points it out as the head-quarters. Houses can be built for nominal sums, the neighbouring hills offer a sanatorium, and due attention to diet and clothing will secure the white man from the inevitable sufferings that result from living near the lower course.

With respect to the exploration of the upper stream, these pages, compared with the records of the "First Congo Expedition," will show the many changes which time has brought with it, and will suggest the steps most likely to forward the traveller's views.

●

I conclude with the hope that the great Nzadi, one of the noblest, and still the least known of the four principal African arteries, will no longer be permitted to flow through the White Blot, a region unexplored and blank to geography as at the time of its creation, and that my labours may contribute something, however small, to clear the way for the more fortunate explorer.

# *from* MR. GLADSTONE
# AND OUR EMPIRE (1877)

*Edward Dicey (1832–1911), a journalist and writer, edited the London* Observer, *Britain's oldest national Sunday paper, in the 1870s and 1880s. In the short piece included here he comments on contemporary debates in Parliament over the future of Britain's growing overseas empire (William Gladstone, to whom the title refers, was head of the Liberal Party at the time Dicey wrote). For Dicey, empire is not simply a matter of politics or economics: it is also about the spread of the English 'race' and its customs, laws, and language.*

It does not logically follow that because a politician objects to any further extension of our Empire he should therefore be in favour of its dismemberment. But if once this country comes to the conclusion that we have had enough of empire, and that we should do wisely to reduce our Imperial liabilities as soon as we can do so consistently with the moral obligations we have undertaken, then the days of our rule as a great Power beyond the four seas are clearly numbered. Englishmen who live out their lives in these small islands, who give the best of their labour to the questions, conflicts, issues of our insular existence, are apt to forget what England is in truth. Take up any gazeteer and you will find there what every schoolboy is supposed to know, but what to scores of Englishmen out of every hundred will read like a new discovery, the dimensions of the Empire of Great Britain. The United Kingdom, with an area of 120,000 square miles and a population of thirty-three millions, rules over eight million square miles of the globe's surface and two hundred millions of the world's inhabitants. Open any map, and glance for one moment at the dominions in which the Union Jack is the standard of the ruling race! Canada, stretching from the Atlantic to the Pacific, the peninsula of India, the continent of Australia, the South of Africa, are only the largest blotches so to speak, in a world chart blurred and dotted over with the stamp marks of British rule. Spread-eagle declamation about the Empire over which the sun never sets is not in accordance with the taste of our day, or the tone of thought which prevails amidst our governing classes. Facts and not fancies are the cry of the age. But it is well to remember that, after all, the existence of the British Empire is a fact and not a fancy. . . . Wherever the Union Jack floats, there the English race rules; English laws prevail; English ideas are dominant: English speech holds the upper hand. Our Empire may or may not be a benefit to England or to the countries over which she holds dominion; but its reality is as certain as its magnitude. . . . All I do assert is that England, like Rome, is the corner-stone of an imperial fabric such as it has fallen to the lot of no other country to erect, or to uphold when erected. This being so—and that it is so even the most fanatical of anti-imperialists will admit—the burden of proof surely rests with those who would pull down this Greater Britain, or allow it to fall to pieces, not with those who would consolidate or, if need be, extend the inheritance handed down to us by the labour, self-sacrifice, and courage of bygone generations of Englishmen.

The general issue of Empire or no Empire is not affected by considerations as to individual augmentations or cessions of territory. I may admit, as a matter of argument, that England gained, rather than lost, by the secession of her American colonies; that the cession of the Ionian Islands was a wise measure and the annexation of Fiji an unwise one. I may even acknowledge that the secession of Canada from the mother country is an event to be looked forward to without regret. Personally I should dissent from most of these conclusions but, even if I accepted them, I should see no cause to alter my view, that the maintenance of the Empire—that is of British authority over a vast outlying territory—ought to be one of the chief, if not the chief, object of British statesmanship. . . . What I want to point out is that our Empire is the result not so much of any military spirit as of a certain instinct of development inherent in our race. We have in us the blood of the Vikings; and the same impulse which sent the Norsemen forth to seek new homes in strange lands has, for century after century, impelled their descendants to wander forth in search of wealth, power, or adventure. 'To be fruitful, and multiply, and replenish the earth', seems to be the mission entrusted to us, as it was to the survivors of the deluge. The Wandering Jew of nations, it is forbidden to us to rest. The history of all our conquests, settlements, annexations, is, with rare exceptions, substantially the same. Attracted by the hope of gain, the love of excitement, or, more still, by the mere migratory instinct, English settlers pitch their tents in some foreign land, and obtain a footing in the country. But, unlike the colonists of other races, they carry England with them; they keep their own tongue, marry amidst their own people; dwell after their own fashion, and, though they may live and die in the land of their adoption, look to the mother country as their home. As their footing becomes established their interests clash with those of the native population. Whether with or without due cause, quarrels ensue; and then, sometimes by their own energy, sometimes by the aid of England, sometimes by both combined, they establish their own supremacy and become the ruling race in the regions which they entered as traders . . . [T]he point I wish to have placed in a clear light is that our Empire is due, not to the ambition of kings, not to the genius of generals, not even to the prevalence of one of those phases of military ardour through which most nations have to pass, but to the silent, constant operation of the instincts, laudable or otherwise, which have filled the world with the sound of the English tongue.

*Ernest Renan*

---

# *from* WHAT IS A NATION? (1882)

*B*orn in France, Ernest Renan (1823–1892) was a philosopher, historian, and scholar of
religion. He originally intended to become a priest, but, in the middle of his seminary
training, he had a crisis of faith and abandoned the Church for an academic career. He
would subsequently scandalize the church hierarchy when, in his opening lecture as the
chair of Hebrew at the Collège de France, he referred to Jesus as "an incomparable man."
Contemporary theorists of nationalism, who have tended to see nations as "imagined communities," have found in Renan a kindred spirit. In the following excerpt from "What Is a
Nation?" Renan views nations as historically contingent rather than eternal, and he sees
them as being dependent on the collective will to preserve them, what he calls "an everyday
plebiscite."

---

A nation is a soul, a spiritual principle. Only two things, actually, constitute this soul,
this spiritual principle. One is in the past, the other is in the present. One is the possession in common of a rich legacy of remembrances; the other is the actual consent,
the desire to live together, the will to continue to value the heritage which all hold in
common. Man, sirs, does not improvise. The nation, even as the individual, is the
end product of a long period of work, sacrifice and devotion. The worship of ancestors is understandably justifiable, since our ancestors have made us what we are. A
heroic past, of great men, of glory (I mean the genuine kind), that is the social principle on which the national idea rests. To have common glories in the past, a common
will in the present; to have accomplished great things together, to wish to do so again,
that is the essential condition for being a nation. One loves in proportion to the sacrifices which one has approved and for which one has suffered. One loves the house
which he has built and which he has made over. The Spartan chant: 'We are what you
make us; we are what you are' is simply the abbreviated hymn of the Fatherland.

   In the past, a heritage of glory and a reluctance to break apart, to realize the same
program in the future; to have suffered, worked, hoped together; that is worth more
than common taxes and frontiers conforming to ideas of strategy; that is what one
really understands despite differences of race and language. I have said 'having suffered together'; indeed, common suffering is greater than happiness. In fact, national

238

sorrows are more significant than triumphs because they impose obligations and demand a common effort.

A nation is a grand solidarity constituted by the sentiment of sacrifices which one has made and those that one is disposed to make again. It supposes a past, it renews itself especially in the present by a tangible deed: the approval, the desire, clearly expressed, to continue the communal life. The existence of a nation (pardon this metaphor!) is an everyday plebiscite; it is, like the very existence of the individual, a perpetual affirmation of life. Oh! I know it, this is less metaphysical than the concept of divine right, less brutal than the so-called historic right. In the order of ideas that I submit to you, a nation has no more right than a king of a province to say: 'You appear to me, I take you.' A province for us is its inhabitants; if anyone in this matter has a right to be considered, it is the inhabitant. A nation never has a real interest in being annexed or holding on to a country despite itself. The desire of nations to be together is the only real criterion that must always be taken into account.

We have traced the politics of metaphysical and theological abstractions. What remains after that? Man remains, his desires, his needs. . . . Human desires change; but what does not change on this earth? Nations are not something eternal. They have begun, they will end. They will be replaced, in all probability, by a European confederation. But such is not the law of the century in which we live. At the present time the existence of nations happens to be good, even necessary. Their existence is a guarantee of liberty, which would be lost if the world had only one law and only one master.

Through their varied, frequently opposing, abilities, nations serve the common cause of civilization; each holds one note in the concert of humanity, which, in the long run, is the highest ideal to which we can aspire. Isolated, they have their weaknesses. I often say to myself that a person who has these defects in quality that nations have, who nourishes himself on vainglory, who is jealous, egotistic and quarrelsome, who could support nothing without fighting; he would be the most intolerable of men. But all these unharmonious details disappear when we are united. Poor humanity! How you have suffered! What ordeals await you yet! Can the spirit of wisdom guide you to prevent the many dangers that line your path?

I continue, sirs. Man is not enslaved, nor is his race nor his language, nor his religion, nor the course of the rivers, nor the direction of the mountain ranges. A great aggregation of men, with a healthy spirit and warmth of heart, creates a moral conscience which is called a nation. When this moral conscience proves its strength by sacrifices that demand abdication of the individual for the benefit of the community, it is legitimate, and it has a right to exist.

—trans. Ida Mae Snyder

# Herbert Spencer

## *from* THE MAN VERSUS THE STATE (1884)

*Herbert Spencer (1820–1903) was an English sociologist and philosopher from a dis-senting, or non-Anglican, religious background. Declining an offer by his uncle to send him to Cambridge, he educated himself. He read widely in the natural sciences, reaching the conclusion that science was preferable to religion. Spencer was an early advocate of evo-lutionary theory and a 'social Darwinist'; that is, he argued that society should conform to Darwinian laws. In the following extract from* The Man versus the State, *he deploys the idea of 'natural selection' and 'the survival of the fittest' to argue for government policies that allow nature to take its course, whether that involves the fighting of poverty at home or the use of military intervention in the cause of imperial expansion.*

The continuance of every higher species of creature depends on conformity, now to one, now to the other, of two radically-opposed principles. The early lives of its members, and the adult lives of its members, have to be dealt with in contrary ways. We will contemplate them in their natural order.

One of the most familiar facts is that animals of superior types, comparatively slow in reaching maturity, are enabled when they have reached it, to give more aid to their offspring than animals of inferior types. The adults foster their young during periods more or less prolonged, while yet the young are unable to provide for themselves; and it is obvious that maintenance of the species can be secured only by a parental care adjusted to the need consequent on imperfection. It requires no proving that the blind unfledged hedge-bird, or the young puppy even after it has acquired sight, would forthwith die if it had to keep itself warm and obtain its own food. The gratuitous parental aid must be great in proportion as the young one is of little worth, either to itself or to others; and it may diminish as fast as, by increasing development, the young one acquires worth, at first for self-sustentation, and by-and-by for sustentation of others. That is to say, during immaturity, benefits received must be inversely as the power or ability of the receiver. Clearly if during this first part of life benefits were proportioned to merits, or rewards to deserts, the species would disappear in a generation.

From this regime of the family-group, let us turn to the regime of that larger group formed by the adult members of the species. Ask what happens when the new

240

individual, acquiring complete use of its powers and ceasing to have parental aid, is left to itself. Now there comes into play a principle just the reverse of that above described. Throughout the rest of its life, each adult gets benefit in proportion to merit—reward in proportion to desert: merit and desert in each case being understood as ability to fulfil all the requirements of life to get food, to secure shelter, to escape enemies. Placed in competition with members of its own species and in antagonism with members of other species, it dwindles and gets killed off, or thrives and propagates, according as it is ill-endowed or well-endowed. Manifestly an opposite regime, could it be maintained, would, in course of time, be fatal to the species. If the benefits received by each individual were proportionate to its inferiority—if, as a consequence, multiplication of the inferior was furthered and multiplication of the superior hindered, progressive degradation would result; and eventually the degenerate species would fail to hold its ground in presence of antagonistic species and competing species.

The broad fact then, here to be noted, is that Nature's modes of treatment inside the family-group and outside the family-group, are diametrically opposed to one another; and that the intrusion of either mode into the sphere of the other, would be fatal to the species either mediately or remotely.

Does any one think that the like does not hold of the human species? He cannot deny that within the human family, as within any inferior family, it would be fatal to proportion benefits to merits. Can he assert that outside the family, among adults, there should not be a proportioning of benefits to merits? Will he contend that no mischief will result if the lowly endowed are enabled to thrive and multiply as much as, or more than, the highly endowed? A society of men, standing towards other societies in relations of either antagonism or competition, may be considered as a species, or, more literally, as a variety of a species; and it must be true of it as of other species or varieties, that it will be unable to hold its own in the struggle with other societies, if it disadvantages its superior units that it may advantage its inferior units. Surely none can fail to see that were the principle of family life to be adopted and fully carried out in social life, were reward always great in proportion as desert was small, fatal results to the society would quickly follow; and if so, then even a partial intrusion of the family regime into the regime of the State, will be slowly followed by fatal results. Society in its corporate capacity, cannot without mediate or remoter disaster interfere with the play of these opposed principles under which every species has reached such fitness for its mode of life as it possesses, and under which it maintains that fitness.

I say advisedly—society in its corporate capacity: not intending to exclude or condemn aid given to the inferior by the superior in their individual capacities. Though when given so indiscriminately as to enable the inferior to multiply, such aid entails mischief; yet in the absence of aid given by society, individual aid, more generally demanded than now, and associated with a greater sense of responsibility, would, on the average, be given with the effect of fostering the unfortunate worthy rather than the innately unworthy: there being always, too, the concomitant social benefit arising from culture of the sympathies. But all this may be admitted while asserting that the radical distinction between family-ethics and State-ethics must be maintained; and that while generosity must be the essential principle of the one, justice must be the essential principle of the other—a rigorous maintenance of those normal relations among citizens under which each gets in return for his labour, skilled or unskilled, bodily or mental, as much as is proved to be its value by the demand for it: such return, therefore, as will enable him to thrive and rear offspring in proportion to the superiorities which make him valuable to himself and others.

And yet, notwithstanding the conspicuousness of these truths, which should strike every one who leaves his lexicons, and his law deeds, and his ledgers, and looks abroad into that natural order of things under which we exist, and to which we must conform, there is continual advocacy of paternal government. The intrusion of family-ethics into the ethics of the State, instead of being regarded as socially injurious, is more and more demanded as the only efficient means to social benefit. So far has this delusion now gone, that it vitiates the beliefs of those who might, more than all others, be thought safe from it.

•

The process of "natural selection," as Mr Darwin called it, co-operating with a tendency to variation and to inheritance of variations, he has shown to be a chief cause (though not, I believe, the sole cause) of that evolution through which all living things, beginning with the lowest and diverging and re-diverging as they evolved, have reached their present degrees of organization and adaptation to their modes of life. So familiar has this truth become that some apology seems needed for naming it. And yet, strange to say, now that this truth is recognized by most cultivated people, now that the beneficent working of the survival of the fittest has been so impressed on them that, much more than people in past times, they might be expected to hesitate before neutralizing its action now more than ever before in the history of the world, are they doing all they can to further survival of the unfittest!

But the postulate that men are rational beings, continually leads one to draw inferences which prove to be extremely wide of the mark.

> "Yes truly; your principle is derived from the lives of brutes, and is a brutal principle. You will not persuade me that men are to be under the discipline which animals are under. I care nothing for your natural-history arguments. My conscience shows me that the feeble and the suffering must be helped; and if selfish people won't help them, they must be forced by law to help them. Don't tell me that the milk of human kindness is to be reserved for the relations between individuals, and that Governments must be the administrators of nothing but hard justice. Every man with sympathy in him must feel that hunger and pain and squalor must be prevented; and that if private agencies do not suffice, then public agencies must be established."

Such is the kind of response which I expect to be made by nine out of ten. In some of them it will doubtless result from a fellow-feeling so acute that they cannot contemplate human misery without an impatience which excludes all thoughts of remote results. Concerning the susceptibilities of the rest, we may, however, be somewhat sceptical. Persons who, now in this case and now in that, are angry if, to maintain our supposed national "interests" or national "prestige," those in authority do not promptly send out some thousands of men to be partially destroyed while destroying other thousands of men whose intentions we suspect, or whose institutions we think dangerous to us, or whose territory our colonists want, cannot after all be so tender in feeling that contemplating the hardships of the poor is intolerable to them. Little admiration need be felt for the professed sympathies of people who urge on a policy which breaks up progressing societies; and who then look on with cynical indifference at the weltering confusion left behind, with all its entailed suffering and death. . . . Indeed, along with this sensitiveness which they profess will not let them look with patience on the pains of "the battle of life" as it quietly goes on around, they appear to have a callousness which not only tolerates but enjoys contemplating the pains of battles of the literal kind; as one sees in the demand for frustrated papers containing scenes of carnage, and in the greediness with which detailed accounts of bloody engagements are read. We may reasonably have our doubts about men whose feelings are such that they cannot bear the thought of hardships borne, mostly by the idle and the improvident, and who, nevertheless, have demanded thirty-one editions of The Fifteen Decisive Battles of the World, in which they may revel in accounts of slaughter. Nay, even still more remarkable is the contrast between the professed tender-heartedness and the actual hard-heartedness of those who would reverse the normal course of things that mediate miseries may be prevented, even at the cost of greater miseries hereafter produced. For on other occasions you may hear them, with utter disregard of bloodshed and death, contend that in the interests of humanity at large it is well that the inferior races should be exterminated and their places occupied by the superior races. So that, marvellous to relate, though they cannot think with calmness of the evils accompanying the struggle for existence as it is carried on without violence among individuals in their own society, they contemplate with contented equanimity such evils in their intense and wholesale forms, when inflicted by fire and sword on entire communities. Not worthy of much respect then, as it seems to me, is this generous consideration of the inferior at home which is accompanied by unscrupulous sacrifice of the inferior abroad.

Still less respectable appears this extreme concern for those of our own blood which goes along with utter unconcern for those of other blood, when we observe its methods. Did it prompt personal effort to relieve the suffering, it would rightly receive approving recognition. Were the many who express this cheap pity like the few who patiently, week after week and year after year, devote large parts of their time to helping and encouraging, and occasionally amusing, those who, in some cases by ill-fortune and in other cases by incapacity or misconduct, are brought to lives of hardship, they would be worthy of unqualified admiration. The more there are of men and women who help the poor to help themselves—the more there are of those whose sympathy is exhibited directly and not by proxy, the more we may rejoice. But the immense majority of the persons who wish to mitigate by law the miseries of the unsuccessful and the reckless, propose to do this in small measure at their own cost and mainly at the cost of others—sometimes with their assent but mostly without. More than this is true; for those who are to be forced to do so much for the distressed, often equally or more require something doing for them. The deserving poor are among those who are burdened to pay the costs of caring for the undeserving poor. . . . In short, men who are so sympathetic that they cannot allow the struggle for existence to bring on the unworthy the sufferings consequent on their incapacity or misconduct, are so unsympathetic that they can, without hesitation, make the struggle for existence harder for the worthy, and inflict on them and their children artificial evils in addition to the natural evils they have to bear!

# *from* THE JEWISH STATE (1896)

*Theodor Herzl (1860–1904), while not the first exponent of Zionism, was certainly the most influential among the early pioneers. Herzl was from an affluent Jewish background and became a journalist and writer. He believed in the promise of the liberal and secular state, a place where Jews could live as integrated members of society without abandoning their faith. The emergence of a new, virulent form of anti-Semitism in the late nineteenth century led him to question such beliefs. He reached the conclusion that the Jews would always be seen as foreigners, and the Jewish questions would never be resolved until they had a state of their own. It is noteworthy that, while 'cultural' Zionists would insist that only Palestine could serve as the foundation of a Jewish state, Herzl was above all interested in creating a safe space for Jews and thus entertained the idea of a Jewish state in Argentina.*

## II.—THE JEWISH QUESTION

No one can deny the gravity of the situation of the Jews. Wherever they live in perceptible numbers, they are more or less persecuted. Their equality before the law, granted by statute, has become practically a dead letter. They are debarred from filling even moderately high positions, either in the army, or in any public or private capacity. And attempts are made to thrust them out of business also: "Don't buy from Jews!"

•

Everything tends, in fact, to one and the same conclusion, which is clearly enunciated in that classic Berlin phrase: *"Juden Raus!"* (Out with the Jews!)

I shall now put the Question in the briefest possible form: Are we to "get out" now and where to?

Or, may we yet remain? And, how long?

•

The common people have not, and indeed cannot have, any historic comprehension. They do not know that the sins of the Middle Ages are now being visited on the nations of Europe. We are what the Ghetto made us. We have attained pre-eminence in finance, because mediaeval conditions drove us to it. The same process is now being repeated. We are again being forced into finance, now it is the stock exchange, by being kept out of other branches of economic activity. Being on the stock exchange, we are consequently exposed afresh to contempt. At the same time we continue to produce an abundance of mediocre intellects who find no outlet, and this endangers our social position as much as does our increasing wealth. Educated Jews without means are now rapidly becoming Socialists. Hence we are certain to suffer very severely in the struggle between classes, because we stand in the most exposed position in the camps of both Socialists and capitalists.

•

## Causes of Anti-Semitism

. . . Modern Anti-Semitism is not to be confounded with the religious persecution of the Jews of former times. It does occasionally take a religious bias in some countries, but the main current of the aggressive movement has now changed. In the principal countries where Anti-Semitism prevails, it does so as a result of the emancipation of the Jews. When civilized nations awoke to the inhumanity of discriminatory legislation and enfranchised us, our enfranchisement came too late. It was no longer possible to remove our disabilities in our old homes. For we had, curiously enough, developed while in the Ghetto into a bourgeois people, and we stepped out of it only to enter into fierce competition with the middle classes. Hence, our emancipation set us suddenly within this middle-class circle, where we have a double pressure to sustain, from within and from without. The Christian bourgeoisie would not be unwilling to cast us as a sacrifice to Socialism, though that would not greatly improve matters.

At the same time, the equal rights of Jews before the law cannot be withdrawn where they have once been conceded. Not only because their withdrawal would be opposed to the spirit of our age, but also because it would immediately drive all Jews, rich and poor alike, into the ranks of subversive parties. Nothing effectual can really be done to our injury. In olden days our jewels were seized. How is our movable property to be got hold of now? . . . The very impossibility of getting at the Jews nourishes and embitters hatred of them. Anti-Semitism increases day by day and hour by hour among the nations; indeed, it is bound to increase, because the causes of its growth continue to exist and cannot be removed. Its remote cause is our loss of the power of assimilation during the Middle Ages; its immediate cause is our excessive production of mediocre intellects, who cannot find an outlet downwards or upwards—that is to say, no wholesome outlet in either direction. When we sink, we become a revolutionary proletariat, the subordinate officers of all revolutionary parties; and at the same time, when we rise, there rises also our terrible power of the purse.

## Effects of Anti-Semitism

. . . I referred previously to our "assimilation." I do not for a moment wish to imply that I desire such an end. Our national character is too historically famous, and, in spite of every degradation, too fine to make its annihilation desirable. We might perhaps be able to merge ourselves entirely into surrounding races, if these were to leave us in peace for a period of two generations. But they will not leave us in peace. For a little period they manage to tolerate us, and then their hostility breaks out again and again. The world is provoked somehow by our prosperity, because it has for many centuries been accustomed to consider us as the most contemptible among the poverty-stricken. In its ignorance and narrowness of heart, it fails to observe that prosperity weakens our Judaism and extinguishes our peculiarities. It is only pressure that forces us back to the parent stem; it is only hatred encompassing us that makes us strangers once more.

Thus, whether we like it or not, we are now and shall henceforth remain, a historic group with unmistakable characteristics common to us all.

We are one people—our enemies have made us one without our consent, as repeatedly happens in history. Distress binds us together, and, thus united, we suddenly discover our strength. Yes, we are strong enough to form a State, and, indeed, a model State. We possess all human and material resources necessary for the purpose.

This is therefore the appropriate place to give an account of what has been somewhat roughly termed our "human material." But it would not be appreciated till the broad lines of the plan, on which everything depends, has first been marked out.

## The Plan

The whole plan is in its essence perfectly simple, as it must necessarily be if it is to come within the comprehension of all.

Let the sovereignty be granted us over a portion of the globe large enough to satisfy the rightful requirements of a nation; the rest we shall manage for ourselves.

The creation of a new State is neither ridiculous nor impossible. We have in our day witnessed the process in connection with nations which were not largely members of the middle class, but poorer, less educated, and consequently weaker than ourselves. The Governments of all countries scourged by Anti-Semitism will be keenly interested in assisting us to obtain the sovereignty we want.

The plan, simple in design, but complicated in execution, will be carried out by two agencies: The Society of Jews and the Jewish Company.

The Society of Jews will do the preparatory work in the domains of science and politics, which the Jewish Company will afterwards apply practically.

The Jewish Company will be the liquidating agent of the business interests of departing Jews, and will organize commerce and trade in the new country.

•

If we wish to found a State today, we shall not do it in the way which would have been the only possible one a thousand years ago. It is foolish to revert to old stages of civilization, as many Zionists would like to do. Supposing, for example, we were obliged to clear a country of wild beasts, we should not set about the task in the fashion of Europeans of the fifth century. We should not take spear and lance and go out singly in pursuit of bears; we would organize a large and active hunting party, drive the animals together, and throw a melinite bomb into their midst. . . .

Should the Powers declare themselves willing to admit our sovereignty over a neutral piece of land, then the Society will enter into negotiations for the possession of this land. Here two territories come under consideration, Palestine and Argentine. In both countries important experiments in colonization have been made, though on the mistaken principle of a gradual infiltration of Jews. An infiltration is bound to end badly. It continues till the inevitable moment when the native population feels itself threatened, and forces the Government to stop a further influx of Jews. Immigration is consequently futile unless we have the sovereign right to continue such immigration.

●

### *Palestine or Argentine?*

Shall we choose Palestine or Argentine? We shall take what is given us, and what is selected by Jewish public opinion. The Society will determine both these points.

Argentine is one of the most fertile countries in the world, extends over a vast area, has a sparse population and a mild climate. The Argentine Republic would derive considerable profit from the cession of a portion of its territory to us. The present infiltration of Jews has certainly produced some discontent, and it would be necessary to enlighten the Republic on the intrinsic difference of our new movement.

Palestine is our ever-memorable historic home. The very name of Palestine would attract our people with a force of marvellous potency. If His Majesty the Sultan were to give us Palestine, we could in return undertake to regulate the whole finances of Turkey. We should there form a portion of a rampart of Europe against Asia, an outpost of civilization as opposed to barbarism. We should as a neutral State remain in contact with all Europe, which would have to guarantee our existence. The sanctuaries of Christendom would be safeguarded by assigning to them an extra-territorial status such as is well-known to the law of nations. We should form a guard of honor about these sanctuaries, answering for the fulfilment of this duty with our existence. This guard of honor would be the great symbol of the solution of the Jewish Question after eighteen centuries of Jewish suffering.

*Gertrude Bell*

## *from* THE DESERT AND THE SOWN (1907)

*Gertrude Bell (1868–1926) took a first in history at Oxford in 1887 and later traveled extensively in Persia, Syria, Iraq, and Arabia. Like earlier travelers such as Richard Burton, she found an exhilarating freedom in travel abroad that she felt was not possible in England. Bell published several books about her travels before the outbreak of the Great War. Her interests were at once cultural and political:* The Desert and the Sown, *which recounts her long journey into Syria in the last years of Ottoman rule, includes photographs and full descriptions of archaeological sites and also detailed notes and speculations on regional political intrigues. During the war Bell was a member of the British administration in Mesopotamia, tasked with furthering British interests amidst the Arab revolt against the Turks; afterwards, during the division of Ottoman territories into new nations, she played an instrumental role in establishing the Hashemite dynasty in power in Iraq. Her continuing passion for Arabia led to her final project: the creation of a national museum in Baghdad to ensure that most of the archaeological treasures being excavated in Iraq would remain there.*

### PREFACE

Those who venture to add a new volume to the vast literature of travel, unless they be men of learning or politicians, must be prepared with an excuse. My excuse is ready, as specious and I hope as plausible as such things should be. I desired to write not so much a book of travel as an account of the people whom I met or who accompanied me on my way, and to show what the world is like in which they live and how it appears to them. And since it was better that they should, as far as possible, tell their own tale, I have strung their words upon the thread of the road, relating as I heard them the stories with which shepherd and man-at-arms beguiled the hours of the march, the talk that passed from lip to lip round the camp-fire, in the black tent of the Arab and the guest-chamber of the Druze, as well as the more cautious utterances of Turkish and Syrian officials. Their statecraft consists of guesses, often shrewd enough, at the results that may spring from the clash of unknown forces, of which the strength and the aim are but dimly apprehended; their wisdom is that of men whose channels of information and standards for comparison are different from ours, and who bring a different set of preconceptions to bear upon the problems laid before them. The Oriental is like a very old child. He is unacquainted with many branches of knowledge which we have come to regard as of elementary necessity; frequently, but not always, his mind is little preoccupied with the need of acquiring them, and he concerns himself scarcely at all with what we call practical utility. He is not practical in our acceptation of the word, any more than a child is practical, and his utility is not ours. On the other hand, his action is guided by traditions of conduct and morality that go back to the beginnings of civilisation, traditions unmodified as yet by any important change in the manner of life to which they apply and out of which they arose. These things apart, he is as we are; human nature does not undergo a complete change east of Suez, nor is it impossible to be on terms of friendship and sympathy with the dwellers in those regions. In some respects it is even easier than in Europe. You will find in the East habits of intercourse less fettered by artificial chains, and a wider tolerance born of greater diversity. Society is divided by caste and sect and tribe into an infinite number of groups, each one of which is following a law of its own, and however fantastic, to our thinking, that law may be, to the Oriental it is an ample and a satisfactory explanation of all peculiarities. A man may go about in public veiled up to the eyes, or clad if he please only in a girdle: he will excite no remark. Why should he? Like every one else he is merely obeying his own law. So too the European may pass up and down the wildest places, encountering little curiosity and of criticism even less. The news he brings will be heard with interest, his opinions will be listened to with attention, but he will not be thought odd or mad, nor even mistaken, because his practices and the ways of his thought are at variance with those of the people among whom he finds himself. "Adat-hu": it is his custom. And for this reason he will be the wiser if he does not seek to ingratiate himself with Orientals by trying to ape their habits, unless he is so skillful that he can pass as one of themselves. Let him treat the law of others respectfully, but he himself will meet with a far greater respect if he adheres strictly to his own. For a woman this rule is of the first importance, since a woman can never disguise herself effectually. That she should be known to come of a great and honoured stock, whose customs are inviolable, is her best claim to consideration.

None of the country through which I went is ground virgin to the traveller, though parts of it have been visited but seldom, and described only in works that are costly and often difficult to obtain. Of such places I have given a brief account, and as many photographs as seemed to be of value. I have also noted in the northern cities of Syria those vestiges of antiquity that catch the eye of a casual observer. There is still much exploration to be done in Syria and on the edge of the desert, and there are many difficult problems yet to be solved. The work has been well begun by de Vogüé, Wetzstein, Brünnow, Sachau, Dussaud, Puchstein and his colleagues, the members of the Princeton Expedition and others. To their books I refer those who would learn how immeasurably rich is the land in architectural monuments and in the epigraphic records of a far-reaching history.

My journey did not end at Alexandretta as this account ends. In Asia Minor I was, however, concerned mainly with archaeology; the results of what work I did there have been published in a series of papers in the *Revue Archeologique*, where, through the kindness of the editor, Monsieur Salomon Reinach, they have found a more suitable place than the pages of such a book as this could have offered them.

I do not know either the people or the language of Asia Minor well enough to come into anything like a close touch with the country, but I am prepared, even on a meagre acquaintance, to lay tokens of esteem at the feet of the Turkish peasant. He is gifted with many virtues, with the virtue of hospitality beyond all others.

I have been at some pains to relate the actual political conditions of unimportant persons. They do not appear so unimportant to one who is in their midst, and for my part I have always been grateful to those who have provided me with a clue to their relations with one another. But I am not concerned to justify or condemn the government of the Turk. I have lived long enough in Syria to realise that his rule is far from being the ideal of administration, and seen enough of the turbulent elements which he keeps more or less in order to know that his post is a difficult one. I do not believe that any government would give universal satisfaction; indeed, there are few which attain that desired end even in more united countries. Being English, I am persuaded that we are the people who could best have taken Syria in hand with the prospect of a success greater than that which might be attained by a moderately reasonable Sultan. We have long recognised that the task will not fall to us. We have unfortunately done more than this. Throughout the dominions of Turkey we have allowed a very great reputation to weaken and decline; reluctant to accept the responsibility of official interference, we have yet permitted the irresponsible protests, vehemently expressed, of a sentimentality that I make bold to qualify as ignorant, and our dealings with the Turk have thus presented an air of vacillation which he may be pardoned for considering perfidious and for regarding with animosity. These feelings, combined with the deep-seated dread of a great Asiatic Empire which is also mistress of Egypt and of the sea, have, I think, led the Porte to seize the first opportunity for open resistance to British demands, whether out of simple miscalculation of the spirit that would be aroused, or with the hope of foreign backing, it is immaterial to decide. The result is equally deplorable, and if I have gauged the matter at all correctly, the root of it lies in the disappearance of English influence at Constantinople. The position of authority that we occupied has been taken by another, yet it is and must be of far deeper importance to us than to any other that we should be able to guide when necessary the tortuous politics of Yildiz Kiosk. The greatest of all Mohammedan powers cannot afford to let her relations with the Khalif of Islam be regulated with so little consistency or firmness, and if the Sultan's obstinacy in the Tabah quarrel can prove to us how far the reins have slipped from our hands, it will have served its turn. Seated as we are upon the Mediterranean and having at our command, as I believe, a considerable amount of goodwill within the Turkish empire and the memories of an ancient friendship, it should not be impossible to recapture the place we have lost.

But these are matters outside the scope of the present book and my *apologia* had best end where every Oriental writer would have begun: "In the name of God, the Merciful, the Compassionate!"

## *FROM* Chapter I

To those bred under an elaborate social order few such moments of exhilaration can come as that which stands at the threshold of wild travel. The gates of the enclosed garden are thrown open, the chain at the entrance of the sanctuary is lowered, with a wary glance to right and left you step forth, and, behold! the immeasurable world.

The world of adventure and of enterprise, dark with hurrying storms, glittering in raw sunlight, an unanswered question and an unanswerable doubt hidden in the fold of every hill. Into it you must go alone, separated from the troops of friends that walk the rose alleys, stripped of the purple and fine linen that impede the fighting arm, roofless, defenceless, without possessions. The voice of the wind shall be heard instead of the persuasive voices of counsellors, the touch of the rain and the prick of the frost shall be spurs sharper than praise or blame, and necessity shall speak with an authority unknown to that borrowed wisdom which men obey or discard at will. So you leave the sheltered close, and, like the man in the fairy story, you feel the bands break that were riveted about your heart as you enter the path that stretches across the rounded shoulder of the earth.

# Vladimir Ilyich Ulyanov (Lenin)

## *from* IMPERIALISM: THE HIGHEST STAGE OF CAPITALISM (1916)

*Vladimir Lenin is arguably the most important revolutionary of the twentieth century. Founder of the Bolshevik or Russian Communist Party, he was the principal leader of the 1917 Russian Revolution, became the first head of the Soviet state, and helped found the international Communist movement or Comintern. His thought, codified by his followers as Marxism-Leninism, inspired Communist movements worldwide. Lenin's* Imperialism: The Highest Stage of Capitalism *was the most important attempt among Marxist revolutionaries to grapple with the rapid proliferation of late nineteenth- and early twentieth-century colonial expansion. It is based on the ideas of J. A. Hobson, an English liberal economist. According to Hobson, imperial expansion did not benefit the nation as a whole, but only part of it: the capitalist class, who thrived on ever expanding markets and investment opportunities. Lenin accepts Hobson's economic emphasis but argues that imperialism represents a particular historical phase of capitalist development, which he labels 'monopoly capitalism'. It would only be vanquished when the capitalist system is overthrown.*

### X. THE PLACE OF IMPERIALISM IN HISTORY

We have seen that in its economic essence imperialism is monopoly capitalism. This in itself determines its place in history, for monopoly that grows out of the soil of free competition, and precisely out of free competition, is the transition from the capitalist system to a higher socio-economic order. We must take special note of the four principal types of monopoly, or principal manifestations of monopoly capitalism, which are characteristic of the epoch we are examining.

Firstly, monopoly arose out of the concentration of production at a very high stage. This refers to the monopolist capitalist associations, cartels, syndicates and trusts. We have seen the important part these play in present-day economic life. At the beginning of the twentieth century, monopolies had acquired complete supremacy in the advanced countries, and although the first steps towards the formation of the cartels were taken by countries enjoying the protection of high tariffs (Germany, America), Great Britain, with her system of free trade, revealed the same basic phenomenon, only a little later, namely, the birth of monopoly out of the concentration of production.

Secondly, monopolies have stimulated the seizure of the most important sources of raw materials, especially for the basic and most highly cartelised industries in capitalist society: the coal and iron industries. The monopoly of the most important sources of raw materials has enormously increased the power of big capital, and has sharpened the antagonism between cartelised and non-cartelised industry.

Thirdly, monopoly has sprung from the banks. The banks have developed from modest middleman enterprises into the monopolists of finance capital. Some three to five of the biggest banks in each of the foremost capitalist countries have achieved the "personal linkup" between industrial and bank capital, and have concentrated in their hands the control of thousands upon thousands of millions which form the greater part of the capital and income of entire countries. A financial oligarchy, which throws a close network of dependence relationships over all the economic and political institutions of present-day bourgeois society without exception—such is the most striking manifestation of this monopoly.

Fourthly, monopoly has grown out of colonial policy. To the numerous "old" motives of colonial policy, finance capital has added the struggle for the sources of raw materials, for the export of capital, for spheres of influence, i.e., for spheres for profitable deals, concessions, monopoly profits and so on, economic territory in general. When the colonies of the European powers, for instance, comprised only one-tenth of the territory of Africa (as was the case in 1876), colonial policy was able to develop by methods other than those of monopoly—by the "free grabbing" of territories, so to speak. But when nine-tenths of Africa had been seized (by 1900), when the whole world had been divided up, there was inevitably ushered in the era of monopoly possession of colonies and, consequently, of particularly intense struggle for the division and the redivision of the world.

The extent to which monopolist capital has intensified all the contradictions of capitalism is generally known. It is sufficient to mention the high cost of living and the tyranny of the cartels. This intensification of contradictions constitutes the most powerful driving force of the transitional period of history, which began from the time of the final victory of world finance capital.

Monopolies, oligarchy, the striving for domination and not for freedom, the exploitation of an increasing number of small or weak nations by a handful of the richest or most powerful nations—all these have given birth to those distinctive characteristics of imperialism which compel us to define it as parasitic or decaying capitalism. More and more prominently there emerges, as one of the tendencies of imperialism, the creation of the "renter state," the usurer state, in which the bourgeoisie to an ever-increasing degree lives on the proceeds of capital exports and by "clipping coupons." It would be a mistake to believe that this tendency to decay precludes the rapid growth of capitalism. It does not. In the epoch of imperialism, certain branches of industry, certain strata of the bourgeoisie and certain countries betray, to a greater or lesser degree, now one and now another of these tendencies. On the whole, capitalism is growing far more rapidly than before; but this growth is not only becoming more and more uneven in general, its unevenness also manifests itself, in particular, in the decay of the countries which are richest in capital (Britain).

In regard to the rapidity of Germany's economic development, Riesser, the author of the book on the big German banks, states:

The progress of the preceding period (1848–70), which had not been exactly slow, compares with the rapidity with which the whole of Germany's national economy, and with it German banking, progressed during this period (1870–1905) in about the same way as the speed of the mail coach in the good old days compares with the speed of the present-day automobile . . . which is whizzing past so fast that it endangers not only innocent pedestrians in its path, but also the occupants of the car.

In its turn, this finance capital which has grown with such extraordinary rapidity is not unwilling, precisely because it has grown so quickly, to pass on to a more "tranquil" possession of colonies which have to be seized—and not only by peaceful methods—from richer nations. In the United States, economic development in the last decades has been even more rapid than in Germany, *and for this very reason,* the parasitic features of modern American capitalism have stood out with particular prominence. On the other hand, a comparison of, say, the republican American bourgeoisie with the monarchist Japanese or German bourgeoisie shows that the most pronounced political distinction diminishes to an extreme degree in the epoch of imperialism—not because it is unimportant in general, but because in all these cases we are talking about a bourgeoisie which has definite features of parasitism.

The receipt of high monopoly profits by the capitalists in one of the numerous branches of industry, in one of the numerous countries, etc., makes it economically possible for them to bribe certain sections of the workers, and for a time a fairly considerable minority of them, and win them to the side of the bourgeoisie of a given industry or given nation against all the others. The intensification of antagonisms between imperialist nations for the division of the world increases this urge. And so there is created that bond between imperialism and opportunism, which revealed itself first and most clearly in Great Britain, owing to the fact that certain features of imperialist development were observable there much earlier than in other countries.

# The Birth of the Modern

In the late nineteenth and first half of the twentieth centuries, there was a second industrial revolution whose impact was greater and whose effects were more widespread than the first one a hundred years before. Germany and the United States displaced Britain as the most innovative and advanced industrial powers. The age of steam was supplanted by the age of electricity. The telephone, the phonograph, the bicycle, the cinema, the sewing machine, the airplane, the typewriter, and the automobile transformed the way that people lived their lives. Family-owned firms, where working people often knew their owner-operators, increasingly gave way to large, impersonal, bureaucratic, and hierarchical corporations. Production in the most modern factories took place on assembly lines, an unparalleled division of the labor process in which individual workers were trained in minute and repetitious tasks. These were the brainchild of the new field of scientific management or Taylorism (named after its founder F. W. Taylor). The second industrial revolution was not, however, simply economic. Taken together, the advent of compulsory education, the extension of voting rights to the working class, and the revolution in mass communications transformed the nature of politics and culture. These changes were responsible for a vigorous mass culture aimed at ordinary working people. (In the late nineteenth century, daily newspapers first achieved circulations of more than a million copies per day.) And they brought about mass politics. On the one hand, existing political parties changed from being informal clubs of the moneyed and propertied classes to bureaucratic and hierarchical organizations that used mass communications to court its membership and appeal to the general public at elections. On the other hand, the working class emerged as an organized force in national politics—in labor and socialist parties and mass trade unions frequently comprising the unskilled workers of the second industrial revolution.

The intellectual and cultural response to this second transformation in the material life of European society is often referred to as 'modernism'. Its tone can be enthusiastic or disparaging, optimistic or gloomy. There were artists and writers who viewed these changes as representing the intensification of the alienation of human beings from themselves and their environments or saw it as the triumph of a soulless society where individuals had become extensions of the machines that they had created. But there were others who had no such ambivalent feelings about the modern world. Just as there are computer junkies in our day who are wildly enthusiastic about cyberspace and the World Wide Web, there were those a hundred years ago who were equally rhapsodic about the machine age.

By the late nineteenth and early twentieth centuries, the idea that men should dominate the public world and women should confine themselves to the domestic sphere began to be challenged. Middle-class women began to enter the workplace as nurses, teachers, social workers, secretaries, and sales clerks. Not only were they more visible in the world of business and the professions, but their status began to change also. Gradually, much sooner in some European nations than in others, they were allowed to own their own property, achieved the right to obtain a divorce, and began to enter higher education (the first women's colleges were established in the 1870s). At the beginning of the twentieth century, a women's suffrage movement challenged the political fabric of English society. Women, who had historically been portrayed as gentle, weak, and passive creatures, embarked on a path of political militancy and violence to force an unyielding government to grant them the right to vote. Emmeline Pankhurst's Women's Social and Political Union led the fight for women's suffrage in England. The suffrage movement failed to budge the government, but it put the issue on the national agenda. It was the First World War, however, that dramatically altered women's status: women increasingly replaced men in the workplace, frequently in positions that conventional wisdom said women could never assume. The idea that women were incapable of exercising independent political judgment was dealt a serious blow. In England and Germany, women won the right to vote following the War; in other European nations they did not achieve that right until the Second World War, or later.

# Charles Baudelaire

# *from* THE PAINTER OF MODERN LIFE (1863)

*Charles Baudelaire (1821–1867) spent most of his life in Paris. Drawn from youth to the life of the urban dandy, he alienated his stepfather, a general, by his spendthrift habits, use of opium, and radical political views. Baudelaire first established himself in the Parisian cultural and intellectual world as an art critic, writing reviews of the annual art Salons. Melancholy in temperament, he found great inspiration in the work of the American writer Edgar Allan Poe, which he translated into French. In 1857, Baudelaire published a collection of poems that achieved immediate notoriety:* Les Fleurs du Mal (Flowers of Evil). *These poems shocked many readers with their misanthropy and frank descriptions of sexuality; several were challenged in court on charges of offending religion or public morality. Their rich language and intense feeling, however, coupled with their striking modernity, would eventually make them his most influential work. In the late essay "The Painter of Modern Life," excerpted here, Baudelaire describes the modern sensibility in more accessible, less startling terms. With the painter Constantin Guys as an example, he describes the modern artist as a* flâneur, *a solitary spectator in the midst of the ever-changing urban multitude.*

Today I want to discourse to the public about a strange man, a man of so powerful and so decided an originality that it is sufficient unto itself and does not even seek approval. Not a single one of his drawings is signed, if by signature you mean that string of easily forgeable characters which spell a name and which so many other artists affix ostentatiously at the foot of their least important trifles. Yet all his works are signed—with his dazzling *soul;* and art-lovers who have seen and appreciated them will readily recognize them from the description that I am about to give.

•

When at last I ran him to earth, I saw at once that it was not precisely an *artist,* but rather a *man of the world* with whom I had to do. I ask you to understand the word *artist* in a very restricted sense, and *man of the world* in a very broad one.

•

His interest is the whole world; he wants to know, understand and appreciate everything that happens on the surface of our globe.

•

Do you remember a picture (it really is a picture!), painted—or rather written—by the most powerful pen of our age, and entitled *The Man of the Crowd*? In the window of a coffee-house there sits a convalescent, pleasurably absorbed in gazing at the crowd, and mingling, through the medium of thought, in the turmoil of thought that surrounds him. But lately returned from the valley of the shadow of death, he is rapturously breathing in all the odours and essences of life; as he has been on the brink of total oblivion, he remembers, and fervently desires to remember, everything. Finally he hurls himself headlong into the midst of the throng, in pursuit of an unknown, half-glimpsed countenance that has, on an instant, bewitched him. Curiosity has become a fatal, irresistible passion!

Imagine an artist who was always, spiritually, in the condition of that convalescent, and you will have the key to the nature of Monsieur G.

•

The crowd is his element, as the air is that of birds and water of fishes. His passion and his profession are to become one flesh with the crowd. For the perfect *flâneur*, for the passionate spectator, it is an immense joy to set up house in the heart of the multitude, amid the ebb and flow of movement, in the midst of the fugitive and the infinite. To be away from home and yet to feel oneself everywhere at home; to see the world, to be at the centre of the world, and yet to remain hidden from the world—such are a few of the slightest pleasures of those independent, passionate, impartial natures which the tongue can but clumsily define. The spectator is a *prince* who everywhere rejoices in his incognito. The lover of life makes the whole world his family, just like the lover of the fair sex who builds up his family from all the beautiful women that he has ever found, or that are—or are not—to be found; or the lover of pictures who lives in a magical society of dreams painted on canvas. Thus the lover of universal life enters into the crowd as though it were an immense reservoir of electrical energy. Or we might liken him to a mirror as vast as the crowd itself; or to a kaleidoscope gifted with consciousness, responding to each one of its movements and reproducing the multiplicity of life and the flickering grace of all the elements of life. He is an 'I' with an insatiable appetite for the 'non-I', at every instant rendering and explaining it in pictures more living than life itself, which is always unstable and fugitive. 'Any man,' he said one day, in the course of one of those conversations which he illumines with burning glance and evocative gesture, 'any man who is not crushed by one of those griefs whose nature is too real not to monopolize all his capacities, and who can yet be *bored in the heart of the multitude,* is a blockhead! a blockhead! and I despise him!'

•

And so away he goes, hurrying, searching. But searching for what? Be very sure that this man, such as I have depicted him—this solitary, gifted with an active imagination, ceaselessly journeying across the great human desert—has an aim loftier than that of a mere *flâneur,* an aim more general, something other than the fugitive pleasure of circumstance. He is looking for that quality which you must allow me to call 'modernity'; for I know of no better word to express the idea I have in mind. He makes it his business to extract from fashion whatever element it may contain of poetry within history, to distil the eternal from the transitory. . . . By 'modernity' I mean the ephemeral, the fugitive, the contingent, the half of art whose other half is the eternal and the immutable. Every old master has had his own modernity; the great majority of fine portraits that have come down to us from former generations are clothed in the costume of their own period. They are perfectly harmonious, because everything—from costume and coiffure down to gesture, glance and smile (for each age has a deportment, a glance and a smile of its own)—everything, I say, combines to form a completely viable whole. This transitory, fugitive element, whose metamorphoses are so rapid, must on no account be despised or dispensed with. By neglecting it, you cannot fail to tumble into the abyss of an abstract and indeterminate beauty, like that of the first woman before the fall of man.

—*trans. Jonathan Mayne*

## Matthew Arnold

# DOVER BEACH (1867)

*Matthew Arnold (see the introduction to* Culture and Anarchy *in section IV for biographical details) developed his ideas about the human condition in the context of the British industrial revolution rather than of the machine age of the late nineteenth and early twentieth century. He is most properly described as a precursor of modernism rather than an example of its full flowering. Arnold's poem "Dover Beach," often cited as one of the first modernist poems, explores the alienation of human beings from an indifferent nature and views the act of love as the only way of avoiding isolation.*

---

The sea is calm to-night.
The tide is full, the moon lies fair
Upon the straits;—on the French coast the light
Gleams and is gone; the cliffs of England stand,
Glimmering and vast, out in the tranquil bay.
Come to the window, sweet is the night-air!
Only, from the long line of spray
Where the sea meets the moon-blanch'd land,
Listen! you hear the grating roar
Of pebbles which the waves draw back, and fling,
At their return, up the high strand,
Begin, and cease, and then again begin,
With tremulous cadence slow, and bring
The eternal note of sadness in.

Sophocles long ago
Heard it on the Ægæan, and it brought
Into his mind the turbid ebb and flow
Of human misery; we
Find also in the sound a thought,
Hearing it by this distant northern sea.

The Sea of Faith
Was once, too, at the full, and round earth's shore
Lay like the folds of a bright girdle furl'd.
But now I only hear
Its melancholy, long, withdrawing roar,
Retreating, to the breath
Of the night-wind, down the vast edges of drear
And naked shingles of the world.
Ah, love, let us be true
To one another! for the world, which seems
To lie before us like a land of dreams,
So various, so beautiful, so new,
Hath really neither joy, nor love, nor light,
Nor certitude, nor peace, nor help for pain;
And we are here as on a darkling plain
Swept with confused alarms of struggle and flight,
Where ignorant armies clash by night.

# *Friedrich Nietzsche*

## *from* THE GAY SCIENCE (1882)

*The German classical scholar, philosopher, and critic of culture, Friedrich Nietzsche (1844–1900) is one of the most influential of all modern thinkers. He was a powerful critic of both Christianity and secularism and is often credited with laying the foundation for twentieth-century existentialism. Nietzsche's parable "The Madman," from* The Gay Science, *is a deceptively simple story about the death of God. What does it mean to murder God? Does the fact that we have murdered God suggest that we have created a world in which the idea of God is no longer necessary? Is the act symbolic of our own spiritual impoverishment? In murdering God have we liberated or condemned ourselves? Why is it a madman who announces God's death?*

---

*The Madman.* Have you not heard of that madman who lit a lantern in the bright morning hours, ran to the market place, and cried incessantly, "I seek God! I seek God!" As many of those who do not believe in God were standing around just then, he provoked much laughter. Why, did he get lost? said one. Did he lose his way like a child? said another. Or is he hiding? Is he afraid of us? Has he gone on a voyage? or emigrated? Thus they yelled and laughed. The madman jumped into their midst and pierced them with his glances.

"Whither is God," he cried. "I shall tell you. *We have killed him*—you and I. All of us are his murderers. But how have we done this? How were we able to drink up the sea? Who gave us the sponge to wipe away the entire horizon? What did we do when we unchained this earth from its sun? Whither is it moving now? Whither are we moving now? Away from all suns? Are we not plunging continually? Backward, sideward, forward, in all directions? Is there any up or down left? Are we not straying as through an infinite nothing? Do we not feel the breath of empty space? Has it not become colder? Is not night and more night coming on all the while? Must not lanterns be lit in the morning? Do we not hear anything yet of the noise of the gravediggers who are burying God? Do we not smell anything yet of God's decomposition? Gods too decompose. God is dead. God remains dead. And we have killed him. How shall we, the murderers of all murderers, comfort ourselves? What was holiest and most powerful of all that the world has yet owned has bled to death under our knives. Who will wipe this blood off us? What water is there for us to clean ourselves? What festivals of atonement, what sacred games shall we have to invent? Is not the greatness of this deed too great for us? Must not we ourselves become gods simply to seem worthy of it? There has never been a greater deed; and whoever will be born after us—for the sake of this deed he will be part of a higher history than all history hitherto."

Here the madman fell silent and looked again at his listeners; and they too were silent and stared at him in astonishment. At last he threw his lantern on the ground, and it broke and went out. "I come too early," he said then; "my time has not come yet. This tremendous event is still on its way, still wandering—it has not yet reached the ears of man. Lightning and thunder require time, the light of the stars requires time, deeds require time even after they are done, before they can be seen and heard. This deed is still more distant from them than the most distant stars—*and yet they have done it themselves.*"

It has been related further that on that same day the madman entered divers churches and there sang his *requiem aeternam deo*. Led out and called to account, he is said to have replied each time, "What are these churches now if they are not the tombs and sepulchers of God?"

—trans. Walter Kaufmann

# *from* THE PROTESTANT ETHIC AND THE SPIRIT OF CAPITALISM (CA. 1904–1905)

*Max Weber (1864–1920) is one of the pioneers of modern sociology, well known for his contributions to sociological methodology and his analysis of modern social phenomena such as bureaucracy. He is perhaps best known for his book* The Protestant Ethic and the Spirit of Capitalism, *in which he seeks to understand how the early Protestant mentality facilitated the growth of modern capitalist society. For Weber, the Protestant work ethic emanates from a religious form of self-denial, which he calls "worldly asceticism." Such beliefs are not materialistic, but they facilitate the development of the idea of accumulating capital for the purposes of investment rather than consumption, an idea crucial to the development of modern capitalism. In the conclusion to the book, Weber argues that what for the Puritans had been a spiritual calling had become in the modern world an empty and vacuous "iron cage": "Specialists without spirit, sensualists without heart; this nullity imagines that it has attained a level of civilization never before achieved."*

One of the fundamental elements of the spirit of modern capitalism, and not only of that but of all modern culture: rational conduct on the basis of the idea of the calling, was born . . . from the spirit of Christian asceticism. . . . The essential elements of the . . . spirit of capitalism are . . . the content of the Puritan worldly asceticism. . . . The idea that modern labour has an ascetic character is of course not new. Limitation to specialized work, with a renunciation of the Faustian universality of man which it involves, is a condition of any valuable work in the modern world; hence deeds and renunciation inevitably condition each other today. This fundamentally ascetic trait of middle-class life, if it attempts to be a way of life at all, and not simply the absence of any, was what Goethe wanted to teach, at the height of his wisdom, in the *Wanderjahren,* and in the end which he gave to the life of his *Faust.* For him the realization meant a renunciation, a departure from an age of full and beautiful humanity, which can no more be repeated in the course of our cultural development than can the flower of the Athenian culture of antiquity.

The Puritan wanted to work in a calling; we are forced to do so. For when asceticism was carried out of monastic cells into everyday life, and began to dominate worldly morality, it did its part in building the tremendous cosmos of the modern economic order. This order is now bound to the technical and economic conditions of machine production which to-day determine the lives of all the individuals who are born into this mechanism, not only those directly concerned with economic acquisition, with irresistible force. Perhaps it will so determine them until the last ton of fossilized coal is burnt. In Baxter's view the care for external goods should only lie on the shoulders of the "saint like a light cloak, which can be thrown aside at any moment." But fate decreed that the cloak should become an iron cage.

Since asceticism undertook to remodel the world and to work out its ideals in the world, material goods have gained an increasing and finally an inexorable power over the lives of men as at no previous period in history. To-day the spirit of religious asceticism—whether finally, who knows?—has escaped from the cage. But victorious capitalism, since it rests on mechanical foundations, needs its support no longer. The rosy blush of its laughing heir, the Enlightenment, seems also to be irretrievably fading, and the idea of duty in one's calling prowls about in our lives like the ghost of dead religious beliefs. Where the fulfilment of the calling cannot directly be related to the highest spiritual and cultural values, or when, on the other hand, it need not be felt simply as economic compulsion, the individual generally abandons the attempt to justify it at all. In the field of its highest development, in the United States, the pursuit of wealth, stripped of its religious and ethical meaning, tends to become associated with purely mundane passions, which often actually give it the character of sport.

No one knows who will live in this cage in the future, or whether at the end of this tremendous development entirely new prophets will arise, or there will be a great rebirth of old ideas and ideals, or, if neither, mechanized petrification, embellished with a sort of convulsive self-importance. For of the last stage of this cultural development, it might well be truly said: "Specialists without spirit, sensualists without heart; this nullity imagines that it has attained a level of civilization never before achieved."

●

Here we have only attempted to trace the fact and the direction of its influence to their motives in one, though a very important point. But it would also further be necessary to investigate how Protestant Asceticism was in turn influenced in its development and its character by the totality of social conditions, especially economic. The modern man is in general, even with the best will, unable to give religious ideas a significance for culture and national character which they deserve. But it is, of course, not my aim to substitute for a one-sided materialistic an equally one-sided spiritualistic causal interpretation of culture and of history. Each is equally possible, but each, if it does not serve as the preparation, but as the conclusion of an investigation, accomplishes equally little in the interest of historical truth.

*—trans. Talcott Parsons*

# AFTER THE RACE,
## *from* DUBLINERS (1904)

*In his story "After the Race," from* Dubliners, *James Joyce (1882–1941) links the new technology of the machine age to the superficial world of status and prestige accompanying an expanding capitalist system. Born in Ireland and one of the influential writers of the twentieth century, Joyce uses a 1903 auto race held outside Dublin (the Gordon Bennet Cup, a predecessor to the Grand Prix) as the occasion for his story. He contrasts the wealth and industry of the Continent with the poverty and passivity of the Irish, who can only enjoy the race as spectators with "the cheer of the gratefully oppressed." The main character, Jimmy Doyle, is an Irish social climber. His ascent rests chiefly on his connections with the Frenchman Charles Seguin. The Frenchman condescends to allow his Irish friend to invest in his newly formed car dealership. Symbolizing Irish aspiration and frustration, Doyle is outmatched by his European friends, suggested by his bad showing at cards. Will his investment in the car dealership turn out any differently? Yet Joyce holds out the possibility that a new day is dawning for underdeveloped nations like Ireland. The final line of the story is "Day-break, gentlemen!"*

The cars came scudding in towards Dublin, running evenly like pellets in the groove of the Naas Road. At the crest of the hill at Inchicore sightseers had gathered in clumps to watch the cars careering homeward and through this channel of poverty and inaction the Continent sped its wealth and industry. Now and again the clumps of people raised the cheer of the gratefully oppressed. Their sympathy, however, was for the blue cars—the cars of their friends, the French.

The French, moreover, were virtual victors. Their team had finished solidly; they had been placed second and third and the driver of the winning German car was reported a Belgian. Each blue car, therefore, received a double round of welcome as it topped the crest of the hill and each cheer of welcome was acknowledged with smiles and nods by those in the car. In one of these trimly built cars was a party of four young men whose spirits seemed to be at present well above the level of successful Gallicism: in fact, these four young men were almost hilarious. They were Charles Ségouin, the owner of the car; André Rivière, a young electrician of Canadian birth; a huge Hungarian named Villona and a neatly groomed young man named Doyle. Ségouin was in good humour because he had unexpectedly received some orders in advance (he was about to start a motor establishment in Paris) and Rivière was in good humour because he was to be appointed manager of the establishment; these two young men (who were cousins) were also in good humour because of the success of the French cars. Villona was in good humour because he had had a very satisfactory luncheon; and besides he was an optimist by nature. The fourth member of the party, however, was too excited to be genuinely happy.

He was about twenty-six years of age, with a soft, light brown moustache and rather innocent-looking grey eyes. His father, who had begun life as an advanced Nationalist, had modified his views early. He had made his money as a butcher in Kingstown and by opening shops in Dublin and in the suburbs he had made his money many times over. He had also been fortunate enough to secure some of the police contracts and in the end he had become rich enough to be alluded to in the Dublin newspapers as a merchant prince. He had sent his son to England to be educated in a big Catholic college and had afterwards sent him to Dublin University to study law. Jimmy did not study very earnestly and took to bad courses for a while. He had money and he was popular; and he divided his time curiously between musical and motoring circles. Then he had been sent for a term to Cambridge to see a little life. His father, remonstrative, but covertly proud of the excess, had paid his bills and brought him home. It was at Cambridge that he had met Ségouin. They were not much more than acquaintances as yet but Jimmy found great pleasure in the society of one who had seen so much of the world and was reputed to own some of the biggest hotels in France. Such a person (as his father agreed) was well worth knowing, even if he had not been the charming companion he was. Villona was entertaining also—a brilliant pianist—but, unfortunately, very poor.

The car ran on merrily with its cargo of hilarious youth. The two cousins sat on the front seat; Jimmy and his Hungarian friend sat behind. Decidedly Villona was in excellent spirits, he kept up a deep bass hum of melody for miles of the road. The Frenchmen flung their laughter and light words over their shoulders and often Jimmy had to strain forward to catch the quick phrase. This was not altogether pleasant for him, as he had nearly always to make a deft guess at the meaning and shout back a suitable answer in the teeth of a high wind. Besides Villona's humming would confuse anybody; the noise of the car, too.

Rapid motion through space elates one; so does notoriety; so does the possession of money. These were three good reasons for Jimmy's excitement. He had been seen by many of his friends that day in the company of these Continentals. At the control Ségouin had presented him to one of the French competitors and, in answer to his confused murmur of compliment, the swarthy face of the driver had disclosed a line of shining white teeth. It was pleasant after that honour to return to the profane world of spectators amid nudges and significant looks. Then as to money—he really had a great sum under his control. Ségouin, perhaps, would not think it a great sum but Jimmy who, in spite of temporary errors, was at heart the inheritor of solid instincts knew well with what difficulty it had been got together. This knowledge had previously kept his bills within the limits of reasonable recklessness and, if he had been so conscious of the labour latent in money when there had been question merely of some freak of the higher intelligence, how much more so now when he was about to stake the greater part of his substance! It was a serious thing for him.

Of course, the investment was a good one and Ségouin had managed to give the impression that it was by a favour of friendship the mite of Irish money was to be included in the capital of the concern. Jimmy had a respect for his father's shrewdness in business matters and in this case it had been his father who had first suggested the investment; money to be made in the motor business, pots of money. Moreover Ségouin had the unmistakable air of wealth. Jimmy set out to translate into days' work that lordly car in which he sat. How smoothly it ran. In what style they had come careering along the country roads! The journey laid a magical finger on the genuine pulse of life and gallantly the machinery of human nerves strove to answer the bounding courses of the swift blue animal.

They drove down Dame Street. The street was busy with unusual traffic, loud with the horns of motorists and the gongs of impatient tram-drivers. Near the Bank Ségouin drew up and Jimmy and his friend alighted. A little knot of people collected on the footpath to pay homage to the snorting motor. The party was to dine together that evening in Ségouin's hotel and, meanwhile, Jimmy and his friend, who was staying with him, were to go home to dress. The car steered out slowly for Grafton Street while the two young men pushed their way through the knot of gazers. They walked northward with a curious feeling of disappointment in the exercise, while the city hung its pale globes of light above them in a haze of summer evening.

In Jimmy's house this dinner had been pronounced an occasion. A certain pride mingled with his parents' trepidation, a certain eagerness, also, to play fast and loose for the names of great foreign cities have at least this virtue. Jimmy, too, looked very well when he was dressed and as he stood in the hall giving a last equation to the bows of his dress tie, his father may have felt even commercially satisfied at having secured for his son qualities often unpurchasable. His father, therefore, was unusually friendly with Villona and his manner expressed a real respect for foreign accomplishments; but this subtlety of his host was probably lost upon the Hungarian, who was beginning to have a sharp desire for his dinner.

The dinner was excellent, exquisite. Ségouin, Jimmy decided, had a very refined taste. The party was increased by a young Englishman named Routh whom Jimmy had seen with Ségouin at Cambridge. The young men supped in a snug room lit by electric candle-lamps. They talked volubly and with little reserve. Jimmy, whose imagination was kindling, conceived the lively youth of the Frenchmen twined elegantly upon the firm framework of the Englishman's manner. A graceful image of his, he thought, and a just one. He admired the dexterity with which their host directed the conversation. The five young men had various tastes and their tongues had been loosened. Villona, with immense respect, began to discover to the mildly surprised Englishman the beauties of the English madrigal, deploring the loss of old instruments. Rivière, not wholly ingenuously, undertook to explain to Jimmy the triumph of the French mechanicians. The resonant voice of the Hungarian was about to prevail in ridicule of the spurious lutes of the romantic painters when Ségouin shepherded his party into politics. Here was congenial ground for all. Jimmy, under generous influences, felt the buried zeal of his father wake to life within him: he aroused the torpid Routh at last. The room grew doubly hot and Ségouin's task grew harder each moment: there was even danger of personal spite. The alert host at an opportunity lifted his glass to Humanity and, when the toast had been drunk, he threw open a window significantly.

That night the city wore the mask of a capital. The five young men strolled along Stephen's Green in a faint cloud of aromatic smoke. They talked loudly and gaily and their cloaks dangled from their shoulders. The people made way for them. At the corner of Grafton Street a short fat man was putting two handsome ladies on a car in charge of another fat man. The car drove off and the short fat man caught sight of the party.

—André.

—It's Farley!

A torrent of talk followed. Farley was an American. No one knew very well what the talk was about. Villona and Rivière were the noisiest, but all the men were excited. They got up on a car, squeezing themselves together amid much laughter. They drove by the crowd, blended now into soft colours, to a music of merry bells. They took the train at Westland Row and in a few seconds, as it seemed to Jimmy, they were walking out of Kingstown Station. The ticket-collector saluted Jimmy; he was an old man:

—Fine night, sir!

It was a serene summer night; the harbour lay like a darkened mirror at their feet. They proceeded towards it with linked arms, singing *Cadet Roussel* in chorus, stamping their feet at every:

—*Ho! Ho! Hohé, vraiment!*

They got into a rowboat at the slip and made out for the American's yacht. There was to be supper, music, cards. Villona said with conviction:

—It is beautiful!

There was a yacht piano in the cabin. Villona played a waltz for Farley and Rivière, Farley acting as cavalier and Rivière as lady. Then an impromptu square dance, the men devising original figures. What merriment! Jimmy took his part with a will; this was seeing life, at least. Then Farley got out of breath and cried *Stop!* A man brought in a light supper, and the young men sat down to it for form's sake. They drank, however: it was Bohemian. They drank Ireland, England, France, Hungary, the United States of America. Jimmy made a speech, a long speech, Villona saying *Hear! hear!* whenever there was a pause. There was a great clapping of hands when he sat down. It must have been a good speech. Farley clapped him on the back and laughed loudly. What jovial fellows! What good company they were!

Cards! cards! The table was cleared. Villona returned quietly to his piano and played voluntaries for them. The other men played game after game, flinging themselves boldly into the adventure. They drank the health of the Queen of Hearts and of the Queen of Diamonds. Jimmy felt obscurely the lack of an audience: the wit was flashing. Play ran very high and paper began to pass. Jimmy did not know exactly who was winning but he knew that he was losing. But it was his own fault for he frequently mistook his cards and the other men had to calculate his I.O.U.'s for him. They were devils of fellows but he wished they would stop: it was getting late. Someone gave the toast of the yacht *The Belle of Newport* and then someone proposed one great game for a finish.

The piano had stopped; Villona must have gone up on deck. It was a terrible game. They stopped just before the end of it to drink for luck. Jimmy understood that the game lay between Routh and Ségouin. What excitement! Jimmy was excited too; he would lose, of course. How much had he written away? The men rose to their feet to play the last tricks, talking and gesticulating. Routh won. The cabin shook with the young men's cheering and the cards were bundled together. They began then to gather in what they had won. Farley and Jimmy were the heaviest losers.

He knew that he would regret in the morning but at present he was glad of the rest, glad of the dark stupor that would cover up his folly. He leaned his elbows on the table and rested his head between his hands, counting the beats of his temples. The cabin door opened and he saw the Hungarian standing in a shaft of grey light:

—Daybreak, gentlemen!

*Filippo Tommaso Marinetti*

# THE FOUNDATION AND MANIFESTO
# OF FUTURISM (1909)

*For the poets and artists who comprised the Italian Futurists, the new world of machinery made everything obsolete, including all previous intellectual and artistic traditions that had come before. They viewed themselves as an* avant-garde, *a cutting-edge movement that was as revolutionary in its implications as the technological transformations that they worshiped. Taking their clues from the new mediums of time-lapse photography and the movies, they attempted to express in paintings and poetry a world of constant motion and speed. In "Foundation and Manifesto of Futurism," Filippo Tommaso Marinetti (1876–1944) pays tribute to the revolutionary power of speed as embodied in the automobile. Equally important, he uses language and imagery in a way that he believes is appropriate to a world that is constantly in flux.*

We had stayed up all night, my friends and I, under hanging mosque lamps with domes of filigreed brass, domes starred like our spirits, shining like them with the prisoned radiance of electric hearts. For hours we had trampled our atavistic ennui into rich oriental rugs, arguing up to the last confines of logic and blackening many reams of paper with our frenzied scribbling.

An immense pride was buoying us up, because we felt ourselves alone at that hour, alone, awake, and on our feet, like proud beacons or forward sentries against an army of hostile stars glaring down at us from their celestial encampments. Alone with stokers reeding the hellish fires of great ships, alone with the black spectres who grope in the red-hot bellies of locomotives launched down their crazy courses, alone with drunkards reeling like wounded birds along the city walls.

Suddenly we jumped, hearing the mighty noise of the huge double-decker trams that rumbled by outside, ablaze with coloured lights, like villages on holiday suddenly struck and uprooted by the flooding Po and dragged over falls and through gorges to the sea.

Then the silence deepened. But, as we listened to the old canal muttering its feeble prayers and the creaking bones of sickly palaces above their damp green beards, under the windows we suddenly heard the famished roar of automobiles.

'Let's go!' I said. 'Friends, away! Let's go! Mythology and the Mystic Ideal are defeated at last. We're about to see the Centaur's birth and, soon after, the first flight of Angels! . . . We must shake the gates of life, test the bolts and hinges. Let's go! Look there, on the earth, the very first dawn! There's nothing to match the splendour of the sun's red sword, slashing for the first time through our millennial gloom!'

We went up to the three snorting beasts, to lay amorous hands on their torrid breasts. I stretched out on my car like a corpse on its bier, but revived at once under the steering wheel, a guillotine blade that threatened my stomach.

The raging broom of madness swept us out of ourselves and drove us through streets as rough and deep as the beds of torrents. Here and there, sick lamplight through window glass taught us to distrust the deceitful mathematics of our perishing eyes.

I cried, 'The scent, the scent alone is enough for our beasts.'

And like young lions we ran after Death, its dark pelt blotched with pale crosses as it escaped down the vast violet living and throbbing sky.

But we had no ideal Mistress raising her divine form to the clouds, nor any cruel Queen to whom to offer our bodies, twisted like Byzantine rings! There was nothing to make us wish for death, unless the wish to be free at last from the weight of our courage!

And on we raced, hurling watchdogs against doorsteps, curling them under our burning tyres like collars under a flatiron. Death, domesticated, met me at every turn, gracefully holding out a paw, or once in a while hunkering down, making velvety caressing eyes at me from every puddle.

'Let's break out of the horrible shell of wisdom and throw ourselves like pride-ripened fruit into the wide, contorted mouth of the wind! Let's give ourselves utterly to the Unknown, not in desperation but only to replenish the deep wells of the Absurd!'

The words were scarcely out of my mouth when I spun my car around with the frenzy of a dog trying to bite its tail, and there, suddenly, were two cyclists coming towards me, shaking their fists, wobbling like two equally convincing but neverthe-less contradictory arguments. Their stupid dilemma was blocking my way—Damn! Ouch! . . . I stopped short and to my disgust rolled over into a ditch with my wheels in the air. . . .

O maternal ditch, almost full of muddy water! Fair factory drain! I gulped down your nourishing sludge; and I remembered the blessed black breast of my Sudanese nurse. . . . When I came up—torn, filthy, and stinking—from under the capsized car, I felt the white-hot iron of joy deliciously pass through my heart!

A crowd of fishermen with handlines and gouty naturalists were already swarm-ing around the prodigy. With patient, loving care those people rigged a tall derrick and iron grapnels to fish out my car, like a big beached shark. Up it came from the ditch, slowly, leaving in the bottom, like scales, its heavy framework of good sense and its soft upholstery of comfort.

They thought it was dead, my beautiful shark, but a caress from me was enough to revive it; and there it was, alive again, running on its powerful fins!

And so, faces smeared with good factory muck—plastered with metallic waste, with senseless sweat, with celestial soot—we, bruised, our arms in slings, but unafraid, declared our high intentions to all the *living* of the earth:

## Manifesto of Futurism

1. We intend to sing the love of danger, the habit of energy and fearlessness.
2. Courage, audacity, and revolt will be essential elements of our poetry.
3. Up to now literature has exalted a pensive immobility, ecstasy, and sleep. We intend to exalt aggressive action, a feverish insomnia, the racer's stride, the mor-tal leap, the punch and the slap.

4. We affirm that the world's magnificence has been enriched by a new beauty: the beauty of speed. A racing car whose hood is adorned with great pipes, like serpents of explosive breath—a roaring car that seems to ride on grapeshot is more beautiful than the *Victory of Samothrace*.

5. We want to hymn the man at the wheel, who hurls the lance of his spirit across the Earth, along the circle of its orbit.

6. The poet must spend himself with ardour, splendour, and generosity, to swell the enthusiastic fervour of the primordial elements.

7. Except in struggle, there is no more beauty. No work without an aggressive character can be a masterpiece. Poetry must be conceived as a violent attack on unknown forces, to reduce and prostrate them before man.

8. We stand on the last promontory of the centuries! . . . Why should we look back, when what we want is to break down the mysterious doors of the Impossible? Time and Space died yesterday. We already live in the absolute, because we have created eternal, omnipresent speed.

9. We will glorify war—the world's only hygiene—militarism, patriotism, the destructive gesture of freedom-bringers, beautiful ideas worth dying for, and scorn for woman.

10. We will destroy the museums, libraries, academies of every kind, will fight moralism, feminism, every opportunistic or utilitarian cowardice.

11. We will sing of great crowds excited by work, by pleasure, and by riot; we will sing of the multicoloured, polyphonic tides of revolution in the modern capitals; we will sing of the vibrant nightly fervour of arsenals and shipyards blazing with violent electric moons; greedy railway stations that devour smoke-plumed serpents; factories hung on clouds by the crooked lines of their smoke; bridges that stride the rivers like giant gymnasts, flashing in the sun with a glitter of knives; adventurous steamers that sniff the horizon; deep-chested locomotives whose wheels paw the tracks like the hooves of enormous steel horses bridled by tubing; and the sleek flight of planes whose propellers chatter in the wind like banners and seem to cheer like an enthusiastic crowd.

It is from Italy that we launch through the world this violently upsetting incendiary manifesto of ours. With it, today, we establish *Futurism,* because we want to free this land from its smelly gangrene of professors, archaeologists, *ciceroni* and antiquarians. For too long has Italy been a dealer in second-hand clothes. We mean to free her from the numberless museums that cover her like so many graveyards.

Museums: cemeteries! . . . Identical, surely, in the sinister promiscuity of so many bodies unknown to one another. Museums: public dormitories where one lies forever beside hated or unknown beings. Museums: absurd abattoirs of painters and sculptors ferociously slaughtering each other with colour-blows and line-blows, the length of the fought-over walls!

That one should make an annual pilgrimage, just as one goes to the graveyard on All Souls' Day—that I grant. That once a year one should leave a floral tribute beneath the *Gioconda,* I grant you that. . . . But I don't admit that our sorrows, our fragile courage, our morbid restlessness should be given a daily conducted tour through the museums. Why poison ourselves? Why rot?

And what is there to see in an old picture except the laborious contortions of an artist throwing himself against the barriers that thwart his desire to express his dream completely? . . . Admiring an old picture is the same as pouring our sensibility into a funerary urn instead of hurling it far off, in violent spasms of action and creation.

Do you, then, wish to waste all your best powers in this eternal and futile worship of the past, from which you emerge fatally exhausted, shrunken, beaten down?

In truth I tell you that daily visits to museums, libraries, and academies (cemeteries of empty exertion, Calvaries of crucified dreams, registries of aborted beginnings!) are, for artists, as damaging as the prolonged supervision by parents of certain young people drunk with their talent and their ambitious wills. When the future is barred to them, the admirable past may be a solace for the ills of the moribund, the sickly, the prisoner. . . . But we want no part of it, the past, we the young and strong *Futurists*!

So let them come, the gay incendiaries with charred fingers! Here they are! Here they are! . . . Come on! set fire to the library shelves! Turn aside the canals to flood the museums! . . . Oh, the joy of seeing the glorious old canvases bobbing adrift on those waters, discoloured and shredded! . . . Take up your pickaxes, your axes and hammers and wreck, wreck the venerable cities, pitilessly.

The oldest of us is thirty: so we have at least a decade for finishing our work. When we are forty, other younger and stronger men will probably throw us in the wastebasket like useless manuscripts—we want it to happen!

They will come against us, our successors, will come from far away, from every quarter, dancing to the winged cadence of their first songs, flexing the hooked claws of predators, sniffing doglike at the academy doors the strong odour of our decaying minds, which will already have been promised to the literary catacombs.

But we won't be there . . . . At last they'll find us—one winter's night—in open country, beneath a sad roof drummed by a monotonous rain. They'll see us crouched beside our trembling aeroplanes in the act of warming our hands at the poor little blaze that our books of today will give out when they take fire from the flight of our images.

They'll storm around us, panting with scorn and anguish, and all of them, exasperated by our proud daring, will hurtle to kill us, driven by a hatred the more implacable the more their hearts will be drunk with love and admiration for us.

Injustice, strong and sane, will break out radiantly in their eyes.

Art, in fact, can be nothing but violence, cruelty, and injustice.

The oldest of us is thirty: even so we have already scattered treasures, a thousand treasures of force, love, courage, astuteness, and raw will-power; have thrown them impatiently away, with fury, carelessly, unhesitatingly, breathless, and unresting. . . . Look at us! We are still untired! Our hearts know no weariness because they are fed with fire, hatred, and speed! . . . Does that amaze you? It should, because you can never remember having lived! Erect on the summit of the world, once again we hurl our defiance at the stars!

You have objections?—Enough! Enough! We know them. . . . We've understood! . . . Our fine deceitful intelligence tells us that we are the revival and extension of our ancestors—Perhaps! . . . If only it were so!—But who cares? We don't want to understand! . . . Woe to anyone who says those infamous words to us again!

Lift up your heads!

Erect on the summit of the world, once again we hurl defiance to the stars!

*—trans. R. W. Flint and Arthur A. Coppotelli*

# Rebecca West

# WOMEN AND WAGES (1912)
# THE SIN OF SELF-SACRIFICE (1913)

*R*ebecca West (1892–1983), born Cicily Fairfield, took her pseudonym from a character *that she played in an Ibsen play while she was still a teenager. Around the same time, she joined the militant suffragette group, the Social and Political Union. Though a supporter of Emeline Pankhurst, the group's founder and leader, West was critical of her support of violent political action: not because West was a pacifist, but because she believed that it was not a useful political tool. West was a socialist-feminist who saw the women's liberation movement of her time as being engaged in the same struggle as the working class. In "Women and Wages," for instance, she views the exploitation of women and of workers as intrinsic to the capitalist mode of production. One reason, in her view, that the capitalist class pays women lower wages is that it keeps the exploited classes divided.*

## WOMEN AND WAGES
### Blacklegging and Timidity

In the *Daily Citizen* of 9 October there was a sentimental quotation, seemingly of feminist import, from *The Shipping World*. A new Act in the States has decreed that every vessel navigating on the American coast or the great lakes must carry a wireless operator; and it furthermore provides that women are eligible to qualify as operators.

And why not? [asks *The Shipping World*]. The invention opens out a new career for women, in which their special abilities can be used to the best advantage. If acuteness of hearing, rapidity of decision and suppleness of wrist and fingers count for anything, then, surely, the Marconi house on the bridge deck seems to be the natural goal for a self-reliant woman with cool nerves and efficient brain.

It is an alluring picture, and one flattering to women. In the mind's eye one sees the Marconi operator sitting gracefully at her work, with a rose in her hair, surrounded by votive offerings from passengers, operating much, much better than any mere man ever did. And, apart from *The Shipping World*'s idealisation of the prospects, it does seem an interesting new occupation for women. Women have had to settle down to occupations which were too tame for men and in which there are few opportunities for the adventurous-minded. The young woman who wants to see over the edge of the world would probably love the life of a wireless operator.

Yet, 'I fear the Greeks even when they bring gifts,' said the one wise Trojan, when he saw his fellow-Trojans dragging the wooden horse into Troy. I fear the Marconi Company even when they bring gifts.

Ah! Here we have it. Here is the powder in the jam, the snake in the grass, the wolf in feminist's clothing. I thought there must be some reason for this sudden lyric outburst of feminist enthusiasm. 'Probably she will be less expensive to the shipowner than the male operator, and quite as reliable.' One might have remembered that the capitalist respects woman in only one capacity; not as the worker or the wife or the mother, but as the blackleg. That takes the pride out of the working woman. If she becomes a Marconi operator on these terms, no matter how efficient and plucky she may be, she is living on the wages of dishonour. She has bought her job with the flesh and blood of her fellow man.

Though it is galling for the woman worker to know that she is not loved for herself alone, she may get a good deal of satisfaction out of the encouraging words that are let fall by the capitalist on the make. For instance, there was that remarkable wave of feminism that passed over local authorities four years ago, when they became obliged to appoint school medical officers. All over the country councillors enthusiastically declared to one another that it was imperative that children should be attended to by women; that men were far too coarse and tactless to deal with them; that every woman (even though she be a doctor) is a mother at heart . . . and that while men doctors were asking £250 a year they could probably get women for £150. The wiles of the municipal seducers were in vain. Women doctors, being in the main middle-class women, had savings and homes to fall back on; so they stood loyally by their male colleagues and refused to blackleg. Not one woman doctor in Great Britain applied for a £150 post. And there was an abrupt subsidence in the wave of feminism among local authorities.

What reason is there that women should play the part of blacklegs? The underpayment of women is one of those 'ninepence for fourpence' tricks that capitalists have ever loved to play on the people whenever they had the chance. Capitalists have said to women: 'We deduct fourpence from your wages so that we can pay men larger wages, and then they can support you as their wives. So in the end you will make at least ninepence out of it.' It is only an excuse for sweating more money out of the people. It pretends that women have no dependents. A woman, according to the capitalist, is an air-bubble blown between earth and sky, with no human ties of any sort. True it is that man recognises that first imperative necessity which is plain to the lowest savage, the duty to provide for the next generation. But there is another duty which is patent only to the more civilised (if one was a really bitter feminist, one might say that that was why it fell to the women), and that is the duty to provide for the old. Miss Grace Neal, of the Domestic Workers' Union, states that it is the rule and not the exception of the members of her Union to send money home to support their parents. And sometimes widowhood lays the burden of both generations on a woman.

Women ought to understand that in submitting themselves to this swindle of underpayment, they are not only insulting themselves, but doing a deadly injury to the community. The capitalist sucks strength out of an exploited class which enables him to exploit other classes. An example of the infectiousness of poverty and the persistence of disease is the terrible economic condition of Edinburgh, which is directly due to the Battle of Flodden Field in 1513. Most of the able-bodied men were killed off and their widows had to set about earning a living for their fatherless children. They got 'woman's wages'. That meant that wages all round were depressed, and capitalism in Edinburgh got a good hold over labour by planting its feet on a solid substratum of the blackest and most helpless poverty. Labour has never shaken itself free.

How can women bear to be willing instruments of this crime against themselves and the community? The industrial women seem to consent to the indignity without resentment. Every woman who has risen from the floral stage of political activity (that is, the Primrose League), or the vegetable stage (that is, the Women's Liberal Association), must admire the suffragettes. Yet we may wish that they had spared a little of their dear irreverence and blessed pluck to stir up the industrial women to revolt. We have clever Miss Pankhurst trying to get the vote and earnest Miss Macarthur trying to organise trade unions; but seemingly we have no women who have read the signs of the times, who have discovered that political power and trade unionism are pin-pricks in the hide of the capitalist monster. Where are our women syndicalists?

Ladies of Great Britain, we are clever, we are efficient, we are trustworthy, we are twice the women that our grandmothers were, but we have not enough devil in us. We are afraid of going back to first causes. We want to earn good wages. But we try to do it by being amenable and competent wage-slaves, and thus pleasing the capitalist. We never try to do it by fighting the capitalist and turning him out of the workshop. The other day Mr. Ramsay MacDonald complained that women do not make good enough socialists for him. The whole trouble is that women make socialists which are just good enough for Mr. Ramsay MacDonald. They accept as doles from the capitalist class what they should take as rights. Wherever one gets a gathering of women socialists, one gets a programme of such charity gifts from the State as free meals and school clinics for children: excellent things, but dangerous unless taken discontentedly as niggardly instalments of a long-due debt. They should watch such things critically lest their children grow up in servitude. A slave is more of a slave when he is well fed than when he is hungry.

It is strange that women who are independent and fearless in private life should not introduce their independence and fearlessness into their public life. This occurs to me especially in connection with elementary-schoolteachers. The cheerfulness with which they have shouldered the responsibilities thrown on them by the free meals and medical examination of schoolchildren explains why the children love their school and their teachers. Yet they submit to being paid salaries of from one-half to two-thirds the amount paid to men for similar work. They submit in spite of the fact that they could end the injustice in a week by a strike. What could the Government do if women teachers struck? There are no hungry teachers walking the streets, so degraded by poverty that—God forgive them and punish the capitalists—they will help to drag their fellows down to poverty, too, by blacklegging. The women teachers of England have their remedy in their own hands.

Yet not only do they not use it, but they consent to remain members of a quaint body called the National Union of Teachers, which, although it exacts an equal subscription from men and women alike, maintains this principle of unequal payment.

The scale which it suggests for certificated class-teachers is quite a humorous little effort. Apparently the male class-teacher is intended to get married at once, as his minimum salary is higher than the female's. True the difference is but £10, but the maintenance of a family can be the only excuse for any difference at all. His maximum salary is £200 against the female's £160. Puzzle: If the NUT thinks a class-teacher can keep a wife on the £10 surplus, how many children does it expect him to rear on the £40 surplus? Surely the birth-rate can't be going down!

I am no teacher, but I don't think much of that Union. I like to get value for my money, and a union that takes my money and does not give me equal benefits with my fellow unionist is no use to me. Decidedly the women members of the NUT ought to withdraw their support from their ungracious colleagues and form a union of their own.

But what is the explanation of the meekness which makes such impositions on women possible? It is perhaps nothing disgraceful to ourselves, nothing that need make us doubt our worthiness as citizens of the ideal State. Nietzsche says that a man who is aiming at Supermanhood passes through three phases: the camel, the lion and the child. At first the soul becomes mastered by the idea of duty and self-sacrifice. It desires to be a preserver of life. Thus far have women gone. They have no time to travel further, having left the home so recently. 'But when the camel is loaded, it goeth to the desert, and there it is transformed into a lion.' The soul finds that the life for which it has sacrificed itself is in its present state hardly worthy of preserving. It turns to rend and destroy life, that out of its wreck it may make a new and more beautiful life. To this stage have men come.

Let women make haste to become lions, and fearlessly attack the social system. So that together men and women may be transformed for the last time into the child, who, untroubled with the consciousness of material things, is concerned only with love and happiness.

*The Clarion,* 18 October 1912

## THE SIN OF SELF-SACRIFICE

The basis of the anti-feminist position is the idea that women ought to sacrifice the development of their own personalities for the sake of men and children: that even if they are fit to vote and to fulfil other activities of men they should not do so, because all their energies should be spent in the service of their families. Such is the view of the governing classes in this country today, and its passionate advocacy by Ellen Key has changed the continental woman's movement from a march towards freedom to a romp towards voluptuous servitude. According to these folk a woman should from her childhood be guarded from the disturbance of intellectual effort and should pass automatically through a serenely sentimental adolescence to a home. There the tranquil flame of her unspoiled soul should radiate purity and nobility upon an indefinitely extended family, exposed to the world's winds only when she goes wisely marketing. Inconceivably incandescent, inconceivably economical, like the advertisement of a motor-lamp come true.

This amounts to a claim to halos for women: for a halo is the only thing I have ever heard of that gives out light yet needs no fuel. Unless a human being is being inspired with wisdom by some supernatural power he can only gain wisdom by an experience compounded of his sensations: that is, the vibration caused by collision between his nerves and external things. We are dependent for the value of this basis of wisdom on the extent to which we lean out of ourselves and adventure among alien things. The only times when a woman's physical feelings are concentrated within herself are when she has indigestion and appendicitis; when she is well she is thinking how warmly the sunlight lies on her face or how sweet the wet loaves smell. Similarly, when a woman's mental feelings are concentrated within herself she must have inflammation of the brain. Only the mad wonder continually whether they are men or poached eggs, and discuss whether the world uses them well or ill. The sane look round on their fellow-men and delight to see who will help them in their work of making the world less madly governed: they walk the earth to choose their battlefields and touch all it contains to find the substance most fit for the forging of weapons. Then they glow with the exhilaration of wisdom and radiate glory. So might many women were they given freedom; but they must remain tinged with no clearer light than the reflection of the kitchen range so long as they are made to ape the self-sufficiency of the maniac. As they are ignorant how can they hope to inspire those who are not ignorant? What influence can a wife who has passed from playing with dolls in her father's house to playing with saucepans and babies in her husband's house hope to have over a man who has been disciplined by years of responsible enterprise among all sorts of men? Her courage has been tried by childbirth, but her character has stood no other test.

It may be said that this is underestimating the value of homekeeping as an occupation. Of course it is. But it is a wild generalisation to say that the majority of wives in Great Britain are homekeepers in the sense of being essential to the existence of the home as was the wife in medieval agricultural England. If she were there would be no need to discuss feminism, for where a woman pays her way by performing labour she usually forces the community (if it be not too corrupt with capitalism) into recognising her equality. While the silk industry made the Burmese women economically independent, they were not submissive to men; but now that this is taken out of their hands they are threatened with that humiliation. And I was recently told by 'A. E.' that there is no need for the preaching of feminism in modern agricultural Ireland, for the farmer and the farmer's wife depend so much on each other's labour that it never occurs to them to imagine that they are different and unequal sorts. The rough home-keeping of the past, and the present in remote districts, presented difficulties which had to be met by skill and determination. Where the cow had to be milked and the churn persuaded, one simply waits for the coming of a milkman who, perhaps, has rarely seen a cow; where jelly had to be forced to jell one buys small packets from some unknown controller of jellies; where one sheared the sheep and spun its wool and wove the cloth and cut out the dress one goes to a shop and buys the finished thing easily, though probably at three times its real cost. It is all very simple and quite artificial. The woman who does these things may fill up her day with them, but the practice of them is hardly a craft. For they are tricks that a performing dog who could count his change might pull off just as well. That there is no interest in the occupation to counterbalance the solitude it entails, in these days of small homes unconnected by any local corporate life, is shown by the numbers of domestic servants who fly from its monotony to the life of the streets. And evidently their mistresses found the home no more educative, for they have not prevented their husbands and sons from preying on these women till, in their misery, they have revenged themselves on society by their disease and drunkenness. Here, in a rather important matter, the home-keeping woman has failed to radiate purity and nobility.

It may be said that the failure of women to create or influence morality does not matter: that their business lies simply with the physical nurture of the race. This is like saying that a doctor has no right to concern himself with the study of poisons because his business is with the preservation of the human body. When the body evolved the mind it evolved a queer, treacherous governor, who never knows what he does with his subject. Just as the African mind, by turning to commerce, has betrayed the African body, because sleeping-sickness travelled along the trade routes as safely as the goods, so the Western mind has betrayed the Western body by inventing the ingenious and in many ways convenient system of capitalism. So long as it persists no wealthy mother can look at her child without remembering that:

> The strongest poison ever known
> Came from Caesar's laurel crown.

No poor mother can hold her healthy child (life is such an indestructible and generous thing that nearly every baby is born healthy) without seeing him the bent extension of a machine. Men have not been able to fight the forces we have in an honest quest for civilisation called up from hell: all the energy of the world is needed to battle with them. The woman who cares merely for the physical nurture of her children is by her softness encouraging the famine that may some day starve them.

The fact is that this idea of sacrificing the individual to the race never works. It hints at a philosophical heresy, such as the belief disproved by Berkeley that matter has a substance apart from its attributes. 'There is nothing behind the facts,' said Chauncey Depew, when offered an idealist system that would 'harmonise' and 'explain' the facts of life. There is nothing behind the race but the individuals. If half the individuals agree to remain weak and undeveloped half the race is weak and undeveloped. And if every alternate link of a chain is weak it matters not how strong the others are: the chain will break all the same. Every nation that has contained a slave class has fallen to dust and ashes in spite of all its military glories and its pride of brains. And I cannot remember that any individual has ever benefited the race by self-sacrifice. I can well believe that St. Simon Stylites did not like perching and the Savonarola's heart bled at his own denunciation of beauty and jollity; but these men saved no race. The people who draw down salvation to earth are the people who insist on self-realisation whether it leads to death or gaiety. Florence Nightingale saved war from its worse disgrace and helped the sick because she hated disorder, not because she thought she ought to do something toilsome. Marx set humanity on its feet because he was interested in economics. Darwin uncovered the significant eyes of truth because he enjoyed zoology.

And truly these are among the saviours of men.

And the recognition of this is the real virtue of the militant suffrage movement. Its later manifestations have seemed to some of us not immoral but pointless and extravagant. Desirable residences are more common than desirable Cabinet Ministers, yet they are sufficiently rare to be preserved. No house is wholly built with hands: it has taken many mental triumphs of the organisation of civilisation to secure that bricklayers shall unmolested lay their bricks and quarrymen convey their stone unrobbed. A house is an achievement not to be burned in a night. And these sporadic attacks on the voter are ineffective, for they create no widespread terror that would cry out to the Government for immediate pacification of the terrorists. They merely make England into a patchwork of irritations. But how admirable is the spirit of the militants! How splendidly selfish they are! There is no doubt that now Mrs. Pankhurst is out of gaol again they will keep her out. All over the country we can help her. There is nothing like sympathetic reference to a lawbreaker for turning the heart of the law to water. We got Jim Larkin out of Mountjoy because we said we liked him. We can keep Mrs. Pankhurst out of Holloway if, remembering what her movement really means, and how it has brought the supreme virtue of selfishness to thousands of English women, we speak well of her.

*The Clarion,* 12 December 1913

*Olive Schreiner*

# THE BUDDHIST PRIEST'S WIFE (1923)

*Olive Schreiner (1855–1920) lived for extended periods in both England and South Africa, the place of her birth, and became politically involved in both localities. She was a supporter of a multi-racial South Africa free of British imperial domination. Upon arriving in England in 1881, she became involved in the emerging feminist movement, and her book* Women and Labour *was referred to by suffragettes as their bible. "The Buddhist Priest's Wife" explores the invisible barriers that prevent women and men from having intimate and equal relations. It raises the question: do men who claim to want close relations with women who are their intellectual equals also want to marry them? The title itself underscores the dilemma: Buddhist priests do not have wives.*

Cover her up! How still it lies! You can see the outline under the white. You would think she was asleep. Let the sunshine come in; it loved it so. She that had travelled so far, in so many lands, and done so much and seen so much, how she must like rest now! Did she ever love anything absolutely, this woman whom so many men loved, and so many women; who gave so much sympathy and never asked for anything in return! Did she ever need a love she could not have? Was she never obliged to unclasp her fingers from anything to which they clung? Was she really so strong as she looked? Did she never wake up in the night crying for that which she could not have? Were thought and travel enough for her? Did she go about for long days with a weight that crushed her to earth? Cover her up! I do not think she would have liked us to look at her. In one way she was alone all her life; she would have liked to be alone now! . . . Life must have been very beautiful to her, or she would not look so young now. Cover her up! Let us go!

Many years ago in a London room, up long flights of stairs, a fire burnt up in a grate. It showed the marks on the walls where pictures had been taken down, and the little blue flowers in the wall-paper and the blue felt carpet on the floor, and a woman sat by the fire in a chair at one side.

Presently the door opened, and the old woman came in who took care of the entrance hall downstairs.

'Do you not want anything to-night?' she said.

'No, I am only waiting for a visitor; when they have been, I shall go.'

'Have you got all your things taken away already?'

'Yes, only these I am leaving.'

The old woman went down again, but presently came up with a cup of tea in her hand.

'You must drink that; it's good for one. Nothing helps one like tea when one's been packing all day.'

The young woman at the fire did not thank her, but she ran her hand over the old woman's from the wrist to the fingers.

'I'll say good-bye to you when I go out.'

The woman poked the fire, put the last coals on, and went.

When she had gone the young one did not drink the tea, but drew her little silver cigarette case from her pocket and lighted a cigarette. For a while she sat smoking by the fire; then she stood up and walked the room.

When she had paced for a while she sat down again beside the fire. She threw the end of her cigarette away into the fire, and then began to walk again with her hands behind her. Then she went back to her seat and lit another cigarette, and paced again. Presently she sat down, and looked into the fire; she pressed the palms of her hands together, and then sat quietly staring into it.

Then there was a sound of feet on the stairs and someone knocked at the door.

She rose and threw the end into the fire and said without moving, 'Come in.'

The door opened and a man stood there in evening dress. He had a great-coat on, open in front.

'May I come in? I couldn't get rid of this downstairs; I didn't see where to leave it!' He took his coat off. 'How are you? This is a real bird's nest!'

She motioned to a chair.

'I hope you did not mind my asking you to come?'

'Oh no, I am delighted. I only found your note at my club twenty minutes ago.'

'So you really are going to India? How delightful! But what are you to do there? I think it was Grey told me six weeks ago you were going, but regarded it as one of those mythical stories which don't deserve credence. Yet I am sure I don't know! Why, nothing would surprise me.'

He looked at her in a half-amused, half-interested way.

'What a long time it is since we met! Six months, eight?'

'Seven,' she said.

'I really thought you were trying to avoid me. What have you been doing with yourself all this time?'

'Oh, been busy. Won't you have a cigarette?'

She held out the little case to him.

'Won't you take one yourself? I know you object to smoking with men, but you can make an exception in my case!'

'Thank you.' She lit her own and passed him the matches.

'But really what have you been doing with yourself all this time? You've entirely disappeared from civilised life. When I was down at the Grahams' in the spring, they said you were coming down there, and then at the last moment cried off. We were all quite disappointed. What is taking you to India now? Going to preach the doctrine of social and intellectual equality to the Hindu women and incite them to revolt? Marry some old Buddhist Priest, build a little cottage on the top of the Himalayas and live there, discuss philosophy and meditate? I believe that's what you'd like. I really shouldn't wonder if I heard you'd done it!'

She laughed and took out her cigarette case.

She smoked slowly.

'I've been here a long time, four years, and I want change. I was glad to see how well you succeeded in that election,' she said. 'You were much interested in it, were you not?'

'Oh, yes. We had a stiff fight. It tells in my favour, you know, though it was not exactly a personal matter. But it was a great worry.'

'Don't you think,' she said, 'you were wrong in sending that letter to the papers? It would have strengthened your position to have remained silent.'

'Yes, perhaps so; I think so now, but I did it under advice. However, we've won, so it's all right.' He leaned back in the chair.

'Are you pretty fit?'

'Oh, yes; pretty well; bored, you know. One doesn't know what all this working and striving is for sometimes.'

'Where are you going for your holiday this year?'

'Oh, Scotland, I suppose; I always do; the old quarters.'

'Why don't you go to Norway? It would be more change for you and rest you more. Did you get a book on sport in Norway?'

'Did you send it me? How kind of you! I read it with much interest. I was almost inclined to start off there and then. I suppose it is the kind of *vis inertiæ* that creeps over one as one grows older that sends one back to the old place. A change would be much better.'

'There's a list at the end of the book,' she said, 'of exactly the things one needs to take. I thought it would save trouble; you could just give it to your man, and let him get them all. Have you still got him?'

'Oh, yes. He's as faithful to me as a dog. I think nothing would induce him to leave me. He won't allow me to go out hunting since I sprained my foot last autumn. I have to do it surreptitiously. He thinks I can't keep my seat with a sprained ankle; but he's a very good fellow; takes care of me like a mother.' He smoked quietly with the firelight glowing on his black coat. 'But what are you going to India for? Do you know anyone there?'

'No,' she said. 'I think it will be so splendid. I've always been a great deal interested in the East. It's a complex, interesting life.'

He turned and looked at her.

'Going to seek for more experience, you'll say, I suppose. I never knew a woman throw herself away as you do; a woman with your brilliant parts and attractions, to let the whole of life slip through your hands, and make nothing of it. You ought to be the most successful woman in London. Oh, yes; I know what you're going to say: "You don't care." That's just it; you don't. You are always going to get experience, going to get everything, and you never do. You are always going to write when you know enough, and you are never satisfied that you do. You ought to be making your two thousand a year, but you don't care. That's just it! Living, burying yourself here with a lot of old frumps. You will never do anything. You could have everything and you let it slip.'

'Oh, my life is very full,' she said. 'There are only two things that are absolute realities, love and knowledge, and you can't escape them.'

She had thrown her cigarette end away and was looking into the fire, smiling.

'I've let these rooms to a woman friend of mine.' She glanced round the room, smiling. 'She doesn't know I'm going to leave these things here for her. She'll like them because they were mine. The world's very beautiful, I think—delicious.'

'Oh, yes. But what do you do with it? What do you make of it? You ought to settle down and marry like other women, not go wandering about the world to India and China and Italy, and God knows where. You are simply making a mess of your life. You're always surrounding yourself with all sorts of extraordinary people. If I hear any man or woman is a great friend of yours, I always say: "What the matter? Lost his money? Lost his character? Got an incurable disease?" I believe the only way in which anyone becomes interesting to you is by having some complaint of mind or body. I believe you worship rags. To come and shut yourself up in a place like this away from everybody and everything! It's a mistake; it's idiotic, you know.'

'I'm very happy,' she said. 'You see,' she said, leaning forwards towards the fire with hands on her knees, 'what matters is that something should need you. It isn't a question of love. What's the use of being near a thing if other people could serve it as well as you can. If they could serve it better, it's pure selfishness. It's the need of one thing for another that makes the organic bond of union. You love mountains and horses, but they don't need you; so what's the use of saying anything about it! I suppose the most absolutely delicious thing in life is to feel a thing needs you, and to give at the moment it needs. Things that don't need you, you must love from a distance.'

'Oh, but a woman like you ought to marry, ought to have children. You go squandering yourself on every old beggar or forlorn female or escaped criminal you meet; it may be very nice for them, but it's a mistake from your point of view.'

He touched the ash gently with the tip of his little finger and let it fall.

'I intend to marry. It's a curious thing,' he said, resuming his pose with an elbow on one knee and his head bent forward on one side, so that she saw the brown hair with its close curls and little tinged with grey at the sides, 'that when a man reaches a certain age he wants to marry. He doesn't fall in love; it's not that he definitely plans anything; but he has a feeling that he ought to have a home and a wife and children. I suppose it is the same kind of feeling that makes a bird build nests at certain times of the year. It's not love; it's something else. When I was a young man I used to despise men for getting married; wondered what they did it for; they had everything to lose and nothing to gain. But when a man gets to be six-and-thirty his feeling changes. It's not love, passion, he wants; it's a home; it's a wife and children. He may have a house and servants; it isn't the same thing. I should have thought a woman would have felt it too.'

She was quiet for a minute, holding a cigarette between her fingers; then she said slowly:

'Yes, at times a woman has a curious longing to have a child, especially when she gets near to thirty or over it. It's something distinct from love for any definite person. But it's a thing one has to get over. For a woman, marriage is much more serious than for a man. She might pass her life without meeting a man whom she could possibly love, and, if she met him, it might not be right or possible. Marriage has become very complex now it has become so largely intellectual. Won't you have another?'

She held out the case to him. 'You can light it from mine.' She bent forward for him to light it.

'You are a man who ought to marry. You've no absorbing mental work with which the woman would interfere; it would complete you.' She sat back, smoking serenely.

'Yes,' he said, 'but life is too busy; I never find time to look for one, and I haven't a fancy for the pink-and-white prettiness so common and that some men like so. I need something else. If I am to have a wife I shall have to go to America to look for one.'

'Yes, an American would suit you best.'

'Yes,' he said, 'I don't want a woman to look after; she must be self-sustaining and she mustn't bore you. You know what I mean. Life is too full of cares to have a helpless child added to them.'

'Yes,' she said, standing up and leaning with her elbow against the fireplace. 'The kind of woman you want would be young and strong; she need not be excessively beautiful, but she must be attractive; she must have energy, but not too strongly marked an individuality; she must be largely neutral; she need not give you too passionate or too deep a devotion, but she must second you in a thoroughly rational manner. She must have the same aims and tastes that you have. No woman has the right to marry a man if she has to bend herself out of shape for him. She might wish to, but she could never be to him with all her passionate endeavour what the other woman could be to him without trying. Character will dominate over all and will come out at last.'

She looked down into the fire.

'When you marry you mustn't marry a woman who flatters you too much. It is always a sign of falseness somewhere. If a woman absolutely loves you as herself, she will criticise and understand you as herself. Two people who are to live through life together must be able to look into each other's eyes and speak the truth. That helps one through life. You would find many such women in America,' she said: 'women who would help you to succeed, who would not drag you down.'

'Yes, that's my idea. But how am I to obtain the ideal woman?'

'Go and look for her. Go to America instead of Scotland this year. It is perfectly right. A man has a right to look for what he needs. With a woman it is different. That's one of the radical differences between men and women.

She looked downwards into the fire.

'It's a law of her nature and of sex relationship. There's nothing arbitrary or conventional about it any more than there is in her having to bear her child while the male does not. Intellectually we may both be alike. I suppose if fifty men and fifty women had to solve a mathematical problem, they would all do it in the same way; the more abstract and intellectual, the more alike we are. The nearer you approach to the personal and sexual, the more different we are. If I were to represent men's and women's natures,' she said, 'by a diagram, I would take two circular discs; the right side of each I should paint bright red; then I would shade the red away till in a spot on the left edge it became blue in the one and green in the other. That spot represents sex, and the nearer you come to it, the more the two discs differ in colour. Well then, if you turn them so that the red sides touch, they seem to be exactly alike, but if you turn them so that green and blue paint form their point of contact, they will seem to be entirely unlike. That's why you notice the brutal, sensual men invariably believe women are entirely different from men, another species of creature; and very cultured, intellectual men sometimes believe we are exactly alike. You see, sex love in its substance may be the same in both of us; in the form of its expression it must differ. It is not man's fault; it is nature's. If a man loves a woman, he has a right to try to make her love him because he can do it openly, directly, without bending. There need be no subtlety, no indirectness. With a woman it's not so; she can take no love that is not laid openly, simply, at her feet. Nature ordains that she should never show what she feels; the woman who had told a man she loved him would have put between them a barrier once and for ever that could not be crossed; and if she subtly drew him towards her, using the woman's means—silence, finesse, the dropped handkerchief, the surprise visit, the gentle assertion she had not thought to see him when she had come a long way to meet him, then she would be damned; she would hold the love, but she would have desecrated it by subtlety; it would have no value. Therefore she must always go with her arms folded sexually; only the love which lays itself down at her feet and implores of her to accept it is love she can ever rightly take up. That is the true difference between a man and a woman. You may seek for love because you can do it openly; we cannot because we must do it subtly. A woman should always walk with her arms folded. Of course friendship is different. You are on a perfect equality with man then; you can ask him to come and see you as I asked you. That's the beauty of the intellect and intellectual life to a woman, that she drops her shackles a little; and that is why she shrinks from sex so. If she were dying perhaps, or doing something equal to death, she might. . . . Death means so much more to a woman than a man; when you knew you were dying, to look round on the world and feel the bond of sex that has broken and crushed you all your life gone, nothing but the human left, no woman any more, to meet everything on perfectly even ground. There's no reason why you shouldn't go to America and look for a wife perfectly deliberately. You will have to tell no lies. Look till you find a woman that you absolutely love, that you have not the smallest doubt suits you apart from love, and then ask her to marry you. You must have children; the life of an old childless man is very sad.'

'Yes, I should like to have children. I often feel now, what is it all for, this work, this striving, and no one to leave it to? It's a blank, suppose I succeed . . . ?'

'Suppose you get your title?'

'Yes; what is it all worth to me if I've no one to leave it to? That's my feeling. It's really very strange to be sitting and talking like this to you. But you are so different from other women. If all women were like you, all your theories of the equality of men and women would work. You're the only woman with whom I never realise that she is a woman.'

'Yes,' she said.

She stood looking down into the fire.

'How long will you stay in India?'

'Oh, I'm not coming back.'

'Not coming back! That's impossible. You will be breaking the hearts of half the people here if you don't. I never knew a woman who had such power of entrapping men's hearts as you have in spite of that philosophy of yours. I don't know,' he smiled, 'that I should not have fallen into the snare myself—three years ago I almost thought I should—if you hadn't always attacked me so incontinently and persistently on all and every point and on each and every occasion. A man doesn't like pain. A succession of slaps damps him. But it doesn't seem to have that effect on other men. . . .

There was that fellow down in the country when I was there last year, perfectly ridiculous. You know his name. . . .' He moved his fingers to try and remember it— 'big, yellow moustache, a major, gone to the east coast of Africa now; the ladies unearthed it that he was always carrying about a photograph of yours in his pocket; and he used to take out little scraps of things you printed and show them to people mysteriously. He almost had a duel with a man one night after dinner because he mentioned you; he seemed to think there was something incongruous between your name and—'

'I do not like to talk of any man who has loved me,' she said. 'However small and poor his nature may be, he has given me his best. There is nothing ridiculous in love. I think a woman should feel that all the love men have given her which she has not been able to return is a kind of crown set up above her which she is always trying to grow tall enough to wear. I can't bear to think that all the love that has been given me has been wasted on something unworthy of it. Men have been very beautiful and greatly honoured me. I am grateful to them. If a man tells you he loves you,' she said, looking into the fire, 'with his breast uncovered before you for you to strike him if you will, the least you can do is to put out your hand and cover it up from other people's eyes. If I were a deer,' she said, 'and a stag got hurt following me, even though I could not have him for a companion, I would stand still and scrape the sand with my foot over the place where his blood had fallen; the rest of the herd should never know he had been hurt there following me. I would cover the blood up, if I were a deer,' she said, and then she was silent.

Presently she sat down in her chair and said, with her hand before her: 'Yet, you know, I have not the ordinary feeling about love. I think the one who is loved confers the benefit on the one who loves, it's been so great and beautiful that it should be loved. I think the man should be grateful to the woman or the woman to the man whom they have been able to love, whether they have been loved back or whether circumstances have divided them or not.' She stroked her knee softly with her hand.

'Well, really, I must go now.' He pulled out his watch. 'It's so fascinating sitting here talking that I could stay all night, but I've still two engagements.' He rose; she rose also and stood before him looking up at him for a moment.

'How well you look! I think you have found the secret of perpetual youth. You don't look a day older than when I first saw you just four years ago. You always look as if you were on fire and being burnt up, but you never are, you know.'

He looked down at her with a kind of amused face as one does at an interesting child or a big Newfoundland dog.

'When shall we see you back?'

'Oh, not at all!'

'Not at all! Oh, we must have you back; you belong here, you know. You'll get tired of your Buddhist and come back to us.'

'You didn't mind my asking you to come and say good-bye?' she said in a childish manner unlike her determinateness when she discussed anything impersonal. 'I wanted to say good-bye to everyone. If one hasn't said good-bye one feels restless and feels one would have to come back. If one has said good-bye to all one's friends, then one knows it is all ended.'

'Oh, this isn't a final farewell! You must come in ten years' time and we'll compare notes—you about your Buddhist Priest, I about my fair ideal American; and we'll see who succeeded best.'

She laughed.

'I shall always see your movements chronicled in the newspapers, so we shall not be quite sundered; and you will hear of me perhaps.'

'Yes, I hope you will be very successful.'

She was looking at him, with her eyes wide open, from head to foot. He turned to the chair where his coat hung.

'Can't I help you put it on?'

'Oh, no, thank you.'

He put it on.

'Button the throat,' she said, 'the room is warm.'

He turned to her in his great-coat and with his gloves. They were standing near the door.

'Well, good-bye. I hope you will have a very pleasant time.'

He stood looking down upon her, wrapped in his great-coat.

She put up one hand a little in the air. 'I want to ask you something,' she said quickly.

'Well, what is it?'

'Will you please kiss me?'

For a moment he looked down at her, then he bent over her.

In after years he could never tell certainly, but he always thought she put up her hand and rested it on the crown of his head, with a curious soft caress, something like a mother's touch when her child is asleep and she does not want to wake it. Then he looked round, and she was gone. The door had closed noiselessly. For a moment he stood motionless, then he walked to the fireplace and looked down into the fender at a little cigarette end lying there, then he walked quickly back to the door and opened it. The stairs were in darkness and silence. He rang the bell violently. The old woman came up. He asked her where the lady was. She said she had gone out, she had a cab waiting. He asked when she would be back. The old woman said, 'Not at all'; she had left. He asked where she had gone. The woman said she did not know; she had left orders that all her letters should be kept for six or eight months till she wrote and sent her address. He asked whether she had no idea where he might find her. The woman said no. He walked up to a space in the wall where a picture had hung and stood staring at it as though the picture were still hanging there. He drew his mouth as though he were emitting a long whistle, but no sound came. He gave the old woman ten shillings and went downstairs.

That was eight years ago.

How beautiful life must have been to it that it looks so young still!

*Virginia Woolf*

# *from* A ROOM OF ONE'S OWN (1929)

*By the time that Virginia Woolf (1882–1941) was writing the books that would make her one of the most important twentieth-century novelists, the majority of English women had won the right to vote. Many now thought that there was no longer a need for feminism. In* A Room of One's Own, *originally given as lectures at Newnham College and Girton College, Cambridge, Woolf reaffirms the continued importance of feminist thinking and suggests that there are more difficult fights for women ahead. At one level, the lectures are feminist explorations into why there had been so few important women writers. They also offer a more general analysis of the inequality in gender relations. According to Woolf, men inflate their own self-image when they see women as being inferior: in their ascribed social role, women act as distorting mirrors, reflecting the figure of men at twice their natural size.*

. . . Life for both sexes—and I looked at them, shouldering their way along the pavement—is arduous, difficult, a perpetual struggle. It calls for gigantic courage and strength. More than anything, perhaps, creatures of illusion as we are, it calls for confidence in oneself. Without self-confidence we are as babes in the cradle. And how can we generate this imponderable quality, which is yet so invaluable, most quickly? By thinking that other people are inferior to oneself. By feeling that one has some innate superiority—it may be wealth, or rank, a straight nose, or the portrait of a grandfather by Romney—for there is no end to the pathetic devices of the human imagination—over other people. Hence the enormous importance to a patriarch who has to conquer, who has to rule, of feeling that great numbers of people, half the human race indeed, are by nature inferior to himself. It must indeed be one of the chief sources of his power. But let me turn the light of this observation on to real life, I thought. Does it help to explain some of those psychological puzzles that one notes in the margin of daily life? Does it explain my astonishment the other day when Z, most humane, most modest of men, taking up some book by Rebecca West and reading a passage in it, exclaimed, "The arrant feminist! She says that men are snobs!" The exclamation, to me so surprising—for why was Miss West an arrant feminist for making a possibly true if uncomplimentary statement about the other sex?—was not merely the cry of wounded vanity; it was a protest against some infringement of his power to believe in himself. Women have served all these centuries as looking-glasses possessing the magic and delicious power of reflecting the figure of man at twice its natural size. Without that power probably the earth would still be swamp and jungle. The glories of all our wars would be unknown. We should still be scratching the outlines of deer on the remains of mutton bones and bartering flints for sheep-skins or whatever simple ornament took our unsophisticated taste. Supermen and Fingers of Destiny would never have existed. The Czar and the Kaiser would never have worn their crowns or lost them. Whatever may be their use in civilised societies, mirrors are essential to all violent and heroic action. That is why Napoleon and Mussolini both insist so emphatically upon the inferiority of women, for if they were not inferior, they would cease to enlarge. That serves to explain in part the necessity that women so often are to men. And it serves to explain how restless they are under her criticism; how impossible it is for her to say to them this book is bad, this picture is feeble, or whatever it may be, without giving far more pain and rousing far more anger than a man would do who gave the same criticism. For if she begins to tell the truth, the figure in the looking-glass shrinks; his fitness for life is diminished. How is he to go on giving judgement, civilising natives, making laws, writing books, dressing up and speechifying at banquets, unless he can see himself at breakfast and at dinner at least twice the size he really is? So I reflected, crumbling my bread and stirring my coffee and now and again looking at the people in the street. The looking-glass vision is of supreme importance because it charges the vitality; it stimulates the nervous system. Take it away and man may die, like the drug fiend deprived of his cocaine. Under the spell of that illusion, I thought, looking out of the window, half the people on the pavement are striding to work. They put on their hats and coats in the morning under its agreeable rays. They start the day confident, braced, believing themselves desired at Miss Smith's tea party; they say to themselves as they go into the room, I am the superior of half the people here, and it is thus that they speak with that self-confidence, that self-assurance, which have had such profound consequences in public life and lead to such curious notes in the margin of the private mind. . . .

. . . women have burnt like beacons in all the works of all the poets from the beginning of time—Clytemnestra, Antigone, Cleopatra, Lady Macbeth, Phèdre, Cressida, Rosalind, Desdemona, the Duchess of Malfi, among the dramatists; then among the prose writers: Millamant, Clarissa, Becky Sharp, Anna Karenina, Emma Bovary, Madame de Guermantes—the names flock to mind, nor do they recall women "lacking in personality and character." Indeed, if woman had no existence save in the fiction written by men, one would imagine her a person of the utmost importance; very various; heroic and mean; splendid and sordid; infinitely beautiful and hideous in the extreme; as great as a man, some think even greater.[1] But this is

[1]"It remains a strange and almost inexplicable fact that in Athena's city, where women were kept in almost Oriental suppression as odalisques or drudges, the stage should yet have produced figures like Clytemnestra and Cassandra, Attosa and Antigone, Phèdre and Medea, and all the other heroines who dominate play after play of the 'misogynist' Euripides. But the paradox of this world where in real life a respectable woman could hardly show her face alone in the street, and yet on the stage woman equals or surpasses man, has never been satisfactorily explained. In modern tragedy the same predominance exists. At all events, a very cursory survey of Shakespeare's work (similarly with Webster, though not with Marlowe or Jonson) suffices to reveal how this dominance, this initiative of women, persists from Rosalind to Lady Macbeth. So too in Racine; six of his tragedies bear their heroines' names; and what male characters of his shall we set against Hermione and Andromaque, Bérénice and Roxane, Phèdre and Athalie? So again with Ibsen: what men shall we match with Solveig and Nora, Hedda and Hilda Wangel and Rebecca West?"—F. L. Lucas, *Tragedy,* pp. 114–15.

woman in fiction. In fact, as Professor Trevelyan points out, she was locked up, beaten and flung about the room.

A very queer, composite being thus emerges. Imaginatively she is of the highest importance; practically she is completely insignificant. She pervades poetry from cover to cover; she is all but absent from history. She dominates the lives of kings and conquerors in fiction; in fact she was the slave of any boy whose parents forced a ring upon her finger. Some of the most inspired words, some of the most profound thoughts in literature fall from her lips; in real life she could hardly read, could scarcely spell, and was the property of her husband.

It was certainly an odd monster that one made up by reading the historians first and the poets afterwards—a worm winged like an eagle; the spirit of life and beauty in a kitchen chopping up suet. But these monsters, however amusing to the imagination, have no existence in fact. What one must do to bring her to life was to think poetically and prosaically at one and the same moment, thus keeping in touch with fact—that she is Mrs. Martin, aged thirty-six, dressed in blue, wearing a black hat and brown shoes; but not losing sight of fiction either—that she is a vessel in which all sorts of spirits and forces are coursing and flashing perpetually. The moment, however, that one tries this method with the Elizabethan woman, one branch of illumination fails; one is held up by the scarcity of facts. One knows nothing detailed, nothing perfectly true and substantial about her. History scarcely mentions her. . . .

. . . Let me imagine, since facts are so hard to come by, what would have happened had Shakespeare had a wonderfully gifted sister, called Judith, let us say. Shakespeare himself went, very probably—his mother was an heiress—to the grammar school, where he may have learnt Latin—Ovid, Virgil and Horace—and the elements of grammar and logic. He was, it is well known, a wild boy who poached rabbits, perhaps shot a deer, and had, rather sooner than he should have done, to marry a woman in the neighbourhood, who bore him a child rather quicker than was right. That escapade sent him to seek his fortune in London. He had, it seemed, a taste for the theatre; he began by holding horses at the stage door. Very soon he got work in the theatre, became a successful actor, and lived at the hub of the universe, meeting everybody, knowing everybody, practising his art on the boards, exercising his wits in the streets, and even getting access to the palace of the queen. Meanwhile his extraordinarily gifted sister, let us suppose, remained at home. She was as adventurous, as imaginative, as agog to see the world as he was. But she was not sent to school. She had no chance of learning grammar and logic, let alone of reading Horace and Virgil. She picked up a book now and then, one of her brother's perhaps, and read a few pages. But then her parents came in and told her to mend the stockings or mind the stew and not moon about with books and papers. They would have spoken sharply but kindly, for they were substantial people who knew the conditions of life for a woman and loved their daughter—indeed, more likely than not she was the apple of her father's eye. Perhaps she scribbled some pages up in an apple loft on the sly, but was careful to hide them or set fire to them. Soon, however, before she was out of her teens, she was to be betrothed to the son of a neighbouring wool-stapler. She cried out that marriage was hateful to her, and for that she was severely beaten by her father. Then he ceased to scold her. He begged her instead not to hurt him, not to shame him in this matter of her marriage. He would give her a chain of beads or a fine petticoat, he said; and there were tears in his eyes. How could she disobey him? How could she break his heart? The force of her own gift alone drove her to it. She made up a small parcel of her belongings, let herself down by a rope one summer's night and took the road to London. She was not seventeen. The birds that sat in the hedge were not more musical than she was. She had the quickest fancy, a gift like her brother's, for the tune of words. Like him, she had a taste for the theatre. She stood at the stage door; she wanted to act, she said. Men laughed in her face. The manager—a fat, loose-lipped man—guffawed. He bellowed something about poodles dancing and women acting—no woman, he said, could possibly be an actress. He hinted—you can imagine what. She could get no training in her craft. Could she even seek her dinner in a tavern or roam the streets at midnight? Yet her genius was for fiction and lusted to feed abundantly upon the lives of men and women and the study of their ways. At last—for she was very young, oddly like Shakespeare the poet in her face, with the same grey eyes and rounded brows—at last Nick Greene the actor-manager took pity on her; she found herself with child by the gentleman and so—who shall measure the heat and violence of the poet's heart when caught and tangled in a woman's body?—killed herself one winter's night and lies buried at some cross-roads where the omnibuses now stop outside the Elephant and Castle.

That, more or less, is how the story would run, I think, if a woman in Shakespeare's day had had Shakespeare's genius. But for my part, I agree with the deceased bishop, if such he was—it is unthinkable that any woman in Shakespeare's day should have had Shakespeare's genius. For genius like Shakespeare's is not born among labouring, uneducated, servile people. It was not born in England among the Saxons and the Britons. It is not born today among the working classes. How, then, could it have been born among women whose work began, according to Professor Trevelyan, almost before they were out of the nursery, who were forced to it by their parents and held to it by all the power of law and custom? Yet genius of a sort must have existed among women as it must have existed among the working classes. Now and again an Emily Brontë or a Robert Burns blazes out and proves its presence. But certainly it never got itself on to paper. When, however, one reads of a witch being ducked, of a woman possessed by devils, of a wise woman selling herbs, or even of a very remarkable man who had a mother, then I think we are on the track of a lost novelist, a suppressed poet, of some mute and inglorious Jane Austen, some Emily Brontë who dashed her brains out on the moor or mopped and mowed about the highways crazed with the torture that her gift had put her to. Indeed, I would venture to guess that Anon, who wrote so many poems without signing them, was often a woman. It was a woman Edward Fitzgerald, I think, suggested who made the ballads and the folk-songs, crooning them to her children, beguiling her spinning with them, or the length of the winter's night.

This may be true or it may be false—who can say?—but what is true in it, so it seemed to me, reviewing the story of Shakespeare's sister as I had made it, is that any woman born with a great gift in the sixteenth century would certainly have gone crazed, shot herself, or ended her days in some lonely cottage outside the village, half witch, half wizard, feared and mocked at. For it needs little skill in psychology to be sure that a highly gifted girl who had tried to use her gift for poetry would have been so thwarted and hindered by other people, so tortured and pulled asunder by her own contrary instincts, that she must have lost her health and sanity to a certainty. . . .

. . . But it is obvious that the values of women differ very often from the values which have been made by the other sex; naturally, this is so. Yet it is the masculine values that prevail. Speaking crudely, football and sport are "important"; the worship of fashion, the buying of clothes "trivial." And these values are inevitably transferred from life to fiction. This is an important book, the critic assumes, because it deals with war. This is an insignificant book because it deals with the feelings of women in a drawing-room. A scene in a battlefield is more important than a scene in a shop—everywhere and much more subtly the difference of value persists. The whole structure, therefore, of the early nineteenth-century novel was raised, if one was a woman, by a mind which was slightly pulled from the straight, and made to alter its clear vision in deference to external authority. One has only to skim those old forgotten novels and listen to the tone of voice in which they are written to divine that the writer was meeting criticism; she was saying this by way of aggression, or that by way of conciliation. She was admitting that she was "only a woman," or protesting that she was "as good as a man." She met that criticism as her temperament dictated, with docility and diffidence, or with anger and emphasis. It does not matter which it was; she was thinking of something other than the thing itself. Down comes her book upon our heads. There was a flaw in the centre of it. And I thought of all the women's novels that lie scattered, like small pock-marked apples in an orchard, about the sec-ondhand book shops of London. It was the flaw in the center that had rotted them. She had altered her values in deference to the opinion of others.

But how impossible it must have been for them not to budge either to the right or to the left. What genius, what integrity it must have required in face of all that criticism, in the midst of that purely patriarchal society, to hold fast to the thing as they saw it without shrinking. Only Jane Austen did it and Emily Brontë. It is another feather, perhaps the finest, in their caps. They wrote as women write, not as men write. Of all the thousand women who wrote novels then, they alone entirely ignored the perpetual admonitions of the eternal pedagogue—write this, think that. They alone were deaf to that persistent voice, now grumbling, now patronising, now dom-ineering, now grieved, now shocked, now angry, now avuncular, that voice which cannot let women alone, but must be at them, like some too conscientious governess, adjuring them, like Sir Egerton Brydges, to be refined; dragging even into the criti-cism of poetry criticism of sex;[2] admonishing them, if they would be good and win, as I suppose, some shiny prize, to keep within certain limits which the gentleman in question thinks suitable: ". . . female novelists should only aspire to excellence by courageously acknowledging the limitations of their sex."[3] That puts the matter in a nutshell, and when I tell you, rather to your surprise, that this sentence was written not in August 1828 but in August 1928, you will agree, I think, that however delight-ful it is to us now, it represents a vast body of opinion—I am not going to stir those old pools, I take only what chance has floated to my feet—that was far more vigorous and far more vocal a century ago. It would have needed a very stalwart young woman in 1828 to disregard all those snubs and chidings and promises of prizes. One must

[2]"[She] has a metaphysical purpose, and that is a dangerous obsession, especially with a woman, for women rarely possess men's healthy love of rhetoric. It is a strange lack in the sex which is in other things more primitive and more materialistic."—*New Criterion,* June 1928.
[3]"If, like the reporter, you believe that female novelists should only aspire to excellence by courageously acknowledging the limitations of their sex (Jane Austen [has] demonstrated how gracefully this gesture can be accomplished). . . ."—*Life and Letters,* August 1928.

have been something of a firebrand to say to oneself, Oh, but they can't buy literature too. Literature is open to everybody. . . .

How can I further encourage you to go about the business of life? Young women, I would say, and please attend, for the peroration is beginning, you are, in my opinion, disgracefully ignorant. You have never made a discovery of any sort of importance. You have never shaken an empire or led an army into battle. The plays of Shakespeare are not by you, and you have never introduced a barbarous race to the blessings of civilisation. What is your excuse? It is all very well for you to say, pointing to the streets and squares and forests of the globe swarming with black and white and coffee-coloured inhabitants, all busily engaged in traffic and enterprise and love-making, we have had other work on our hands. Without our doing, those seas would be unsailed and those fertile lands a desert. We have borne and bred and washed and taught, perhaps to the age of six or seven years, the one thousand six hundred and twenty-three million human beings who are, according to statistics, at present in existence, and that, allowing that some had help, takes time.

There is truth in what you say—I will not deny it. But at the same time may I remind you that there have been at least two colleges for women in existence in England since the year 1866; that after the year 1880 a married woman was allowed by law to possess her own property; and that in 1919—which is a whole nine years ago—she was given a vote? May I also remind you that the most of the professions have been open to you for close on ten years now? When you reflect upon these immense privileges and the length of time during which they have been enjoyed, and the fact that there must be at this moment some two thousand women capable of earning over five hundred a year in one way or another, you will agree that the excuse of lack of opportunity, training, encouragement, leisure and money no longer holds good. Moreover, the economists are telling us that Mrs. Seton has had too many children. You must, of course, go on bearing children, but, so they say, in twos and threes, not in tens and twelves.

Thus, with some time on your hands and with some book learning in your brains—you have had enough of the other kind, and are sent to college partly, I suspect, to be uneducated—surely you should embark upon another stage of your very long, very laborious and highly obscure career. A thousand pens are ready to suggest what you should do and what effect you will have. My own suggestion is a little fantastic, I admit; I prefer, therefore, to put it in the form of fiction.

I told you in the course of this paper that Shakespeare had a sister; but do not look for her in Sir Sidney Lee's life of the poet. She died young—alas, she never wrote a word. She lies buried where the omnibuses now stop, opposite the Elephant and Castle. Now my belief is that this poet who never wrote a word and was buried at the crossroads still lives. She lives in you and in me, and in many other women who are not here tonight, for they are washing up the dishes and putting the children to bed. But she lives; for great poets do not die; they are continuing presences; they need only the opportunity to walk among us in the flesh. This opportunity, as I think, it is now coming within your power to give her. For my belief is that if we live another century or so—I am talking of the common life which is the real life and not of the little separate lives which we live as individuals—and have five hundred a year each of us and rooms of our own; if we have the habit of freedom and the courage to write exactly what we think; if we escape a little from the common sitting-room and see human beings not always in their relation to each other but in relation to reality; and the sky, too, and the trees or whatever it may be in themselves; if we look past Milton's bogey, for no human being should shut out the view; if we face the fact, for it is a fact, that there is no arm to cling to, but that we go alone and that our relation is to the world of reality and not only to the world of men and women, then the opportunity will come and the dead poet who was Shakespeare's sister will put on the body which she has so often laid down. Drawing her life from the lives of the unknown who were her forerunners, as her brother did before her, she will be born. As for her coming without that preparation, without that effort on our part, without that determination that when she is born again she shall find it possible to live and write her poetry, that we cannot expect, for that would be impossible. But I maintain that she would come if we worked for her, and that so to work, even in poverty and obscurity, is worth while.

# SECTION VII

# Global War

The two world wars of the twentieth century are often thought of as discrete events. Yet it is also possible to think of them as comprising one epoch of global war, the interwar years representing a pause rather than a resolution of the initial conflict. However it is conceived, the result was the end of the European era. It is not for nothing that Europeans refer to the period prior to 1914 as *la belle epoque*.

One of the principles that Marinetti embraces in the "Futurist Manifesto" (found in the previous section) is the glorification of war, one of "the beautiful ideas worth dying for" and "the destructive gesture of freedom-bringers." Published in 1909, five years prior to the First World War (the Great War, as Europeans call it), Marinetti's praise of military combat reminds us of how eagerly many Europeans on both sides plunged into combat. Yet those who had hopes and dreams of performing heroic acts in the name of national honor were soon disappointed. They expected a short and limited war that would produce an early diplomatic settlement. What they got was one of the most devastating and far-reaching conflicts ever experienced: a 'total war' that affected whole populations, was the first global conflict in human history, involved unparalleled technological sophistication, and was responsible for death and destruction on an unprecedented scale. Overall there were 37.5 million casualties, including 8.5 million dead. In Germany and France, the two nations that suffered the most, it seemed as if an entire generation of young men had been wiped out.

Many intellectuals, poets, and artists were pessimistic about the human condition following the First World War. But there were others who hoped that lessons learned from the War would make it possible to produce a lasting peace. For some, the Bolshevik Revolution of 1917, which developed in the context of the Russia war experience under the Czar, represented the dawn of a new historical epoch. They regarded it as the first genuinely egalitarian society in human history, and they believed that it could serve as a model worldwide. Moreover, with the return of economic prosperity in the later part of the 1920s, there was renewed optimism about the European future. But just as it appeared that there was a return to peace, growth, and normalcy, the greatest economic downturn of the twentieth century—the Great Depression—swept through the capitalist world with unprecedented speed and intensity, placing unbearable strains on already fragile societies.

The most famous casualty was the German Weimar Republic. Germany's first experiment in liberal democracy, shaped in the power vacuum created by a defeated and discredited regime in 1918, would have found it difficult to succeed under the best of circumstances. But from the onset, it faced conditions that seriously undermined its authority. In the public imagination—exploited by the Nazis—it was responsible for the humiliation of Germany at the postwar peace talks. The Weimar Republic was blamed for the crushing reparations that Germany had to pay the victorious Allies; and it was never forgiven for its recognition (forced upon it) of German responsibility for the War. It managed to survive the out-of-control inflation of the early 1920s, when an egg cost 150 billion marks, only to be destroyed by the economic devastation of the 1930s, when unemployment hovered at 25%.

One of the first signs of decay was the disintegration of the political center. As conditions in Germany worsened, the forces that stood for compromise and moderation gave way to those preaching confrontation and radical change. Among those who benefited, though it proved to be short-lived, was the German Communist party. A group of dedicated revolutionaries composed of intellectuals and workers, it saw the Great Depression as the final crisis of capitalism predicted by Marx in *The Communist Manifesto*. The Soviet Regime—which proved immune to the Depression—appeared to them as the wave of the future. Of course, the real story of the thirties was the rapid growth of the radical right—particularly the National Socialist or Nazi Party—which used the economic collapse as an avenue to move from the periphery to the mainstream of German politics.

National Socialism was a tributary of a broader 'fascist' stream. The word *fascism* comes from the Latin *fasces*, a word signifying the bundle of rods with ax head carried by Roman magistrates. The fascist parties of the interwar years were simultaneously anticapitalist and anticommunist, seeing the 'total state' as an alternative to the chaos of liberalism and the internationalism preached by the Bolsheviks. Fascists embraced a nationalist rhetoric that they delivered in a highly-charged emotional form. Central to their success was their skill at exploiting the new means of mass communications—such as radio and film—for propaganda purposes and their ability to create tightly-knit party organizations. The fascist parties saw themselves as being engaged in a war over the culture of Europe: the maintenance of 'traditional' values was as important as industrial growth and development.

The "final solution" or the Holocaust was National Socialism's grimmest legacy. So much has been written about this darkest of all European episodes that it is virtually impossible to say anything about it that hasn't been said before. Yet in a book about the "trials of modernity" it is perhaps worth pointing out how 'modern' the death camps were—how 'rational', 'scientific', and 'efficient' the methods of extermination. Indeed, the Holocaust is as much a part of the modern experience as is a scientific breakthrough in fighting a disease or a revolutionary technological development such as the automobile or the computer. In addition, while the Jews suffered more than any other group—six million of them perished in the camps—they were not the only victims. As many as five million others—including Slavs, Soviet prisoners of war, communists, gypsies, and homosexuals—were victims as well.

Fascism was effective because it was able to prey on the worst side of human beings. But its success was not universal, and no picture of the period is complete without reference to those men and women who refused to accept it, either by covert resistance or by helping those who were potentially its victims. The European Resistance has been romanticized; its numbers have been inflated; and its impact has been exaggerated. This does mean it is not important. The Resistance reiterated the most basic moral truths at a time when mainstream European society all but forgot them.

# CALL TO THE WOMEN
# OF ALL NATIONS (1915)

*Women's organizations and congresses in the late nineteenth and twentieth centuries came to see promoting peace as a logical extension of their fight for suffrage, full legal rights for women, and safe living and working conditions for women and children. In 1915, in the midst of the First World War, prominent women's leaders long involved in these causes met at the Hague for a conference on peace. Dr. Aletta Jacobs, the first woman to have been admitted to university in the Netherlands and director of the first family planning clinic in Europe (founded in 1882), issued the call for the International Congress of Women. American social reformer Jane Addams chaired the meeting, and participants came from both embattled and neutral nations. The selection here includes the initial conference announcement and the Resolutions of the Conference.*

## HOLLAND, 1915

From many countries appeals have come asking us to call together an International Women's Congress to discuss what the women of the world can do and ought to do in the dreadful times in which we are now living.

We women of the Netherlands, living in a neutral country, accessible to the women of all other nations, therefore take upon ourselves the responsibility of calling together such an International Congress of Women. We feel strongly that at a time when there is so much hatred among nations, we women must show that we can retain our solidarity and that we are able to maintain a mutual friendship.

Women are waiting to be called together. The world is looking to them for their contribution towards the solution of the great problems of to-day.

Women, whatever your nationality, whatever your party, your presence will be of great importance.

The greater the number of those who take part in the Congress, the stronger will be the impression its proceedings will make.

Your presence will testify that you, too, wish to record your protest against this horrible war, and that you desire to assist in preventing a recurrence of it in the future.

Let our call to you not be in vain!

## SOME PRINCIPLES OF A PEACE SETTLEMENT

### *1. Plea for Definition of Terms of Peace*

Considering that the people in each of the countries now at war believe themselves to be fighting not as aggressors, but in self-defence and for their national existence, this International Congress of Women urges the Governments of the belligerent countries publicly to define the terms on which they are willing to make peace, and for this purpose immediately to call a truce.

### *2. Arbitration and Conciliation*

This International Congress of Women, believing that war is the negation of all progress and civilisation, declares its conviction that future international disputes should be referred to arbitration or conciliation, and demands that in future these methods shall be adopted by the Governments of all nations.

### *3. International Pressure*

This International Congress of Women urges the Powers to come to an agreement to unite in bringing pressure to bear upon any country which resorts to arms without having referred its case to arbitration or conciliation.

### *4. Democratic Control of Foreign Policy*

War is brought about not by the peoples of the world, who do not desire it, but by groups of individuals representing particular interests.

This International Congress of Women demands, therefore, that foreign politics shall be subject to democratic control, and at the same time declares that it can only recognise as democratic a system which includes the equal representation of men and women.

### *5. Transference of Territory*

That there should be no transference of territory without the consent of the men and women in it.

### *6. Protest*

War, the ultima ratio of the statesmanship of men, we women declare to be a madness, possible only to a people intoxicated with a false idea; for it destroys everything the constructive powers of humanity have taken centuries to build up.

### *7. Women's Responsibility*

This International Congress of Women is convinced that one of the strongest forces for the prevention of war will be the combined influence of the women of all countries, and that therefore upon women as well as men rests the responsibility for the outbreak of future wars. But as women can only make their influence effective if they have equal political rights with men, this Congress declares that it is the duty of the women of all countries to work with all their force for their political enfranchisement.

### 8. Women's Sufferings in War

This International Congress of Women protests against the assertion that war means the protection of women. Not forgetting their sufferings as wives, mothers, and sisters, it emphasises the fact that the moral and physical sufferings of many women are beyond description, and are often of such a nature that by the tacit consent of men the least possible is reported. Women raise their voices in commiseration with those women wounded in their deepest sense of womanhood and powerless to defend themselves.

### 9. Women Delegates to Conference of Powers

Believing that it is essential for the future peace of the world that representatives of the people should take part in the conference of the Powers after the war, this International Women's Congress urges that among the representatives women delegates should be included.

### 10. Woman Suffrage Resolution

This International Women's Congress urges that, in the interests of civilisation, the conference of the Powers after the war should pass a resolution affirming the need in all countries of extending Parliamentary franchise to women.

### 11. Promotion of International Good Feeling

This International Women's Congress, which is in itself an evidence of the serious desire of women to bring together mankind in the work of building up our common civilisation, considers that every means should be used for promoting mutual understanding and goodwill between the nations, and for resisting any tendency towards a spirit of hatred and revenge.

### 12. Education of Children

Realising that for the prevention of the possibility of a future war every individual should be convinced of the inadmissibility of deciding disputes by force of arms, this International Congress of Women urges the necessity of so directing the education of children as to turn their thoughts and desires towards the maintenance of peace, and to give them a moral education so as to enable them to act on this conviction whatever may happen.

# *Aleksandra Kollontay*

## *from* COMMUNISM AND THE FAMILY (1918)

*Aleksandra Kollontay (1872–1952) was born to a life of privilege as the daughter of a general in the Imperial Russian Army. She left that life in 1898, however, when she joined the Russian Social Democratic Workers' Party and became an activist for the causes of socialism, women's emancipation, and pacifism. In 1915 she joined the Bolsheviks, and when they assumed power in Russia in 1917 she became the first Soviet commissar of public welfare. Kollontay used this position to advocate reforms in traditional family structure that would free women from conventional burdens for a new mode of life, one in which they would be workers and comrades fully equal to men. She describes these social goals in* Communism and the Family, *published in London in 1918. Kollontay later served as Soviet minister to Norway, Mexico, and Sweden. In her seventies, she conducted the armistice negotiations between Finland and the Soviet Union late in the Second World War.*

In Soviet Russia, owing to the care of the Commissariats of Public Education and of Social Welfare, great advances are being made, and already many things have been done in order to facilitate for the family the task of bringing up and supporting the children. There are homes for very small babies, day nurseries, kindergarten, children's colonies and homes, infirmaries, and health resorts for sick children, restaurants, free lunches at school, free distribution of text books, of warm clothing, of shoes to the pupils of the educational establishments—does all this not sufficiently show that the child is passing out of the confines of the family and being placed from the shoulders of the parents on those of collectivity?

The care of children by the parents consisted of three distinct parts: (1) the care necessarily devoted to the very young babies; (2) the bringing up of the child; (3) the instruction of the child. As for the instruction of children in primary schools and later in gymnasiums and universities, it has become a duty of the State, even in capitalist society. The other occupations of the working class, its conditions of life, imperatively dictated, even to capitalist society, the creation for the purposes of the young, of playgrounds, infants' schools, homes, etc., etc. The more the workers became conscious of their rights, the better they were organized in any specific State, the more society would show itself to be concerned with relieving the family of the care of the children. But bourgeois society was afraid of going too far in this matter of meeting the interests of the working class, lest it contribute in this way to the disintegration of the family. The capitalists themselves are not unaware of the fact that the family of old, with the wife a slave and the man responsible for the support and well-being of the family, that the family of this type is the best weapon to stifle the proletarian effort toward liberty, to weaken the revolutionary spirit of the working man and working woman. Worry for his family takes the backbone out of the worker, obliges him to compromise with capital. The father and the mother, what will they not do when their children are hungry? Contrary to the practice of capitalist society, which has not been able to transform all education of youth into a truly social function, a State work, Communist society will consider the social education of the rising generation as the very basis of its laws and customs, as the corner stone of the new edifice. Not the family of the past, petty and narrow, with its quarrels between the parents, with its exclusive interests in its own offspring, will mould for us the man of the society of tomorrow. Our new man, in our new society, is to be moulded by Socialist organizations such as playgrounds, gardens, homes, and many other such institutions, in which the child will pass the greater part of the day and where intelligent educators will make of him a Communist who is conscious of the greatness of this sacred motto: solidarity, comradeship, mutual aid, devotion to the collective life.

## THE MOTHER'S LIVELIHOOD ASSURED

But now, with the bringing up gone and with the instruction gone, what will remain of the obligations of the family toward its children, particularly after it has been relieved also of the greater portion of the material cares involved in having a child, except for the care of a very small baby while it still needs its mother's attention, while it is still learning to walk, clinging to its mother's skirt? Here again the Communist State hastens to the aid of the working mother. No longer shall the child-mother be bowed down with a baby in her arms! The Workers' State charges itself with the duty of assuring a livelihood to every mother, whether she be legitimately married or not, as long as she is suckling her child, of creating all over maternity houses, of establishing in all the cities and all the villages, day nurseries and other similar institutions in order thus to permit the woman to serve the State in a useful manner and simultaneously to be a mother.

## MARRIAGE NO LONGER A CHAIN

Let the working mothers be re-assured. The Communist Society is not intending to take the children away from the parents nor to tear the baby from the breast of its mother; nor has it any intention of resorting to violence in order to destroy the family as such. No such thing! Such are not the aims of the Communist Society. What do we observe today? The outworn family is breaking. It is gradually freeing itself from all the domestic labors which formerly were as so many pillars supporting the family as a social unit. Housekeeping? It also appears to have outlived its usefulness. The children? The parent-proletarians are already unable to take care of them; they can assure them neither subsistence nor education. This is the situation from which both parents and children suffer in equal measure. Communist Society therefore approaches the working woman and the working man and says to them: "You are young, you love each other. Everyone has the right to happiness. Therefore live your life. Do not flee happiness. Do not fear marriage, even though marriage was truly a chain for the working man and woman of capitalist society. Above all, do not fear, young and healthy as you are, to give to your country new workers, new citizen-children. The society of the workers is in need of new working forces; it hails the arrival of every newborn child in the world. Nor should you be concerned because of the future of your child; your child will know neither hunger nor cold. It will not be unhappy nor abandoned to its fate as would have been the case in capitalist society. A subsistence ration and solicitous care are assured to the child and to the mother by the Communist Society, by the Workers' State, as soon as the child arrives in the world. The child will be fed, it will be brought up, it will be educated by the care of the Communist Fatherland; but this Fatherland will by no means undertake to tear the child away from such parents as may desire to participate in the education of their little ones. The Communist Society will take upon itself all the duties involved in the education of the child, but the paternal joys, the maternal satisfaction—such will not be taken away from those who show themselves capable of appreciating and understanding these joys." Can this be called a destruction of the family by means of violence? or a forcible separation of child and mother?

## THE FAMILY A UNION OF AFFECTION AND COMRADESHIP

There is no escaping the fact: the old type of family has seen its day. It is not the fault of the Communist State, it is the result of the changed conditions of life. *The family is ceasing to be a necessity of the State, as it was in the past;* on the contrary, it is worse than useless, since it needlessly holds back the female workers from a more productive and far more serious work. Nor is it any longer necessary to the members of the family themselves, since the task of bringing up the children, which was formerly that of the family, is passing more and more into the hands of the collectivity. But, on the ruins of the former family we shall soon behold rising a new form which will involve altogether different relations between men and women, and which will be *a union of affection and comradeship, a union of two equal persons of the Communist Society, both of them free, both of them independent, both of them workers.* No more domestic "servitude" for women! No more inequality within the family. No more fear on the part of the woman to remain without support or aid with little ones in her arms if her husband should desert her. The woman in the Communist city no longer depends on her husband but on her work. It is not her husband but her robust arms which will support her. There will be no more anxiety as to the fate of her children. The State of the Workers' will assume responsibility for these. Marriage will be purified of all its material elements, of all money calculations, which constitute a hideous blemish on family life in our days. Marriage is henceforth to be transformed into a sublime union of two souls in love with each other, each having faith in the other; this union promises to each working man and to each working woman simultaneously, the most complete happiness, the maximum of satisfaction which can be the lot of creatures who are conscious of themselves and of the life which surrounds them. *This free union*, which is strong in the comradeship with which it is inspired, *instead of the conjugal slavery of the past—that is what the Communist Society of tomorrow offers to both men and women.*

*Wilfred Owen*

---

# Dulce et Decorum Est (1920)

*Wilfred Owen (1893–1918) served as an officer at the Battle of the Somme and, as a result of shell shock, was sent to a hospital near Edinburgh to recover. He had already written poetry prior to the War. But his war experiences, and his meeting the poet Siegfried Sassoon, a fellow patient at the hospital, transformed his writing. Owen's poetry gave expression to continual nightmares that he endured during his recovery. In the following poem, the title, "Dulce et Decorum Est," is a fragment from a sentence in Horace's* Odes: *"It is sweet and meet to die for one's country. Sweet! And decorous!" The poem itself explores the discrepancy between the language glorifying war and patriotism and the reality of what it is like to fight under modern conditions. Despite the option of staying in Britain, Owen returned to France in August 1918 as a company commander. He received the Military Cross prior to being killed a week before the armistice.*

---

Bent double, like old beggars under sacks,
Knock-kneed, coughing like hags, we cursed through sludge,
Till on the haunting flares we turned our backs
And towards our distant rest began to trudge.
Men marched asleep. Many had lost their boots,
But limped on, blood-shod. All went lame; all blind;
Drunk with fatigue; deaf even to the hoots
Of tired, outstripped Five-Nines that dropped behind.

Gas! GAS! Quick, boys!—An ecstasy of fumbling,
Fitting the clumsy helmets just in time;
But someone still was yelling out and stumbling,
And flound'ring like a man in fire or lime . . .
Dim, through the misty panes and thick green light,
As under a green sea, I saw him drowning.

In all my dreams before my helpless sight,
He plunges at me, guttering, choking, drowning.

If in some smothering dreams you too could pace
Behind the wagon that we flung him in,

And watch the white eyes writhing in his face,
His hanging face, like a devil's sick of sin;
If you could hear, at every jolt, the blood
Come gargling from the froth-corrupted lungs,
Obscene as cancer, bitter as the cud
Of vile, incurable sores on innocent tongues,—
My friend, you would not tell with such high zest
To children ardent for some desperate glory,
The old Lie: Dulce et decorum est
Pro patria mori.

October 1917–March 1918

# THE SECOND COMING (1920)

*William Butler Yeats (1865–1939) is among the finest modern poets writing in English. Born in Ireland, from a Protestant background, he was the central figure in the Irish literary renaissance of the late nineteenth and twentieth centuries, which played a central role in defining the Irish nationalist sensibility that would overthrow British rule following World War I. His poem "The Second Coming" views this war less as an event in itself than as a symbol of the collapse and fragmentation of European civilization. Yeats believes that the War represents the end of a historical cycle, but he is apprehensive about what will come next. He once wrote: "we may be about to accept the most implacable authority the world has known." In retrospect, such words seem like a prophesy of the authoritarian movements that came to dominate the politics of interwar Europe.*

Turning and turning in the widening gyre
The falcon cannot hear the falconer;
Things fall apart; the centre cannot hold;
Mere anarchy is loosed upon the world,
The blood-dimmed tide is loosed, and everywhere
The ceremony of innocence is drowned;
The best lack all conviction, while the worst
Are full of passionate intensity.

Surely some revelation is at hand;
Surely the Second Coming is at hand.
The Second Coming! Hardly are those words out
When a vast image out of *Spiritus Mundi*
Troubles my sight: somewhere in the sands of the desert
A shape with lion body and the head of a man,
A gaze blank and pitiless as the sun,
Is moving its slow thighs, while all about it
Reel shadows of the indignant desert birds.
The darkness drops again; but now I know
That twenty centuries of stony sleep
Were vexed to nightmare by a rocking cradle,
And what rough beast, its hour come round at last,
Slouches towards Bethlehem to be born?

# Adolf Hitler

## *from* MEIN KAMPF (1925–1926)
## *from* SPEECH DEDICATING THE HOUSE OF GERMAN ART (1937)

*A*dolf Hitler (1889–1945), son of a Hapsburg civil servant, spent his childhood in Austria. When his attempts to be admitted to the Academy of Fine Arts failed, he worked at temporary jobs and moved to Munich. After war broke out in 1914, he joined the German army, where he served as a headquarters runner, was wounded and gassed, and was decorated twice with the Iron Cross. Like many in defeated Germany, Hitler was dismayed by the terms of the Treaty of Versailles. He responded by immersing himself in political work, joining an unknown party that in 1920 renamed itself the National-sozialistische Deutsche Arbeiterpartei (the Nazi party). Seeking to build a mass movement, Hitler and the party, which he soon led, held public meetings and published a propaganda paper. In 1923, they attempted to seize power in Munich and start a national revolution; when that failed, Hitler was sentenced to jail. There he wrote the first volume of Mein Kampf (My Struggle), a manifesto combining autobiography, political demagoguery, and racist invective. His ideas contradicted modern scientific thought and were expressed illogically, but they nonetheless found an audience that would further his rise to power. Ten years after the failure in Munich, he became chancellor of Germany.

The importance that Hitler attached to the struggle over culture is evident in his speech dedicating the House of German Art in July 1937. The museum was the first public building project of the Third Reich. Designed by Hitler's favorite architect at the time, Paul Ludwig Troost, in a style of monumental classicism, it visually proclaimed that the Reich represented the culmination of Western Civilization. In the present context, what interests us about Hitler's speech are not only the 'traditional' and 'nationalist' values in art that he embraces, but the 'modernist' ones that he condemns. Hitler uses the occasion to denounce modernism in painting and architecture, movements to which German artists and architects were major contributors. He lumps together modernism, the Jews, and the Bolsheviks, seeing them all as different expressions of the same 'decadence'. And he wonders whether artists who have such twisted, distorted visions should be allowed to produce offspring. As farfetched as this might sound, Hitler was reiterating what was already established Nazi policy. In 1933, one of the first legislative acts of the Third Reich declared that compulsory sterilization of 'undesirables' was necessary to ensure the elimination of inferior genes. In all, four hundred thousand undesirables—both men and women—became the victims of forced sterilization.

## *FROM* MEIN KAMPF

There are some truths which are so obvious that for this very reason they are not seen or at least not recognized by ordinary people. They sometimes pass by such truisms as though blind and are most astonished when someone suddenly discovers what everyone really ought to know. Columbus's eggs lie around by the hundreds of thousands, but Columbuses are met with less frequently.

Thus men without exception wander about in the garden of Nature; they imagine that they know practically everything and yet with few exceptions pass blindly by one of the most patent principles of Nature's rule: the inner segregation of the species of all living beings on this earth.

Even the most superficial observation shows that Nature's restricted form of propagation and increase is an almost rigid basic law of all the innumerable forms of expression of her vital urge. Every animal mates only with a member of the same species. The titmouse seeks the titmouse, the finch the finch, the stork the stork, the field mouse the field mouse, the dormouse the dormouse, the wolf the she-wolf, etc.

Only unusual circumstances can change this, primarily the compulsion of captivity or any other cause that makes it impossible to mate within the same species. But then Nature begins to resist this with all possible means, and her most visible protest consists either in refusing further capacity for propagation to bastards or in limiting the fertility of later offspring; in most cases, however, she takes away the power of resistance to disease or hostile attacks.

This is only too natural.

Any crossing of two beings not at exactly the same level produces a medium between the level of the two parents. This means: the offspring will probably stand higher than the racially lower parent, but not as high as the higher one. Consequently, it will later succumb in the struggle against the higher level. Such mating is contrary to the will of Nature for a higher breeding of all life. The precondition for this does not lie in associating superior and inferior, but in the total victory of the former. The stronger must dominate and not blend with the weaker, thus sacrificing his own greatness. Only the born weakling can view this as cruel, but he after all is only a weak and limited man; for if this law did not prevail, any conceivable higher development of organic living beings would be unthinkable.

The consequence of this racial purity, universally valid in Nature, is not only the sharp outward delimitation of the various races, but their uniform character in themselves. The fox is always a fox, the goose a goose, the tiger a tiger, etc., and the difference can lie at most in the varying measure of force, strength, intelligence, dexterity, endurance, etc., of the individual specimens. But you will never find a fox who in his inner attitude might, for example, show humanitarian tendencies toward geese, as similarly there is no cat with a friendly inclination toward mice.

Therefore, here, too, the struggle among themselves arises less from inner aversion than from hunger and love. In both cases, Nature looks on calmly, with satisfaction, in fact. In the struggle for daily bread all those who are weak and sickly or less determined succumb, while the struggle of the males for the female grants the right or opportunity to propagate only to the healthiest. And struggle is always a means for improving a species' health and power of resistance and, therefore, a cause of its higher development.

If the process were different, all further and higher development would cease and the opposite would occur. For, since the inferior always predominates numerically over the best, if both had the same possibility of preserving life and propagating, the inferior would multiply so much more rapidly that in the end the best would inevitably be driven into the background, unless a correction of this state of affairs were undertaken. Nature does just this by subjecting the weaker part to such severe living conditions that by them alone the number is limited, and by not permitting the remainder to increase promiscuously, but making a new and ruthless choice according to strength and health.

No more than Nature desires the mating of weaker with stronger individuals, even less does she desire the blending of a higher with a lower race, since, if she did, her whole work of higher breeding, over perhaps hundreds of thousands of years, night be ruined with one blow.

Historical experience offers countless proofs of this. It shows with terrifying clarity that in every mingling of Aryan blood with that of lower peoples the result was the end of the cultured people. North America, whose population consists in by far the largest part of Germanic elements who mixed but little with the lower colored peoples, shows a different humanity and culture from Central and South America, where the predominantly Latin immigrants often mixed with the aborigines on a large scale. By this one example, we can clearly and distinctly recognize the effect of racial mixture. The Germanic inhabitant of the American continent, who has remained racially pure and unmixed, rose to be master of the continent; he will remain the master as long as he does not fall a victim to defilement of the blood.

The result of all racial crossing is therefore in brief always the following:

(a) Lowering of the level of the higher race;

(b) Physical and intellectual regression and hence the beginning of a slowly but surely progressing sickness.

To bring about such a development is, then, nothing else but to sin against the will of the eternal creator.

And as a sin this act is rewarded.

When man attempts to rebel against the iron logic of Nature, he comes into struggle with the principles to which he himself owes his existence as a man. And this attack must lead to his own doom.

Here, of course, we encounter the objection of the modern pacifist, as truly Jewish in its effrontery as it is stupid! 'Man's rôle is to overcome Nature!'

Millions thoughtlessly parrot this Jewish nonsense and end up by really imagining that they themselves represent a kind of conqueror of Nature; though in this they dispose of no other weapon than an idea, and at that such a miserable one, that if it were true no world at all would be conceivable.

But quite aside from the fact that man has never yet conquered Nature in anything, but at most has caught hold of and tried to lift one or another corner of her immense gigantic veil of eternal riddles and secrets, that in reality he invents nothing but only discovers everything, that he does not dominate Nature, but has only risen on the basis of his knowledge of various laws and secrets of Nature to be lord over those other living creatures who lack this knowledge—quite aside from all this, an idea cannot overcome the preconditions for the development and being of humanity, since the idea itself depends only on man. Without human beings there is no human idea in this world, therefore, the idea as such is always conditioned by the presence of human beings and hence of all the laws which created the precondition for their existence.

And not only that! Certain ideas are even tied up with certain men. This applies most of all to those ideas whose content originates, not in an exact scientific truth, but in the world of emotion, or, as it is so beautifully and clearly expressed today, reflects an 'inner experience.' All these ideas, which have nothing to do with cold logic as such, but represent only pure expressions of feeling, ethical conceptions, etc., are chained to the existence of men, to whose intellectual imagination and creative power they owe their existence. Precisely in this case the preservation of these definite races and men is the precondition for the existence of these ideas. Anyone, for example, who really desired the victory of the pacifistic idea in this world with all his heart would have to fight with all the means at his disposal for the conquest of the world by the Germans; for, if the opposite should occur, the last pacifist would die out with the last German, since the rest of the world has never fallen so deeply as our own people, unfortunately, has for this nonsense so contrary to Nature and reason. Then, if we were serious, whether we liked it or not, we would have to wage wars in order to arrive at pacifism. This and nothing else was what Wilson, the American world savior, intended, or so at least our German visionaries believed—and thereby his purpose was fulfilled.

In actual fact the pacifistic-humane idea is perfectly all right perhaps when the highest type of man has previously conquered and subjected the world to an extent that makes him the sole ruler of this earth. Then this idea lacks the power of producing evil effects in exact proportion as its practical application becomes rare and finally impossible. Therefore, first struggle and then we shall see what can be done. Otherwise mankind has passed the high point of its development and the end is not the domination of any ethical idea but barbarism and consequently chaos. At this point someone or other may laugh, but this planet once moved through the ether for millions of years without human beings and it can do so again some day if men forget that they owe their higher existence, not to the ideas of a few crazy ideologists, but to the knowledge and ruthless application of Nature's stern and rigid laws.

Everything we admire on this earth today—science and art, technology and inventions—is only the creative product of a few peoples and originally perhaps of *one* race. On them depends the existence of this whole culture. If they perish, the beauty of this earth will sink into the grave with them.

However much the soil, for example, can influence men, the result of the influence will always be different depending on the races in question, The low fertility of a living space may spur the one race to the highest achievements; in others it will only be the cause of bitterest poverty and final undernourishment with all its consequences. The inner nature of peoples is always determining for the manner in which outward influences will be effective. What leads the one to starvation trains the other to hard work.

All great cultures of the past perished only because the originally creative race died out from blood poisoning.

The ultimate cause of such a decline was their forgetting that all culture depends on men and not conversely; hence that to preserve a certain culture the man who creates it must be preserved. This preservation is bound up with the rigid law of necessity and the right to victory of the best and stronger in this world.

Those who want to live, let them fight, and those who do not want to fight in this world of eternal struggle do not deserve to live.

Even if this were hard—that is how it is! Assuredly, however, by far the harder fate is that which strikes the man who thinks he can overcome Nature, but in the last analysis only mocks her. Distress, misfortune, and diseases are her answer.

The man who misjudges and disregards the racial laws actually forfeits the happiness that seems destined to be his. He thwarts the triumphal march of the best race and hence also the precondition for all human progress, and remains, in consequence, burdened with all the sensibility of man, in the animal realm of helpless misery.

—*trans. Ralph Manheim*

## *FROM* SPEECH DEDICATING THE HOUSE OF GERMAN ART

Four years ago, when the festive cornerstone-laying ceremonies for this structure took place, we were all aware that not only was a stone being laid in place for a building, but that the ground had to be prepared for a new and truly German art. It was imperative to bring about a turning point in the development of all German cultural activity. . . .

The collapse and general decline of Germany was, as we know, not only economic and political but, possibly to a greater extent, cultural. Moreover, these proceedings were not to be explained solely through the fact of a lost war. Such catastrophes have often affected states and peoples, and it has been those which have not infrequently been the stimulus for purification and, thereby, inner uplifting. That flood of slime and filth which the year 1918 vomited to the surface was not created by the loss of the war, but was instead only released by it. A body tainted inherently, through and through, discovered only through defeat the total extent of its own decomposition. . . .

Certainly the economic decline had naturally been felt the most because its effect alone was emphatically able to reach the awareness of the great masses. The political decline, on the other hand, was either flatly denied by countless Germans or at the least not recognized, while the cultural decline was neither seen nor understood by the majority of the people. It is noteworthy that during this time of general decline and collapse catchwords and phrases simultaneously began to make their triumphant appearance. . . . But the general distress, especially the misery of the millions of unemployed, could not be denied, and neither could the consequences for those affected be excused. It was therefore more difficult to hide the economic than the political collapse of the nation with catchwords or phrases.

In the political sphere for a time the democratic and Marxist phraseology of the November [i.e., Weimar] Republic, as well as continual references to various aspects of international solidarity and the effectiveness of international institutions, and so on, was able to veil from the German people the unparalleled decline and collapse. . . . Far more successful and, above all, far more enduring was the effect of these phrases and catchwords in the cultural field, where they created complete confusion concerning the essential character of culture in general and about German cultural life in particular. . . . In this sphere, more than in others, the Jews employed all means and devices that shape and guide public opinion. The Jews were especially clever in utilizing their control of the press and with the aid of so-called art critics were able not only to create confusion about the character and purpose of art but were also able to destroy generally sound perceptions. . . .

Art was said to be an experience of the international community; and thus all understanding of its essential association with a people was destroyed. Art was said to be associated with a particular age, so that there was no actual art of a people or of a race, but only an art form of a certain period. According to this theory the Greeks did not create Greek art, but instead it was the expression of a certain age. The same was said to be true of Rome. . . . So today there is no German, French, Japanese, or Chinese art, but there is only simply "modern" art. . . . According to such a theory art and artistry is put on the same level as the craftsmanship of our modern tailor shops and fashion studios, according to the principle of something different every year. One time Impressionism, then Futurism, Cubism, perhaps even Dadaism. . . . If it were not so tragic, it would be almost comical to find out how many catchwords and phrases these so-called students of art used during recent years to describe and interpret their wretched creations.

It was sad to experience how these catchwords and this verbal nonsense created not only a general feeling of uncertainty in the appraisal of artistic achievement or endeavor but contributed to the intimidation of those who might otherwise have protested against this cultural Bolshevism. . . . And so, just as today clothes are judged not by their beauty but only according to whether or not they are modern, so are the old masters simply rejected because they are not modern and it is not fashionable to admire them or to acquire their works.

But true art is and remains eternal, it does not follow the law of seasonal fashion assessment of works created in dress design studios. It merits appreciation because it is an eternal revelation arising from the depths of the essential character of a people. . . .

. . . But those whose works do not have eternal value do not like to speak of eternities. They prefer to dim the radiance of these giants who reach from out of the past into the future, in order that contemporaries might discover their own tiny flames. These lightweight smear artists are at best only the products of a day. Yesterday they did not exist, today they are modern, and the day after tomorrow they will be forgotten. These littlest producers of art were overjoyed by the Jewish discovery that art was connected to a certain period. Lacking all qualifications for eternal value, their art could now at least be the art of the present time. . . .

It is these artistic dwarfs who themselves demand the greatest tolerance in the judgment of their own works, but who in turn are extremely intolerant in their valuation of the works of others, be they artists from the past or the present. Just as in politics, there was here, too, a conspiracy of incapacity and mediocrity against better works of the past, present, and the anticipated future. . . . These miserable art-critiquing windbags were always able to take advantage of the cowardice and insecurity of our so-called wealthy citizens because these nouveau-riche types were too uncultivated to pass their own judgment on art. . . . These types of art creators and art dealers loved nothing better than to play into each other's hands, and to characterize all those who saw through their scheme as "uncultivated philistines." But where the parvenu was concerned, the favored and surest method to counteract any latent doubts and resistance was to emphasize right from the beginning that the artwork in question was not easy for just anyone to understand and that because of that its price was set correspondingly high. These so-called art connoisseurs have grown rich by these methods, but no one understandably wants to be told by one of these types that he lacks appreciation for art, or does not have the money to pay for it. This type of buyer often judged the quality of a work simply by the amount of the price being asked for it. And when this nonsense was then also praised in obscure phrases, it became all the easier to come up with the money. In the end, one could still secretly hope that the thing that one did not understand oneself, one's neighbor most certainly would not understand either. . . .

Here today I want to make the following declaration: until the seizure of power by National Socialism, there existed in Germany a so-called modern art; that is, as the word implies—almost every year there was a new one. National Socialist Germany, however, desires to have again a "German art," which, like all creative works of a people, should and will be an eternal one. When the cornerstone was laid for this building it signaled the beginning of the construction of a temple for art; not for a so-called modern art, but for an eternal German art; better yet: a House of Art for the German people, and not for an international art for the year 1937, '40, '50, or '60. Art is not dependent on an age but on a people. . . . Time changes, the years come and go . . . but the people are a constant point within the entire range of phenomena. . . . There can therefore be no standard of yesterday and today, of modern and unmodern, but only of "valueless" or "valuable," or of "eternal" or "transitory." . . . And therefore when I speak of German art—for which this House was built—what I want to see is the standard for that art in the German people, in their character and their life, in their feeling, their emotions, and in their development.

From the history of the development of our race we know that it is composed of a number of more or less distinct races that in the course of thousands of years, thanks to the formative influence of a certain outstanding racial kernel, produced that mixture we see before us in our people today. This force, which formed the people in time past and which still today continues to shape it, stems from the same Aryan branch of mankind we recognize not only as the carrier of our own civilization but of the earlier civilizations of the ancient world.

The way in which our race was composed has produced the manysidedness of our own cultural development. . . . But nonetheless, we the German people, as the end result of this historical development, wish to have an art that corresponds to the ever-increasing homogeneity of our racial composition, and that would then in itself present the characteristics of unity and homogeneity. The question has often been posed, to define just what it means "to be German." Among all the many definitions that have been put forth, it appears to me that the most praiseworthy are those that have not attempted to arrive at a definition but have instead chosen to state a law. The most fitting law I would propose has already been expressed by a great German: "To be German is to be clear." What this means is that to be German is to be logical and above all, to be true. . . . The deepest inner desire to have such a truly German art is reflected in this law of clarity, and has always been present in our people. It has inspired our great painters, our sculptors, our architects, our thinkers and poets, and above all our musicians. . . .

During the long years of planning the formation of a new Reich, I thought much about the tasks that would confront us in the cultural cleansing of the people's life, because Germany was to have not only a political and economic rebirth, but above all else, Germany was to undergo a cultural renaissance. . . .

. . . I was convinced, after our collapse, that a people that have stumbled and from then on have been trampled on by the whole world have all the greater duty consciously to assert their own value toward their oppressors. There can be no greater proof of the highest rights of a people to their own life than immortal cultural achievements. I was therefore always determined that if fate should one day give us power I would debate these issues with no one, but would make my own decisions. Because an understanding for such great tasks has not been granted to everyone. . . .

Among the countless plans that floated through my mind both during the war and in the period following the collapse was the thought of building in Munich, the city with the greatest tradition of cultural exhibits, a great new exhibition palace. This was needed in view of the totally undignified condition of the old building. Years ago I also thought about the location where this building now stands. . . . In 1931, the seizure of power by National Socialism still appeared to be in the distant future, and there was little prospect of reserving for the Third Reich the building of a new exhibition palace. For a time it actually did look as though the men of November wanted to create an art exhibit building in Munich which had very little in common with art, but which would have corresponded to the Bolshevik tenor of the times. Possibly some of you remember the plans that were drawn up during those days. . . . The intended building was difficult to define, and could easily have served as a Saxon yarn factory, a market hall of a town, or possibly even a train station or [an indoor] swimming pool . . . but the lack of resolve of my former political enemies [to carry out this project] gave me joy and provided the only hope that in the end the erection of the new building . . . might still fall to the Third Reich, and that it would become its first task. . . .

This new building we have conceived is, you will no doubt agree, of a truly bold and artistic design. It is so unique and so individual that it cannot be compared with anything else. . . . It is, I daresay, a true monument for this city and, beyond that, for German art. . . . This House that has arisen here possesses proper dignity and will enable the highest artistic achievements to present themselves to the German people. This House represents a turning point; it brings to an end the era of chaotic, incompetent architecture. This, the first of the new buildings, will take its place among the immortal achievements of our German artistic life.

But you understand now that it is not enough merely to provide the House . . . the exhibit itself must also bring about a turning point. . . . If I presume to make a judgment, speak my opinion, and act accordingly. I do this not just because of my outlook on German art, but I claim this right because of the contribution I myself have made to the restoration of German art. Because our present state, which I and my comrades in the struggle have created, has alone provided German art with the conditions for a new, vigorous flowering.

It was not Bolshevik art collectors or their literary henchmen who laid the foundation for a new art or even secured the continued existence of art in Germany. No, we were the ones who created this state and have since then provided vast sums for the encouragement of art. We have given art great new tasks. . . . I declare here and now that it is my irrevocable resolve that just as in the sphere of political bewilderment, I am going to make a clean sweep of phrases in the artistic life of Germany. "Works of art" which cannot be comprehended and are validated only through bombastic instructions for use . . . from now on will no longer be foisted upon the German people!

We are more interested in ability than in so-called intent. An artist who is counting on having his works displayed, in this House or anywhere else in Germany, must possess ability. Intent is something that is self-evident. These windbags have tried to make their works more palatable by representing them as expressions of a new age; but they need to be told that art does not create a new age, that it is the general life of peoples which fashions itself anew and therefore often seeks to express itself anew. . . . Men of letters are not the creators of new epochs; it is the fighters, those who truly shape and lead peoples, who make history. . . . Aside from that, it is either impudent effrontery or an inscrutable stupidity to exhibit to our own age works that might have been made ten or twenty thousand years ago by a man of the Stone Age. They talk of primitive art, but they forget that it is not the function of art to retreat backward from the level of development a people has already reached. The function of art can only be to symbolize the vitality of this development.

The new age of today is at work on a new human type. Tremendous efforts are being made in countless spheres of life in order to elevate our people, to make our men, boys, lads, girls, and women more healthy and thereby stronger and more beautiful. From this strength and beauty streams forth a new feeling of life, and a new joy in life. Never before was humanity in its external appearance and perceptions closer to the ancient world than it is today.

This type of human, which we saw last year during the Olympic games . . . exuding proud physical strength—this my good prehistoric art-stutterers—this is the "type" of the new age. But what do you manufacture? Deformed cripples and cretins, women who inspire only disgust, men who are more like wild beasts, children who, if they were alive, would be regarded as God's curse! . . . Let no one say that that is how these artists see things. From the pictures submitted for exhibition, I must assume that the eye of some men shows them things different from the way they really are. There really are men who can see in the shapes of our people only decayed cretins; who feel that meadows are blue, the heavens green, clouds sulphur-yellow. They like to say that they experience these things in this way.

I do not want to argue about whether or not they really experience this. But in the name of the German people I only want to prevent these pitiable unfortunates, who clearly suffer from defective vision, from attempting with their chatter to force on their contemporaries the results of their faulty observations, and indeed from presenting them as "art." Here there are only two possibilities open: either these so-called artists really do see things this way and believe in that which they create—and if so, one has to investigate how this defective vision arose—if it is a mechanical problem or if it came about through heredity. The first case would be pitiable, while the second would be a matter for the Ministry of the Interior, which would then deal with the problem of preventing the perpetuation of such horrid disorders. Or they them-selves do not believe in the reality of such impressions, but are for different reasons attempting to annoy the nation with this humbug. If this is the case, then it is a mat-ter for a criminal court.

This House, in any case, was not planned or built for the works of art incompe-tents or for maltreaters of art. A thousand workmen did not labor for four and a half years on this building only to have creations exhibited here by people who are lazy to excess and who spend but five hours bespattering a canvas, while hoping confidently that the boldness of the pricing would produce the desired effect and result in the hailing of the work as the most brilliant lightning-birth of a genius. No, the hard work of the builders of this House demands equally hard work from those who want to exhibit here. I do not care in the least if these pseudo-artists then are left to cackle over each other's eggs!

The artist does not create for the artist, but for the people! We will see to it that from here on the people will be called on to judge their own art. No one must say that the people have no appreciation for a truly valuable enrichment of its cultural life. Long before the critics did justice to the genius of a Richard Wagner he had the people on his side. For their part, however, during the last few years the people have had no affinity for the so-called modern art that was placed before them. The mass of the people moved through our art exhibits in a completely uninterested fashion or stayed away altogether. The people's healthy perceptions recognized that all these smearings of canvas were really the outcome of an impudent and unashamed arro-gance or of a simply shocking lack of skill. Millions of people felt instinctively that these art-stammerings of the last few decades were more like the achievements that might have been produced by untalented children of from eight to ten years old and could under no circumstances be regarded as the expression of our own time or of the German future.

Since we know today that the development of millions of years repeats itself in every individual but is compressed into a few decades, we have the proof that an artis-tic creation that does not surpass the achievement of eight-year-old children is not "modern" or even "futuristic" but is, on the contrary, highly archaic. It probably is not as developed as the art of the Stone Age period, when the people scratched pictures of their environment on the walls of caves. . . .

I know, therefore, that when the *Volk* passes through these galleries it will recog-nize in me its own spokesman and counselor . . . it will draw a sigh of relief and joy-ously express its agreement with this purification of art. And this is decisive, for an art that cannot count on the ready inner agreement of the broad, healthy mass of the people, but which must instead rely on the support of small, partially indifferent cliques, is intolerable. . . . We are convinced that the German people will again fully support and joyously appreciate the future truly great artists from within their ranks. . . .

This exhibition then is but a beginning. . . . But the opening of this exhibit is also the beginning of the end of the stultification of German art and the end of the cultural destruction of our people. . . . Many of our young artists will recognize the path they will have to take; they will draw inspiration from the greatness of the time in which we all live, and they will draw the courage to work hard and will in the end complete the task. And when a sacred conscientiousness at last comes into its own, then, I have no doubt, the Almighty will lift from this mass of decent creators of art, several individuals who will rise to the eternal star-covered heaven of immortal, God-favored artists of great ages. . . . We believe that especially today, when in so many spheres the highest individual achievements are standing the test, so also in the sphere of art will the highest value of personality again emerge to assert itself.

—*trans. Dieter Kuntz*

# SHOOTING AN ELEPHANT (1936)

*George Orwell (1903–1950) was born Eric Arthur Blair in Bengal, to a family of British civil servants and minor merchants. He attended Eton on scholarship and was drawn to writing but, heeding family expectations, entered the imperial service. His first posting, in 1922, was to Burma as an assistant superintendent in the Indian Imperial Police. Blair's experiences there, separated from the people he governed by officially-accepted barriers of race and class, changed his life. In 1927 he returned to England and made the dramatic decision to resign his position for an uncertain future as a writer. His first book,* Down and Out in Paris and London *(1933), marked this change: he signed this sympathetic account of life in the slums of Paris and working-class East End of London with a new name, George Orwell. Orwell, whose opposition to imperialism in any form led him to become a socialist, would eventually be best known for the novels* Animal Farm *(1945) and* Nineteen Eighty-four *(1949), which explore the fragility of egalitarian ideals in a world where dictatorship seems to thrive. "Shooting an Elephant" is one of Orwell's finest essays. In it he recounts an incident that occurred while he was with the Imperial Police.*

---

In Moulmein, in Lower Burma, I was hated by large numbers of people—the only time in my life that I have been important enough for this to happen to me. I was sub-divisional police officer of the town, and in an aimless, petty kind of way anti-European feeling was very bitter. No one had the guts to raise a riot, but if a European woman went through the bazaars alone somebody would probably spit betel juice over her dress. As a police officer I was an obvious target and was baited whenever it seemed safe to do so. When a nimble Burman tripped me up on the football field and the referee (another Burman) looked the other way, the crowd yelled with hideous laughter. This happened more than once. In the end the sneering yellow faces of young men that met me everywhere, the insults hooted after me when I was at a safe distance, got badly on my nerves. The young Buddhist priests were the worst of all. There were several thousand of them in the town and none of them seemed to have anything to do except stand on street corners and jeer at Europeans.

All this was perplexing and upsetting. For at that time I had already made up my mind that imperialism was an evil thing and the sooner I chucked up my job and got out of it the better. Theoretically—and secretly, of course—I was all for the Burmese and all against their oppressors, the British. As for the job I was doing, I hated it more bitterly than I can perhaps make clear. In a job like that you see the dirty work of Empire at close quarters. The wretched prisoners huddling in the stinking cages of the lock-ups, the grey, cowed faces of the long-term convicts, the scarred buttocks of the men who had been flogged with bamboos—all these oppressed me with an intolerable sense of guilt. But I could get nothing into perspective. I was young and ill-educated and I had had to think out my problems in the utter silence that is imposed on every Englishman in the East. I did not even know that the British Empire is dying, still less did I know that it is a great deal better than the younger empires that are going to supplant it. All I knew was that I was stuck between my hatred of the empire I served and my rage against the evil-spirited little beasts who tried to make my job impossible. With one part of my mind I thought of the British Raj as an unbreakable tyranny, as something clamped down, in *saecula saeculorum*, upon the will of prostrate peoples; with another part I thought that the greatest joy in the world would be to drive a bayonet into a Buddhist priest's guts. Feelings like these are the normal by-products of imperialism; ask any Anglo-Indian official, if you can catch him off duty.

One day something happened which in a roundabout way was enlightening. It was a tiny incident in itself, but it gave me a better glimpse than I had had before of the real nature of imperialism—the real motives for which despotic governments act. Early one morning the sub-inspector at a police station the other end of the town rang me up on the 'phone and said that an elephant was ravaging the bazaar. Would I please come and do something about it? I did not know what I could do, but I wanted to see what was happening and I got on to a pony and started out. I took my rifle, an old .44 Winchester and much too small to kill an elephant, but I thought the noise might be useful *in terrorem*. Various Burmans stopped me on the way and told me about the elephant's doings. It was not, of course, a wild elephant, but a tame one which had gone "must." It had been chained up, as tame elephants always are when their attack of "must" is due, but on the previous night it had broken its chain and escaped. Its mahout, the only person who could manage it when it was in that state, had set out in pursuit, but had taken the wrong direction and was now twelve hours' journey away, and in the morning the elephant had suddenly reappeared in the town. The Burmese population had no weapons and were quite helpless against it. It had already destroyed somebody's bamboo hut, killed a cow and raided some fruit-stalls and devoured the stock; also it had met the municipal rubbish van and, when the driver jumped out and took to his heels, had turned the van over and inflicted violences upon it.

The Burmese sub-inspector and some Indian constables were waiting for me in the quarter where the elephant had been seen. It was a very poor quarter, a labyrinth of squalid bamboo huts, thatched with palm-leaf, winding all over a steep hillside. I remember that it was a cloudy, stuffy morning at the beginning of the rains. We began questioning the people as to where the elephants had gone and, as usual, failed to get any definite information. That is invariably the case in the East; a story always sounds clear enough at a distance, but the nearer you get to the scene of events the vaguer it becomes. Some of the people said that the elephant had gone in one direction, some said that he had gone in another, some professed not even to have heard of any elephant. I had almost made up my mind that the whole story was a pack of lies, when we heard yells a little distance away. There was a loud, scandalized cry of "Go away, child! Go away this instant!" and an old woman with a switch in her hand came round the corner of a hut, violently shooing away a crowd of naked children. Some more women followed, clicking their tongues and exclaiming; evidently there was something that the children ought not to have seen. I rounded the hut and saw a man's dead body sprawling in the mud. He was an Indian, a black Dravidian coolie, almost naked, and he could not have been dead many minutes. The people said that the elephant had come suddenly upon him round the corner of the hut, caught him with its trunk, put its foot on his back and ground him into the earth. This was the rainy season and the ground was soft, and his face had scored a trench a foot deep and a couple of yards long. He was lying on his belly with arms crucified and head sharply twisted to one side. His face was coated with mud, the eyes wide open, the teeth bared and grinning with an expression of unendurable agony. (Never tell me, by the way, that the dead look peaceful. Most of the corpses I have seen looked devilish.) The friction of the great beast's foot had stripped the skin from his back as neatly as one skins a rabbit. As soon as I saw the dead man I sent an orderly to a friend's house nearby to borrow an elephant rifle. I had already sent back the pony, not wanting it to go mad with fright and throw me if it smelt the elephant.

The orderly came back in a few minutes with a rifle and five cartridges, and meanwhile some Burmans had arrived and told us that the elephant was in the paddy fields below, only a few hundred yards away. As I started forward practically the whole population of the quarter flocked out of the houses and followed me. They had seen the rifle and were all shouting excitedly that I was going to shoot the elephant. They had not shown much interest in the elephant when he was merely ravaging their homes, but it was different now that he was going to be shot. It was a bit of fun to them, as it would be to an English crowd; besides they wanted the meat. It made be vaguely uneasy. I had no intention of shooting the elephant—I had merely sent for the rifle to defend myself if necessary—and it is always unnerving to have a crowd following you. I marched down the hill, looking and feeling a fool, with the rifle over my shoulder and an ever-growing army of people jostling at my heels. At the bottom, when you got away from the huts, there was a metalled road and beyond that a miry waste of paddy fields a thousand yards across, not yet ploughed but soggy from the first rains and dotted with coarse grass. The elephant was standing eight yards from the road, his left side towards us. He took not the slightest notice of the crowd's approach. He was tearing up bunches of grass, beating them against his knees to clean them and stuffing them into his mouth.

I had halted on the road. As soon as I saw the elephant I knew with perfect certainty that I ought not to shoot him. It is a serious matter to shoot a working elephant—it is comparable to destroying a huge and costly piece of machinery—and obviously one ought not to do it if it can possibly be avoided. And at that distance, peacefully eating, the elephant looked no more dangerous than a cow. I thought then and I think now that his attack of "must" was already passing off; in which case he would merely wander harmlessly about until the mahout came back and caught him. I decided that I would watch him for a little while to make sure that he did not turn savage again, and then go home.

But at that moment I glanced round at the crowd that had followed me. It was an immense crowd, two thousand at the least and growing every minute. It blocked the road for a long distance on either side. I looked at the sea of yellow faces above the garish clothes—faces all happy and excited over this bit of fun, all certain that the elephant was going to be shot. They were watching me as they would watch a conjurer about to perform a trick. They did not like me, but with the magical rifle in my hands I was momentarily worth watching. And suddenly I realized that I should have to shoot the elephant after all. The people expected it of me and I had got to do it; I could feel their two thousand wills pressing me forward, irresistibly. And it was at this moment, as I stood there with the rifle in my hands, that I first grasped the hollowness, the futility of the white man's dominion in the East. Here was I, the white man with his gun, standing in front of the unarmed native crowd—seemingly the leading actor of the piece; but in reality I was only an absurd puppet pushed to and fro by the will of those yellow faces behind. I perceived in this moment that when the white man turns tyrant it is his own freedom that he destroys. He becomes a sort of hollow, posing dummy, the conventionalized figure of a sahib. For it is the condition of his rule that he shall spend his life in trying to impress the "natives," and so in every crisis he has got to do what the "natives" expect of him. He wears a mask, and his face grows to fit it. I had got to shoot the elephant. I had committed myself to doing it when I sent for the rifle. A sahib has got to act like a sahib; he has got to appear resolute, to know his own mind and do definite things. To come all that way, rifle in hand, with two thousand people marching at my heels, and then to trail feebly away, having done nothing—no, that was impossible. The crowd would laugh at me. And my whole life, every white man's life in the East, was one long struggle not to be laughed at.

But I did not want to shoot the elephant. I watched him beating his bunch of grass against his knees, with that preoccupied grandmotherly air that elephants have. It seemed to me that it would be murder to shoot him. At that age I was not squeamish about killing animals, but I had never shot an elephant and never wanted to. (Somehow it always seems worse to kill a *large* animal.) Besides, there was the beast's owner to be considered. Alive, the elephant was worth at least a hundred pounds, possibly. But I had got to act quickly. I turned to some experienced-looking Burmans who had been there when we arrived, and asked them how the elephant had been behaving. They all said the same thing: he took no notice of you if you left him alone, but he might charge if you went too close to him.

It was perfectly clear to me what I ought to do. I ought to walk up to within, say, twenty-five yards of the elephant and test his behavior. If he charged, I could shoot; if he took no notice of me, it would be safe to leave him until the mahout came back. But also I knew that I was going to do no such thing. I was a poor shot with a rifle and the ground was soft mud into which one would sink at every step. If the elephant charged and I missed him, I should have about as much chance as a toad under a steam-roller. But even then I was not thinking particularly of my own skin, only of the watchful yellow faces behind. For at that moment, with the crowd watching me, I was not afraid in the ordinary sense, as I would have been if I had been alone. A white man mustn't be frightened in front of "natives"; and so, in general, he isn't frightened. The sole thought in my mind was that if anything went wrong those two thousand Burmans would see me pursued, caught, trampled on and reduced to a grinning corpse like that Indian up the hill. And if that happened it was quite probable that some of them would laugh. That would never do. There was only alternative. I shoved the cartridges into the magazine and lay down on the road to get a better aim.

The crowd grew very still, and a deep, low, happy sigh, as of people who see the theatre curtain go up at last, breathed from innumerable throats. They were going to have their bit of fun after all. The rifle was a beautiful German thing with cross-hair sights. I did not then know that in shooting an elephant one would shoot to cut an imaginary bar running from ear-hole to ear-hole. I ought, therefore, as the elephant was sideway on, to have aimed straight at his ear-hole; actually I aimed several inches in front of this, thinking the brain would be further forward.

When I pulled the trigger I did not hear the bang or feel the kick—one never does when a shot goes home—but I heard the devilish roar of glee that went up from the crowd. In that instant, in too short a time, one would have thought, even for the bullet to get there, a mysterious, terrible change had come over the elephant. He neither stirred nor fell, but every line of his body had altered. He looked suddenly stricken, shrunken, immensely old, as though the frightful impact of the bullet had paralyzed him without knocking him down. At last, after what seemed a long time—it might have been five seconds, I dare say—he sagged flabbily to his knees. His mouth slobbered. An enormous senility seemed to have settled upon him. One could have imagined him thousands of years old. I fired again into the same spot. At the second shot he did not collapse but climbed with desperate slowness to his feet and stood weakly upright, with legs sagging and head drooping. I fired a third time. That was the shot that did for him. You could see the agony of it jolt his whole body and knock the last remnant of strength from his legs. But in falling he seemed for a moment to rise, for as his hind legs collapsed beneath him he seemed to tower upward like a huge rock toppling, his trunk reaching skywards like a tree. He trumpeted, for the first and only time. And then down he came, his belly towards me, with a crash that seemed to shake the ground even where I lay.

I got up. The Burmans were already racing past me across the mud. It was obvious that the elephant would never rise again, but he was not dead. He was breathing very rhythmically with long rattling gasps, his great mound of a side painfully rising and falling. His mouth was wide open—I could see far down into caverns of pale pink throat. I waited a long time for him to die, but his breathing did not weaken. Finally I fired my two remaining shots into the spot where I thought his heart might be. The thick blood welled out of him like red velvet, but still he did not die. His body did not even jerk when the shots hit him, the tortured breathing continued without a pause. He was dying, very slowly and in great agony, but in some world remote from me where not even a bullet could damage him further. I felt that I had got to put an end to that dreadful noise. It seemed dreadful to see the great beast lying there, powerless to move and yet powerless to die, and not even to be able to finish him. I sent back for my small rifle and poured shot after shot into his heart and down his throat. They seemed to make no impression. The tortured gasps continued as steadily as the ticking of a clock.

In the end I could not stand it any longer and went away. I heard later that it took him half an hour to die. Burmans were bringing dahs and baskets even before I left, and I was told they had stripped his body almost to the bones by the afternoon.

Afterwards, of course, there were endless discussions about the shooting of the elephant. The owner was furious, but he was only an Indian and could do nothing. Besides, legally I had done the right thing, for a mad elephant has to be killed, like a mad dog, if its owner fails to control it. Among the Europeans opinion was divided.

The older men said I was right, the younger men said it was a damn shame to shoot an elephant for killing a coolie, because an elephant was worth more than any damn Coringhee coolie. And afterwards I was very glad that the coolie had been killed; it put me legally in the right and it gave me a sufficient pretext for shooting the elephant. I often wondered whether any of the others grasped that I had done it solely to avoid looking a fool.

# Stefan Zweig

## *from* THE WORLD OF YESTERDAY (1942)

*Stefan Zweig (1881–1942) was born in Vienna, capital of the Austro-Hungarian Empire. Influenced by the ideas of his compatriot Sigmund Freud, Zweig achieved renown for his psychologically astute biographical studies of such figures as Mary Stuart, Charles Dickens, Fyodor Dostoevsky, and Friedrich Nietzsche. He also published fiction and poetry; his work appeared in over thirty languages. Zweig's most enduring work, however, is* The World of Yesterday, *an autobiography that describes in rich, elegiac tones the social and intellectual life of his generation. Writing after the Nazis drove him into exile, he attempts to describe the utter separation between "our today and our yesterday":*

> *My literary work . . . was burned to ashes in the same land where my books made friends of millions of readers. And so I belong nowhere, and everywhere am a stranger, a guest at best. Europe, the homeland of my heart's choice, is lost to me, since it has torn itself apart suicidally a second time. . . . Against my will I have witnessed the most terrible defeat of reason and the wildest triumph of brutality in the chronicle of the ages.*

I had now lived through ten years of the new century and had seen India, Africa and part of America; it was with a new, more informed pleasure that I began to look at our Europe. I never loved that old earth more than in those last years before the First World War, never hoped more ardently for European unity, never had more faith in its future than then, when we thought we saw a new dawning. But in reality it was the glare of the approaching world conflagration.

It may perhaps be difficult to describe to the generation of today, which has grown up amidst catastrophes, collapses, and crises, to which war has been a constant possibility and even a daily expectation, that optimism, that trustfulness in the world which had animated us young people since the turn of the century. Forty years of peace had strengthened the economic organism of the nations, technical science had given wings to the rhythm of life, and scientific discoveries had made the spirit of that generation proud; there was sudden upsurge which could be felt in almost identical measure in all countries of Europe. The cities grew more beautiful and more populous from year to year. The Berlin of 1905 no longer resembled the city that I had known in 1901; the capital had grown into a metropolis and, in turn, had been magnificently overtaken by the Berlin of 1910. Vienna, Milan, Paris, London, and Amsterdam on each fresh visit evoked new astonishment and pleasure. The streets became broader and more showy, the public buildings more impressive, the shops more luxurious and tasteful. Everything manifested the increase and spread of wealth. Even we writers experienced it in the editions of our works which, within some ten years, had increased three-, five- and ten-fold. New theaters, libraries, and museums sprang up everywhere; comforts such as bathrooms and telephones, formerly the privilege of the few, became the possession of the more modestly placed, and the proletariat emerged, now that working hours had been shortened, to participate in at least the small joys and comforts of life. There was progress everywhere. Whoever ventured, won. Whoever bought a house, a rare book, or a painting saw it increase in value; the more daring and the larger the scale on which an enterprise was founded, the more certain a profit. A wondrous unconcernedness had thus spread over the world, for what could interrupt this rapid ascent, restrict the *élan,* which constantly drew new force from its own soaring? Never had Europe been stronger, richer, more beautiful, or more confident of an even better future. None but a few shriveled graybeards bemoaned, in the ancient manner, the "good old days."

Not only the cities, the people too looked handsomer and healthier because of sports, better nutrition, shorter working hours, and a closer tie with Nature. Winter, formerly a dreary time which men spent in ill-humor at cards in the cafés, or bored in over-heated rooms, had been rediscovered on the mountain-tops as a fount of filtered sunshine, as nectar for the lungs, as delight for the flushed and ruddy skin. The mountains, the lakes, the ocean were no longer as far away as formerly; the bicycle, the automobile, and the electric trains had shortened distances and had given the world a new spaciousness. On Sundays thousands and tens of thousands in gaudy sport coats raced down the snowbanks on skis and toboggans; sport-palaces and swimming pools appeared everywhere, and it was just in the pools that the transformation was most noticeable; whereas in my youth a really well-built man attracted attention among the thick necks, the fat bellies and the sunken chests, now persons athletic, lithe, browned by the sun and steeled through sport vied with one another in gay competition as in the days of antiquity. None but the very poorest remained at home on Sundays, and all of youth hiked, climbed and gamboled, schooled in every type of sport. People on vacation no longer restricted themselves to some nearby resort or at best to the Salzkammergut, as in the days of my parents, for they had become curious about the world, curious to see whether it was as beautiful everywhere, and whether there were varieties of beauty. Whereas formerly only the privileged few had ventured abroad, now bank clerks and small trades-people would visit France and Italy. Traveling had become cheaper and more comfortable. But above all it was the new courage, the new spirit of adventure that made people more daring in their travels, and less fearful and parsimonious in their living; one was even ashamed to appear anxious. The world began to take itself more youthfully and, in contrast to the world of my parents, was proud of being young. Suddenly beards began to disappear among the young, then the elders followed lest they appear old. To be young and fresh, and to get rid of pompous dignity, was the watchword of the day. The women threw off the corsets which had confined their breasts, and abjured parasols and veils since they no longer feared air and sunshine. They shortened their skirts so that they could use their legs freely at tennis, and were no longer bashful about displaying them if they were pretty ones. Fashions became more natural; men wore breeches, women dared to ride astride and people no longer covered up and hid themselves from one another. The world had become not only more beautiful, but more free.

This health and self-confidence of the generation that succeeded mine won for itself freedom in modes and manners as well. For the first time girls were seen without governesses on excursions with their young friends, or participating in sports in frank, self-assured comradeship; they were no longer timid or prudish, they knew what they wanted and what they did not want. Freed from the anxious control of their parents, earning their own livelihood as secretaries or office workers, they seized the right to live their own lives. Prostitution, the only love institution which the old world sanctioned, declined markedly, for because of this newer and healthier freedom all manner of false modesty had become old-fashioned. In the swimming places the wooden fences which had inexorably separated the women's section from the men's were torn down, and men and women were no longer ashamed to show how they were built. More freedom, more frankness, more spontaneity had been regained in these ten years than in the previous hundred years.

For a different rhythm prevailed in the world. None could foretell all that might happen in a single year! One discovery, one invention, followed another, and instantly was directed to the universal good; for the first time the nations sensed in common that which concerned the commonweal. On the day that the Zeppelin made its first flight I happened to be in Strassburg on my way to Belgium when, amidst the jubilant roaring of the crowd, it circled the cathedral as if to pay homage to the thousand-year-old edifice. That night at Verhaeren's in Belgium came the news that the ship had crashed in Echterdingen. Verhaeren had tears in his eyes and was terribly moved. He was not indifferent to the German catastrophe as if, being a Belgian, it concerned him less, but as a European of our time he shared the common victory over the elements as he now did the common trial. In Vienna we shouted with joy when Blériot flew over the Channel as if he had been our own hero; because of our pride in the successive triumphs of our technics, our science, a European community spirit, a European national consciousness was coming into being. How useless, we said to ourselves, are frontiers when any plane can fly over them with ease, how provincial and artificial are customs-duties, guards and border patrols, how incongruous in the spirit of these times which visibly seeks unity and world brotherhood! This soaring of our feelings was no less wonderful than that of the planes, and I pity those who were not young during those last years of confidence in Europe. For the air about us is not dead, is not empty, it carries in itself the vibration and the rhythm of the hour, it presses them unknowingly into our blood and directs them deep into our heart and brain. In those years each one of us derived strength from the common upswing of the time and increased his individual confidence out of the collective confidence. Perhaps, thankless as we human beings are, we did not realize then how firmly and surely the wave bore us. But whoever experienced that epoch of world confidence knows that all since has been retrogression and gloom.

●

Today's generation, which has only observed the outbreak of the Second World War, may ask: why was our experience different? Why did not the masses in 1939 flare up with the same rapturous madness as in 1914? Why did they respond to the call only with the gravity and determination, fatalistically and in silence? Was it not the same thing, were not even holier and higher aims at stake in our present war, which is one of ideas and not merely concerned with frontiers and colonies?

The answer is simple: because the world of 1939 does not possess so much childishly naïve credulity as did that of 1914. Then the people had unqualified confidence in their leaders; no one in Austria would have ventured the thought that the all-high ruler Emperor Franz Josef, in his eighty-third year, would have called his people to war unless from direct necessity, would have demanded such a sacrifice of blood unless evil, sinister, and criminal foes were threatening the peace of the Empire. The Germans, on the other hand, had read the telegrams of their Emperor to the Tsar in which he struggled for peace; a mighty respect for the "authorities," the ministers, the diplomats, and for their discernment and honesty still animated the simple man. If war had come, then it could only have come against the wishes of their own statesmen; they themselves were not at fault, indeed no one in the entire land was at fault. Therefore the criminals, the war mongers must be the other fellows; we had taken up arms in self-defense against a villainous and crafty enemy, who had "attacked" peaceful Austria and Germany without the slightest provocation. In 1939, however, this almost religious faith in the honesty or at least in the capacity of one's own government had disappeared throughout Europe. Diplomacy was despised, since one had seen with bitterness how the possibility of a lasting peace had been betrayed at Versailles; nations remembered all too clearly how they had been shamefully cheated of the promises of disarmament and the abolition of secret diplomacy. In truth, there was not a single statesman in 1939 for whom anyone had respect and none in whom one would confidently entrust his destiny. The humblest French crossing-sweeper ridiculed Daladier, and in England, since Munich—"peace in our time"—all confidence in Chamberlain's perspicacity had vanished; in Italy and in Germany the masses looked upon Mussolini and Hitler with anxiety: Where will he drive us now? To be sure, they had no choice, the Fatherland was at stake: and so the soldiers shouldered their guns, the women let their children go, but not with the unswerving belief of other times that this sacrifice had been unavoidable. They obeyed but without rejoicing. They went to the front, but without the old dream of being a hero; the people, and each individual, already knew that they were naught but the victims either of mundane, political stupidity or of an incomprehensible and malicious force of destiny.

Besides, what did the great mass know of war in 1914, after nearly half a century of peace? They did not know war, they had hardly given it a thought. It had become legendary, and distance had made it seem romantic and heroic. They still saw it in the perspective of their school readers and of paintings in museums; brilliant cavalry attacks in glittering uniforms, the fatal shot always straight through the heart, the entire campaign a resounding march of victory—"We'll be home at Christmas," the recruits shouted laughingly to their mothers in August of 1914. Who in the villages and the cities of Austria remembered "real" war? A few ancients at best, who in 1866 had fought against Prussia, which was now their ally. But what a quick, bloodless, far-off war that had been, a campaign that had ended in three weeks with a few victims and before it had well started! A rapid excursion into the romantic, a wild, manly adventure—that is how the war of 1914 was painted in the imagination of the simple man, and the young people were honestly afraid that they might miss this most wonderful and exciting experience of their lives; that is why they hurried and thronged to the colors, and that is why they shouted and sang in the trains that carried them to the slaughter; wildly and feverishly the red wave of blood coursed through the veins of the entire nation. But the generation of 1939 knew war. It no longer deceived itself. It knew that it was not romantic but barbaric. It knew that it would last for years and years, an irretrievable span of time. It knew that men did not storm the enemy, decorated with oak leaves and ribbons, but hung about for weeks at a time in trenches or quarters covered with vermin and mad with thirst and that men were crushed and mutilated from afar without ever coming face to face with the foe. The newspapers and cinemas had already made the new and devilish techniques of destruction familiar: people knew how the giant tanks ground the wounded under in their path, and how airplanes destroyed women and children in their beds. They knew that a World War of 1939, because of its soulless mechanization, would be a thousand times more cruel, more bestial, more inhuman than all of the former wars of mankind. Not a single individual of the generation of 1939 believed any longer in a God-decreed justice of war: and what was worse they no longer believed in the justice and permanence of the peace it was to achieve. For they remembered all too well the disappointments that the last war had brought; impoverization instead of riches, bitterness instead of contentment, famine, inflation, revolts, the loss of civil rights, enslavement by the State, nerve-destroying uncertainty, distrust of each against all.

That is what made the difference. The war of 1939 had a spiritual meaning, a question of freedom and the preservation of moral possessions; and to fight for an idea makes man hard and determined. The war of 1914, on the other hand, knew nothing of realities, it still served a delusion, the dream of a better, a righteous and peaceful world. And it is only delusion, and not knowledge, that bestows happiness. That is why the victims, crowned with flowers and with oak leaves in their helmets, marched jubilating on their way to the shambles through streets that rumbled and sparkled as if on a holiday.

# Leon Ginsburg

# THE ORDEAL (1993)

*Both the extent of Jewish suffering and the fact that others suffered also is suggested in the stirring account by Leon Ginsburg (b. 1932–) of his effort to escape capture and certain death during the Nazi occupation of the Ukraine. Ginsburg's story is so extraordinary that a fictionalized version could hardly be more dramatic. He is one of countless survivors who endured because of a remarkable will to live and an extraordinary degree of luck at crucial moments. Many survivors went on to live fruitful and productive lives, but they are permanently marked by their experiences and have told their stories so that we will never forget.*

*Leon Ginsburg, sixty, is slim and wiry in a neat, dark-gray suit, striped shirt, and flowered tie. An electrical engineer, Leon owns a company that manufactures high-tech dental equipment for which he holds several patents. The home he shares with his wife in Rockland County, New York, is impeccably neat—except for Leon's study, a small room crammed to the gills with stacks of Holocaust-related material, including pictures, maps, books, and his own personal notes. "This is where I go to steal away from everything," he explains. "Sometimes we think of forgetting. Some people want to forget, but I feel more than ever now that we need to remember."*

"I was born in 1932 in Maciejow, a small town at the border where Poland ends and Russia begins. Our community was basically Hasidic. We all kept our heads covered, and the older men wore beards. The Ukrainians who ruled that part of Poland were viciously anti-Semitic, but we were unprepared for the Germans and their absolute policy of getting rid of the Jews. I was on the street the day the Germans marched into town. As a gesture of friendship the rabbi was sitting at a little table on the street with bread and salt, the traditional way of saying welcome. Suddenly one of the Germans pushed the table over and told the rabbi to get out of there. I didn't understand what was happening.

"Shortly after that an SS group settled in the town. The first thing they did was to order all the men between sixteen and sixty to report. The SS made it clear that anyone who didn't go could be killed. So most of the people reported. But once they lined up, they couldn't get out; they were covered by machine guns. I was just a little boy, but I saw what was happening, and I got out of that area quickly. Later I heard the shots. All those people had been marched inside the headquarters and killed.

After that the killing was at random, but for us Jews normal life was over. We had a six P.M. curfew. If you were caught outside after that, you were shot. I would hear the German patrols marching on the cobblestone streets a block away.

"One night we were all at my grandparents' house on the outskirts of town when they began rounding up Jews. I woke up and saw a light from outside on the ceiling. Yelling in German, the soldiers pounded on the door. My grandfather's name was Yakov, and they were calling his name. 'Yakov, open up!' My brother was afraid to go, but I opened the door, and they came in with flashlights. Right away they asked me where the women were. Almost in a crying way, I said, 'I don't know, they took them away! Maybe *you* can tell *me*!'

"Ignoring me, the soldiers began to search. One of them ran down to the basement. Then he came up and asked me where the attic was. I pointed. He said, 'Anybody up there?' My mother, sister, grandmother, and aunts were all up there, but I said no. Then the soldier took out his gun and put it to my head and cocked it. He said, If we find somebody there, you're 'caput.' He asked me again, 'Anybody there?' I said, 'No.' And you know what? When I think of it now, I feel sorry for that young child I was with my little round red cheeks that all the relatives loved to pinch. Either I didn't understand fear or maybe I didn't think that they would really do anything to me. Luckily the attic was big, and everyone up there was hiding in a corner, blocked off from view so that the Germans never saw them.

"That roundup was over in a week. After that things were quiet until 1942, when Hitler became so maddened and poisoned with his wish to get rid of Jews that he ordered complete annihilation. Our town was one of three in a row. They concentrated first on killing twenty-four thousand Jews in Kovel, one of the other towns. They dug big ditches or graves. They would just take the people there, shoot them on the spot, and push them in. We weren't allowed to move from our town, but a Polish woman who came from Kovel talked about corpses in the street.

"Our turn came in August. There was a feeling in the air that something was going to happen, so my mother arranged for a hiding place in a basement we entered through a tunnel under an outside toilet. We slept there that night. There must have been fifty people in that place. Early the next morning we heard voices. It seemed that the Ukrainians and the Germans were going through all the houses looking for Jews.

"We stayed quiet and were safe that day, but there was one woman with us who had five children, including a little girl who wouldn't stop crying. When that little girl finally fell asleep, her mother carried her up to the house above our hiding place. That was a tremendous decision to make; it was certain death for that little girl. Of course, if she'd stayed below with us, then we'd all have been caught.

"However, the plan backfired. When the little girl woke up, the Ukrainians were in the house and asked where her mother was. The little girl ran to the area where the toilet was, but the soldiers couldn't understand her. They searched inside the house for hours. Finally they realized that this girl was pointing to the toilet, so they touched it and realized it moved. Then they found our place—and that was basically it. We were trapped! People started filing out.

"There was a space boarded up where there had once been a window. As most of the people were going out, my mother suddenly ripped off one piece of board. She whispered for me to get in there and put the board back. When I got in, I had to hold the nail in place with my hand. Then my mother hid under some bedding. By then it was dark, and the police were lighting matches. One had a rifle with a bayonet on it. He was right next to me. Suddenly he took that bayonet and stabbed my mother, who was still hiding under the bedding. She screamed. I didn't know how badly she was hurt, but they took her away. I sat there frozen! They were only inches away from me—so close I had to stop breathing.

"I don't know how long I sat like that. Probably for hours. Then I heard someone speaking Yiddish. I peeked out and I recognized one of the Jews from the town. He said he was looking for a pair of galoshes. He was going into the woods and he was worried about mud! I followed him up to the attic of his house. Then we heard a noise. The man peered down—right into the face of a Ukrainian militiaman with a gun. The militiaman saw the Jew and grabbed him. I stayed hidden as the Jewish man was taken away.

"I sat there stunned, not knowing what to do. I felt like a tiny fish swimming in a sea of danger. Everybody was ready to grab me. Where was I supposed to go? What was I supposed to do? As I sat there, I heard a wagon pull up. Then I realized that soldiers were looting the house, which was the practice. I had to get out. Fortunately I remembered my mother mentioning another hiding place a few houses away, so I went to it, and there I found a little opening, just big enough to crawl through. Suddenly I was dizzy and I almost fainted. Someone hiding in there pulled me in and poured a little whiskey on my lips, which revived me. At last I felt safe! I stayed there for the next few days. These people had a barrel of water, but when we needed more, we had to sneak out to the well, which was the chain type that you crank, and it made a lot of noise squeaking. One of us had to do it very carefully, while someone else watched.

"Soon, however, food became a problem. I volunteered to go get some fruit from the orchard right next to the German headquarters. I chose a Sunday when I knew that most people would be in church. Then I sneaked over there. When the old woman at the orchard saw me, she crossed herself; she couldn't believe any Jewish kid was still alive. She was afraid the Ukrainian workers would see me, so she gave me some fruit and hid me in her attic. She told me to wait until dark, when it would be safe. However, I was scared to wait, so I put the fruit inside my shirt, crept out the window and down to the ground below.

"In order to get back to the hiding place where I had been staying, I had to go through town. Before I knew it, there was somebody in a wagon yelling, 'Jew!' It was a fifteen-year-old boy who lived next door to my grandfather, so I acted casual, not running. Then this teenager jumped off the wagon and started chasing me. As I ran, he grabbed me. He yelled, 'I got you.' A second later I put my hand in my pocket as if I had a gun. I said, 'Are you going to let me go or not?'

"Amazingly he fell for the trick! This kid, who was five years older and so much bigger than I, said in a cringing tone, 'You know I didn't mean anything.' All he had to do was hold me for another thirty seconds, because the other guys were coming around the corner. But I just said, 'I gotta go.' I ran as fast as I could. When I came close to the hiding place, nobody was chasing me anymore, so I dashed back in. A minute later I heard my pursuers running by. They didn't know where I went! We managed to stay in that hiding place another week. Meanwhile the Ukrainians were going around boarding up the houses, convinced that the Jews were gone. They had hatchets and they were hitting the walls.

"When I realized they were about to break into our hiding place, I crawled out a little window. I heard people yelling, 'Jews!' and at first I thought they meant me. I looked down and saw that nobody was paying attention to me, so with a carefully contrived show of nonchalance I walked away. I kept walking, right out of town and all the way to the next village.

"I knew a farmer in that village who had been friendly with my grandfather. I greeted him, but he told me to stay in the bushes because it was dangerous. It seemed that his whole village was collaborating with the Germans. He couldn't take me in, but he advised me to go twenty miles farther, to a town called Luboml, where there was still a Jewish ghetto and where I had some relatives. My uncle, who lived in Luboml, had a big house filled with people who had fled from surrounding areas, including two aunts who had left our town earlier. When I reached his place, I went to sleep exhausted. In the morning, the day when I tried to get up, my legs were so swollen from all the walking I had done the day before, I couldn't move them.

"A few days later my brother showed up, telling a horrible story. He had been caught and taken to the synagogue in our town, and they were about to shoot him, when he and another boy managed to crawl into a big stove. The police shot into the oven and killed the other boy. My brother was wounded in the leg, but the police didn't see him. When it was dark and the coast was clear, my brother sneaked out and made his way to my uncle's place. That night my brother and I slept, holding each other, and he said, 'I will never leave you again.'

"We had been there for about a week when I woke up at four A.M. to the sound of gunfire. I knew what was going on: They were rounding up Jews, just as they had done in our town. I looked out, and sure enough I saw the Germans and Ukrainians with guns, bayonets, and dogs. Quickly we all went to hide in a room that was boarded up except for the entrance, through a fireplace that moved. I was packed in there with my father's first cousin, his wife and two children, and other people as well. We stayed there all night.

"It must have been on the second day that one of the cousins wanted some water. He opened up the secret door. That alerted two Ukrainian militiamen, who shot into the wall, right next to me. I realized that this was about to be a repetition of what had happened in the other basement when my mother was taken. But I had gone through it already, so I knew what to do.

"The other people were all saying, 'Close it up!' But my logic said, 'Close up what? They've got us.' I said, 'No,' and started to crawl out. The militiaman pushed me back. He wanted gold. I crawled in again with a hat, to collect everybody's jewelry. Then I crawled out again and I gave the militiaman the hat with everything in it. The soldier's eyes bugged out! He was so excited by the gold, he wasn't pushing me back anymore . . . and I was able to get out of the hole! I pulled my brother behind me. He was petrified; he couldn't move. I actually had to pull him by the hair, and then we were both out. I looked at the soldier, who was still busy with the gold. I inched over to a window. Now I was sitting on the window ledge. I motioned to my brother to get up there with me. Suddenly the militiaman saw us, pointed his rifle, and ordered us down.

"At that moment someone from the hiding place handed them more valuables, and the Ukrainian militiaman got distracted. We ran up some steps to the next floor and dashed into a bedroom and hid under a bed. One of the militiamen ran after us and searched the rooms, but he didn't find us.

"When it seemed safe at last, we headed out the window. My brother went first, to help me down, but we were spotted. We had to run back up a ladder into the attic of the house next door. A militiaman was already in that house! He tried to push open the attic door, but my brother and I were sitting on it, holding on and pushing. The soldier saw it wasn't opening, so he left. We stayed in the attic. Within an hour I heard them leading out the people from our former hiding place at my uncle's. My father's cousin's little girl, who was eight, asked, 'Mommy are they going to shoot us?' I couldn't hear what her mother answered because so many people were crying.

"That evening my brother and I were hungry. I said I'd go down and get something, but my brother very firmly said, 'You're not going anywhere.' Later I looked around the attic and I didn't see him. Assuming that he had gone to look for food, I decided to go too. I went back to the old hiding place. I couldn't find anything, but while I was looking, I heard voices yelling in German. The Nazis had found the attic—and my brother *was* still in there! I never saw him again.

"That night I met Esther, a cousin of mine who was nineteen and kind of a leader, heading off to the woods with six others, so I followed. It was so dark that I had to hold on to somebody. We had to pass the main railroad area, which was brightly lit up to make sure no Jews got out. When there was a minute between flares, we crossed the tracks. We walked and walked and finally we sat down to rest near a Ukrainian cemetery. The moment I sat down, I fell asleep. When I woke up, everyone was gone.

"Right away my mind started working: What do you do next? I was scared of cemeteries! Kids were always talking about ghosts, and I believed in them. I didn't want to go into the cemetery to look for my companions. I calculated the real risk, and I said to myself, You're afraid, but don't be afraid. Nobody kills people in a cemetery. I climbed the stone wall and dropped down into the cemetery. I was shaking as I searched among the graves. I softly called, 'Isaac,' who was one of the boys with us.

"There was no answer. It was pitch-dark. Then I saw something a little darker, and I went in that direction. When I got a little closer, I saw it was a farm. I looked for the barn and made my way to the stall where a cow slept. I thought, A cow is a nice, friendly animal. So I lay down and slept next to the cow's head. I felt its warm, comforting breath. Just before dawn I woke up and saw a hayloft. It was high up, but I managed to jump up and grab one of the boards and pull myself up—quite an amazing feat for a little boy! Later the farmer's wife came to milk the cow. I coughed to get her attention. She was scared. I said, 'Don't be afraid.' I told her I was lost and I promised I would leave soon.

"She said, 'Don't leave now. Wait until the shepherd comes and takes the cows out.' She brought me a glass of milk and piece of bread. But while I hid, I heard talk about 'Jews hiding in the graveyard with gold.' I figured those must be my relatives and I'd better warn them. Without a sound I sneaked out to the cemetery, which wasn't far. Sure enough I found my cousins hiding under bushes. Now it seemed our lives were balanced on a hair.

"Our plan was to go to the next town, where there were Jews still in the ghetto. It was a long walk. One night we slept in the woods, and it was so cold, my clothes were frozen stiff. Amazingly I didn't catch cold. Now when I walk without shoes on cold tile, I get sick. But then? Being cold was the least of my problems!

"At one point I volunteered to go into the woods to find one of my cousins. I got lost and walked most of the day. Finally I got back, but I was tired and lagging behind the others. All of a sudden I heard a noise behind me, and when it got closer, I could see it was a guy on a bicycle with a rifle. He passed me and stopped. Then he took off his rifle, shot it in the air, and yelled. I lay down and started crawling away. Elated, I realized that he hadn't even seen me. Then I heard more Nazis coming. I started running, and they started shooting at me. A bullet went through my legs, grazed my shoe, and burned my foot a little bit.

"Wondering what to do, I spotted a drainage pipe that went under the road. I crawled in there. Luckily it didn't go straight, so the Nazis couldn't see me when they looked in. Then I heard them taking my cousins away. I was sitting there in water, afraid to get out. After a while I lifted my head and peeked. There was nobody around. Soaking wet, I climbed out and started walking. By the time I reached a farm, I was so tired, I made a hole in the nearest haystack, burrowed in, and immediately dropped off to sleep.

"I awoke with a start: The woman of the farm was jabbing me with a pitchfork. She was cursing me. Evidently she thought I was some kind of animal! Afraid she'd kill me, I put out my hand. The woman ran screaming for her husband. He was there in a moment, yanking me out and demanding to know who I was. Truthfully I told him, 'Ginsburg from Luboml is my uncle.' The farmer nodded. My uncle, who had owned a bar, had gotten along well with the farmers, who came to town on market day. Now this farmer gave me milk and bread and directions to the home of another farmer named Sliva, who had also known my uncle.

"As I started out, I passed a wagon full of drunk militia with guns. They were rowdy, but I had to play 'You guys don't bother me.' While they were passing, I was paying attention to the other side of the road. It took two days to reach the Sliva farm. When I arrived, the woman there said I couldn't stay. The Slivas had been helping Jews, so they were suspect. They let me stay one night, but advised me to join some other Jews hiding in the woods.

"The next day I found the place they told me to go, but the people were eaten up with all kinds of vermin. It was horrible! As it happened, the Ukrainians found them and killed them with hand grenades. So it was good I didn't stay! Sliva told me that farmers don't always lock the barns. He said, 'Like, for instance, I have a little door that I never lock.' Now I knew there was a place I could sneak in at night and sleep in the hay. When I heard the roosters, that was my alarm clock!

"In this particular farm colony most of the people were not Catholics, but Seventh-Day Adventists. Their philosophy, their mentality, was different. In other words they may still have had anti-Semitism ingrained in them, but they would not betray a Jew. So I was safer. Finally I found a family who said they would keep me if I gave them something. I decided to go to the ghetto of Vlodzimiez Volinsk and see what I could find.

"Mr. Sliva was going in that direction by horse and wagon. Together we left at four A.M. with plans to meet a week later for the trip back. Mr. Sliva dropped me off near the ghetto. He showed me the gate, where they let me walk right in. I saw a Ukrainian militiaman with a gun, and I realized I was in a ghetto surrounded by barbed wire and soldiers. I understood with surprise and dismay that I was trapped, with no way to get out.

"I went to the empty, cleaned-out part of the ghetto in search of clothes. All I could find was a ripped sheepskin. A woman sewed it up for me. I found two shoes—

both left feet—lost or abandoned by a Russian soldier. They were too big, but I took them anyway . . . and started planning. How would I get out? There seemed to be no way. Finally I had an idea: I put that sheepskin and those big shoes on to make myself look bigger. I waited until the line of people going out to work in the morning all got counted. Then I got in line, and somehow, once outside, I got away.

"That was Tuesday morning. When I got to the meeting place, Sliva wasn't there. I waited a while but knew it would be dangerous to hang around too long. The important thing was not to draw attention to myself, as they were still killing Jews all over the place. Finally I started walking, and eventually I did meet up with Sliva, who took me to the folks who had agreed to keep me. To my surprise those people already had another six Jews hiding in their barn and under the kitchen.

"I spent the whole next winter there. It was the first time since I lost my mother that I felt safe enough to cry. I felt so sorry that I hadn't gotten out to help her. Theoretically there was nothing I could have done, and if I'd tried, I would have just died too. At least I took some comfort from the fact that when my mother went to her death, she knew that they hadn't gotten me. That was a victory for her!

"When spring came, I felt I ought to earn my keep, so I took a job as a shepherd and worked until summer. At this time the Ukrainians decided that the Jews were all gone, and they started attacking Polish villages. Some of these Seventh-Day Adventists believed, as many Jews did, that God would intercede and smite the Germans. Just like the Jews, those Protestants and Catholic Poles were taken to their death—forty thousand of them! Some of them didn't want to run away. I knew of one family that was killed except for one boy who ran away. He saw the Ukrainians kill everyone in his family, bayoneting children to the walls, just like they'd done with the Jews before.

"Where was I to run now? The family I was staying with knew the attack was to come, and they sent me out on the road to watch, like a spy. When I heard shots, they almost left me there, but we ended up hiding on church property. After that there were many close calls. One day that teenager who'd chased me in the city when I got away by pretending that I had a gun appeared. He stared at me and said, 'I know you.' It had only been about a year. I tried to get away, but he followed me. Desperate, I played the game, acting cool. Finally he went away.

"On another occasion two German officers had taken over half the farmhouse where I was working. They took a liking to me. They thought I was Christian. Every time they got their rations, they would give me the candy. When they saw what a hard worker I was, they said that their mother had a farm in Germany and they wanted to send me to her. I got scared because that was all I needed! I knew if I got to Germany, they would give me an inspection and I'd be finished. I had to tell them, 'No, I'm waiting here. My parents may be alive.' Somehow I got out of that.

"Finally the war and my hiding ordeal were over. I was brought to the United States in a group of orphans. I went to live with an aunt. I spoke no English, but always resourceful, I managed to excel in school, earning grades of ninety-five and higher. Later I put myself through college, first with a job selling ice cream and candy in the subways and then with a part-time job in a factory. Now, four decades later, I have a beautiful wife who was also hidden as a child, three successful children, and even a grandchild.

"I'm certainly grateful to the United States, my adopted country, for the freedom and opportunity I've had to contribute and belong. For example, I'm an electrical engineer. A long while ago I came up with a new and much better way of making a furnace that processes dental porcelain. It was something I figured out. A manufacturer who was the king of the industry at that time looked at my plans and smiled. He said, 'It'll never work.' However, he was wrong: I had virtually revolutionized the process, and I got the patent.

"Fortunately I never lost my wartime ability to size up a situation and know what to do. Not long ago I was at my factory in the Bronx, having just come back from the bank with the payroll. When I walked in the door, there was a big guy ready to hit me with a lead pipe. Bang! He brought the pipe down on my head, but I moved so fast, the blow was cushioned. I fought with him. He must have thought I was crazy. Maybe I *was* at that point! Moments later I had his hat in my hand, and I was chasing him down the street. I ended up with some bruises, but thanks to my very, very fast reaction, I was—once again—the clever little boy outsmarting the bully who wanted me dead.

"When I look back at what happened to me during the war, it all seems so crazy. I've read a great deal about the Holocaust, and I've made a lot of notes. But up until now I've kept my own story to myself. In fact I haven't even shared it fully with my three children, even though my daughter is a psychiatrist. It's still such a soft and vulnerable part of me. When I think about all my relatives who died, I'm afraid I might cry, and that is something I don't allow myself to do.

"However, lately I'm feeling that I can't stay quiet any longer. I was just reading about an organization that's been putting ads in college newspapers, claiming that the Holocaust never happened. In response I wrote an article, giving a little of my background. I sent it to the editor of the Rutgers University newspaper. I felt I had to go on record. I realize that the older survivors are passing away, and I'm getting older myself. When I'm gone, there will be very few people left with any firsthand experience. So what can I do but tell the truth?"

# Jean-Paul Sartre

## *from* EXISTENTIALISM IS A HUMANISM (1946)

*Jean-Paul Sartre (1905–1980) is perhaps the most important French thinker of the twentieth century. Sartre was a philosopher, novelist, playwright, essayist, and political activist. He joined the French army in 1939 and was taken prisoner in Alsace during the German invasion. After nine months in a prisoner-of-war camp—an experience that made him optimistic about human solidarity—he went to Paris and took part in the Resistance movement, writing for clandestine publications such as* Combat. *Sartre is arguably the most famous proponent of the philosophy of* existentialism, *and in his essay "Existentialism is a Humanism" he provides a famous definition of it: "existence precedes essence." Equally important, the essay demonstrates his Resistance experience. Writing in the aftermath of the war, Sartre denies that existentialism is a pessimistic philosophy but does not portray human beings as being inherently good. He stresses individual moral responsibility.*

---

What can be said from the very beginning is that by existentialism we mean a doctrine which makes human life possible and, in addition, declares that every truth and every action implies a human setting and a human subjectivity.

As is generally known, the basic charge against us is that we put the emphasis on the dark side of human life. . . . we are said to be naturalists; and if we are, it is rather surprising that in this day and age we cause so much more alarm and scandal than does naturalism, properly so called. The kind of person who can take in his stride such a novel as Zola's *The Earth* is disgusted as soon as he starts reading an existentialist novel. . . .

. . . There are still . . . the people who say, "It's only human!" whenever a more or less repugnant act is pointed out to them . . . these are the people who accuse existentialism of being too gloomy, and to such an extent that I wonder whether they are complaining about it, not for its pessimism, but much rather its optimism. Can it be that what really scares them in the doctrine I shall try to present here is that it leaves to man a possibility of choice? To answer this question, we must re-examine it on a strictly philosophical plane. What is meant by the term *existentialism*? . . .

. . . What complicates matters is that there are two kinds of existentialists; first, those who are Christian, among whom I would include Jaspers and Gabriel Marcel, both Catholic; and on the other hand the atheistic existentialists among whom I class

Heidegger, and then the French existentialists and myself. What they have in common is that they think that existence precedes essence, or, if you prefer, that subjectivity must be the starting point.

. . . Atheistic existentialism, which I represent . . . states that if God does not exist, there is at least one being in whom existence precedes essence, a being who exists before he can be defined by any concept, and that this being is man. . . . What is meant here by saying that existence precedes essence? It means that, first of all, man exists, turns up, appears on the scene, and, only afterwards, defines himself. If man, as the existentialist conceives him, is indefinable, it is because at first he is nothing. Only afterward will he be something, and he himself will have made what he will be. Thus, there is no human nature, since there is no God to conceive it. Not only is man what he conceives himself to be, but he is also only what he wills himself to be after this thrust toward existence.

Man is nothing else but what he makes of himself. Such is the first principle of existentialism. . . . if existence really does precede essence, man is responsible for what he is. Thus, existentialism's first move is to make every man aware of what he is and to make the full responsibility of his existence rest on him. And when we say that a man is responsible for himself, we do not only mean that he is responsible for his own individuality, but that he is responsible for all men. . . .

. . . When we say that man chooses his own self, we mean that every one of us does likewise; but we also mean by that that in making this choice he also chooses all men. In fact, in creating the man that we want to be, there is not a single one of our acts which does not at the same create an image of man as we think he ought to be. To choose to be this or that is to affirm at the same time the value of what we choose, because we can never choose evil. We always choose the good, and nothing can be good for us without being good for all.

If . . . existence precedes essence, and if we grant that we exist and fashion our image at one and the same time, the image is valid for everybody and for our whole age. Thus, our responsibility is much greater than we might have supposed, because it involves all mankind. If I am a workingman and choose to join a Christian trade-union rather than be a communist, and if by being a member I want to show that the best thing for man is resignation, that the kingdom of man is not of this world, I am not only involving my own case—I want to be resigned for everyone. As a result, my action has involved all humanity. To take a more individual matter, if I want to marry, to have children; even if this marriage depends solely on my own circumstances or passion or wish, I am involving all humanity in monogamy and not merely myself. Therefore, I am responsible for myself and for everyone else. I am creating a certain image of man of my own choosing. In choosing myself, I choose man.

This helps us understand what the actual content is of such rather grandiloquent words as anguish, forlornness, despair. As you will see, it's all quite simple.

First, what is meant by anguish? The existentialists say at once that man is anguish. What that means is this: the man who involves himself and who realizes that he is not only the person he chooses to be, but also a lawmaker who is, at the same time, choosing all mankind as well as himself, can not help escape the feeling of his total and deep responsibility. Of course, there are many people who are not anxious; but we claim that they are hiding their anxiety, that they are fleeing from it. Certainly, many people believe that when they do something, they themselves are the only ones involved, and when someone says to them, "What if everyone acted that way?" they shrug their shoulders and answer, "Everyone doesn't act that way." But really, one should always ask himself, "What would happen if everybody looked at things that way?" There is no escaping this disturbing thought except by a kind of double-dealing. A man who lies and makes excuses for himself by saying "Not everybody does that," is someone with an uneasy conscience, because the act of lying implies that a universal value is conferred upon the lie.

Anguish is evident even when it conceals itself. . . .

When we speak of forlornness . . . we mean only that God does not exist and that we have to face all the consequences of this. . . .

. . . all possibility of finding values in a heaven of ideas disappears along with Him; there can no longer be an *a priori* Good, since there is no infinite and perfect consciousness to think it. Nowhere is it written that the Good exists, that we must be honest, that we must not lie; because the fact is we are on a plane where there are only men. Dostoievsky said, "If God didn't exist, everything would be possible." That is the very starting point of existentialism. Indeed, everything is permissible if God does not exist, and as a result man is forlorn, because neither within him nor without does he find anything to cling to. He can't start making excuses for himself.

If existence really does precede essence, there is no explaining things away by reference to a fixed and given human nature. In other words, there is no determinism, man is free, man is freedom. On the other hand, if God does not exist, we find no values or commands to turn to which legitimize our conduct. So, in the bright realm of values, we have no excuse behind us, nor justification before us. We are alone, with no excuses.

That is the idea I shall try to convey when I say that man is condemned to be free. Condemned, because he did not create himself, yet, in other respects is free; because, once thrown into the world, he is responsible for everything he does. . . .

As for despair. . . . It means that we shall confine ourselves to reckoning only with what depends upon our will, or on the ensemble of probabilities which make our action possible. . . . The moment the possibilities I am considering are not rigorously involved by my action, I ought to disengage myself from them, because no God, no scheme, can adapt the world and its possibilities to my will. When Descartes said, "Conquer yourself rather than the world," he meant essentially the same thing. . . .

. . . Quietism is the attitude of people who say, "Let others do what I can't do." The doctrine I am presenting is the very opposite of quietism, since it declares, "There is no reality except in action." Moreover, it goes further, since it adds, "Man is nothing else than his plan; he exists only to the extent that he fulfills himself; he is therefore nothing else than the ensemble of his acts, nothing else than his life."

According to this, we can understand why our doctrine horrifies certain people. Because often the only way they can bear their wretchedness is to think, "Circumstances have been against me. What I've been and done doesn't show my true worth. . . ."

. . . A man is involved in life, leaves his impress on it, and outside of that there is nothing. To be sure, this may seem a harsh thought to someone whose life hasn't been a success. But, on the other hand, it prompts people to understand that reality alone is what counts, that dreams, expectations, and hopes warrant no more than to define a man as a disappointed dream, as miscarried hopes, as vain expectations. In other words, to define him negatively and not positively. . . . What we mean is that a man is nothing else than a series of undertakings, that he is the sum, the organization, the ensemble of the relationships which make up these undertakings.

When all is said and done, what we are accused of, at bottom, is not our pessimism, but an optimistic toughness. If people throw up to us our works of fiction in which we write about people who are soft, weak, cowardly, and sometimes even downright bad, it's not because these people are soft, weak, cowardly, or bad; because if we were to say, as Zola did, that they are that way because of heredity, the workings of environment, society, because of biological or psychological determinism, people would be reassured. They would say, "Well, that's what we're like, no one can do anything about it." But when the existentialist writes about a coward, he says that this coward is responsible for his cowardice. He's not like that because he has a cowardly heart or lung or brain; he's not like that on account of his physiological make-up; but he's like that because he has made himself a coward by his acts. . . . what makes cowardice is the act of renouncing or yielding. . . .

What the existentialist says is that the coward makes himself cowardly, that the hero makes himself heroic. There's always a possibility for the coward not to be cowardly any more and for the hero to stop being heroic. What counts is total involvement; some one particular action or set of circumstances is not total involvement. . . .

. . . if it is impossible to find in every man some universal essence which would be human nature, yet there does exist a universal human condition. It's not by chance that today's thinkers speak more readily of man's condition than of his nature. By condition they mean, more or less definitely, the *a priori* limits which outline man's fundamental situation in the universe. Historical situations vary; a man may be born a slave in a pagan society or a feudal lord or a proletarian. What does not vary is the necessity for him to exist in the world, to be at work there, to be there in the midst of other people, and to be mortal there. . . . And though the configurations may differ, at least none of them are completely strange to me, because they all appear as attempts either to pass beyond these limits or recede from them or deny them or adapt to them. Consequently, every configuration, however individual it may be, has a universal value.

Every configuration, even the Chinese, the Indian, or the Negro, can be understood by a Westerner. "Can be understood" means that by virtue of a situation that he can imagine, a European of 1945 can, in like manner, push himself to his limits and reconstitute within himself the configuration of the Chinese, the Indian, or the African. Every configuration has universality in the sense that every configuration can be understood by every man. This does not at all mean that this configuration defines man forever, but that it can be met with again. There is always a way to understand the idiot, the child, the savage, the foreigner, provided one has the necessary information.

In this sense we may say that there is a universality of man; but it is not given, it is perpetually being made. I build the universal in choosing myself; I build it in understanding the configuration of every other man, whatever age he might have lived in. . . .

. . . Existentialism isn't so atheistic that it wears itself out showing that God doesn't exist. Rather, it declares that even if God did exist, that would change nothing. There you've got our point of view. Not that we believe that God exists, but we think that the problem of His existence is not the issue. In this sense existentialism is optimistic, a doctrine of action, and it is plain dishonesty for Christians to make no distinction between their own despair and ours and then to call us despairing.

# Simone de Beauvoir

# *from* THE SECOND SEX (1949)

*S*imone de Beauvoir (1908–1986), born into a conservative Catholic family in Paris, studied philosophy at the Sorbonne and became a leading figure among French intellectuals. In her novels and memoirs, she explored the experiences of women and men and the formation of the self in a modern, existential world. Beauvoir is best known for her monumental treatise The Second Sex, which examines women's subordination to men throughout European history, particularly the ways women are socialized and the contradictions between myths about women and the realities of women's lives. "One is not born, but rather becomes, a woman," Beauvoir argues, for what we have understood the term 'woman' to stand for is something artificial, man-made, rather than natural. 'Woman' is the second sex because she has been "defined and differentiated with reference to man and not he with reference to her; she is the incidental, the inessential as opposed to the essential. He is the Subject, he is the Absolute—she is the Other." A landmark work in both feminist and existentialist thought, The Second Sex remains one of the most influential books published since the Second World War.

## *FROM* CHAPTER XI

### *Myth and Reality*

The myth of woman plays a considerable part in literature; but what is its importance in daily life? To what extent does it affect the customs and conduct of individuals? In replying to this question it will be necessary to state precisely the relations this myth bears to reality.

There are different kinds of myths. This one, the myth of woman, sublimating an immutable aspect of the human condition—namely, the "division" of humanity into two classes of individuals—is a static myth. It projects into the realm of Platonic ideas a reality that is directly experienced or is conceptualized on a basis of experience; in place of fact, value, significance, knowledge, empirical law, it substitutes a transcendental Idea, timeless, unchangeable, necessary. This idea is indisputable because it is beyond the given: it is endowed with absolute truth. Thus, as against the dispersed, contingent, and multiple existences of actual women, mythical thought opposes the Eternal Feminine, unique and changeless. If the definition provided for this concept is contradicted by the behavior of flesh-and-blood women, it is the latter who are wrong: we are told not that Femininity is a false entity, but that women concerned are not feminine. The contrary facts of experience are impotent against the myth. In a way, however, its source is in experience. Thus it is quite true that woman is other than man, and this alterity is directly felt in desire, the embrace, love; but the real relation is one of reciprocity; as such it gives rise to authentic drama. Through eroticism, love, friendship, and their alternatives, deception, hate, rivalry, the relation is a struggle between conscious beings each of whom wishes to be essential, it is the mutual recognition of free beings who confirm one another's freedom, it is the vague transition from aversion to participation. To pose Woman is to pose the absolute Other, without reciprocity, denying against all experience that she is a subject, a fellow human being.

In actuality, of course, women appear under various aspects; but each of the myths built up around the subject of woman is intended to sum her up *in toto;* each aspires to be unique. In consequence, a number of incompatible myths exist, and men tarry musing before the strange incoherencies manifested by the idea of Femininity. As every woman has a share in a majority of these archetypes—each of which lays claim to containing the sole Truth of woman—men of today also are moved again in the presence of their female companions to an astonishment like that of the old sophists who failed to understand how man could be blond and dark at the same time! Transition toward the absolute was indicated long ago in social phenomena: relations are easily congealed in classes, functions in types, just as relations, to the childish mentality, are fixed in things. Patriarchal society, for example, being centered upon the conservation of the patrimony, implies necessarily, along with those who own and transmit wealth, the existence of men and women who take property away from its owners and put it into circulation. The men—adventurers, swindlers, thieves, speculators—are generally repudiated by the group; the women, employing their erotic attraction, can induce young men and even fathers of families to scatter their patrimonies, without ceasing to be within the law. Some of these women appropriate their victims' fortunes or obtain legacies by using undue influence; this role being regarded as evil, those who play it are called "bad women." But the fact is that quite to the contrary they are able to appear in some other setting—at home with their fathers, brothers, husbands, or lovers—as guardian angels; and the courtesan who "plucks" rich financiers is, for painters and writers, a generous patroness. It is easy to understand in actual experience the ambiguous personality of Aspasia or Mme de Pompadour. But if woman is depicted as the Praying Mantis, the Mandrake, the Demon, then it is most confusing to find in woman also the Muse, the Goddess Mother, Beatrice.

As group symbols and social types are generally defined by means of antonyms in pairs, ambivalence will seem to be an intrinsic quality of the Eternal Feminine. The saintly mother has for correlative the cruel stepmother, the angelic young girl has the perverse virgin: thus it will be said sometimes that Mother equals Life, sometimes that Mother equals Death, that every virgin is pure spirit or flesh dedicated to the devil.

Evidently it is not reality that dictates to society or to individuals their choice between the two opposed basic categories; in every period, in each case, society and the individual decide in accordance with their needs. Very often they project into the myth adopted the institutions and values to which they adhere. Thus the paternalism that claims woman for hearth and home defines her as sentiment, inwardness, immanence. In fact every existent is at once immanence and transcendence; when one offers the existent no aim, or prevents him from attaining any, or robs him of his victory, then his transcendence falls vainly into the past—that is to say, falls back into immanence. This is the lot assigned to woman in the patriarchate; but it is in no way a vocation, any more than slavery is the vocation of the slave. The development of this mythology is to be clearly seen in Auguste Comte. To identify Woman with Altruism is to guarantee to man absolute rights in her devotion, it is to impose on women a categorical imperative. . . .

Few myths have been more advantageous to the ruling caste than the myth of woman: it justifies all privileges and even authorizes their abuse. Men need not bother themselves with alleviating the pains and the burdens that physiologically are women's lot, since these are "intended by Nature"; men use them as a pretext for increasing the misery of the feminine lot still further, for instance by refusing to grant woman any right to sexual pleasure, by making her work like a beast of burden.

Of all these myths, none is more firmly anchored in masculine hearts than that of the feminine "mystery." It has numerous advantages. And first of all it permits an easy explanation of all that appears inexplicable; the man who "does not understand" a woman is happy to substitute an objective resistance for a subjective deficiency of mind; instead of admitting his ignorance, he perceives the presence of a "mystery" outside himself: an alibi, indeed, that flatters laziness and vanity at once. A heart smitten with love thus avoids many disappointments: if the loved one's behavior is capricious, her remarks stupid, then the mystery serves to excuse it all. And finally, thanks again to the mystery, that negative relation is perpetuated which seemed to Kierkegaard infinitely preferable to positive possession; in the company of a living enigma man remains alone—alone with his dreams, his hopes, his fears, his love, his vanity. This subjective game, which can go all the way from vice to mystical ecstasy, is for many a more attractive experience than an authentic relation with a human being. What foundations exist for such a profitable illusion? . . .

. . . Mystery is never more than a mirage that vanishes as we draw near to look at it.

We can see now that the myth is in large part explained by its usefulness to man. The myth of woman is a luxury. It can appear only if man escapes from the urgent demands of his needs; the more relationships are concretely lived, the less they are idealized. The fellah of ancient Egypt, the Bedouin peasant, the artisan of the Middle Ages, the worker of today has in the requirements of work and poverty relations with his particular woman companion which are too definite for her to be embellished with an aura either auspicious or inauspicious. The epochs and the social classes that have been marked by the leisure to dream have been the ones to set up the images, black and white, of femininity. But along with luxury there was utility; these dreams were irresistibly guided by interests. Surely most of the myths had roots in the spontaneous attitude of man toward his own existence and toward the world around him. But going beyond experience toward the transcendent Idea was deliberately used by patriarchal society for purposes of self-justification; through the myths this society imposed its laws and customs upon individuals in a picturesque, effective manner; it is under a mythical form that the group-imperative is indoctrinated into each conscience. Through such intermediaries as religion, traditions, language, tales, songs, movies, the myths penetrate even into such existences as are most harshly enslaved to material realities. Here everyone can find sublimation of his drab experiences: deceived by the woman he loves, one declares that she is a Crazy Womb; another, obsessed by his impotence, calls her a Praying Mantis; still another enjoys his wife's company: behold, she is Harmony, Rest, the Good Earth! The taste for eternity at a bargain, for a pocket-sized absolute, which is shared by a majority of men, is satisfied by myths. The smallest emotion, a slight annoyance, becomes the reflection of a timeless Idea—an illusion agreeably flattering to the vanity.

The myth is one of those snares of false objectivity into which the man who depends on ready-made valuations rushes headlong. Here again we have to do with the substitution of a set idol for actual experience and the free judgments it requires. For an authentic relation with an autonomous existent, the myth of Woman substitutes the fixed contemplation of a mirage. . . .

## FROM CHAPTER XII

### Childhood

One is not born, but rather becomes, a woman. No biological, psychological, or economic fate determines the figure that the human female presents in society; it is civilization as a whole that produces this creature, intermediate between male and eunuch, which is described as feminine. Only the intervention of someone else can establish an individual as an *Other*.

## FROM CHAPTER XIII

### The Young Girl

Beyond the lack of initiative that is due to women's education, custom makes independence difficult for them. If they roam the streets, they are stared at and accosted. I know young girls who, without being at all timid, find no enjoyment in taking walks alone in Paris because, importuned incessantly, they must be always on the alert, which spoils their pleasure. If girl students run in gay groups through the streets, as boys do, they make a spectacle of themselves; to walk with long strides, sing, talk, or laugh loudly, or eat an apple, is to give provocation; those who do will be insulted or followed or spoken to. Careless gaiety is in itself bad deportment; the self-control that is imposed on women and becomes second nature in "the well-bred young girl" kills spontaneity; her lively exuberance is beaten down. The result is tension and ennui.

This ennui is catching: young girls quickly tire of one another; they do not band together in their prison for mutual benefit; and this is one of the reasons why the company of boys is necessary to them. This incapacity to be self-sufficient engenders a timidity that extends over their entire lives and is marked even in their work. They believe that outstanding success is reserved for men; they are afraid to aim too high. We have seen that little girls of fourteen, comparing themselves with boys, declared that "the boys are better." This is a debilitating conviction. It leads to laziness and mediocrity. A young girl, who had no special deference for the stronger sex, was reproaching a man for his cowardice; it was remarked that she herself was a coward. "Oh, a woman, that's different!" declared she, complacently.

The fundamental reason for such defeatism is that the adolescent girl does not think herself responsible for her future; she sees no use in demanding much of herself since her lot in the end will not depend on her own efforts. Far from consigning herself to man because she recognizes her inferiority, it is because she is thus consigned to him that, accepting the idea of her inferiority, she establishes its truth.

And, actually, it is not by increasing her worth as a human being that she will gain value in men's eyes; it is rather by modeling herself upon their dreams. When still inexperienced, she is not always aware of this fact. She may be as aggressive as the boys; she may try to make their conquest with a rough authority, a proud frankness; but this attitude almost surely dooms her to failure. All girls, from the most servile to the haughtiest, learn in time that to please they must abdicate. Their mothers enjoin upon them to treat the boys no longer as comrades, not to make advances, to take a passive role. If they wish to start a friendship or a flirtation, they must carefully avoid seeming to take the initiative in it; men do not like *garçons manqués,* or bluestockings, or brainy women; too much daring, culture, or intelligence, too much character, will frighten them. In most novels, as George Eliot remarks, it is the blonde and silly heroine who is in the end victorious over the more mannish brunette; and in *The Mill on the Floss* Maggie tries in vain to reverse the roles; but she finally dies and the blonde Lucy marries Stephen. In *The Last of the Mohicans* the vapid Alice gains the hero's heart, not the valiant Clara; in *Little Women* the likable Jo is only a childhood playmate for Laurie: his love is reserved for the insipid Amy and her curls.

To be feminine is to appear weak, futile, docile. The young girl is supposed not only to deck herself out, to make herself ready, but also to repress her spontaneity and replace it with the studied grace and charm taught to her by her elders. Any self-assertion will diminish her femininity and her attractiveness. The young man's journey into existence is made relatively easy by the fact that there is no contradiction between his vocation as human being and as male; and this advantage is indicated even in childhood. Through self-assertion in independence and liberty, he acquires his social value and concurrently his prestige as male: the ambitious man, like Balzac's Rastignac, aims at wealth, celebrity, and women in one and the same enterprise; one of the stereotypes which stimulate his effort is that of the powerful and famous man whom women adore.

But for the young woman, on the contrary, there is a contradiction between her status as a real human being and her vocation as a female. And just here is to be found the reason why adolescence is for a woman so difficult and decisive a moment. Up to this time she has been an autonomous individual: now she must renounce her sovereignty. Not only is she torn, like her brothers, though more painfully, between the past and the future, but in addition a conflict breaks out between her original claim to be subject, active, free, and, on the other hand, her erotic urges and the social pressure to accept herself as passive object. Her spontaneous tendency is to regard herself as the essential: how can she make up her mind to become the inessential? But if I can accomplish my destiny only as the *Other,* how shall I give up my Ego? Such is the painful dilemma with which the woman-to-be must struggle. Oscillating between desire and disgust, between hope and fear, declining what she calls for, she lingers in suspense between the time of childish independence and that of womanly submission. It is this uncertainty that, as she emerges from the awkward age, gives her the sharp savor of a fruit still green.

—*trans. H.M. Parshley*

# SECTION VIII

# NEW IDENTITIES

In some ways it is difficult to generalize about the last half-century because it is still so much a part of the present. Only recently have most European nations selected political leaders from the generation raised after the Second World War; only in the last decade has the postwar division of Europe into East and West begun to be dismantled; only as they have become elderly have many children of the Holocaust told their stories. In the half-century since the war, Europeans have continued to revisit issues that have concerned Europe for centuries; they have also addressed new issues that were virtually unimaginable in the past.

To understand late twentieth-century Europe it is necessary to think globally. For five hundred years, Europe understood itself to be the center of the world—culturally, intellectually, politically, economically. The literalness with which we have taken that metaphor is embodied in the words commonly used in English (until very recently) to name different areas on the globe. Geographical designations such as 'West Indies' and 'East Indies,' 'Near East,' 'Middle East,' and 'Far East' sound reasonable if you are standing in London, but quite illogical if you stand in Delhi, Tokyo, or Los Angeles. Traditional notions of center and periphery had to give way as nations once considered by Europeans to be peripheral—particularly the United States and the Soviet Union—became major participants in European history. This de-centering of Europe, furthered by world wars at home and revolutionary movements abroad, led inevitably to a difficult and often violent process of decolonization. Since 1945, over 50 independent nations have been established where representatives of a few European empires once governed.

From our vantage point, Munch's *The Scream* seems a prescient response to the cataclysmic events of the twentieth century—the Great War, the Second World War, the Holocaust, the atom bomb. These events irrevocably shattered nineteenth-century optimism that the world was progressing and becoming increasingly civilized, and that science could provide the answers to all human questions. It is not surprising that Sartrean existentialism, born in part out of the war experience, rejected the assumption that human beings are inherently good for an emphasis on responsibility and action. In the decades since the Second World War, people in many parts of the globe have reconsidered their European cultural legacies and faced unavoidable questions. What is the legacy of the scientific revolution—the atom bomb? What remains of enlightenment after the final solution? How can cultures, and cultural differences, best be understood after the discrediting of social Darwinism and the end of empires? As women and men question a legacy of differentiation based on gender, race, and class, what new forms of social order and new philosophies may, or should, develop? Are there basic human rights that should never be violated? If so, how are they to be guaranteed? What new identities are authentically possible in a postmodern, postcolonial world?

Establishing European cultural institutions in colonies was part of the process of imperialism; rethinking and, in many cases, dismantling those institutions has been part of the program of decolonization. The stakes here are high, and complex. Modernization has its origins in Europe, but has substantially affected every part of the world; figuring out which modern institutions and European practices serve the needs of a particular culture, and which do not, is a difficult and controversial process. As the readings in this section demonstrate, it is impossible to separate the personal stories of the twentieth century from this larger history to which, in the words of English novelist Penelope Lively, we are "shackled . . . like it or not." Europe's past continues to shape the present lives of people around the world: in the nations of Europe, whose boundaries have changed through local revolutions and global wars; in new nations established out of the ruins of empire; and in other nations such as the United States, where a majority of citizens trace their ancestry to nineteenth- and twentieth-century immigrants from Europe and its former colonies.

As the introduction to this reader notes, contemporary thinkers have begun to question whether the cultural condition or epoch called 'modernity' continues to exist today. One form this questioning takes is the characterization of the present historical moment as 'postmodern.' Whether 'postmodern' means 'beyond modernism,' 'beyond modernity,' 'the last wave of modernism,' or something else has been the topic of much debate. A common thread in each definition of postmodernism is the sense that modernity has played out all its variations, that it is in need of critique, that it is exhausted or bankrupt. Certainly its many achievements have come at high cost. For some, then, postmodernism is a cultural stance that rejects the grand narratives that once offered modern, cutting-edge explanations of history. For others, it is a political stance related to the fight against imperialism. For still others, it is a state of mind, a way of engaging the past ironically as we create the present. Donna Haraway proposes the cyborg, an image from science fiction, as a liberating image of a new kind of identity—postmodern, postcolonial, and beyond gender distinctions—for the world of the future.

# Mohandas K. Gandhi

## *from* HIND SWARAJ
## OR INDIAN HOME RULE (1938)

*Mohandas K. Gandhi (1869–1948)—or Mahatma, "the Great Souled"—led the Indian nationalist movement against British rule, which produced independence in 1948. Educated in India and England, Gandhi developed a form of political resistance, Swaraj, often translated as 'passive resistance', but according to Gandhi himself closer to 'truth-force' or 'soul-force'. In practice it meant disobeying laws that were immoral or illegitimate and accepting the consequences of that action. In addition, his vision of Indian renewal rejected Western materialism and modernization in favor of returning to India's deepest religious and spiritual values. Ironically, Gandhi's own path to embracing these views was partially indebted to the socialists and humanitarians that he knew in England in the late 1880s. Following independence, India was wracked by civil war between Hindus and Muslims. Gandhi, who sought to negotiate between the two sides, increasingly alienated the intransigent groups of both. A Hindu militant assassinated him while he was kneeling during his morning prayer.*

READER: . . . Will you tell me something of what you have read and thought of [modern] civilization?

EDITOR: Let us first consider what state of things is described by the word "civilization." Its true test lies in the fact that people living in it make bodily welfare the object of life. We will take some examples. The people of Europe today live in better-built houses than they did a hundred years ago. This is considered an emblem of civilization, and this is also a matter to promote bodily happiness. Formerly, they wore skins, and used spears as their weapons. Now, they wear long trousers, and, for embellishing their bodies, they wear a variety of clothing, and, instead of spears, they carry with them revolvers containing five or more chambers. If people of a certain country, who have hitherto not been in the habit of wearing much clothing, boots, etc., adopt European clothing, they are supposed to have become civilized out of savagery. Formerly, in Europe, people ploughed their lands mainly by manual labour. Now, one man can plough a vast tract by means of steam engines and can thus amass great wealth. This is called a sign of civilization. Formerly, only a few men wrote valuable books. Now, anybody writes and prints anything he likes and poisons people's minds. Formerly, men travelled in waggons. Now, they fly though the air in trains at a rate of four hundred and more miles per day. This is considered the height of civilization. It has been stated that, as men progress, they shall be able to travel in airships and reach any part of the world in a few hours. Men will not need the use of their hands and feet. They will press a button, and they will have their clothing by their side. They will press another button, and they will have their newspaper. A third, and a motor-car will be in waiting for them. They will have a variety of delicately dished up food. Everything will be done by machinery. Formerly, when people wanted to fight with one another, they measured between them their bodily strength; now it is possible to take away thousands of lives by one man working behind a gun from a hill. This is civilization. Formerly, men worked in the open air only as much as they like. Now thousands of workmen meet together and for the sake of maintenance work in factories or mines. Their condition is worse than that of beasts. They are obliged to work, at the risk of their lives, at most dangerous occupa-tions, for the sake of millionaires. Formerly, men were made slaves under physical compulsion. Now they are enslaved by temptation of money and of the luxuries that money can buy. There are now diseases of which people never dreamt before, and an army of doctors is engaged in finding out their cures, and so hospitals have increased. This is a test of civilization. Formerly, special messengers were required and much expense was incurred in order to send letters; today, anyone can abuse his fellow by means of a letter for one penny. True, at the same cost, one can send one's thanks also. Formerly, people had two or three meals consisting of home-made bread and vege-tables; now, they require something to eat every two hours so that they have hardly leisure for anything else. What more need I say? All this you can ascertain from sev-eral authoritative books. These are all true tests of civilization. And if anyone speaks to the contrary, know that he is ignorant. This civilization takes note neither of morality nor of religion. Its votaries calmly state that their business is not to teach religion. Some even consider it to be a superstitious growth. Others put on the cloak of religion, and prate about morality. But, after twenty years' experience, I have come to the conclusion that immorality is often taught in the name of morality. Even a child can understand that in all I have described above there can be no inducement to morality. Civilization seeks to increase bodily comforts, and it fails miserable even in doing so.

READER: . . . What, then, is [true] civilization?

EDITOR: The answer to that question is not difficult. I believe that the civiliza-tion India has evolved is not to be beaten in the world. Nothing can equal the seeds sown by our ancestors. Rome went, Greece shared the same fate; the might of the Pharaohs were broken; Japan has become westernized; of China nothing can be said; but India is still, somehow or other, sound at the foundation. The people of Europe learn their lessons from the writings of the men of Greece or Rome, which exist no longer in their former glory. In trying to learn from them, the Europeans imagine that they will avoid the mistakes of Greece and Rome. Such is their pitiable condi-tion. In the midst of all this India remains immoveable and that is her glory. It is a charge against India that her people are so uncivilized, ignorant and stolid, that it is not possible to induce them to adopt any changes. It is a charge really against our merit. What we have tested and found true on the anvil of experience, we dare not change. Many thrust their advice upon India, and she remains steady. This is her beauty; it is in the sheet-anchor of our hope.

Civilization is that mode of conduct which points out to man the path of duty. Performance of duty and observance of morality are convertible terms. To observe morality is to attain mastery over our mind and our passions. So doing, we know ourselves. The Gujarati equivalent for civilization means "good conduct."

If this definition be correct, then India, as so many writers have shown, has nothing to learn from anybody else, and this is as it should be. We notice that the mind is a restless bird; the more it gets the more it wants, and still remains unsatisfied. The more we indulge our passions the more unbridled they become. Our ancestors, therefore, set a limit to our indulgences. They saw that happiness was largely a mental condition. A man is not necessarily happy because he is rich, or unhappy because he is poor. The rich are often seen to be unhappy, the poor to be happy. Millions will always remain poor. Observing all this, our ancestors dissuaded us from luxuries and pleasures. We have managed with the same kind of plough as existed thousands of years ago. We have retained the same kind of cottages that we had in former times and our indigenous education remains the same as before. We have had no system of life-corroding competition. Each followed his own occupation or trade and charged a regulation wage. It was not that we did not know how to invent machinery, but our forefathers knew that, if we set our hearts after such things, we would become slaves and lose our moral fibre. They, therefore, after due deliberation decided that we should only do what we could with our hands and feet. They saw that our real happiness and health consisted in a proper use of our hands and feet. They further reasoned that large cities were a snare and a useless encumbrance and that people would not be happy in them, that there would be gangs of thieves and robbers, prostitution and vice flourishing in them and that poor men would be robbed by rich men. They were, therefore, satisfied with small villages. They saw that kings and their swords were inferior to the sword of ethics, and they, therefore, held the sovereigns of the earth to be inferior to the Rishis and the Fakirs. A nation with a constitution like this is fitter to teach others than to learn from others. This nation had courts, lawyers and doctors, but they were all within bounds. Everybody knew that these professions were not particularly superior; moreover, these vakils and vaids did not rob people; they were considered people's dependents, not their masters. Justice was tolerably fair. The ordinary rule was to avoid courts. There were no touts to lure people into them. This evil, too, was noticeable only in and around capitals. The common people lived independently and followed their agricultural occupation. They enjoyed true Home Rule.

And where this cursed modern civilization has not reached, India remains as it was before. The inhabitants of that part of India will very properly laugh at your new-fangled notions. The English do not rule over them, nor will you ever rule over them. Those in whose name we speak we do not know, nor do they know us. I would certainly advise you and those like you who love the motherland to go into the interior that has yet been not polluted by the railways and to live there for six months; you might then be patriotic and speak of Home Rule.

Now you see what I consider to be real civilization. Those who want to change conditions such as I have described are enemies of the country and are sinners.

•

READER: If Indian civilization is, as you say, the best of all, how do you account for India's slavery?

EDITOR: This civilization is unquestionably the best, but it is to be observed that all civilizations have been on their trial. That civilization which is permanent outlives it. Because the sons of India were found wanting, its civilization has been placed in jeopardy. But its strength is to be seen in its ability to survive the shock. Moreover, the whole of India is not touched. Those alone who have been affected by Western civilization have become enslaved. We measure the universe by our own miserable foot-rule. When we are slaves, we think that the whole universe is enslaved. Because we are in an abject condition, we think that the whole of India is in that condition. As a matter of fact, it is not so, yet it is as well to impute our slavery to the whole of India. But if we bear in mind the above fact, we can see that if we become free, India is free. And in this thought you have a definition of Swaraj. It is Swaraj when we learn to rule ourselves. It is, therefore, in the palm of our hands. Do not consider this Swaraj to be like a dream. There is no idea of sitting still. The Swaraj that I wish to picture is such that, after we have once realized it, we shall endeavour to the end of our life-time to persuade others to do likewise. But such Swaraj has to be experienced, by each one for himself. One drowning man will never save another. Slaves ourselves, it would be a mere pretension to think of freeing others. Now you will have seen that it is not necessary for us to have as our goal the expulsion of the English. If the English become Indianized, we can accommodate them. If they wish to remain in India along with their civilization, there is no room for them. It lies with us to bring about such a state of things.

•

READER: . . . You know that what the English obtained in their own country they obtained by using brute force. I know you have argued that what they have obtained is useless, but that does not affect my argument. They wanted useless things and they got them. My point is that their desire was fulfilled. What does it matter what means they adopted? Why should we not obtain our goal, which is good, by any means whatsoever, even by using violence?

EDITOR: . . . Two kinds of force can back petitions. "We shall hurt you if you do not give this," is one kind of force; it is the force of arms, whose evil results we have already examined. The second kind of force can thus be stated: "If you do not concede our demand, we shall be no longer your petitioners. You can govern us only so long as we remain the governed; we shall no longer have any dealings with you." The force implied in this may be described as love-force, soul-force, or, more popularly, but less accurately, passive resistance. This force is indestructible. He who uses it perfectly understands his position. We have an ancient proverb which literally means: "One negative cures thirty-six diseases." The force of arms is powerless when matched against the force of love or the soul.

•

READER: When you speak of driving out Western civilization, I suppose you will also say that we want no machinery?

EDITOR: . . . Machinery has begun to desolate Europe. Ruination is now knocking at the English gates. Machinery is the chief symbol of modern civilization; it represents a great sin.

The workers in the mills of Bombay have become slaves. The condition of the women working in the mills is shocking. When there were no mills, these women were not starving. If the machinery craze grows in our country, it will become an unhappy land. It may be considered a heresy, but I am bound to say that it were better for us to send money to Manchester [England] and to use flimsy Manchester cloth that to multiply mills in India. By using Manchester cloth we only waste our money; but by reproducing Manchester in India, we shall keep our money at the price of our blood, because our very moral being will be sapped, and I call in support of my statement the very mill-hands as witnesses. And those who have amassed wealth out of factories are not likely to be better than other rich men. It would be folly to assume that an Indian Rockefeller would be better than the American Rockefeller. Impoverished India can become free, but it will be hard for any India made rich through immorality to regain its freedom. I fear we shall have to admit that moneyed men support British rule; their interest is bound up with its stability. Money renders a man helpless. The other thing which is equally harmful is sexual vice. Both are poison. A snake-bite is a lesser poison than these two, because the former merely destroys the body but the latter destroy body, mind and soul. We need not, therefore, be pleased with the prospect of the growth of the mill-industry.

•

READER: What, then, would you say to the English?

EDITOR: To them I would respectfully say: "I admit you are my rulers. It is not necessary to debate the question whether you hold India by the sword or by my consent. I have no objection to your remaining in my country, but although you are the rulers, you will have to remain as servants of the people. It is not we who have to do as you wish, but it is you who have to do as we wish. You may keep the riches that you have drained away from this land, but you may not drain riches henceforth. Your function will be, if you so wish, to police India; you must abandon the idea of deriving any commercial benefit from us. We hold the civilization that you support to be the reverse of civilization. We consider our civilization to be far superior to yours. If you realize this truth, it will be to your advantage and, if you do not, according to your own proverb, you should only live in our country in the same manner as we do. You must not do anything that is contrary to our religions. It is your duty as rulers that for the sake of the Hindus you should eschew beef, and for the sake of Mahomedans you should avoid bacon and ham. We have hitherto said nothing because we have been cowed down, but you need not consider that you have not hurt our feelings by your conduct. We are not expressing our sentiments either through base selfishness or fear, but because it is our duty now to speak out boldly. We consider your schools and law courts to be useless. We want our own ancient schools and courts to be restored. The common language of India is not English but Hindi. You should therefore, learn it. We can hold communication with you only in our national language.

"It is likely that you will laugh at all this in the intoxication of your power. We may not be able to disillusion you at once; but if there be any manliness in us, you will see shortly that your intoxication is suicidal and that your laugh at our expense is an aberration of intellect. We believe that at heart you belong to a religious nation. We are living in a land which is the source of religions. How we came together need not be considered, but we can make mutual good use of our relations.

●

"You, English, who have come to India are not good specimens of the English nation, nor can we, almost half-Anglicized Indians, be considered good specimens of the real Indian nation. If the English nation were to know all you have done, it would oppose many of your actions. The mass of the Indians have had few dealings with you. If you will abandon your so-called civilization and search into your own scriptures, you find that our demands are just. Only on condition of our demands being fully satisfied may you remain in India; and if you remain under those conditions, we shall learn several things from you and you will learn many from us. So doing we shall benefit each other and the world. But that will happen only when the root of our relationship is sunk in a religious soil."

## *The United Nations*

# UNIVERSAL DECLARATION OF HUMAN RIGHTS (1948)

*The United Nations was chartered in 1945 at a conference in San Francisco attended by representatives of fifty nations from around the world. Born out of discussions among the Allied powers during the Second World War, its purpose was to provide a framework for international relations in the postwar world. The UN Charter described its ends: "to save succeeding generations from the scourge of war, . . . and to reaffirm faith in fundamental human rights, . . . and to establish conditions under which justice and respect for the obligations arising from treaties and other sources of international law can be maintained, and to promote social progress and better standards of life in larger freedom." Three years later, the UN adopted the Universal Declaration of Human Rights. In the spirit of the French Declaration of the Rights of Man and Citizen and the American Bill of Rights, it proclaims as a common international standard the kinds of civil and political rights that have been sought in modern Western nations.*

## PREAMBLE

*Whereas* recognition of the inherent dignity and of the equal and inalienable rights of all members of the human family is the foundation of freedom, justice and peace in the world,

*Whereas* disregard and contempt for human rights have resulted in barbarous acts which have outraged the conscience of mankind, and the advent of a world in which human beings shall enjoy freedom of speech and belief and freedom from fear and want has been proclaimed as the highest aspiration of the common people,

*Whereas* it is essential, if man is not to be compelled to have recourse, as a last resort, to rebellion against tyranny and oppression, that human rights should be protected by the rule of law,

*Whereas* it is essential to promote the development of friendly relations between nations,

*Whereas* the peoples of the United Nations have in the Charter reaffirmed their faith in fundamental human rights, in the dignity and worth of the human person and in the equal rights of men and women and have determined to promote social progress and better standards of life in larger freedom,

*Whereas* Member States have pledged themselves to achieve, in cooperation with the United Nations, the promotion of universal respect for and observance of human rights and fundamental freedoms,

*Whereas* a common understanding of these rights and freedoms is of the greatest importance for the full realization of this pledge,

*Now, therefore,*

*The General Assembly*

*Proclaims* this Universal Declaration of Human Rights as a common standard of achievement for all peoples and all nations, to the end that every individual and every organ of society, keeping this Declaration constantly in mind, shall strive by teaching and education to promote respect for these rights and freedoms and by progressive measures, national and international, to secure their universal and effective recognition and observance, both among the peoples of Member States themselves and among the peoples of territories under their jurisdiction.

## Article 1

All human beings are born free and equal in dignity and rights. They are endowed with reason and conscience and should act towards one another in a spirit of brotherhood.

## Article 2

Everyone is entitled to all the rights and freedoms set forth in this Declaration, without distinction of any kind, such as race, colour, sex, language, religion, political or other opinion, national or social origin, property, birth or other status.

Furthermore, no distinction shall be made on the basis of the political, jurisdictional or international status of the country or territory to which a person belongs, whether it be independent, trust, non-self-governing or under any other limitation of sovereignty.

## Article 3

Everyone has the right to life, liberty and the security of person.

## Article 4

No one shall be held in slavery or servitude; slavery and the slave trade shall be prohibited in all their forms.

## Article 5

No one shall be subjected to torture or to cruel, inhuman or degrading treatment or punishment.

## Article 6

Everyone has the right to recognition everywhere as a person before the law.

## Article 7

All are equal before the law and are entitled without any discrimination to equal protection of the law. All are entitled to equal protection against any discrimination in violation of this Declaration and against any incitement to such discrimination.

## *Article 8*

Everyone has the right to an effective remedy by the competent national tribunals for acts violating the fundamental rights granted him by the constitution or by law.

## *Article 9*

No one shall be subjected to arbitrary arrest, detention or exile.

## *Article 10*

Everyone is entitled in full equality to a fair, and public hearing by an independent and impartial tribunal, in the determination of his rights and obligations and of any criminal charge against him.

## *Article 11*

1. Everyone charged with a penal offence has the right to be presumed innocent until proved guilty according to law in a public trial at which he has had all the guarantees necessary for his defence.
2. No one shall be held guilty of any penal offence on account of any act or omission which did not constitute a penal offence, under national or international law, at the time when it was committed. Nor shall a heavier penalty be imposed than the one that was applicable at the time the penal offence was committed.

## *Article 12*

No one shall be subjected to arbitrary interference with his privacy, family, home or correspondence, nor to attacks upon his honour and reputation. Everyone has the right to the protection of the law against such interference or attacks.

## *Article 13*

1. Everyone has the right to freedom of movement and residence within the borders of each State.
2. Everyone has the right to leave any country, including his own, and to return to his country.

## *Article 14*

1. Everyone has the right to seek and to enjoy in other countries asylum from persecution.
2. This right may not be invoked in the case of prosecutions genuinely arising from non-political crimes or from acts contrary to the purposes and principles of the United Nations.

## *Article 15*

1. Everyone has the right to a nationality.
2. No one shall be arbitrarily deprived of his nationality nor denied the right to change his nationality.

## Article 16

1. Men and women of full age, without any limitation due to race, nationality or religion, have the right to marry and to found a family. They are entitled to equal rights as to marriage, during marriage and at its dissolution.
2. Marriage shall be entered into only with the free and full consent of the intending spouses.
3. The family is the natural and fundamental group unit of society and is entitled to protection by society and the State.

## Article 17

1. Everyone has the right to own property alone as well as in association with others.
2. No one shall be arbitrarily deprived of his property.

## Article 18

Everyone has the right to freedom of thought, conscience and religion; this right includes freedom to change his religion or belief, and freedom, either alone or in community with others and in public or private, to manifest his religion or belief in teaching, practice, worship and observance.

## Article 19

Everyone has the right to freedom of opinion and expression; this right includes freedom to hold opinions without interference and to seek, receive and impart information and ideas through any media and regardless of frontiers.

## Article 20

1. Everyone has the right to freedom of peaceful assembly and association.
2. No one may be compelled to belong to an association.

## Article 21

1. Everyone has the right to take part in the government of his country, directly or through freely chosen representatives.
2. Everyone has the right of equal access to public service in his country.
3. The will of the people shall be the basis of the authority of government; this will shall be expressed in periodic and genuine elections which shall be by universal and equal suffrage and shall be held by secret vote or by equivalent free voting procedures.

## Article 22

Everyone, as a member of society, has the right to social security and is entitled to realization, through national effort and international co-operation and in accordance with the organization and resources of each State, of the economic, social and cultural rights indispensable for his dignity and the free development of his personality.

## Article 23

1. Everyone has the right to work, to free choice of employment, to just and favourable conditions of work and to protection against unemployment.

2. Everyone, without any discrimination, has the right to equal pay for equal work.
3. Everyone who works has the right to just and favourable remuneration ensuring for himself and his family an existence worthy of human dignity, and supplemented, if necessary, by other means of social protection.
4. Everyone has the right to form and to join trade unions for the protection of his interests.

## *Article 24*

Everyone has the right to rest and leisure, including reasonable limitation of working hours and periodic holidays with pay.

## *Article 25*

1. Everyone has the right to a standard of living adequate for the health and well-being of himself and of his family, including food, clothing, housing and medical care and necessary social services, and the right to security in the event of unemployment, sickness, disability, widowhood, old age or other lack of livelihood in circumstances beyond his control.
2. Motherhood and childhood are entitled to special care and assistance. All children, whether born in or out of wedlock, shall enjoy the same social protection.

## *Article 26*

1. Everyone has the right to education. Education shall be free, at least in the elementary and fundamental stages. Elementary education shall be compulsory. Technical and professional education shall be made generally available and higher education shall be equally accessible to all on the basis of merit.
2. Education shall be directed to the full development of the human personality and to the strengthening of respect for human rights and fundamental freedoms. It shall promote understanding, tolerance and friendship among all nations, racial or religious groups, and shall further the activities of the United Nations for the maintenance of peace.
3. Parents have a prior right to choose the kind of education that shall be given to their children.

## *Article 27*

1. Everyone has the right freely to participate in the cultural life of the community, to enjoy the arts and to share in scientific advancement and its benefits.
2. Everyone has the right to the protection of the moral and material interests resulting from any scientific, literary or artistic production of which he is the author.

## *Article 28*

Everyone is entitled to a social and international order in which the rights and freedoms set forth in this Declaration can be fully realized.

## *Article 29*

1. Everyone has duties to the community in which alone the free and full development of his personality is possible.

2. In the exercise of his rights and freedoms, everyone shall be subject only to such limitations as are determined by law solely for the purpose of securing due recognition and respect for the rights and freedoms of others and of meeting the just requirements of morality, public order and the general welfare in a democratic society.

3. These rights and freedoms may in no case be exercised contrary to the purposes and principles of the United Nations.

## Article 30

Nothing in this Declaration may be interpreted as implying for any State, group or person any right to engage in any activity or to perform any act aimed at the destruction of any of the rights and freedoms set forth herein.

# Milovan Djilas

# *from* THE NEW CLASS (1957)

*M*ilovan Djilas (1911–1995) was born into poverty in Montenegro and studied law at *the University of Belgrade. After serving time in prison in the 1930s for opposing the roy-alist government, he became a member of the Yugoslavian Communist leadership. During the Second World War, he fought with the partisan resistance against the Nazi occupation. Following the war he became one of the most powerful men in Yugoslavia, now governed by Communist Josip Tito, and served as a cabinet minister, a vice president, and later head of the assembly. Djilas' open criticism of Tito's increasingly restrictive regime and the extravagance of high Communist officials, however, led to an abrupt end to his power: he was dismissed from office and forced from the party. Djilas then turned to publishing his political analyses, for which he would be sent to prison several times. In 1957* The New Class *was published in the West. In this work, Djilas explains how the ideals that had drawn his generation to Communism had failed: Stalinism, he writes, did not destroy exploitation but simply replaced capitalist domination with the authoritarian apparatus of the state.*

Everything happened differently in the U.S.S.R. and other communist countries from what the leaders—even such prominent ones as Lenin, Stalin, Trotsky, and Bukharin—anticipated. They expected that the state would rapidly wither away, that democracy would be strengthened. The reverse happened. They expected a rapid improvement in the standard of living—there has been scarcely any change in this respect, and in the subjugated East European countries, the standard has even declined. In every instance, the standard of living has failed to rise in proportion to the rate of industrialization, which was much more rapid. It was believed that the dif-ferences between cities and villages, between intellectual and physical labor, would slowly disappear; instead these differences have increased. Communist anticipations in other areas—including their expectations for developments in the noncommunist world—have also failed to materialize.

The greatest illusion was that industrialization and collectivization in the U.S.S.R., and destruction of capitalist ownership, would result in a classless society. In 1936, when the new [Soviet] constitution was promulgated, Stalin announced that the "exploiting class" had ceased to exist. The capitalist and other classes of ancient origin had in fact been destroyed, but a new class, previously unknown to history, had been formed.

It is understandable that this class, like those before it, should believe that the establishment of its power would result in happiness and freedom for all men. The only difference between this and other classes was that it treated the delay in the realization of its illusions more crudely. It thus affirmed that its power was more complete than the power of any other class before in history, and its class illusions and prejudices were proportionally greater.

This new class, the bureaucracy, or more accurately the political bureaucracy, has all the characteristics of earlier ones as well as some new characteristics of its own. Its origin had its special characteristics also, even though in essence it was similar to the beginnings of other classes.

Other classes, too, obtained their strength and power by the revolutionary path, destroying the political, social, and other orders they met in their way. However, almost without exception, these classes attained power *after* new economic patterns had taken shape in the old society. The case was the reverse with new classes in the communist systems. It did not come to power to *complete* a new economic order but to *establish* its own and, in so doing, to establish its power over society.

In earlier epochs the coming to power of some class, some part of a class, or of some party, was the final event resulting from its formation and its development. The reverse was true in the U.S.S.R. There the new class was definitely formed after it attained power. Its consciousness had to develop before its economic and physical powers, because the class had not taken root in the life of the nation. This class viewed its role in relation to the world from an idealistic point of view. Its practical possibilities were not diminished by this. In spite of its illusions, it represented an objective tendency toward industrialization. Its practical bent emanated from this tendency. The promise of an ideal world increased the faith in the ranks of the new class and sowed illusions among the masses. At the same time it inspired gigantic physical undertakings.

Because this new class had not been formed as a part of the economic and social life before it came to power, it could only be created in an organization of a special type, distinguished by a special discipline based on identical philosophic and ideological views of its members. A unity of belief and iron discipline was necessary to overcome its weaknesses.

The roots of the new class were implanted in a special party, of the Bolshevik type. Lenin was right in his view that his party was an exception in the history of human society, although he did not suspect that it would be the beginning of a new class.

To be more precise, the initiators of the new class are not found in the party of the Bolshevik type as a whole but in that stratum of professional revolutionaries who made up its core even before it attained power. It was not by accident that Lenin asserted after the failure of the 1905 revolution that only professional revolutionaries—men whose sole profession was revolutionary work—could build a new party of the Bolshevik type. It was still less accidental that even Stalin, the future creator of a new class, was the most outstanding example of such a professional revolutionary. The new ruling class has been gradually developing from this very narrow stratum of revolutionaries. These revolutionaries composed its core for a long period. Trotsky noted that in prerevolutionary professional revolutionaries was the origin of the future Stalinist bureaucrat. What he did not detect was the beginning of a new class of owners and exploiters.

This is not to say that the new party and the new class are identical. The party, however, is the core of that class, and its base. It is very difficult, perhaps impossible, to define the limits of the new class and to identify its members. The new class may be said to be made up of those who have special privileges and economic preference because of the administrative monopoly they hold.

As in other owning classes, the proof that it is a special class lies in its ownership and its special relations to other classes. In the same way, the class to which a member belongs is indicated by the material and other privileges which ownership brings to him.

As defined by Roman law, property constitutes the use, enjoyment, and disposition of material goods. The communist political bureaucracy uses, enjoys, and disposes of nationalized property.

If we assume that membership in this bureaucracy or new owning class is predicated on the use of privileges inherent in ownership—in this instance nationalized material goods—then membership in the new party class, or political bureaucracy, is reflected in a larger income in material goods and privileges than society should normally grant for such functions. In practice, the ownership privilege of the new class manifests itself as an exclusive right, as a party monopoly, for the political bureaucracy to distribute the national income, to set wages, direct economic development, and dispose of nationalized and other property. This is the way it appears to the ordinary man who considers the communist functionary as being very rich and as a man who does not have to work.

The ownership of private property has, for many reasons, proved to be unfavorable for the establishment of the new class's authority. Besides, the destruction of private ownership was necessary for the economic transformation of nations. The new class obtains its power, privileges, ideology, and its customs from one specific form of ownership—collective ownership—which the class administers and distributes in the name of the nation and society.

The new class maintains that ownership derives from a designated social relationship. This is the relationship between the monopolists of administration, who constitute a narrow and closed stratum, and the mass of producers (farmers, workers, and intelligentsia) who have no rights. But that is not all, since the communist bureaucracy also has complete monopolistic control over material assets.

Every substantive change in the social relationship between those who monopolize administration and those who work is inevitably reflected in the ownership relationship. Social and political relations and ownership—the totalitarianism of government and the monopoly of ownership—are being more fully brought into accord in communism than in any other political system.

To divest communists of their ownership rights would be to abolish them as a class. To compel them to relinquish their other social powers, so that workers may participate in sharing the profits of their work—which capitalists have had to permit as a result of strikes and parliamentary action—would mean that communists were being deprived of their monopoly over property, ideology, and government. This would be the beginning of democracy and freedom in communism, the end of communist monopolism and totalitarianism. Until this happens, there can be no indication that important, fundamental changes are taking place in communist systems, at least not in the eyes of men who think seriously about social progress.

The ownership privileges of the new class and membership in that class are the privileges of *administration*. This privilege extends from state administration and the administration of economic enterprises to that of sports and humanitarian organizations. Political, party, or so-called general leadership is executed by the core. This position of leadership carries privileges with it. In his *Stalin au pouvoir*, published in Paris in 1951, Orlov states that the average pay of a worker in the U.S.S.R. in 1935 was 1,800 rubles annually, while the pay and allowances of the secretary of a rayon committee amounted to 45,000 rubles annually. The situation has changed since then for both workers and party functionaries, but the essence remains the same. Other authors have arrived at the same conclusions. Discrepancies between the pay of workers and party functionaries are extreme; this could not be hidden from persons visiting the U.S.S.R. or other communist countries in the past few years.

Other systems, too, have their professional politicians. One can think well or ill of them, but they must exist. Society cannot live without a state or a government, and therefore it cannot live without those who fight for it.

However, there are fundamental differences between professional politicians in other systems and in the communist system. In extreme cases, politicians in other systems use the government to secure privileges for themselves and their cohorts, or to favor the economic interests of one social stratum or another. The situation is different with the communist system where the power and the government are identical with the use, enjoyment, and disposition of almost all the nation's goods. He who grabs power grabs privileges and indirectly grabs property. Consequently, in communism, power or politics as a profession is the ideal of those who have the desire or the prospect of living as parasites at the expense of others.

Membership in the Communist party before the revolution meant sacrifice. Being a professional revolutionary was one of the highest honors. Now that the party has consolidated its power, party membership means that one belongs to a privileged class. And at the core of the party are the all-powerful exploiters and masters.

For a long time the communist revolution and the communist system have been concealing their real nature. The emergence of the new class has been concealed under socialist phraseology and, more important, under the new collective forms of property ownership. The so-called socialist ownership is a disguise for the real ownership by the political bureaucracy. And in the beginning this bureaucracy was in a hurry to complete industrialization, and hid its class composition under that guise.

No class is established by deliberate design, even though its ascent is accompanied by an organized and conscious struggle. This holds true for the new class in communism, but it also embodies some special characteristics. Since the hold of the new class on economic life and on the social structure was fairly precarious, and since it was fated to arise within a specific party, it required the highest possible degree of organization, as well as a consistent effort to present a united, balanced, class-conscious front. This is why the new class is better organized and more highly class conscious than any class in recorded history.

This proposition is true only if it is taken relatively; consciousness and organizational structure being taken in relation to the outside world and to other classes, powers, and social forces. No other class in history has been as cohesive and single-minded in defending itself and in controlling that which it holds—collective and monopolistic ownership and totalitarian authority.

On the other hand, the new class is also the most deluded and least conscious of itself. Every private capitalist or feudal lord was conscious of the fact that he belonged to a special discernible social category. He usually believed that this category was destined to make the human race happy and that without this category chaos and general ruin would ensue. A communist member of the new class also believes that without his party, society would regress and founder. But he is not conscious of the fact that he belongs to a new ownership class, for he does not consider himself an owner and does not take into account the special privileges he enjoys. He thinks that he belongs to a group with prescribed ideas, aims, attitudes, and roles. That is all he sees. He cannot see that at the same time he belongs to a special social category: the *ownership* class.

The new class instinctively feels that national goods are, in fact, its property, and that even the terms *socialist, social,* and *state* property denote a general legal fiction. The new class also thinks that any breach of its totalitarian authority might imperil its ownership. Consequently, the new class opposes *any* type of freedom, ostensibly for the purpose of preserving "socialist" ownership. Criticism of the new class's monopolistic administration of property generates the fear of a possible loss of power. The new class is sensitive to these criticisms and demands depending on the extent to which they expose the manner in which it rules and holds power.

This is an important contradiction. Property is legally considered social and national property. But, in actuality, a single group manages it in its own interest. The discrepancy between legal and actual conditions continuously results in obscure and abnormal social and economic relationships. It also means that the words of the leading group do not correspond to its actions and that all actions result in strengthening its property holdings and its political position.

This contradiction cannot be resolved without jeopardizing the class's position. Other ruling, property-owning classes could not resolve this contradiction either, unless forcefully deprived of monopoly of power and ownership. Wherever there has been a higher degree of freedom for society as a whole, the ruling classes have been forced, in one way or another, to renounce monopoly of ownership. The reverse is true also: Wherever monopoly of ownership has been impossible, freedom, to some degree, has become inevitable.

In defending its authority, the ruling class must execute reforms every time it becomes obvious to the people that the class is treating national property as its own. Such reforms are not proclaimed as being what they really are but, rather, as part of the "further development of socialism" and "socialist democracy." The groundwork for reforms is laid when the discrepancy mentioned above becomes public. From the historical point of view the new class is forced to fortify its authority and ownership constantly, even though it is running away from the truth. It must constantly demonstrate how it is successfully creating a society of happy people, all of whom enjoy equal rights and have been freed of every type of exploitation. The new class cannot avoid falling continuously into profound internal contradictions; for in spite of its historical origin it is not able to make its ownership lawful, and it cannot renounce ownership without undermining itself. Consequently, it is forced to try to justify its increasing authority, invoking abstract and unreal purposes.

This is a class whose power over men is the most complete known to history. For this reason it is a class with very limited views, views which are shaky because they are based on falsehoods. Closely knit, isolated, and in complete authority, the new class must unrealistically evaluate its own role and that of the people around it.

Having achieved industrialization, the new class can now do nothing more than strengthen its brute force and pillage the people. It ceases to create. Its spiritual heritage is overtaken by darkness.

While the revolution can be considered an epochal accomplishment of the new class, its methods of rule fill some of the most shameful pages in history. Men will marvel at the grandiose ventures it accomplished and will be ashamed of the means it used.

When the new class leaves the historical scene—and this must happen—there will be less sorrow over its passing than there was for any other class before it. Smothering everything except what suited its ego, it has condemned itself to failure and shameful ruin.

# *Frantz Fanon*

# *from* THE WRETCHED OF THE EARTH (1961)

*Frantz Fanon (1925–1961) was born in Martinique, an overseas territory of France, and served in the French army during the Second World War. Later he completed studies in medicine at the University of Lyon, specializing in psychiatry. His psychiatric work in the Antilles led to his first book,* Black Skin, White Masks *(1952), a study of the psychological effects of racism. From 1953 to 1956, Fanon served as head of psychiatry at a hospital in Algeria, where a revolutionary movement was fighting for independence from France. While there he joined the rebel movement and became editor of its newspaper and, in 1960, ambassador to Ghana from the Provisional Government.* The Wretched of the Earth *was published just before Fanon died from cancer at 36. Speaking from his experiences as psychiatrist, revolutionary, and member of a colonized people, Fanon issued an impassioned analysis of the process of decolonization sweeping across the Third World. Imperialism had been so violent, he argued, that only violence would undo its effects. Fanon's book spoke powerfully to colonized peoples and European intellectuals: in Jean-Paul Sartre's words, he was "the first since Engels to bring the processes of history into the clear light of day."*

National liberation, national renaissance, the restoration of nationhood to the people, commonwealth: whatever may be the headings used or the new formulas introduced, decolonization is always a violent phenomenon. At whatever level we study it—relationships between individuals, new names for sports clubs, the human admixture at cocktail parties, in the police, on the directing boards of national or private banks—decolonization is quite simply the replacing of a certain "species" of men by another "species" of men. Without any period of transition, there is a total, complete, and absolute substitution. It is true that we could equally well stress the rise of a new nation, the setting up of a new state, its diplomatic relations, and its economic and political trends. But we have precisely chosen to speak of that kind of *tabula rasa* which characterizes at the outset all decolonization. Its unusual importance is that it constitutes, from the very first day, the minimum demands of the colonized. To tell the truth, the proof of success lies in a whole social structure being changed from the bottom up. The extraordinary importance of this change is that it is willed, called for, demanded. The need for this change exists in its crude state, impetuous

369

and compelling, in the consciousness and in the lives of the men and women who are colonized. But the possibility of this change is equally experienced in the form of a terrifying future in the consciousness of another "species" of men and women: the colonizers.

Decolonization, which sets out to change the order of the world, is, obviously, a program of complete disorder. But it cannot come as a result of magical practices, nor of a natural shock, nor of a friendly understanding. Decolonization, as we know, is a historical process: that is to say that it cannot be understood, it cannot become intelligible nor clear to itself except in the exact measure that we can discern the movements which give it historical form and content. Decolonization is the meeting of two forces, opposed to each other by their very nature, which in fact owe their originality to that sort of substantification which results from and is nourished by the situation in the colonies. Their first encounter was marked by violence and their existence together— that is to say the exploitation of the native by the settler—was carried on by dint of a great array of bayonets and cannons. The settler and the native are old acquaintances. In fact, the settler is right when he speaks of knowing "them" well. For it is the settler who has brought the native into existence and who perpetuates his existence. The settler owes the fact of his very existence, that is to say, his property, to the colonial system.

Decolonization never takes place unnoticed, for it influences individuals and modifies them fundamentally. It transforms spectators crushed with their inessentiality into privileged actors, with the grandiose glare of history's floodlights upon them. It brings a natural rhythm into existence, introduced by new men, and with it a new language and a new humanity. Decolonization is the veritable creation of new men. But this creation owes nothing of its legitimacy to any supernatural power; the "thing" which has been colonized becomes man during the same process by which it frees itself.

In decolonization, there is therefore the need of a complete calling in question of the colonial situation. If we wish to describe it precisely, we might find it in the well-known words: "The last shall be first and the first last." Decolonization is the putting into practice of this sentence. That is why, if we try to describe it, all decolonization is successful.

The naked truth of decolonization evokes for us the searing bullets and blood-stained knives which emanate from it. For if the last shall be first, this will only come to pass after a murderous and decisive struggle between the two protagonists. That affirmed intention to place the last at the head of things, and to make them climb at a pace (too quickly, some say) the well-known steps which characterize an organized society, can only triumph if we use all means to turn the scale, including, of course, that of violence.

You do not turn any society, however primitive it may be, upside down with such a program if you have not decided from the very beginning, that is to say from the actual formulation of that program, to overcome all the obstacles that you will come across in so doing. The native who decides to put the program into practice, and to become its moving force, is ready for violence at all times. From birth it is clear to him that this narrow world, strewn with prohibitions, can only be called in question by absolute violence.

The colonial world is a world divided into compartments. It is probably unnecessary to recall the existence of native quarters and European quarters, of schools for natives and schools for Europeans; in the same way we need not recall apartheid in South Africa. Yet, if we examine closely this system of compartments, we will at least be able to reveal the lines of force it implies. This approach to the colonial world, its ordering and its geographical layout will allow us to mark out the lines on which a decolonized society will be reorganized.

The colonial world is a world cut in two. The dividing line, the frontiers are shown by barracks and police stations. In the colonies it is the policeman and the soldier who are the official, instituted go-betweens, the spokesmen of the settler and his rule of oppression. In capitalist societies the educational system, whether lay or clerical, the structure of moral reflexes handed down from father to son, the exemplary honesty of workers who are given a medal after fifty years of good and loyal service, and the affection which springs from harmonious relations and good behavior—all these aesthetic expressions of respect for the established order serve to create around the exploited person an atmosphere of submission and of inhibition which lightens the task of policing considerably. In the capitalist countries a multitude of moral teachers, counselors and "bewilderers" separate the exploited from those in power. In the colonial countries, on the contrary, the policeman and the soldier, by their immediate presence and their frequent and direct action maintain contact with the native and advise him by means of rifle butts and napalm not to budge. It is obvious here that the agents of government speak the language of pure force. The intermediary does not lighten the oppression, nor seek to hide the domination; he shows them up and puts them into practice with the clear conscience of an upholder of the peace; yet he is the bringer of violence into the home and into the mind of the native.

The zone where the natives live is not complementary to the zone inhabited by the settlers. The two zones are opposed, but not in the service of a higher unity. Obedient to the rules of pure Aristotelian logic, they both follow the principle of reciprocal exclusivity. No conciliation is possible, for of the two terms, one is superfluous. The settlers' town is a strongly built town, all made of stone and steel. It is a brightly lit town; the streets are covered with asphalt, and the garbage cans swallow all the leavings, unseen, unknown and hardly thought about. The settler's feet are never visible, except perhaps in the sea; but there you're never close enough to see them. His feet are protected by strong shoes although the streets of his town are clean and even, with no holes or stones. The settler's town is a well-fed town, an easygoing town; its belly is always full of good things. The settlers' town is a town of white people, of foreigners.

The town belonging to the colonized people, or at least the native town, the Negro village, the medina, the reservation, is a place of ill fame, peopled by men of evil repute. They are born there, it matters little where or how; they die there, it matters not where, nor how. It is a world without spaciousness; men live there on top of each other, and their huts are built one on top of the other. The native town is a hungry town, starved of bread, of meat, of shoes, of coal, of light. The native town is a crouching village, a town on its knees, a town wallowing in the mire. It is a town of niggers and dirty Arabs. The look that the native turns on the settler's town is a look of lust, a look of envy; it expresses his dreams of possession—all manner of possession: to sit at the settler's table, to sleep in the settler's bed, with his wife if possible. The colonized man is an envious man. And this the settler knows very well; when their glances meet he ascertains bitterly, always on the defensive, "They want to take our place." It is true, for there is no native who does not dream at least once a day of setting himself up in the settler's place.

This world divided into compartments, this world cut in two is inhabited by two different species. The originality of the colonial context is that economic reality, inequality, and the immense difference of ways of life never come to mask the human realities. When you examine at close quarters the colonial context, it is evident that what parcels out the world is to begin with the fact of belonging to or not belonging to a given race, a given species. In the colonies the economic substructure is also a superstructure. The cause is the consequence; you are rich because you are white, you are white because you are rich. This is why Marxist analysis should always be slightly stretched every time we have to do with the colonial problem.

Everything up to and including the very nature of precapitalist society, so well explained by Marx, must here be thought out again. The serf is in essence different from the knight, but a reference to divine right is necessary to legitimize this statutory difference. In the colonies, the foreigner coming from another country imposed his rule by means of guns and machines. In defiance of his successful transplantation, in spite of his appropriation, the settler still remains a foreigner. It is neither the act of owning factories, nor estates, nor a bank balance which distinguishes the governing classes. The governing race is first and foremost those who come from elsewhere, those who are unlike the original inhabitants, "the others."

The violence which has ruled over the ordering of the colonial world, which has ceaselessly drummed the rhythm for the destruction of native social forms and broken up without reserve the systems of reference of the economy, the customs of dress and external life, that same violence will be claimed and taken over by the native at the moment when, deciding to embody history in his own person, he surges into the forbidden quarters. To wreck the colonial world is henceforward a mental picture of action which is very clear, very easy to understand and which may be assumed by each one of the individuals which constitute the colonized people. To break up the colonial world does not mean that after the frontiers have been abolished lines of communication will be set up between the two zones. The destruction of the colonial world is no more and no less that the abolition of one zone, its burial in the depths of the earth or its expulsion from the country.

*—trans. Constance Farrington*

# C.L.R. James

## *from* OLD SCHOOL-TIE (1963)

*C.L.R. James (1901–89) was a playwright, historian, literary critic, journalist, revolutionary Marxist, and pan-Africanist. Born and educated in Trinidad, he also spent significant periods of time in Britain, the United States, and Ghana. For three months in 1948, he lived at the Pyramid Lake Divorce Ranch in Northern Nevada, where, while waiting for his divorce, he wrote a book on the philosopher Hegel. His work on the manuscript was only interrupted by trips to Reno where he played and lost on the slot machines. James was passionate about cricket, and, during his original stay in England in the 1930s, he wrote on cricket matches for the* Manchester Guardian. *For James, cricket was more than a game: originally English, it was a cultural practice on which the Caribbean had placed its own stamp. Similarly, as he suggests in "Old School-Tie," his own identity was multicultural. A passionate opponent of the British Empire, he was nonetheless steeped in English values, as his observations of American culture suggest.*

What was it that so linked my Aunt Judith with cricket as I, a colonial, experienced it? The answer is in one word: Puritanism; more specifically, restraint, and restraint in a personal sense. But that restraint, did we learn it only on the cricket field, in *The Captain* and the *Boy's Own Paper*, in the pervading influence of the university men who taught me, as I once believed? I don't think so. I absorbed it from Judith and from my mother—it was in essence the same code—and I was learning it very early from my *Vanity Fair*.

•

I laughed without satiety at Thackeray's constant jokes and sneers and gibes at the aristocracy and at people in high places. Thackeray, not Marx, bears the heaviest responsibility for me.

But the things I did not notice and took for granted were more enduring: the British reticence, the British self-discipline, the stiff lips, upper and lower.

•

If Judith [like a Thackeray character] had been a literary person that is the way she would have spoken. The West Indian masses did not care a damn about this. They shouted and stamped and yelled and expressed themselves fully in anger and joy then, as they do to this day, whether they are in Bridgetown or Birmingham. But they knew the code as it applied to sport, they expected us, the educated, the college boys, to maintain it; and if any English touring team or any member of it fell short they were merciless in their condemnation and shook their heads over it for years afterwards. Not only the English masters, but Englishmen in their relation to games in the colonies held tightly to the code as example and as a mark of differentiation.

I was an actor on a stage in which the parts were set in advance. I not only took it to an extreme, I seemed to have been made by nature for nothing else. There were others around me who did not go as far and as completely as I did. There was another cultural current in the island, French and Spanish, which shaped other characters. I have heard from acute observers that in Barbados, an island which has known no other strain but British, the code was unadulterated and even more severe. . . . In an article welcoming the West Indies team of 1957 E. W. Swanton has written in the *Daily Telegraph* that in the West Indies the cricket ethic has shaped not only the cricketers but social life as a whole. It is an understatement. There is a whole generation of us, and perhaps two generations, who have been formed by it not only in social attitudes but in our most intimate personal lives, in fact there more than anywhere else. The social attitudes we could to some degree alter if we wished. For the inner self the die was cast. But that is not my theme except incidentally. The coming West Indies novelists will show the clash between the native temperament and environment, and this doctrine from a sterner clime.

The depth psychologists may demur. I can help them. Long before I had begun my immersion into *Vanity Fair*, when I was so small that I had to be taken to school, I would refuse to leave the school grounds with the older child who brought me in the morning. I would fight and resist in order to watch the big boys playing cricket, and I would do this until my grandmother came for me and dragged me home protesting. I was once knocked down by a hard on-drive, my ear bled for a day or two and I carefully hid it by exemplary and voluntary washings. Later, when reading elementary English history books, I became resentful of the fact that the English always won all, or nearly all, of the battles and read every new history book I could find, searching out and noting the battles they had lost. I would not deny that early influences I could know nothing about had cast me in a certain mould or even that I was born with certain characteristics. That could be. What interests me, and is, I think, of general interest, is that as far back as I can trace my consciousness the original found itself and came to maturity within a system that was the result of centuries of development in another land, was transplanted as a hot-house flower is transplanted and bore some strange fruit.

Along with restraint, not so much externally as in internal inhibitions, we learnt loyalty. It is good to be loyal to what you believe in—that, however, may be tautology. Loyalty to what is wrong, outmoded, reactionary is mischievous. To that in general all will agree, even the reactionary. The most profound loyalty can co-exist with a jealously critical attitude. Should loyalty be taught? Can it be taught? Or must it be learned? I don't know the answers to these questions, and perhaps they are too abstract. I am not asking them as a syllogistic exercise. The national characteristics of great nations are involved. Here are the concrete facts.

At the school we learnt not only to play with the team. We were taught and learnt loyalty in the form of loyalty to the school. As with everything else in those days, I took it for granted. It was only long afterwards, after gruesome experience in another country, that I saw it for the specifically British thing that it was.

•

My attitude to the code was not merely critical. It was, if anything, contemptuous. I had said good-bye to all that. I didn't know how deeply the early attitudes had been ingrained in me and how foreign they were to other peoples until I sat at baseball matches with friends, some of them university men, and saw and heard the howls of anger and rage and denunciation which they hurled at the players as a matter of course. I could not understand them and they could not understand me either—they asked anxiously if I were enjoying the game. I was enjoying the game; it was they who were disturbing me. And not only they. Managers and players protested against adverse decisions as a matter of course, and sometimes, after bitter quarrels, were ordered off the field, fined and punished in other ways. When I played in some friendly games, from the start the players shouted and yelled at one another, even at their own side. One day I explained cricket to friends at a camp and at their request organized a little game with bats hacked from pieces of wood, and a rubber ball. As soon as the fielders took position, they burst out with hue and cry, and when a ball was hit towards a fieldsman his own side seemed to pursue him like the hounds of heaven until he had gathered the ball and thrown it in.

All this seemed natural to them. It was very strange to me. However, I ignored it as differences of national character and outlook. If they played that way that was their way.

Then in 1950 came a series of events which I could not ignore. Day after day there appeared in the Press authenticated reports that university basketball teams had sold out games or played for results arranged beforehand, in return for money from bookmakers. The reports continued until an astounding number of teams from the best schools in the United States had been found guilty of these crimes. One case which particularly struck me was that of a boy who had taken the money, had hidden it in the basement of his house and left it there. When questioned, it appeared from his answers that he had had no idea of what to do with so large a sum and so had put it away and out of his mind. My usual restraint vanished and I expressed my horror to my friends with an unaccustomed freedom that astonished them. Unaccustomed, because from the first day of my stay in the United States to the last I never made the mistake that so many otherwise intelligent Europeans make of trying to fit that country into European standards. Perhaps for one reason, because of my colonial background, I always saw it for what it was and not for what I thought it ought to be. I took in my stride the cruelties and anomalies that shocked me and the immense vitality, generosity and audacity of these strange people. But this was too much—how could these young men behave in that way? Before I could choose my words I found myself saying that adults in Trinidad or in Britain, in the world of business or private life, could or would do anything, more or less. But in the adult world of sport, certainly in cricket, despite the tricks teams played upon one another, I had never heard of any such thing and did not believe it possible. That young men playing for school or university should behave in this way on such a scale was utterly shocking to me.

Shock succeeded shock. My friends and associates were chiefly political people. Some of them, young university graduates or students themselves, had demonstrated that they could not be shifted from their political and social principles by threats of gaol or promise of any material benefit. Some of them had rejected all the bribes offered by wealthy parents to return to the fold of Democrats or Republicans. But to my outburst they shrugged their shoulders and could not understand what I was talking about. The boys were wrong in being caught, that was all. The school? Why should they put 'the school' above what they wanted? Would one of them do such a thing? After some brief thought the answer was always: 'No. I am not interested in that sort of business. I don't want to get money from a bookie or to help him with money from another bookie or from the public. But if the bookie wants to and the players want to, I couldn't care less.'

As one of the older ones, I was among those responsible for the general education of these young people. I didn't press the matter, but it would not let me rest. I found, too, that the unusual definiteness of my views, my instinctive repulsion, had made some impression upon some of them. They felt for the first time that something was wrong with their own attitude, though what it was they could not say.

Periodically we returned to it. Older ones and I exchanged the practices, events and ideas of our early days. I left the United States, but the discussion continued, and we have arrived at some conclusions. These young people had no loyalties to school because they had no loyalties to anything. They had a universal distrust of their elders and preceptors, which had begun with distrust of their teachers. Each had had to work out his own individual code. Too many of them have assured me of this as true, not only of themselves but of their friends, for it to be the quirk of a few egotistic individuals. In 1956 Hollywood, as Hollywood will today, stated the case in that revealing film *Rebel Without a Cause:* though, as Hollywood does, it dodged any serious attempt to investigate either causes or conclusions. So do I. This is not the place for it. I merely record the immensity of the gulf that suddenly opened between me and people to whom I was so closely bound, speaking the same language, reading the same books and both of us ready when we had nothing better to do to make our jokes at the old school-tie.

When the discussions began they had looked at me a little strangely. I, a colonial born and bred, a Marxist, declared enemy of British imperialism and all its ways and works, was the last person they had expected that sort of thing from. By the time we had discussed for some little while I was looking at myself a little strangely. At the age of fifty I was questioning what from the time I had met it forty years before I had accepted and never questioned. I could be ribald about the old school-tie but the school itself had done me no harm. I hadn't allowed it to. I had read the stories of boys who had been unhappy at school. My Puritan soul had not been too sympathetic to them. But that there were people of my own way of thinking in the important things of my life who were utterly indifferent as to whether the boys in their old school or any other school sold games for money or not, that had never crossed my provincial mind. Where, I asked myself, would they want to send their own children to school? Where indeed? Not only they had to answer it. I too had to give some answer.

# Christa Wolf

# *from* A CHANGING VIEWPOINT (1970)

*Christa Wolf (1929–) grew up in the Nazi era in central Germany. Her semiautobio-
graphical novel about this period begins with these words: "What is past is not dead; it is
not even past. We cut ourselves off from it; we pretend to be strangers." After the Second
World War, Wolf and her family lived in the German Democratic Republic (East Germany), where she attended the universities of Jena and Leipzig. In her thirties, she
achieved success as a novelist whose works received attention in both East and West Germany. Her best-known novel,* The Quest for Christa T. *(1968), concerns a woman's
reflections on the effects of socialism on the individual; praised in the West, it was banned
at home. Wolf's later work deals with feminist and pacifist themes and the compromises
she and other writers made to survive in a police state. In the piece excerpted here, "A
Changing Viewpoint," Wolf deals with a familiar theme: the inextricable intertwining of
individual stories, national histories, and politics. Told from the viewpoint of a young
German refugee fleeing from the advancing Russian army, it describes the day of "liberation" at the war's end.*

•

I am to write about liberation, the hour of liberation. Nothing easier, I thought. After
all these years, that hour still stands clearly before me, ready in my memory, and if
there have been reasons not to touch it until today, then twenty-five years should have
wiped them out or at least softened them. I needed only to give the word and the
machine would begin to work and everything would appear on paper, a sequence of
clear, exact pictures, as if of their own free will. Unexpectedly, I got stuck with the
question of what my grandmother was wearing on the way; from there I got to the
stranger who had changed me into himself and who is now someone else again and
passes different judgments, and finally I have to admit that nothing will come of the
sequence of pictures; the memory is not like a set of folding pictures, liberation does not
depend on a date or accidental movements of the Allied troops but surely, too, on difficult and long-drawn-out movements within oneself. And if time wipes out some reasons
it certainly brings forth others, again and again, and makes it more and more difficult to
decide on a specific hour. It is necessary to state clearly what one was liberated from and

perhaps, too, if one is conscientious, for what purpose. The next thing one recalls is the end of a childhood fear—Storekeeper Rambow, who was no doubt a worthy man—and looks for a new starting point, which is again only a bit nearer, so one leaves it at that. The end of my fear of low-flying planes. You've made your bed, now you must lie in it, Kalle would say, if he were still alive, but I suppose he is dead, like many of the people concerned (yes, death wipes out reasons).

Dead like Foreman Wilhelm Grund, when a low-flying plane shot him in the stomach. That was the first death I saw, at sixteen, pretty late for those days, I should add. (I don't count the infant I handed up in a stiff bundle to a refugee woman on a truck. I didn't see it, I only heard its mother scream, and ran away.) It was a pure accident that Wilhelm Grund was in my place, for nothing but chance had kept my uncle in the barn with a sick horse that morning, instead of our going on with the others as usual in Grund's oxcart. We ought to have been there, too, I said to myself, and not where people were safe, although we heard the firing and the fifteen horses stamping about wildly. Since then I've always been afraid of horses, but I've been more afraid of the faces of people who are forced to see what no human being should see. Gerhard Grund, the farm boy, had a face like that when he pushed open the barn door, took a couple of steps and then collapsed: Herr Volk, what have they done to my father?

He was my age. His father lay in the dust at the side of the road beside his oxen, staring up, into heaven, you might say if you insisted. I could see that nothing would ever change that stare, not his wife's moans or the whimpering of his three children. This time they forgot to tell us not to look. Quick, said Herr Volk, we must get away from here. They might have seized me and dragged me over to the edge of the wood just as they seized that dead man by the arms and legs. Any one of us, myself included, would have had a tarpaulin from the barn floor instead of a coffin. I should have gone down into the grave without a prayer or a song, like the farmer, Wilhelm Grund. They would have wept for me, too, and then moved on, because we could not stay there. They wouldn't have wanted to talk for a long time, and we didn't either, and then they would have had to think what to do to keep themselves alive and, as we did then, they would have broken off long birch boughs and spread them over our cart, as if moving birchwood could have held off those foreign pilots. Everything, everything would have been the same, only I no longer would have been there. And the difference that meant everything to me meant almost nothing to most of the others. Gerhard Grund took his father's place and whipped up the oxen, and Herr Volk nodded to him: Good boy. Your father died like a soldier.

I didn't really believe this. A soldier's death wasn't described like that in school readers or in the newspapers. I told the last court with which I was in constant contact, and which I called God, although with some scruples and reservations, that according to my convictions a father of four children or anyone else for that matter, shouldn't end like that. It's war, after all, said Herr Volk, and that was true and it had to be, but I could plead that this was true and it had to be, but I could plead that this was a deviation from the ideal of death for Führer and Reich, and I didn't ask whom my mother meant when, putting her arms around Frau Grund, she said aloud: The criminals. The accursed criminals.

It fell to me, because I happened to have the watch, to signal with a whistle the next attack, two American fighters. The birchwood could be seen far and wide, as I had thought, as easy prey on the empty road. Everyone who could jumped off the cart and threw himself into the ditch. I did, too, but this time I didn't bury my face in the sand but lay on my back and went on eating my sandwich. I didn't want to die and I certainly wasn't defying death and I knew what fear was better than I could have wished. But you don't die twice on one day. I wanted to see who shot at me, for the thought struck me that there were a couple of individuals in each plane. First I saw the white star under the wings, then as they throttled the engines for another dive I saw the pilots' helmets quite clearly and finally even the bare white spots of their faces. I had seen prisoners, but this was the attacking enemy face to face; I knew I should hate them, and it seemed queer that I wondered for a moment if they enjoyed what they were doing. In any case, they soon gave it up.

When we got back to the cart one of the oxen, the one they called Heinrich, fell to his knees before us. The blood shot out of his neck. My uncle and my grandfather took off his harness and grandfather, who hadn't opened his mouth when he stood beside the dead Wilhelm Grund, began pouring curses out of his toothless mouth. An innocent creature, he said hoarsely, the bastards, damn them, the damned dogs, all of them, every damned one of them. I was afraid he was going to weep and wanted him to get it all off his chest. I forced myself to look at the dying ox for a full minute. It couldn't be reproach in his eyes, but why did I feel guilty? Herr Volk handed my uncle his hunting gun and showed him the place behind the ox's ear. We were sent away. I turned round when the shot rang out. The ox fell heavily on his side. The women were busy all evening preparing the meat. It was already dark when we sat in the straw eating our stew. Kalle, who had complained bitterly of being hungry, supped greedily out of his bowl, wiped his mouth on his sleeve and began to sing croakily: All mops dogs bark, all mops dogs bark, only little rollmops doesn't . . . The devil take you, you meshuge old man, my grandfather shouted at him. Kalle fell back on the straw and drew his jacket over his head.

•

You needn't be afraid when everyone else is afraid. It is certainly reassuring to know this, but liberation came first and I shall write down today what I can find in my memory. It was the morning of May 5th, a glorious day. Panic broke out again when it appeared that we were surrounded by Soviet tanks. The word came—quick march to Schwerin, the Americans are there, and anyone who was still able to think should have wondered why we all pushed on towards the enemy that had been chasing us for days. None of what was now possible seemed to me desirable or even bearable, but the world obstinately refused to come to an end and we were not prepared to find our way about after it had failed to do so. So I understood the gruesome answer a woman gave when they told her that the Führer's long-awaited miracle weapon could only destroy us all together now, enemies and Germans. Well, let it, said the woman.

A sandy path led past the houses in the village. Outside a red-brick farmhouse a soldier was washing himself at the pump. He had rolled up the sleeves of his white undershirt. He stood there legs astraddle and called out to us: The Führer's dead, as if he were saying: Nice day today.

The tone he used upset me more than the knowledge that he was speaking the truth.

I trotted along beside the cart, hearing the driver's hoarse shouts of encouragement to the exhausted horses. I saw the smoldering fire by the roadside where Wehrmacht officers had burnt their papers, saw piles of guns and hand grenades lined up ghost-like in the ditches, saw typewriters, suitcases, radios and all sorts of valuable war matériel pointlessly lining our path and I had to keep on reminding myself of the tone of a remark that ought to have reverberated between heaven and earth, I thought, instead of sounding so ordinary.

Then came the paper. Suddenly the road was snowed under with it; they were tossing it wildly out of Wehrmacht cars: forms, mobilization orders, documents, minutes of court cases, command headquarters orders, top secret papers, statistics of casualties from double-locked safes that no one bothered about anymore now that they were thrown down in front of them. As if there were something disgusting about all this confused mass of paper I didn't stop to pick up a single sheet, something I regretted later on, but I did pick up the cans of food a truck driver threw down to me. The sweep of his arm reminded me of the way I had swung my arm so often that summer of 1939 when I had thrown packs of cigarettes at the dusty column of vehicles as they rolled eastward day and night past our house. That was six years ago and I had ceased to be a child since then, summer had come again, but I had no idea what I should do with it.

A Wehrmacht unit had abandoned its supplies on a side road. Whoever came past took what he could carry. The caravan broke up, people went mad with greed just as before they had been mad with fear. Only Kalle laughed as he heaved a great block of butter over to our cart, clapped his hands and shouted gaily: Hey, you little devil! It's enough to make you kick up your heels in sheer madness.

Then we saw concentration camp inmates. The rumor that the prisoners of Oranienburg were being herded along behind us had haunted us like a specter. It did not occur to me then that we, too, were fleeing from them. They stood at the edge of the wood and peered at us. We could have signaled to them that the way was clear, but no one did so. They approached the road cautiously. They did not look like any-one I had ever seen before and that we all involuntarily edged away from them did not surprise me. But this edging away betrayed us; whatever we might tell ourselves or each other: we knew about them. All of us wretched people who had been driven away from our possessions, our farms or big country houses, our stores and stuffy bedrooms and polished drawing rooms with pictures of the Führer on the walls, all of us knew we had abandoned these people to their fate, these people who had been dubbed animals and were now advancing slowly upon us to avenge themselves. These ragged, starving people would now put on our clothes, shove their bleeding feet into our shoes, snatch at the butter and flour and sausage that we had just carried off. And I felt with horror that this was only right and just and, for a fraction of a second, knew that we were guilty. I forgot it again.

The concentration camp inmates did not snatch at the food but at the guns in the ditches. They loaded themselves down with them, crossed the road without tak-ing any notice of us, climbed painfully up the slope on the other side and took up posts above, their guns at the ready. They looked down at us in silence. I could not bear to go on looking at them. Why don't they scream, I thought, or shoot into the air or at us, for God's sake? But they stood quietly there. I saw that some of them were swaying on their feet and could only just manage to hold their guns and stand upright. Perhaps they had longed for this moment, day and night. I could not help them and they could not help me. I did not understand them and did not need them and everything about them was wholly strange to me.

A call came back to us that everyone except the drivers was to get down from the carts. This was an order. A deep sigh swept through the caravan, for it could mean only one thing: the last steps into freedom were before us.

Before we could get moving again the Polish drivers jumped down, slung their reins round the supports, laid their whips on the seats, gathered together in a small group and began to move back towards the east, up and away. Herr Volk turned purple with rage and blocked the way. He spoke quietly to them first but soon began to shout at them, a put-up job, a plot, refusal to work and so on. I saw a Polish forced laborer shove a German landowner aside. The world was certainly topsy-turvy now, but Herr Volk didn't know it. He snatched up his whip, as usual, but the blow was arrested in mid-air, someone seized his arm, the whip fell to the ground and the Poles went on their way. Herr Volk pressed his hand to his heart, leaned heavily against a cart and let his tightlipped wife and the stupid little dackel Sweetypie comfort him while Kalle shouted down at him: Dirty bastard! Dirty bastard! The Frenchmen who stayed with us called farewells to the Poles, who didn't understand their words any more than I did, but they understood the feeling behind the words, and so did I, and it hurt me to be excluded from their calls and hand-waving and cap-throwing, from their joy and their language. But it had to be. The world consisted of victors and vanquished. The victors could give free rein to their feelings. The others, we others, would have to keep ours locked up inside us in future. The enemy should not see us weak.

And there it came. A fire-spitting dragon would have been more to my taste than that light jeep with the gum-chewing driver and the three indifferent officers who despised us so thoroughly that they didn't even have their holsters open. I tried to look right through them with a wooden face and told myself that their easy smiles, their clean uniforms, their indifferent glances, all this damned victors' behavior had certainly been ordered for our special humiliation.

People round me began to hide their rings and watches; I unstrapped my wrist-watch, too, and stuck it carelessly into my coat pocket. With a wave of the hand the guard at the end of the narrow path, a tall, slouching fellow with the impossible steel helmet we had always jeered at in the newsreels, showed the few armed men where they were to throw down their arms, and others frisked us civilians with a firm, prac-ticed police grip. Stiff with indignation I submitted to being searched, secretly proud that they thought I might have a weapon. Your watch? my overworked guard asked in a businesslike voice. So he wanted my watch—the victor. But he didn't get it, for I managed to take him in by saying his comrade had already got it. As far as the watch was concerned I got away unshorn. Then my sharpened ear caught the sound of a plane approaching. It was none of my business, but as usual I held on to the direction of approach and a reflex action impelled me to throw myself down as it dived. Once more that horrible shadow that darted quickly across grass and trees, once more that sickening sound as bullets struck the ground. Still? I thought, astounded, and realized from one second to the next, that one could get used to being out of danger. With malicious satisfaction I saw American artillery men set up an American machine gun and fire at an American plane which then rose hastily and disappeared behind the forest.

One should be able to describe what it was like when all was quiet. I stayed lying behind a tree for a while. I think I didn't care that from that moment onwards no bomb or burst of MG fire might ever again descend on me. I had no curiosity about what was going to happen. I couldn't see what use a dragon would be once it stopped spitting fire. I had no idea how the horned Siegfried would behave if the dragon asked him for his watch instead of gobbling him up hair and hide. I had not the faintest desire to see how Mr. Dragon and Mr. Siegfried would get on together in private life. Nor had I any wish to go to the Americans in the villas they occupied to ask for every pail of water we needed, and I certainly didn't want to get into an argument with black-haired Lieutenant Davidson from Ohio at the end of which I was forced to explain that my pride commanded me to hate him.

I had no desire, either, to talk to the concentration camp man who sat at our fire peering at us through his bent wire spectacles and saying the shocking word Communist as if it were an everyday, permitted word like hate or war or destruction. No. And least of all did I want to hear the sorrow and consternation in his voice when he asked us: Where have you been all these years?

I had no desire for liberation. I lay under my tree and it was quiet. I was lost and I thought I should hold in my mind's eye the branches of the tree against the glory of the May sky. Then my tall sergeant came up the hill after his stretch of duty and he had a giggling German girl on each arm. All three moved off towards the villas, and at last I had a reason to turn away and weep.

—*trans. Joan Becker*

# Stuart Hall

## *from* MINIMAL SELVES (1987)
## *from* THE MEANING OF NEW TIMES (1989)

*Stuart Hall (1932–) was born in Jamaica and has lived in England since 1951, when he attended Oxford University as a Rhodes scholar. Hall has simultaneously been an intellectual and political activist. He was one of the founders of the British new left, active in the Campaign for Nuclear Disarmament, a supporter of student protests in the late 1960s, and a commentator on black politics in the British media. His portrait is in the collection of the National Portrait Gallery in London. Hall is among the pioneers of 'cultural studies'—an interdisciplinary field in the humanities whose resonance has been international. His recent work has been concerned with the multiple and hybrid nature of identity in a world that has been transformed by globalization. In "Minimal Selves," Hall draws on his own experience to draw a picture of identity as being historically contingent, unstable, and continually in flux.*

### *FROM* MINIMAL SELVES

A few adjectival thoughts only . . .

Thinking about my own sense of identity, I realize that it has always depended on the fact of being a *migrant*, on the *difference* from the rest of you. So one of the fascinating things about this discussion is to find myself centered at last. Now that, in the postmodern age, you all feel so dispersed, I become centered. What I've thought of as dispersed and fragmented comes, paradoxically, to be *the* representative modern experience! This is "coming home" with a vengeance! Most of it I much enjoy—welcome to migranthood. It also makes me understand something about identity which has been puzzling me in the last three years.

I've been puzzled by the fact that young black people in London today are marginalized, fragmented, unenfranchised, disadvantaged, and dispersed. And yet, they look as if they own the territory. Somehow, they too, in spite of everything, are centered, in place: without much material support, it's true, but nevertheless, they occupy a new kind of space at the center. And I've wondered again and again: what is it about that long discovery-rediscovery of identity among blacks in this migrant situation which allows them to lay a kind of claim to certain parts of the earth which aren't theirs, with quite that certainty? I do feel a sense of—dare I say—envy surrounding them. Envy is a very funny thing for the British to feel at this moment in time—to want to be black! Yet I feel some of you surreptitiously moving toward that marginal identity. I welcome you to that, too.

Now the question is: is this centering of marginality really *the* representative postmodern experience? I was given the title "the minimal self." I know the discourses which have theoretically produced that concept of "minimal self." But my experience now is that what the discourse of the postmodern has produced is not something new but a kind of recognition of where identity always was at. It is in that sense that I want to redefine the general feeling which more and more people seem to have about themselves—that they are all, in some way, *recently migrated*, if I can coin that phrase.

The classic questions which every migrant faces are twofold: "Why are you here?" and "When are you going back home?" No migrant ever knows the answer to the second question until asked. Only then does she or he know that really, in the deep sense, she/he's never going back. Migration is a one-way trip. There is no "home" to go back to. There never was. But "why are you here?" is also a really interesting question, which I've never been able to find a proper answer to either. I know the reasons one is supposed to give: "for education," "for the childrens' sake," "for a better life, more opportunities," "to enlarge the mind," etc. The truth is, I am here because it's where my family is not. I really came here to get away from my mother. Isn't that the universal story of life? One is where one is to try and get away from somewhere else. That was the story which I could never tell anybody about myself. So I had to find other stories, other fictions, which were more authentic or, at any rate, more acceptable, in place of the Big Story of the endless evasion of patriarchal family life. Who I am—the "real" me—was formed in relation to a whole set of other narratives. I was aware of the fact that identity is an invention from the very beginning, long before I understood any of this theoretically. Identity is formed at the unstable point where the "unspeakable" stories of subjectivity meet the narratives of history, of a culture. And since he/she is positioned in relation to cultured narratives which have been profoundly expropriated, the colonized subject is always "somewhere else:" doubly marginalized, displaced always *other* than where he or she is, or is able to speak from.

It wasn't a joke when I said that I migrated in order to get away from my family. I did. The problem, one discovers, is that since one's family is always already "in here," there is no way in which you can actually leave them. Of course, sooner or later, they recede in memory, or even in life. But these are not the "burials" that really matter. I wish they were still around, so that I didn't have to carry them around, locked up somewhere in my head, from which there is no migration. So from the first, in relation to them, and then to all the other symbolic "others," I certainly was always aware of the self as only constituted in that kind of absent-present contestation with something else, with some other "real me," which is and isn't there.

If you live, as I've lived, in Jamaica, in a lower-middle-class family that was trying to be a middle-class Jamaican family trying to be an upper-middle-class Jamaican family trying to be an English Victorian family . . . I mean the notion of displacement as a place of "identity" is a concept you learn to live with, long before you are able to spell it. Living with, living through difference. I remember the occasion when I returned to Jamaica on a visit sometime in the early 1960s, after the first wave of migration to England, my mother said to me: "Hope they don't think you are one of those immigrants over there!" And of course, at that point I knew for the first time I was an immigrant. Suddenly in relation to that narrative of migration, one version of the "real me" came into view. I said: "Of course, I'm an immigrant. What do you think I am?" And she said in that classic Jamaican middle-class way, "Well, I hope the people over there will shove all the immigrants off the long end of a short pier." (They've been shoving ever since.)

The trouble is that the instant one learns to be "an immigrant," one recognizes one can't be an immigrant any longer: it isn't a tenable place to be. I, then, went through the long, important, political education of discovering that I am "black." Constituting oneself as "black" is another recognition of self through difference: certain clear polarities and extremities against which one tries to define oneself. We constantly underestimate the importance, to certain crucial political things that have happened in the world, of this ability of people to constitute themselves, psychically, in the black identity. It has long been thought that this is really a simple process: a recognition—a resolution of irresolutions, a coming to rest in some place which was always there waiting for one. The "real me" at last!

The fact is "black" has never been just there either. It has always been an unstable identity, psychically, culturally, and politically. It, too, is a narrative, a story, a history. Something constructed, told, spoken, not simply found. People now speak of the society I come from in totally unrecognizable ways. Of course Jamaica is a black society, they say. In reality it is a society of black and brown people who lived for three or four hundred years without ever being able to speak of themselves as "black." Black is an identity which had to be learned and could only be learned in a certain moment. In Jamaica that moment is the 1970s. So the notion that identity is a simple—if I can use the metaphor—black or white question, has never been the experience of black people, at least in the diaspora. These are "imaginary communities"—and not a bit the less real because they are also symbolic. Where else could the dialogue of identity between subjectivity and culture take place?

Despite its fragmentations and displacements, then, "the self" does relate to a real set of histories. But what are the "real histories" to which so many at this conference have "owned up"? How new is this new condition? It does seem that more and more people now recognize themselves in the narratives of displacement. But the narratives of displacement have certain conditions of existence, real histories in the contemporary world, which are not only or exclusively psychical, not simply "journeys of the mind." What is that special moment? Is it simply the recognition of a general condition of fragmentation at the end of the twentieth century?

It may be true that the self is always, in a sense, a fiction, just as the kinds of "closures" which are required to create communities of identification—nation, ethnic group, families, sexualities, etc.—are arbitrary closures; and the forms of political action, whether movements, or parties, or classes, those too, are temporary, partial, arbitrary. I believe it is an immensely important gain when one recognizes that all identity is constructed across difference and begins to live with the politics of difference.

•

Now I perfectly recognize that this recognition of difference, of the impossibility of "identity" in its fully unified meaning, does, of course, transform our sense of what politics is about. It transforms the nature of political commitment. Hundred-and-one percent commitment is no longer possible. But the politics of infinitely advancing while looking over the shoulder is a very dangerous exercise. You tend to fall into a hole. Is it possible, acknowledging the discourse of self-reflexivity, to constitute a *politics* in the recognition of the necessarily fictional nature of the modern self, and the necessary arbitrariness of the closure around the imaginary communities in relation to which we are constantly in the process of becoming "selves"?

•

You see, I don't think it's true that we've been driven back to a definition of identity as the "minimal self." Yes, it's true that the "grand narratives" which constituted the language of the self as an integral entity don't hold. But actually, you know, it isn't just the "minimal selves" stalking out there with absolutely no relation to one another. Let's think about the question of nation and nationalism. One is aware of the degree to which nationalism was/is constituted as one of those major poles or terrains of articulation of the self. I think it is very important the way in which some people now (and I think particularly of the colonized subject) begin to reach for a new conception of ethnicity as a kind of counter to the old discourses of nationalism or national identity.

Now one knows these are dangerously overlapping terrains. All the same they are not identical. Ethnicity *can* be a constitutive element in the most viciously regressive kind of nationalism or national identity. But in our times, as an imaginary community, it is also beginning to carry some other meanings, and to define a new space for identity. It insists on difference—on the fact that every identity is placed, positioned, in a culture, a language, a history. Every statement comes from somewhere, from somebody in particular. It insists on specificity, on conjuncture. But it is not necessarily armor-plated against other identities. It is not tied to fixed, permanent, unalterable oppositions. It is not wholly defined by exclusion.

I don't want to present this new ethnicity as a powerless, perfect universe. Like all terrains of identification, it has dimensions of power in it. But it isn't quite so framed by those extremities of power and aggression, violence and mobilization, as the older forms of nationalism. The slow contradictory movement from "nationalism" to "ethnicity" as a source of identities is part of a new politics. It is also part of the "decline of the West"—that immense process of historical relativization which is just beginning to make the British, at least, feel just marginally "marginal."

## *FROM* The Meaning of New Times

How new are these 'new times'? Are they the dawn of a New Age or only the whisper of an old one? What is 'new' about them? How do we assess their contradictory tendencies—are they progressive or regressive? These are some of the questions which the ambiguous discourse of 'new times' poses.

•

### *The Return of the Subject*

One boundary which 'new times' has certainly displaced is that between the 'objective' and subjective dimensions of change. This is the so-called 'revolution of the subject' aspect. The individual subject has become more important, as collective social subjects—like that of class or nation or ethnic group—become more segmented and 'pluralised'. As social theorists have become more concerned with how ideologies actually function, and how political mobilization really takes place in complex societies, so they have been obliged to take the *'subject'* of these processes more seriously.

●

This is novel conceptual or theoretical terrain. But these vicissitudes of 'the subject' also have their own histories which are key episodes in the passage to 'new times'. They include the cultural revolution of the 1960s; '1968' itself, with its strong sense of politics as 'theatre' and its talk of 'will' and 'consciousness'; feminism, with its insistence that 'the personal is political'; the renewed interest in psychoanalysis, with its rediscovery of the unconscious roots of subjectivity; the theoretical revolutions of the 1960s and 1970s—with their concern for language, discourse and representation.

'Postmodernism' is the preferred term which signals this more *cultural* character of 'new times'. 'Modernism', it argues, which dominated the art and architecture, the cultural imagination, of the early decades of the 20th century, and came to represent the look and experience of 'modernity' itself, is at an end. It has declined into the International Style characteristics of the freeway, the wall-of-glass skyscraper and international airports. Modernism's revolutionary impulse—which could be seen in surrealism, Dada, constructivism, the move to an abstract and non-figurative visual culture—has been tamed and contained by the museum. It has become the preserve of an avant-garde élite, betraying its revolutionary and 'populist' impulses.

●

'Postmodernism', by contrast, celebrates the penetration of aesthetics into everyday life and the ascendancy of popular culture over the High Arts. Theorists like Fredric Jameson and Jean-François Lyotard agree on many of the characteristics of 'the postmodern condition.' They remark on the dominance of image, appearance, surface-effect over depth (was Ronald Reagan a president or just a B-movie actor, real or cardboard cut-out, alive or Spitting Image?). They point to the blurring of image and reality in our media-saturated world (is the Contra war real or only happening on TV?). They note the preference for parody, nostalgia, kitsch and pastiche—the continual re-working and quotation of past styles—over more positive modes of artistic representation, like realism or naturalism. They note, also, a preference for the popular and the decorative over the brutalist or the functional in architecture and design. 'Postmodernism' also has a more philosophical aspect. Lyotard, Baudrillard and Derrida cite the erasure of a strong sense of history, the slippage of hitherto stable meanings, the proliferation of difference, and the end of what Lyotard calls the 'grand narratives' of progress, development, Enlightenment, Rationality, and Truth which, until recently, were the foundations of Western philosophy and politics.

Jameson, however, argues very persuasively that postmodernism is also 'the new cultural logic of capital'—'the purest form of capital yet to have emerged, a prodigious expansion into hitherto uncommodified areas.'

*Jamaica Kincaid*

# *from* A SMALL PLACE (1988)

*Jamaica Kincaid (1949–) was born Elaine Potter Richardson in Antigua, then a British colony. At seventeen she moved to New York, where she worked as an au pair; in her twenties she took a pen name and began writing essays about Caribbean culture and fiction. In 1976 she became a staff writer for the* New Yorker; *in 1985, she accepted a teaching position at Bennington College in Vermont. Kincaid's fiction and essays, known for their direct, spare prose, deal primarily with the devastating personal and cultural damage wrought by colonialism. In* A Small Place, *she writes with passion and indignation of the tiny island of her childhood, discovered by Columbus in 1493, turned into a site of slave plantations by Europeans, and then left to work out its own postcolonial future.*

The Antigua that I knew, the Antigua in which I grew up, is not the Antigua you, a tourist, would see now. That Antigua no longer exists. That Antigua no longer exists partly for the usual reason, the passing of time, and partly because the bad-minded people who used to rule over it, the English, no longer do so. (But the English have become such a pitiful lot these days, with hardly any idea what to do with themselves now that they no longer have one quarter of the earth's human population bowing and scraping before them. They don't seem to know that this empire business was all wrong and they should, at least, be wearing sackcloth and ashes in token penance of the wrongs committed, the irrevocableness of their bad deeds, for no natural disaster imaginable could equal the harm they did. Actual death might have been better. And so all this fuss over empire—what went wrong here, what went wrong there—always makes me quite crazy, for I can say to them what went wrong: they should never have left their home, their precious England, a place they loved so much, a place they had to leave but could never forget. And so everywhere they went they turned it into England; and everybody they met they turned English. But no place could ever really be England, and nobody who did not look exactly like them would ever be English, so you can imagine the destruction of people and land that came from that. The English hate each other and they hate England, and the reason they are so miserable now is that they have no place else to go and nobody else to feel better than.) But let me show you the Antigua that I used to know.

In the Antigua that I knew, we lived on a street named after an English maritime criminal, Horatio Nelson, and all the other streets around us were named after some other English maritime criminals. There was Rodney Street, there was Hood Street, there was Hawkins Street, and there was Drake Street. There were flamboyant trees and mahogany trees lining East Street. Government House, the place where the Governor, the person standing in for the Queen, lived, was on East Street. Government House was surrounded by a high white wall—and to show how cowed we must have been, no one ever wrote bad things on it; it remained clean and white and high. (I once stood in hot sun for hours so that I could see a putty-faced Princess from England disappear behind these walls. I was seven years old at the time, and I thought, She has a putty face.) There was the library on lower High Street, above the Department of the Treasury, and it was in that part of High Street that all colonial government business took place. In that part of High Street, you could cash a cheque at the Treasury, read a book in the library, post a letter at the post office, appear before a magistrate in court. (Since we were ruled by the English, we also had their laws. There was a law against using abusive language. Can you imagine such a law among people for whom making a spectacle of yourself through speech is everything? When West Indians went to England, the police there had to get a glossary of bad West Indian words so they could understand whether they were hearing abusive language or not.) It was in that same part of High Street that you could get a passport in another government office. In the middle of High Street was the Barclays Bank. The Barclay brothers, who started Barclays Bank, were slave-traders. That is how they made their money. When the English outlawed the slave trade, the Barclay brothers went into banking. It made them even richer. It's possible that when they saw how rich banking made them, they gave themselves a good beating for opposing an end to slave trading (for surely they would have opposed that), but then again, they may have been visionaries and agitated for an end to slavery, for look at how rich they became with their banks borrowing from (through their savings) the descendants of the slaves and then lending back to them. But people just a little older than I am can recite the name of and the day the first black person was hired as a cashier at this very same Barclays Bank in Antigua. Do you ever wonder why some people blow things up? I can imagine that if my life had taken a certain turn, there would be the Barclays Bank, and there I would be, both of us in ashes. Do you ever try to understand why people like me cannot get over the past, cannot forgive and cannot forget? There is the Barclays Bank. The Barclay brothers are dead. The human beings they traded, the human beings who to them were only commodities, are dead. It should not have been that they came to the same end, and heaven is not enough of a reward for one or hell enough of a punishment for the other. People who think about these things believe that every bad deed, even every bad thought, carries with it its own retribution. So do you see the queer thing about people like me? Sometimes we hold your retribution.

And then there was another place, called the Mill Reef Club. It was built by some people from North America who wanted to live in Antigua and spend their holidays in Antigua but who seemed not to like Antiguans (black people) at all, for the Mill Reef Club declared itself completely private, and the only Antiguans (black people) allowed to go there were servants. People can recite the name of the first Antiguan (black person) to eat a sandwich at the clubhouse and the day on which it happened; people can recite the name of the first Antiguan (black person) to play golf on the golf course and the day on which the event took place. In those days, we Antiguans thought that the people at the Mill Reef Club had such bad manners, like pigs; they were behaving in a bad way, like pigs. There they were, strangers in someone else's home, and then they refused to talk to their hosts or have anything human, anything intimate, to do with them. I believe they gave scholarships to one or two bright people each year so they could go overseas and study; I believe they gave money to children's charities; these things must have made them seem to themselves very big and good, but to us there they were, pigs living in that sty (the Mill Reef Club). And what were these people from North America, these people from England, these people from Europe, with their bad behaviour, doing on this little island? For they so enjoyed behaving badly, as if there was pleasure immeasurable to be had from not acting like a human being. Let me tell you about a man; trained as a dentist, he took it on himself to say he was a doctor, specialising in treating children's illnesses. No one objected—certainly not us. He came to Antigua as a refugee (running away from Hitler) from Czechoslovakia. This man hated us so much that he would send his wife to inspect us before we were admitted into his presence, and she would make sure that we didn't smell, that we didn't have dirt under our fingernails, and that nothing else about us—apart from the colour of our skin—would offend the doctor. (I can remember once, when I had whooping cough and I took a turn for the worse, that my mother, before bundling me up and taking me off to see this man, examined me carefully to see that I had no bad smells or dirt in the crease of my neck, behind my ears, or anywhere else. Every horrible thing that a housefly could do was known by heart to my mother, and in her innocence she thought that she and the doctor shared the same crazy obsession—germs.) Then there was a headmistress of a girls' school, hired through the colonial office in England and sent to Antigua to run this school which only in my lifetime began to accept girls who were born outside a marriage; in Antigua it had never dawned on anyone that this was a way of keeping black children out of this school. This woman was twenty-six years old, not too long out of university, from Northern Ireland, and she told these girls over and over again to stop behaving as if they were monkeys just out of trees. No one ever dreamed that the word for any of this was racism. We thought these people were so ill-mannered and we were so surprised by this, for they were far away from their home, and we believed that the farther away you were from your home the better you should behave. (This is because if your bad behaviour gets you in trouble you have your family not too far off to help defend you.) We thought they were un-Christian-like; we thought they were small-minded; we thought they were like animals, a bit below human standards as we understood those standards to be. We felt superior to all these people; we thought that perhaps the English among them who behaved this way weren't English at all, for the English were supposed to be civilised, and this behaviour was so much like that of an animal, the thing we were before the English rescued us, that maybe they weren't from the real England at all but from another England, one we were not familiar with, not at all from the England we were told about, not at all from the England we could never be from, the England that was so far away, the England that not even a boat could take us to, the England that, no matter what we did, we could never be of. We felt superior, for we were so much better behaved and we were full of grace, and these people were so badly behaved and they were so completely empty of grace. (Of course, I now see that good behaviour is the proper posture of the weak, of children.) We were taught the names of the Kings of England. In Antigua, the twenty-fourth of May was a holiday—Queen Victoria's official birthday. We didn't say to ourselves, Hasn't this extremely unappealing person been dead for years and years? Instead, we were glad for a holiday. Once, at dinner (this happened in my present life), I was sitting across from an Englishman, one of those smart people who know how to run things that England still turns out but who now, since the demise of the empire, have nothing to do; they look so sad, sitting on the rubbish heap of history. I was reciting my usual litany of things I hold against England and the English, and to round things off I said, "And do you know that we had to celebrate Queen Victoria's birthday?" So he said that every year, at the school he attended in England, they marked the day she died. I said, "Well, apart from the fact that she belonged to you and so anything you did about her was proper, at least you knew she died." So that was England to us—Queen Victoria and the glorious day of her coming into the world, a beautiful place, a blessed place, a living and blessed thing, not the ugly, piggish individuals we met. I cannot tell you how angry it makes me to hear people from North America tell me how much they love England, how beautiful England is, with its traditions. All they see is some frumpy, wrinkled-up person passing by in a carriage waving at a crowd. But what I see is the millions of people, of whom I am just one, made orphans: no motherland, no fatherland, no gods, no mounds of earth for holy ground, no excess of love which might lead to the things that an excess of love sometimes brings, and worst and most painful of all, no tongue. (For isn't it odd that the only language I have in which to speak of this crime is the language of the criminal who committed the crime? And what can that really mean? For the language of the criminal can contain only the goodness of the criminal's deed. The language of the criminal can explain and express the deed only from the criminal's point of view. It cannot contain the horror of the deed, the injustice of the deed, the agony, the humiliation inflicted on me. When I say to the criminal, "This is wrong, this is wrong, this is wrong," or, "This deed is bad, and this other deed is bad, and this one is also very, very bad," the criminal understands the word "wrong" in this way: It is wrong when "he" doesn't get his fair share of profits from the crime just committed; he understands the word "bad" in this way: a fellow criminal betrayed a trust. That must be why, when I say, "I am filled with rage," the criminal says, "But why?" And when I blow things up and make life generally unlivable for the criminal (is my life not unlivable, too?) the criminal is shocked, surprised. But nothing can erase my rage—not an apology, not a large sum of money, not the death of the criminal—for this wrong can never be made right, and only the impossible can make me still: can a way be found to make what happened not have happened?

●

Are you saying to yourself, "Can't she get beyond all that, everything happened so long ago, and how does she know that if things had been the other way around her ancestors wouldn't have behaved just as badly, because, after all, doesn't everybody behave badly given the opportunity?"

Our perception of this Antigua—the perception we had of this place ruled by these bad-minded people—was not a political perception. The English were ill-mannered, not racists; the school headmistress was especially ill-mannered, not a racist; the doctor was crazy—he didn't even speak English properly, and he came from a strangely named place, he also was not a racist; the people at the Mill Reef Club were puzzling (why go and live in a place populated mostly by people you cannot stand), not racists.

Have you ever wondered to yourself why it is that all people like me seem to have learned from you is how to imprison and murder each other, how to govern badly, and how to take the wealth of our country and place it in Swiss bank accounts? Have you ever wondered why it is that all we seem to have learned from you is how to corrupt our societies and how to be tyrants? You will have to accept that this is mostly your fault. Let me just show you how you looked to us. You came. You took things that were not yours, and you did not even, for appearances' sake, ask first. You could have said, "May I have this, please?" and even though it would have been clear to everybody that a yes or no from us would have been of no consequence you might have looked so much better. Believe me, it would have gone a long way. I would have had to admit that at least you were polite. You murdered people. You imprisoned people. You robbed people. You opened your own banks and you put our money in them. The accounts were in your name. The banks were in your name. There must have been some good people among you, but they stayed home. And that is the point. That is why they are good. They stayed home. But still, when you think about it, you must be a little sad. The people like me, finally, after years and years of agitation, made deeply moving and eloquent speeches against the wrongness of your domination over us, and then finally, after the mutilated bodies of you, your wife, and your children were found in your beautiful and spacious bungalow at the edge of your rubber plantation—found by one of your many house servants (none of it was ever yours; it was never, ever yours)—you say to me, "Well, I wash my hands of all of you, I am leaving now," and you leave, and from afar you watch as we do to ourselves the very things you used to do to us. And you might feel that there was more to you than that, you might feel that you had understood the meaning of the Age of Enlightenment (though, as far as I can see, it had done you very little good); you loved knowledge, and wherever you went you made sure to build a school, a library (yes, and in both of these places you distorted or erased my history and glorified your own). But then again, perhaps as you observe the debacle in which I now exist, the utter ruin that I say is my life, perhaps you are remembering that you had always felt people like me cannot run things, people like me will never grasp the idea of Gross National Product, people like me will never be able to take command of the thing the most simpleminded among you can master, people like me will never understand the notion of rule by law, people like me cannot really think in abstractions, people like me cannot be objective, we make everything so personal. You will forget your part in the whole setup, that bureaucracy is one of your inventions, that Gross National Product is one of your inventions, and all the laws that you know mysteriously favour you. Do you know why people like me are shy about being capitalists? Well, it's because we, for as long as we have known you, *were* capital, like bales of cotton and sacks of sugar, and you were the commanding, cruel capitalists, and the memory of this is so strong, the experience so recent, that we can't quite bring ourselves to embrace this idea that you think so much of. As for what we were like before we met you, I no longer care. No periods of time over which my ancestors held sway, no documentation of complex civilisations, is any comfort to me. Even if I really came from people who were living like monkeys in trees, it was better to be that than what happened to me, what I became after I met you.

# *from* AFRICAN LAUGHTER:
# FOUR VISITS TO ZIMBABWE (1992)

*Doris Lessing (1919– ) was born in Persia, where her father served as an officer in the British Army, and spent her childhood on a family farm in the British colony of Rhodesia. In 1949, she settled in London. A communist in her early years, Lessing's primary focus has been her unusually prolific and varied career as a writer of fiction, essays, poetry, and plays. Her works include several novels about whites living in colonial Africa; a science fiction series; numerous short stories, many dealing with personal relationships between men and women; and a novel about revolutionaries in London. The Golden Notebook (1962) is a complex novel about a writer attempting to come to terms with contemporary history and the social roles expected of women. Seen by many as her most significant fictional work, it is often cited as a feminist landmark. In later life, Lessing has written autobiographical essays and books. The selections here, from* African Laughter, *deal with her visit to Zimbabwe (formerly Rhodesia) in 1982, two years after it became an independent nation.*

## A LITTLE HISTORY

Southern Rhodesia was a shield-shaped country in the middle of the map of Southern Africa, and it was bright pink because Cecil Rhodes had said the map of Africa should be painted red from Cape to Cairo, as an outward sign of its happy allegiance to the British Empire. The hearts of innumerable men and women responded with idealistic fervour to his clarion, because it went without saying that it would be good for Africa, or for anywhere else, to be made British. At this point it might be useful to wonder which of the idealisms that make our hearts beat faster will seem wrongheaded to people a hundred years form now.

In 1890, just over a hundred years from when this book is being written, the Pioneer Column arrived in grassy plains five thousand feet up from the distant sea: a dry country with few people in it. The one hundred and eighty men, and some policemen, had a bad time of it, travelling hundreds of miles up from the Cape through a landscape full of wild beasts and natives thought of as savages. They were journeying into the unknown, for while explores, hunters and missionaries had come this way, homesteaders—people expecting to settle—had not. They were on this adventure for the sake of the Empire, for Cecil Rhodes whom they knew to be a great man, for the Queen, and because they were of the pioneering breed, people who had to see horizons as a challenge. Within a short time there was a town with banks, churches, a hospital, schools and, of course, hotels of the kind whose bars, then as now, were as important as the accommodations. This was Salisbury, a white town, British in feel, flavour and habit.

The progress of the Pioneer Column was watched by the Africans, and it is one record they laughed at the sight of the white men sweating in their thick clothes. A year later came Mother Patrick and her band of Dominican nuns, wearing thick and voluminous black and white habits. They at once began their work of teaching children and nursing the sick. Then, and very soon, came the women, all wrapped about and weighed down in their clothes. Respectable Victorian women did not discard so much as a collar, a petticoat or a corset when travelling.

•

At all times and everywhere invaders with superior technology have subjugated countries while in pursuit of land and wealth and the Europeans, the whites, are only the most recent of them. Having taken the best land for themselves, and set up an efficient machinery of domination, the British in Southern Rhodesia were able to persuade themselves—as is common among conquerors—that the conquered were inferior, that white tutelage was to their advantage, that they were bound to be the grateful recipients of a superior civilization. The British were so smug about themselves partly because they never went in for general murder, did not attempt to kill out an entire native population, as did the New Zealanders, and is happening now in Brazil where Indian tribes are being murdered while the world looks on and does nothing. They did not deliberately inject anyone with diseases, nor use drugs and alcohol as aids to domination. On the contrary, there were always hospitals for black people, and white man's liquor was made illegal, for it had been observed what harm firewater had done to the native peoples of North America.

If it is asked, How did these people, no more or less intelligent than ourselves, manage to accommodate so many incompatibles in their minds at the same time, then this belongs to a wider query: How and why do we all do it, often not noticing what we do? I remember as a child hearing farmers remark, with the cynical good nature that is the mark of a certain kind of bad conscience: 'One of these days they are all going to rise and drive us into the sea.' This admission clearly belonged in a different part of the brain from that where dwelled the complacencies of Empire.

By 1900 there was Southern Rhodesia, bright pink all over, inside its neat boundaries, with Mozambique, or Portuguese East Africa on one side, Angola (Portuguese West Africa) and the Bechuanaland Protectorate (pink) on the other, and Northern Rhodesia (pink) just above it.

The Transvaal, arena for the Boer War, was to the south.

The same neat shape is now stamped Zimbabwe. The trouble is that these boundaries ignore a good deal of history, mainly to do with the Portuguese influence, for Portuguese traders, adventurers, explorers, travelled and sometimes lived in areas that later were painted pink. There were no frontiers then, and if any European country were to claim the territory by right of precedence, it should have been Portugal. These histories are in Portuguese archives, not so much in the British, and school children were not taught about the Portuguese in Monomotapa or the kingdom of Lo Magondi. Yet that the Portuguese had been before them could hardly have been overlooked by the British adventurers. There is a certain wonderfully fertile valley, still full of citrus groves planted by the Portuguese, who also brought in maize and other crops.

The boundaries also ignore the pre-European politics of the Shona—for instance the Mutapa state which is the sixteenth century included much of central Mozambique.

The picture of Mashonaland presented as history to the heirs of the Pioneer Column went something like this: When we whites came we found the Matabele, an off-shoot from the Zulus. They had travelled north to escape from murderous Zulu kings, and taken land from the Mashona, whom they harried and raided. The Mashona were groups of loosely related clans always on the move, for they stayed in one place only long enough to exhaust the soil and scare away the animals. We, the British, brought the Mashona people peace as well as White Civilization.

In fact the Mashona were skilled farmers and miners, whose techniques are only now being investigated by researchers. It was necessary for the British to see them as ignorant savages who owed everything to their conquerors.

●

Meanwhile the nationalist movements of Southern Rhodesia, encouraged by the success of their northern allies, fomented 'trouble' most successfully, everywhere. Already in 1956 I met a couple of young men, whose names I was not told, who described an underground life smuggling political literature, of police harassment and arbitrary arrest, beatings, imprisonment. This underground war, still minor, did not find its way into the newspapers, though people spoke of it. Throughout the 1960s the writing on the wall became ever more visible, but the whites, who had learned nothing from Kenya, chose to ignore it. The War of Independence in Southern Rhodesia, like many other wars, need not have happened. The whites numbered 250,000 at their maximum. Of these, nay, if differently led, I believe would have compromised and shared power with the blacks. But a minority of the whites, led by Ian Smith, were determined to fight for White Supremacy. There was no date for the start of that war, which slowly simmered into one of the nastiest conflicts of our time. The opposing armies were not neatly separated into black and white. On the white side fought black soldiers and black police. The whites, far from united at the start, became united by the passions of war, and the few who thought the War was a mistake, and should be ended, and could not be won (for look what was happening in Mozambique where the whites were thrown out after a terrible war) were treated with hysterical hatred, were persecuted, victimized, vilified. The backs, too, were infinitely divided. Not only were there different armies with different leaders and ideas, there was division in the armies themselves.

●

The War was fought with cruelty on both sides. People living in the villages had a hard time, for both the government forces and the black armies punished them for aiding the other side, but they had to help whichever soldiers arrived and demanded it. Large numbers of villagers were taken by force from their homes and put into what amounted to concentration camps—of course 'for their own protection'. Young men and girls, as soon as they were old enough, ran away to join guerrilla armies, in Zambia, or Mozambique, or even the forests of Southern Rhodesia itself, for there at least they would not be subjected to harassment, torture or death by the government troops. Part of a whole generation of black youth was educated in guerrilla armies, sometimes to the accompaniment of marxist slogans, but always unified by their hatred of the whites.

The War over, the atrocities on both sides were gently allowed to be forgotten, for when the black population voted—for the first time in their lives—it was Robert Mugabe they chose, and he at once announced a multi-racial society and the end of the race hatred.

●

The young nation Zimbabwe came into being in 1980. That is to say, from the arrival of the Pioneer Column at the foot of the small hill that would mark the beginnings of Salisbury, called the Kopje, to Independence, took ninety years. Ninety years—nothing. Yet in that time the culture of the large area—roughly the size of Spain—had been destroyed; the people had been kept subdued by all the power of modern weapons, policing, propaganda; finally they had rebelled against armies equipped with the most advanced weaponry, and they had won. Now they had to take power as equals in a modern world.

●

The best of the Zimbabwe story is the vigour, the optimism, the determination of the people. You may return from a several-weeks' visit to Zimbabwe and realize, finding yourself again in the enervating airs of Europe, that you have been day and night with people, white and black, who talk of nothing else but how to make Zimbabwe work, of new ideas that may be adopted there, and who have an identification with the processes of government and of administration that means nothing can happen which does not at once attract the most passionate reactions, for or against. People are coming to Zimbabwe after Mozambique, or Zambia, where nothing is a success, where cynicism poisons everything, say their faith in Africa is restored, and that Zimbabwe, for whatever reason, is unique in Africa because of the creative energies of its people. They are proud of themselves . . . thus you may hear a black person remark of Zambia, or of Mozambique: 'They don't know how to do anything, we shall have to show them.' This self-respecting, or perhaps one might say, bumptious, attitude is a continuation of the Southern Rhodesian white love of themselves and 'their' country, which goes on though the country is no longer theirs.

●

## 1982

When I returned to the country where I had lived for twenty-five years, arriving as a child of five and leaving as a young woman of thirty, it was after an interval of over twenty-five years. This was because I was a Prohibited Immigrant. An unambiguous status, one would think: either a good citizen or a bad one, Prohibited or Unprohibited.

But is was not so simple. I was already a Prohibited Immigrant in 1956 but did not know it. It never crossed my mind I could be: the impossibility was a psychological fact, nothing to do with daylight realities. You cannot be forbidden the land you grew up in, so says the web of sensations, memories, experience, that binds you to that landscape. In 1956 I was invited to go to the Prime Minister's office. This was Garfield Todd. Striding about an office he clearly felt confined him, a rugged and handsome man in style rather like Abraham Lincoln, he said, 'I have stretched my hand over you, my child.' He was then ten years older than I was. I attributed his proprietorial style to the fact he had been a missionary, and did not really hear what he was saying: he was welcoming me to Southern Rhodesia because he knew I could give Federation a good write-up. 'I have let you in . . .' I said I could not approve of Federation. We argued energetically and with good feeling for a couple of hours. Later I asked to interview Lord Malvern who, as Doctor Huggins, had been the family doctors, and told him I wanted to visit Northern Rhodesia and Nyasaland, then full of riots, dissidents, social disorder, and other mani-festations of imminent Independence. He said, 'Oh you do, do you!' During the course of arguments much less good-natured than those with Garfield Todd, he said, 'I wasn't going to have you upsetting our natives.' I still did not hear what was being said. Finally he said I could go to Northern Rhodesia and Nyasaland for two weeks. 'I don't suppose you can do much harm in that time.' It goes without saying this flattered me: people who see themselves as recorders and observers are always surprised to be seen as doers and movers. (These long-ago events are of interest now only when I try to come to terms with the irrationality of my reactions.) I came back to London and then began to think there was something here I could be seeing. That I had been Prohibited in North-ern Rhodesia and Nyasaland, countries where I had never been, did not affect me, but I could not 'take in' the fact that I could be Prohibited in the country I had been brought up in. At last I asked a lawyer to come with me to Southern Rhodesia House where an official, peevish with what he clearly felt was a false position, said, 'Oh drat it, you have forced my hand.' In this way was I finally informed that I was a Prohibited Immigrant. Prime Minister Huggins had ruled long ago, when I left home to come home, that I must not be allowed to upset his natives.*

As the convention was, I was proud to be Prohibited. Since then it has become clear that countries with the levels of purity of motive high enough to match our idea of ourselves as world citizens are not many.

I did not want to live in Southern Rhodesia, for if its climate was perfection, probably the finest in the world, and its landscape magnificent, it was provincial and tedious. I wanted to live in London. What this Prohibition amounted to was that I would be prevented from visiting relatives and friends. They, however, might visit London. These rational considerations did not reach some mysterious region of myself that was apparently an inexhaustible well of tears, for night after night I wept in my sleep and woke knowing I was unjustly excluded from my own best self. I dreamed the same dream, night after night. I was in the bush, or in Salisbury, but I was there illegally, without papers. 'My' people, that is, the whites, with whom after all I had grown up, were coming to escort me out to the country, while to 'my' people, the blacks, amiable multitudes, I was invisible. This went on for months. To most people at some point it comes home that inside our skins we are not made of a uni-form and evenly distributed substance, like a cake-mix or mashed potato, or even sadza, but rather accommodate several mutually unfriendly entities. It took me much longer to ask myself the real question: what effect on our behaviour, our decisions, may these subterranean enemies have? That lake of tears, did it slop about, or seep, or leak, secretly making moist what I thought I kept dry?

Now I see that refusal, that inability to 'take in' my exclusion, as a symptom of innate babyishness: mine, and, too, the inhabitants of privileged countries, safe countries, for there are more and more people in the world who have had to leave, been driven from, a country, the valley, the city they call home, because of war, plague, earthquake, famine. At last they return, but these places may not be there, they have been destroyed or eroded; for if at first glance, like a child's recognition of its mother's face when she has been absent too long, everything is as it was, then slowly it has to be seen that things are not the same, there are gaps and holes or a thinning of the substance, as if a light that suffused the loved street or valley has drained away. Quite soon the people who have known one valley or town all their lives will be the rare ones, and there are even those who speculate how humanity will have to leave the planet with plans to return after an interval to allow it to regenerate itself, like a sick or poisoned organism, but when they return after long generations they find . . .

## AIR ZIMBABWE

In 1982 I booked the seat on Air Zimbabwe, made arrangements, with more than usually mixed feelings.

As I seated myself inappropriate emotions began, all much too strong. For a start, the stewardesses were black, once impossible. Since nearly all the passengers were white, and these black girls had no reason to expect courtesy from them, they were defensive and would not look at anyone. The atmosphere was unpleasant. I had hoped to sit next to a black person, so as to hear what was being thought, but was beside a white race-horse owner, a man of forty or so, who grumbled obsessively for the ten hours of the flight about the new black government. I had heard this note of peevish spite before: at the Independence celebrations in Zambia the white officials of an administration which had done nothing to train blacks for responsibility, recited examples of inefficiency while their faces shone with triumphant malice. Here it was again. This man insisted in one sentence that this was still God's Own Country, and he could raise and train race-horses more cheaply and better here than anywhere in the world; he and his family enjoyed a wonderful life and he wouldn't leave for anything—but the black government . . . I listened with half an ear, thinking that soon, when I had paid my dues to the white world, I could leave it and find out about the new Zimbabwe. Meanwhile I disliked this man with an impatience identical to that I had felt all those years ago, growing up here. Childish, spoiled, self-indulgent, spiteful . . . yes, he was all this, they were all like this, or most of them, but what of it, and why should I remain so involved?

While he grumbled about the deprivations they suffered in the way of food, breakfast was served, slabs of bacon, scrambled eggs, sausage, fried bread, a meal to fuel farm labourers or gravediggers.

The little airport was unchanged: I hardly saw it. The smells, the colours of the earth had undone me, and my emotional balance was gone. Immigration was a shy young man, hesitant, inexperienced, who asked if I planned to come and live here now: too many of 'our friends' had left because of the old government. He enquired about my passport: for I had been born in Persia, and I explained that one could—loosely—equate Persia and Iran with Southern Rhodesia and Zimbabwe. When I changed my money at the airport bank the official asked if I was the author and welcomed me in the name of Zimbabwe. I went out into the dry scented air and wept. And there was the young man who had brought the hired car to the airport. So occupied was I in admonishing my tear-ducts that I hardly saw the streets. I left the young man at the car-hire firm and parked. I was on my own in the streets of the town that was once my big city.

# Donna J. Haraway

## *from* A CYBORG MANIFESTO: SCIENCE, TECHNOLOGY, AND SOCIALIST-FEMINISM IN THE LATE TWENTIETH CENTURY (1991)

*Donna Haraway (1944– ) completed her doctorate in cell biology at Yale University. A graduate student in the late 1960s, she was strongly influenced by the counter-culture movements of the era. Her interdisciplinary research interests include the history of science; ideologies about gender, race, and nature; and relations between humans and animals. Haraway is Professor in the History of Consciousness program at the University of California, Santa Cruz. Her essay "A Cyborg Manifesto: Science, Technology, and Socialist-Feminism in the Late Twentieth Century," excerpted here, has been widely influential. In it Haraway proposes that the science-fiction figure of the cyborg can serve as an icon for a new kind of identity, one that draws upon technology but is not overrun by it: a postmodern, post-Western hybrid figure of liberation.*

This chapter is an effort to build an ironic political myth faithful to feminism, socialism, and materialism. Perhaps more faithful as blasphemy is faithful, than as reverent worship and identification. Blasphemy has always seemed to require taking things very seriously. I know no better stance to adopt from within the secular-religious, evangelical traditions of the Untied States politics, including the politics of socialist feminism. Blasphemy protects one from the moral majority within, while still insisting on the need for community. Blasphemy is not apostasy. Irony is about contradictions that do not resolve into larger wholes, even dialectically, about the tension of holding incompatible things together because both or all are necessary and true. Irony is about humour and serious play. It is also a rhetorical strategy and a political method, one I would like to see more honoured within socialist-feminism. At the centre of my ironic faith, my blasphemy, is the image of the cyborg.

A cyborg is a cybernetic organism, a hybrid of machine and organism, a creature of social reality as well as a creature of fiction. Social reality is lived social relations, our most important political construction, a world-changing fiction. The international women's movements have constructed 'women's experience', as well as uncovered or discovered this crucial collective object. This experience is a fiction and fact of the most crucial, political kind. Liberation rests on the construction of the consciousness, the imaginative apprehension, of oppression, and so of possibility. The cyborg is a matter of fiction and lived experience that changes what counts as women's experience in the late twentieth century. This is a struggle over life and death, but the boundary between science fiction and social reality is an optical illusion.

Contemporary science fiction is full of cyborgs—creatures simultaneously animal and machine, who populate worlds ambiguously natural and crafted. Modern medicine is also full of cyborgs, of couplings between organism and machine, each conceived as coded devices, in an intimacy and with a power that was not generated in the history of sexuality. Cyborg 'sex' restores some of the lovely replicative baroque of ferns and invertebrates (such nice organic prophylactics against heterosexism). Cyborg replication is uncoupled from organic reproduction. Modern production seems like a dream of cyborg colonization work, a dream that makes the nightmare of Taylorism seem idyllic. And modern war is a cyborg orgy, coded by C³I, command-control-communication-intelligence, and $84 billion item in 1984's US defence budget. I am making an argument for the cyborg as a fiction mapping our social and bodily reality and as an imaginative resource suggesting some very fruitful couplings. Michael Foucault's biopolitics is a flaccid premonition of cyborg politics, a very open field.

By the late twentieth century, our time, a mythic time, we are all chimeras, theorized and fabricated hybrids of machine and organism; in short, we are cyborgs. The cyborg is our ontology; it gives us our politics. The cyborg is a condensed image of both imagination and material reality, the two joined centres structuring any possibility of historical transformation. In the traditions of 'Western' science and politics—the tradition of racist, male-dominant capitalism; the tradition of progress; the tradition of the appropriation of nature as resource for the productions of culture; the tradition of reproduction of the self from the reflections of the other—the relation between organism and machine has been a border war. The stakes in the border war have been the territories of production, reproduction, and imagination. This chapter is an argument for *pleasure* in the confusion of boundaries and for *responsibility* in their construction. It is also an effort to contribute to socialist-feminist culture and theory in a postmodernist, non-naturalist mode and in the utopian tradition of imagining a world without gender, which is perhaps a world without genesis, but maybe also a world without end. The cyborg incarnation is outside salvation history. Nor does it mark time on an oedipal calendar, attempting to heal the terrible cleavages of gender in oral symbiotic utopia or post-oedipal apocalypse. As Zoe Sofoulis argues in her unpublished manuscript on Jacques Lacan, Melanie Klein, and nuclear culture, *Lacklein,* the most terrible and perhaps the most promising monsters in cyborg worlds are embodied in non-oedipal narratives with a different logic of repression, which we need to understand for our survival.

The cyborg is a creature in a post-gender world; it has no truck with bisexuality, pre-oedipal symbiosis, unalienated labour, or other seductions to organic wholeness through a final appropriation of all the powers of the parts into a higher unity. In a sense, the cyborg has no origin story in the Western sense—a 'final' irony since the cyborg is also the awful apocalyptic *telos* of the 'West's' escalating dominations of abstract individuation, an ultimate self untied at last from all dependency, a man in space. An origin story in the 'Western', humanist sense depends on the myth of original unity, fullness, bliss and terror, represented by the phallic mother from whom all humans must separate, the task of individual development and of history, the twin potent myths inscribed most powerfully for us in psychoanalysis and Marxism.

Hilary Klein has argued that both Marxism and psychoanalysis, in their concepts of labour and of individuation and gender formation, depend on the plot of original unity out of which difference must be produced and enlisted in a drama of escalating domination of woman/nature. The cyborg skips the step of original unity, of identification with nature in Western sense. This is its illegitimate promise that might lead to subversion of its teleology as star wars.

The cyborg is resolutely committed to partiality, irony, intimacy, and perversity. It is oppositional, utopian, and completely without innocence. No longer structured by the polarity of public and private, the cyborg defines a technological polis based partly on a revolution of social relations in the *oikos,* the household. Nature and culture are reworked; the one can no longer be the resource for appropriation or incorporation by the other. The relationships for forming wholes from parts, including those of polarity and hierarchical domination, are at issue in the cyborg world. Unlike the hopes of Frankenstein's monster, the cyborg does not expect its father to save it through a restoration of the garden; that is, through the fabrication of a heterosexual mate, through its completion in a finished whole, a city and cosmos. The cyborg does not dream of community on the model of the organic family, this time without the oedipal project. The cyborg would not recognize the Garden of Eden; it is not made of mud and cannot dream of returning to dust. Perhaps that is why I want to see if cyborgs can subvert the apocalypse of returning to nuclear dust in the manic compulsion to name the Enemy. Cyborgs are not reverent; they do not re-member the cosmos. They are wary of holism, but needy for connection—they seem to have a natural feel for united front politics, but without the vanguard party. The main trouble with cyborgs, of course, is that they are the illegitimate offspring of militarism and patriarchal capitalism, not to mention state socialism. But illegitimate offspring are often exceedingly unfaithful to their origins. Their fathers, after all, are inessential.

●

To recapitulate, certain dualisms have been persistent in Western traditions; they have all been systemic to the logics and practices of domination of women, people of colour, nature, workers, animals—in short, domination of all constituted as others, whose task is to mirror the self. Chief among these troubling dualisms are self/other, mind/body, culture/nature, male/female, civilized/primitive, reality/appearance, whole/part, agent/resource, maker/made, active/passive, right/wrong, truth/illusion, total/partial, God/man. The self is the One who is not dominated, who knows that by the service of the other, the other is the one who holds the future, who knows that by the experience of domination, which gives the lie to the autonomy of the self. To be One is to be autonomous, to be powerful, to be God; but to be One is to be an illusion, and so to be involved in a dialectic of apocalypse with the other. Yet to be other is to be multiple, without clear boundary, frayed, insubstantial. One is too few, but two are too many.

High-tech culture challenges these dualisms in intriguing ways. It is not clear who makes and who is made in the relation between human and machine. It is not clear what is mind and what body in machines that resolve into coding practices. In so far as we know ourselves in both formal discourse (for example, biology) and in daily practice (for example, the homework economy in the integrated circuit), we find ourselves to be cyborgs, hybrids, mosaics, chimeras. Biological organisms have become biotic systems, communications devices like others. There is no fundamental, ontological separation in our formal knowledge of machine and organism, of technical and organic. The replicant Rachel in the Ridley Scott film *Blade Runner* stands as the image of a cyborg culture's fear, love, and confusion.

●

There are several consequences to taking seriously the imagery of cyborgs as other than our enemies. Our bodies, ourselves; bodies are maps of power and identity. Cyborgs are no exception. A cyborg body is not innocent; it was not born in a garden; it does not seek unitary identity and so generate antagonistic dualisms without end (or until the world ends); it takes irony for granted. One is too few, and two is only one possibility. Intense pleasure in skill, machine skill, ceases to be a sin, but an aspect of embodiment. The machine is not an *it* to be animated, worshipped, and dominated. The machine is us, our processes, an aspect of our embodiment. We can be responsible for machines; *they* do not dominate or threaten us. We are responsible for boundaries; we are they. Up till now (once upon a time), female embodiment seemed to be given, organic, necessary; and female embodiment seemed to mean skill in mothering and its metaphoric extensions. Only by being out of place could we take intense pleasure in machines, and then with excuses that this was organic activity after all, appropriate to females. Cyborgs might consider more seriously the partial, fluid, sometimes aspect of sex and sexual embodiment. Gender might not be global identity after all, even if it has profound historical breadth and depth.

The ideologically charged question of what counts as daily activity, as experience, can be approached by exploiting the cyborg image. Feminists have recently claimed that women are given to dailiness, that women more than men somehow sustain daily life, and so have a privileged epistemological position potentially. There is a compelling aspect to this claim, one that makes visible unvalued female activity and names it as the ground of life. But *the* ground of life? What about all the ignorance of women, all the exclusions and failures of knowledge and skill? What about men's access to daily competence, to knowing how to build things, to take them apart, to play? What about other embodiments? Cyborg gender is a local possibility taking a global vengeance. Race, gender, and capital require a cyborg theory of wholes and parts. There is no drive in cyborgs to produce total theory, but there is an intimate experience of boundaries, their construction and deconstruction. There is a myth system waiting to become a political language to ground one way of looking at science and technology and challenging the informatics of domination—in order to act potently . . .

Cyborg imagery can suggest a way out of the maze of dualisms in which we have explained our bodies and our tools to ourselves. This is a dream not of a common language, but of a powerful infidel heteroglossia. It is an imagination of a feminist speaking in tongues to strike fear into the circuits of the super-savers of the new right. It means both building and destroying machines, identities, categories, relationships, space stories. Though both are bound in the spiral dance, I would rather be a cyborg than a goddess.